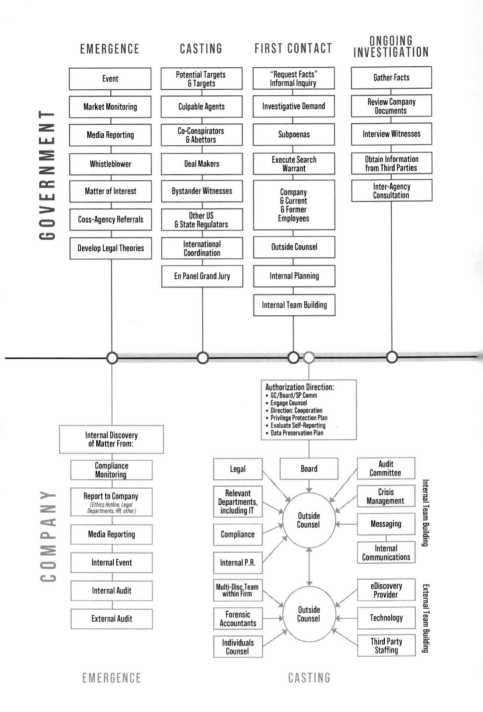

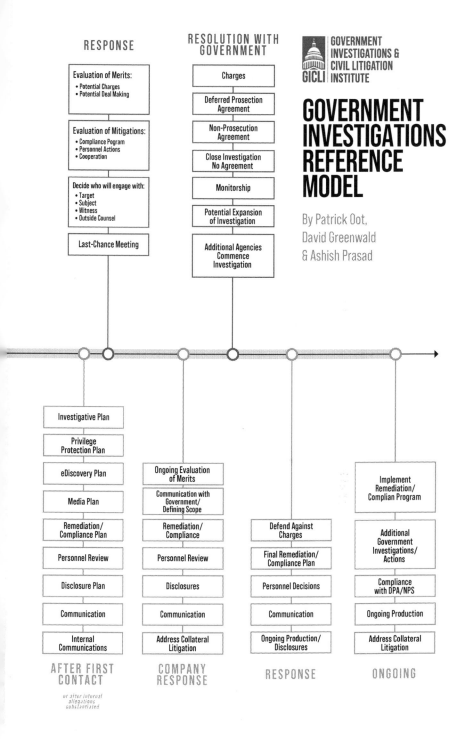

RESPONSE

Evaluation of Merits:
- Potential Charges
- Potential Deal Making

Evaluation of Mitigations:
- Compliance Pogram
- Personnel Actions
- Cooperation

Decide who will engage with:
- Target
- Subject
- Witness
- Outside Counsel

Last-Chance Meeting

RESOLUTION WITH GOVERNMENT

- Charges
- Deferred Prosection Agreement
- Non-Prosecution Agreement
- Close Investigation No Agreement
- Monitorship
- Potential Expansion of Investigation
- Additional Agencies Commence Investigation

GOVERNMENT INVESTIGATIONS & CIVIL LITIGATION
GICLI INSTITUTE

GOVERNMENT INVESTIGATIONS REFERENCE MODEL

By Patrick Oot,
David Greenwald
& Ashish Prasad

AFTER FIRST CONTACT
or after internal allegations substantiated

- Investigative Plan
- Privilege Protection Plan
- eDiscovery Plan
- Media Plan
- Remediation/ Compliance Plan
- Personnel Review
- Disclosure Plan
- Communication
- Internal Communications

COMPANY RESPONSE

- Ongoing Evaluation of Merits
- Communication with Government/ Defining Scope
- Remediation/ Compliance
- Personnel Review
- Disclosures
- Communication
- Address Collateral Litigation

RESPONSE

- Defend Against Charges
- Final Remediation/ Compliance Plan
- Personnel Decisions
- Communication
- Ongoing Production/ Disclosures

ONGOING

- Implement Remediation/ Complian Program
- Additional Government Investigations/ Actions
- Compliance with DPA/NPS
- Ongoing Production
- Address Collateral Litigation

THE

GENERAL COUNSEL'S GUIDE TO GOVERNMENT INVESTIGATIONS

FOURTH EDITION

WWW.GICLI.ORG

Copyright © 2024 by
The Government Investigations & Civil Litigation Institute

Published by:
The Government Investigations & Civil Litigation Institute
401 E. Las Olas Boulevard, Suite 130-275
Fort Lauderdale, FL 33301

ISBN-13: 979-8867152451

Cover Photos Credit Copyright Contribution:
Josiah Grandfield

The General Counsel's Guide to Government Investigations

Fourth Edition

Editor-in-Chief: Patrick Oot
Executive Editor: Ashish Prasad
Assistant Editor: Ashley B. Hayes

Fourth Edition Editorial Board:

EXECUTIVE DIRECTOR
Barbara Hanahan

GICLI ANNUAL MEETING CO-CHAIRS EMERITUS

Brian Chebli (2023)
Executive Director & Assistant General Counsel
JP Morgan Chase & Co.

Larissa Eustice (2023)
Senior Assistant General Counsel
Bayer US

Laura Kibbe (2022)
VP, Deputy General Counsel, Global Head of Legal Operations &
Chief of Staff to the General Counsel
Unisys

Sonia Zeledon (2022)
Assistant General Counsel, Ethics, Compliance and Data Privacy
The Hershey Company

Ann Claire Phillips (2021)
Chief Government Investigative Counsel
U.S. Bank

Kate Shrout (2021)
Director, Legal - Investigations
ServiceNow

Heather Capell Bramble (2019)
Head of Regulatory Affairs, Safety
Mattel, Inc.

Kelly Clay (2019)
Global eDiscovery Counsel & Head of Information Governance
GlaxoSmithKline

Marc Fishman (2018)
Vice President, Associate General Counsel
Novo Nordisk, Inc.

LaTanya Langley (2018)
Chief Legal Officer
Edgewell Personal Care

Rishi Chhatwal (2017)
Managing Director
Alvarez & Marsal Holdings

David Orensten (2017)
Director, Corporate Counsel – Litigation
Starbucks

TABLE OF CONTENTS

C.   Avoid Voluntary Disclosure Without
      Fully Understanding the
      Requirements.................................602
D.   Avoid Giving Insufficient *Upjohn*
      Warnings 603
E.   Avoid Failing to Preserve Records
      and Electronically Stored Information
     603

VIII.   CONCLUSION 604

Chapter 25 Insider Trading 606

I.   INTRODUCTION...............................606
II.   THEORIES OF INSIDER TRADING:
        CLASSICAL V. MISAPPROPRIATION..607

        A.   The Classical Theory of Insider
              Trading....................................607
        B.   The Misappropriation Theory of
              Insider Trading.........................608

III.   TIPPER AND TIPPEE LIABILITY..........611
IV.   SANCTIONS FOR INSIDER TRADING.616
V.   RULE 10B5-1 PLANS..........................616
VI.   INSIDER TRADING CONTROLS..........619
VII.   CONCLUSION 621

Chapter 26 Computer Forensics: An Investigation Begins
       623

I.   ASSESS THE SCOPE AND TYPE OF
        INVESTIGATION: MUNDANE
        MISBEHAVIOR 623

        A.   Collecting ESI in a Simple
              Investigation.............................624
        B.   More Serious Investigations.........626

Preface

By: The GICLI Advisory Board

"The Regulators Always Ring Twice"

As regulatory complexity grows in the face of surging enforcement, corporate counsel and litigators are expected to continually buttress their knowledge base and expertise with respect to regulatory oversight and litigation. With adequate preparation, research, and an exploration of the intricacies and particularities of regulatory matters, corporate counsel and litigators can ensure they are well prepared. Guidance and resources compiled by, and for, corporate legal teams and litigators can often prove invaluable in navigating the regulatory landscape.

This Guide contains a wide array of content from a wealth of contributors and co-authors across many industries and sectors. The chapters touch upon the most significant aspects of regulatory investigations in a shifting legislative environment, and provide insights on how counsel can best prepare for the inevitable and the unexpected developments in that environment. The Guide encapsulates the thorough summaries of regulatory investigations from the perspective of key agencies and regulatory bodies, and includes important case law, best practices, and strategies that litigators can revisit as their matters require.

The introductory chapter leads us through an overview of the corporate regulatory enforcement environment, addressing the benefits which adequate response affords too many corporations, while also touching upon the pitfalls that befall other corporations. From there follows an in-depth review of Department of Justice investigations, written with the aim of assisting internal company lawyers in asking the right questions, managing attendant risks, and ensuring effective collaboration with the DOJ.

The ensuing content provides a look at the structure, statutory framework, and nature of SEC enforcement actions, while also delving into the SEC's investigative process and best practices for response. Following that is a similar overview of FTC investigations, which highlights the fact that comprehensive discovery planning, litigation holds, and preservation can assist in demonstrating collaboration and cooperation with the FTC, and can reduce complexity and costs. These chapters are followed by an-depth look at CFTC and FINRA investigations, looking at agency structure, significant case law, and recent advisories.

A review of government investigations under the False Claims Act and FIRREA highlights the essential fact that an adequate approach and response at the investigation stage increases the odds of a successful outcome, including narrowing the allegations or even resolving the matter in its entirety. An overview of the intricacies of the FCPA is then followed with insights on state-level attorney general investigations and litigation.

Key concepts in investigations are also addressed in this volume: there are in-depth analyses of the role of compliance in government investigations, eDiscovery, forensic accounting, board of directors and audit committee issues, and ethical issues in investigations.

Finally, a thorough treatment of additional considerations in government investigations is provided, especially those which have grown in prominence over the past 10 – 15 years. These include: international investigations and cross-border issues in an ever more globalized world; the representation of individuals tied to corporate malfeasance; and a look at computer forensics and the handling of electronically stored information (ESI) in investigations, especially as the volume of ESI has changed the way that technology is approached in the practice of law.

When investigators ring, a well-prepared answer to that call is essential. Our hope is that, with reference to this volume, corporate litigators and legal teams will be in a position to efficiently and effectively narrow the scope of investigations, collaborate effectively with regulators, and work toward consistently successful outcomes.

Chapter 1

The Government Investigation Reference Model (GIRM) Project Overview

By: Patrick L. Oot[1]

Found in the first few pages of this Guide, The GIRM represents a conceptual view of the investigative process that will improve the management and efficiency of investigations. It also provides an iterative framework which allows the user to focus and analyze some or all of the steps in a government investigation. Originally developed by three practitioners and launched at the Government Investigations & Civil Litigation Institute (GICLI) Third Annual Meeting, The GIRM is an attempt to develop a roadmap to assist both sides of the investigative process in a cooperative path to successful resolution of disputes. Each year, GICLI advisory board, the authors of this book and the designers of the GIRM invite practitioners from corporations, private practice and the government from around the world to provide input on the ongoing developments of the GIRM. We hope you find it useful, and appreciate your input on the next version at girm@gicli.org

I.   INTRODUCTION

For the unwary, the uncooperative, or simply the unprepared, being subject to a government investigation can be the worst possible scenario for the fate of yourself or your company. All too often, a company's lack of wherewithal can derail the course of governmental investigative proceedings to catastrophic proportion. On the government side, unprepared and unresponsive attorneys

---

[1] Patrick Oot is a Partner at Shook, Hardy & Bacon, LLP in Washington, DC and founder of The Government Investigations & Civil Litigation Institute. Prior to joining the firm, Patrick was Senior Special Counsel in the Office of General Counsel at the Securities and Exchange Commission. Prior to joining the S.E.C., Patrick was Director and Senior Litigation Counsel at Verizon in Washington, DC.

4

only frustrate the goals of the investigation and potentially paints an inadvertent picture of culpability.

Whether or not you choose to cooperate, being under a government investigation is almost universally negative. Being under investigation is bad enough; but, you can compound the negative repercussions of any investigation by not knowing what you have gotten yourself into and, therefore, not having an understanding of what a government investigation is going to involve and how to respond in a manner most conducive to your own interests.

The aim of this Guide is twofold. First, it is to educate those that have a limited understanding of government investigations and to give them a "Government Investigations 101." But it is also to give practitioners who deal with these issues on a regular basis a stronger, more comprehensive understanding of how to manage these situations more effectively. It is not intended to be the end-all of legal advice – each side might have unique tools and special circumstances that allow for diversion from these high-level thoughts. Moreover, the GIRM will and should change over time – as the law develops – so will the GIRM.

Take Mark Cuban – entrepreneurial and successful as he is, he recently made seven years of his life incredibly difficult (and spent millions of dollars unnecessarily) because he didn't understand the way government investigations run. Responding to SEC charges against his companies for insider trading, he – from the outset – refused to take them seriously. In his own words, Cuban made a "huge mistake" because he didn't "take it seriously upfront." He assumed he would be able to satisfy the SEC with "one sit-down."[2] Had Cuban, or others similarly situated, understood the basic mechanics of how a government investigation works, in all likelihood, they could have ultimately used their knowledge to their advantage to expend *less* time and money and probably ascertain a better final outcome.

---

[2] Natalie Posgate, The Behind-The-Scenes Story in Mark Cuban's Insider Trading Trial, THE TEXAS LAWBOOK (March 7, 2014).

This is the solution that this Guide and the GIRM endeavours to provide. It attempts to equip practitioners with the knowledge necessary to be adequately prepared and responsive to governmental investigations. It seeks to avoid leaving those who care to understand how these systems work "high and dry." The remainder of this chapter aims to give you an index of sorts to create a baseline understanding of the terms, phrases, concepts, and actors that are at play in the lifespan in various types of government investigations – all of which are more fully explored in the subsequent chapters of this Guide.

II.   GIRM TERMS

A.   Emergence: How an Issue Comes About

In broad terms, **emergence** represents the idea that "red flags" have been raised – either internally or externally; from the respondent, third parties or the government. It is indicia of sufficient importance to merit follow up action, either through closer attention or actual, direct examination.

1.   Government

From the government perspective, what may constitute a "**matter under inquiry**" or "**matter of interest**" can vary widely from one agency to another or from one U.S. Attorney to the next. Typically, a "matter of interest" is going to be largely defined by the focus and priorities of whomever is at the head of a particular office or agency and how they exercise their broad prosecutorial discretion in the use of their available resources. A matter of interest, then, satisfies two basic criteria of being both an issue of particular concern to a given government entity and having some appearance of merit or legitimacy.

A common way by which the government first learns of potential wrongdoing is through whistle blowers. A **whistle blower** is, as the name implies, someone who is "blowing the whistle" on an illegal or unethical conduct or practice in the hopes that their disclosure will lead to government intervention. As discussed in the False Claims Act and other chapters, a whistle blower may also stand to benefit financially if their exposure of bribery, waste, or other wrongdoing leads to the eventual recovery of public funds lost to fraud. Moreover, if the whistle blower was involved in the misconduct, being the first to inform the government of that misconduct may potentially enable that individual to avoid prosecution or mitigate their punishment.

In addition to learning of a matter of interest through their own day-to-day operations and from whistle blowers, the government also often learns of matters of interest through **cross agency referrals**. Governmental agencies will refer matters of interest to other governmental agencies for a number of reasons. For instance, a matter that may not be a particular concern for one agency may be of high priority for another. Alternately, a matter of interest may be outside the bounds of one agency's jurisdiction but squarely within the bounds of another. For example, while investigating an act of terror, the Federal Bureau of Investigation (FBI) may learn of a financial crime that is more suitable for investigation by the Securities Exchange Commission (SEC).

Matters of interest can also derive from obvious sources, such as a notable public **events**, news, and **media reporting**, and—for agencies like the SEC that deal with financial matters—careful monitoring of financial markets ("**market monitoring**") and review of corporate disclosures.

From the perspective of the company, emergence represents the internal discovery of anything that would potentially expose the company to civil or criminal harm. These sorts of flags may be raised by myriad sources, both internal and external to the company. The formal program specifying a company's internal policies, procedures, and actions in a process to help it prevent and detect violations of laws and regulations and other misconduct is known as **compliance monitoring**. While there is no "one-size-fits-all" prescription, the United States Federal Sentencing Guidelines broadly articulate the following elements as comprising the framework for an effective compliance program:

- Leadership commitment: Buy in an active participation in development and operation of compliance program.

- Effective management: A successful compliance program demands adequate commitment of funds and personnel to ensure successful operation.

- Oversight: Develop and implement protocol for detecting criminal activity and ensuring that employees abide by internal corporate standards of conduct and policies, and comply with the law. More specifically, part of virtually any effective compliance program should include having a company-wide **ethics hotline** that employees can call to report potential legal or policy violations without fear of retaliation.

- Awareness: Ensure that all employees are adequately apprised of the compliance program and their rights and obligations under it. This includes implementing effective and ongoing training at all levels of the company and requires involvement by all stakeholders. Two of the most critical divisions to a successful compliance program are necessarily the **legal** and **human resources departments**. Other parts of the company that could identify risks or potential misconduct include the government affairs department, who may learn of impending statutory or regulatory changes that could have an effect on the company's future decision-making. Likewise, the day-to-day operation of the finance department may detect irregularities that call for an internal audit.

- Risk monitoring and assessment: Follow through with all steps of the program to ensure prompt detection of incidents and risks. **Risk monitoring** is committing to review your compliance program on an ongoing, real-time basis and reacting quickly to remediate them. The primary goal of monitoring is to identify and address gaps or issues in your program on a regular, consistent basis. Conduct frequent, unscheduled **internal audits** and potentially the occasional **external audit** as well should also be done. Audits are more limit reviews targeting some specific business component in a particular timeframe for the purpose of evaluating or detecting certainly risks, especially in connections with financial records.

- Enforcement and incident management: Appropriately respond to potential incidents by applying the established course of corrective action. Comprehensively investigate potential incidents of non-compliance.

- On-going evaluation: A compliance program is not static; it should be regularly evaluated and continue evolving to better prevent and detect violations.

2. Company

From within a company, matters of interest can be identified from a wide range of sources. Reports can derive from virtually any company department or division. Ideally, potential misconduct will not first be brought to the attention of a company through **media reporting**. Realistically, however, a violation may first surface in the news. Therefore, companies should strive to remain vigilant in their monitoring of media sources to ensure that, in the event that misconduct is first exposed in the public news, they are made immediately aware of it.

9

B.   Casting: Individuals Involved in an Investigation

1.   Government

As a part of every criminal or regulatory government investigation, a wide variety of actors will be involved.

Subjects are people or organizations whose conduct puts them within the scope of the government's investigation. A subject is not, however, necessarily a **target** of an investigation. A target is a person or organization believed to have some level of culpability that may warrant prosecution. Whether one's status changes from being a subject of an investigation to being one of its targets can derive from a variety of factors, depending on both the law and prosecutorial discretion. The terms "subject" and "target" do not, themselves, have any technical legal significance.

The same is true for a **witness** in an investigation; witnesses are those individuals in a corporation with relevant information about the alleged misconduct, but are generally understood to lack potential criminal exposure themselves.

Potential targets include not only those individuals responsible for the "final act" of the commission of misconduct; the category of targets also extends to individuals who participated in the misconduct at some point along the way; these types of people include **conspirators** and **accomplices**. Conspirators are simply defined as two or more people who have agreed to commit a crime; their conspiracy is what makes each conspirator a principle offender. An accomplice is someone who did not necessarily conspire or even agree to participate in the crime itself, but they have taken action to advance its commission, completion, or even its cover-up.

A **culpable agent** is someone who has committed wrongdoing within a corporation. Their actions thereby may implicate potential liability for the corporation—if they were committed within the scope of their employment. The culpable agent may still be personally liable as well.

A **deal maker** can be any actor with some sort of potential culpability for a crime who provides the government with information relevant to their investigation in exchange for their cooperation.

For further discussion of these categories of potential targets, see the chapter titled "DOJ Investigations Overview."

C.   First Contact

1.   Government

Upon learning of a matter of interest, a government agency may first issue an **informal inquiry** to the company to request facts regarding the incident. Participation in an informal inquiry is voluntary, but cooperation has the potential to lead to termination of an investigation without an enforcement action or indictment. Receipt of a **civil investigative demand** signals that the government has opened a False Claims investigation. Upon its receipt, a company has immediate and often broad obligations. While an investigative demand is a tool for the government to determine whether sufficient evidence exists to warrant the filing of a complaint, the requests themselves can demand a wide range of documentary evidence. Voluntarily offering cooperation will not necessarily result in leniency or immunity.

A **subpoena** is, generally, a court-order mandating compliance with its request. As elaborated on in Section III of our chapter titled "DOJ Investigations Overview," a subpoena may require a person to appear in court and testify as a witness at trial or before a grand jury, to produce documents, or to appear at a deposition.

Unlike a subpoena, which requires a witness to appear on a specific date and time and provide testimony or documents, a **search warrant** is issued by a judge and authorizes law enforcement personnel to search and seize property or arrest a person. A search warrant is delivered contemporaneous with its execution and is only issued upon satisfaction of the probable cause standard.

During the course of an investigation, the government may approach current or formal employees outside of the workplace requesting an informal interview. These **informal employee interviews** do not require cooperation on the part of the employee, but without prior instruction, an unprepared employee might not recognize that they are required to participate, or that their subsequent statement can be later used against them or their employer.

Upon learning of a government investigation, companies can take certain **internal planning** steps to prepare their employees for how best to respond, manage, internalize, and handle the receipt of a subpoena, search warrant, or request for informal interview. This includes instructing employees on their legal rights and what employees should or should not say to the government, how that they can ensure that privileged company information is protected and that the government actions are properly undertaken.

2.   <u>Company</u>

From the company's side, once a matter of interest significant enough to potentially implicate individuals or organizations for criminal or regulatory liability has emerged, the people who will *necessarily* need to be notified—if not become actively involved—are the company's **President**, its **General Counsel**, and the **Board of Directors**, as well as the members of any potential **Special Committee**. Some internal investigations are handled or managed by a company's Board of Directors, but under certain circumstances where allegations of wrongdoing are either beyond the Board's capacity to investigate or implicate the ability to conduct an independent investigation, the Board may create an independent **Special Committee** to manage the investigation on its own.

Depending on the preliminary results of an internal or Special Committee investigation, the company may need to **engage outside counsel**, who will have the experience, resources and independence necessary to lead a thorough investigation and communicate, when needed, with the government.

If the company's initial fact-gathering investigation does, in fact, unearth misconduct, the inquiry should expand to allow those conducting it to fully understand the evidence and address the misconduct. The results of the company's preliminary investigation will also help inform its plans for responding to its findings. A major consideration for those at the helm of the company will be deciding the direction to take going forward in undertaking further investigation; in particular, this will be the time the company's leadership decides the extent of **cooperation**, if any, it plans to engage in with the government.

To ensure that communication and documentation produced during an internal investigation are protected under the attorney-client privilege, companies must establish and follow a **privilege protection plan**. The plan is implemented for the purpose of showing that the investigation is being undertaken for the purpose of obtaining legal advice.

If outside counsel is necessary to respond to an ongoing matter involving misconduct, their role will put them at the center of managing to distinct teams of actors: external and internal. **Internal team building** invariably involves members of the in-house legal department and the Board. Where applicable, outside counsel will also engage with members of the **compliance** department along with any internal and external **audit committees**. Depending upon the circumstances and the type of misconduct at issue, outside counsel may also need to coordinate with and direct the actions of specific divisions or departments within the company implicated by the allegations. Based on the misconduct alleged, the department or departments where it arose will become **relevant departments** in these proceedings.

Outside counsel will also need to engage with a company's **internal public relations** and, where applicable, **crisis management** departments to coordinate the company's response if allegations of illegality are made public. To this end, they will need to devise a **messaging** strategy that represents the company in a coherent manner before the public. Outside counsel will likewise need to oversee the development of a framework for managing **internal communications** to avoid unintended disclosures.

The second part of outside counsel's team-building leadership role is coordinating various entities external to the company (*i.e.* **external team building**). This may consist of groups of individuals within outside counsel's own firm, such as experts in the fields of Discovery, litigation, regulatory affairs, etc. Outside counsel will also, if necessary, be expected to lead the collection of electronic discovery through a **third-party Discovery vendor**. Depending on whether the underlying misconduct pertains to a financial, outside counsel will engage with **forensic accounting** firm. As the chapter titled "Forensic Accounting Issues" explains in greater detail, forensic accountants use "accounting skills to investigate fraud or embezzlement and to analyze financial information for us in legal proceedings." Finally, when individuals within the company retain their own counsel, outside counsel must liaise with those **individuals' counsel** as part of the external team building process.

Outside the central sphere of interested actors are **interested third parties**; namely, parties who may also have a stake in or other connection to the controversy. Such individuals might include: **elected officials**, the **media**, company **shareholders**, **plaintiffs' attorneys**, **victims**, and the **public** at large.

D.   Ongoing Investigation

1.   Government

The government's approach to a particular investigation will rely heavily on the circumstances at issue. However, any investigation will generally involve a predictable set of steps, beginning with **fact gathering**. The fact gathering stage may entail the issuance of subpoenas, requests for information, or service of search warrants. Indeed, an investigation may be months along before a company is even aware that it is under investigation.

A key government tool at the fact gathering stage is the **grand jury**. The principal function of an empanelled grand jury is to determine whether there is probable cause to believe that a federal offense has been committed. To aid in this determination, grand juries can subpoena for the government financial records and other documentary evidence, testimony from witnesses, as well as targets of an investigation. Federal grand juries consist of 16-23 members and generally meet on a monthly basis for a certain period of time, generally between 6-18 months.

Upon receipt of documents from a company, whether through voluntary production or through required production—*i.e.*, a subpoena or search warrant—the government will then **review the company documents**. This step is central to the government's ability to fully assess the merit of the misconduct at issue under investigation.

Either concurrent with or subsequent to document review, the government may **interview witnesses**. People who have or may have knowledge necessary or of interest to the investigation are likely candidates for these witness interviews.

Obtain Information: This is also the point at which the government agency tasked with carrying out this investigation would obtain information from other agencies that may have concurrently been investigating the same company (or individuals within a company) and correspond with them in order to have a more comprehensive understanding of the information acquired in relation to a matter. In the event that two or more government agencies are simultaneously pursuing an investigation against a company or individuals involved with a company, this is the stage at which those government agencies would coordinate their parallel investigations to the extent that it would allow them to share and exchange mutually helpful information.

> **E.** **After First Contact or Internal Allegations are Substantiated**
>
> 1. Company

After first contact—or when the government announces a formal investigation, or a company has substantiated allegations of wrongdoing—the next task is to assemble an **investigative plan** and team. A key initial step will be to educate management on the issues that are likely to arise during the course of the investigation.

Unless the company was previously aware of potential misconduct, the initial government contact is the point in time at which the company must quickly institute a defensible **Discovery plan**. The plan will entail a litigation hold and the litigation processing and review of electronic documents.

Government investigations can attract intense public attention. If not handled properly, the story can be controlled by the media rather than the company. Instituting an early action **media plan** can help ensure a coherent company message that minimizes the company's negative exposure. Ideally, such a plan will be developed and put into place before the public exposure.

Remediation/Compliance Plan: An investigation can reveal remedial actions that can be implemented to allow for early detection and prevention of future issues (or misconduct) identified by the investigation and imparting safeguards to ensure that the company can maintain compliance going forward. Such remedial measure should include a **personnel review**, which should identify any of the persons involved in the improper conduct and taking appropriate disciplinary action, up to and including the immediate termination. The company objective, once wrongdoing or misconduct is identified, the investigative team must move swiftly to ensure that whatever the substance of that misconduct was has been effectively contained and brought to a halt in order to mitigate the company's company going forward.

Following the completion of an internal investigation, the company needs to decide how it wishes to disclose its findings—*i.e.* its **disclosure plan**. Depending on the nature of the misconduct, the company may not necessarily be under an obligation to reveal its findings to the government. However, even if not obligated to disclose its findings, the company and outside counsel should closely consider the potential advantages of voluntary disclosure. Voluntary disclosure may assist in rehabilitation of public image and help avoid indictment or other further governmental punitive actions.

The measures a company must undertake to qualify for cooperation credit are outlined in the "Filip Factors," detailed in the chapter titled "DOJ Investigations Overview."

F.   Government Response

Evaluation of Merits: Prosecutors and other investigators are guided in their determination of the merits of a prosecution or other enforcement action by factors enumerated in their respective departments. For example, the U.S. Attorney's Manual provides a non-exhaustive list of ten factors for a prosecutor to consider when deciding on whether to bring charges against a corporate target. These include:

- The seriousness of the offense

- The pervasiveness of the wrongdoing

- The company history of misconduct

- The company's willingness to cooperate

At this point in its evaluation of the potential charges, the government will consider who are the potential **targets** of its investigation, identify who are the necessary **witnesses** it will need to engage with, and determine what the potential charges, or **subject actions,** will be. And at this point, the government will need to first reach out to and **engage with the company's outside counsel.**

Whether and which charges the government will bring are also guided by the steps a company has taken to mitigate the harm of potential internal misconduct or wrongdoing. "Cooperation is a mitigating factor, by which a corporation [ ] can gain credit in a case that otherwise is appropriate for indictment and prosecution."

See also U.S.A.M. § 9-28.700 (The Value of Corporation); See Chap. 16 re: FSGO (fn. 6-7)

Beyond these factors, decisions regarding **potential charges** will be guided by what is statutorily set forth. Certain conduct, while perhaps appearing to have been improper, may not fit within the scope of any given criminal or regulatory violation. At this point, rather than putting the time and effort into preparing a case for indictment, prosecutors may first wish to reach out to the company to discuss a pre-charge settlement. This will, of course, depend upon the type of misconduct at issue and the agency's priorities.

G.   Company Response

At this stage, the company has already commenced **communication with the government** agency handling its investigation into the matter. As previously, the company will need to **establish an internal protocol** for dealing with the government's involvement. In essence, this is a negotiation process with the government. The company, when it is meeting with the government at this stage, will be trying to acquire the information that the government has, what it has collected, what it is focused on looking for, who the potential targets are, the **areas of additional or particular interest**, the **pace and direction of its investigation**. Broadly, the company's goal here is to develop a closer understanding of what the government knows and what they intend to do with the information they have.

This is also the company's opportunity to **present mitigation**; this means trying to explain its side of the story, show the company any efforts it has already undertaking to effectuate **remediation** through its own measures.

In contrast to the initial stage, the company by this point should have a better grasp on the government's case and its facts, and it should also have a better understanding of what has happened from an internal perspective as well. In light of its improved understanding of and ability to assess the situation, the company will now begin considering potential avenues for taking **corrective action** by asking itself: what do we need to do to make sure this does not happen again? Relatedly, it will undertake a **personnel review**, determining whether it has all the right people, in the right places, doing the right things to make sure things are being (and continue to be) handled as effectively as possible going forward.

Another important part of the company's response after first contact has been made will fine-tuning a comprehensive, step-by-step **disclosure plan** for how they are going to interact with the government during the investigation. This will include considerations such as how, when, and what **documents to produce**, as well as how, when, and which **witnesses to make available**. More broadly, the company will have to determine who, from within the company; it is willing to or wants to allow the government to interview. The company will need to think ahead about what its document production obligations are going to be and put in place a plan for how it will proceed with document productions. It will have to consider not only the present, **ongoing production** obligations in the **instant government investigation**, but also any potential production obligations in the event that a future, **ancillary government investigation** or even a **civil action** commences. Such civil actions might include, though are not limited to, possible **shareholder litigation** or **class actions**.

At this point, it will also be critically important for counsel – either outside or in-house, depending on how the company has decided to structure the legal component of the proceedings – to communicate to members of the Board, members of any special investigative company (where applicable), and other company employees *"Upjohn"* **warnings** to make sure that they are aware that counsel represents the company, not the individual employees. *For detailed discussion on Upjohn warnings, see Section III of the chapter titled "DOJ Investigations Overview."*

The company will also now need to **implement** its **media plan**. This is also possibly the first time that things have been made public, so the company needs to be mindful of any publicity surrounding the matter in view of news coverage.

H.   Resolution with Government: USAM § 9-28.1300 (Adequacy of the Prosecution of Individuals)

A **Deferred Prosecution Agreement** (or "DPA") is, as the U.S. Attorney's Manual defines it: a written agreement between a government agency and a potential cooperating individual or company in which the agency files an enforcement action but agrees to forego prosecution of that action if that individual or company agrees to, among other things, (1) cooperate with the agency's investigation, (2) enter into a long-term tolling agreement, and (3) agree to admit underlying facts that the agency could use to establish a violation of the federal laws. DPAs should not exceed five years. If the individual or company complies with all obligations during the term of the agreement, the agency will dismiss its enforcement action and not pursue any further action regarding the matter in the agreement. Conversely, if the individual or company violates the agreement during its term, the agency may pursue its enforcement action against the individual or company." *USAM §§ 9-28.200 (General Considerations of Corporate Liability), 9-28.1100 (Collateral Consequences).*

A **Non-Prosecution Agreement**, (or "NPA"), as set out in sections 9-28.200 and 9-28.1100 of the U.S. Attorney's Manual and also discussed at further length in Section III of the chapter titled "DOJ Investigations Overview," is defined as: "a written agreement between a government agency and a potential cooperating individual or company which the government agency agrees not to file an enforcement action against that individual or company if the individual or company agrees to cooperate fully and abide by certain terms. If the agreement is violated, the agency may recommend an enforcement action against the individual or company."

Close Investigation; No Agreement: This denotes that the government has decided not to take any current action but is not way precluded from reopening the investigation in the future, should additional evidence or information arise that should warrant further examination.

I.   Ongoing

As part of the resolution of a government investigation, the
government may require a company to engage a **monitor** to
oversee efforts to oversee compliance and remediation efforts.

Potential Expansion of Investigation: Additional Agencies—At
some point in an investigation, issues may arise that require the
original investigating agency to engage the help of another agency.
On one hand, people may come forward with additional
information. Or the investigation could simply spiral into
something unanticipated at the outset. It may result in a larger
scope than originally anticipated due to evidence revealed in the
investigatory process.

J.   Potential Responses

Final Remediation/Compliance Plan: Going forward, the
company must institute a plan to ensure that its continuing
compliance obligations are fulfilled and that it achieves the
remediation goals required of it, either by court order or in
fulfilment of its compliance obligations (or both).

Personnel Decisions: The company needs to re-evaluate its hiring
and training protocols to ensure that the people that it hires to
replace company employees terminated as a result of prior
misconduct are adequately educated and trained to avoid future
compliance infractions, and to monitor their adherence to the
instituted protocols on an ongoing basis.

Additional Government Investigations/Actions: What a
government investigation and even prosecution reveals may not be
the end of the story for a company in terms of its liability for
misconduct; in the course of its investigation, the government can
uncover information that exposes the company to potential liability
giving rise to **shareholder litigation** or **consumer litigation**.

Compliance with DPA/NPA: These agreements have time limits
(usually of five years) that require a company to continue its

diligence with respect to **ongoing monitorship** and **providing required reporting to the government.**

Implement Remediation/Compliance Program: You had your original compliance program established early on, but you need to ensure that, as detailed earlier, it remains static and responsive to the demands of your company as they arise.

K. Conclusion

Again, there are many paths an investigation can take and the authors of this Guide and designers of the GIRM hope that it will facilitate improved management and efficiency in investigations. Ideally, those involved in an investigation stay ahead of the requests and attempt to anticipate what a requesting party might ask before the request has actually been received. We hope that you join practitioners from corporations, private practice and the government at our next annual meeting to provide input on the ongoing developments of the GIRM. We appreciate your input on the next version at girm@gicli.org.

Chapter 2

Government Enforcement Agencies: An Overview

By: John Kosmidis[3] and Yasir Sadat[4]

The U.S. government divides its enforcement powers among multiple departments, agencies, and bureaus. These enforcers have distinct jurisdictions and priorities, though one pattern of conduct can draw the attention of more than one enforcer. Increasingly, enforcers pool their resources, coordinate investigations, and work closely with their international counterparts. Understanding the histories, structures, and jurisdictions of the many enforcing arms of the U.S. Government allows companies to gain insights into who is investigating alleged misconduct and what their goals are.

The U.S. government has what feels like countless enforcement arms. This introduction is not intended to cover all government enforcement agencies in the U.S. It is focused only on those federal agencies most likely to conduct investigations and bring enforcement actions against corporations and/or their executives that represent large risks and require the use of significant resources.

---

[3] John Kosmidis is a Trial Attorney in the Fraud Section at U.S. Department of Justice. This chapter was written while he was a Partner in the White-collar Defense Practice at Baker & McKenzie, LLP. The statements of this article do not reflect positions of the government.

[4] Yasir Sadat is a Special Assistant United States Attorney in the Eastern District of North Carolina. This chapter was written while he was an Associate at Baker & McKenzie LLP. He works on behalf of companies conducting business in emerging and frontier markets. Yasir has assisted companies across various industries on a variety of legal compliance matters. The statements of this article do not reflect positions of the government. Ashley B. Hayes contributed to this chapter with updates for this edition.

I.   THE DEPARTMENT OF JUSTICE ("DOJ")

A.   History / Background

The Department of Justice ("DOJ") was officially created on July 1, 1870, transforming from a one-person part-time position into an entire department.[5] The DOJ is responsible for enforcing federal criminal law and defending the interests of the United States.[6] The mission of the DOJ is: "to enforce the law and defend the interests of the United States according to the law; to ensure public safety against threats foreign and domestic; to provide federal leadership in preventing and controlling crime; to seek just punishment for those guilty of unlawful behavior; and to ensure fair and impartial administration of justice for all Americans."[7]

B.   Structure

The DOJ is comprised of over fifty agencies, bureaus, and divisions.[8] The Deputy Attorney General oversees all of the agencies', bureaus', and divisions' activities.[9] The Deputy Attorney General reports to the Attorney General.[10] The President nominates the Attorney General and the Senate confirms the nominee.[11] Each of the agencies, bureaus, and divisions within the DOJ is responsible for investigating and prosecuting a specific area

---

[5] Department of Justice ("DOJ"), About DOJ, https://www.justice.gov/about (last visited June 30, 2019).

[6] Id.

[7] Id.

[8] DOJ, Organizational Chart, https://www.justice.gov/agencies/chart/map (last updated December 5, 2022).

[9] Id.

[10] Id.

[11] DOJ, Meet the Attorney General, https://www.justice.gov/ag/staff-profile/meet-attorney-general (last updated November 15, 2022).

of federal criminal or civil law, but they cooperate frequently if the target offense impacts more than one area of law.[12]

C.   Jurisdiction / Types of Cases

The DOJ has jurisdiction over the investigation and prosecution of federal civil and criminal law. To understand the jurisdictional scope of the DOJ, it is vital to understand the roles of the major divisions within the DOJ: the Office of the United States Attorneys, the Criminal Division, the Civil Division, the National Security Division, the Antitrust Division, and the Tax Division.

The Office of the United States Attorneys ("USAO") investigates and enforces cases involving the federal government in the 94 judicial districts throughout the country.[13] The United States Attorneys conduct a majority of the trial work in cases involving the federal government as a party and they act as the chief federal law enforcement officer within their respective jurisdictions.[14] The United States Attorneys are statutorily mandated to: 1) prosecute criminal cases brought by the federal government; 2) prosecute and defend civil cases in which the federal government is a party; and 3) collect debts owed to the federal government that are administratively uncollectible.[15]

The Criminal Division "develops, enforces, and supervises the application of all federal criminal law" except when an area of law is specifically designated to another division.[16] The Criminal Division is composed of many sections that focus on prosecuting

---

[12] DOJ, Organizational Chart, https://www.justice.gov/agencies/chart/map (last updated December 5, 2022).

[13] DOJ - Office of the United States Attorneys, *Mission*, https://www.justice.gov/usao/mission (last updated September 22, 2016) (noting that one United States Attorney covers both Guam and the Northern Mariana Islands).

[14] *Id.*

[15] *Id.*; 28 U.S.C. § 547.

[16] DOJ, *About the Criminal Division*, https://www.justice.gov/criminal/about-criminal-division (last updated January 18, 2017).

cases in their specialty.[17] Each section prosecutes nationally significant cases in addition to formulating and implementing enforcement policy.[18] The Fraud Section is a section within the Criminal Division and is tasked with investigating and prosecuting complex white-collar crime cases.[19]

The Civil Division represents the federal government and its agencies in affirmative and defensive civil litigation.[20] These cases generally involve national policy, national or foreign courts, removal of illegal aliens, cases involving multiple jurisdictions, and cases that are "so massive and span so many years that they would overwhelm…any individual field office."[21] The Civil Division returns hundreds of millions of dollars to federal programs each year while defending billions of dollars of claims against the federal government.[22]

The National Security Division was created in 2006 by the USA Patriot Reauthorization and Improvement Act.[23] The National Security Division is responsible for investigating and prosecuting threats to national security as well as designing and proposing national security laws.[24] The National Security Division

---

[17] DOJ, *Criminal Division - Sections/Offices,* https://www.justice.gov/criminal/sectionsoffices (last visited August 1, 2023).

[18] *Id.*

[19] DOJ, *Criminal Division - About the Fraud Section,* https://www.justice.gov/criminal-fraud (last visited August 1, 2023).

[20] DOJ, *About the Civil Division,* https://www.justice.gov/civil/about (last updated January 19, 2023).

[21] *Id.*

[22] *Id.*

[23] DOJ, *National Security Division,* https://www.justice.gov/nsd/about-national-security-division-nsd (last visited August 1, 2023).

[24] *Id.*

encompasses many sections, which focus on "protect[ing] the United States from threats to our national security."[25]

The Antitrust Division has jurisdiction over the enforcement of federal antitrust laws. Its mission is to "promote economic competition through enforcing and providing guidance on antitrust laws and principles."[26] The Antitrust Division works closely with foreign antitrust agencies, state attorney generals, and the Federal Trade Commission.[27] The Antitrust Division prosecutes violations of antitrust laws that can result in significant fines and jail time.[28]

The Tax Division employs more than 350 attorneys in 14 civil, criminal, and appellate sections.[29] The Division litigates all civil and criminal cases to ensure compliance with IRS laws.[30] Civil cases usually collecting unpaid assessments, and foreclosing and prioritizing federal tax liens.[31] Criminal cases, on the other hand, involve tax evasion, wilful failure to file returns, submission of false tax forms, and other forms of fraud.[32]

---

[25] DOJ, *NSD Organization Chart*, https://www.justice.gov/nsd/national-security-division-organization-chart (last visited August 1, 2023).

[26] DOJ, *Antitrust Division - Mission*, https://www.justice.gov/atr/mission (last updated June 5, 2023).

[27] *Id.*

[28] *Id.*

[29] DOJ, *Tax Division - About the Division*, https://www.justice.gov/tax/about-division (last updated April 4, 2023).

[30] *Id.*

[31] *Id.*

[32] *Id.*

II. THE SECURITIES AND EXCHANGE COMMISSION ("SEC")

A. History / Background

Before the Great Crash of 1929, the federal government did not actively regulate the securities market.[33] Congress passed the Securities Act of 1933 and the Securities Exchange Act of 1934 to restore the public's faith in the capital markets by providing transparent and reliable information alongside "clear rules of honest dealing."[34] The mission of the SEC is to "protect investors, maintain fair, orderly, and efficient markets, and facilitate capital formation" and the Commission "strives to promote a market environment that is worthy of the public's trust."[35]

The SEC oversees, among other entities and individuals, stock issuers, securities brokers and dealers, investment advisors, and mutual funds by bringing hundreds of civil enforcement actions each year.[36] The SEC is responsible for interpreting and enforcing federal securities laws, issuing rules and amending current rules, overseeing the inspection of securities institutions and organizations, and coordinating securities regulation with state, federal, and foreign law enforcement.[37] The SEC emphasizes educating investors as it relies on these investors to provide information on potential violations of federal securities laws.[38] The SEC also relies on cooperation from Congress, the stock

---

[33] U.S. Securities and Exchange Commission (SEC), *What We Do*, https://www.sec.gov/Article/whatwedo.html#create (last visited August 1, 2023).

[34] U.S. Securities and Exchange Commission (SEC), *The Laws that Govern the Securities Industry*, https://www.sec.gov/about/about-securities-laws (last visited August 1, 2023).

[35] SEC, *About the SEC*, https://www.sec.gov/about.shtml (last updated November 22, 2016).

[36] *Id.*

[37] *Id.*

[38] *Id.*

exchanges, state securities regulators, various federal agencies, and private sector organizations.[39]

B.   Structure

The SEC consists of five Commissioners, eleven regional offices, five divisions, twenty-four Offices, and approximately 4,600 employees.[40] The five Commissioners are appointed by the U.S. President and confirmed by the Senate to serve five-year terms.[41] They may serve an additional 18 months after their term expires if they have not been replaced by then.[42] Only three of the five Commissioners can be of the same political party.[43] Additionally, the President designates one of the five Commissioners to serve as Chairman.[44]

C.   Jurisdiction / Types of Cases

As a civil agency, the SEC does not have the power to impose criminal penalties, such as imprisonment. Instead, the SEC can impose injunctions and statutory civil penalties, require disgorgement of ill-gotten gains, or it can seek other forms of relief in administrative proceedings and federal court.[45] The most common cases involve insider trading, accounting fraud, and providing false or misleading information about securities and the companies that issue these securities. Section 10(b) of the Exchange Act and Rule 10b-5 primarily regulate the most common

---

[39] *Id.*

[40] *Id.*

[41] SEC, *Current SEC Commissioners*, https://www.sec.gov/Article/about-commissioners.html (last updated December 29, 2020).

[42] *Id.*

[43] *Id.*

[44] *Id.*

[45] U.S Securities and Exchange Commission, *Inflation Adjustments to the Civil Monetary Penalties Administered by the Securities and Exchange Commission (as of January 15, 2023)*, https://www.sec.gov/enforce/civil-penalties-inflation-adjustments (last updated January 17, 2023)

violations.[46] Additionally, the SEC is empowered to enforce periodic reporting of information by companies with publicly traded securities.[47] Lastly, the SEC enforces the registration of market participants, such as exchanges, brokers, dealers, transfer agents, and clearing agencies.[48] Registration requires that these participants file disclosure documents, which are to be updated regularly.[49]

III.   THE FEDERAL TRADE COMMISSION ("FTC")

A.   History / Background

The FTC's mission is to "protect consumers and competition by preventing anticompetitive, deceptive, and unfair business practices through law enforcement, advocacy, and education without unduly burdening legitimate business activity."[50] The FTC was created in 1914 with the passage of the Federal Trade Commission Act.[51]

B.   Structure

The FTC consists of five Commissioners, three bureaus, and ten offices in addition to various regional offices.[52] The five Commissioners are appointed by the President and confirmed by

---

[46] 15 U.S.C. § 78j(b); 17 C.F.R. § 240.10b-5.

[47] U.S. Securities and Exchange Commission (SEC), *The Laws that Govern the Securities Industry*, https://www.sec.gov/about/about-securities-laws (last visited August 1, 2023).

[48] 15 U.S.C. § 78o(a).

[49] U.S. Securities and Exchange Commission (SEC), *The Laws that Govern the Securities Industry*, https://www.sec.gov/about/about-securities-laws (last visited August 1, 2023).

[50] Federal Trade Commission ("FTC"), *About the FTC*, https://www.ftc.gov/about-ftc (last visited August 1, 2023).

[51] FTC, *Our History*, https://www.ftc.gov/about-ftc/our-history (last visited August 1, 2023).

[52] FTC, *About the FTC*, https://www.ftc.gov/about-ftc/bureaus-offices (last visited August 1, 2023).

the Senate to serve seven-year terms.[53] Only three of the five
Commissioners can be of the same political party.[54] Additionally,
the President designates one of the five Commissioners to serve as
Chairman.[55]

C.   Jurisdiction / Types of Cases

In addition to the FTC Act, the FTC enforces over 70 other statutes
including the Telemarketing Sale Rule, Identity Theft Act, Fair
Credit Reporting Act, and Clayton Act.[56] The FTC has the power
to investigate and enforce laws against "any person, partnership, or
corporation engaged in or whose business affects commerce,
excepting banks, savings, and loan institutions…federal credit
unions…and common carriers."[57]

The FTC has dual mandates. First, the FTC seeks to protect
consumers by enforcing Section 5 of the FTC Act's prohibition
against unfair or deceptive acts or practices.[58] Second, the FTC
seeks to prohibit unfair methods of competition.[59] Eliminating
methods of unfair competition is primarily enforced through
Section 5 of the FTC Act, Sections 1 and 2 of the Sherman Act,
and Section 7 of the Clayton Act.[60] The Sherman Act is invoked
most often to enforce prohibitions on monopolization and

---

[53] FTC, *Commissioners*, https://www.ftc.gov/about-ftc/commissioners (last
visited August 1, 2023).

[54] *Id.*

[55] *Id.*

[56] FTC, *Statutes Enforced or Administered by the Commission*,
https://www.ftc.gov/enforcement/statutes (last visited August 1, 2023).

[57] 15 U.S.C. § 46(a).

[58] FTC, *A Brief Overview of the Federal Trade Commission's Investigative, Law
Enforcement, and Rulemaking Authority*, https://www.ftc.gov/about-ftc/what-we-
do/enforcement-authority (last visited August 1, 2023).

[59] *Id.*

[60] *Id.*

collusion while the Clayton Act is invoked to prevent mergers and acquisitions that would reduce competition.[61]

IV.   THE COMMODITY FUTURES TRADING COMMISSION ("CFTC")

A.   History / Background

The CFTC's mission is to "deter and prevent price manipulation or any other disruptions to market integrity; to ensure the financial integrity of all transactions subject [to its authority]...and the avoidance of systemic risk; to protect all market participants from fraudulent or other abusive sales practices and misuses of customer assets; and to promote responsible innovation and fair competition among...markets and market participants."[62]

The CFTC was created in 1974 under the Commodity Futures Trading Commission Act.[63] Originally operating primarily in the agricultural sector, the CFTC now regulates a more varied futures market ranging from energy and metals to interest rates and stock indexes.[64] The Commodity Exchange Act ("CEA") and the CFTC Regulations establish the regulatory framework for the CFTC to oversee derivatives clearing organizations, contract markets, commodity pool operators, and many other entities.[65] The CFTC's regulatory authority was further enhanced after the 2008 Financial Crisis with the Dodd-Frank Wall Street Reform and Consumer Protection Act ("Dodd-Frank Act"), granting the CFTC authority

---

[61] *Id*; 15 U.S.C. § 18.

[62] 7 U.S.C. § 5(b).

[63] U.S. Commodity Futures Trading Commission ("CFTC"), *Mission & Responsibilities*, https://www.cftc.gov/About/MissionResponsibilities/index.htm (last visited August 1, 2023).

[64] *Id.*

[65] 7 U.S.C. § 1; 17 C.F.R., Part I; CFTC, *Mission & Responsibilities*, https://www.cftc.gov/About/MissionResponsibilities/index.htm (August 1, 2023).

to regulate the more than $400 trillion swaps market.[66] The swaps market is approximately twelve times the size of the futures market.[67]

B. Structure

The CFTC consists of five Commissioners, the ten offices of the Chairman, and the agency's four operating units.[68] The five Commissioners are appointed by the President and confirmed by the Senate to serve five-year terms.[69] Only three of the five Commissioners can be of the same political party.[70] Additionally, the President designates one of the five Commissioners to serve as Chairman.[71]

C. Jurisdiction / Types of Cases

The Division of Enforcement ("DOE") has discretionary authority to investigate violations of the CEA and the CFTC Regulations.[72] The CFTC has sole jurisdiction over regulating futures and options on commodities.[73] A "commodity" includes any article, good, interest, or service "in which contracts for future delivery are presently or in the future dealt in."[74] The CFTC has the power to "administer oaths and affirmations, subpoena witnesses, compel their attendance, take evidence, and require the production of any

---

[66] CFTC, *The Commodity Exchange Act (CEA)*, https://www.cftc.gov/LawRegulation/CommodityExchangeAct/index.htm (last visited August 1, 2023)

[67] *Id.*

[68] CFTC, *Chairman & Commissioners*, https://www.cftc.gov/About/Commissioners/index.htm (last visited August 1, 2023).

[69] *Id*; 7 U.S.C. § 2(a)(2)(A).

[70] *Id.*

[71] *Id.*

[72] 17 C.F.R. § 11.2(a).

[73] 7 U.S.C. §§ 2(a)(1)(A), 2(c)(2).

[74] 7 U.S.C. § 2(a)(1)(A).

[records] that the [CFTC] deems relevant or material to the inquiry."[75]

Accordingly, the CFTC also retains the power to recommend administrative proceedings or sanctions as well as to refer a matter to the DOJ for prosecution.[76] The most common charges arising under the CFTC's jurisdiction are fraud, manipulation, manipulative and deceptive devices, disruptive trading, false reports and false statements.[77]

V. THE FINANCIAL INDUSTRY REGULATORY AUTHORITY ("FINRA")

A. History / Background

FINRA is a not-for-profit organization authorized by Congress to "protect America's interests by making sure the broker-dealer industry operates fairly and honestly."[78] FINRA accomplishes this by enforcing rules regarding all registered broker-dealer firms and registered brokers, investigating firm compliance, promoting market transparency, and providing education to investors.[79]

The Maloney Act of 1938, an amendment to the Securities Exchange Act of 1934, created FINRA.[80] The Maloney Act charged FINRA to "protect investors and the public interest, and remove the impediments to and perfect the mechanism of a free

---

[75] 7 U.S.C. § 9(5).

[76] CFTC, *Enforcement*, https://www.cftc.gov/LawRegulation/Enforcement/OfficeofDirectorEnforcement.html (last visited August 1, 2023).

[77] 7 U.S.C. § 6b(a); 7 U.S.C. § 9(3); 7 U.S.C. § 9(1); 7 U.S.C. § 6c(a)(5); 7 U.S.C. § 9(2).

[78] Financial Industry Regulatory Authority ("FINRA"), About FINRA, http://www.finra.org/about (last visited August 1, 2023).

[79] *Id.*

[80] FINRA, *FINRA Marks 75th Anniversary of Protecting Investors*, FINRA Marks 75th Anniversary of Protecting Investors (last updated September 18, 2014).

and open market."[81] In 2020, FINRA "brought 808 disciplinary actions against registered brokers and firms for unethical behavior, levied $57 million in fines, ordered $25.2 million in restitution to harmed investors, and referred more than 970 fraud and insider trading cases to the SEC and other agencies for litigation and/or prosecution." [82]

B.   Structure

FINRA's organization appears similar to other not-for-profit companies. FINRA is composed of a Board of Governors, executives, standing committees, advisory committees, regional committees, and ad hoc committees.[83] The Board of Governors governs body of the corporation, oversees management in the administration of FINRA's affairs and the promotion of FINRA's welfare, objectives and purposes.[84] The Board consists of 24 members – 10 of which are industry members, 13 are public members, and one is the Chief Executive Officer.[85] Additionally, FINRA has more than 3,600 employees across 19 offices.[86] FINRA supervises 624,000 brokers across the country, resulting in billions being processed every day in transactions.[87]

---

[81] *Id.*

[82] FINRA, *What We Do*, http://www.finra.org/about/what-we-do (last visited August 1, 2023).

[83] FINRA, *Governance*, http://www.finra.org/about/governance (last visited August 1, 2023).

[84] FINRA, *FINRA Board of Governors*, http://www.finra.org/about/finra-board-governors (last visited August 1, 2023).

[85] *Id.*

[86] FINRA, *Locations*, https://www.finra.org/about/locations (last visited August 1, 2023).

[87] FINRA, *About FINRA*, http://www.finra.org/about (last visited August 1, 2023).

C. Jurisdiction / Types of Cases

FINRA's jurisdiction only extends to broker-dealers and their affiliated persons and representatives.[88] Therefore, individuals no longer registered or associated with a broker-dealer are not under the jurisdiction of FINRA. However, FINRA's jurisdiction over these affiliated persons lasts for a two-year period following termination of their registration status.[89] Typical cases with FINRA involve securities fraud, failure to detect and prevent fraudulent schemes, and charging customers unfair and unreasonable prices and excessive markups.[90] Additionally, FINRA maintains the largest forum for dispute resolution for securities-related disputes between investors, securities firms, and individual brokers.[91] FINRA has 70 hearing locations and handles nearly 100 percent of arbitrations and mediations regarding securities.[92]

VI. ADDITIONAL ENFORCEMENT AGENCIES

A. Office of Foreign Assets Control ("OFAC")

OFAC is a branch of the U.S. Department of the Treasury and is responsible for administering and enforcing economic and trade sanctions based on U.S. foreign policy and national security goals.[93] OFAC was established in 1950 during the Korean War when President Truman sought to block all Chinese and North Korean

---

[88] 15 U.S.C. § 78o.

[89] FINRA, *Retention of Jurisdiction*, https://www.finra.org/rules-guidance/rulebooks/corporate-organization/retention-jurisdiction-0 (last visited August 1, 2023).

[90] FINRA, *What We Do*, http://www.finra.org/about/what-we-do (last visited August 1, 2023).

[91] *Id.*

[92] FINRA, *Arbitration & Mediation*, https://www.finra.org/arbitration-mediation/overview (last visited August 1, 2023).

[93] U.S. Department of the Treasury, *About Office of Foreign Assets Control*, https://www.treasury.gov/about/organizational-structure/offices/pages/office-of-foreign-assets-control.aspx (last visited August 1, 2023).

assets in the U.S.[94] OFAC is granted its powers pursuant to the President's national emergency powers as well as specific legislation.[95] OFAC's jurisdiction includes cases dealing with the proliferation of weapons of mass destruction, terrorists, and international narcotics trafficking.[96] OFAC imposes sanctions in the form of controls on transactions and freezing of assets under U.S. jurisdiction. Many of these sanctions are mandated by the United Nations and other international organizations; therefore, requiring close cooperation with other governments.[97]

B.   Financial Crimes Enforcement Network ("FinCEN")

FinCEN is another branch of the U.S. Department of the Treasury. FinCEN's mission is to "safeguard the financial system from illicit use, combat money laundering, and promote national security through the strategic use of financial authorities and the collection, analysis, and dissemination of financial intelligence."[98] FinCEN performs their mission by receiving and maintaining financial transactions data and using that data to cooperate with foreign and international organizations to enforce compliance.[99] FinCEN receives its power under the Currency and Financial Transactions Reporting Act of 1970 and the Bank Secrecy Act.[100]

---

[94] *Id.*

[95] *Id.*

[96] *Id.*

[97] *Id.*

[98] Financial Crimes Enforcement Network, *Mission*, https://www.fincen.gov/about/mission (last visited August 1, 2023).

[99] FinCEN, *What We Do*, https://www.fincen.gov/what-we-do (last visited August 1, 2023).

[100] *Id.*

Chapter 3

Introduction to Corporate Investigations

By: Claudius O. Sokenu[101]

Federal enforcement agencies and regulators have long abandoned their passive approach to investigations, under which they were content to mete out sanctions after discovering violations.[102] The government now proactively seeks out evidence of corporate misconduct, demanding that corporations act aggressively to identify and self-report potential misconduct. Federal agencies have instituted and formalized a clear carrot-and-stick approach promising lighter punishments for companies that cooperate by conducting thorough investigations early on and fully disclosing the results, while threatening harsh penalties for companies that fail on either count. The worst of these penalties include substantial civil and criminal penalties for corporate executives, and even the demise of the target corporation. Cooperation efforts that begin only when the government arrives on the scene are often insufficient to head off the harshest of sanctions. Accordingly,

---

[101] Claudius Sokenu is the EVP, Chief and Compliance Officer, & Corporate Secretary at Avantor. Until recently, Mr. Sokenu was the General Counsel, Corporate Secretary and Chief Administrative Officer at Unisys; a SVP, Deputy General Counsel, Global Head of Litigation, Labor & Employment, and Legal Operations, ad Chief of Staff to the General Counsel at Cognizant; Deputy General Counsel, Global Head of Litigation, Investigations, Ethics and Compliance at Andeavor; a Partner in the New York and Washington, DC offices of Shearman & Sterling LLP; and a former Senior Counsel with the Securities and Exchange Commission, Division of Enforcement, in Washington, DC.

[102] *See, e.g.*, Michael Piwowar, Acting Chairman, U.S. Securities and Exchange Comm'n, Remarks Before the 27th International Institute for Securities Market Growth and Development (Mar. 27, 2017), *available at* https://www.sec.gov/news/speech/remarks-27th-international-institute-securities-market-growth-and-development; Robert Khuzami, Director, Division of Enforcement, U.S. Securities and Exchange Comm'n, Remarks Before the Consumer Federation of America's Financial Services Conference (Dec. 1, 2011), *available at* https://www.sec.gov/news/speech/2011/spch120111rk.htm; Stephen M. Cutler, Remarks Before the District of Columbia Bar Association (Feb. 11, 2004), *available at* http://www.sec.gov/news/speech/spch021104smc.htm [hereinafter "Cutler Remarks"].

corporate counsel face substantial pressure to conduct corporate investigations earlier, dig deeper, and disclose more broadly than ever before. The inevitable result is that the corporate internal investigation is increasingly tied to both corporate punishment and corporate survival. The disclosures demanded by the government will almost always ensure the imposition of some sanctions, but the same disclosures, corporate counsel are told, will stave off the worst sanctions. Section I of this chapter describes the recent changes that have reshaped the corporate enforcement environment, and with it, the role of the corporate internal investigation. Section II details some of the benefits that have accrued to corporations that have successfully responded to this new enforcement environment, while Section III describes potential pitfalls.

I.   SOURCES OF PRESSURE TO CONDUCT INTERNAL INVESTIGATIONS

Since 2001, legislative and regulatory initiatives have combined to markedly increase incentives to conduct internal investigations when allegations of corporate malfeasance surface. These developments include the passage of the Sarbanes-Oxley Act of 2002 ("Sarbanes-Oxley"), the Dodd-Frank Wall Street Reform and Consumer Protection Act of 2010 ("Dodd-Frank"), the issuance of policy statements concerning cooperation by the Department of Justice ("DOJ" or "Justice Department"), the Securities and Exchange Commission (the "SEC" or the "Commission"), and follow-on undertakings on the part of the New York Stock Exchange ("NYSE" or the "Exchange") and the Financial Industry Regulatory Authority ("FINRA").

A.   The Sarbanes-Oxley Act of 2002

Sarbanes-Oxley,[103] passed in response to numerous corporate and accounting scandals that had diminished public trust in financial reporting practices, helped reshape the role of the internal investigation in at least two respects. First, § 404 of Sarbanes-

---

[103] Pub. L. No. 107-204, 116 Stat. 745 (codified at 15 U.S.C. § 7201 *et seq.*).

Oxley amended the audit requirements governing public companies. Second, § 307 of Sarbanes-Oxley imposed new reporting obligations on inside and outside counsel when evidence or suspicions of illegal activity are reported to its chief legal counsel.[104]

1. Section 404 of Sarbanes-Oxley

Under § 404 of Sarbanes-Oxley, a public company audit must include an assessment of the internal accounting controls the company employs to ensure the accuracy of its statements. Management is required, therefore, to acknowledge its responsibility for maintaining adequate internal controls,[105] including antifraud programs and a system to provide reasonable assurance that transactions are properly authorized and recorded.[106] In addition, Sarbanes-Oxley requires audit committees to establish procedures for (1) the receipt, retention, and treatment of complaints received regarding accounting, internal accounting controls, or auditing matters, and (2) the confidential, anonymous submission by employees of concerns regarding questionable accounting or auditing matters.[107] Audit committees have also become the primary overseer for investigations into financial reporting and accounting issues, charged with the oversight and responsibility for all aspects of the investigation, including the decision whether, when and how to report to the Commission.[108] Because the decision to conduct an internal investigation will often lead to the hiring of outside counsel,[109] Sarbanes-Oxley requires

[104] See, e.g., 15 U.S.C. § 78j-1.

[105] See 15 U.S.C. § 7262; Donald K. McConnell Jr. & George Y. Banks, *How Sarbanes-Oxley Will Change the Audit Process*, J. ACCOUNTANCY, Sept. 2003, available at http://www.aicpa.org/pubs/jofa/sep2003/mcconn.htm.

[106] See id.

[107] 15 U.S.C. § 78j-1(m)(4).

[108] 15 U.S.C. § 78j-l(b)(3); see also Michaela Dohoney & Win Minot, *The Financial Restatement Process*, SARBANES-OXLEY COMPLIANCE JOURNAL, April 19, 2006, available at http://www.s-ox.com/news/detail.cfm?articleID=1783.

[109] See id.

the audit committee to have authority to engage independent counsel and other advisers as it deems necessary to carry out its duties.[110]

2.   <u>Section 307 of Sarbanes-Oxley</u>

Section 307 of Sarbanes-Oxley provides additional impetus for internal investigations by requiring a company's attorneys to report suspicions of possible material violations of law up the corporate ladder to the company's chief legal officer and chief executive officer.[111] If, after conducting an appropriate investigation,[112] the chief legal officer believes that no violation has occurred, that determination must be presented to the attorney who initially reported the possible violation and the basis for that determination.[113] The reporting attorney must then decide whether the chief legal officer and CEO "have provided an appropriate response within a reasonable time."[114] If not, the reporting attorney must submit his or her evidence concerning the possible violation to (a) the audit committee, or, if the company has no audit committee, (b) the company's outside directors or, if there are no outside directors, (c) the entire board.[115] These requirements essentially require a company's chief legal officer to initiate a

---

[110] 15 U.S.C. § 78j-1(m)(5)-(6).

[111] *See* 17 C.F.R. § 205.3(b)(1) ("If an attorney, appearing and practicing before the Commission in the representation of an issuer, becomes aware of evidence of a material violation by the issuer or by any officer, director, employee, or agent of the issuer, the attorney shall report such evidence to the issuer's chief legal officer . . . or to both the issuer's chief legal officer and its chief executive officer."). Where appropriate, this evidence may also be reported directly to the company's legal compliance committee. *See* 17 C.F.R. § 205.3(c)(1).

[112] *See* 17 C.F.R. § 205.3(b)(2). Alternatively, the chief legal officer may refer the matter immediately to the company's legal compliance committee. *See* 17 C.F.R. § 205.3(b)(2).

[113] *See id.*

[114] *See* 17 C.F.R. § 205.3(b)(3).

[115] *See* 17 C.F.R. § 205.3(b)(3). The reporting attorney may also turn directly to these persons if he or she believes it would be futile to first turn to the chief legal officer and chief executive officer. *See* 17 C.F.R. § 205.3(b)(4).

formal investigatory process in response to any allegation of wrongdoing that comes to the attention of any in-house lawyer.

B. The Dodd-Frank Act of 2010

The Dodd–Frank Wall Street Reform and Consumer Protection Act ("Dodd–Frank")[116] puts additional pressure on companies to conduct internal investigations by further strengthening legal protections for whistle-blowers and providing them with financial incentives.

Building on Sarbanes–Oxley,[117] Dodd–Frank expanded protections against both direct and indirect retaliation[118] for whistle-blowers who reasonably believe[119] their employer engaged in a violation of federal securities law[120] and provide "original information" regarding such violation.[121] These include rules that prohibit a company from using confidentiality agreements to restrict its employees' ability to communicate with government authorities.[122] A whistle blower's initial disclosure need not

---

[116] Pub. L. No. 111-203 (2010).

[117] 18 USC § 1514A.

[118] *Compare* 15 U.S.C. § 78u-6(h)(1)(A) (Dodd–Frank covers all retaliation broadly) *with* 26 18 U.S.C. § 1514A(a) (Sarbanes–Oxley protects against prescribed formal categories retaliation).

[119] 18 U.S.C. § 1514A(a)(1); *see also Day v. Staples, Inc.*, 555 F.3d 42, 54 (1st Cir. 2009); *Ashmore v. Cgi Cgp.*, 138 F. Supp. 3d 329, 344 (S.D.N.Y. 2015) (that belief must be both subjectively held and objectively reasonably based).

[120] 15 U.S.C. § 78u-6(a)(6).

[121] US Securities and Exchange Commission Office of the Whistleblower, Frequently Asked Questions, https://www.sec.gov/about/offices/owb/owb-faq.shtml. Unlike Sarbanes-Oxley, Dodd–Frank's protections are not limited to any class of persons, such as employees at reporting companies.

[122] 17 C.F.R. § 240.21F-17 (2011) ("No person may take any action to impede an individual from communicating directly with the Commission staff about a possible securities law violation, including enforcing, or threatening to enforce, a confidentiality agreement . . . with respect to such communications."). This rule has been broadly interpreted by the SEC and has resulted in several recent SEC enforcement actions. *See* Exchange Act Release No. 74619; *see also In the Matter of KBR, Inc.*, Admin. Proc. 3-16466 (charging military and industrial contractor KBR, Inc. with violating the whistleblower protection rule), *available at* https://www.sec.gov/litigation/admin/2015/34-74619.pdf.

necessarily be to the SEC to enjoy the benefits of Dodd-Frank,[123] as its whistle-blower protections may attach even when the disclosure is purely internal.[124]

The Dodd-Frank Act also provides financial incentives for whistle-blowers with its so-called "bounty-hunter" provision. The SEC pays monetary awards to individuals that meet the following criteria:[125] The individual must "voluntarily"[126] provide "original information"[127] that "leads to"[128] an enforcement action in which over a million dollars in sanctions is ordered,[129] and the individual

---

[123] The date of a whistleblower's initial internal report will be treated as the date of disclosure to the SEC, provided the whistleblower makes a report to the SEC within 120 days of the internal report. 17 C.F.R. § 240.21F-4(b)(7).

[124] The SEC has taken the position that internal whistleblowers that have not reported outside of the company are covered by Dodd-Frank's whistleblower protections, but courts are split. *See* Whistleblower Provisions of § 21F of the Securities Exchange Act of 1934, Exchange Act Release No. 34-64545 (May 25, 2011) (DFA Implementation Release) at 16-17; *compare Berman v. Neo@Ogilvy LLC*, 801 F.3d 145, 146 (2d Cir. 2015) (deference to the SEC's interpretive rule granting whistleblower status to internally reporting employees) *with Asadi v. GE Energy (USA), LLC*, 720 F.3d 620, 625 (5th Cir. 2013) (internal whistleblowers are not protected) *and Wagner v. Bank of Am. Corp.*, 2013 WL 3786643, at *5 (D. Colo. 19 July 2013) *aff'd*, 571 F. App'x 698 (10th Cir. 2014) (same).

[125] 15 U.S.C. §§ 78u-6(j), 78u-7(a) (2012); SEC Rules Implementing the Whistleblower Provisions of § 21F of Securities Exchange Act of 1934, SEC Release No. 34-64545, 76 Fed. Reg. 34,300, 34,307 (May 25, 2011).

[126] 17 C.F.R. § 240.21F-4(a)(1)–(2) (2013). Whistleblower's submission must be made before the SEC, an Attorney General, the Public Company Accounting Oversight Board or other regulatory entity requests information related to the subject matter of the submission directly from the whistleblower or the whistleblower's representative. The mere fact that a whistleblower's employer received a request from one of these authorities related to the whistleblower's subsequent submission does not, however, render the submission involuntary.

[127] U.S. Securities and Exchange Commission Office of the Whistleblower, Frequently Asked Questions, https://www.sec.gov/about/offices/owb/owb-faq.shtml. Unlike Sarbanes–Oxley, Dodd–Frank's protections are not limited to any class of persons, such as employees at reporting companies.

[128] 17 C.F.R. § 240.21F-4(c)(1) ("based in whole or in part on conduct that was the subject of [the] original information.").

[129] *See* 15 U.S.C. § 78u-6. Dodd-Frank also imposed a similar regime under the Commodity Exchange Act. *See* 7 U.S.C. § 26. SEC may aggregate the monetary

must not otherwise be ineligible for an award (for example, by having obtained the information illegally, being an employee of a government regulator or a family member of one, or being convicted of a related criminal violation).[130] Awards may range from 10-30% of the amount collected.[131]

C. The SEC's Statements on Cooperation

1. The Seaboard Report

On October 23, 2001, the SEC issued the Seaboard Report, which outlined some of the criteria that it would consider in deciding whether to bring an enforcement action against a company.[132] The report identified four broad factors that influence the SEC's evaluation of a company's cooperation: (i) self-policing prior to the discovery of the misconduct, including the establishment of effective compliance procedures and an appropriate tone with respect to compliance at the top of the organization; (ii) self-reporting of misconduct upon discovery, including conducting a thorough review of the nature, extent, origins and consequences of the misconduct, and prompt, complete, and effective disclosure to the public, regulators, and self-regulatory organizations; (iii) remediation, including the dismissal or appropriate discipline of individual wrongdoers, the modification of internal controls and compliance procedures to prevent recurrence, and the compensation of those adversely affected; and (iv) cooperation

---

sanctions in two or more separately captioned SEC actions, if the proceedings arise from the "same nucleus of operative facts." 17 C.F.R. §§ 240.21F-4(c)(2), 240.21F-4(d)(1).

[130] 17 C.F.R. §§ 240.21F-4(c)(3), 240.21F-8(c)(1)–(7).

[131] See https://www.sec.gov/whistleblower/; see also SEC Rel. No. 34-63237 at 58-59 ("foreign officials" not eligible).

[132] Report of Investigation Pursuant to § 21(a) of the Securities Exchange Act of 1934 and Commission Statement on the Relationship of Cooperation to Agency Enforcement Decisions, Rel. No. 34-44969 (Oct. 23, 2001), available at http://www.sec.gov/litigation/investreport/34-44969.htm [hereinafter "Seaboard Report"]. The Seaboard Report outlined in detail the steps taken by Seaboard Corporation, the company that was the subject of the SEC's investigation, after it discovered that it may have violated the federal securities laws.

with law enforcement authorities, including providing the Commission staff with all information relevant to the underlying violations and the company's remedial efforts.[133]

The Commission indicated that where a company takes the steps outlined in the Seaboard Report, it may "credit" the company for its remedial efforts. Such "credit for cooperative behavior," the Commission says, "may range from the extraordinary step of taking no enforcement action at all to bringing reduced charges, seeking lighter sanctions, or including mitigating language in documents the Commission uses to announce and resolve enforcement actions."[134]

---

[133] Press Release, SEC Issues Report of Investigation and Statement Setting Forth Framework for Evaluating Cooperation in Exercising Prosecutorial Discretion (Oct. 23, 2001), *available at* http://www.sec.gov/news/headlines/prosdiscretion.htm. In addition to the four broad factors outlined above, the Seaboard Report lists thirteen additional criteria that the Commission will consider in deciding whether to recommend enforcement action against a company. These criteria are: (i) the nature of the misconduct; (ii) the way in which the misconduct arose; (iii) the locus of the misconduct within the organization; (iv) the duration of the misconduct; (v) the level of harm inflicted upon investors and other corporate constituencies, and whether the company's share price dropped significantly upon its disclosure; (vi) the manner in which the misconduct was detected, and who uncovered it; (vii) the rapidity of the company's post-discovery response; (viii) the steps taken by the company upon learning of the misconduct; (ix) the processes followed by the company in resolving the issues raised by its discovery; (x) whether the company fully and expeditiously committed to learning the truth; (xi) whether the company promptly reported the results of its review to the SEC staff and provided sufficient documentation reflecting its response to the situation; (xii) whether there are assurances that the misconduct is unlikely to recur; and (xiii) whether the company in which the misconduct occurred has undergone a fundamental corporate change such as a merger or bankruptcy reorganization.

[134] *See In re Baker Hughes Inc.*, Rel. No. 34-44784 (Sept. 12, 2001), for an example of one of the first enforcement actions in which the Commission included mitigating language in the document used to announce and resolve the action. *See also* Press Release, SEC Charges Texas-Based Layne Christensen Company with FCPA Violations, Rel. No. 2014-240 (Oct. 27, 2014) (crediting cooperation in determining penalties); *In the Matter of PTC Inc.*, Admin Proc. File No. 3-17118 (Feb. 16, 2016) (order instituting cease-and-desist proceedings), *available at* https://www.sec.gov/litigation/admin/2016/34-77145.pdf (crediting cooperation in determining penalties); Press Rel. No. 2013-174, SEC Charges Former Vice President of Investor Relations With Violating Fair Disclosure Rules

The Seaboard Report demystifies the SEC's decision-making process and provides companies facing potential enforcement problems with new confidence to actively seek out the Commission and self-report. Acknowledging as much, then-Director of Enforcement Stephen Cutler said the Commission "will bring in more cases and use fewer resources" thereby offering "more protection for investors."[135] The SEC's posture after the Seaboard Report can be viewed as encouraging collaboration between the public and private sectors in promoting and enhancing the securities markets.

2.   The Penalties Statement

On January 4, 2006, in the aftermath of vociferous complaints by two Republican commissioners, the business community, and the defense bar about multi-million dollar penalties, the Commission took the unusual step of issuing a press release announcing the principles that it will consider when determining whether, and to

---

(Sept. 6, 2013) (noting declination as to a public issuer due to its cultivation of an environment of compliance as well as its self-reporting, remediation, and cooperation), *available at* http://www.sec.gov/News/PressRelease/Detail/PressRelease/1370539799034; *compare* Complaint, *SEC v. Raffle et al.*, Case No. 11-Civ.-540 (W.D. Tex. June 27, 2011) (charging certain former executives with aiding and abetting violations by an issuer of the antifraud provisions), *available at* http://www.sec.gov/litigation/complaints/2011/comp22027.pdf, *with* Order Instituting Cease-and-Desist Proceedings, *In re Arthrocare Corp.*, Sec. Exch. Act. Rel. No. 63833 (Feb. 9, 2011) (ordering the issuer to cease and desist from violations of books and records and other provisions, and noting that the issuer's remedial acts and cooperation were taken into account in determining to accept its offer to settle to such charges), *available at* https://www.sec.gov/litigation/admin/2011/34-63883.pdf.

[135] Press Release, Statement of the Securities and Exchange Commission Concerning Financial Penalties (Jan. 4, 2006), *available at* http://www.sec.gov.news/press/2006-4.htm [hereinafter "Penalties Statement"]; *see also* Daniel M. Gallagher, Remarks at Columbia Law School Conference (Hot Topics: Leading Current Issues in Securities Regulation and Enforcement) (Nov. 15, 2013), *available at* https//www.sec.gov/news/speech/2013-spch111513dmg (discussing the enduring importance of the Penalties Statement).

what extent, such penalties should be imposed (the "Penalties Statement").[136]

In his speech announcing the Penalties Statement, former Chairman Christopher Cox emphasized that it is the Commission's "intention that these principles will establish objective standards that will provide the maximum degree of investor protection."[137]

This Penalties Statement outlined two principal factors that it will take into account in deciding whether to impose monetary penalties, along with seven other secondary factors.[138] The first is the presence or absence of a direct benefit to the corporation as a result of the violation.[139] According to the Commission, the "fact that a corporation has received a direct and material benefit from the offense, for example through reduced expenses or increased revenue, weighs in support of the imposition of a [monetary] penalty. Similarly, a monetary penalty would be appropriate if the issuer is in any other way 'unjustly enriched,'"[140] or where shareholders have "received an improper benefit as a result of the violation."[141] At the other end of the continuum lie cases in which the affected company's shareholders are the "principal victims of the [federal] securities law violation." In the Commission's view,

---

[136] Press Release, Statement of the Securities and Exchange Commission Concerning Financial Penalties (Jan. 4, 2006), *available at* http://www.sec.gov/news/press/2006-4.htm [hereinafter "Penalties Statement"]; *see also* Daniel M. Gallagher, Remarks at Columbia Law School Conference (Hot Topics: Leading Current Issues in Securities Regulation and Enforcement) (Nov. 15, 2013), *available at* https://www.sec.gov/news/speech/2013-spch111513dmg (discussing the enduring importance of the Penalties Statement).

[137] *See* Christopher Cox, Chairman, U.S. Securities and Exchange Comm'n, Statement of Chairman Cox Concerning Objective Standards for Corporate Penalties (Jan. 4, 2006), *available at* http://www.sec.gov/news/speech/spch010406cc.htm.

[138] *See generally* Penalties Statement, *supra* n.136.

[139] *Id.*

[140] *Id.*

[141] *Id.*

the case for the imposition of a monetary penalty is at its weakest in these circumstances.[142]

The second principal factor is the degree to which the penalty will recompense or further harm the injured shareholders.[143] With respect to this factor, the Commission stated that, notwithstanding that the "imposition of a penalty on the corporation itself carries with it the risk that shareholders who are innocent of the violation will nonetheless bear the burden of the penalty," in certain cases, it is appropriate to seek a monetary penalty because the penalty may be "used as a source of funds to recompense the injury suffered by victims of the [federal] securities law violations."[144] However, the "likelihood a corporate penalty will unfairly injure investors, the corporation, or third parties weighs against its use as a sanction."[145] In other words, "[b]ecause the protection of innocent investors is a principal objective of the [federal] securities laws," the Commission will not seek to impose a monetary penalty on an issuer where such a penalty is likely to disproportionately harm innocent investors.[146]

Leaning heavily on the Commission's statutory authority to seek monetary penalties, the Penalties Statement outlined seven other factors that will influence its decision to impose monetary penalties in settled enforcement actions. Two of these factors bear directly on whether a company should decide to conduct an internal investigation.[147] First, echoing the Seaboard Report, the

---

[142] *Id.*

[143] Penalties Statement, *supra* n.136.

[144] *Id.*

[145] Penalties Statement, *supra* n.136.

[146] *Id.*

[147] The other five secondary factors identified by the Commission were: (1) the need to deter the particular type of offense charged and the capacity of a monetary penalty to achieve that result; (2) the extent of injury to innocent parties; (3) whether the allegedly unlawful conduct was widespread, or instead committed by a small group of corporate actors; (4) the level of intent on the part of the responsible individuals; and (5) the difficulty of detecting the unlawful behavior. *Id.*

Commission stated that it will look to whether the issuer took remedial steps.[148] Second, again drawing on the principles articulated in the Seaboard Report, the Commission stated that when "[federal] securities law violations are discovered, it is incumbent upon management to report them to the Commission and to other appropriate law enforcement authorities."[149]

There has been some question as to how closely the Commission adhered to the Penalties Statement during the Obama administration. While Obama-era Chairwoman Mary Jo White had praised the Penalties Statement shortly after taking office as providing "a useful, non-exclusive list of factors that may guide a Commissioner's consideration of corporate penalties," she emphasized that it is "not a binding policy" and that "each Commissioner has the discretion... to reach his or her own judgment on whether a corporate penalty is appropriate and how high it should be."[150] Commissioner Michael S. Piwowar, a Republican, expressed concern that the Commission's staff has increasingly disregarded the Penalties Statement, and that such "fail[ure] to follow our own publicly-announced framework for monetary penalties" risked depriving parties of "appropriate due process."[151]

3. The Enforcement Cooperation Initiative

On January 13, 2010, the Commission's then-Director of Enforcement, Robert Khuzami, announced the "Enforcement Cooperation Initiative," a set of policies designed to encourage

---

[148] Penalties Statement, *supra* n.136; *see also* Seaboard Report, *supra* n.132; Richard A. Spehr & Claudius O. Sokenu, *SEC Self-Policing Policy Presents Benefits and Pitfalls*, 7 ANDREWS SEC. LIT. & REG. REP. 17 (Feb. 27, 2002).

[149] *Id.*

[150] Mary Jo White, Chairwoman, Securities and Exchange Commission, Speech at Council of Institutional Investors fall conference in Chicago, IL (Sept. 26, 2013), *available at* https://www.sec.gov/News/Speech/Detail/Speech/1370539841202.

[151] Michael S. Piwowar, Commissioner, Securities and Exchange Commission, Remarks to the Securities Enforcement Forum 2014, Washington, D.C. (Oct. 14, 2014), *available at* https://www.sec.gov/News/Speech/Detail/Speech/1370543156675.

"individuals and companies to fully and truthfully cooperate and assist with SEC investigations and enforcement actions."[152] As part of the initiative, the Enforcement Division amended its enforcement manual to give its staff more authority to reward companies and individuals who provide substantial cooperation with more lenient treatment. These incentives, which mirror incentives used by the Justice Department, include: (a) "cooperation agreements," by which the Enforcement Division agrees to recommend that a cooperator receive credit if it provides "substantial assistance" to an investigation; (b) "deferred prosecution agreements," under which the Commission agrees to forego an enforcement action if the cooperating party agrees "to cooperate fully and truthfully and to comply with express prohibitions and undertakings during a period of deferred prosecution"; and (c) "non-prosecution agreements," under which the Commission agrees to not initiate an enforcement action if the cooperate agrees to "cooperate fully and truthfully and comply with express undertakings."[153] The Commission also simplified its process for submitting witness immunity requests to the Justice Department for witnesses "who have the capacity to assist in its investigations and related enforcement actions."[154]

In addition to the new tools given to its staff, the Cooperation Initiative explained the factors it would consider in deciding to reward cooperation by individuals. Drawing off of the Seaboard Report, which, as explained above, outlines the factors considered in evaluating cooperation by companies, the Cooperation Initiative identifies four factors by which the Commission evaluates cooperation by individuals, namely: (a) the assistance provided by the cooperator; (b) the importance of the underlying matter in which the individual cooperated; (c) the societal interest in ensuring that the individual is held accountable for his misconduct;

---

[152] Press Release, U.S. Securities and Exchange Comm'n, SEC Announces Initiative to Encourage Individuals and Companies to Cooperate and Assist in Investigations (Jan. 13, 2010), *available at* https://www.sec.gov/news/press/2010/2010-6.htm.

[153] *Id.*

[154] *Id.*

and (d) the appropriateness of cooperation credit based upon the cooperator's risk profile.[155]

D. Federal Sentencing Guidelines

The Federal Sentencing Guidelines (the "Guidelines")—like the Seaboard Report, and the NYSE and NASD guidelines—place significant emphasis on cooperation and compliance programs in determining the penalties that corporations will face for violations of federal criminal laws.[156] Section 8B2.1, entitled "Effective Compliance and Ethics Program," provides that, to have a compliance and ethics program that will factor favorably into a sentencing decision, an organization shall "[e]xercise due diligence to prevent and detect criminal conduct," and promote a culture that encourages ethical conduct and compliance with the law.[157] Section 8B2.1(b) identifies in detail the minimum requirements for an effective compliance program.[158]

Section 8C2.5, entitled "Culpability Score," provides a methodology that district courts must consider in deciding whether to impose a fine on a corporation,[159] and provides for reduced penalties for companies that timely self-report wrongdoing,[160] fully cooperate,[161] and/or have effective compliance programs.[162] Just as the Guidelines reward good behavior, however, they also punish

---

[155] Id.

[156] See U.S. Sentencing Comm'n, U.S. SENTENCING GUIDELINES MANUAL, § 8B2.1 (2004).

[157] Id. § 8C2.1.

[158] See id. § 8C2.1(b).

[159] See id. § 8C2.5.

[160] Id. § 8C2.5(g)(1).

[161] Id. § 8C2.5(g)(2). The application notes clarify that to qualify for a reduction for self-reporting or cooperation under Section 8C2.5(g)(1) or (g)(2), cooperation must be "timely and thorough." Id. § 8C2.5 cmt. n.12.

[162] Id. § 8C2.5(f).

corporations found to have obstructed justice and impeded a government investigation.[163]

While the Guidelines no longer require a company to waive its attorney-client privilege to receive a culpability reduction under § 8C2.5(g),[164] in practice, corporations still face tremendous pressure to waive privilege in connection with federal criminal investigations, as described more fully below.

E.   The New York Stock Exchange

On September 14, 2005, the NYSE issued Information Memo 05-65 (the "Cooperation Memorandum").[165] The Cooperation Memorandum not only makes clear that cooperation with the Exchange is an obligation of member firms, but that only a record of "proactive and exceptional" cooperation, such as, *inter alia*, the waiver of attorney-client privilege, can serve to mitigate sanctions.[166]

---

[163] *See id.* § 8C2.5(e).

[164] *Id.* § 8C2.5(g), cmt. n.12 (Nov. 2004). The waiver requirement had appeared for the first time just two years earlier on the tails of the Seaboard Report and the Thompson Memorandum. *See infra* Part I.F (discussing the Thompson Memorandum).

[165] *See* Memorandum from Susan Merrill, Exec. V.P., NYSE Div. of Enforcement, to All Members, Member Orgs. and COOs, NYSE Info. Memo No. 05-65 (Sept. 14, 2005), *available at* http://apps.nyse.com/commdata/PubInfoMemos.nsf/AllPublishedInfoMemosNyse Com/85256FCB005E19E88525707C004C6DE0/$FILE/Microsoft%20Word%20-%20Document%20in%2005-65.pdf [hereinafter "Cooperation Memorandum"].

[166] *Id.* at 3. *See also* Memorandum from Susan Merrill, NYSE Div. of Enforcement, to All Members, Member Orgs. and COOs, NYSE Information Memo 05-77, at 4 (Oct. 7, 2005) ("No additional credit will be given for doing what is required by Exchange Rules. However, where a respondent can demonstrate a record of disclosure and cooperation that is proactive and exceptional, the Enforcement Division will, in appropriate circumstances, give this factor weight in its consideration of a sanction. Conversely, a respondent's failure to cooperate fully and completely will support an increased sanction."), *available at* http://apps.nyse.com/commdata/PubInfoMemos.nsf/AllPublishedInfoMemosNyse

The NYSE has made it abundantly clear that it considers waiver to be the centerpiece of cooperation, and that any corporation facing an NYSE investigation must be prepared to waive its privilege or find an alternative way to disclose all of the information that NYSE investigators might find relevant. Corporations that do not cooperate in these ways will risk severe sanctions for their failure to comply with the NYSE's expectations.

F.   Financial Industry Regulatory Authority

Not to be outdone, FINRA also announced in 2008 that it will place significant emphasis on a member firm's level of cooperation in determining whether, and to what extent, sanctions will be levied, and listed four factors it would take into account in deciding to grant cooperation credit, including: (1) self-reporting before regulators are aware of the issue; (2) extraordinary steps to correct deficient procedures and systems; (3) extraordinary remediation to customers; and (4) providing substantial assistance to FINRA's investigation.[167] For self-reporting to count, it must be

---

Com/85256FCB005E19E88525709200068314A/$FILE/Microsoft%20Word%20-%20Document%20in%2005-77.pdf.

https://www.finra.org/sites/default/files/NoticeDocument/p117452.pdf.

[167] *Id.* at 2.

[167] *Id.*

[167] *Id.* at 2–3.

[167] *Id.* at 3–4. FINRA's guidance goes on to note that "[w]hen on-going violative conduct has numerous participants yet is difficult to uncover, collaboration with the regulator can have a dramatic impact on regulatory consequences. This can include apprising FINRA of wrongdoing beyond the scope of the original investigation and alerting staff to industrywide, systemic problems. When a firm or individual brings to the regulator's attention a pattern or practice of which the regulator was unaware, or is the first to come forward to cooperate in a widespread, industry-wide investigation and thereby assists the regulator in understanding, scoping and resolving the investigation, this assistance should be credited." *Id.*

[167] *See* Larry D. Thompson, Deputy Attorney General, Principles of Federal Prosecution of Business Organizations (Jan. 20, 2003) ("Thompson Memorandum"), *available at* http://www.usdoj.gov/dag/cftf/corporate_guidelines.htm.

"prompt, detailed, complete and straightforward... beyond that which is otherwise required to be reported pursuant to regulatory reporting requirements."[168] Correcting deficient procedures may garner cooperation credit if done *before* detection by FINRA, though post-detection corrections may be credited "in appropriate circumstances."[169] FINRA expects remediation efforts to "promptly and immediately identify[] injured customers and make such investors whole," as well as "proactively identif[y] and provide[ ] restitution to customers that goes beyond the universe of customers and transactions covered by the staff's investigation."[170] Finally, FINRA will credit "substantial assistance" with its investigation if the firm provides access to individuals or documents outside FINRA's jurisdiction, undertakes "comprehensive internal investigations" and shares findings with FINRA, and helps FINRA "to uncover substantial industry wrongdoing."[171]

---

[167] *See* Mem. From Dep. Att'y Gen. Paul J. McNulty to Heads of Dep't Components and U.S. Att'ys, *Principles of Federal Prosecution of Business Organizations* 1-2 (Dec. 12, 2006) ("McNulty Memorandum"), *available at* https://www.justice.gov/sites/default/files/dag/legacy/2007/07/05/mcnulty_memo.pdf.

[167] The Thompson Memorandum's Effect on the Right to Counsel in Corporate Investigations: Hearing Before the United States Senate Committee on the Judiciary, 109th Cong. (Sept. 12, 2006) [hereinafter "Senate Hearings"]

[167] FINRA Regulatory Notice 08-70, FINRA Investigations: FINRA Provides Guidance Regarding Credit for Extraordinary Cooperation (Nov. 2008), *available at* https://www.finra.org/sites/default/files/NoticeDocument/p117452.pdf.

[168] *Id.* at 2.

[169] *Id.*

[170] *Id.* at 2–3.

[171] *Id.* at 3–4. FINRA's guidance goes on to note that "[w]hen on-going violative conduct has numerous participants yet is difficult to uncover, collaboration with the regulator can have a dramatic impact on regulatory consequences. This can include apprising FINRA of wrongdoing beyond the scope of the original investigation and alerting staff to industrywide, systemic problems. When a firm or individual brings to the regulator's attention a pattern or practice of which the regulator was unaware, or is the first to come forward to cooperate in a widespread, industry-wide investigation and thereby assists the regulator in

FINRA's regime of cooperation mirrors that of the NYSE and the SEC. Since both the NYSE and FINRA are regulated by the SEC, it is no surprise that both thought it reasonable and appropriate to follow in the footsteps of the SEC.

G.   Filip and Yates Memoranda

Historically, the DOJ and SEC have granted increased cooperation "credit" to companies that waive attorney-client privilege. The Justice Department formalized this policy in the Thompson Memorandum of 2003[172] and revised it in the McNulty Memorandum of 2006.[173] Both the Thompson and McNulty Memorandums have been widely criticized as creating a coercive "culture of waiver," in which "governmental agencies believe it is reasonable and appropriate to expect a corporation under investigation to broadly waive [its] attorney client privilege."[174] In response to this criticism, the Justice Department withdrew these guidelines in 2008 and replaced them with the Principles of

---

understanding, scoping and resolving the investigation, this assistance should be credited." *Id.*

[172] *See* Larry D. Thompson, Deputy Attorney General, Principles of Federal Prosecution of Business Organizations (Jan. 20, 2003) ("Thompson Memorandum"), *available at* http://www.usdoj.gov/dag/cftf/corporate_guidelines.htm.

[173] *See* Mem. From Dep. Att'y Gen. Paul J. McNulty to Heads of Dep't Components and U.S. Att'ys, *Principles of Federal Prosecution of Business Organizations* 1-2 (Dec. 12, 2006) ("McNulty Memorandum"), *available at* https://www.justice.gov/sites/default/files/dag/legacy/2007/07/05/mcnulty_memo.pdf.

[174] The Thompson Memorandum's Effect on the Right to Counsel in Corporate Investigations: Hearing Before the United States Senate Committee on the Judiciary, 109th Cong. (Sept. 12, 2006) [hereinafter "Senate Hearings"] (testimony of Edwin Meese III). A related criticism was that the emphasis placed on privilege waiver threatened to create a counterproductive climate of distrust between corporations and their employees, and could undermine companies' internal compliance programs and procedures. As noted by the ABA, "[b]ecause the effectiveness of these internal mechanisms depends in large part on the ability of the individuals with knowledge to speak candidly and confidentially with lawyers, any attempt to require routine waiver of attorney-client and work product protections will seriously undermine systems that are crucial to compliance and have worked well." Id. (testimony of Karen J. Mathis).

Federal Prosecution of Business Organizations, also known as the "Filip Memorandum" after then-Deputy Attorney General Mark R. Filip.[175] Under the Filip Memorandum, a company's "[e]ligibility for cooperation credit is not predicated upon waiver of attorney-client privilege or work product protection."[176] Instead, the most important factor DOJ will consider is "disclosure of the relevant facts concerning [the alleged] misconduct."[177] Thus, DOJ may ask the corporation to disclose all relevant facts learned through an internal investigation, including "factual information acquired through [witness] interviews," but the company need not produce the interview notes or memoranda themselves,[178] nor is it expected to disclose legal advice.[179]

In 2015, the Justice Department revised and replaced the Filip Memorandum with new guidelines for "Individual Accountability for Corporate Wrongdoing," also known as the Yates Memorandum, after then-Deputy Attorney General Sally Yates, who authored the memorandum.[180] The Yates Memorandum

---

[175] Memorandum from Mark R. Filip, Deputy Att'y Gen., U.S. Dep't of Justice, to Heads of Department Components and United States Attorneys, regarding Principles of Federal Prosecution of Business Organizations (Aug. 28, 2008) ("Filip Memorandum"), *available at* https://www.justice.gov/sites/default/files/dag/legacy/2008/11/03/dag-memo-08282008.pdf.

[176] *Id.* at 9.

[177] *Id.*

[178] *Id.* at 10 n.3.

[179] *Id.* at 11–12 ("Separate from (and usually preceding) the fact-gathering process in an internal investigation, a corporation, through its officers, employees, directors, or others, may have consulted with corporate counsel regarding or in a manner that concerns the legal implications of the putative misconduct at issue. Communications of this sort, which are both independent of the fact-gathering component of an internal investigation and made for the purpose of seeking or dispensing legal advice, lie at the core of the attorney-client privilege. . . . Except [where an advice of counsel defense is at issue or the crime-fraud exception to privilege applies], a corporation need not disclose and prosecutors may not request the disclosure of such communications as a condition for the corporation's eligibility to receive cooperation credit.").

[180] Memorandum from Sally Quillian Yates, Deputy Att'y Gen., U.S. Dep't of Justice, to Heads of Department Components and United States Attorneys,

memorialized DOJ's new focus on targeting individuals for prosecution for corporate wrongdoing and emphasized that a corporation's eligibility for cooperation credit will depend on the assistance it provides to DOJ in its investigation of individual executives and employees. While the Filip Memorandum noted that assistance with identifying individual wrongdoers is just one factor in deciding whether to prosecute a corporation,[181] the Yates Memorandum makes it a prerequisite. In other words, "to be eligible for any credit for cooperation, [a] company must identify all individuals involved in or responsible for the misconduct at issue."[182] Moreover, "[i]f a company seeking cooperation credit declines to learn of such facts or to provide the [Justice] Department with complete factual information about individual wrongdoers, its cooperation will not be considered a mitigating factor."[183] The emphasis on disclosing "all relevant facts" and identifying culpable individuals raises the question of whether a company can satisfy DOJ without waiving privilege or work-product production.

There is some scepticism over whether the Yates Memorandum's emphasis on pushing companies to implicate individuals will lead to more prosecutions of individual executives and employees. Yate's immediate predecessor, former Deputy Attorney General James Cole, criticized the Yates Memorandum as "impractical" and not based on "reality."[184] Cole noted that emphasizing a company's assistance with prosecuting individuals is nothing new, but suggested that individual prosecutions have been rare because it is "very difficult" to find evidence that a single individual

---

regarding Individual Accountability for Corporate Wrongdoing (Sept. 9, 2015) ("Yates Memorandum"), *available at* https://www.justice.gov/dag/file/769036/download.

[181] Filip Memorandum, *supra* n.175, at 4.

[182] Yates Memorandum, *supra* n.80, at 3.

[183] *Id.*

[184] ABA News, *Former deputy AG James Cole says DOJ's new white-collar crime policy is 'impractical'* (Nov. 24, 2015), *available at* http://www.americanbar.org/news/abanews/aba-news-archives/2015/11/former_deputy_agjam.html.

possessed the "requisite intent."[185] Cole believed the practical consequences of the Yates Memorandum would not be more individual prosecutions, but longer, more expensive investigations, in which employees are less willing to cooperate with the company's investigation.[186]

II. THE BENEFITS OF CONDUCTING CORPORATE INTERNAL INVESTIGATIONS

In response to the demands described above by federal prosecutors, civil enforcement agencies and self-regulatory organizations, many corporations now go to great lengths to take whatever steps they believe are necessary to avoid indictment and minimize penalties, including waiving privilege, requiring employees to make themselves accessible to enforcement agencies, providing the results of internal investigations and interviews, and revamping compliance programs.[187] In return, companies might

---

[185] *Id.*

[186] *Id.*

[187] *See, e.g., Stein I*, 435 F. Supp. 2d 330 (chronicling the numerous actions taken by KPMG in its efforts to avoid indictment); Deferred Prosecution Agreement, *United States v. AIG-FP Pagic Equity Holding Corp.* (W.D. Pa. filed Nov. 30, 2004) [hereinafter "AIG Agreement"]; Deferred Prosecution Agreement, *United States v. Computer Assocs. Int'l*, Cr. No. 04-837 (ILG) (E.D.N.Y. filed Sept. 24, 2004) [hereinafter "CA Agreement"]; Deferred Prosecution Agreement, *United States v. Am. Online, Inc.*, Crim. No. 1:04 M 1133 (E.D. Va. filed Dec. 15, 2004) [hereinafter "AOL Agreement"]; Siobhan Hughes, *Prudential Will Pay $600 Million*, WALL ST. J., Aug. 29, 2006, at C11; Press Release, DOJ, Schnitzer Steel Industries Inc.'s Subsidiary Pleads Guilty to Foreign Bribes and Agrees to Pay a $7.5 Million Criminal Fine (Oct. 16, 2006), *available at* http://www.usdoj.gov/criminal/press_room/press_releases/2006_4809_10-16-06schnitzerfraud.pdf [hereinafter "Schnitzer Press Release"]; Press Release, DOJ, Bristol-Myers Squibb Charged with Conspiring to Commit Securities Fraud; Prosecution Deferred for Two Years (June 15, 2005), *available at* http://www.usdoj.gov/usao/nj/press/files/bms0615_r.htm; Press Release, DOJ, PNC ICLC Corp. Enters into Deferred Prosecution Agreement with the United States (June 2, 2003), *available at* http://www.usdoj.gov/opa/pr/2003/June/03_crm_329.htm [hereinafter "PNC Press Release"]; U.S. District Attorney's Office, Eastern District of New York, "The Bank of New York Resolves Parallel Criminal Investigations Through Non-Prosecution Agreement With The United States" (Nov. 8, 2005), *available at* http://www.justice.gov/usao/nye//pr/2005/2005nov08.html.

hope for leniency in the form of reduced fines, deferrals of prosecution,[188] or non-prosecution agreements.[189]

In cases of extraordinary cooperation, the government declines to take any action against a company, seeking no guilty plea, deferred prosecution agreement, non-prosecution agreement, settlement or fine. For example, in 2015, the DOJ declined to prosecute PetroTiger Ltd., a British Virgin Islands oil and gas company, for alleged violations of the Foreign Corrupt Practices Act ("FCPA") because it "self-reported and fully cooperated" with DOJ's investigation, made sure that DOJ received "all relevant information... quickly," and the company's cooperation helped

---

[188] In a typical deferred prosecution agreement, the government files a criminal complaint against the corporation, and the corporation accepts and acknowledges responsibility for the allegedly unlawful conduct. Based on the corporation's acceptance of responsibility, and as long as the corporation complies with all of the obligations set forth in the deferred prosecution agreement – which can include, *inter alia*, the payment of fines and penalties, extensive cooperation with the Justice Department's investigation, appointment of an independent monitor, establishment of internal compliance programs, and waiver of the attorney-client and work product protections – the government will defer prosecution for a period of time (often between twelve and twenty-four months). If the corporation complies with its obligation under the deferred prosecution agreement, the complaint is dismissed with prejudice at the end of the deferral period. *See, e.g.,* SEC Press Release, SEC Charges Three RMBS Traders With Defrauding Investors, Rel. No. 2015-181 (Sept. 8, 2015), *available at* http://www.sec.gov/news/pressrelease/2015-181.html; Complaint, *SEC v. Shapiro, et al.,* No. 15-cv-07045(S.D.N.Y. Sept. 8, 2015). Recently, the SEC entered into its first-ever FCPA DPA with an individual in connection with an enforcement action brought against a technology company and its foreign subsidiaries. *In the Matter of PTC, Inc.,* Admin. Proc. File No. 3-17118 (Feb. 16, 2016), (order instituting cease-and-desist proceedings), *available at* https://www.sec.gov/litigation/admin/2016/34-77145.pdf; Deferred Prosecution Agreement, Nov. 18, 2015, *available at* https://www.sec.gov/litigation/admin/2016/34-77145-dpa.pdf (the first ever such agreement with an individual).

[189] A typical non-prosecution agreement imposes similar obligations on the corporation, and places the corporation in a probationary period; if the corporation fails to comply with the obligations of the non-prosecution agreement, it can be prosecuted. *See, e.g.,* Nortek, Inc. Non Prosecution Agreement (May 3, 2016), *available at* https://www.sec.gov/news/press/2016/2016-109-npa-nortek.pdf.

59

DOJ obtain the conviction of senior executives, including a former CEO and the general counsel.[190]

Even without cooperation as extensive as PetroTiger's, the government is still willing to reward cooperation. For example, in February 2016, Dutch telecommunications company VimpelCom Ltd. settled allegations that it violated the FCPA for $460 million, a 45% reduction off the lowest suggested fine in the Sentencing Guidelines.[191] Even though VimpelCom did not voluntarily self-disclose, the DOJ nonetheless decided that such "significant credit" was warranted because of the company's "prompt acknowledgement of wrongdoing after being informed of the department's investigation, for [its] willingness to promptly resolve their criminal liability on an expedited basis and for [its] extensive cooperation with the [D]epartment's investigation."[192]

Similarly, the DOJ in February 2016 reached a non-prosecution agreement with the Chinese subsidiaries of PTC, Inc., a U.S. software company, concerning allegations that the subsidiaries violated the FCPA.[193] The DOJ commended the company for providing "all relevant facts known to them, including information

---

[190] Leslie R. Caldwell, Assistant Attorney General, U.S. Dep't of Justice, Remarks at the New York City Bar Association's Fourth Annual White-collar Crime Institute (May 12, 2015), *available at* https://www.justice.gov/opa/speech/assistant-attorney-general-leslie-r-caldwell-delivers-remarks-new-york-city-bar-0; *see also* Press Release, U.S. Dep't of Justice, Former Chief Executive Officer of Oil Services Company Pleads Guilty to Foreign Bribery Charge (June 15, 2015), *available at* https://www.justice.gov/opa/pr/former-chief-executive-officer-oil-services-company-pleads-guilty-foreign-bribery-charge.

[191] Press Release, U.S. Dep't of Justice, VimpelCom Limited and Unitel LLC Enter into Global Foreign Bribery Resolution of More than $795 Million (Feb. 18, 2016), *available at* https://www.justice.gov/opa/pr/vimpelcom-limited-and-unitel-llc-enter-global-foreign-bribery-resolution-more-795-million.

[192] *Id.* DOJ suggested that VimpelCom would have been eligible for even more cooperation credit had it voluntarily self-disclosed.

[193] Press Release, U.S. Dep't of Justice, PTC Inc. Subsidiaries Agree to Pay More Than $14 Million to Resolve Foreign Bribery Charges (Feb. 16, 2016), *available at* https://www.justice.gov/opa/pr/ptc-inc-subsidiaries-agree-pay-more-14-million-resolve-foreign-bribery-charges.

about individuals involved in the FCPA misconduct,"[194] which undoubtedly led the DOJ to agree to a non-prosecution agreement as opposed to a deferred prosecution agreement or a guilty plea. PTC nonetheless did not receive full cooperation credit or credit for voluntary disclosure because its initial disclosure failed to include all relevant facts that the company had learned through a prior internal investigation.[195] PTC ultimately agreed to pay a criminal fine of $14.54 million to the DOJ, plus an additional $13.6 million to the SEC in disgorgement and prejudgment interest.[196]

Should a company decline to cooperate, the government has made clear that such companies can expect severe punishment, especially if the company's non-cooperation "thwart[s] the [D]epartment's ability to bring charges against responsible individuals."[197] Then-Assistant Attorney General Leslie Caldwell cited the prosecution of BNP Paribas, a French bank, for violation of U.S. sanctions on Sudan, Iran and Cuba as an example of how not to handle an investigation. "BNPP not only failed to cooperate with our investigation at the outset, but affirmatively hindered the investigation by dragging its feet, based in part on assertions regarding data privacy laws."[198] BNP Paribas agreed to the largest criminal penalty ever to be imposed at the time of settlement (2014), $8.9 billion.[199] Additionally, BNP Paribas pled guilty and

---

[194] *Id.*

[195] *Id.*

[196] *Id.*

[197] Leslie R. Caldwell, Assistant Attorney General, U.S. Dep't of Justice, Remarks at the New York City Bar Association's Fourth Annual White-collar Crime Institute (May 12, 2015), *available at* https://www.justice.gov/opa/speech/assistant-attorney-general-leslie-r-caldwell-delivers-remarks-new-york-city-bar-0.

[198] *Id.*

[199] Press Release, U.S. Dep't of Justice, BNP Paribas Agrees to Plead Guilty and to Pay $8.9 Billion for Illegally Processing Financial Transactions for Countries Subject to U.S. Economic Sanctions (June 30, 2014), *available at* https://www.justice.gov/opa/pr/bnp-paribas-agrees-plead-guilty-and-pay-89-billion-illegally-processing-financial.

agreed to a five-year probationary period. A similar fate befell French power and transportation company Alstom S.A. in 2015, when it paid the largest FCPA fine to date, totalling $772 million, in addition to entering a guilty plea.[200] Assistant Attorney General Caldwell noted that in the face of Alstom's initial refusal to cooperate, DOJ was still able to proceed with its own investigation and bring charges against individual executives.[201] Alstom's settlement was justified by Alstom's "failure to voluntarily disclose misconduct, even though it was aware of it, and the company's refusal to fully cooperate with our investigation for years until they saw the writing on the wall as their top executives began to be charged."[202]

III. POTENTIAL PITFALLS OF COOPERATION

Although cooperation yields many benefits, including the potential to avoid prosecution and minimize financial penalties, lawyers for corporations and other business organizations nevertheless should proceed with caution.

Considerations When Waiving Privileges. One measure of a corporation's cooperation has been the corporation's willingness to waive claims of attorney-client privilege and work product protection. Although, as discussed above, privilege waivers are no longer a prerequisite for earning cooperation credit, there is no prohibition against rewarding voluntary waivers. In addition to the Justice Department's enforcement policies, the SEC's Seaboard

---

[200] Press Release, U.S. Dep't of Justice, Alstom Sentenced to Pay $772 Million Criminal Fine to Resolve Foreign Bribery Charges (Nov. 13, 2015), *available at* https://www.justice.gov/opa/pr/alstom-sentenced-pay-772-million-criminal-fine-resolve-foreign-bribery-charges.

[201] Leslie R. Caldwell, Assistant Attorney General, U.S. Dep't of Justice, Remarks at the New York City Bar Association's Fourth Annual White-collar Crime Institute (May 12, 2015), *available at* https://www.justice.gov/opa/speech/assistant-attorney-general-leslie-r-caldwell-delivers-remarks-new-york-city-bar-0.

[202] *Id.*

Report encourages waiver,[203] although since 2013, the SEC has required approval of the Director or Deputy Director of the Enforcement Division before such waiver may be demanded.[204]

Notwithstanding the obvious benefits of cooperation, voluntary disclosure of protected information, even when disclosed pursuant to a confidentiality agreement, is fraught with pitfalls that often can have dire consequences for a corporation, not the least of which is that the results of the internal investigation provides a roadmap to plaintiffs' lawyers. The decision whether to waive therefore is one that must be considered in light of all of the current and future litigation that the corporation may face.[205]

For these reasons, the decision to waive attorney-client privilege or work product privilege must be approached with caution, particularly in the early days of an investigation that could take several years to resolve, and could be accompanied by third-party

---

[203] *Report of Investigation Pursuant to Section 21(a) of the Securities Exchange Act of 1934 and Commission Statement on the Relationship of Cooperation to Agency Enforcement Decisions*, Rel. No. 34-44969, at n.3 (Oct. 23, 2001) ("In some cases, the desire to provide information to the Commission staff may cause companies to consider choosing not to assert the attorney-client privilege, the work product protection and other privileges, protections and exemptions with respect to the Commission."), *available at* http://www.sec.gov/litigation/investreport/34-44969.htm.

[204] U.S. Securities and Exchange Commission Division of Enforcement, *Enforcement Manual* (Oct. 9, 2013), *available at* http://www.sec.gov/divisions/enforce/enforcementmanual.pdf.

[205] While in some jurisdictions a confidentiality agreement might go some way to protect privileged information, at least three circuits have held that the disclosure of privileged information operates as a waiver notwithstanding the existence of a confidentiality agreement. *See In re Qwest Communications Int'l, Inc.*, 450 F.3d 1179, 1194 (10th Cir. 2006), *cert. denied*, 127 S. Ct. 584 (2006) (dismissing notion that confidentiality agreements with enforcement agencies warranted selective waiver rule under the circumstances); *In re Columbia/HCA Healthcare Corp. Billing Practices Litig.*, 293 F.3d 289, 307 (6th Cir. 2002) (rejecting notion of selective waiver under circumstances, notwithstanding confidentiality agreement); *In re Chrysler Motors Corp. Overnight Evaluation Program Litig.*, 860 F.2d 844, 847 (8th Cir. 1988) (holding that agreement with adversary not to disclose work product materials to a third party could not protect the materials from waiver).

63

litigation. Where possible, counsel should cooperate fully with the government investigation while preserving the corporation's privilege, and should consider whether alternatives to waiver may be acceptable.[206] In cases where it becomes necessary to disclose privileged information, a strong confidentiality agreement is critical.[207]

Deputizing Corporate Counsel to Conduct Internal Investigations. On April 9, 2004, Ira Zar ("Zar"), the former chief financial officer of Computer Associates International, Inc., pleaded guilty to federal charges of securities fraud, conspiracy to commit securities fraud, and conspiracy to obstruct justice, based on allegations that he and others engaged in a scheme to fraudulently report fiscal quarter revenues by artificially extending months for accounting purposes, and to conceal this practice from outside auditors.[208] The government based its obstruction of justice charge not on representations by Zar to the United States Attorney's office, but rather on Zar's communications with lawyers employed by Computer Associates and its audit committee. According to the government, Zar provided false justifications for the illegal accounting practices "to the [c]ompany's [l]aw [f]irm and the [a]udit [c]ommittee's [l]aw [f]irm knowing and with the intent that they would, in turn, be presented to the United States Attorney's Office, the SEC and the FBI."[209]

The government's obstruction of justice charge against Zar highlights both ethical and legal concerns. First, counsel must

[206] See Sheila Finnegan, THE FIRST 72 HOURS OF A GOVERNMENT INVESTIGATION: A GUIDE TO IDENTIFYING ISSUES AND AVOIDING MISTAKES 40 (Nat'l Legal Ctr. for the Public Interest, Vol. 10, No. 2, Feb. 2006).

[207] Richard A. Spehr and Claudius O. Sokenu, SEC Self-Policing Policy Presents Benefits and Pitfalls, 7 Andrews Sec. Lit. & Reg. Rep. 17 (Feb 27, 2002), at 4.

[208] See Kenneth N. Gilpin, Guilty Pleas in Computer Associates Case, INT'L HERALD TRIB., Apr. 9, 2004, at 11; see also Information ¶¶ 10-17, at 5-9, United States v. Ira Zar, Cr. No. 04-331 (ILG) (E.D.N.Y. Apr. 8, 2004), available at http://www.usdoj.gov/dag/cftf/chargingdocs/zarinfo.pdf [hereinafter Zar Information].

[209] Zar Information, supra n.208, ¶ 33.

remain vigilant in upholding her duty as a zealous advocate for her client, while ensuring that the current and former employees clearly understand that the corporation's counsel does not represent them individually.[210] An *Upjohn* warning therefore is imperative at the outset of an employee interview.[211] Depending on the relationship between the government and the corporation, counsel must also consider giving a so-called Zar warning, in which the employee is warned that the information provided may be turned over to the government, exposing the employee to the possibility of obstruction of justice charges in the event that the employee's statements are deemed to be untruthful.[212] While giving a Zar warning may actually create the potential for an obstruction charge where it might not otherwise have existed in the absence of a warning,[213] the Yates Memorandum's directive that companies turn over "all relevant facts" pertaining to misconduct by individual employees makes it increasingly likely that the company will share employee interviews with the government,[214] necessitating a Zar warning.

Deferred Prosecution Agreements. Part I of this chapter discussed how deferred prosecution and non-prosecution agreements are becoming increasingly popular methods for corporations to avoid criminal prosecution. However, counsel should consider the pitfalls that may arise from entering into such agreements. First, entering into a deferred prosecution or non-prosecution agreement will have significant implications in the event of parallel investigations and subsequent litigation. Such agreements will almost always contain a stipulation of facts that the target of the criminal investigation must agree it will not

---

[210] *See, e.g.*, N.Y. Rules of Prof'l Conduct 1.7 (governing concurrent conflicts of interests).

[211] *See Upjohn Co. v. United States*, 449 U.S. 383, 394-96 (1981); *see also* Finnegan, *supra* n.206, at 30 (discussing *Upjohn* warnings).

[212] Finnegan, *supra* n.206, at 32.

[213] *Id.*

[214] *See supra*, Section I.F.

contradict.[215] Thus, these agreements provide a roadmap to further liability, with little the corporation can do to defend itself. Second, a corporation that enters into a deferred prosecution or non-prosecution agreement faces severe consequences if it is found to be in breach of the agreement. A breach will subject the corporation to prosecution, which is likely to result in a conviction since the corporation had already stipulated to the government's recitation of the facts.[216]

Selection of Counsel. While in-house counsel may conduct minor investigations, a corporation may wish to turn to outside counsel for more serious and complex matters. If outside counsel is chosen, the corporation should consider that government enforcement agencies will tend to view investigations conducted by outside attorneys without prior ties to the corporation as more credible than those conducted by regular outside counsel. For example, the SEC's Seaboard Report states that the SEC will ask: "Did

---

[215] *See, e.g.*, Yu Kai Yuan, Deferred Prosecution Agreement, at ¶ 1 (Dec. 10, 2015) ("Respondent has offered to accept full responsibility for his conduct and to not contest or contradict the factual statements contained in Paragraph 6 in any future Commission enforcement action in the event he breaches this Agreement."), *available at* https://www.sec.gov/litigation/admin/2016/34-77145-dpa.pdf; PBSJ Corporation, Deferred Prosecution Agreement at ¶ 1 (Jan. 21, 2015) (same), *available at* https://www.sec.gov/news/press/2015/2015-13-dpa.pdf; Scott Jonathan Herckis, Deferred Prosecution Agreement, at ¶ 1 (Nov. 8, 2013) (same), *available at* https://www.sec.gov/news/press/2013/2013-241-dpa.pdf; Tenaris, S.A., Deferred Prosecution Agreement, at ¶ 1 (May 17, 2011) (same), *available at* https://www.sec.gov/news/press/2011/2011-112-dpa.pdf.*United States v. Computer Associates Int'l*, Cr. No. 04-837 (ILG), Deferred Prosecution Agreement ¶ 27 (E.D.N.Y. Sept. 24, 2004) [hereinafter "CA Deferred Prosecution Agreement"] ("CA agrees that it shall not, through its attorneys, Board of Directors, agents, officers or employees, make any public statement, in litigation or otherwise, contradicting its acceptance of responsibility or the allegations set forth in the Information or Stipulation of Facts."); *see also United States v. America Online, Inc.*, Crim. No. 1:04 M 1133 (E.D. Va.), Deferred Prosecution Agreement ¶ 3 [hereinafter AOL Deferred Prosecution Agreement]; *United States v. AIG-FP Pagic Equity Holding Corp.*, Deferred Prosecution Agreement ¶ 4 (W.D. Pa. Nov. 30, 2004) [hereinafter "AIG-FP Pagic Deferred Prosecution Agreement"].

[216] *See, e.g.*, CA Deferred Prosecution Agreement, *supra* n.215, ¶¶ 25-26; *see also* AOL Deferred Prosecution Agreement, *supra* n.215, ¶ 17-18; AIG-FP Pagic Deferred Prosecution Agreement, *supra* n.215, ¶ 4.

company employees or outside persons perform the review? If outside persons, had they done other work for the company? Where the review was conducted by outside counsel, had management previously engaged such counsel?"[217] In the case of Symbol Technologies, Inc. ("Symbol"), the company initially hired one of its regular outside law firms to conduct an internal investigation after being notified by the SEC of an anonymous letter alleging fraud.[218] After the law firm reported that no accounting fraud had occurred, the SEC expressed its dissatisfaction with the investigation, and Symbol Technologies replaced its regular firm with another outside law firm that was independent of Symbol. During the second investigation, Symbol dismissed a senior vice president of finance who was deemed to be a ringleader in obstructing the initial investigation, agreed to share the substance of its interviews with current and former employees and customers with the government, made witnesses available to the government, and produced hundreds of thousands of documents and e-mail communications. Based on the manner in which the second investigation was conducted, the SEC reached a settlement with Symbol, twelve Symbol executives were charged with accounting fraud, and the Department of Justice announced that it would not charge Symbol with criminal wrongdoing.[219]

The government thus may view regular outside counsel as less willing to make difficult decisions, such as recommending discipline and/or termination of uncooperative employees.[220] Other considerations include whether regular outside counsel gave legal advice regarding the transaction in question, whether regular outside counsel may be subpoenaed as a witness, and whether

---

[217] Seaboard Report, *supra* n.132.

[218] *See* Andrew Longstreth, In the New Era of Internal Investigations, Defense Lawyers Have Become Deputy Prosecutors, 27 AM. LAW. 68 (Feb. 2005); *see also SEC v. Symbol Technologies, Inc.*, Lit. Rel. 18734 (SEC June 30, 2004).

[219] *Id.*

[220] *See id.* The Filip Memorandum articulates that corporate compliance programs should be designed, *inter alia*, to prevent and detect misconduct. Filip Memorandum, *supra* n.175, at 14–16.

67

regular outside counsel and the corporation have a close and long-standing relationship.[221]

Determining Scope of Investigation. An internal investigation that is too narrow or overly broad in scope may lead to inaccurate findings, or, possibly, allegations that the corporation attempted to conceal wrongdoing.[222] Both the SEC and DOJ scrutinize the sufficiency of an internal investigation's scope. The SEC considers an investigation's scope, among other factors, in determining whether to bring an enforcement action: "Did the company commit to learn the truth, fully and expeditiously? Did it do a thorough review of the nature, extent, origins and consequences of the conduct and related behavior?"[223] The DOJ, in assessing a corporation's level of cooperation, will consider "whether the corporation has engaged in conduct intended to impede the investigation," including "making presentations or submissions that contain misleading assertions or material omissions."[224]

To minimize the chance that the government will view an investigation's scope as too narrow or overly broad, an investigation should, at a minimum, mirror that of the government, unless reason exists to broaden it further.[225] In addition, counsel may wish to ensure that the investigation thoroughly addresses the criteria identified in the Seaboard Report and the Filip Memorandum, including the nature of the misconduct, how the misconduct arose, where in the organization the misconduct occurred, how long it lasted, the harm that the misconduct has inflicted upon investors and other corporate constituencies, and how (and by whom) the misconduct was detected.[226]

---

[221] Longstreth, *supra* n.218.

[222] *See also* Finnegan, *supra* n.206, at 27.

[223] Seaboard Report, *supra* n.132.

[224] Filip Memorandum, *supra* n.175, at 12.

[225] Finnegan, *supra* n.206, at 27.

[226] *See id.* at 28-29; Seaboard Report, *supra* n.132; Filip Memorandum, *supra* n.175.

68

Joint Defense Agreements. If, after weighing all of the circumstances, counsel decides that the interests of the corporation and management are closely aligned, counsel may choose to obtain separate representation for management and enter into a joint defense agreement. Such an arrangement will achieve two objectives. First, obtaining separate counsel for management at an early stage avoids the need to continually reassess the propriety of joint representation down the road, particularly when it is likely that the corporation's interests may diverge from those of its employees.[227] Second, implementation of a joint defense agreement will facilitate the sharing of information. Nevertheless, counsel should be aware that entry into a joint defense agreement may constrain the availability of strategic options available to the corporation. A corporation that has obtained information from an employee may be foreclosed from sharing this information if the parties have signed a joint defense agreement.[228] Counsel therefore should weigh carefully the costs of entering into a joint defense agreement against any prospective benefits.

Implications of Rule 408 for Settlement Offers Made in Civil Negotiations. Federal Rule of Evidence 408—which normally prohibits evidence of compromises and offers to compromise from being introduced in court—contains an exception for criminal cases that permits introduction of statements or conduct during negotiations of a civil dispute involving a government regulatory, investigative, or enforcement agency.[229] In essence, Rule 408 allows prosecutors to introduce evidence of settlement offers made during civil negotiations as evidence of criminal liability. This exception raises an important issue for counsel considering whether to engage in settlement negotiations with the government,

---

[227] *See* N.Y. Rules of Prof'l Conduct 1.7, 1.13.

[228] *See United States v. LeCroy*, 348 F. Supp. 2d 375, 384-85 (E.D. Pa. 2004) (observing that company was bound by joint defense agreement and could not turn over notes and memoranda of discussions with employees to the government unless and until it withdrew from joint defense agreement); *see also* Finnegan, *supra* n.206, at 24 n.28; *United States v. Henke*, 222 F.3d 633, 637 (9th Cir. 2000) (finding an "implied attorney-client relationship with the co-defendant" arising out of a joint-defense agreement).

[229] *See* Fed. R. Evid. 408.

69

and should inform decisions such as whether a client should file a Wells submission. Because Rule 408 does not prevent prosecutors from introducing any settlement offer contained in a Wells submission for purposes of showing liability in a criminal proceeding, it is crucial that counsel engage in civil settlement negotiations with government officials with an eye toward the possibility that such negotiations could resurface in a criminal trial.[230]

Evidence Preservation Obligations. Once a corporation has learned that it may be under investigation, counsel must take immediate action to suspend document destruction practices and avoid the inadvertent destruction of relevant documents and electronic data.[231] Even the inadvertent destruction of relevant materials can result in serious consequences for a corporation that has been subpoenaed by the government, including obstruction of justice charges. The criminal obstruction statute contained in § 802 of the Sarbanes-Oxley Act of 2002 is notable when compared to other federal obstruction statutes because it criminalizes—without requiring either the existence of an official proceeding or a wilful or corrupt state of mind—the destruction, alteration, or falsification of records with the intent to impede a federal investigation.[232] Even if the government concludes that an obstruction charge is not warranted, the inadvertent destruction of pertinent documents undoubtedly will call into question, in the current enforcement environment, a corporation's efforts to cooperate.

Electronic data presents particularly unique preservation challenges, including the difficult task of determining where relevant electronic data exists and what must be done to preserve

---

[230] *Cf. United States v. Prewitt*, 34 F.3d 436, 439 (7th Cir. 1994) (holding, under an interpretation consistent with proposed Amended Rule 408, that Rule 408 did not prohibit the introduction into evidence of the defendant's statements made during civil compromise negotiations with the Securities Division of the Indiana Secretary of State).

[231] *See generally* Finnegan, *supra* n.206, at 2.

[232] *See* 18 U.S.C. § 1519.

it. Counsel should ensure that it can determine all sources of stored information, including personal computers, network drives, and materials stored under the employees' individual control. The complexity of determining where responsive electronic materials may exist warrants consideration of hiring a discovery expert in the early stages of an internal investigation.[233] Counsel should also address the existence of the corporation's disaster recovery backup tapes early in an investigation. Backup tapes routinely are recycled by companies, thus causing data on the tapes to be overwritten from time to time. Therefore, once a corporation learns of circumstances that are likely to lead to a government investigation, counsel must determine whether the corporation should continue to recycle its backup tapes. While a corporation need not preserve every single e-mail and backup tape when litigation is threatened,[234] the Committee Notes to Federal Rule of Civil Procedure 37(f) suggest that affirmative steps may be required to preserve backup tapes where the tapes may be the only source of certain relevant and discoverable information. In light of the harsh penalties associated with document destruction, if the internal investigation is in response to a government action, counsel's best course of action is to negotiate with the government at the beginning of the investigation, as the government's view of what must be preserved likely will vary from that of the corporation.

The Federal Rules of Civil Procedure emphasize the importance of outside counsel gaining an early and complete understanding of client systems, data sources, and retention policies and practices in civil litigation. For example, Rule 26(a)(1)(B) requires that initial disclosures include a description of all electronically stored information that may be used to support the party's claims or defenses.[235] Rule 26(f) requires the parties to confer on issues related to preserving discoverable information and develop a discovery plan that includes proposals concerning, *inter alia*, the

---

[233] *See generally* Finnegan, *supra* n.206, at 4.

[234] *Chin v. Port Auth. of N.Y. & N.J.*, 685 F.3d 135, 162 (2d Cir. 2012); *Sekisui Am. Corp. v. Hart*, 945 F. Supp. 2d 494 (S.D.N.Y. 2013); *Zubulake v. UBS Warburg LLC*, (*Zubulake IV*), 220 F.R.D. 212, 217 (S.D.N.Y. 2003).

[235] FED. R. CIV. P. 26(a)(1)(B).

form in which electronically stored information should be produced.[236] Rule 34 permits the party requesting documents to specifically request electronically stored information."[237]

Administrative proceedings and case law illustrate the role that document retention and production can play in dealings with the government. For example, in assessing a $7.5 million penalty against Halliburton Company ("Halliburton"), the SEC cited "unacceptable lapses in the company's conduct during the course of the [SEC's] investigation, which had the effect of delaying the production of information and documentation necessary to the staff's expeditious completion of its investigation."[238] Conversely, the SEC credited the NYSE's cooperation and effective document production when investigating the NYSE's alleged failure to properly detect, investigate and discipline unlawful proprietary trading by specialists on the floor of the NYSE.[239] In accepting the NYSE's settlement offer, the SEC specifically cited the NYSE's cooperation with the SEC, which included the production, without service of notice or subpoena, of documents and other relevant information.[240]

The SEC's investigations of American International Group, Inc. ("AIG") and Brightpoint, Inc. ("Brightpoint") further illustrate how important it is to preserve documents when a government investigation is afoot.[241] Brightpoint cooperated with the SEC's investigation, including the production of documents, interviews, waiving privilege, and testimony.[242] By contrast, AIG erroneously

---

[236] Fed. R. Civ. P. 26(f)(3).

[237] FED. R. CIV. P. 34(b).

[238] *Id.* at *9 & n.11.

[239] *In re New York Stock Exch., Inc.*, Rel. No. 34-51524, 2005 WL 840452, at *1 (SEC Apr. 12, 2005).

[240] *Id.* at *11.

[241] *See In the Matter of American Int'l Group, Inc.*, Rel. No. 34-48477, 2003 WL 22110366 (Sept. 11, 2003); *In the Matter of Brightpoint, Inc.*, Rel. No. 34-48474, 2003 WL 22110368 (Sept. 11, 2003).

[242] *See In the Matter of Brightpoint, Inc., supra* n.241, at *15.

certified that production of subpoenaed documents was complete when, in fact, AIG had not produced all responsive documents.[243] Under their respective settlements, Brightpoint was forced to pay a $450,000 civil penalty, whereas AIG was required to pay a $10 million civil penalty and disgorge $100,000 plus prejudgment interest.[244]

IV.   CONCLUSION

Today's enforcement environment is in many ways highly uncertain, and will no doubt continue to evolve. The climate of heightened cooperation has been a learning experience for corporations and regulators alike. In this environment, counsel must navigate through the various pitfalls while not forgoing her obligations to the corporation. This task will require close scrutiny of the options available to the client, and consideration of how decisions will impact (or limit) a corporation's options many years down the road in parallel government investigations, private litigation, or congressional hearings.

---

[243] *See In the Matter of American Int'l Group, Inc.*, *supra* n.241, at *11.

[244] *See In the Matter of Brightpoint, Inc.*, *supra* n.241, at *16 & n.10 (imposing a $450,000 civil penalty on Brightpoint); *In the Matter of American Int'l Group, Inc.*, *supra* n.241, at *15-*16 & n.11 (imposing payment of disgorgement, prejudgment interest, and civil sanctions).

Chapter 4

Department of Justice (DOJ) Investigations Overview

By: Andrew Hruska[245]

I.   INTRODUCTION

Every sizable business engaged in commerce in the United States will confront issues of federal criminal law enforcement, either as a witness, victim, or subject in an investigation, or as a criminal defendant. Sometimes a company's role in an investigation—and the nature of the investigation itself—will remain unclear until that process has reached an advanced stage. To effectively confront the virtual inevitability of facing federal enforcement issues, it is crucial to understand the structure and nature of the various components of the Department of Justice, the common patterns and pitfalls involved in handling investigations, and the overarching emerging issues and trends.

While companies will always want to hire experienced external counsel who can help lead them through the threatening prospect of involvement in a federal enforcement investigation, attention to these concepts at the outset will help internal company lawyers ask the right questions and design their collaboration in a focused and effective way.

II.   STRUCTURE OF DOJ

The United States Department of Justice ("DOJ" or the "Department") is the primary agency responsible for enforcing federal criminal law in the United States. The Department is comprised of over fifty divisions and agencies, ranging from the United States Attorneys' Offices to the Federal Bureau of Prisons

---

[245] Andrew Hruska is a Partner in the New York office of King & Spalding, LLP, where he leads the government investigations practice. He served as the Chief Assistant U.S. Attorney in the Eastern District of New York and as the Senior Counsel to the U.S. Deputy Attorney General. Jack Leahey, Harvard Law School J.D. Candidate 2023, assisted significantly in updating this chapter.

to the Office of Tribal Justice. All of these divisions and agencies report to the Deputy Attorney General ("DAG"), who is tasked with the general oversight of their respective affairs. The DAG, in turn, reports to the Attorney General.

Within DOJ's broader structure, this chapter focuses on the work of several of its components: the U.S. Attorney's Offices ("USAOs"), the Criminal Division, the Civil Division, the Antitrust Division, the Environment and Natural Resources Division ("ENRD"), the Tax Division, and the National Security Division ("NSD").[246] Each DOJ component has a leading role in the investigation and prosecution of criminal and civil enforcement matters under federal law. Additionally, collaboration between these units, both informally and through a growing number of interagency taskforces (*e.g.*, Task Force KleptoCapture on evasion of sanctions imposed on Russia in 2022 and the COVID-19 Fraud Enforcement Task Force), is increasingly common.

A.   U.S. Attorney's Offices

The United States Attorneys are the principal litigators on behalf of the United States and under the direction of the Attorney General. Each of the 94 federal districts has a USAO in its territory. Each district's office is overseen by a United States Attorney ("U.S. Attorney"), who is appointed by the President and confirmed by the Senate.

USAOs are typically divided into Criminal and Civil Divisions, and may further be broken down into units that handle particular types of investigations or enforcement actions, such as white-collar crime or financial fraud. These divisions generally correspond to the three statutory responsibilities assigned to USAOs under Title 28: (1) criminal prosecution, (2) civil defense and prosecution, and (3) debt collection.[247] Generally, USAOs have substantial autonomy to decide when to initiate an investigation and bring

---

[246] U.S. Dept. of Justice, Agency Organization Chart (2021), https://www.justice.gov/agencies/chart.

[247] 28 U.S.C. § 547 (2018).

charges. In some instances, however, USAOs must seek prior approval from the DOJ to prosecute, such as cases arising under the Foreign Corrupt Practices Act ("FCPA"), and, in even fewer cases, the USAOs must defer entirely to the DOJ for prosecution (*e.g.*, cases under federal antitrust laws).

B. Criminal Division

The DOJ Criminal Division is tasked with enforcing all federal criminal laws. Within the Division, various Sections specialize in prosecuting cases in priority areas. For example, the Money Laundering and Asset Recovery Section ("MLARS") focuses on cases involving money laundering and seizure of assets used in or derived from criminal activity. MLARS also manages the DOJ program that distributes proceeds from seized assets to law enforcement and the public.

The Fraud Section is the Division's largest and is responsible for investigating and prosecuting complex white-collar crime cases throughout the nation. In this capacity, the Fraud Section has extensive experience dealing with sophisticated and often multi-jurisdictional fraud schemes. In 2021, the Fraud Section's areas of focus included: reviewing the effectiveness of corporate compliance programs and monitorships; holding individuals accountable for their roles in corporate fraud; continued interagency efforts to enforce U.S. anti-corruption treaty obligations through FCPA actions against U.S.-based companies and individuals; and a willingness, spurred on by unprecedentedly large recoveries, to bring financial and healthcare fraud cases on its own initiative in addition to action on *qui tam* (*i.e.*, "whistle-blower") complaints under the False Claims Act. Most expect the Fraud Section will reemphasize these focus areas in 2023.

The Fraud Section consists of three main litigating units relevant to corporate criminal enforcement issues: the FCPA Unit; the Health Care Fraud ("HCF"); and the Market Integrity and Major Frauds Unit ("MIMF") Unit. The MIMF Unit focuses on prosecuting large-scale and sophisticated securities, commodities, cryptocurrency, and other financial fraud cases, ranging from insider trading to market manipulation to accounting fraud, which account for a significant portion of wrongdoing a corporation encounters. In connection with its investigation and prosecution of these frauds, the MIMF Unit works closely with other regulators, such as the SEC and CFTC. In 2021, the MIMF Unit charged 105 individuals, obtained the conviction of 105 individuals, and negotiated 6 corporate resolutions that resulted in $2.82B in criminal fines, forfeiture, restitution, and other compensation payments. These convictions and penalties followed 5 corporate resolutions and $578.2M in corporate penalties in 2020, indicating that this unit will continue to be one of the most active and productive for the Criminal Division. Corporate counsel are quickly learning that the ceiling has now become the new floor with regard to these penalty amounts.

C.   Civil Division

The Civil Division represents the United States, including its departments and agencies, in both defensive and affirmative civil litigation. Like the Criminal Division, the Civil Division also contains a Fraud Section, which falls within its Commercial Litigation Branch. This section works with USAOs nationwide to litigate cases involving financial fraud against the Federal Government. While its largest caseload involves fraud against federal healthcare programs, the Civil Fraud Section also investigates allegations involving illegal kickbacks, deceptive or illegal marketing practices, conflicts of interest, and bribery. Of particular interest, the False Claims Act, which imposes liability on persons for defrauding governmental programs, allows private citizens to file suits on behalf of the government against those who have defrauded the government. The private citizens, called relators, who bring these actions successfully may receive a portion of the government's recovery. As a result of this incentive, many Fraud Section investigations and lawsuits result from relator (*qui tam*) actions.

D.   Antitrust Division

The Antitrust Division is the sole criminal enforcer of federal antitrust laws. The Antitrust Division focuses on investigating and prosecuting *per se* violations of antitrust law—*e.g.*, price fixing, bid rigging, and market allocation schemes—that can support felony convictions, fines in excess of $100M for corporations, and up to ten years' imprisonment for individuals. A hallmark of the Antitrust Division is its unique Leniency Program, which guarantee no criminal prosecution to the first entity and/or individual that self-reports violations of federal antitrust laws. Other requirements for leniency under the Antitrust Division's Programs include truthful admission of wrongdoing, agreement of full cooperation with the Division's investigation, and payment of restitution to victims.

E.   Tax Division

The Tax Division enforces federal tax laws through criminal and civil litigation. The Civil Trial Section promotes compliance with internal revenue laws by investigating and litigating unpaid assessments and tax liens, and it enforces any Internal Review Service ("IRS") summons, including those for books, records, and other documentary data. The Criminal Enforcement Section ("CES") focuses on tax fraud and tax evasion by uncovering the promotion and facilitation of illegal tax sheltering transactions conducted through foreign banks. CES also prioritizes enforcement of employment tax, where companies have a legal responsibility to collect and turn over federal taxes withheld from employees' wages, as well as paying their own share. In partnership with the IRS and USAOs, the Tax Division seeks monetary judgments, injunctions, and criminal convictions, which often involve restitution, financial penalties, and other sanctions against those who, for example, prepare false tax returns, are involved in tax fraud and tax evasion schemes, and abuse the bankruptcy system for tax purposes.

F.   Environment and Natural Resources Division

ENRD enforces pollution control and wildlife protection laws, and collaborates with the Department of Labor on worker endangerment matters. ENRD mainly focuses on pollution control laws by utilizing regional criminal task forces with USAOs, as well as state and local law enforcement officials, to investigate and prosecute these violations. ENRD also collaborates with state agencies to bring joint civil enforcement cases, many of which have resulted in record-setting financial awards. ENRD cases, particularly those involving violations of pollution control laws, are usually resolved through consent decrees filed in federal court. While these decrees may involve no admission of guilt or liability by a company, they do mandate specific performances in adherence with the decree. For example, ENRD utilized a consent decree to resolve all federal civil claims, damages, and penalties against BP for its role in the 2010 Gulf of Mexico Oil Spill, as well as using it to both implement BP's Gulf Coast restoration plan and settle the related economic damage claims brought by States and municipalities.

G.   National Security Division

NSD oversees federal law enforcement activities related to counterterrorism, counterintelligence, and foreign investment. Of note for U.S.-based companies maintaining international business relationships or operations, NSD is the division primarily responsible for initiating investigations and bringing enforcement actions for suspected violations of export controls and sanctions regimes. Sanctions enforcement, in particular, has become a major DOJ focus. In what she called a "sea change" in DOJ enforcement priorities in a June 2022 speech, DAG Lisa Monaco characterized sanctions as the "new FCPA."[248] NSD also oversees the administration and enforcement of the Foreign Agents Registration Act ("FARA"), a federal statute that imposes disclosure requirements and other legal obligations on persons engaging in political advocacy work on behalf of "foreign principals." Covered entities and individuals have redoubled their FARA compliance efforts following a substantial uptick in enforcement activity in recent years.

---

[248] U.S. DEP'T OF JUSTICE, "Deputy Attorney General Lisa O. Monaco Delivers Keynote Remarks at 2022 GIR Live: Women in Investigations" (June 16, 2022), tinyurl.com/47jmnt5p.

III. ANATOMY OF A DOJ INVESTIGATION

While certain unique factors—such as subject matter, scope, and timeline—may vary greatly from investigation to investigation, DOJ investigations generally share a standard path from inception to charging decision. Understanding that path allows a company to better chart out its responses to government requests and develop a parallel investigative plan. This chapter notes some of the standard elements of a DOJ investigation, while touching on related issues and concerns.

A. Preliminary Matters

The Department generally learns of potential wrongdoing in one of two key ways before a formal investigation commences. First, the government may conduct its own, independent investigation of wrongdoing after it is alerted to questionable conduct by either a whistle-blower, in the form of a current or former employee, or through its review of data, such as trading activity. Second, the government may become aware of potential wrongdoing through voluntary disclosure by a company. For example, a corporation may approach the government with findings of its own internal investigation, following a trigger, such as a hotline complaint, employee misconduct, or a newsworthy accident or incident relating to the company.

Once the DOJ learns of wrongdoing, it will then determine which entities and/or individuals that should be investigated. The Department may choose to enforce federal laws against a corporation, its employees, or both (as is frequently the case). However, the facts necessary for prosecutors to eliminate certain of these options may not be available at the inception of an investigation. In investigating corporations, for example, the success of future charges often turns on whether the government can establish the elements for *respondent superior* liability, a legal doctrine that holds an employer liable for its employee's or agent's actions under certain circumstances, as well as evidence of certain factors delineated in the Justice Manual Principles of Federal

Prosecution of Business Organizations.[249] As reflected in the Justice Manual, to hold a corporation liable for unlawful acts of its employees, the government must show the employee's acts were (1) within the scope of the employee's duties, and (2) intended (at least in part) to benefit the corporation.[250] However, at the early stages of an investigation, the government may not know the full scope of the conduct at issue, let alone the motives of the individuals responsible for it. Moreover, even if the preliminary facts available to the DOJ indicate corporate liability is unlikely, a fulsome investigation may show otherwise.

As a result, the Department frequently errs on the side of caution, investigating both the corporation (as an independent entity) and its employees in order to fully understand the landscape of the criminal conduct. Because the investigation may encompass a criminal or fraudulent scheme, prosecution of the company ensures that widespread conduct is adequately addressed. That said, the Department's investigation of a corporation differs very little structurally from that of an individual—the Department must still develop key facts, such as the timing of the alleged misconduct, the manner in which the conduct was carried out, and the individuals that approved of or participated in the conduct. On a parallel track, a company should begin its own internal investigation. In the case of a regulatory inquiry, a company may be suited to handle the investigation with its own resources. On the other hand, if a company believes it is the subject of a DOJ investigation, it should consider engaging outside counsel to assist with the internal investigation and to communicate with the assigned prosecutor.

B.   Fact Gathering

Once a civil or criminal investigation is opened, the DOJ has several tools at its disposal to gather relevant information from knowledgeable parties, such as search warrants, witness interviews, consensual monitoring, and electronic surveillance

---

[249] *See infra* §§ III(c)(i) and IV(a) for further discussion of these principles.

[250] U.S. Dep't of Justice, Justice Manual § 9-28.210 [JM].

through informants.[251] Since the law and practices surrounding each of these tools could fill their own chapters, we focus here on two of the government's preferred methods for developing a factual record: (1) subpoenas and (2) witness communications. For each, we provide a few key recommendations for corporate counsel in handling these matters.

1. Subpoenas

The Department's subpoena power is the primary mechanism that enables it to request and obtain information related to an initiated investigation. A subpoena is best defined as a court order mandating compliance with its request. The Department may either issue a subpoena for testimony (subpoena *ad testificandum*) or a subpoena for documents (subpoena *duces tecum*); the latter is far more commonly received by a company. The main form of subpoena is a grand jury subpoena, which is issued under the supervision of a federal prosecutor who is able to negotiate its terms, and is used exclusively for criminal investigations. Grand jury subpoenas have a vast reach, where documents, tangible objects, and testimony may be subpoenaed if there is a reasonable possibility that the materials sought will provide generally relevant information. In contrast, a company may receive an administrative subpoena, which is limited to documents and does not require prior approval of a grand jury or court. Administrative subpoenas (sometimes characterized as "Civil Investigations Demands" (or "CIDs")), however, are issued pursuant to the authority of a federal agency, such as the DOJ. Such a subpoena may be used in civil investigations, but cannot be used in criminal investigations.

Assuming the Department has learned of potential wrongdoing from an independent source, the Department may issue either an administrative or grand jury subpoena, depending on the nature of the investigation, to both the company and its employees. In a civil

---

[251] This section focuses on strategies specifically directed to the targets or subjects of an investigation. Of course, any whistleblower or corporation that is already cooperating with the government is likely to remain a significant source of relevant information throughout the ensuing investigation. Similarly, federal agents and victims are also sources of leads and information.

investigation, the issuance of an administrative subpoena for documents will set in motion a lengthy document collection, review, and production process, during which the scope of the subpoena is narrowed, custodians of relevant documents are identified, and documents are reviewed for responsiveness to the subpoena and content protected by the attorney-client privilege. The issuance of a grand jury subpoena, used solely for criminal investigations, will often initiate a conversation with the assigned prosecutor to determine the "status" of the employee, and, in turn, the course of the investigation and the extent of cooperation with the government.

In general, an employee may be characterized in one of three categories: (1) witness, (2) subject, or (3) target—either at the inception of the Department's investigation, or as the investigation evolves and the factual record is established. Per the JM,[252] a "subject" of an investigation is defined as "a person whose conduct is within the scope of the grand jury's subpoena." A "target" is "a person as to whom the prosecutor or the grand jury has substantial evidence linking him or her to the commission of a crime and who, in the judgment of the prosecutor, is a putative defendant. An officer or employee of an organization which is a target is not automatically considered a target even if such officer's or employee's conduct contributed to the commission of the crime by the target organization. The same lack of automatic target status holds true for organizations which employ, or employed, an officer or employee who is a target." Individuals in a corporation who possess relevant information regarding the alleged wrongdoing, but who are generally understood to lack potential criminal exposure themselves, are considered "witnesses."

2. Witness Communications

In addition to grand jury and administrative subpoenas, it is useful for corporate counsel to understand the significance of the types of

---

[252] JM § 9-11.151.

communication the government may have with company employees, such as interviews or testimony.

Interviews versus Testimony. Before speaking with the government, counsel must ascertain the conditions under which its employees or executives will be sharing information. The employee may be offered no protection from future prosecution, with the understanding that cooperation still may yield lenient treatment, or the employee may be afforded some level of immunity. The easiest and simplest form of immunity is a "proffer agreement," sometimes known as a "queen for a day." A proffer agreement generally allows an individual to provide the government with information through an informal interview while receiving limited protections regarding the potential use of such information against the individual in later proceedings. While a proffer generally offers the individual protection against use of statements by the government in its case, should an action against the individual ultimately be pursued, the proffer also may allow the government to impeach an individual at trial with statements made during the proffer session, should the individual choose to testify.

When the government is requesting or conducting employee interviews, counsel should be aware of any rights the company enjoys and any professional rules at play. As a starting point, government attorneys are bound by the same local rules and state laws on professional conduct as other attorneys practicing in a jurisdiction (*e.g.*, the well-known "no-contact" rule forbidding attorneys from directly contacting another attorney's client on the subject of the client's case). Rules and laws may vary by jurisdiction, but company counsel generally have a right to be present at government interviews—and the government generally cannot bypass company counsel and directly contact employees—when the contact or interviewee is a current employee and the communication or interview relates to the matter of his representation.[253] These rights are generally weaker, if not absent, where the person contacted or interviewed is a former employee,

---

[253] *See, e.g.*, Cal. Rules Prof. Conduct 4.2 (2021); NY Rules Prof. Conduct 4.2 cmt. 7 (2021); DC Rules Prof. Conduct 4.2 cmt. 3 (2007); *accord* Model Rules of Prof. Conduct 4.2 (Am. Bar Ass'n 1983).

the employee initiates contact with the government, or the communication relates to a confidential informant operation, service of a subpoena, or is otherwise authorized by law to be directed to the employee.[254] But company counsel generally do have the right to be present at the interview of a former employee to invoke, where appropriate, attorney client privilege and attorney work product claims.

Employee Interviews. To prepare for these communications with the government, it is wise to extensively prepare the employee or executive for an interview or testimony, particularly given most employees inexperience with the legal system. Employee interviews performed during the course of the company's internal investigation allow the company to gain an understanding of the critical facts and players, while also exposing employees to the formatting of the government's questioning and the types of documents the individual may be shown. These in-person preparation sessions, conducted either by the company's internal legal department, or, more often, by experienced outside counsel, further serve to refresh the witness's recollection of events (or even their own educational and work background), focus the witness on the questions being asked and their overall demeanor, and engage in the type of questioning that may be conducted by the government in a more formal setting.

These sessions may then be supplemented by the occasional call or email with the witness to discuss topics explored in other employees' testimony or to clarify his or her understanding about a particular document. Due to the document-heavy focus of these sessions, it is imperative that counsel thoroughly understand the chronology of key facts, anticipate the government's areas of interest and potential questions, and compile a relevant set of documents related to the witness's role in the events at issue. For this reason, the significance of the document collection and review process, discussed briefly above, cannot be overemphasized, as

---

[254] *See* discussion of professional rules and case law in JOHN IRVING, "Can Company Counsel Be at Gov't Interviews of Employees?" (Dec. 12, 2017), https://tinyurl.com/yckfh8wt.

these materials become critical during the internal witness interview process.

***Upjohn* Warnings.** The DOJ will also consider a company's willingness to disclose the results of a thorough internal investigation, including the facts learned through employee interviews, in part because such an investigation avoids the duplication of efforts by the Department and conserves government resources. Because of this consideration, it is important that individual employees or executives be given an *Upjohn* warning by company lawyers at the outset of an individual investigation.[255] The *Upjohn* warning serves to identify the circumstances under which employee communications with corporate counsel qualify as protected attorney-client communications. It should consist of the following elements:

Elements of *Upjohn* Warning

✓ "I represent the company."

✓ "I don't represent you."

✓ "I am conducting this interview to gather facts in order to provide legal advice to the company."

✓ "The conversation is privileged."

✓ "The privilege belongs to the company."

✓ "In order for this conversation to be privileged, it must be kept in confidence."

✓ "The company can choose to waive its privilege later and disclose information learned to the government or other third parties."

✓ "Do you understand my explanation, and are you willing to proceed under these ground rules?"

---

[255] *See Upjohn Co. v. United States*, 449 U.S. 383 (1981).

C.   Charging & Cooperation Determinations

1.   Potential Resolutions

Once DOJ has received both collected documents and transcripts of witness interviews, it may decide, despite a company's best efforts to cooperate and voluntarily disclose wrongdoing, to charge either the corporation or its employees, or in some instances, both. The JM mandates that corporations "should not be treated leniently because of their artificial nature nor should they be subject to harsher treatment."[256] The JM thus provides eleven factors[257]—the evolution of which will be discussed later in this chapter—for prosecutors to consider in determining whether to charge a business entity:

1. The nature and seriousness of the offense (JM 9-28.400);

2. The pervasiveness of wrongdoing within the corporation (JM 9-28.500);

3. The corporation's history of similar conduct (JM 9-28.600);

4. The corporation's willingness to cooperate in the investigation of its agents (JM 9-28.700);

5. The existence and effectiveness of the corporation's compliance program (JM 9-28.800);

6. The timely and voluntary disclosure of wrongdoing (JM 9-28.900);

7. Remedial actions (JM 9-28.1000);

---

[256] JM § 9-28.200.

[257] *See* JM § 9-28.300.

8. Collateral consequences (JM 9-28.1100);

9. The adequacy of non-criminal remedies (JM 9-28.1200);

10. The adequacy of the prosecution of individuals (JM 9-28.1300); and

11. The interests of any victims (JM 9-28.1400).

The weight assigned to each of these factors is subject to prosecutorial discretion. Since cooperation is a factor often within a company's control, the government is at liberty to offer leniency, such as opting for civil instead of criminal charges, or granting a reduction in penalties, based on the company's level of cooperation. The totality of these factors, along with advocacy papers and presentations to the government, may also yield a decision to decline to prosecute or to seek a non-prosecution (NPA) or deferred prosecution agreement (DPA)—or, in some cases, to insist on a corporate guilty plea as a condition of a negotiated resolution.

A NPA indicates that no formal charges will be filed so long as the company or individual complies with the terms of the agreement. Alternatively, a DPA involves the filing of criminal charges by the prosecutor against the entity, and the agreement is approved by a federal judge. Upon satisfaction of the DPA's terms, which, for example, may include the appointment of a monitor to oversee efforts to enhance the company's compliance program or require certain reporting requirements, the charges are dismissed. While these alternatives may sound enticing, a guilty plea may actually be the preferred method for a corporation to achieve the immediate closure of an investigation and to avoid continuing obligations under a plea agreement. This is particularly true given that any of these potential resolutions can include a monetary component, including the forfeiture of certain funds or assets, or a sanction, ranging from a financial penalty to restitution. Furthermore, a parent company and its subsidiaries may elect different resolutions. In 2013, UBS Securities Japan Co. Ltd. pleaded guilty to LIBOR manipulation, whereas its parent company, UBS AG, entered an NPA for the same underlying behavior.[258]

2. Cooperation Credit

Since 2015, cooperation has become inextricably linked to the tenth factor listed in the JM—the prosecution of individuals. In September 2015, former Deputy Attorney General Sally Quillian Yates released a memorandum entitled "Individual Accountability for Corporate Wrongdoing," announcing the DOJ's commitment to prosecuting corporate misconduct by pursuing wrongdoing by individuals in an organization. Targeting individuals is not, of course, an entirely new objective. Based on the Principles articulated in the Yates Memo, the JM advises that "[p]rosecution of a corporation is not a substitute for the prosecution of criminally culpable individuals," and that "regardless of the ultimate corporate disposition, a separate evaluation must be made with respect to potentially liable individuals."[259] In fact, the DOJ historically built its cases on individual wrongdoing, with the transition to prosecution of corporations intensifying in the early 2000s. With this transition came an increase in guilty pleas from corporations, later to be replaced by plea agreements and a downswing in corporate prosecution. That said, the emphasis that the DOJ has placed on developing cases against individuals, particularly in the civil context, is new by its own admission, but is perhaps another cycle in the DOJ's ever-changing stance on prosecution priorities.[260]

The Yates Memo thus promulgated six principles to govern criminal and civil investigations into wrongdoing. Certain principles, such as the fact that criminal and civil attorneys

---

[258] Press Release, UBS Securities Japan Co. Ltd Sentenced for Long-running Manipulation of Libor (Sept. 18, 2013) (on file with the Department of Justice).

[259] See, e.g., JM § 9-28.210.

[260] For a further discussion, see generally BRANDON L. GARRETT, "Structural Reform Prosecution," 93 VA. L. REV. 853 (June 2007); DAVID M. UHLMANN, "The Pendulum Swings: Reconsidering Corporate Criminal Prosecution," 49 U.C. DAVIS L. REV. 1235 (2016).

handling corporate investigations should be in routine communication with each other, are familiar. Other principles, such as the fact that to be eligible for any cooperation credit, corporations must provide DOJ with all relevant facts about the individuals involved in corporate misconduct, have heightened employee fears that a company will throw him or her under the proverbial bus to receive cooperation credit.[261] That focus on fact-gathering on culpable individuals is further emphasized in DOJ's supplementary, offense-specific guidelines on cooperation credit, such as in its guidance for cases involving the False Claims Act, the FCPA, export controls, and sanctions.[262]

Following the publication of the Yates Memo, the JM's "9-28.010 Foundational Principles of Corporate Prosecution" introduction was updated to explicitly instruct federal prosecutors to "focus on wrongdoing by individuals from the very beginning of any investigation." The JM explains that this new approach will allow the Department to: (1) increase its ability to identify the full extent of corporate misconduct; (2) increase the likelihood that those with knowledge of the corporate misconduct are identified and provide information about the individuals involved; and (3) maximize the

---

[261] *See, e.g.*, U.S. DEP'T OF JUSTICE, "Deputy Attorney General Sally Q. Yates Delivers Remarks at the 33rd Annual International Conference on Foreign Corrupt Practices Act" (Nov. 30, 2016), http://tinyurl.com/lbxj2j7; U.S. DEP'T OF JUSTICE, "Principal Deputy Associate Attorney General Bill Baer Delivers Remarks at Society of Corporate Compliance and Ethics Conference" (Sept. 27, 2016), http://tinyurl.com/zq5nkeh; U.S. DEP'T OF JUSTICE, "Deputy Attorney General Sally Q. Yates Delivers Remarks at the New York City Bar Association White-collar Crime Conference" (May 10, 2016), http://tinyurl.com/honqdq2. In 2018, then-DAG Rod Rosenstein walked back this "all-or-nothing" approach to cooperation credit, but the change in policy was temporary: DAG Lisa Monaco reinstated the Yates Memo's approach in October 2021. *See* Memorandum from Lisa Monaco, Deputy Attorney General, to Heads of Department Components and United States Attorneys, "Corporate Crime Advisory Group and Initial Revisions to Corporate Criminal Enforcement Policies" (Oct. 28, 2021), https://tinyurl.com/3hvcp2ff.

[262] *See, e.g.*, JM § 4-4.112 (Guidelines for Taking Disclosure, Cooperation, and Remediation into Account in False Claims Act Matters); JM § 9-47.120 (FCPA Corporate Enforcement Policy); JM § 9-90.625 (Export Control and Sanctions Enforcement Policy for Business Organizations).

likelihood that the final resolution includes charges against culpable individuals and not just the corporation.

In view of the tension that stems from the focus on individual liability, the next section of this chapter addresses issues that companies will face when deciding how to balance the demands of cooperation against its own interests and the interests of its employees.

IV.   EMERGING TRENDS & ISSUES

This final section focuses on a few areas where the DOJ's policies on cooperation credit and charging determinations may raise thorny decisions for corporate counsel to resolve. Companies have strong incentives to demonstrate cooperation to prosecutors—to expedite the investigation process (and minimize its impact on operations), lessen resulting charges and penalties, or avoid prosecution altogether. However, DOJ is not beholden to a statutory definition of "cooperation" and, thus, a cooperative company is one that provides the type of information in the manner and timeframe that the DOJ deems most useful, a judgment which the DOJ may change at its discretion.

While companies may generally want to demonstrate cooperation to prosecutors, doing so in some cases may require waiving privileges, postponing internal investigation activities, or ceding control over compliance policies going forward. Why cooperate in these particular situations? In short, most charging and cooperation policies across the DOJ constrain a company's ability to engage in this kind of case-by-case decision making while still being seen as cooperative overall. In a process where the stakes are high, and the measure of success is increasingly all or nothing, companies will feel compelled always to err on the government's side.

A.   Waiving the Attorney-Client & Work Product Protections

The attorney-client privilege and attorney work product protection can play important parts in a company's ability to prevent, identify, and respond to matters that may warrant an internal investigation. Effective compliance systems, for example, rely on employees to rapidly escalate events that could give rise to civil or criminal liability to a company's legal advisors. The assurance that any information reported will be protected from disclosure encourages employees to be forthcoming and candid, characteristics equally beneficial during interviews once a problem has been identified. However, these boons to companies can be burdens to prosecutors interested in uncovering potentially unlawful conduct and the individuals responsible for it. This tension is clear from the DOJ's shifting approach—articulated in four memoranda published between 1999 and 2006—to requests that companies waive the attorney-client and work product privileges as a condition to receiving cooperation credit.

First, in 1999, then-DAG Eric H. Holder published "Bringing Criminal Charges Against Corporations," or the Holder Memo, which set out eight discretionary factors for prosecutors to use in "reaching a decision as to the proper treatment of a corporate target"—*i.e.*, whether to bring criminal charges, award cooperation credit, and so on.[263] Among these factors was "[t]he corporation's timely and voluntary disclosure of wrongdoing and its willingness to cooperate in the investigation of its agents, including, if necessary, *the waiver of the corporate attorney-client and work product privileges*[.]"[264] In connection with this factor, the Holder Memo authorized prosecutors to request privilege waivers, though a corporation's willingness to do so was not made "an absolute requirement" for non-prosecution.[265]

Then, in 2003, DAG Larry D. Thompson published a slightly modified version of the Holder Memo, "Principles of Federal Prosecution of Business Organizations," a name that stuck in

---

[263] Memorandum from Eric H. Holder, Deputy Attorney General to All Component Heads and United States Attorneys, "Bringing Criminal Charges Against Corporations" § II, ¶A (June 16, 1999), http://tinyurl.com/k2usplh.

[264] *Id.* at § II, ¶A(4) (emphasis added).

[265] 28 U.S.C. § 547 (2012); *Id.* at § VI, ¶A.

subsequent revisions.[266] The Thompson Memo required prosecutors to assess whether a corporation should be charged for individual employees' violations, but it did not change the Holder Memo's original language on privilege waivers.[267]

The practical application by prosecutors of the waiver provisions in DOJ policy was criticized by members of the bar and Congress, citing a perceived infringement on these privileges.[268] Many companies facing investigations were reluctant to resist DOJ attorneys seeking privileged communications, at the risk of prompting an indictment. Employees, in turn, may have become less forthcoming in interviews during internal investigations, knowing whatever information they provided was likely to be turned over. Additionally, disclosure to DOJ often resulted in a waiver of privilege as to unrelated public and private third parties, encompassing the particular documents disclosed or all documents related to the relevant subject matter, thereby vastly increasing companies' exposure in lawsuits brought by others.[269]

---

[266] Memorandum from Larry D. Thompson, Deputy Attorney General, to Heads of Department Components and United States Attorneys, "Principles of Federal Prosecution of Business Organizations" (Jan. 20, 2003), http://tinyurl.com/m3p4pww.

[267] Compare id. §§ II, VI, and III(c)(i) and IV(a), with Holder Memo, supra note 19, at §§ II, VI, and 28 U.S.C. § 547 (2012).

[268] See, e.g., Letter from Former Attorneys General, Deputy Attorneys General, and Solicitor Generals to Alberto Gonzales, Attorney General (Sept. 5, 2006), http://tinyurl.com/k5o5yuq; The Thompson Memorandum's Effect on the Right to Counsel in Corporate Investigations: Hearing Before the Senate Judiciary Committee, 109th Cong., 2d Sess. (Sept. 12, 2006), http://tinyurl.com/lax6u39.

[269] It is important to keep in mind that the risk of third-party waiver can vary significantly from one federal agency to another. One example arises in the banking context, where common law and statutory privileges can protect a financial institution against third-party waivers of confidential information and communications shared with certain regulators. See, e.g., 12 U.S.C. § 1828(x); Disclosure of non-public OCC information, 12 C.F.R. § 4.36 (1999); Purpose and scope (FDIC), 12 C.F.R. § 309.1 (2011). Some agencies have also adopted aspects of the protections against inadvertent and subject matter waivers that Congress included in the 2008 addition of Rule 502 to the Federal Rules of Evidence. See, e.g., Withholding requested material (CFBC), 12 C.F.R.

The DOJ responded in 2006 with DAG Paul J. McNulty's revisions to the Principles of Federal Prosecution of Business Organizations, or the McNulty Memo, which made clear that *voluntary* privilege waiver was permitted, though it was not a prerequisite for obtaining cooperation credit.[270] The McNulty Memo also required prosecutors requesting privilege waiver to show a "legitimate need" for the material on the basis of a four-part standard and that the waiver sought be the "least intrusive" means necessary to "a complete and thorough investigation."[271]

When the McNulty Memo failed to stem legislative efforts to further limit privilege waivers in government investigations, DOJ issued its final policy response—the August 2008 revisions of DAG Mark Filip to the Principles.[272] The Filip Memo emphasizes that the touchstone for cooperation credit is the disclosure of relevant facts regarding the conduct under investigation.[273] "Accordingly, a corporation should receive the same credit for disclosing facts contained in materials that are not protected by the attorney-client privilege or attorney work product as it would for disclosing identical facts contained in materials that are so protected."[274] Elaborating on this Filip Memo policy in the important context of internal investigations, the JM clarifies that the company does not need to produce, and the government may not request, notes and memoranda generated through interviews

---

§ 1080.8(c) (2012); General discovery provisions (FTC), 16 C.F.R. § 3.31(g) (2011).

[270] Memorandum from Paul J. McNulty, Deputy Attorney General, to Heads of Department Components and United States Attorneys, "Principles of Federal Prosecution of Business Organizations" (Dec. 12, 2006), http://tinyurl.com/mvl9mrb.

[271] *Id.* at § VII.B.2.

[272] Memorandum from Mark R. Filip, Deputy Attorney General, to Heads of Department Components and United States Attorneys, "Principles of Federal Prosecution of Business Organizations" (Aug. 28, 2008), http://tinyurl.com/m38f6l4.

[273] *Id.* at 8; *see also* JM § 9-28.710 ("The critical factor is whether the corporation has provided the facts about the events[.]").

[274] Filip, *supra* note 28; JM §9-28.720(a).

conducted in an internal investigation and protected by attorney-client privilege or the work product doctrine. However, the government is free to request, and the company must produce, "relevant factual information acquired through those interviews, unless the identical information has otherwise been provided."[275] In practice and despite the thrust of the written policy, DOJ and many other federal agencies may still put pressure on to waive their privilege and work-product protections by conditioning cooperation credit or other benefits on such a waiver.[276]

DOJ's policy approach to privilege waivers has remained constant since 2008. In light of the continued uncertainty about whether to voluntarily waive privilege to reduce potential charges and penalties, the following are some of the practical considerations that companies should account for to resolve this difficult question in the best possible manner:

> **Key Considerations for Privilege Waivers**
> 1. Engage counsel early on to increase the likelihood that the privileges will apply to work arising from an internal investigation.
>
> 2. Returning to the distinction between Category I and II information, make every effort to conduct "dual-track" investigations, where privileged material is kept separate from the underlying facts.[277]
>
> 3. In deciding whether to disclose privileged information, companies should consider making use of legal tools designed to prevent a disclosure from operating as a waiver of privilege—for example, through an agreement to seek a court order preserving privilege under Federal Rule

---

[275] JM § 9-28.720, n.2.

[276] *See generally* "Federal Agency Policies that Erode the Attorney-Client Privilege," AM. BAR ASS'N, https://tinyurl.com/2p9e9ywa.

[277] A concrete example is witness interviews. Summaries that may be turned over to the government should contain only what the witness reported. Reports distilling and analyzing one or more witness interviews, and reflecting counsel's legal theories and commentary, should be prepared and maintained separately.

of Evidence 502(d) or through a contractual agreement with the government under 502(e).[278]

4. If the decision to waive has been reached instead, operate on the assumption that privilege will also be lost as to other public and private litigants; most circuits do not recognize selective waiver at all or allow it only in very limited circumstances.[279]

5. Once a decision to waive is reached, focus on ensuring that the scope of the material turned over does not exceed the specific needs of the government, and consider requesting a confidentiality agreement on the issue of third-party sharing.

B.   Managing the Internal Investigation Process

Many DOJ policies acknowledge that whether to conduct an internal investigation is ordinarily a matter for companies and their legal advisors to decide. The same is true for resolving how an investigation will proceed—its proper scope, the order in which

---

[278] For a recent case illustrating the consequences of not having a legal mechanism in place to preserve privilege in disclosing information to the government, consider *United States v. Coburn.* 2022 WL 357217 (D.N.J. Feb. 1, 2022). In that case, which involved no such mechanism, a judge ruled that a company's selective disclosure of "detailed oral downloads" from its internal investigation to DOJ as part of its cooperation with the government's investigation waived privilege as to the entire internal investigation. *See id.*; *see also In re: Ex Parte Application of financialright GmbH*, 2017 WL 2879696 (S.D.N.Y. June 23, 2017) (declining to find waiver of attorney-client privilege and protections of work product doctrine where company had previously entered into agreement with DOJ to voluntarily shared privileged information on condition of confidentiality).

[279] *See In re Pacific Pictures*, 679 F.3d 1121 (9th Cir. 2012); *In re Qwest Communications International Inc.*, 450 F.3d 1179 (10th Cir. 2006); *In re Columbia/HCA Healthcare Corporation Billing Practices Litig.*, 293 F.3d 289 (6th Cir. 2002); *U.S. v. Mass. Institute of Technology*, 129 F.3d 681 (1st Cir. 1997); *In re Steinhardt Partners, L.P.*, 9 F.3d 230 (2d Cir. 1993); *Westinghouse Electric Corp. v. Republic of the Philippines*, 951 F.2d 1414 (3d Cir. 1991); *Permian Corp. v. U.S.*, 665 F.2d 1214 (D.C. Cir. 1981); *see also Dellwood Farms, Inc. v. Cargill, Inc.*, 128 F.3d 1122, 1127 (7th Cir. 1997) ("The cases, however, generally reject a right of 'selective waiver,'" and collecting cases).

relevant facts are gathered, the assignment of responsibilities to attorneys versus non-attorneys, etc.[280] However, the government can try to influence these decisions, particularly with respect to company employees, to align with its own prosecutorial objectives.

Being too actively involved in company investigations has created problems for DOJ in the past.[281] Where DOJ has strongly influenced a company's conduct during the course of an internal investigation, the company's own actions can threaten constitutional protections designed to constrain DOJ. In a stark example, *United States v. Stein*, the Second Circuit affirmed the dismissal of an indictment against thirteen former KPMG employees based on Sixth Amendment violations that KPMG caused at the direction of government prosecutors.[282]

---

[280] *See* JM § 9-28.720(a) ("Exactly how and by whom the facts are gathered is for the corporation to decide."); U.S. DEP'T OF JUSTICE, "Assistant Attorney General Leslie R. Caldwell Delivers Remarks at New York University Law School's Program on Corporate Compliance and Enforcement" (Apr. 17, 2015) ("Let me be clear, however, the Criminal Division does not dictate how a company should conduct an investigation. . . . [A] company must determine how best to conduct its own internal investigation. Although we can provide guideposts, the manner in which an internal investigation is conducted is an internal corporate decision."); JM § 9-28-720(a) ("Exactly how and by whom the facts are gathered is for the corporation to decide"), http://tinyurl.com/zw3z5fz.

[281] On the general subject of constitutional concerns raised by excessive government involvement in internal investigations, the Manhattan federal district court caused a stir with its 2019 decision in *United States v. Connolly*, 2019 WL 2120523 (S.D.N.Y. May 2, 2019). In that case, the court found government involvement in an independent law firm's internal investigation so thorough that it had effectively become the government's "outsourced" investigation, raising Fifth Amendment concerns over statements made in the internal investigation. However, that decision, which was reversed on appeal on other grounds, has not turned out to be quite the watershed some expected, with no courts reaching similar conclusions in its wake. *See, e.g.*, MICHAEL M. SAWERS, LEVI GIOVANETTO, SOPHIE H. GOTLIEB, AND DANIEL J. COLLINS, "Watershed White Collar Decision? Assessing the Impact of *U.S. v. Connolly* One Year Later" (July 28, 2020), https://tinyurl.com/55tuz646; *United States v. Vorley*, 2020 WL 1166185 (N.D. Ill. Mar. 11, 2020) (rejecting *Connolly* argument that statements in internal investigation were compelled in violation of Fifth Amendment).

[282] *United States v. Stein*, 541 F.3d 130 (2d Cir. 2008) (*affirming United States v. Stein*, 435 F. Supp. 2d 330 (S.D.N.Y. 2006)). The opinion of Judge Kaplan in the district court is thorough and well-reasoned. We focus here primarily on the

97

Stein found that DOJ's cooperation approach had effectively caused KPMG to alter a longstanding policy of covering all employee legal fees for conduct arising within the scope of their employment. Prosecutors relied on an instruction in DOJ policy that "promise[s] of support to culpable employees and agents," including "through the advancing of attorneys['] fees," could be considered in deciding "the extent and value of a corporation's cooperation" in their refusal to sign-off on KPMG's adherence to the fee policy.[283] In response, KPMG capped coverage at a preset amount, conditioned advancement on cooperation with the government (including employees not pleading the Fifth Amendment), and terminated coverage upon indictment, all with the tacit approval of prosecutors.[284] Following adoption of the revised policy, prosecutors also instructed KPMG on what to tell employees prior to meetings with the government, including that they did not need to retain counsel, and informed KPMG of employees who—in the government's view— refused to fully participate with the investigation so that KPMG could suspend fee advancement. In addition to supporting a finding of state action, the Court concluded the prosecutors' conduct, coupled with the DOJ policy, reflected a "desire to minimize the involvement of defense attorneys."[285]

The result in *Stein* and subsequent revisions to the Principles of Federal Prosecution of Business Organizations make it less likely that future cases involving coerced corporate action will center on prosecutorial meddling in fee arrangements. However, the potential for a corporation's interests to align with the DOJ's, and to diverge from those of its employees, is alive and well.[286] In fact,

---

Second Circuit's opinion because of its binding effect on the lower courts, citing to portions of the lower court opinion as needed for relevant facts.

[283] *Stein*, 541 F.3d at 137-38; *cf. supra* note 26 at § VI.

[284] *Stein*, 541 F.3d at 139.

[285] *Id.* at 143, 146-47.

[286] *See* JM § 9-28.730 ("In evaluating cooperation, however, prosecutors should not take into account whether a corporation is advancing or reimbursing attorneys' fees or providing counsel to employees, officers, or directors under investigation or indictment.").

since the release of the Yates Memo[287] and related policies, it has become an accepted practice for the government to involve itself in internal investigations, dictating what companies should *not* do to be seen as cooperative.

One example of this new involvement is an increase in DOJ requests that companies withhold information from current and former employees under investigation. Though not unheard of before Yates, such requests were rare and narrowly tailored to serve particular objectives, like a credible concern of ongoing fraud. Absent such an articulable need, satisfying these requests risks preventing employees from fully preparing their defense by reviewing relevant information, often contained in their own documents and emails, and also may prevent companies from developing an understanding of the factual record through interviews with employees about this information. As some commentators have observed, the restriction on information sharing may also undermine joint defense and common interest agreements, whose efficacy partly depends on the flow of information between company counsel and counsel for individuals.[288]

A more recent trend is the "de-confliction" request. As used here, de-confliction refers to the deferral of one party's witness interview until another party has completed its own. Until 2016, use of the term in DOJ's public documents was reserved for information sharing and joint investigations among government agencies, not cooperation between the government and private parties.[289] That has since changed, most notably in 2019 with DOJ's publication of the FCPA Corporate Enforcement Policy, which became part of the JM and remains in effect.

---

[287] *See supra* § III(c)(ii).

[288] WILLIAM F. JOHNSON, "DOJ's Increasing Involvement in Internal Investigations" (July 5, 2017), tinyurl.com/3u6djfc7.

[289] ANDREW WEISSMANN, Chief, Fraud Section, U.S. Dep't of Justice, "The Fraud Section's Foreign Corrupt Practices Act Enforcement Plan and Guidance" at 2 (Apr. 5, 2016) (emphasis added).

The Policy provides greater transparency about requirements for companies seeking mitigation credit for voluntarily self-disclosing misconduct, fully cooperating with an investigation, and implementing timely and appropriate remediation measures. Under the Policy, each of the bases for credit—self-disclosure, cooperation, and remediation—is treated separately, with its own list of cooperation "items," and the credit available to companies depends on their satisfaction of those "items."[290] One item of the five listed for full cooperation is: "[w]here requested and appropriate, de-confliction of witness interviews and other investigative steps that a company intends to take as part of its internal investigation with steps that the Department intends to take as part of its investigation[.]"[291]

Conditioning cooperation credit on counsel not meeting with knowledgeable employees for any extended period approaches the "desire to minimize [] involvement of defense attorneys" criticized in *Stein*. This issue also creates tension with other parts of the cooperation analysis. For example, the JM provides that "[e]xactly how and by whom the facts are gathered is for the corporation to decide,"[292] and identifies only making witnesses available, not making them available to the government first, let alone exclusively, as relevant to assessing cooperation.[293] Delaying interviews can also impede a company's obligation to disclose all relevant facts about individuals, and failure to disclose can itself result in greater penalties.[294]

The DOJ has offered little clarification about the circumstances in which de-confliction requests are appropriate, nor has it explained the impact failing to heed them will have on the penalties

[290] JM § 9-47.120 (under the voluntary self-disclosure prong, "[t]he Department will *require* the following items for a company to receive credit for voluntary self-disclosure of wrongdoing . . .") (emphasis added).

[291] JM § 9-47.120(3)(b).

[292] JM § 9-28-720(a).

[293] *See* JM § 9-28.720, n.1.

[294] Press Release, State Street Corporation Agrees to Pay More than $64 Million to Resolve Fraud Charges (Jan. 18, 2017) (on file with the Department of Justice).

companies face. The only reported comment to date, from a former Criminal Division AAG, is that de-confliction requests should be "rare," though some evidence from 2017 suggested that requests were increasing in frequency.[295] As to penalties, compliance with de-confliction requests has not been mentioned in any DOJ settlement press releases. For its part, the FCPA Corporate Enforcement Policy indicates that companies "will be eligible for some cooperation credit if they meet the criteria of JM 9-28.700 . . . but the credit generally will be markedly less than for full cooperation."[296] For companies facing millions of dollars in potential penalties, this language makes earning full cooperation credit all the more imperative. For example, a former deputy chief of the DOJ's Fraud Section once stated in a speech that if the target-company of its investigation, Alstom, had self-disclosed its conduct and cooperated with the investigation, the DOJ would have sought a penalty as low as $207 million, which stands in stark contrast to the $772 million assessed as part of Alstom's FCPA settlement.[297]

C. Compliance Counsel – Management of Company Operations

In 2015, the DOJ announced its hiring of a compliance counsel, who would report to the Chief of the Fraud Section, to assist DOJ prosecutors in evaluating the effectiveness of companies' corporate compliance programs. Specifically, the DOJ's press release revealed that the newly appointed position would scrutinize any compliance program that a company had in place during the conduct giving rise to the prospect of criminal charges and whether the corporation had taken meaningful remedial action, such as implementing new compliance measures to detect and prevent

---

[295] ROGER HAMILTON-MARTIN, "Leslie Caldwell: 'deconfliction' requests should be rare" (Apr. 28, 2016), http://tinyurl.com/m5yzods.

[296] Weissmann, *supra* note 45, at § A.2 pp. 6-7.

[297] JIMMY HOOVER, *Feds Say Sky-High Fines Show Perks of FCPA Self-Reporting,* Law 360 (Mar. 12, 2015), https://www.law360.com/articles/631116/feds-say-sky-high-fines-show-perks-of-fcpa-self-reporting.

future wrongdoing. Together with more recent developments (*e.g.*, the 2022 hiring of a former chief compliance officer, Hewlett-Packard's Glenn Leon, to lead the Criminal Division's Fraud Section), this announcement emphasizes the importance the DOJ now places on compliance programs in assessing whether to charge a company for failing to detect or prevent criminal wrongdoing by its employees.

While this chapter has largely focused on a company's ability to react to a DOJ investigation, it would serve any company well to proactively assess its compliance program on an annual basis, perhaps in consultation with outside counsel. The JM contains a wide range of factors for counsel to consider in determining whether compliance programs are well-designed, applied in good faith, and effective in more than just name. In addition, the Fraud Section published updated guidance in June 2020, entitled "Evaluation of Corporate Compliance Programs," which outlines general "sample topics and questions" that the DOJ has found particularly relevant in evaluating corporate compliance programs. The topics range from analysis and remediation of underlying conduct—including what the "root cause" of the misconduct was, and how "systemic were the issues"—to compliance policies and procedures, encompassing such questions as how a program was designed and implemented.

As part of its compliance program, a company should ensure that there are appropriate guidelines for remedial action in the case of employee misconduct, even when such conduct does not rise to the level of violating the law. The company's attempts to remedy and correct such behavior could result in more lenient treatment from the government. In remarks he delivered in March 2022, Assistant Attorney General Kenneth Polite made it known that companies with strong compliance programs can expect such leniency when they otherwise find themselves in the DOJ's sights: "The Department is committed to rewarding responsible companies and financial institutions that promote ethical corporate culture and invest in effective compliance programs."[298] In the past, the DOJ has even announced decisions to not prosecute based on a "company's robust compliance program," noting that a major investment bank was a "compliance success story."

With this guidance in hand, the simple step of evaluating a company's compliance program could potentially avoid employee misconduct from the outset—and save the company millions of dollars in penalties on the back-end—should the DOJ initiate an investigation.

---

[298] U.S. DEP'T OF JUSTICE, "Assistant Attorney General Kenneth A. Polite Jr. Delivers Remarks at ACAMS 2022 Hollywood Conference" (Mar. 22, 2022), https://tinyurl.com/2han32e5.

Chapter 5

Department of Justice (DOJ) Antitrust Division Investigations

By: Jason C. Murray and David Griffith[299]

A DOJ antitrust investigation can be an imposing and trying experience for any company. From criminal cartels to merger reviews, DOJ antitrust investigations often involve millions of documents, multiple parties, dozens of witnesses, complex economics, and conduct spanning a decade or more. They are expensive, disruptive to business, and can take years to resolve. Even figuring out where to begin under such circumstances can be daunting.

Further, not all antitrust investigations are alike—even those within the Antitrust Division's purview. A criminal cartel investigation is very different from a merger investigation, which is different from a civil non-merger investigation. And aside from the type of investigation, an investigation will differ considerably depending on each party's role. For instance, in the realm of merger investigations, the burden, cost, and responsibilities of the merging parties certifying substantial compliance with a Second Request are very different from those of a third party complying with a Civil Investigative Demand.

This chapter is intended to assist in-house attorneys in understanding the key strategies for navigating a DOJ antitrust investigation.

I. JURISDICTION OF THE ANTITRUST DIVISION OF THE DEPARTMENT OF JUSTICE

<u>Criminal Investigations</u>: The Antitrust Division of the United States Department of Justice (DOJ) has exclusive responsibility for

---

[299] Jason C. Murray is a Partner at Crowell & Moring LLP in Los Angeles and co-chairs the firm's Antitrust and Competition Group. David Griffith is an Associate in Crowell's Antitrust and Competition, and White Collar and Regulatory Enforcement Groups.

criminal enforcement of the federal antitrust laws. DOJ prosecutes criminal antitrust violations, and these prosecutions can lead to large fines and lengthy jail sentences. A Sherman Act violation carries a statutory maximum penalty of $100 million for corporations, and $1 million and 10 years of imprisonment for individuals.[300] The prescribed statutory maximum fines may be further enhanced under the Sentencing Reform Act, 18 U.S.C. § 3571. For example, in the long-running investigation into automotive parts, it was reported that DOJ has charged 47 companies and 65 executives with fines totalling more than $2.9 billion.[301] At least nine of these fines have exceeded $100 million.[302]

Civil Investigations: DOJ also has jurisdiction over civil antitrust violations. Most civil cases get settled by consent decrees but, DOJ can and does file civil actions seeking a court order forbidding future violations of the law and requiring companies to remedy the anticompetitive effects of past violations. The range of conduct that may be investigated civilly is broad, ranging from exclusionary conduct, information sharing, invitations to collude, and other conduct. Indeed, the Antitrust Civil Process Act of 1976 broadly defines the term "antitrust investigation" to mean "any inquiry conducted by any antitrust investigator for the purpose of ascertaining whether any person is or has been engaged in any antitrust violation..."[303]

---

[300] 15 U.S.C. § 1.

[301] DOJ Antitrust Division, *Japanese Auto Parts Company Agrees to Plead Guilty to Antitrust Conspiracy Involving Steel Tubes* (Nov. 8, 2016), *available at* https://www.justice.gov/opa/pr/japanese-auto-parts-company-agrees-plead-guilty-antitrust-conspiracy-involving-steel-tubes.

[302] DOJ Antitrust Division, *Sherman Act Violations Yielding a Corporate Fine of $10 Million or More* (Feb. 16, 2017), *available at* https://www.justice.gov/atr/sherman-act-violations-yielding-corporate-fine-10-million-or-more.

[303] 15 U.S.C. § 1311(c).

Merger Investigations: DOJ—and the Federal Trade
Commission—review proposed mergers, acquisitions, and joint
ventures under the Hart-Scott-Rodino Improvements Act of 1976,
as amended (the "HSR Act") and Section 7 of the Clayton Act.

- The HSR Act requires that parties to proposed
  stock or asset acquisitions exceeding certain
  thresholds (and not exempt under the HSR act) file
  premerger notification reports with the FTC and
  then observe a statutorily prescribed waiting
  period prior to closing the transaction. Once the
  parties file their merger notification report, the
  FTC and DOJ confer as to which agency will have
  exclusive jurisdiction to review the merger. This is
  the internal agency clearance process. Once a
  merger is "cleared" to DOJ or FTC, the agency
  can then review the transaction. DOJ and FTC
  typically allocate proposed mergers based on the
  historical experience of each agency in addressing
  specific sectors, which was last outlined in a
  Memorandum of Agreement entered into on
  March 5, 2002.[304] For example, DOJ has
  historically reviewed telecom mergers, while the
  FTC has reviewed oil and gas mergers.

- Section 7 of the Clayton Act prohibits mergers and
  acquisitions where the effect "may be substantially
  to lessen competition, or to tend to create a
  monopoly." Under Section 7 of the Clayton Act,
  DOJ also has jurisdiction to investigate mergers or
  joint ventures, which do not require an HSR
  premerger notification. DOJ, and FTC, often
  investigate such mergers if they are likely to
  substantially lessen competition.

---

[304] Federal Trade Commission, *FTC and DOJ Announce New Clearance
Procedures for Antitrust Matters* (Mar. 5, 2002), *available at*
https://www.ftc.gov/news-events/press-releases/2002/03/ftc-and-doj-announce-
new-clearance-procedures-antitrust-matters.

II.   CRIMINAL ANTITRUST INVESTIGATIONS

A.   Antitrust Division Organization

The Assistant Attorney General of the Antitrust Division bears ultimate responsibility in federal criminal antitrust matters. The Deputy Assistant Attorney General (DAAG) for Criminal Enforcement and the Director of Criminal Enforcement oversee the Antitrust Division's criminal enforcement program. These positions typically are filled by career Antitrust Division prosecutors and not politically appointed DAAGs.

The DAAG for Criminal Enforcement, in turn, oversees trial lawyers from the Division's two criminal sections (Criminal I and Criminal II) in Washington, DC, and three other regional field offices. Criminal I and II trial attorneys' sole focus is criminal antitrust investigations and prosecutions. Field office attorneys mostly conduct criminal investigations and prosecutions, but can also assist in civil and merger investigations.

Antitrust Division trial attorneys assigned to criminal matters work closely with special agents from the FBI and other federal agency investigators, depending on the subject matter of the investigation. They also coordinate with the DOJ Criminal Division and U.S. Attorneys' offices, as well as with staff attorneys from foreign antitrust agencies in cross border criminal cartel investigations.

B.   Subject Matter of Criminal Investigations

The Antitrust Division published an Antitrust Primer describing the most common antitrust violations and events that may indicate anticompetitive collusion.[305] Criminal antitrust prosecutions involve clear per se violations of the antitrust laws, such as price

---

[305] DOJ Antitrust Division, Price Fixing, Bid Rigging, and Market Allocation Schemes: What They Are and What to Look For, (revised February 2021), *available at* https://www.justice.gov/atr/price-fixing-bid-rigging-and-market-allocation-schemes.

fixing, bid rigging, or market division. These restraints may take several forms, such as the following:

- Agreeing to raise, fix, or stabilize prices;

- Eliminating or reducing discounts;

- Adopting a standard formula for computing prices;

- Maintaining certain price differentials between different types, sizes, or quantities of products;

- Adhering to a minimum fee or price schedule;

- Bid suppression (one competitor agrees to refrain from bidding);

- Complementary bidding (one competitor agrees to submit a bid that will not be accepted);

- Bid rotation (competitors take turns being the low bidders);

- Subcontracting (competitors agree to not bid as principal against each other); and

- Dividing markets or customers.

In addition to the types of anticompetitive activity in the Antitrust Primer delineated above, the Biden administration issued an executive order in late 2021 instructing federal agencies to promote competition in specific sectors of the US economy[306]:

---

[306] Executive Order 14036, Promoting Competition in the American Economy (July 15, 2021), https://www.whitehouse.gov/briefing-room/presidential-actions/2021/07/09/executive-order-on-promoting-competition-in-the-american-economy/.

108

- Technology

- Healthcare

- Labor markets

- Agriculture/Food

- Aviation

- Defense/Government Contracts

- Real Estate

Criminal investigations target both companies and culpable individuals. Unless the conduct comes to the attention of the company through internal sources, the company typically learns of the investigation from the service of a grand jury subpoena, the execution of a search warrant, or DOJ attorneys approaching current or former company employees to request informal interviews.

C.   Penalties

DOJ historically has aggressively pursued criminal cartels—both in terms of penalties imposed and criminal charges filed but the enforcement landscape appears to be evolving. Every year, DOJ publishes statistics on criminal enforcement fines and individual charged.[307]

As the table below indicates, DOJ enforcement significantly decreased towards the tail end of the last decade:

[307] DOJ Antitrust Division, Criminal Enforcement: Trends Charts Through Fiscal Year 2021, *available at* https://www.justice.gov/atr/criminal-enforcement-fine-and-jail-charts.

Year	Corporations Charged	Individuals Charged	Total Fines
2015	20	66	$3.6 billion
2016	19	52	$399 million
2017	8	27	$67 million
2018	5	28	$172 million
2019	13	15	$365 million
2020	11	22	$529 million
2021	14	29	$151 million

However, despite the downturn in enforcement, criminal antitrust fines can still be staggeringly high. As of February 16, 2017, there had been 138 fines or penalties that have exceeded $10 million, with 32 of these exceeding $100 million.[308] And while most fines are the result of DOJ settlements, a few cases go to trial. In the *LCD* case, AU Optronics was found guilty by a jury and sentenced to pay a then-record fine of $500 million.

In addition to the recent decrease in corporate fines and penalties there has been a slight decrease in average prison sentences for individuals who committed criminal antitrust violations. From 1990 through 1999, the average prison sentence for individuals was 8 months. From 2000 through 2009, the average sentence increased to 20 months, and from 2010 through 2019, the average sentence decreased to 18 months. It remains DOJ's stated position that "the most effective deterrent to cartel offenses is to impose jail sentences on the individuals who commit them."[309] More generally, focusing on individual accountability for corporate wrongdoing continues to be the policy of the Department of Justice as a whole despite differing administrations. In September 2015, then Deputy Attorney General Sally Yates stated that "[it is our obligation at the Justice Department to ensure that we are holding lawbreakers accountable regardless of whether they commit their

---

[308] *Supra*, note 4.

[309] Scott D Hammond, Deputy Ass't Att'y Gen., Antitrust Div., Dep't of Justice, Charting New Waters in International Cartel Prosecutions, Speech before the ABA Criminal Justice Section's Twentieth Annual National Institute on White-collar Crimes (March 2, 2016).

crimes on the street corner or in the boardroom. In the white-collar context, that means pursuing not just corporate entities, but also the individuals through which these corporations act."[310] Ms. Yates further codified this policy in what is now known as the Yates Memo.[311] The Yates Memo was subsequently adopted by DOJ under both Trump and Biden, but as the chart above indicates, the significant downturn in enforcement beginning the final year of the Obama administration, serves as a reminder that DOJ's priorities and enforcement decisions may be influenced by the priorities of the administration in power at the time.[312]

D.   DOJ's Leniency Regime

The DOJ leniency program is the cornerstone of its criminal enforcement efforts and the source of many cartel investigations. It has been a very successful whistle-blower program, which has been adopted by many antitrust agencies worldwide. The leniency program allows a company to self-report antitrust crimes in exchange for significant benefits including no criminal

---

[310] Sally Q. Yates, Deputy Att'y Gen., Dept't of Justice, Remarks at New York University School of Law Announcing New Policy in Individual Liability in Matters of Corporate Wrongdoing (Sept. 10, 2015), http://www.justice.gov/opa/speech/deputy-attorney-general-sally-quillian-yates-delivers-remarks-new-york-university-school.

[311] Memorandum from Sally Yates, Deputy Att'y Gen., Dep't of Justice, to Assistant Att'y Gen., Antitrust Div., et al. (Sept. 9, 2015), http://www.justice.gov/dag/file/769036/download.

[312] Indeed, certain provisions of the Yates Memo were subsequently walked back by the Trump administration in 2018, and then reinstituted by the Biden administration in 2021. See Deputy Attorney General Rod J. Rosenstein Delivers Remarks at the American Conference Institute's 35th International Conference on Foreign Corrupt Practices Act, Office of Public Affairs, US Dep't of Justice (Nov. 29, 2018), https://www.justice.-gov/archives/dag/file/769036/download; see also Lisa O. Monaco, Deputy Att'y Gen., Dept't of Justice, Keynote Address at ABA's 36th National Institute on White Collar Crime (October 28, 2021) ("Accountability starts with the individuals responsible for criminal conduct … this department's first priority in corporate criminal matters to prosecute the individuals who commit and profit from corporate malfeasance."), https://www.justice.gov/opa/speech/deputy-attorney-general-lisa-o-monaco-gives-keynote-address-abas-36th-national-institute.

convictions, no fines, and no jail time for employees.[313] Being the "amnesty applicant" in a cartel case requires a company to reach out to DOJ very quickly as only one company can be the "first in the door" to obtain amnesty. A second-in company—even if it is only second by a matter of minutes—may see its employees prosecuted and face substantial fines. For that reason, even when companies have not yet completed their internal investigations, they often seek leniency as soon as it becomes apparent that a criminal antitrust violation was committed. Company counsel will call the Antitrust Division to obtain a "marker" to keep its place in line, and, hopefully first, in the DOJ investigation. DOJ will ordinarily provide a company additional time to perfect its leniency application—with 30 days being common, but more or less time being possible based on factors such as the location and number of company employees, the number of documents, and whether DOJ currently has an ongoing investigation.

The leniency regime has four basic components:

1. A company will automatically be granted "Type A" leniency if DOJ has *not yet begun an investigation* and the following conditions are met:

   - The corporation is the first to come forward with information about the cartel.

   - The corporation must terminate its part in the illegal activity.

   - The corporation must truthfully and completely report the violation promptly after its discovery.

---

[313] Another benefit is that a successful leniency applicant will not have pay treble damages in follow-on civil litigation if they cooperate with the plaintiffs in those cases. Under the Antitrust Criminal Penalty Enhancement and Reform Act of 2004 ("ACPERA"), the civil liability of a leniency applicant is limited to the actual damages attributable to the entity's conduct rather than the usual joint-and-several treble damages faced by antitrust defendants.

- The corporation must cooperate fully and completely with DOJ during the course of the entire investigation.

- The corporation must confess as a corporation and not just isolated individuals.

- The corporation must make restitution to injured parties, if possible.

- The corporation cannot have coerced other parties to participate in the cartel and cannot have been the ringleader or originator of the cartel.

2. Alternatively, the Division has the discretion to grant "Type B" leniency *after it commenced an investigation* if the following conditions are met:

- The corporation must be the "first-in" to cooperate.

- The corporation must promptly terminate its part in the illegal activity.

- The corporation must truthfully and completely report the violation promptly after its discovery.

- The corporation must cooperate fully and completely with DOJ during the course of the entire investigation.

- The corporation must confess as a corporation and not just isolated individuals.

- The corporation must make restitution to injured parties, if possible.

- When the corporation comes forward, DOJ must not yet have evidence against the applicant that is likely to result in a sustainable conviction.

- A grant of leniency must not be unfair to others, considering the nature of the illegal activity, the corporation's role in it, and when the corporation comes forward.

3. Where a company qualifies for leniency, all directors, officers, and employees of the corporation who admit their involvement in the illegal activity, as part of the corporate confession, will receive leniency in the form of not being charged criminally for the illegal activity. In other words, the individuals will face no jail time or individual criminal fines.

4. In addition, the leniency policy for individuals applies to individuals who approach DOJ on their own behalf, not as part of a corporate proffer.[314]

E. Best Practices Upon Learning of the Investigation

1. <u>Dawn Raid/Execution of Search Warrant</u>

The most jarring way a company can learn of a criminal investigation is when DOJ trial attorneys and FBI agents execute a search warrant through an official dawn raid.

Few companies expect a raid. To the extent practicable, at least one lawyer at each company facility should have been trained regarding the proper response to a search warrant. Management at facilities without a company lawyer should know whom to call in

---

[314] For more information on the Leniency Program, *see* the DOJ's Corporate Leniency Policy, *available at* https://www.justice.gov/atr/page/file/1490246/downloadand the Frequently Asked Questions About the Antitrust Division's Leniency Program, *available at* https://www.justice.gov/atr/page/file/1490311/download..

the event of a search. Here are some do's and don'ts in the event of such a raid:

The company *should*:

>Meet with the lead agent and learn the identity of the supervising prosecutor;
>
>Ask for a copy of the warrant and review it carefully;
>
>Determine whether agents are attempting to interview employees;
>
>Advise employees of their rights and obligations—remind them they do not have to speak with the agents and may consult with an attorney prior to doing so;
>
>Consider sending non-essential employees home;
>
>Object to the seizure of privileged documents;
>
>Make a careful record of events;
>
>Ask to be present when agents make an inventory of seized materials;
>
>Ask for copies of seized computer files; and
>
>Advise the lead agent of any classified or potentially privileged documents that are seized (if applicable).

The company *should not*:

>Interfere with the search;
>
>Allow anyone to alter, hide, or destroy documents;

Consent to the search of any area or the seizure of
any materials beyond the scope of the warrant;

Volunteer substantive information;

Instruct or encourage anyone not to speak with the
agents.

2. "Informal" Coordinated Visits

Another tactic frequently employed by DOJ is the informal—or
"drop in"—visit to company employees. Such visits frequently
occur simultaneously. For example, a DOJ attorney and FBI agent
may show up at several employees' houses in the morning or
evening without a warrant or subpoena, hoping to talk about the
subject of the investigation. While the company may ultimately
determine to cooperate with the DOJ investigation, it is generally
preferable to delay these interviews until a legal strategy has been
determined. If employees are approached at their home, they
should contact in-house counsel immediately for further
instruction. And it may be preferable that any interview should
proceed only with counsel present, or should not occur at all.

3. Receipt of Grand Jury Subpoena

Alternatively, a company may first learn of an investigation upon
receipt of a grand jury subpoena. Companies should observe
certain best practices when they receive a grand jury subpoena,
including:

- Promptly notifying employees who may possess
  the documents at issue;

- Issuing a document preservation (or "hold") notice
  to all relevant employees;

- Notifying IT personnel and getting them involved
  early in compliance efforts; and

- Suspending any scheduled document destruction or deletion protocols.

It is imperative to make clear to employees that any document destruction, hiding, alteration, or manipulation is strictly prohibited and could result in criminal charges. Further, the company should not immediately start searching through files or physically removing any documents in response to the subpoena. Instead, it is preferable to have to have a team of legal and forensic experts supervise this process, as they will know how to respect the form of e-Discovery production to DOJ and make the document production to DOJ a smoother process.

F.   Immediate Response to Investigation

After learning of a DOJ investigation, the company should begin to very quickly gather relevant facts about the alleged conduct. Of utmost importance is the decision to seek leniency, which, as described above, must be done promptly if the company hopes to be first in. Even if another company already conditionally holds the amnesty position, the company will still need to determine whether it wants to cooperate. While a second-in company may still face criminal charges and the attending fines and prison exposure for employees, the company can receive more lenient treatment based on early cooperation through lower fines and more individuals "carved in" to—that is, protected by—the company's plea. In any event, the company should promptly identify the relevant employees and begin interviews to understand the facts. And counsel should be able to perform targeted searches of electronically stored information to quickly gather documents to assist in these interviews—for example, by searching for any correspondence with competitors.

Upon learning of the investigation, counsel for the company should reach out to the DOJ investigation team to understand the scope of the investigation and the nature of the alleged conduct. Counsel should inquire as to whether the company as well as any employees are considered a subject or a target of the investigation:

- A target is "a person as to whom the prosecutor or the grand jury has substantial evidence linking him or her to the commission of a crime and who, in the judgment of the prosecutor, is a putative defendant."[315]

- A subject is "a person whose conduct is within the scope of the grand jury's investigation."[316]

It is incumbent on corporate counsel to provide proper *Upjohn* warnings clearly and early during these interviews. If at any point it becomes clear that an individual is a target or is likely to become a target of the investigation, it may become advisable to retain separate counsel for that individual as soon as practicable. This will help avoid actual or potential conflicts of interest, which can frequently arise when, for instance, a company chooses to plead guilty but certain employees do not (and vice versa), or when employees within the company attempt to cast blame on one another.

G. Complying with Investigation

Document production: If the company believes the subpoena is overbroad or overly burdensome, the company may attempt to negotiate with DOJ to narrow the scope and reduce its burden. For example, the company can work with DOJ to produce high-value documents early on, which may help to narrow DOJ's focus. This can ultimately result in a lighter burden for the company. Even if the company is not cooperating, it is most often unproductive to threaten a motion to quash the subpoena during its negotiations with DOJ. The Antitrust Division's Guidelines state that it is the "policy and practice of the Antitrust Division to defend its subpoenas vigorously against motions to quash."[317]

---

[315] U.S. Attorneys' Manual § 9-11.151 (1997).

[316] *Id.*

[317] U.S. Department of Justice, *Antitrust Division Manual* § III.F.4.a (5th ed. 2015).

118

<u>Witness Interviews:</u> If the company is cooperating—as either an amnesty applicant or a later-in company—DOJ will want to interview employees to help build its case. For company employees who are not targets or potential targets, this should not be a problem, but for individuals who are targets, more care must be taken in deciding whether and how to make the individual available. For individuals on the cusp, a candid interview that assists the DOJ's investigation may be the tipping point between that individual being carved in to the company's plea agreement and being carved out and facing potential individual criminal exposure. But individuals who are clear targets—or have even already been informed they will be carved out—stand to gain little from voluntarily appearing for such an interview.

DOJ may also subpoena individuals to testify before a grand jury. Individuals who have been called to testify before the grand jury may not have counsel present, although they may step outside to confer with counsel if necessary. Further, individuals may exercise their Fifth Amendment right during their testimony by refusing to answer questions if a truthful answer would be incriminatory. DOJ guidelines counsel that when a witness is subpoenaed, the witness should be made aware of their status as a target.[318]

As the DOJ staff gathers evidence during its investigation, it will determine what type of case, if any, will be recommended. Throughout the course of the investigation, it is possible that individuals or companies may agree to plead guilty and be charged by criminal information. For companies or individuals who do not plead guilty, DOJ guidelines counsel that the staff attorneys provide notification to any prospective defendant's counsel so that they have an opportunity to present their views prior to any recommendation to the Front Office that a criminal indictment be pursued. If the views of the staff attorneys do not change, there may be an opportunity for attorneys to also meet with the Director of Criminal Enforcement of the Front Office as an "appeal." If, on the other hand, the DOJ concludes that no charges should be

---

[318] *Id.* § III.F.4.b.

brought, it will notify the subjects of the investigation that the investigation has been closed.

III.   CIVIL NON-MERGER INVESTIGATIONS

A.   Scope

Some of the Division's highest-profile matters in recent years have been civil, including the investigations and subsequent litigation against Google for its advertising practices, Apple in the e-books case, and against American Express regarding the use of anti-steering rules and non-discrimination provisions.

In civil investigations, DOJ ordinarily does not seek civil fines (outside of HSR violations), but most often seeks injunctive relief to enjoin illegal conduct from occurring again. Exceptionally, DOJ has sought and received disgorgement of profits due to anticompetitive conduct.[319] This is rare, as DOJ tends to defer to private parties to seek monetary relief.

A company may first learn of a civil investigation through a voluntary request for information or the receipt of a civil investigative demand (CID), the compulsory process tool most commonly used by DOJ. CIDs require the production of documents, responses to interrogatories, or deposition testimony.

B.   Best Practices

Many of the same considerations pertaining to criminal investigations apply to civil investigations with equal force, particularly since the line between civil and criminal behavior may

---

[319] *United States v. Keyspan Corp.*, 763 F. Supp. 2d 633, 638-41 (S.D.N.Y. 2011) (concluding, as a matter of first impression, that disgorgement was available to remedy a Sherman Act violation); See Competitive Impact Statement at 10-12, *United States v. Twin America*, No. 1:12-cv-08989 (S.D.N.Y. 2015) ([T]his case involves a consummated joint venture that resulted in actual and substantial consumer harm. . . . By awarding disgorgement of Defendants' ill-gotten gain, the proposed Final Judgment will prevent Defendants from being unjustly enriched by their conduct and deter Defendants and others from engaging in similar conduct in the future.").

be blurry in some cases. Upon receipt of a CID, the company should:

- Immediately issue a preservation notice;

- Avoid document destruction or alteration; and

- Ensure that any automatic deletion protocols are suspended.

Any efforts to interfere with or obstruct a civil investigation can turn a civil investigation into a criminal one.

The company should promptly identify the relevant employees and begin interviews. Even in civil investigations, it is always good practice to provide individuals with *Upjohn* warnings. While DOJ historically has not targeted individuals in separate civil complaints, the focus always is on conduct committed by individual employees or executives. The Yates Memo noted that "civil attorneys should consistently focus on individuals as well as the company and evaluate whether to bring suit against an individual based on considerations beyond that individual's ability to pay."[320]

It is also true in civil investigations that separate representation for individuals may be advisable if it becomes clear to the company that individuals may face exposure or run into conflicts with the company.

1.   Narrowing the Scope of the CID

There are certain modifications to the CID a company can request to try to ease the burden of complying with a CID. Any meritorious objections on burden, breadth, and relevance grounds typically can likely be resolved through dialogue with the DOJ

---

[320] Brent Snyder, *Individual Accountability for Antitrust Crimes* (Feb. 19, 2016), *available at* https://www.justice.gov/opa/file/826721/download.

staff attorneys. But a wholesale challenge to the issuance of the CID through a motion to quash is unlikely to succeed.

Such discussions with the DOJ staff attorneys are also useful in that they may help inform the company of the Division's focus or priorities. To that end, early in the process, the company should:

- Negotiate with the staff attorneys to try and agree on a list of custodians whose documents will be searched and the relevant time period. In the ESI age, limiting the number of custodians and narrowing the time period by even a few months can substantially reduce e-discovery costs.

- Explain why a specific request for documents or data is burdensome and unlikely to yield useful information. If a document or data request seems unlikely to lead to any information useful to the investigation, DOJ staff attorneys are frequently willing to consider narrowing or modifying the request.

- Follow DOJ best practices and engage DOJ staff attorneys regarding the use of search terms, predictive coding, or other methods of technology-assisted review. DOJ has issued guidance regarding the use of such discovery practices, such as the DOJ Model Second Request, which requires a company to submit a written description of the methods used to conduct any part of the search for documents. If search terms are used, the company must submit: (1) a list of the proposed terms; (2) a tally of all the terms that appear in the collection and the frequency of each term (that is, a hit report); (3) a list of stop words and operators for the platform being used; and (4) a glossary of industry and company terminology. If predictive coding is used, it requires the company to submit: (1) confirmation that subject-matter experts will be reviewing the seed set and training rounds; (2) recall, precision, and confidence level statistics (or an equivalent); and (3) a validation process that allows the Division to review statistically-significant samples of documents categorized as non-responsive.[321]

- Because the initial return date in a CID is frequently unrealistic, counsel should attempt to negotiate a rolling production of documents with a more realistic compliance date—perhaps prioritizing certain document requests at the agency's request. The Division will routinely grant reasonable requests for extensions of time.

Strategies for responding to data requests or interrogatories do not materially differ. Counsel should confer with the staff attorneys and try to determine the agency's priorities in an effort to develop a workable schedule and attempt to negotiate modifications for interrogatories that are overly broad and unlikely to assist the investigation. A dialogue with the staff attorneys can cut to the heart of what they are looking for and save the company time and expense.

One area that frequently poses an enormous burden is the creation of a privilege log. Antitrust cases frequently involve millions of documents. Further complicating matters is that large companies may employ individuals who perform dual business and legal responsibilities. In larger investigations, a privilege log can contain tens of thousands of entries. Given the expense and time associated with compiling a privilege log of this magnitude, it behooves companies to work with DOJ staff attorneys to explore ways this

---

[321] Request for Additional Information and Documentary Material Issued to [Weebyewee Corporation], *available at* https://www.justice.gov/atr/file/706636/download. A collection of speeches and memoranda given by Division personnel dealing with e-discovery issues such as technology-assisted review—albeit in their personal capacity—can be found here: https://www.justice.gov/atr/electronic-discovery. These documents provide additional insight into how the Division may deal with these issues.

burden can be minimized. Certain strategies include, but are not limited to: seeking to omit conversations with outside counsel; seeking to omit or not providing descriptions for conversations with in-house counsel who have an exclusively legal role; and, seeking to limit the time period for which a privilege log must be provided. In any event, extra care should be paid to privilege log entries in which no attorney is present. These will attract the attention of the DOJ staff attorneys, and further negotiation may be complicated if unmeritorious claims of privilege have been asserted.

2.   Interviews and Depositions

During the course of the civil investigation, it is common for DOJ to first request informal interviews of certain individuals—particularly those that are not primary subjects (or targets) of the investigation. It is important to note that intentionally lying or withholding information during these interviews may constitute a criminal offense under 18 U.S.C. § 1505 if the information provided is construed as an attempt to evade or obstruct compliance with the CID. Counsel is typically always present at these interviews. Eventually, the investigators will also likely want to depose the relevant individuals. This testimony is taken under oath and is transcribed.

3.   Advocacy

There are several ways to advocate before DOJ in an antitrust investigation, including through in-person meetings with the staff attorneys or the front office and the submission of written advocacy through targeted letters or white papers.

One key question is when to submit such written advocacy. A common strategy is to proactively submit white papers to DOJ. There are pros and cons to submitting white papers early in the investigation. The submission of a white paper can successfully narrow the scope of the investigation or have the unintended consequence of expanding it. If the investigation is wide-ranging and it has not yet coalesced around a theory, submitting a white paper can help the agency back down from certain theories. But it can also expand the investigation in an area that was not an initial focus.

That is why companies often seek informal feedback from the DOJ staff attorneys as to which business area or legal or factual topic is crucial to the investigation. And the DOJ staff attorneys routinely ask the parties to submit white papers on specific topics, including the factual record, discrete legal issues, or economic analysis. Anticipating these topics early so that the parties can quickly respond to such requests may accelerate and focus the investigation.

C.   Resolution / Consent Decree Negotiation

Ultimately, staff attorneys will recommend whether a suit should be filed or whether the investigation should be closed with no further action. DOJ may close the investigation if it believes that no wrongdoing has occurred, it will not be able to meet its burden at trial, or any other number of reasons. If DOJ believes wrongdoing has occurred, it may recommend further action being taken—either in the form of a consent agreement or, if the parties are unwilling to enter into a such a consent decree, by filing a complaint in federal court.

Before DOJ actually files a complaint, the parties will have an opportunity to meet with the Assistant Attorney General of the Antitrust Division, or one of his or her Deputies, in what is commonly referred to as a "last rites" meeting. In most cases, while companies take this opportunity to further advocate with DOJ, a last rites meeting is unlikely to change DOJ's position on key issues. By the time of the last rites meeting, there have been many opportunities for the parties to present their positions to the DOJ staff attorneys, and these positions have been relayed to the front office. Then, the front office has pressure tested the staff and the parties' arguments with the staff. If the front office disagrees with the staff on a key issue, that issue would no longer be on the table by the time of the last rites meeting.

Most DOJ civil antitrust investigations conclude with a consent decree entered between DOJ and the parties. If the parties decide

to enter into a consent decree, DOJ staff attorneys will typically
take the first draft of the decree and share it with the parties for
comments. At this stage, there is some opportunity for negotiations
on the terms of the consent decree, such the conduct enjoined by
the decree, the "carve-outs"—that is, conduct that is not enjoined
by the decree—the compliance provisions, or the duration of the
decree.

Finally, the Antitrust Procedures and Penalties Act (commonly
known as the "Tunney Act") provides for judicial review of
proposed consent decrees. Before entering the consent decree, the
court must determine whether entry of the decree is in the public
interest. The court assesses the proposed decree's competitive
impact, including the duration of the relief sought, the anticipated
effects of alternative remedies, and the impact of the consent
decree "upon the public generally and individuals alleging specific
injury" from the violations stated in the complaint.[322]

IV.   MERGER INVESTIGATIONS

Unlike criminal or civil investigations, companies should be able
to anticipate the focus and scope of a DOJ merger investigation. In
most cases, merging parties will anticipate whether a particular
transaction will trigger a merger investigation and devise a strategy
to comply with the investigation. While a thorough presentation of
DOJ merger investigations is beyond the scope of this article, here
are four best practices that merging parties should consider before
signing the merger agreement.

1.   Know your antitrust risk: The merging parties should
assess, with specificity, the level of antitrust risk and DOJ scrutiny
that a transaction may yield. Is it likely to prompt an initial DOJ
investigation?[323] Is this investigation likely to be satisfied in the

---

[322] 15 U.S.C. § 16(e)(2).

[323] Both DOJ and FTC are actively reviewing the 2010 Horizontal Merger
Guidelines and the 2020 Vertical Merger Guidelines. Most recently, in early
2022, DOJ and FTC sought public input aimed at modernizing the Merger
Guidelines to better detect and prevent anticompetitive deals. However, although

first 30 days of the HSR waiting period? Rather, is it likely that it would require a "pull and refile" of the HSR notification (which would add 30 days)? Will it trigger a protracted Second Request investigation? And if it does, would the antitrust concerns be fixed via a remedy that would be acceptable to DOJ?

These questions may seem obvious, but there may be strategic impediments to thorough antitrust diligence pre-signing. For example, the buyer may not want to engage in detailed discussions with the seller regarding antitrust issues before signing in an effort to avoid bearing significant antitrust risk. Further, there may be practical impediments. In many instances, the parties' subject matter experts on the competitive landscape may not be "in the tent" and aware of the parties' negotiations. All that said, the merging parties should try to answer these questions as best they can *before* signing the merger agreement.

2.   Know your antitrust evidence: The merging parties should try to get a good sense of the key evidence that would become relevant to the DOJ investigation. Some of this evidence may be difficult to fully gather pre-signing. For example, while an acquirer may have access to its own strategic documents on the nature of competition—and such documents may not focus on competition with the target company—it is possible that the target company's documents focus heavily on the acquirer. There could be documents which state that the merging companies are the only competitive options for a subset of customers. That is precisely why the acquirer should try to review some of these key documents from the Target before entering into the merger agreement.

Also, the parties should try to review, and possibly have their legal and economic experts review, the key quantitative evidence on the competition between the merging parties, such as win-loss databases or spreadsheets. This qualitative and quantitative

---

rescinded by the FTC, the 2020 Vertical Merger Guidelines are still in effect at DOJ.

evidence would inform the degree of antitrust risk for a particular transaction.

3. Anticipate the process: The merging parties may want to devote e-discovery and legal resources to anticipate compliance with a Second Request investigation in an effort to quickly identify and collect documents and data likely to be requested in a Second Request. For example, the parties can, before the issuance of a Second Request:

- Draft a "mock Second Request" to guide document review efforts based on Second Requests issued in prior transactions or the model DOJ/FTC Second Request;

- Create an organizational matrix of the likely document custodians in the DOJ investigation;

- Interview these custodians and collect their documents;

- Retain an e-discovery vendor with experience in Second Request investigations;

- Gather data and start drafting mock interrogatory responses; and

- Assign a privilege team to focus on the privilege review and privilege log.

4. Anticipate litigation or settlement: Finally, before they engage in mergers likely to raise significant antitrust issues, the parties should decide early whether and how they want to pursue settlement and litigation strategies. Both DOJ and the FTC have proven that they are "litigation-ready" and that they will not hesitate to challenge transactions in court. The agencies often have separate investigation and litigation teams. Similarly, merging parties often allocate separate investigation/settlement and litigation teams.

The settlement analysis should focus early on one fundamental question—if often overlooked—can the transaction actually be fixed? Is there a remedy that would satisfy DOJ? More specifically, how likely is it that DOJ will determine that a set of assets needs to be divested, or that another remedy must be imposed? Once this threshold question has been answered, several questions of equal importance quickly follow: who would be the buyer of these assets? Would such a buyer be viewed as a viable competitor going forward? If at all possible, this analysis should be pursued before signing the merger agreement. All these questions were front and center in many high-profile M&A transactions recently challenged by DOJ, or abandoned following DOJ opposition. These transactions included American Airlines/JetBlue's Northeast Alliance, Visa/Plaid, Penguin Random House/Simon & Schuster, and UnitedHealth Group/Change Healthcare. To avoid such results, the parties should thoroughly investigate any possible weakness of the antitrust remedy. They should assess internally whether the assets to be divested and potential divestiture buyers would pass muster at DOJ or whether divesture is a remedy the DOJ is willing to accept.[324] The parties might want to focus on the weaknesses of the remedy and create an internal "red team" if need be to vet and question the effectiveness of the proposed remedy. The parties may also want to develop a strategy to understand customer reactions to the remedy. DOJ will market test the proposed remedy with the merging parties' top customers. Anticipating customer reactions earlier in the process will minimize the risk of agency delays or opposition to a divestiture buyer.

---

[324] In a January 24, 2022 speech, Jonathan Kanter, DOJ Antitrust Division Head, suggested that DOJ will be less willing to accept divestiture as a remedy for mergers his office views as likely to lessen competition. In these cases, the appropriate step is to "seek a simple injunction to block the transaction" instead of agreeing on a remedy. See Jonathan Kanter, Ass't Att'y Gen., Dep't of Justice, Antitrust Div., Remarks to the New York State Bar Association Antitrust Section (Jan. 24, 2022), https://www.justice.gov/opa/speech/assistant-attorney-general-jonathan-kanter-antitrust-division-delivers-remarks-new-york.

V.   THIRD PARTY INVESTIGATIONS

Third parties, such as customers, suppliers, or competitors, often play a critical role in DOJ investigations. In many cases, DOJ investigations are initiated by unsolicited complaints from customers or competitors.

Even without a third-party complaint, DOJ will routinely request third parties' assistance with an investigation. Despite not being the target or subject of an investigation, responding to these requests can still be extraordinarily burdensome and costly: DOJ may ask for documents and data from the company and may even ask the company to provide witnesses for an interview or deposition. For example, in a cartel case, the DOJ may be interested in obtaining a large customer's transactional data as well as understanding their purchase process during a specific time period. Likewise, in a merger investigation, DOJ will hear from competitors and customers about the current state of the market and how they think the merger will affect competition.

There are several ways that third parties can minimize burden and costs. First, it is critical to quickly liaise with the DOJ staff attorney to explain the burden incurred by the CID. It is equally important to get a sense from the DOJ staff attorney of what exactly constitutes a "must have" piece of data or document for the DOJ case versus less critical information. Second, understanding where the third party fits in the DOJ investigation is equally critical. For example, DOJ may be more amenable to modify a subpoena of a small customer of the merging parties rather than top-5 customers who frequently play one of the merging parties against the other.

VI.   CONCLUSION

One overarching trend in all DOJ antitrust investigations is that they are only getting more complex, lengthy, and burdensome. This is true for complex merger, cartel, and civil DOJ investigations. This trend is unlikely to abate any time soon. In addition to refreshing and updating their antitrust compliance programs to avoid criminal or civil antitrust liability, companies would do well to spend compliance and legal resources to refresh their standard operating plan on how to respond and manage antitrust investigations. The time and resources spent on such an effort upfront will bear dividends if DOJ comes knocking on their door.

Chapter 6

Responding To and Managing Risk In Department of Justice (DOJ) Civil Division Investigations

By:

Bradley A. Klein
Paul A. Solomon
Douglas J. DeBaugh
Barri Dean
Kiki Griffith[325]

I.   INTRODUCTION

The United States Department of Justice ("DOJ") has often been described as the largest law firm in the world. With over 110,000 employees at Main Justice and in the United States Attorneys' Offices, and multiple investigative agencies such as the Federal Bureau of Investigation, and coordinating investigative authorities such as the Inspectors General of administrative agencies, the scope, reach and sweep of the DOJ has virtually no limit. While the Criminal Division's authority extends throughout the States and abroad, even the Civil Division's investigative authority enjoys broad investigative license.

Responding to investigations initiated by the Civil Division of the DOJ presents significant risks for individuals and corporations, including the risk of a civil investigation evolving into a criminal investigation and prosecution. And while the DOJ's authority is broad and its investigative measures may be intrusive, constitutional, statutory and regulatory protections do exist and, in

---

[325] Mr. Klein is a Partner with Skadden, Arps, Slate, Meagher & Flom LLP's ("Skadden") Litigation, Government Enforcement and White Collar Crime, and Cross-Border Investigations Practice Groups. Mr. Solomon is a Counsel with Skadden's Litigation Practice Group. Mr. DeBaugh, Ms. Dean, and Ms. Griffith are Associates with Skadden's Litigation Practice Group. The views expressed by the authors are their own and do not necessarily represent the views of the firm or any of its clients.

appropriate circumstances, may curtail certain DOJ techniques, investigative demands, and adverse resolution of the investigation.

As a guide to corporations and individuals working for corporations in responding to DOJ investigations, this chapter will afford a review of the DOJ Civil Division's organization, legal authority and investigative practices. Because much of the Civil Division's work is conducted in coordination with federal regulatory agencies, we will refer to certain agencies' roles and practices in DOJ investigations as well.

The initial responses to a DOJ inquiry can be critical to appropriate and successful resolution of an investigation. Managing communications, engaging legal counsel, preserving documents and privileges, and avoiding further potential liability in the course of responding to a DOJ investigation will be addressed in the following sections.

Additionally, there are some strategic measures to consider from the commencement of an investigation to its resolution. Among these are managing a company's public disclosure obligations, assessing individual officer and employee responsibilities, whether and how to cooperate with the DOJ investigation and possible voluntary disclosure and repayment measures. This chapter will examine the legal and procedural elements of these strategic considerations.

Finally, the ultimate resolution of a DOJ investigation can vary from closure of the investigation by the DOJ, to settlement involving millions of dollars, to initiation of civil litigation. Successful management of a DOJ investigation may encompass any or all of these outcomes depending on the circumstances. And there is also the risk that a civil investigation becomes a criminal investigation and prosecution if the DOJ were to conclude that there has been obstruction of its investigative efforts, perjury, or the civil investigation yields evidence of criminal wrongdoing. So the stakes in a civil investigation may be substantially greater than suggested by an early assessment that the matter is "only civil" in nature. Planning for and managing the course and outcome of the investigation requires a thorough understanding of the process, the protections afforded, and the integrity of the corporate response.

II.   OVERVIEW OF THE DOJ'S CIVIL DIVISION

The DOJ's Civil Division represents the United States, its agencies and departments, officers, employees, and members of Congress in certain areas of civil litigation. The Civil Division's branches include the Appellate Staff, the Commercial Litigation Branch, the Federal Programs Branch, the Office of Immigration Litigation, the Consumer Protection Branch, and the Torts Branch.[326]

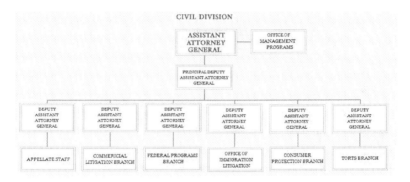

Most relevant to this guide are the Commercial Litigation Branch's Fraud Section, which investigates and brings False Claims Act ("FCA") litigation, and the Consumer Protection Branch, which has responsibility for enforcing the Food, Drug and Cosmetic Act ("FDCA") and the Consumer Product Safety Act, among other statutes.

The Civil Division coordinates its activities with the U.S. Attorneys' Offices ("USAOs") across the country and delegates certain responsibilities to the USAOs. The Civil Division's attorneys typically handle large and complex litigation matters that may overburden the resources and staffing of a particular USAO or which involve multiple jurisdictions. The USAOs generally have authority to file suits and settle claims asserted by the United

---

[326] *See* About the Civil Division, U.S. Dep't of Justice, https://www.justice.gov/civil/about.

States in all matters where the gross amount of the original claim asserted by the United States does not exceed $10,000,000.[327] With regard to fraud and FCA cases, however, the Director of the Fraud Section of the Commercial Litigation Branch determines, after discussion with the USAO, whether a particular case should be delegated to the USAO, handled by the Fraud Section, or jointly handled by the Fraud Section and the USAO.[328] The Director of the Fraud Section may choose not to delegate a specific FCA case to the USAO if that case presents a novel question of law or policy or if the disposition of that case will influence the disposition of claims in other cases that total more than $10,000,000.[329] The Civil Division and the USAO may also coordinate their actions with the DOJ's Criminal Division and federal regulatory agencies that have responsibility for certain industries or conduct. For example, the DOJ may partner with the U.S. Health and Human Services Office of Inspector General when investigating allegations of Medicare or Medicaid fraud or violations of the FDCA.

Although a full discussion of parallel civil and criminal proceedings is beyond the scope of this chapter, companies should be aware that such proceedings typically raise numerous issues involving discovery, Fifth Amendment privilege, and double jeopardy concerns that a company should discuss with outside counsel.[330]

---

[327] *See* Redelegation of Authority to Deputy Assistant Attorneys General, Branch Directors, Heads of Offices, and United States Attorneys in Civil Division Cases, 80 Fed. Reg. 31,998 (June 5, 2015) (codified in 28 C.F.R. pt. 0, subpt. Y, app. (Civil Directive No. 1-15, § 1(b) (June 1, 2015))); *accord Justice Manual* ("JM"), Civil Resource Manual ch. 46 (updated Nov. 2016) (reprinting Civil Division Directive No. 1-15, § 1(b) (June 1, 2015)), https://www.justice.gov/jm/civil-resource-manual-46-redelegation-authority-compromise-civil-claims.

[328] Redelegation of Authority, 80 Fed. Reg. at 31,999 (codified in 28 C.F.R. pt. 0, subpt. Y, app. (Civil Directive No. 1-15, § 1(e)(2)); *accord* Civil Resource Manual ch. 46, *supra* note 3.

[329] *Id.* at 31,998-99 (codified in 28 C.F.R. pt. 0, subpt. Y, app. (Civil Directive No. 1-15, § 1(a)(1), (c)(1), (e)(1)(i), (ii))).

[330] Please see other chapters for a fuller discussion of the issues arising from potential parallel proceedings.

III.   INITIAL CONTACT BY THE DOJ

A company may first learn of a DOJ investigation in multiple ways:

- **Letter inquiry.** The DOJ may issue a letter seeking voluntary production of documents or information on certain topics. Although compliance is voluntary, cooperating with the DOJ is generally advised to expedite resolution of the DOJ's inquiry and foster a working relationship with the government as the investigation proceeds.

- **Civil investigative demand ("CID").** Receipt of a CID is a strong indicator that the recipient is the subject of an FCA investigation. The Civil Division and the USAO may issue CIDs if they have "reason to believe" that any person or entity may be in possession of documents relevant to an FCA investigation. A CID may require the production of significant volumes of documents and information. A CID can also require responses to interrogatories and oral testimony.[331] If a CID recipient does not respond, the DOJ can petition a federal district court for an order enforcing compliance.[332]

- **Subpoenas.** Federal departments and agencies, through their offices of inspector general, have the authority to issue subpoenas to compel production of documents or oral testimony. If the subpoena

---

[331] *See* 31 U.S.C. § 3733(a)(1)-(2) (discussing requirements and conditions for CID).

[332] *Id.* § 3733(j)(1).

target fails to comply, the subpoena is enforceable through an order from a federal district court.[333]

- **Employees, press and third parties**. The Civil Division may conduct its investigation covertly or under seal. Absent a letter inquiry, CID, or subpoena, little public information may be available indicating that an investigation is underway. Nevertheless, reports from employees, vendors, and the general press can reveal that the DOJ has begun an investigation. For example, the DOJ may seek to interview or gather information from company employees. Companies should ask their employees to contact the legal or compliance departments immediately if they receive any communication from the DOJ so that company counsel can be present during those conversations. Use caution to avoid the appearance that advice to employees could be construed as an instruction not to cooperate with the DOJ personnel as such instructions could lead to obstruction of justice charges. Instead, it may be best to inform employees, in writing, that if they are contacted and they choose to speak with the DOJ, they must be truthful and can insist on certain conditions such as having counsel or company counsel present for interviews or questioning. Press reports could also indicate that the DOJ is investigating

---

[333] *See* Inspector General Act of 1978, Pub. L. No. 95-452, 92 Stat. 1101 (1978) (establishing inspectors general offices in various federal departments and agencies); *see also* Inspector General Act of 1978 § 6(a), 5 U.S.C. App. § 6(a) (as amended through The Whistleblower Protection Coordination Act, Pub. L. No. 115-192 (2018)) ("In addition to the authority otherwise provided by this Act, each Inspector General, in carrying out the provisions of this Act, is authorized . . . to require by subpoena the production of all information, documents, reports, answers, records, accounts, papers, and other data in any medium (including electronically stored information), as well as any tangible thing and documentary evidence necessary in the performance of the functions assigned by this Act, which subpoena, in the case of contumacy or refusal to obey, shall be enforceable by order of any appropriate United States district court . . . .").

the company or its industry, as could reports from company vendors. Upon hearing these reports, the company should strongly consider undertaking the initial steps outlined below.

IV. MANAGING COMMUNICATIONS WITH THE DOJ

At the outset of an investigation, it is important to establish clear lines of communication with DOJ representatives and to identify a consistent authorized voice to speak for the company regarding the investigation. Companies must be mindful of how their actions and words will be viewed by DOJ investigators. The government will understandably be skeptical of certain claims regarding innocence, lack of documents, unavailability of witnesses and even assertion of attorney-client privilege for company communications.

In addition, the DOJ may have information available to it *before the company is aware of the investigation.* This information may have been supplied by whistleblowers or obtained through covert investigative techniques, including interviews of company employees and other witnesses. Only rarely will the DOJ commence an investigation without some prior background information. Consequently, in some cases the DOJ may know more than company management or legal counsel about an issue, and the DOJ may have formed a firm belief about suspected legal violations. It is important for the company's credibility and effectiveness in responding to an identified investigation to be cautious in initial statements to the DOJ. Early communications by the company will be carefully assessed by the DOJ for accuracy and possible intent to mislead. Moreover, the DOJ investigators may have confidential sources within the company or even information from a parallel criminal investigation that informs their views.

A.   Communicating with the DOJ

A few precautionary measures will assist the company in the early stages of and throughout an investigation:

1. *Speak with one voice—the company's designated representative, preferably outside counsel, should be the primary, if not the exclusive, voice in communications with the DOJ.* Management statements, including those of the General Counsel, will be viewed as binding on the company and will be difficult to retract with credibility should they later prove to be inaccurate. Such communications pose risks to the company and to management representatives and must be carefully reviewed for legal and factual accuracy before being conveyed to DOJ investigators.

2. *Avoid factual representations to the DOJ before reviewing all the available information and talking with personnel in the company with knowledge of the apparent issues.* The DOJ will understand in most cases that a company may have to conduct an internal review before responding substantively to its inquiries. Protestations of innocence or claims of a failure by the DOJ to understand the issues will be unavailing in the absence of evidence. Facts asserted before a thorough internal evaluation of the circumstances will lack credibility.

3. *Get the DOJ to disclose as much as possible regarding the focus of their investigation, including whether any individuals are of interest or face potential personal liability.* This serves to expedite the search for information responsive to DOJ investigative demands and to guard against inadvertent waiver of privileged materials. If individuals are an independent focus of the DOJ inquiry, that must be known to avoid conflicts for the company and its counsel and to determine whether such individuals should be afforded indemnity or advancement of fees for retention of

separate legal counsel. See discussion in **Section VIII**.

4. *Identify the DOJ representatives who will be in charge of the investigation.* At the outset of an investigation there may be multiple government agents and agencies in contact with the company. Request the DOJ to designate its key contacts for the investigation and to limit contacts with the company to such persons in the absence of some independent basis for multiple communications by government representatives.

5. *Manage expectations of DOJ investigators.* Promising more in response to investigative demands than can be provided within the specified time or scope of the request can damage the company's credibility and may prejudice the effectiveness of the company's response or legal defenses. Most DOJ representatives will understand that the 20 – 30-day response period typically set by a subpoena or other request is not a realistic deadline for significant document production. Negotiating a more realistic but still timely production should be the goal. *See* discussion in **Section VII**.

6. *Initiate a document preservation protocol and advise the DOJ of its implementation.* As discussed further at **Section V.C.**, the government will closely scrutinize the circumstances involving any loss of information, data, or communications, including email. Implementation of a "litigation hold" is among the most important initial responses to a DOJ investigation. It is not typically necessary to document such efforts to the satisfaction of the DOJ, and there may be privilege issues associated with such measures. Simply acknowledging the need for and the establishment

of such preservation efforts, however, will enhance the company's credibility and may avoid more intrusive investigative measures by DOJ investigators concerned with loss or spoliation of evidence.

B. "Cooperating" with a DOJ Investigation

Companies choosing to cooperate with a DOJ investigation often do so based on a number of factors, including the desire to be viewed as a good corporate citizen and to obtain "credit" from the DOJ for cooperating with its investigation. Failure or refusal to cooperate with a DOJ investigation can have severe consequences for a company, including greater fines and punishment than a company might otherwise have faced. Adhering to the above measures will support a company's efforts in the DOJ's evaluation of its level of cooperation with an investigation, whether the company self-disclosed conduct or began cooperating after a DOJ-initiated inquiry. Under DOJ protocols, before the DOJ will evaluate the company's "credit" for cooperating, a company must first satisfy the DOJ that it has provided all relevant facts regarding potential individual misconduct.

1. *A company's eligibility for cooperation credit is predicated on the company's provision of "all relevant facts about the individuals who were involved in the misconduct."*[334] Since Deputy Attorney General Sally Quillian Yates issued the "Yates Memorandum" in September 2015, the DOJ has required that, in order to receive cooperation credit, companies provide "all relevant facts" to the DOJ about any individuals involved in potential corporate misconduct, including the identities of those individuals regardless of their role in the organization.[335] This

---

[334] JM § 9-28.720; *see also id.* §§ 4-3.100(3), 9-28.700.

[335] Memorandum from Sally Quillian Yates, Deputy Att'y Gen. on Individual Accountability for Corporate Wrongdoing at 3 (Sept. 9, 2015) (the "Yates Memorandum"), https://www.justice.gov/dag/file/769036/download; JM § 9-

requirement applies equally to civil and criminal investigations.[336] Further, the DOJ encourages its attorneys to focus on individual misconduct from the start of any corporate investigation – and coordinate any such parallel criminal and civil proceedings. The Justice Manual ("JM") incorporates the Yates Memorandum terms and provides:[337]

- "[c]ivil corporate investigations should focus on individuals" from the inception of an investigation;[338]

28.720(a). DOJ announced in November 2018 that companies wishing to receive maximum cooperation credit in a civil case need only identify individuals "substantially involved in or responsible for . . . misconduct." Rod Rosenstein, Deputy Att'y Gen., U.S. Dep't of Justice, Remarks at the American Conference Institute's 35th International Conference on the Foreign Corrupt Practices Act (Nov. 29, 2018), https://www.justice.gov/opa/speech/deputy-attorney-general-rod-j-rosenstein-delivers-remarks-american-conference-institute-0. Current DOJ policy, however, has returned to the requirements of the Yates Memorandum, and "cooperating companies will now be required to provide the government with *all* non-privileged information about individual wrongdoing." Lisa Monaco, Deputy Attorney Gen., U.S. Dep't of Justice, Keynote Address at ABA's 36th National Institute on White Collar Crime (Oct. 28, 2021) (emphasis added), https://www.justice.gov/opa/speech/deputy-attorney-general-lisa-o-monaco-gives-keynote-address-abas-36th-national-institute.

[336] Yates Memorandum at 3. Emphasizing its application to civil investigations, the Yates Memorandum provided, as an example, that "the Department's position on 'full cooperation' under the False Claims Act, 31 U.S.C. § 3729(a)(2), will be that, at a minimum, all relevant facts about responsible individuals must be provided." *Id.* at 4.

[337] On November 16, 2017, Attorney General Jeff Sessions issued a memorandum prohibiting the issuance of guidance documents that "purport to create rights or obligations binding on persons or entities outside the Executive Branch" and directing a review of previously issued guidance documents. Memorandum from Jeff Sessions, Att'y Gen. on Prohibition on Improper Guidance Documents (Nov. 16, 2017), https://www.justice.gov/opa/press-release/file/1012271/download.

[338] JM § 4-3.100(1); *see id.* § 9-28.210. If, at the conclusion of a corporate investigation in which a resolution is reached or charges are pursued against the corporation, a decision is made not to bring criminal or civil charges against the individuals who committed the misconduct, U.S. Attorneys are required to

- civil attorneys should "be in routine communication" with criminal attorneys during a corporate investigation to aid in the pursuit of cases against individuals;[339]

- resolutions against companies ought not provide individuals with protection from civil or criminal liability, absent "extraordinary circumstances";[340]

- prosecutors ought to have "a clear plan to resolve" cases against individuals before resolving a corporate case;[341] and

- if "civil attorneys believe that an individual identified in the course of their corporate investigation should be the subject of a criminal inquiry, that matter should promptly be referred to criminal prosecutors, regardless of the current status of the civil corporate investigation."[342]

2. *Cooperation credit is measured based on a number of factors related to the company's communications with the DOJ and compliance and remediation activities.* Only when a company has disclosed relevant facts related to potential wrongdoing by individuals can the company be eligible for credit based on the DOJ's assessment

---

memorialize this decision and obtain approval "by the United States Attorney or Assistant Attorney General whose office handled the investigation, or their designees." *Id.* §§ 4-3.100(5), 9-28.210(B).

[339] *See id.* § 4-3.100(2).

[340] *See id.* §§ 4-3.100(4), 9-28.210(A).

[341] *See id.* § 4-3.100(5).

[342] *See id.* § 4-3.100(2). In addition, the Yates Memorandum made clear that "[p]ursuit of civil actions against culpable individuals should not be governed solely by those individuals' ability to pay." Yates Memorandum at 6.

of traditional factors the DOJ has used to assess a company's level of cooperation (e.g., thoroughness and speed of an internal investigation, timeliness of the cooperation, voluntary disclosure of the wrongdoing, availability of witnesses, the proactive nature of the cooperation, a company's existing compliance program and remediation efforts).[343]

3. *Companies choosing to disclose facts to the DOJ should carefully consider the manner, scope and timing of reporting.*[344] Oral presentations can be beneficial because they avoid use of potentially discoverable work product, but can lead to miscommunications and written presentations may be preferable to the government. Often, during early stages of an investigation, oral presentations may be preferable through meetings or telephone calls while written presentations may be beneficial during advanced stages of an investigation. The DOJ expects clear and complete reporting and often asks a company to analyze key factual

---

[343] *See id.* §§ 4-3.100(3), 9-28.300, 9-28.700, 9-28.720, 9-28.900; *see also* Claire McCusker Murray, Principal Assoc. Att'y Gen., U.S. Dep't of Justice, Remarks at Compliance Week Annual Conference (May 20, 2019), https://www.justice.gov/opa/speech/remarks-principal-deputy-associate-attorney-general-claire-mccusker-murray-compliance (describing newly issued guidance for crediting cooperation of False Claims Act defendants and highlighting recent False Claims Act settlements); JM § 4-4.112 (identifying types of cooperation eligible for credit in False Claims Act matters).

[344] The decision to disclose facts requires careful consideration of the timing of such disclosure and how it might impact cooperation credit. Yates explained that the DOJ's policy was revised to "recognize the significant value of early, voluntary self-reporting," by separating such self-reporting from the concept of cooperation as distinct charging factors. Sally Q. Yates, Deputy Att'y Gen., U.S. Dep't of Justice, Remarks at the New York City Bar Association White-collar Crime Conference (May 10, 2016), https://www.justice.gov/opa/speech/deputy-attorney-general-sally-q-yates-delivers-remarks-new-york-city-bar-association. Yates stated that this decision was made to "account for the difference between a company raising its hand and voluntarily disclosing misconduct and a company simply agreeing to cooperate once it gets caught." *Id.*

findings and remedial measures, sometimes with interim or regular updates. Effective reports also present a balanced view of the conduct, including by dealing with facts that may not be favorable to the company but also presenting opportunities to produce exculpatory evidence.

4. *"Cooperation" does not mean that a company must waive attorney-client or work product protections.* In fact, federal prosecutors have been directed to refrain from seeking waivers of privilege and to focus on obtaining relevant facts.[345] Moreover, as a former Assistant Attorney General publicly stated, if a company has been "unable to identify the culpable individuals following" a thorough and appropriately tailored review, cooperation credit will not be precluded so long as the company aided the DOJ in obtaining evidence and provided relevant facts.[346]

With cooperation comes greater potential for conflict between a company and its officers, directors, and employees. As discussed in **Section VIII**, companies will need to consider whether to provide counsel to individuals throughout an investigation as new facts are learned, and recognize that a company's ability to fully cooperate with government requests may be affected by an individual's independent counsel.

V. KEY STEPS IN RESPONDING TO A DOJ INVESTIGATION

Successful management of a DOJ investigation begins with consideration of the following initial actions:

---

[345] *See* JM §§ 9-28.700(A), 9-28.710, 9-28.720.

[346] Leslie R. Caldwell, Assistant Att'y Gen., U.S. Dep't of Justice, Remarks at the Second Annual Global Investigations Review Conference (Sept. 22, 2015), https://www.justice.gov/opa/speech/assistant-attorney-general-leslie-r-caldwell-delivers-remarks-second-annual-global-0.

A. Retain Competent Outside Counsel to Manage the Investigation

Engaging outside counsel allows a company to tap the knowledge of those who have significant experience responding to and managing DOJ investigations. It also can ensure the investigative process is protected under the attorney-client privilege and/or the work product doctrine.[347] For example, if the company general counsel manages company employees outside of the legal department in the normal course of business, a court could interpret this reporting structure as an ongoing business relationship that does not fall within the attorney-client privilege parameters. To avoid confusion in this respect, a company can remove such non-legal employees from the legal reporting chain and engage outside counsel to manage the investigation, making clear that the primary purpose of the investigation is to gather facts to provide legal advice.

B. Consider a Public Relations Consultant to Protect the Brand

Given the complexity and potential impact of a DOJ investigation, hiring outside public relations ("PR") consultants may help protect

---

[347] *See, e.g., Parneros v. Barnes & Noble, Inc.*, No. 18 Civ. 7834, 2019 WL 4891213, at *1, *6-8, *11-12 (S.D.N.Y. Oct. 4, 2019) (holding, among other things, that (i) documents prepared by the general counsel and by a non-lawyer acting at the direction of the general counsel were "protected by the attorney-client privilege"; (ii) emails and draft press releases circulated among non-attorneys were not protected by the work product doctrine as there was no evidence that the non-attorneys prepared the documents; and (iii) a memorandum provided to the Board, together with redacted Board meeting minutes and related communications were protected by the attorney-client privilege as the general counsel testified that he had engaged and regularly communicated with outside counsel, who provided legal advice in the Board memorandum and attended the Board meeting, and the general counsel had prepared the minutes of the meeting); *Beasley v. Rowan Cos., Inc.*, No. 18-CV-00365, 2019 WL 1676017, at *2-3 (E.D. La. Apr. 17, 2019) (holding that the work product doctrine did not protect from discovery an investigation report and interview notes prepared during internal investigations that were not conducted by counsel or at counsel's direction but were conducted "in the ordinary course of business" and "not primarily in anticipation of litigation").

a company's public image. While many companies have sophisticated media relations and shareholder relations departments, responding to the press regarding a DOJ investigation may require additional expertise and experience. Although PR professionals may work closely with attorneys conducting an internal investigation, steps should be taken to safeguard communications under the attorney-client privilege and/or the work product doctrine. At a minimum, consider the following guidelines:

1. Outside counsel—rather than the company itself—should retain the PR firm and an engagement letter should expressly provide that the PR firm is being retained to provide assistance in connection with threatened or anticipated litigation.

2. Do not hire a PR firm previously retained by the company, nor ask the PR firm to perform any general media relations functions not related to anticipated litigation.

3. Outside counsel should be present for all communications with the PR firm and make clear that such communications are intended to aid counsel in providing legal advice to the company.[348]

---

[348] *Compare In re Grand Jury Subpoenas Dated Mar. 24, 2003 Directed to (A) Grand Jury Witness Firm & (B) Grand Jury Witness*, 265 F. Supp. 2d 321, 330-31 (S.D.N.Y. 2003) (concluding that communications between the PR consultants and defense attorneys were privileged because they "were directed at giving or obtaining legal advice" and not to provide general media relations advice), *with 12W RPO, LLC v. Victaulic Co.*, No. 3:15-cv-01411-MO, 2017 WL 7312758, at *3-6 (D. Or. Mar. 7, 2017) (holding that communications between a public relations firm and counsel were not protected by attorney-client privilege or work product doctrine because the communications were to "help [Plaintiff] communicate about this litigation with [third-parties], not to assist [it] in preparing the case or to advise on matters like change of venue or how potential jurors might react to Plaintiffs' allegations"); *see also Universal Standard Inc. v. Target Corp.*, 331 F.R.D. 80, 92 (S.D.N.Y. 2019) (distinguishing *In re Grand Jury Subpoenas* on the grounds that counsel was not "using a public relations

C.   Initiate Document Preservation Efforts

When a company learns of—or reasonably anticipates—a government investigation, it must implement a document preservation effort to ensure that relevant information is not destroyed. Also known as a "litigation hold" or "freeze directive," this notice instructs company personnel and representatives to preserve documents relevant to a particular subject matter or matters.[349] The company's duty to preserve relevant documents may extend to such documents that are in the possession or custody of third parties, such as vendors, consultants and outside counsel, if the company has control over the documents.[350]

---

consultant to implement a specific legal strategy that required the use of a public relations consultant"). Because *In re Grand Jury Subpoenas* involved an individual, the court's opinion does not draw a distinction between outside counsel and in-house counsel. However, given the careful scrutiny with which courts are likely to analyze the relationship between a PR firm and the Company, where outside counsel has been retained, it would be prudent for outside counsel to retain the PR firm. *See In re Signet Jewelers Ltd. Secs. Litig.*, 332 F.R.D. 131, 133, 135-38 (S.D.N.Y. 2019) (concluding that none of a party's relevant communications with two PR firms were protected by the attorney-client privilege even where outside counsel had retained the PR firms because the PR firms "were not called upon to perform a specific litigation task that the attorneys needed to accomplish in order to advance their litigation goals" but instead "were involved in public relations activities aimed at burnishing [the party's] image"), *aff'd*, 16 Civ. 6728 (CM) (SDA), 2019 WL 5558081 (S.D.N.Y. Oct. 23, 2019).

[349] *See, e.g.*, Fed R. Civ. P. 37(e) (describing measures a court can take "[i]f electronically stored information that should have been preserved in the anticipation or conduct of litigation is lost because a party failed to take reasonable steps to preserve it, and it cannot be restored or replaced through additional discovery"); The SEDONA CONFerence, *Commentary on Legal Holds*, Second Edition: The Trigger & The Process, 20 SEDONA CONF. J. 341, 347 (2019) (recognizing that organizations have a duty to preserve data when litigation is reasonably anticipated and "use of a 'legal hold' has become a common means by which organizations initiate meeting their preservation obligations").

[350] *See, e.g.*, *Funk v. Belneftekhim*, 2019 WL 7603139, at *6 (E.D.N.Y. Jan. 17, 2019) (finding that a party had "control" over documents and a duty to preserve where the party had a "practical ability to direct [a third-party] to preserve the Originals or to preserve them themselves"); *Pine Top Receivables of Ill., LLC v. Banco de Seguros del Estado*, No. 12 C 6357, 2013 WL 3776971, at *2-3 (N.D. Ill. July 18, 2013) (finding that plaintiff had a duty to preserve relevant documents in the physical possession of a third-party because the plaintiff had "a

Relevant information is not limited to hard-copy documents or files located on the company computer servers.[351] As employees increasingly use personal devices (*e.g.*, laptops and smartphones) and cloud-based accounts (*e.g.*, email and data storage accounts) for business purposes, a company must evaluate whether such media may contain relevant information and whether the company has a duty to preserve the data.[352] Moreover, a company must ensure that automatic document destruction policies do not inadvertently destroy relevant documents by suspending routine data management practices (*e.g.*, electronic email deletion programs or the routine overwriting of back-up storage).[353] With

---

contractual right to access" the documents); *Haskins v. First Am. Title Ins. Co.*, Civil No. 10-5044 (RMB/JS), 2012 WL 5183908, at *4-5 (D.N.J. Oct. 18, 2012) (same); *GenOn Mid-Atl., LLC v. Stone & Webster, Inc.*, 282 F.R.D. 346, 353-56 (S.D.N.Y. 2012) (finding that plaintiff had a duty to preserve relevant documents in the physical possession of its litigation consultant because it had the practical ability to obtain the documents on demand), *aff'd*, No. 11 CV 1299(HB), 2012 WL 1849101 (S.D.N.Y. May 21, 2012).

[351] *See, e.g.*, *Hollis v. CEVA Logistics U.S., Inc.*, No. 19 CV 50135, --- F. Supp. 3d ---, 2022 WL 1591731, at *4 (N.D. Ill. May 19, 2022) (holding defendant had duty to preserve security camera recordings following notice from terminated employee).

[352] *See, e.g.*, *Shaffer v. Gaither*, Docket No. 5:14-cv-00106-MOC-DSC, 2016 WL 6594126, at *2 (W.D.N.C. Sept. 1, 2016) (holding that relevant text messages and other data on a cell phone must be preserved when litigation is reasonably anticipated); *Selectica, Inc. v. Novatus, Inc.*, No. 6:13-cv-1708-Orl-40TBS, 2015 WL 1125051, at *1, 4-5 (M.D. Fla. Mar. 12, 2015) (finding that the defendant had a duty to preserve relevant files on the personal cloud-based data storage account of its employee because it had the practical ability to access the files saved in the storage account); *In re Pradaxa (Dabigatran Etexilate) Prods. Liab. Litig.*, MDL No. 2385, 3:12-md-02385-DRH-SCW, 2013 WL 6486921, at *17-18 (S.D. Ill. Dec. 9, 2013) (finding that the defendant's preservation directive applied to relevant business-related texts messages on its employees' personal cell phones), *order rescinded in part on other grounds sub nom. In re Boehringer Ingelheim Pharms., Inc.*, 745 F.3d 216 (7th Cir. 2014).

[353] *See, e.g.*, *Hice v. Lemon*, 19-cv-4666 (JMA)(SIL), 2021 WL 6053812, at *5 (E.D.N.Y. Nov. 17, 2021) ("To meet its preservation obligations, each party 'must suspend its routine document retention/destruction policy and put in place a "litigation hold" to ensure the preservation of relevant documents.'" (citation omitted)), *report and recommendation adopted*, 19-cv-4666 (JMA)(SIL), 2021 WL 6052440 (E.D.N.Y. Dec. 21, 2021); *Ramos v. Swatzell*, No. ED CV 12-1089-BRO (SPx), 2017 WL 2857523, at *5 (C.D. Cal. June 5, 2017) ("Once the duty to preserve attaches, a party must suspend any existing policies related to deleting or

these technological pitfalls in mind, it is axiomatic that early involvement by the company's records managers and information technology ("IT") personnel in the document preservation process is critical. Accordingly, the document preservation notice should be communicated in writing to records managers and IT personnel in addition to other relevant employees.

D. Initiate and Conduct an Internal Investigation

As previously discussed, to maximize credibility and flexibility and not foreclose any strategic responses to a DOJ inquiry, it is important that an internal investigation be properly scoped and scaled, use appropriate processes, and proceed in an unbiased and untainted manner. In contemplating such an approach, a company should consider how an internal investigation will be perceived by the government at the end of the process, including whether the process and findings of the internal investigation should be credited, and that the company acted appropriately upon learning of potential misconduct. Generally, a company maximizes the likelihood of a favorable reception by ensuring that any internal investigation is conducted in a full, fair, and candid manner. Determinations as to who will conduct the investigation (whether inside counsel, outside counsel, or some combination thereof) and who will oversee the investigation (whether an independent committee of the board of directors or company officers) are equally important decisions that may shape the government's opinion.

Regarding the scope of any internal investigation, danger lies at both ends of the spectrum. If too narrow, the government will distrust the investigation's findings and conclusions, and the company is unlikely to receive much credit for its efforts. If too

---

destroying files and preserve all relevant documents related to the litigation." (citation omitted)), *report and recommendation adopted,* No. ED CV-121089-BRO (SPx), 2017 WL 2841695 (C.D. Cal. June 30, 2017); *Apple Inc. v. Samsung Elecs. Co.,* 888 F. Supp. 2d 976, 991 (N.D. Cal. 2012) (same). Depending on the nature of the crisis and the company's electronic systems and back-up policies, it may be prudent to pull and preserve the set of back-up data made immediately prior to the crisis.

broad, the government may become frustrated with the delay in producing results, which in turn would undermine the company's credibility. To avoid either scenario, as well as the economic cost of an ineffective investigation, the company should communicate with the government at the outset of an investigation to agree upon or at least give notice of the intended scope and set expectations.

Ultimately, the company must show that its investigation was unbiased, untainted and sensible—capable of identifying misconduct in connection with the relevant subject matter. The end goal in any internal investigation should be the same: the company wants to be in a position where it has earned credit from the government for conducting an impartial, thorough, and accurate investigation, which is appropriate for the circumstances and which produces results upon which the company and the government can reasonably rely.[354] In some cases, such a review may even satisfy the DOJ that no civil case can or should be brought against the company.

E. Determine Public Disclosure Obligations Regarding the DOJ Investigation

Separate from the issue of disclosure to the government, a public company managing a DOJ inquiry—or a related internal investigation—also must consider its ongoing public disclosure obligations. The company should consider whether a duty to disclose arises in the context of periodic filings, or where the company or a knowledgeable insider purchases or sells shares of the company.[355] Further, even if one aspect of the investigation may not lead to a disclosure obligation, the combination or interaction of events may lead to an obligation to disclose a

---

[354] The DOJ's Civil and Criminal Divisions have documented factors their attorneys consider in determining credit to provide to entities and individuals upon voluntary disclosure of conduct and cooperation with investigations. *See, e.g.,* JM §§ 4-4.112 (discussing guidelines on considering disclosure, cooperation and remediation in FCA cases), 9-28.700 (discussing the value of cooperation, including "early voluntary disclosure").

[355] *See Chiarella v. United States*, 445 U.S. 222, 228-29 (1980).

potentially material impact of the investigation on the company's finances or operations.

The company should also carefully consider whether the disclosure of the existence of a government investigation is prudent even if such disclosure is not required. One primary consideration is the likelihood that such information will ultimately leak to the public and to significant third parties. For example, if the government seeks information from third parties, it could cause those parties to infer that an investigation is underway. In any event, a company must be careful not to falsely deny the existence of an investigation.

Further, a company may determine that an early, voluntary disclosure about a potential issue would benefit the company by acclimating the market and minimizing the risk of a strong reaction later. However, a company should be mindful of its duties to update the market so as not to mislead investors, *i.e.*, that supplemental disclosure may be required if the investigation changes track unexpectedly and prior disclosures no longer accurately reflect the state of affairs.

And in the final analysis, the company must assess the impact of its public disclosure on the DOJ's perception of the company and its response to the investigation.

VI.   PRESERVING ATTORNEY-CLIENT PRIVILEGE AND WORK PRODUCT PROTECTIONS

A.   Conduct an Internal Investigation Under Privilege Through Outside Counsel

As discussed above, an internal investigation is often critical to the successful and timely resolution of a DOJ investigation. If the internal investigation is conducted by in-house or outside counsel, the attorney-client privilege and the attorney work product doctrine generally protect the communications and materials prepared in connection with the investigation.[356]

The internal investigation or review helps to determine the extent of any potential legal liability to the company or its employees. An internal investigation may also aid in assessing potential liability from any follow-on government investigation by other state or federal regulatory authorities or from any private litigation. The company can also use the facts developed during its investigation to institute appropriate remedial measures and decide whether to take personnel actions. A thorough internal investigation is also necessary to qualify for cooperation credit from the DOJ.[357] And the DOJ does not require a waiver of that privilege as part of its evaluation of the company's level of cooperation.[358]

B.   Take Precautions to Protect Communications with Professionals and Experts

Communications and materials shared with third-parties specifically retained to assist counsel with an investigation, including accountants, information technology vendors, public relations firms, and other specialists and consultants, are typically also protected from disclosure.[359] A company should consider the

---

[356] See generally Fed. R. Evid. 502(g); Upjohn Co. v. United States, 449 U.S. 383 (1981); FTC v. Boehringer Ingelheim Pharms., Inc., 892 F.3d 1264 (D.C. Cir. 2018); In re Kellogg Brown & Root, Inc., 756 F.3d 754 (D.C. Cir. 2014).

[357] See JM §§ 9-28.700(A), 9-28.720.

[358] See id. § 9-28.710. Individuals and organizations cooperating with a DOJ investigation should be careful about disclosing internal investigation materials to the government. See United States v. Coburn, No. 2:19-cr-00120, 2022 WL 357217, at *7 (D.N.J. Feb. 1, 2022) (holding that the organization could not "claim privilege over materials that it furnished to the Government" because the disclosures were made "to the Government while under threat of prosecution [and the organization] handed these materials to a potential adversary and destroyed any confidentiality they may have had, undermining the purpose of both attorney-client and work-product privileges").

[359] See, e.g., United States v. Kovel, 296 F.2d 918, 920-23 (2d Cir. 1961) (applying privilege to communications between client and accountant to help lawyer provide legal advice); In re Grand Jury Subpoenas, 265 F. Supp. 2d at

consequences of using these consultants in other capacities during and after the investigation. Facts or data considered by a testifying expert in forming his opinions may be discoverable, so if, for example, an accountant hired to assist counsel in an internal investigation is also designated as the company's testifying expert in civil litigation on the same issues addressed in the investigation, facts or data considered by the accountant in forming his opinions may be discoverable by adverse parties and privilege is waived.[360] Retention of and materials shared with a consulting expert witness, however, may remain protected as work product in appropriate circumstances, even if the consulting expert later becomes a testimonial expert.[361] If the company expects to preserve the privilege over the investigation materials and communications, the company should plan to secure other experts for related state court

---

330-31 (concluding that the attorney-client privilege covered communications between client and PR firm aimed at obtaining or giving legal advice).

[360] *See* Fed. R. Civ. P. 26(b)(4)(B)-(C); *see also* Fed. R. Civ. P. 26 advisory committee's notes (2010 amendments) (explaining that protection of attorney-expert communications is "limited" to communications between a testifying expert required to provide a report under Rule 26(a)(2)(B) and "does not . . . protect communications between counsel and other expert witnesses" such as non-testifying experts (for whom communications can be sought only under Rule 26(b)(4)(D)) and non-reporting experts designated under Rule 26(a)(2)(C)); *U. S. ex rel. Scott v. Humana Inc.*, 2021 WL 3909906, at *3-6 (W.D. Ky. Aug. 31, 2021) (discussing Rule 26(b)(4) and requiring disclosure of communications between a relator's consulting expert—who was later designated a testifying expert—and the government, including communications made prior to the expert's designation as a testifying expert).

[361] *See* Fed. R. Civ. P. 26(b)(4)(D); *see also Republic of Ecuador v. Mackay*, 742 F.3d 860, 869 (9th Cir. 2014) ("[T]he amended rule 'provide[s] work-product protection against discovery regarding draft expert disclosures or reports and— with three specific exceptions—communications between expert witnesses and counsel.'" (citation omitted)); *Scott*, 2021 WL 3909906, at *5 (describing the "objective test" embraced by courts requiring disclosure of "anything received, reviewed, read, or authored by the expert, before or in connection with the forming of his opinion if the subject matter relates to the facts or opinions expressed"); *Soukhaphonh v. Hot Topic, Inc.*, No. CV 16-5124-DMG (AGRx), 2017 WL 10378493, at *3-5 (C.D. Cal. Sept. 14, 2017) (noting that "compliance with Rule 26(b)(4)(C)" by producing a consultant-turned-testifying witness's emails with counsel should not be construed "as a waiver of all work product protection").

litigation, however, and strictly limit the documents shared with them.[362]

C. Communications with Independent Auditors May Not be Protected

In the ordinary course, sharing communications and materials with independent auditors may lead a court to conclude that there has been a waiver of the attorney-client privilege or the attorney work product protection. Several federal courts have held that disclosure of attorney-client communications to an independent auditor waives the privilege with respect to those communications.[363] Although some states have codified—or have developed common law supporting—client-accountant and client-auditor privileges that extend privilege protection to communications that are disclosed to independent auditors,[364] federal common law generally does not recognize such an extension of the privilege. In contrast, some federal courts have concluded that disclosure of attorney work product to an independent auditor does not waive the protection because an auditor does not represent the type of adversarial relationship necessary to constitute waiver.[365] Still, the

---

[362] Not all state jurisdictions have adopted the expert discovery provisions of Federal Rule of Civil Procedure 26, which limits disclosure of counsel's communications with testifying experts to communications regarding the expert's compensation, facts or information counsel asked the expert to consider, and any assumptions from counsel the expert relied upon.

[363] *E.g.*, *United States v. Deloitte LLP*, 610 F.3d 129, 139-40 (D.C. Cir. 2010) (noting that voluntary disclosure to an auditor waives the attorney-client privilege); *Cantu v. TitleMax, Inc.*, No. 5:14-CV-628 RP, 2015 WL 5944258, at *5 (W.D. Tex. Oct. 9, 2015) (concluding that "disclosure of a document to an outside auditor destroys attorney-client privilege for that document"); *In re Juniper Networks, Inc. Secs. Litig.*, Nos. C 06-4327 JW (PVT), C 08-00246 JW (PVT), 2009 WL 4644534, at *2 (N.D. Cal. Dec. 9, 2009) (noting that disclosure to an auditor waives the attorney-client privilege); *Westernbank P.R. v. Kachkar*, Civil No. 07-1606 (ADC/BJM), 2009 WL 530131, at *3 (D.P.R. Feb. 9, 2009) (holding that disclosure to an auditor waives the attorney-client privilege).

[364] *See, e.g.*, Fla. Stat. Ann. § 90.5055 (West 1999); Tex. Occ. Code Ann. § 901.457 (West Supp. 2016); 63 Pa. Stat. and Cons. Stat. Ann. § 9.11a (West 2010).

[365] *Compare Medinol, Ltd. v. Bos. Sci. Corp.*, 214 F.R.D. 113-17 (S.D.N.Y. 2002) (holding that disclosure of attorney work product to an auditor waives the

law is far from settled, and care must be taken to evaluate the risk of waiver while a DOJ investigation is pending.

In order to shore up support against any waiver argument, a company should ensure that the auditor engagement letter contains confidentiality provisions. Further, it is important to regularly evaluate whether to share the results of an internal review with the company's auditor, including weighing factors such as the likely harm from waiver versus the benefits of disclosure to the auditor. If a determination is made to share communications or materials with an auditor, it may be helpful to limit the briefing to the underlying facts and not include any of the analyses or impressions of counsel.

---

protection), *with Merrill Lynch & Co. v. Allegheny Energy, Inc.*, 229 F.R.D. 441, 445-49 (S.D.N.Y. 2004) (holding that disclosure of attorney work product to an auditor does not waive the protection because an independent auditor is not an adversary within the meaning of the attorney work product doctrine); *see also Breuder v. Board of Trustees*, No. 15 CV 9323, 2021 WL 4283464, at *9 (N.D. Ill. Sept. 21, 2021 (recognizing that although the defendant "concedes [that] disclosure of privileged information to an independent auditor typically results in a waiver of the attorney-client privilege," the "disclosure does not waive the Board's work-product privilege unless the disclosure was made 'in a manner which substantially increases the opportunity for potential adversaries to obtain the information'") (citations omitted)); *First Horizon Nat'l Corp. v. Hous. Cas. Co.*, No. 2:15-cv-2235-SHL-dkv, 2016 WL 5867268, at *10 (W.D. Tenn. Oct. 5, 2016) (citing *Medinol* approvingly and holding that disclosure of privileged communications to public auditor waived attorney-client and work product protection); *SEC v. Berry*, No. C07-04431 RMW (HRL), 2011 WL 825742, at *7 (N.D. Cal. Mar. 7, 2011) (quoting *SEC v. Schroeder*, No. C07–03798 JW (HRL), 2009 WL 1125579, at *9 (N.D. Cal. Apr. 27, 2009), which stated that *Merrill Lynch* correctly concluded that disclosure to an outside auditor does not represent the type of adversarial relationship necessary to constitute waiver of the attorney work product protection); *Westernbank P.R.*, 2009 WL 530131, at *4-8 (holding that disclosure of attorney work product to an auditor does not waive the protection and noting that *Medinol* has been "roundly criticized"); *cf. United States v. Baker*, Cause No. A-13-CR-346-SS, 2014 WL 722097, at *2 (W.D. Tex. Feb. 21, 2014) (explaining that voluntary disclosure to an outside auditor "does not necessarily" waive the work product protection because such disclosure does not always "undercut the adversary process" (citing *Deloitte*, 610 F.3d at 140)).

VII.   RESPONDING TO DOJ INVESTIGATIVE REQUESTS

As discussed in **Section III**, DOJ requests for information in a civil investigation may take a variety of forms, from simple letter inquiries to civil investigative demands and subpoenas. Each form of request imposes distinct obligations under the law, and each requires a truthful and non-misleading response even if the response is to decline to provide the information requested or seek judicial intervention and relief.

Generally, a company's interests are best served by a candid and cooperative response to DOJ requests, but there are a number of issues and concerns that may temper a company's willingness to respond or respond in full to a DOJ inquiry. And these concerns may go to the form of the inquiry as well as the scope and other terms of the demand. These concerns include the following.

A.   Scope of Information Requested – Relevance and Burden

DOJ inquiries are often wide-ranging in time and subject matter. Seeking agreement with the DOJ on narrowing the time period and subject areas of these inquiries can alleviate significant burden and disruption to the company and its employees. For example, demands for transactional information or conduct outside the applicable statute of limitations may be excessive, although the request may not be legally confined by the limitations period. Offering valid reasons for restricting the search due to excessive burden or lack of relevance may be persuasive. The scope of most investigative demands, including CIDs and administrative subpoenas, will be evaluated by a reviewing court under the standards applicable to a grand jury subpoena or discovery requests under the Federal Rules of Civil Procedure.[366] Thus, as in

---

[366] *See* 31 U.S.C. § 3733(b)(1)(A) and (B); *United States v. Seitz*, No. MS2-93-063, 1993 WL 501817, at *3 (S.D. Ohio Aug. 26, 1993) ("The False Claims Act CID provisions expressly state that a demand recipient may not be forced to produce documents protected from production by standards applicable to grand jury subpoenas or by 'standards applicable to discovery requests under the Federal Rules of Civil Procedure, to the extent that the application of such

civil litigation, the scope of information requested by a civil investigative request may exceed norms of evidentiary "relevance" but must be reasonably proportionate to the needs for the inquiry.[367]

B. Scope of Information Requested – Authority of DOJ Challenged

Challenges to investigative demands that exceed the authority of the DOJ or the subject agency or applicable statute may be necessary. Note that such civil investigative inquiries, in various forms, are typically administrative actions and not self-enforcing. That is, if a party declines to provide the information demanded by the inquiry, the DOJ must seek a court order to enforce the subpoena or CID through a motion to compel or petition for enforcement; no contempt sanction is available to the DOJ prior to a valid court order.[368] A company may challenge the CID by petitioning a federal district court to modify or set aside the CID.[369] Such challenges, however, to the extent they are considered administrative inquiries, may be difficult to sustain.[370]

---

standards to any such demand is appropriate and consistent with the provisions and purposes of this section.'" (quoting 31 U.S.C. § 3733(b)(1)(A) and (B))), *aff'd*, 53 F.3d 332 (6th Cir. 1995) (per curiam) (unpublished table decision); *see also Cleveland Clinic Found. v. United States*, No. 1:11MC14, 2011 WL 862027, at *1-2 (N.D. Ohio Mar. 9, 2011) (denying petition to modify or set aside CID following application of standards applicable to subpoenas issued by a court of the United States to aid in a grand jury investigation and the standards applicable to discovery requests under the Federal Rules of Civil Procedure).

[367] *See* Fed. R. Civ. P. 26(b)(1); *CFPB v. Accrediting Council for Indep. Colls. & Schs.*, 854 F.3d 683, 688 (D.C. Cir. 2017) ("In determining whether to enforce a CID, courts consider only whether '[(1)] the inquiry is within the authority of the agency, [(2)] the demand is not too indefinite and [(3)] the information sought is reasonably relevant.'" (quoting *FTC v. Ken Roberts Co.*, 276 F.3d 583, 586 (D.C. Cir. 2001))).

[368] *See, e.g.*, 31 U.S.C. § 3733(j)(1) (requiring the DOJ to petition a federal district court to enforce a CID).

[369] *See, e.g.*, 31 U.S.C. § 3733(j)(2).

[370] *See United States v. Markwood*, 48 F.3d 969, 976, 979 (6th Cir. 1995) (holding that a CID issued by the DOJ under 31 U.S.C. § 3733 is an "administrative subpoena" and that a federal district court's task is limited to determining whether

In determining whether the DOJ or its client agency has the legal authority to compel production, reviewing courts typically look to whether the inquiry is reasonably within the scope of authority delegated to the DOJ or the agency by the enabling legislation.[371] And courts will defer to agency interpretation of such authority in most cases where such interpretation is reasonable.[372]

C. Form of Investigative Request for Information – Request for Voluntary Production or Interview of Company Representative

Although civil investigations often entail issuance of subpoenas or CIDs, many investigations are initiated by the DOJ through correspondence requesting a voluntary production of information by the company. Essentially, these simply represent a request that the company produce certain information and cooperate with the DOJ's inquiries while under no legal compulsion to do so on the part of the company. As noted, the scope and timing of such productions may be subject to negotiation, and the request is often issued with the admonition that legally compulsory investigative demands may be issued if the request is refused by the company.

Companies often find such requests to be considerably more beneficial and manageable than requiring the DOJ to go through more formal procedures. For example, many companies would prefer to be engaged in a dialogue with the DOJ than having to

---

the subpoena or CID, and the enforcement process, was authorized by Congress, "whether the information sought is relevant to the agency's investigation," and "whether or not the investigation and enforcement of the subpoena is an abuse of the court's process").

[371] *See, e.g., Accrediting Council for Indep. Colls. & Schs.*, 854 F.3d at 688 (citation omitted).

[372] *See id.* at 689; *see also Ken Roberts Co.*, 276 F.3d at 587 ("[W]e have held that enforcement of an agency's investigatory subpoena will be denied only when there is 'a patent lack of jurisdiction' in an agency to regulate or to investigate." (quoting *CAB v. Deutsche Lufthansa Aktiengesellschaft*, 591 F.2d 951, 952 (D.C. Cir. 1979))).

report publicly the receipt of an investigative subpoena directed to corporate activities or transactions.

Even when production is voluntary, however, certain conditions prevail. First and foremost, the production and representations about the production of information must be truthful and accurate. Even in the absence of any required certification of compliance with the DOJ request, federal law imposes sanctions for misleading or obstructing DOJ investigations, and misrepresentations of facts in such productions may give rise to criminal liability.[373]

Voluntarily affording the DOJ an opportunity to interview company officials or witnesses also is possible but carries significant risks for a company. The DOJ has no independent authority to compel persons to submit to an interview.[374] Therefore, declining such a request in a civil investigation does not generally involve a calculation of whether the DOJ would seek to compel an interview or deposition. And the terms and conditions of such an interview can vary widely, from a meeting in a controlled setting where the witness can decline to answer or the company's counsel objects to any answer, to a more formal interrogation before a court reporter and under oath.

There are times when such an interview may prove dispositive of the outcome of an investigation and benefit a company, but the opposite is equally true. Very careful consideration must be given before any agreement to put a company representative in such a voluntary interview setting, including the individual risk such a witness faces from possible later obstruction, perjury or misrepresentation allegations by the DOJ.

---

[373] *See, e.g.*, 18 U.S.C. § 1001 (prohibiting making false statements to federal officials); 18 U.S.C. § 1505 (prohibiting the obstruction of a pending federal proceeding).

[374] *See, e.g.*, 31 U.S.C. § 3733(j)(1) (requiring DOJ to petition a federal district court to enforce a CID to compel oral testimony).

D. Form of Investigative Request – CIDs for Documents

Certain statutes, such as the FCA, allow the DOJ to issue demands for documents related to an investigation of possible violations of that Act. Legally they have the same status as agency subpoenas, and are enforceable by the DOJ through a court order upon application of a petition to enforce the CID. Importantly, such CIDs are typically subject to the Federal Rules of Civil Procedure for reasonableness of scope, relevancy, and burden of production.

In some circumstances, companies may prefer to voluntarily produce information rather than have to respond to a CID. That is within the discretion of the DOJ, however, and it may prefer the formality of a CID and the obligations imposed by such a request.

E. Form of Investigative Request – CID for Interrogatory Responses

Also, under the FCA and federal antitrust laws,[375] the DOJ may issue CIDs for interrogatory responses. Like civil discovery interrogatories, written responses to CID interrogatories are provided under oath or verification by a witness for the company or by an individual.

As with all CID-based demands, they are treated as administrative agency requests, are not self-executing, and are subject to the Federal Rules of Civil Procedure in their scope and obligations.

F. Form of Investigative Request – CID for Deposition Testimony

Under the FCA, CIDs for deposition of a company witness may include employees, officers and other representatives. Additionally, the CID may demand production of a company representative to testify to company practices, conduct, policy or

---

[375] *See* 31 U.S.C. § 3733(a), (g) (FCA); 15 U.S.C. § 1312(a)-(b), (h) (Antitrust).

other relevant matters.[376] Such depositions are among the most potentially dangerous for a company and on occasion the DOJ has resisted certain procedural protections during such depositions including providing transcripts, opportunity for examination by company counsel, and offers of immunity for deposition witnesses.

Judicial intervention and remedies, as with all CIDs and DOJ subpoenas, typically require a motion to compel or petition for enforcement by the DOJ, and parties served with a CID or subpoena may also petition a federal district court to modify or set aside a CID or subpoena.[377]

VIII.   RETAINING SEPARATE COUNSEL FOR OFFICERS, EMPLOYEES AND BOARD MEMBERS

Given the DOJ's focus on identifying and potentially pursuing actions against individuals involved in misconduct (*see* **Section IV.B.**), it is not surprising that investigations often require determination of whether to retain separate individual counsel for current or former employees, officers or board members. These decisions include determining whether to advance fees or indemnify current or former personnel and potential cooperation among defense counsel.

A.   Engage Separate Counsel When There Are Conflicts

Separate counsel ought to be engaged whenever there is reason to anticipate or have knowledge that the interests of the company and current or former personnel diverge.[378] Until that scenario, it can

---

[376] *See* 31 U.S.C. § 3733(a)(1)(C), (h) (granting authority to issue a CID for oral testimony and prescribing procedures for oral examination, including that testimony may be taken consistent with the Federal Rules of Civil Procedure).

[377] *See* 31 U.S.C. § 3733(j)(1) (requiring the DOJ to petition a federal district court to enforce a CID); 31 U.S.C. § 3733(j)(2) (permitting persons in receipt of a CID to petition a federal district court to modify or set aside the CID).

[378] The risk of conflicts between a company and its personnel is exacerbated by the JM and the Federal Sentencing Guidelines for Organizations of the U.S. Sentencing Commission. *See* JM §§ 4-3.100(3), 9-28.700, 9-28.720 (providing, in

be appropriate for outside counsel to represent both a company and individual personnel, although the DOJ may take issue with joint representation if it calls witnesses before a grand jury or where the company may have reason to avoid even the appearance that it might be attempting to influence a witness's testimony.

A company also may decide to retain a single outside firm to represent many or all employees in need of representation. Doing so can reduce fees and can aid in leveraging counsel's factual knowledge. Before making such a decision a company should consider the: (i) likelihood that individual personnel's interests may diverge as additional facts are developed, particularly where pertinent facts involve conduct of individuals with diverse roles within an organization (*e.g.*, there may be greater chance of conflicts, for example, when considering obtaining counsel for a sales executive on the one hand and a compliance officer on the other); (ii) ethical considerations such as obtaining clients' informed consent following consultation; and (iii) likelihood the DOJ or other investigative authorities might object to joint representation. Courts have disqualified attorneys seeking to undertake joint representation "even after full disclosure has been made and consent of clients obtained," "[b]ecause an attorney's joint representation of two adverse parties in a legal proceeding is fraught with potential for irreconcilable conflict."[379]

---

pertinent part, that a company is eligible to receive cooperation credit only when it discloses "all relevant facts" of individual misconduct); U.S. Sentencing Guidelines Manual § 8C2.5(g) (U.S. Sentencing Comm'n 2021), https://www.ussc.gov/sites/default/files/pdf/guidelines-manual/2021/GLMFull.pdf (a significant factor in reducing a company's "culpability score" for purposes of sentencing is whether the company reported to the government the misconduct of its employees); *see also* Yates Memorandum, *supra* note 11, at 4 (directing DOJ attorneys to "focus on individual wrongdoing from the very beginning of any investigation of corporate misconduct").

[379] *Booth v. Cont'l Ins. Co.*, 634 N.Y.S.2d 650, 656 (Sup. Ct. 1995) (citation omitted). Attorneys seeking to undertake joint representation may equally run afoul of the Model Rules of Professional Conduct. *See* American Bar Association, Model Rules of Professional Conduct at Rule 1.7 Conflict of Interest ("Concurrent conflicts of interest can arise from the lawyer's responsibilities to

B. Advancing or Paying Fees For Separate Counsel Can Be Appropriate

When identifying separate individual counsel, a company should consider whether to pay for its current or former personnel's attorneys' fees, which would enable its personnel to retain high quality and experienced counsel. Arrangements to indemnify or advance funds for personnel's attorneys' fees and other related expenses generally are permitted and may be required under state law, company bylaws or partnership agreements, or other relevant employment contracts. The JM specifies that prosecutors may not request that companies refrain from paying employees' attorneys' fees and provides that, "[i]n evaluating cooperation... prosecutors should not take into account whether a corporation is advancing or reimbursing attorneys' fees or providing counsel to employees, officers, or directors under investigation or indictment."[380]

Companies may decide to advance fees or include indemnification clauses in employment contracts when trying to attract executives or other top talent. A company's decision to advance attorneys' fees for its personnel can be made subject to an undertaking agreement with the employee, officer or board member obligating them to repay fees if it is later determined that indemnification is inappropriate or unavailable, such as when it is discovered that the individual engaged in wrongdoing. Companies also should consider whether any director and officer insurance policies contain coverage for applicable defense costs.

When a company identifies counsel for individuals and agrees to advance attorneys' fees or pay the attorneys' fees pursuant to an indemnification clause, the company's counsel should exercise caution to avoid influencing—or the perception of influencing—an individual's counsel. The United States Supreme Court has indicated that a conflict of interest may result if "counsel was

---

another client, a former client or a third person or from the lawyer's own interests.").

[380] JM § 9-28.730.

164

influenced in his basic strategic decisions by the interests of the employer who hired him."[381]

C.   Cooperation Among Defense Counsel

A company can benefit from entering into joint defense or common interest agreement with counsel for individuals or with counsel for other companies involved in an investigation. The DOJ has been directed to respect that the "mere participation by a corporation in a joint defense agreement does not render the corporation ineligible to receive cooperation credit, and prosecutors may not request that a corporation refrain from entering into such agreements."[382] Key considerations in deciding whether to enter into a joint defense or common interest agreement with other defense counsel include:

- Whether to enter into a written confidentiality agreement between the attorneys for the company and the employees to allow for the sharing of information and documents among counsel and to make the joint defense privilege applicable to communications between the lawyers and their clients. Courts vary in their consideration of whether written agreements are required and in many instances no written agreement is needed.[383]

See Wood v. Georgia, 450 U.S. 261, 272 (1981).

[382] JM § 9-28.730.

[383] *Compare Lugosch v. Congel*, 219 F.R.D. 220, 237 (N.D.N.Y. 2003) (advising that documenting a joint-defense agreement would be prudent given the "vagaries of an oral agreement"); *In re Rivastigmine Patent Litig.*, No. 05 MD 1661 (HB/JCF), 2005 WL 2319005, at *4 (S.D.N.Y. Sept. 22, 2005) (finding insufficient evidence of a common interest agreement and noting that "parties relying on an oral agreement run the risk that the Court can not determine when or if an agreement was reached." (citation omitted)), *aff'd*, No. 05 MD 1661 (HB), 2005 WL 3159665 (S.D.N.Y. Nov. 22, 2005), *with Kansas City Power & Light Co. v. United States*, 139 Fed. Cl. 546, 563 (2018) (explaining that a joint-defense agreement can be "written or unwritten").

- If a written agreement is employed, the agreements ought to include a non-disclosure provision reflecting that shared information covered by the attorney-client privilege and work product doctrine shall not be disclosed to non-parties without the prior consent of the party who made the information available and should memorialize the understanding among counsel with respect to the common defense of their clients.

- The likelihood that one of the represented parties might be directly implicated in improper conduct. Courts have held that the privilege may be asserted so long as the parties have a common legal interest or are involved in a "joint defense effort or strategy."[384]

- Understanding that the temporal nature of the privilege varies by state jurisdictions. Some states expressly limit the doctrine to communications made during the time period when the parties shared a common interest: communications made before a common interest agreement or the parties' interests align are not protected and communications made after the parties no longer share a common interest also are not protected (although communications occurring during the time a common interest existed do not lose their

---

[384] *United States v. Krug*, 868 F.3d 82, 86 (2d Cir. 2017) (quoting *United States v. Schwimmer*, 892 F.2d 237, 243 (2d Cir. 1989)). Notably, the majority view is that "threat of litigation is not a prerequisite to the common interest doctrine." *United States v. BDO Seidman, LLP*, 492 F.3d 806, 816 (7th Cir. 2007) (collecting authorities). *But see In re Santa Fe Int'l Corp.*, 272 F.3d 705, 711 (5th Cir. 2001) ("[T]here must be a palpable threat of litigation at the time of the communication . . . before communications between one possible future co-defendant and another . . . could qualify for protection.").

privileged status upon the expiry of a common interest).[385]

- When considering a joint defense agreement with another company involved in an investigation, a company ought to refrain from inter-company disclosures until a common legal goal can be identified as the parties must have a stake in the same resolution to a legal question, not merely share commercial interests.[386]

IX. AVOIDING INVESTIGATION-RELATED LIABILITIES

Action or inaction taken by a company or its representatives during a DOJ inquiry may give rise to civil and criminal liability separate from and in addition to the civil liability for actions underlying the investigation. For example, failing to preserve documents relevant to the investigation may give rise to both civil and criminal liability, regardless of whether such destruction was intentional or the result of the routine operation of an electronic information system. The consequences of failing to preserve relevant documents are serious and could include:

- Loss of credibility with the government;

- Monetary sanctions; and

---

[385] *See Citizens for Ceres v. Super. Court*, 159 Cal. Rptr. 3d 789, 792 (Cal. Ct. App. 2013) (holding that "the common-interest doctrine . . . does not protect otherwise privileged communications disclosed" between parties prior to the period when their interests aligned); *Zirn v. VLI Corp.*, CIV. A. No. 9488, 1990 WL 119685, at *8 (Del. Ch. Aug. 13, 1990) (holding pre-common interest discussions were not protected).

[386] *See, e.g., Bank Brussels Lambert v. Credit Lyonnais (Suisse) S.A.*, 160 F.R.D. 437, 447 (S.D.N.Y. 1995) ("[T]he common interest doctrine does not encompass a joint business strategy which happens to include as one of its elements a concern about litigation.").

- Obstruction of justice charges.[387]

Additional investigation-related liabilities that may arise include criminal liability for perjury by a company's employees or representatives and, where the investigative target is a government contractor, a DOJ-initiated suspension and/or debarment action to preclude future procurements, grants, and other government funding mechanisms.[388]

X. RESOLVING THE INVESTIGATION

A. Voluntary Self-Disclosure Considerations

Some federal agencies have developed self-disclosure programs that allow companies to bring potential violations of federal law to the government's attention proactively.[389] And the terms of the

---

[387] *See* 18 U.S.C. § 1505 (providing that "[w]hoever corruptly . . . obstructs, or impedes or endeavors to influence, obstruct, or impede the due and proper administration of the law under which any pending proceeding is being had before any department or agency of the United States . . . [s]hall be fined . . . imprisoned not more than 5 years or, if the offense involves international or domestic terrorism . . . imprisoned not more than 8 years, or both"); *see also United States v. Caldwell*, 581 F. Supp. 3d 1, 17 (D.D.C. 2021) (citation omitted) ("As used in [18 U.S.C. § 1505], the term 'corruptly' means acting with an improper purpose, personally or by influencing another, including making a false or misleading statement, or withholding, concealing, altering, or destroying a document or other information.").

[388] *See generally* Debarment, Suspension, and Ineligibility, 48 C.F.R. § 9.402; *see also* Office of Inspector Gen., U.S. Dep't of Justice, *Audit of Statutory Suspension and Debarment Activities within the Department of Justice*, Audit Report 12-25 (June 2012), https://oig.justice.gov/reports/2012/a1225.pdf.

[389] *See* Office of Inspector Gen., U.S. Dep't of Health & Human Servs., *Updated OIG's Provider Self-Disclosure Protocol* (2013) ("OIG HHS Self-Disclosure Protocol"), https://oig.hhs.gov/compliance/self-disclosure-info/files/Provider-Self-Disclosure-Protocol.pdf. Other agencies may also use similar self-disclosure protocols. *See, e.g.*, Office of Inspector Gen., *Contractor Disclosure Program,* U.S. Dep't of Defense, http://www.dodig.mil/Programs/Contractor-Disclosure-Program/ (last visited Sept. 16, 2022); The Special Inspector General for Pandemic Recovery, Self-Disclosure Reporting, https://www.sigpr.gov/report-fraud-waste-abuse/self-disclosure-reporting (last visited Sept. 16, 2022) (SIGPR was established by the CARES Act and maintains a hotline for whistleblowers and a self-disclosure page on its website to afford program participants the option

FCA allow the DOJ and federal district courts to consider voluntary disclosures and reduce the potential damages.[390] Similarly, under the U.S. Department of Health and Human Services' Office of Inspector General ("OIG") Self-Disclosure Protocol, health care providers can disclose violations of the federal healthcare laws and, in return, resolve any supposed violations on an expedited basis and potentially on more favorable terms than if a whistleblower or the government raised the issue independently. Further, an ongoing government inquiry does not automatically prohibit use of the Self-Disclosure Protocol, as long as the disclosure is made in good faith and not for avoiding another governmental inquiry.[391] If an internal investigation in response to a governmental inquiry reveals potentially improper acts, the company may want to consider self-reporting if such a program is available.

B.   Settlement Considerations

While this chapter does not address the full range of issues a company may encounter during settlement, here are several key topics that deserve close scrutiny:

- **Scope of released conduct**. Once the DOJ has released the company from liability for certain conduct, then neither it nor private *qui tam* plaintiffs under the FCA can seek any further

---

to self-report potential violations); Bureau of Industry and Security, U.S. Dep't of Commerce, Voluntary Self Disclosures, https://www.bis.doc.gov/index.php/enforcement/oee/voluntary-self-disclosure (last visited Sept. 16, 2022); Environmental Protection Agency, eDisclosure, https://www.epa.gov/compliance/epas-edisclosure (last visited Sept. 16, 2022).

[390] 31 U.S.C. § 3729(a)(2) (stating that "the court may assess not less than 2 times the amount of damages which the Government sustains because of the act of" the defendant upon a finding that (i) the defendant who violated the FCA provided to the government "all information known to such person about the violation within 30 days after the date on which the defendant first obtained the information," (ii) the defendant fully cooperated with a government investigation, and (iii) no criminal, civil or administrative action was pending at the time of the disclosures to the government).

[391] OIG HHS Self-Disclosure Protocol at 3.

recovery for that same conduct. It is to the company's advantage to negotiate a broad scope of released conduct that covers all matters addressed during the investigation to minimize the potential for future liabilities.[392]

- **Admissions of liability**. The DOJ typically does not require admissions of liability in civil settlements, but if the DOJ requests them, the company should consider that such admissions will likely be admissible in any future civil, administrative, or criminal proceeding, regardless of the context.[393] The company must carefully consider the potential impact of any such admission in the context of its own regulatory

---

[392] For example, in 2012, Wells Fargo Bank N.A. signed a consent judgment with the government and paid $5 billion to settle allegations of having submitted false annual certifications of compliance in Federal Housing Administration-insured mortgage loans. *See United States v. Bank of Am.*, 922 F. Supp. 2d 1, 4 (D.D.C. 2013), *affirmed per curiam, United States v. Bank of Am. Corp.*, 753 F.3d 1335 (D.C. Cir. 2014). Shortly thereafter, the government filed another suit against Wells Fargo in a different district court alleging violations of the FCA. *Bank of Am.*, 922 F. Supp. at 4-5. Wells Fargo sought enforcement of the consent judgment, arguing, among other things, that the new lawsuit alleged "claims arising from conduct covered by" the earlier settlement. *Id.* at 7. The district court analyzed the terms of the consent judgment and denied the motion. *Id.* at 7-11. Wells Fargo later settled the action for $1.2 billion. *See* DOJ Press Release, *Wells Fargo Bank Agrees to Pay $1.2 Billion for Improper Mortgage Lending Practices*, Apr. 8, 2016, https://www.justice.gov/opa/pr/wells-fargo-bank-agrees-pay-12-billion-improper-mortgage-lending-practices (last visited Sept. 16, 2022).

[393] *See, e.g.*, DOJ Press Release, *Bayer to Pay $40 Million to Resolve the Alleged Use of Kickbacks and False Statements Relating to Three Drugs*, Sept. 2, 2022, https://www.justice.gov/opa/pr/bayer-pay-40-million-resolve-alleged-use-kickbacks-and-false-statements-relating-three-drugs (last visited Sept. 16, 2022) ("The claims settled by this agreement are allegations only, and there has been no admission of liability"); Settlement Agreement in *U.S. ex rel. Simpson v. Bayer Pharm. Corp.*, No. 05-cv-3895 (D. N.J.), at ¶ F, https://www.justice.gov/opa/press-release/file/1530771/download (last visited Sept. 16, 2022) (stating that the settlement is "neither an admission of liability by Bayer nor a concession by the United States that its claims are not well founded").

environment, including the risk of debarment or other agency sanctions.

- **Ongoing monitoring.** The DOJ and its client agencies will sometimes ask companies to retain compliance experts or independent monitors to ensure that certain remedial actions are implemented. Use of these monitors and consultants may depend upon the breadth of the company's cooperation and remediation during the investigation. Such "corporate integrity agreements" are commonly negotiated with the relevant agency, but the DOJ has independently required these in some cases. These obligations typically continue for several years.[394]

- **Other government actions.** The announcement of a DOJ settlement may also trigger additional inquiries from other government regulators. Moreover, in considering corporate resolutions, the DOJ now adheres to a policy encouraging coordination among enforcement authorities in reaching resolutions.[395] The policy, titled, "Coordination of Corporate Resolution Penalties in Parallel and/or Joint Investigations and Proceedings Arising from the Same Misconduct,"[396] identifies four main principles:

---

[394] *See, e.g.*, DOJ Press Release, *Essilor Agrees to Pay $16.4 Million to Resolve Alleged False Claims Act Liability for Paying Kickbacks*, Aug. 23, 2022, https://www.justice.gov/opa/pr/essilor-agrees-pay-164-million-resolve-alleged-false-claims-act-liability-paying-kickbacks (last visited Sept. 16, 2022) (stating that the settlement included a five-year Corporate Integrity Agreement with HHS-OIG requiring such measures as hiring of "an independent review organization to review [the company's] systems, policies, processes and procedures for ensuring that any discounts, rebates, or other reductions in price offered to providers comply with the Anti-Kickback Statute").

[395] *See* JM § 1-12.100.

[396] The policy has been popularly referred to as the policy against "piling on." *See* Rod Rosenstein, Deputy Attorney Gen., U.S. Dep't of Justice, Remarks to the

171

- "Department attorneys should remain mindful of their ethical obligation not to use criminal enforcement authority unfairly to extract, or to attempt to extract, additional civil or administrative monetary payments."

- Where "multiple Department components are investigating... the same misconduct, Department attorneys should coordinate with one another to avoid the unnecessary imposition of duplicative fines, penalties, and/or forfeiture against the company... with the goal of achieving an equitable result."

- The DOJ "should also endeavor, as appropriate, to coordinate with and consider the amount of fines, penalties, and/or forfeiture paid to other federal, state, local, or foreign enforcement authorities that are seeking to resolve a case with a company for the same misconduct."

- Finally, in "determining whether coordination and apportionment between [DOJ] components and with other enforcement authorities allows the interests of justice to be fully vindicated," the DOJ should consider factors, including, but not limited to, "the egregiousness of a company's

New York City Bar White Collar Crime Institute (May 9, 2018), https://www.justice.gov/opa/speech/deputy-attorney-general-rod-rosenstein-delivers-remarks-new-york-city-bar-white-collar (Deputy Attorney General Rod Rosenstein announced the policy on May 9, 2018, referring to the phrase in football as the act of players jumping onto a pile of other players after the ball carrier has been tackled.).

misconduct; statutory mandates regarding penalties, fines, and/or forfeitures; the risk of unwarranted delay in achieving a final resolution; and the adequacy and timeliness of a company's disclosures and its cooperation with the Department."[397]

The company also should consider retaining a public relations firm to assist with framing the company's position for the media and responding to additional government inquiries.

C.   Preparing for Litigation

If settlement is not a possibility, a company must prepare for litigation with the DOJ. Although not an exhaustive list, the following are several issues a company should consider:

- **Retaining local counsel.** While not previously required during the investigation phase, a company should consider retaining local counsel to provide insight on the local rules of practice and the preferences of the local bench.

- **Refresh document preservation instructions.** To guard against any document spoliation, a company should consider refreshing or re-issuing a document preservation notice to remind employees of their obligations. The notice can also address any new topics or issues for retention that arose since the original notice.

- **Prepare for discovery.** Some jurisdictions allow the parties to delay discovery until motions to dismiss are resolved, but others require the parties to begin discovery while motions are still pending. Regardless, the company should consider what information it wants from the government's or a

---

[397] *See* JM § 1-12.100.

qui tam relator's files and begin preparing discovery requests accordingly. Recent amendments to the Federal Rules of Civil Procedure allow parties to deliver Rule 34 Requests for Production beginning 21 days after the complaint and summons are served.[398] To the extent not already done, the company should coordinate with counsel to retain an e-discovery vendor to assist with document review and production.

- **Experts.** If damages or other experts will be necessary, the company may also want to retain appropriate testifying or consulting experts sooner rather than later. As noted earlier, materials provided to consulting experts are treated as work product if not otherwise privileged. And consulting experts can assist with document discovery and help counsel frame complicated fact issues for the court. In some cases, these experts may even become testimonial experts for the defense.

In conclusion, complex and significant risks for individuals and corporations come with navigating investigations initiated by the Civil Division of the DOJ. It is imperative that corporations and individuals understand the scope and reach of the power of the relevant government authorities, the process and protections afforded by relevant laws and regulations, and the importance of maintaining the integrity of their response. Stakeholders will be aided by effectively managing communications with the DOJ and the public, appropriately preserving documents and safeguarding privileges, and planning for and managing the outcome of the investigation.

---

[398] *See* Fed. R. Civ. P. 26(d)(2).

Chapter 7

Department of Justice (DOJ) Criminal Division Investigations

By: Ann Claire Phillips[399]

The Department of Justice's Criminal Division includes attorneys handpicked to join the Department and handle significant criminal investigations and prosecutions. Criminal Division attorneys are formidable opponents in an investigation or courtroom, and it can be helpful for a general counsel or other corporate attorney to understand how the Division is staffed, what its priorities are, and what to anticipate, should their company receive an inquiry or notice of investigation from the Division.

I.   HISTORY OF THE CRIMINAL DIVISION

The origins of the Criminal Division date back to 1915, when Government attorneys who worked in the practice area were listed under the Office of the Assistant Attorney General William Wallace, Jr. in the Department of Justice Register. Later, in 1919, the Attorney General formally organized the Division, describing it in the Report of the Attorney General as follows: "The present division of the work of the department assigns to this division all criminal matters arising under Federal laws except prosecutions under the food bill, the antitrust act, and violations of the war-time prohibition bill (act of Nov. 21, 1918)." To date, the mission of the Criminal Division remains relatively intact and, in 2019, the Division will celebrate its centennial anniversary.

---

[399] Ann Claire Phillips is the Chief Government Investigations Counsel and Chief Risk Officer, Legal for U.S. Bank National Association and previously served as an Assistant United States Attorney for nine years. The views expressed in this chapter are her own, do not necessarily represent the views of the Bank, and should not be considered legal advice. Ashley B. Hayes is an attorney in the Washington, D.C. office of Shook, Hardy and Bacon, L.L.P. and contributed to this chapter.

II.   STAFFING OF THE CRIMINAL DIVISION

In recent years, the Criminal Division has been staffed with attorneys handpicked for their skills and expertise in particular, and often specialized, areas of criminal law. Most Division attorneys are experienced criminal lawyers, and some are extremely senior counsel with decades of practice under their belts. Serving as a Criminal Division attorney is a prestigious position that brings with it significant responsibility and a unique skillset, and it can often springboard an attorney into a partnership at a large law firm, a senior in-house position, or even a position within the federal judiciary. As such, competition for positions with the Division can be stiff. Only a small percentage of applicants are interviewed, and an even smaller percentage are offered a position. Open positions with the Division are advertised on the USAJobs website (www.usajobs.gov).

The exceptions to this procedure are attorneys hired through the Department of Justice Honors Program (hereafter, the "Honors Program"), which places certain members in the Criminal Division. Through the Honors Program, entry-level candidates can join the Division, as well as other sections of the Department of Justice. However, it is rare that a member of the Honors Program would lead a Criminal Division investigation into a corporation: it is much more common for such a junior attorney to work under the tutelage of a more senior Criminal Division attorney.

The personnel structure of the Criminal Division is much more egalitarian than that of a law firm. There are no "partners" or "associates," for example. Rather, the Criminal Division has certain subsections, which are detailed below. The leadership of these sections, and the Division as a whole, tends to fluctuate over time, and senior positions can change with political administrations. Movement between the Criminal Division and a United States Attorney's Office (USAO) is also common. However, an attorney within the Criminal Division is a part of the General Schedule (GS) pay scale, whereas an Assistant United States Attorney (AUSA) falls under the Administratively Determined (AD) pay scale.

III.   CRIMINAL DIVISION DUTIES

Generally speaking, the Criminal Division is responsible for developing, enforcing, and supervising the application of all federal criminal laws, excluding those specifically assigned to other Department of Justice divisions. The Criminal Division works closely with the 93 United States Attorneys and their offices to oversee all federal criminal matters. Most nationally significant cases are handled by the Criminal Division, often in conjunction with one (or more) USAO.

The Criminal Division is also responsible for formulating and implementing criminal enforcement policies and providing legal advice on criminal matters. This may take the form of approving and/or monitoring certain sensitive areas, such as the use of electronic surveillance or participation in the Witness Security Program. The Criminal Division provides advice on matters of criminal law to the White House, Congress, Attorney General, and the Office of Management and Budget. Additionally, the Criminal Division serves as a resource and provides assistance to federal investigative agencies and prosecutors, including AUSAs. This often takes the form of leading and coordinating joint investigations and enforcement matters, both internationally and within the United States.

IV.   STRUCTURE OF THE CRIMINAL DIVISION

The Criminal Division is headed by Kenneth A Polite, Jr., who was confirmed as Assistant Attorney General for the Criminal Division on July 20, 2021.[400] The Office of the Assistant Attorney General (OAAG) and the 93 USAOs oversee criminal investigations and prosecutions of crimes under more than 900 statutes. The OAAG also advises the Attorney General, Congress, the White House, and the Office of Management and Budget on criminal matters. The Assistant Attorney General for the Criminal Division is supported by the Principal Deputy Assistant Attorney

---

[400] The United States Department of Justice, *Assistant Attorney General Kenneth A. Polite, Jr.*, https://www.justice.gov/criminal/meet-aag (last updated March 30, 2022).

177

General, who, in turn, is supported by the Chief of Staff/Counselor to the Assistant Attorney General, to whom the Office of Administration and Office of Policy and Legislation report.

Six Deputy Assistant Attorneys General report to the Principal Deputy Assistant Attorney General. They are responsible for, respectively:

- Office of Enforcement Operations; Narcotic and Dangerous Drug Section

- Money Laundering and Asset Recovery Section; Public Integrity Section

- Office of International Affairs; International Criminal Investigative Training Assistance Program; Office of Overseas Prosecutorial Development, Assistance and Training.

- Fraud Section; Appellate Section.

- Computer Crime and Intellectual Property Section; Child Exploitation and Obscenity Section

- Human Rights and Special Prosecutions Section; Organized Crime and Gang Section; Capital Case Section.[401]

Each of these sections overseen by the six Deputy Assistant Attorneys General has separate areas of expertise, as described below.[402]

Appellate Section: The Appellate Section prepares briefs, argues cases in the United States Courts of Appeal, and makes

[401] This Organizational Structure was implemented by then-Attorney General William P. Barr on July 24, 2019.

[402] The United States Department of Justice, *Sections/Offices*, https://www.justice.gov/criminal/sectionsoffices (last visited August 2, 2023).

recommendations to the Solicitor General as to whether further
review is warranted on adverse decisions in federal courts. The
Section also drafts briefs and certiorari petitions for filing in the
United States Supreme Court.

Capital Case Section: The Capital Case Section oversees all
capital cases prosecuted by the Criminal Division and the 93
USAOs.

Child Exploitation and Obscenity Section: The Child
Exploitation and Obscenity Section (CEOS), along with the 93
USAOs, prosecutes all violations of federal laws related to the
exploitation of children, including offenses related to child
pornography and interstate and international travel to abuse
children sexually. It also prosecutes international parental
kidnapping.

Computer Crime and Intellectual Property Section: The
Computer Crime and Intellectual Property Section (CCIPS)
handles computer and intellectual property crimes, including
electronic penetrations, data breaches and thefts, and cybercrimes.

Fraud Section: The Fraud Section investigates and prosecutes
complex white-collar criminal cases across the United States. It
frequently assists with complex multi-district litigation. It also has
the ability to assist evolving law enforcement priorities and
geographic spikes in crime. The Fraud Section is also instrumental
in setting the Department of Justice's policy as to the prosecution
of economic crime.

Human Rights and Special Prosecutions Section: The Human
Rights and Special Prosecutions (HRSP) Section evolved from
what had been two separate sections, the Domestic Security
Section and the Office of Special Investigations. This newer,
combined section handles matters in the areas of human rights,
international violent crime and war crimes, and immigration
crimes.

**International Criminal Investigative Training Assistance
Program:** The International Criminal Investigative Training

Assistance Program works hand-in-hand with foreign governments to develop law enforcement programs and reduce the threat of terrorism and transnational crime.

Money Laundering and Asset Recovery Section: The Money Laundering and Asset Recovery Section (MLARS) manages the Department of Justice's asset recovery program and provides managerial direction to the 93 USAOs and other components involved in prosecuting money laundering.

Narcotics and Dangerous Drug Section: The Narcotics and Dangerous Drug Section investigates and prosecutes international and national drug trafficking organizations.

Office of Administration: The Office of Administration provides administrative assistance to all components of the Criminal Division.

Office of Enforcement Operations: The Office of Enforcement Operations (OEO) reviews and approves the Criminal Division's work in approximately forty different subject areas, including reviewing wiretap requests, consulting on electronic surveillance, administering the Federal Witness Security Program, handling subpoenas from the media, and reviewing requests for witness immunity.

Office of International Affairs: The Office of International Affairs (OIA) coordinates the extradition/legal rendition of international fugitives, coordinates international evidence gathering, and provides assistance on international criminal matters.

Office of Overseas Prosecutorial Development, Assistance, and Training: The Office of Overseas Prosecutorial Development, Assistance, and Training (ODAT) helps develop foreign sector justice institutions and their law enforcement personnel, with a goal of partnering with the Department of Justice in combatting human trafficking, organized crime, corruption, financial and cybercrimes, and terrorism.

Office of Policy and Legislation: The Office of Policy and Legislation develops and comments on pending legislation affecting the federal criminal justice system, represents the Department of Justice before the U.S. Sentencing Commission on sentencing-related matters, and represents the Department before the Judicial Conference's Advisory Committees on Criminal Rules and Evidence regarding the Federal Rules of Criminal Procedure and Federal Rules of Evidence.

Organized Crime and Gang Section: The Organized Crime and Gang Section works with the 93 USAOs and other agencies to disrupt and dismantle significant gangs and organized crime entities.

Public Integrity Section: The Public Integrity Section has exclusive jurisdiction over investigations and cases involving alleged criminal misconduct by federal judges and monitors election and conflict of interest cases. This section frequently partners with the particular USAO that is prosecuting a case against one or more federal, state, or local officials.

V.   CRIMINAL DIVISION TASK FORCES

The Criminal Division is also responsible for coordinating and leading specialized task forces. These have included task forces related to specific events, such as the Disaster Fraud Task Force established after Hurricane Katrina, as well as more generalized task forces designed to combat specific crimes. One of the latter is the Financial Fraud Enforcement Task Force, which was designed to investigate and prosecute individuals and institutions that helped bring about the most recent United States financial crisis and, as a part thereof, attempted to take advantage of the country's efforts at economic recovery.

One significant task force is the Intellectual Property Task Force, which is part of a Department of Justice-wide initiative to combat intellectual property crimes in the United States and internationally. This task force has grown as technological advances have occurred and is chaired by the Deputy Attorney General.

On July 22, 2018, former President Trump signed Executive Order 13844, which established a new Task Force on Market Integrity and Consumer Fraud. This Task Force is designed to combat fraud conducted against consumers, in particular, the elderly, military service members and veterans, as well as investigate and prosecute corporate fraud of which the Government and/or general public may be victims.

One of the largest task forces in the Criminal Division is the Organized Crime Drug Enforcement Task Forces (OCDETF) Program, which dates back to 1982. OCDETF attorneys and agents use Department resources to combat organized drug traffickers, including, but not limited to, the cartels.

It is important to remember that the Department of Justice's resources allocated to these various task forces, as well as assigned to new ones, vary over time. The OCDETF program, for example, has been robust for decades, with at least one specialized OCDETF prosecutor assigned to each USAO. Criminal Division OCDETF attorneys work hand-in-hand with these district OCDETF AUSAs, as well as with federal, state, and local agents. The Criminal Division plays a significant role in this area of investigation and prosecution, as it frequently coordinates work by assorted offices on large international and domestic narcotics cases. Additionally, the Criminal Division plays a role on such task forces by providing specialized expertise that junior AUSAs, AUSAs in smaller Districts, or AUSAs who have not practiced in the area before might not possess.

VI.   THE FREEDOM OF INFORMATION ACT AND THE CRIMINAL DIVISION

Like each federal agency, the Criminal Division handles its own Freedom of Information Act (FOIA) requests and processes its own responsive records. As such, and before making a request to the Criminal Division, you should determine if the Division is likely to have the records you seek. The Department of Justice's webpage contains a reference guide listing components of the Department, as well as instructions for how to make a request and to whom to direct it.[403] Similarly, before disclosing documents to the Criminal Division, you should consider including a "Confidentiality and FOIA Statement" with your production. Such statements are commonly included at the conclusion of a production letter.

VII.   CRIMINAL DIVISION INVESTIGATIONS

As you can see from the above, the Criminal Division tends to be involved in specialty investigations and often works with USAOs on large, complex, or significant matters. In terms of investigative style and timing, investigations led by the Criminal Division proceed in the normal federal course. Specifically, one or more federal government agencies, sometimes along with state or local authorities, conduct an investigation, followed by presentation of the investigative file to the Criminal Division, along with a request for consideration for prosecution.

Investigations may begin informally, with a request for documents or information sent to a company, frequently to its general counsel or chief risk officer. Such requests may at times, include a request to meet with employees familiar with a particular subject. Identifying the individual most familiar with the particular area who should be produced is most often left to the company, and the resulting meeting will likely not be formal (*i.e.*, testimony taken under oath). Rather, the meeting will likely include more open-ended questions, designed to familiarize the Criminal Division attorney with the company's practices and procedures. In-house and/or outside counsel can and, except in rare cases, should accompany the employee to ensure topics of discussion and questioning do not veer into areas contrary to the company's interest.

Companies should evaluate such informal requests extremely carefully. It may or may not be in a company's interest to cooperate in an informal fashion, rather than demanding formal

---

[403] The United States Department of Justice, *CRM Freedom of Information Act*, https://www.justice.gov/criminal/crm-freedom-information-act (last updated July 25, 2023).

requests. Such formal requests will often involve the convening of a grand jury on a matter and the issuance of grand jury subpoenas for production of documents and/or testimony. At times, certain agencies working with the Criminal Division may issue administrative subpoenas as well, but grand jury subpoenas are far more common. One potential drawback is that subpoenas bring with them time deadlines and more formalized procedures for responding to the Criminal Division's requests.

PRACTICE TIP: It is important to remember that a grand jury subpoena can only demand existing documents or testimony. A company is not required to create documents to respond to a grand jury subpoena.

A grand jury subpoena may also demand testimony from a particular individual determined by the Criminal Division or a subject matter expert to be designated by the company. Caution is again advised, as grand jury testimony is sworn and on the record. Individuals who testify before a grand jury are not entitled to bring counsel into the grand jury proceeding. Rather, counsel must wait outside, but the witness may seek leave for a break to confer with counsel. Should a company find itself in this situation, it should strongly consider retaining experienced outside counsel familiar with Criminal Division grand jury proceedings and the federal criminal process.

After an investigation is complete, the Criminal Division must make a charging decision. As the Criminal Division has no judicial district of its own, it has the ability to bring a case wherever jurisdiction lies, which might afford the Division several choices. While at least one local AUSA usually becomes involved in the matter, as discussed further below, charging and dispositive decisions remain firmly in the hands of the Criminal Division's attorneys in matters on which Division attorneys are lead counsel.

VIII. RESOLUTION OF CRIMINAL DIVISION INVESTIGATIONS

Criminal Division investigations can conclude in many ways. In some cases, a federal agent or Criminal Division attorney will inform a company that the investigation is complete and no further action will occur. This often takes the form of a letter sent to the company's outside or in-house counsel.

In other cases, a company will comply with all requests, whether informal or formal, and simply never hear from the investigating agents again. This frequently occurs because the company was not originally, or over time transitioned from, the focus of the investigation. Such investigations can be frustrating for companies and costly in terms of time and financial expenditures. However, despite the resources required to respond, a resolution of this type is a positive outcome. Put simply, no news is often good news when a significant period of silence follows an active Criminal Division investigation.

Sometimes, it will become clear from agents or Criminal Division attorneys that the company is the target of the investigation. In such instances, it is important for a company to consider hiring outside counsel experienced with the Department of Justice, in particular the Criminal Division. Attorneys with experience serving as a Criminal Division attorney or AUSA are located in nearly all major cities and are familiar with the Division and its methods of operation. The bar of attorney alumni of the Criminal Division and USAO tends to be small, and relationships form, which can prove beneficial to a company under investigation, in terms of obtaining information, avoiding pitfalls, and negotiating the scope of investigative requests and, potentially, charges and settlements.

Unfortunately, Criminal Division investigations can go on for years as the Division evaluates a matter and, if it is moving forward, perfects its case. Because of the significance of many of these investigations, they will be reviewed by several lawyers within the Division (line attorneys and supervisors) before a decision as to how to proceed is made.

In the end, some cases may be handled by the Department of Justice's Civil Division (a sister division to the Criminal Division)—for example, when the Civil Division proceeds with a False Claims Act case rather than the Criminal Division indicting a company for bank, wire, or mail fraud. Ultimately, most cases investigated by the Criminal Division that proceed to charging are prosecuted by the Division itself and, with regard to companies, are frequently settled before trial or, at times, even indictment. Settlements may take the form of a non-prosecution agreement (NPA), deferred prosecution agreement (DPA), or formal criminal charges, which must be resolved through a guilty plea. Of course, in some instances, a company will decide to proceed to trial and be acquitted or convicted by a jury or judge.[404] In such cases, the Criminal Division attorney traditionally assumes the lead prosecutorial role. These cases are discussed in greater detail below.

IX.   JURISDICTION

As noted above, the Criminal Division is free to bring a case in whatever jurisdiction with ties to the matter that the Division chooses. This can prove problematic, as the case may ultimately be brought in a district far from the company's headquarters or any corporate locale. Travel costs can mount quickly in such cases.

Criminal Division attorneys frequently include a local AUSA to assist and serve as de facto local counsel. Adding a local AUSA to the team provides the Criminal Division attorneys handling the case with information about the district, its judges, and its juries that the Division might not otherwise possess.

PRACTICE TIP: Hiring experienced local counsel, either to lead a defense or to serve in a secondary capacity, can help level the playing field.

X.   CRIMINAL DIVISION PROSECUTIONS

Criminal Division cases follow the same progression as all other criminal cases in federal court. First, the Criminal Division will charge a company, at times along with one or more individuals,

---

[404] In rare instances, a jury trial can result in a hung jury.

frequently former or current employees. Charging can occur in several fashions.

A federal magistrate judge may issue a criminal complaint, pursuant to Rule 3 of the Federal Rules of Criminal Procedure. A criminal complaint is a written statement of the key facts constituting the charged offense. The federal magistrate judge must find probable cause based on sworn information presented by the Criminal Division before the judge issues the criminal complaint. This information is presented in a supporting sworn affidavit, which will contain sufficient information to establish probable cause. These affidavits are nearly always signed by an agent or law enforcement officer, rather than the Criminal Division attorney or AUSA.

A criminal complaint is accompanied by an arrest warrant or summons, pursuant to Rule 4 of the Federal Rules of Criminal Procedure. A summons is more commonly used in white-collar cases, where the defendant is neither a danger to himself nor others. A summons should be taken seriously—if a defendant fails to appear pursuant to the summons, the Criminal Division attorney may request, and will usually obtain, an arrest warrant from the Court. Arrest warrants are exactly what they sound like—authorizations for law enforcement to arrest an individual on the spot and bring him to court. After an individual is arrested or summoned, he makes his initial appearance in federal district court, pursuant to Rule 5 of the Federal Rules of Criminal Procedure.

Initial appearances are held before federal magistrate judges. The purpose of an initial appearance is to inform a defendant of the charges filed against him and of his right to counsel. Additionally, an individual charged by criminal complaint may demand a preliminary hearing, which must occur, under Federal Rule of Criminal Procedure 5.1, no later than fourteen days after the defendant's initial appearance if he is in custody, and not more than 21 days after his initial appearance if the defendant is not in custody.

Thereafter, the defendant is arraigned, where he is presented with the charges lodged against him. After reviewing the charges, the defendant must enter a plea of guilty or not guilty. In rare instances, a defendant may plea *nolo contendere*, but the Criminal Division discourages such pleas.

PRACTICE TIP: After a criminal complaint is issued, the Criminal Division has thirty days to present its case to a federal grand jury and obtain an indictment. Otherwise, the charges should be dismissed under the law.

An indictment is another means by which the Criminal Division can charge a case. Criminal Division attorneys obtain an indictment by presenting evidence, in the form of testimony and, at times, documents, to a federal grand jury sitting in the district. Grand jury meetings are secret and are limited to the members of the grand jury, a court reporter, and the Criminal Division attorneys or AUSAs presenting a matter. At times, a witness may be present for the limited purpose of presenting testimony, along with an interpreter (if necessary).

Following an indictment, the procedure for arrest, pursuant to a summons or arrest warrant, is the same as for a criminal complaint. The process for a defendant's initial appearance and arraignment is also the same. A defendant charged by indictment is not entitled to a preliminary hearing.

PRACTICE TIP: A grand jury must find that evidence has been presented that establishes "probable cause" that a criminal offense has occurred to indict a company or defendant. Indictments are fairly easy to obtain – there is a reason for the old joke that a grand jury would indict a ham sandwich!

Finally, a defendant may be charged by a criminal bill of information. A bill of information requires a defendant to waive his right to be prosecuted by indictment. A bill of information is frequently used when a company or individual and the Criminal Division have reached an agreement as to a charge and plea ahead of the "normal" charging event. In most "information" cases, a defendant makes one court appearance, at which time he has his initial appearance, detention hearing, arraignment, and Rule 11 (plea) hearing.

The goal of any criminal prosecution is to obtain a conviction, either by a guilty plea or by a trial verdict of "guilty." The standard of proof for a conviction is "beyond a reasonable doubt," which is a higher standard than a "preponderance of the evidence" or "probable cause."

XI. CRIMINAL DIVISION GUIDANCE – CORPORATE COMPLIANCE PROGRAMS

In February of 2017 and with little fanfare, the Criminal Division's Fraud Section issued guidance on the "Evaluation of Corporate Compliance Programs," (hereinafter Compliance Guidance) which has since been updated. It was designed to form the basis for the Criminal Division's decision regarding conducting an investigation, bringing charges, and negotiating an NPA, DPA, or plea agreement.

While worded differently, the 2017 Compliance Guidance factors were very similar to the principles set forth in the Filip Factors Memorandum, promulgated by former Deputy Attorney General Mark Filip in 2008. The Filip Factors Memo outlined measures a company must undertake to qualify for cooperation credit. Under the Filip Factors Memorandum, prosecutors are required to consider the following factors:[405]

1. The nature and seriousness of the offense, including the risk of harm to the public, and applicable policies and priorities, if any, governing the prosecution of corporations for particular categories of crime.

2. The pervasiveness of wrongdoing within the corporation, including the complicity in, or the

---

[405] The factors that follow are taken verbatim from the Filip Factors Memorandum, as codified in the then-United States Attorney's Manual (USAM).

condoning of, the wrongdoing by corporate management.

3. The corporation's history of similar misconduct, including prior criminal, civil, and regulatory enforcement actions against it.

4. The corporation's willingness to cooperate in the investigation of its agents.

5. The existence and effectiveness of the corporation's pre-existing compliance program.

6. The corporation's timely and voluntary disclosure of wrongdoing.

7. The corporation's remedial actions, including any efforts to implement an effective corporate compliance program or to improve an existing one, to replace responsible management, to discipline or terminate wrongdoers, to pay restitution, and to cooperate with the relevant government agencies.

8. Collateral consequences, including whether there is disproportionate harm to shareholders, pension holders, employees, and others not proven personally culpable, as well as impact on the public arising from the prosecution.

9. The adequacy of remedies such as civil or regulatory enforcement actions.

10. The adequacy of the prosecution of individuals for the corporation's malfeasance.

Much of the information contained in the 2017 Compliance Guidance is not really "new"—most was included in the Filip Factors Memorandum, as well as previous policy statements by the Department of Justice.

In May of 2019, AAG Benczkowski announced updated guidance for DOJ attorneys and AUSAs (hereafter, "2019 Compliance Guidance"), which expanded on the 2017 Compliance Guidance. The 2019 Compliance Guidance aimed to ensure consistency with the DOJ's principles for corporate prosecution and appeared to be a part of the DOJ's broader effort to ensure transparency in white-collar enforcement matters by articulating the benefits of responsible corporate approaches to misconduct.

The 2019 Compliance Guidance follows the "fundamental questions" that the DOJ Justice Manual encourages prosecutors to review when assessing the efficacy of corporate compliance programs. There are three parts to the 2019 Compliance Guidance. First, was the corporate compliance program well-designed? Second, was the corporate compliance program implemented in good faith? And third, did the corporate compliance program work in a practical sense? The 2019 Compliance Guidance contains a number of topics and subtopics regarding whether a company under investigation will be prosecuted; the size of any financial penalties that might be imposed; and whether any resolution will require an in-company compliance monitor.

Additionally, the 2019 Compliance Guidance emphasized two new areas. First, it stressed that corporate compliance programs must be ever-evolving and appropriate for a particular company's current risks, taking into account on any prior incidents that may have occurred at that particular company. As the DOJ will be examining whether a company learned from its past actions and updated its compliance program accordingly, it is crucial that companies periodically review and update their compliance programs and maintain clear records of any improvements thereto, in case they are called upon to document the same.

Second, the 2019 Compliance Guidance directed prosecutors to assess data in their decision-making regarding the effectiveness of a particular company's compliance program. The 2019 Compliance Guidance suggested that prosecutors use metrics when assessing corporate training practices and programs, internal controls, tracking mechanisms, internal investigations related to potential misconduct, and incentive compensation related to promoting good corporate citizenship. As such, it would be a good practice for companies to review their methods of collecting and using compliance data, both with an eye to the direction set forth in the 2019 Compliance Guidance and the clear signals from the DOJ that it will consider corporate compliance programs in making charging decisions and determining the penalties associated therewith.

As of March 2023, the Compliance Guidance has been continues to outline the Division's view of an effective corporate compliance program. The 2023 Compliance Guidance includes three fundamental questions prosecutors should ask themselves when evaluating a company's performance on various topics. The topics and subtopics contained in the 2023 Compliance Guidance[406] are noted below:

1. Is the corporation's compliance program well designed?

   a. Risk Assessment

   b. Policies and Procedures

   c. Training and Communications

   d. Confidential Reporting Structure and Investigation Process

   e. Third Party Management

   f. Mergers and Acquisitions (M&A)

---

[406] The sample topics and broad question areas contained in the 2023 Compliance Guidance are noted word-for-word herein. The sub-questions are not included herein but may be viewed in the full document, linked on the Criminal Division's website.

2. Is the program being applied and in good faith? In other words, is the program adequately resourced and empowered to function effectively?

    a. Commitment by Senior and Middle Management

    b. Autonomy and Resources

    c. Compensation Structures and Consequence Management

3. Does the corporation's compliance program work in practice?

    a. Continuous Improvement, Periodic Testing, and Review

    b. Investigation of Misconduct

    c. Analysis and Remediation of Any Underlying Misconduct

PRACTICE TIP: Legal websites, such as Law360, frequently disseminate key points from new guidance issued by the Criminal Division, along with providing analysis and interpretation. Subscriptions to legal websites and news services can be very helpful to staying current on the latest Criminal Division activities, as some policies, such as the Compliance Guidance, are rolled out with little fanfare. Additionally, the Criminal Division, at times, comments on policies at conferences and other events, articles about which are frequently published on these websites.

XII. COLLATERAL CONSEQUENCES OF CRIMINAL DIVISION INVESTIGATIONS AND PROSECUTIONS

Like all investigations, those by the Criminal Division can have significant consequences for a company. Financial risk is one obvious consequence. Reputational risk is another consideration.

Cases brought by the Criminal Division tend to be complex, large, and newsworthy. A company must carefully consider how to handle media inquiries and when and if to make public statements. Depending on the scope of the matter and size of the company, it may be worth engaging outside assistance from crisis management or media relations firms. Certainly, at the appropriate time, the General Counsel or another senior company representative will want to brief other senior leaders and the Board as to the nature of the investigation and the risk associated therewith.

Finally, Criminal Division investigations and cases may also entail specialized reporting requirements. Depending on the industry, a company may need to report to its regulators that it is under investigation or being prosecuted by the Criminal Division.

XIII.   CONCLUSION

Hopefully, your company will never be involved in a Criminal Division investigation or prosecution. However, if your company does find itself in the crosshairs of the Criminal Division, it is important to be proactive early on in making decisions about counsel and cooperation. For the reasons set forth above, such decisions can have a significant effect on the ultimate outcome of an investigation, matter, or case.

Retaining outside counsel who have experience with the Department of Justice in general, and the Criminal Division in particular, can be a wise move. While this chapter serves as a brief introduction to the Criminal Division and its work, experienced outside counsel can consider your company's particular industry and assist you with the nuances of your particular matter. Unfortunately, when it comes to the Criminal Division, there is no "one size fits all" —the proper response will vary widely based on the factors discussed in this chapter and elsewhere in this volume.

Chapter 8

Department of Justice/US Attorney Office Investigations

By:

Steve Brody
Mary Pat Brown
Samantha E. Miller[407]

I.   INTRODUCTION AND OVERVIEW OF THE DEPARTMENT OF JUSTICE'S INVESTIGATION PROCESS

Early in the Biden Administration, the Department of Justice ("DOJ" or the "Department") announced that it would strengthen the way that it responded to corporate crime, ushering in an era of increased focus on, and resources for, investigating suspected corporate wrongdoing.[408] And while the Department has stated that

---

[407] Steve Brody is a Partner at O'Melveny & Myers LLP in Washington, DC, where Mary Pat Brown is Of Counsel. Samantha Miller is a Counsel in the firm's New York office. Steve serves as firmwide Co-Chair of O'Melveny's Product Liability & Mass Torts Group and frequently works on government investigations impacting pharmaceutical and medical device companies. He is also Co-Chair of the firm's Attorney General Investigations and Litigation practice. Mary Pat is a member of the White-collar Defense and Corporate Investigations Practice. Before joining O'Melveny, Mary Pat was a Deputy Assistant Attorney General for the Criminal Division at the U.S. Department of Justice. During her 23 years with the U.S. Attorney's Office for the District of Columbia and the Department of Justice, she held numerous additional leadership positions, including Chief of the Criminal Division at the U.S. Attorney's Office and head of the Justice Department's Office of Professional Responsibility. Samantha represents individuals and companies in internal investigations, white collar criminal investigations, and regulatory matters. She was previously seconded to Morgan Stanley, where she worked with the US Litigation group and Special Investigations Unit on various investigations and litigation matters. Former O'Melveny associates Eileen Brogan and Dave Dorey also contributed drafting and research to earlier versions of this chapter.

[408] *See* Attorney General Merrick B. Garland Delivers Remarks to the ABA Institute on White Collar Crime, (March 3, 2022), *available at* https://www.justice.gov/opa/speech/attorney-general-merrick-b-garland-delivers-remarks-aba-institute-white-collar-crime.

the prosecution of individuals responsible for criminal conduct is its top priority in corporate criminal matters, it has also made it abundantly clear that it "will not hesitate to hold companies accountable."[409]

With of the prosecution of corporate crime as an enforcement priority for the Department, government investigations remain a constant possibility, and a likely ever-increasing presence, in the corporate world. These investigations can and often do last for years, and can visit untold financial and human capital costs upon targets, subjects, and witnesses. Knowing when and how to respond to indications that the government suspects wrongdoing protects corporate interests and prevents waste by effectively deploying legal resources to minimize litigation risk and negative exposure for a company and its employees. Further, should an investigation uncover misconduct, knowing the Department's expectations for disclosure, cooperation, remediation, and effective compliance programs can put a company in the best possible position to negotiate the best possible resolution with the government.

Department of Justice and U.S. Attorney's Office investigations can be triggered by whistle-blower disclosures, reporting inconsistencies, unauthorized employee action, media or legislative scrutiny, agency referrals (e.g., inspectors general), information learned from cooperating witnesses, or even anonymous tips. The investigative jurisdiction and the investigative process will vary by the alleged criminal activity. For example, DOJ's Antitrust Division must approve an AUSA's preliminary inquiry into suspected antitrust violations. In other circumstances, the FBI will conduct the investigation and involve a division of Justice only once additional evidence has been collected.

---

[409] Deputy Attorney General Lisa O. Monaco Gives Keynote Address at ABA's 36th National Institute on White Collar Crime (October 28, 2021) *available at* https://www.justice.gov/opa/speech/deputy-attorney-general-lisa-o-monaco-gives-keynote-address-abas-36th-national-institute.

The government seeks to hold companies criminally and civilly responsible in order to ensure corporations do not profit from corporate malfeasance, obtain restitution for victims, encourage remediation and corporate accountability, and deter further wrongdoing by that company, individuals within it, or other individuals or companies. Recognition of this investigative purpose should inform a company's response when it discovers potential wrongdoing or learns that such an investigation is underway. Corrective action, identification of wrongdoing, disclosure, and forward-looking compliance reforms will help limit liability.

This chapter is designed to be a brief aide to assist the general counsel's office in appropriately and effectively responding to internal and external indications that misconduct is occurring or that your business is under government investigation. It is not comprehensive. Any decisions made with respect to these issues should be done in consultation with subject matter experts, guided by in-house or outside counsel. It does not constitute legal advice, and it should be used only as a starting reference.

II. YOUR COMPANY IS BEING INVESTIGATED BY THE GOVERNMENT. WHAT NOW?

The most critical action a company can take in response to internal suspicion or external indications that it is under investigation is to involve both its in-house and outside counsel. In cases when a company has an early indication that an investigation is happening and can marshal resources *before* it is contacted by the government, a united legal team with clear direction and purpose can transform invasive investigative techniques into a more manageable negotiation with the government without admitting criminal liability or risking outsized penalties. It will also allow a company to consider availing itself of some of the benefits voluntarily self-disclosure and cooperation may afford.

Regardless of when or how a company discovers that it is under investigation, you must make every effort to preserve privilege and work product protection, retain relevant documents and email communication, and avoid even the appearance of the obstruction

of justice. Government investigations require extensive legal
responses often before the extent of company and employee
involvement is clear, and early retention of outside counsel helps
prevent duplicative legal costs and efforts.

In certain circumstances, it may be advisable to retain separate
counsel for individual employees, particularly when a company
wants to preserve its ability to obtain leniency for its cooperation.
Revised DOJ policy states that it is no longer sufficient for
cooperating companies to disclose only the individuals it considers
to be *substantially* involved. Rather, companies must disclose all
non-privileged information about any employee involved in or
responsible for the misconduct, regardless of the nature or degree
that employee's involvement.[410]

> **A.**   **What to do if you receive a civil subpoena,
>   grand jury subpoena, or Civil Investigative
>   Demand.**

Whether you receive a civil subpoena, a grand jury subpoena, or a
Civil Investigative Demand, your response should be the same.
Compliance is mandatory, although outside counsel can help
negotiate with the government about the scope of subpoenas or
Demands, or prepare motions to quash or modify a subpoena if
necessary. If the receipt of a subpoena or similar demand is the
first point of contact with the government, outside counsel can, and
should, request that DOJ explicitly state how it views a company
in its investigation—as a target, a subject, or a witness.

Issue a Document Hold Notice. If you discover for the first time
via receipt of a subpoena that your company is being investigated,
the investigation has likely already progressed to a point that
document preservation is immediately necessary. First, issue a
hold notice to all employees and contact your IT department about
halting any automated document deletion. When crafting your

---

[410] *See* Deputy Attorney General Lisa O. Monaco Gives Keynote Address at
ABA's 36th National Institute on White Collar Crime (October 28, 2021)
available at https://www.justice.gov/opa/speech/deputy-attorney-general-lisa-o-
monaco-gives-keynote-address-abas-36th-national-institute.

document preservation notice, consider whether there are likely to be responsive communications on employees' mobile devices and ephemeral messaging applications and ensure the hold is drafted to include those potentially responsive materials. Contact outside counsel for assistance with document retention as well as consideration of the production issues set forth below.

Preserve Attorney-Client Privilege and Attorney Work Product Protection. When producing documents to DOJ or any other regulator pursuant to a subpoena, be sure to do so without compromising privileged materials. Preserving attorney-client privilege and attorney work product protection is critical to a company's ability to effectively defend against allegations and actions brought against it, and is also an ethical obligation of your counsel. By providing or producing documents and other information that are privileged, a company risks waiving its privilege claim over the subject matter discussed in those materials. Attorney-client privilege and work product protection only protect documents or information shared in the course of giving or obtaining legal advice or prepared in anticipation of litigation. Waiver of these protections is not necessary, and prosecutors are not permitted to affirmatively seek waivers, even if a company seeks to benefit from cooperating with the government.

All legal communications about or in response to receipt of the subpoena should be labelled with appropriate designations: "Privileged & Confidential—Attorney-Client Communication"; "Confidential—Attorney Work Product." Be sure all electronic communications contain these designations as well. Limit their distribution and instruct others not to forward or disclose them. When informing employees of legal responses to the subpoena or giving employees *Upjohn*[411] warnings, be sure they understand that privileges and/or protections require vigilance to maintain and that

---

[411] *Upjohn Co. v. United States*, 449 U.S. 383 (1981). *Upjohn* warnings are giving to employees in the corporate context to inform them that in-house counsel and outside counsel represent the company as a whole rather than the individual employee. These warnings are also sometimes called corporate Miranda warnings.

those privileges – and the decision to waive them – belong to the company, and not the individual employee.

Recognize that attorney-client privilege is often destroyed by disclosure to third parties. Disclosures to auditors, insurers, regulators, government agents, whistle-blowers, and other third parties should be examined and considered in order to protect privilege. Only in some situations can you share privileged information with third parties without waiving the privilege. The joint defense privilege protects litigation-related information disclosed to a co-defendant or a co-defendant's lawyer. Third-party disclosures may also be protected when they are made under the common interest doctrine, which allows for the disclosure of privileged materials when parties who share a common legal interest share information in the service of that interest.

Document Preservation and Production of Records. Every subpoena will contain some indication, however slight, of the government's purpose in investigating—whether that be by expressing interest in certain types of transactions or business, certain regions where a company does business, or even particular employees or third-party agents. After issuing the hold notice mentioned above, a company will eventually have to produce responsive documents, unless the subpoena is quashed, modified, or otherwise negotiated away. During production, be sure to label and withhold and/or redact documents that are privileged or protected, disclosing only a log of the withheld or redacted materials and an indication of the relevant privilege or protection. Also be sure to make clear what, if any, confidentiality protections a document is entitled to. For example, if a document is being produced pursuant to a federal grand jury subpoena, be sure that each page of the responsive productions indicates that it is being produced subject to Federal Rule of Criminal Procedure 6(e), which governs the secrecy of federal grand jury proceedings. Similarly, where appropriate, be sure to request that the government afford the appropriate FOIA treatment to the productions.

Consider using outside counsel to help scope the potential universe of responsive documents that require review and analysis, to thoroughly review documents to ensure compliance with production requests, and to guard against inadvertent attorney-client or work product privilege waivers. In order to identify the appropriate universe of documents and materials to assess for responsiveness, it will be necessary to identify the appropriate custodians and sources of those documents. It will sometimes be necessary to involve third parties including former employees, board members, outside consultants, temporary employees, or vendors to be sure that all responsive documents are identified and reviewed for production.

Working with the IT department, create a preservation protocol for deleted or archived data as well as active data. The need for deleted and archived data will vary, and its preservation can be costly, but it is important to evaluate. Indeed, such information may prove to be exculpatory. Also consider the company's policies for preserving business-related messages on mobile devices and ephemeral messaging applications. As mobile messaging becomes increasingly relied upon to conduct business, it is important to consider how the company requires such communications to be retained should it need to retrieve them at any point in the future.

The government may consider delayed or incomplete production of requested documents as conduct that obstructs justice. For this reason, consider as appropriate retaining outside counsel to handle such e-discovery efforts.

Preparing for Witness Testimony. A subpoena may request testimony rather than, or in addition to, the production of documents. If the subpoena calls for testimony, consultation with counsel is a critical first step. Criminal penalties for false statements are severe, and misstatements under oath can lead to perjury and/or obstruction of justice charges. Further, producing an unprepared witness relying only on a limited and imperfect recollection could result in inaccurate testimony that is harmful to the company's position, particularly when that testimony has to be provided before the company has had an opportunity to conduct a thorough internal investigation. Obtain legal advice to ensure that testimony attributable to the company or to its employees does not admit wrongdoing or contain inaccuracies. Because the company does not enjoy a Fifth Amendment right against self-incrimination, those testifying must well understand the importance of accurate and circumscribed statements.

B.   What to do if the government contacts you by phone or by "target letter."

Say nothing and immediately contact outside counsel and relay the contents of the phone call or a copy of the letter. Outside counsel may contact the investigating government agent to determine the scope of the investigation and your suspected role in any wrongdoing. Such contact should *only* be made by outside counsel in order to avoid any argument that the company has made a "party admission" that may later be offered into evidence as an exception to the hearsay rule. In addition, when outside counsel contacts the government, it serves as notice to the prosecutor that the right to counsel has been invoked and therefore corporate representatives and employees should not be contacted without the presence of an attorney.

Internal Determinations of Wrongdoing. Jointly determine with outside counsel if this government contact requires the company to conduct an internal investigation to determine the extent of wrongdoing. DOJ policy grants prosecutors wide latitude in determining whether to prosecute companies for wrongdoing. Prosecutors weigh the same eleven factors when determining whether to charge a company that they do when considering whether to bring charges against an individual for corporate misconduct. Among those factors are the pervasiveness of the wrongdoing, including the complicity or condoning of the wrongdoing by management, the nature and seriousness of the offense, the adequacy of the prosecution of the individuals responsible for the misconduct, and the adequacy and effectiveness of the company's compliance program, both at the time of the offense and at the time of the charging decision.[412] Even where the criminal activity itself is relatively minor, DOJ may decide to prosecute companies for that misconduct where it is found to be pervasive, condoned by management, or the result of an ineffective compliance program. Where a company can demonstrate that the misconduct was limited to isolated acts by a rogue employee, despite the existence of an effective compliance program, the government may be less inclined to prosecute a corporate entity, or at least be more willing to consider an alternative resolution, such as a non-prosecution or deferred prosecution agreement.

An internal determination of the breadth of wrongdoing will help inform any contacts with the government as the investigation moves forward, including whether it is in the company's best interest to cooperate with the government's investigation and seek the cooperation credit it may earn as a result. It will also govern the procedures outlined below to protect privilege and respond appropriately. As with a subpoena, preserve attorney-client privilege and attorney work product protection not only to shield documents that might otherwise be obtained by the investigators, but also to facilitate effective representation if charges are brought against the company.

Employee Interviews. When contact by a government agent indicates that the government is investigating a company, it likely will not be clear whether this contact is unrelated to the company itself, is an initial inquiry into suspected wrongdoing, or is a final determination as to whether a formal investigation is required. It follows that company responses may more easily mitigate or aggravate the situation while the government's position is fluid. Employee discretion is necessary in such interactions, as the government agents are likely to attempt to interview employees both at and outside of work. Consider arming these employees with counsel to ensure they are not left to navigate these

---

[412] *See* JM 9-28.300 "Factors to Be Considered" *available at* https://www.justice.gov/jm/jm-9-28000-principles-federal-prosecution-business-organizations#9-28.200_ftn1.

conversations with government agents on their own and advise
your employees of their rights if approached for an interview:

- Advise employees that they may call in-house counsel immediately, and provide contact information.

- Employees have a right to refuse the interview. However, the company cannot prevent employees from communicating with the government or giving interviews.

- Employees may not lie. If employees are giving interviews, inform them that separate criminal penalties exist for false statements made to government agents—if an employee agrees to an interview, he or she must tell the truth and refrain from stating facts not known to them.

- Each employee has a right to have counsel present while the interview is conducted. Advise employees that they may call in-house counsel, and provide them with that contact information. The company may be willing to provide outside counsel for employee interviews. If so, employees have a right to know whether provided counsel represents the company or the individual.

It is best to communicate this guidance over email or in writing so that the company has a clear record that it did nothing to obstruct the investigation.

Considering Voluntary Self-Disclosure and Cooperation. DOJ's policy is clear that the voluntarily self-disclosure of discovered misconduct is the clearest path to avoiding a guilty plea or indictment and is considered an indication that a company has an effective compliance program.[413] The policy is designed to act as

---

[413] Deputy Attorney General Lisa O. Monaco Delivers Remarks on Corporate Criminal Enforcement (September 15, 2022) *available at*

an incentive and provide benefits to companies that promptly self-disclose misconduct. DOJ announced common principles that will apply across the Department's self-disclosure policies, including that, absent aggravating circumstances, it will not seek a guilty plea where a company has self-disclosed, cooperated, and remediated. Further, DOJ will not impose a compliance monitor as part of a corporate resolution where a self-disclosing company, at the time of resolution, has implemented and tested an effective compliance program.[414]

Policies on amnesty differ by agency. The Securities and Exchange Commission, the Environmental Protection Agency, and DOJ's Division of Environmental and Natural Resources require self-reporting and voluntary disclosures to qualify for amnesty. In DOJ's Antitrust Division, only the first corporate entity to report is entitled to amnesty. Amnesty is never guaranteed, it is therefore best to consult an attorney who deals with a given agency frequently if your organization is seeking amnesty. Every component of DOJ has been directed to implement a formal policy for voluntarily self-disclosure that makes clear to companies (i) what self-disclosure to that division requires and (ii) the benefits companies can expect if they do self-disclose.

Voluntary self-disclosure and cooperation are not the same. Even where a company does not self-disclose misconduct, it can still opt to cooperate with the government's investigation. To be eligible for any cooperation credit, as a threshold matter, the company must identify and turn over all non-privileged relevant information about *all* individuals involved in, or responsible for, the misconduct at issue. The amount of cooperation credit a company receives is based on a number of factors, including the diligence, thoroughness and speed of its internal investigation, the timeliness of its cooperation, and the proactive nature of the cooperation.

In 2018, the government addressed a practice referred to commonly as "piling on," where a company can be subject to fines

---

https://www.justice.gov/opa/speech/deputy-attorney-general-lisa-o-monaco-gives-keynote-address-abas-36th-national-institute.

[414] *Id.*

and penalties by various law enforcement agencies and regulators because of the same misconduct. At that time, DOJ directed its prosecutors to avoid over-enforcement by discouraging parallel corporate criminal enforcements by multiple agencies and regulators.[415] But recently, the Attorney General – in announcing the prosecution of corporate crime as a Justice Department priority – referred to DOJ's partnerships with other federal regulators, as well as with state, local, Tribal, and territorial law enforcement agencies, as a "force multiplier" that would bolster DOJ's ability to prosecute corporate crime.[416] These remarks could be seen as a shift away from the spirit of 2018's "anti-piling on" policy.

Executing and Testing an Effective Compliance Program. DOJ announced that it "[t]o the extent that prior Justice Department guidance suggested that monitorships are disfavored or are the exception, [it] rescind[ed] that guidance."[417] Now, the Department is expected to impose a compliance monitor wherever it deems necessary to ensure that a company is meeting is compliance and disclosure obligations pursuant to any negotiated resolution.[418] DOJ has issued ten factors for prosecutors to consider when evaluating whether the imposition of a compliance monitor is necessary to reduce the risk of further misconduct and correct any compliance lapses.[419] These factors look both to the state of the

---

[415] *See* Deputy Attorney General Rod Rosenstein's Remarks to the New York City Bar White-collar Crime Institute, (May 9, 2018), *available at* https://www.justice.gov/opa/speech/deputy-attorney-general-rod-rosenstein-delivers-remarks-new-york-city-bar-white-collar.

[416] *See* Attorney General Merrick B. Garland Delivers Remarks to the ABA Institute on White Collar Crime, (March 3, 2022), *available at* https://www.justice.gov/opa/speech/attorney-general-merrick-b-garland-delivers-remarks-aba-institute-white-collar-crime.

[417] Deputy Attorney General Lisa O. Monaco Gives Keynote Address at ABA's 36th National Institute on White Collar Crime (October 28, 2021) *available at* https://www.justice.gov/opa/speech/deputy-attorney-general-lisa-o-monaco-gives-keynote-address-abas-36th-national-institute.

[418] *Id.*

[419] Memorandum from Deputy Attorney General Lisa O. Monaco to Head of Department Components and United States Attorneys, "Further Revisions to Corporate Criminal Enforcement Policies Following Discussions with Corporate Crime Advisory Group" at p. 12 (September 15, 2022) *available at* https://www.justice.gov/opa/speech/file/1535301/download.

compliance program at the time of the resolution and at the time of the misconduct, and a heavy emphasis is placed on the testing of the relevant compliance controls. With outside counsel, a company should identify and evaluate the compliance controls that should have prevented the alleged misconduct and identify the compliance personnel responsible for those controls to evaluate the strength of the compliance program, and identify gaps that need to be remediated.

C. What to do if the government serves you with a search warrant.

Do Not Consent to a Search. Withhold consent and courteously ask the government to delay searching until counsel arrives. Although the warrant obviates the need for consent from the government's perspective, withholding it ensures that if the warrant is defective, the company retains its ability to object to the legality of the search at a later time. Do not leave offices or the premises unattended; outside counsel may observe the search. Inform law enforcement that the company does not consent to the search and that no employee has the authorization to consent to any search or the seizure of any materials. Dismiss non-essential or uninvolved employees for the day or, if possible, for the duration of the search. Obviously, discretion must be exercised to ensure that the facility continues to operate at an acceptable level.

Review the Search Warrant and Identify the Agents. You have the right to obtain a copy of and review the search warrant before the search begins. Ask the lead law enforcement agent for a copy of the warrant while maintaining the company's objection to the search. Fax or scan and email a copy of the warrant to outside counsel immediately.

Review the warrant for inaccuracies. A warrant must always be limited in time and scope. It must indicate with specificity areas to be searched and documents and objects to be seized. Where the address is incorrect, the warrant is more than 10 days old, or the terms are overly broad, you have a right to delay the search and to seek relief from a prosecutor, the judge who issued the warrant, or a judge who is on duty at the time. Because the execution of a search warrant creates a stressful atmosphere, having outside counsel present or reachable by phone can help in identifying such inaccuracies. You may also ask for a copy of the affidavit providing the probable cause to issue the search warrant, but the agent is not required to give it to you.

In addition, verify the identification of all law enforcement personnel present and conducting the search. If any agent seeks to conduct a search, he or she must be authorized by the terms of the search warrant. If outside counsel is not present, collect business cards from each agent or a list of names and contact information for each agent.

Instructions to Employees. You should have on file a draft email to send in response to government action such as the execution of a search warrant. If you do not, contact legal counsel to advise and assist in the creation of such an email that can go out if a search were to take place at your company. Generally, you will not have the time to carefully draft an email or to inform all employees on how best to comply once the agents appear. When you send a copy of the search warrant to outside counsel, you should send the search procedure email to all affected employees.

Any advice to employees given the day of or during the search should be consistent with the directions sent by email. Employees should do nothing to impede law enforcement officers or their efforts. Be sure that employees know that they are not authorized to consent to a search or a seizure and that they should not represent to any agent that they are able to consent.

The government will often attempt to interview employees during the search. Employees have a legal right to refuse to talk with agents, but take care on this point: instructing employees not to speak with agents puts the company at risk of being charged with obstruction of justice. Inform employees of their right to counsel, and make an attorney available to employees who would like to confer with counsel before, or have an attorney present when, speaking with agents.

It is critical that employees do not destroy or modify any documents or records. Any destroyed or altered document will be presumed to have been relevant and the burden will be on the company to show that evidence was not destroyed. Finally, remind employees that they are not required to sign any written statements presented during the search, and that they should not make any comments to the media about or related to the search.

Monitor the Execution of the Search Warrant. First, consider asking outside counsel to contact the prosecutor to negotiate an alternative to the search in the form of discovery production. In the event of a search, you have no obligation to assist the government, but should truthfully answer questions about the location of documents if asked.

Attempt to document the search either by taking photographs or videotaping (although do not interfere with the search), and request copies of any photographs or videotapes taken by agents on the scene. Additionally, request permission to copy all documents or data seized before the government removes it from the premises. If permission is denied, ask the agent for an inventory list of everything seized. Although the agents can refuse the request to copy, they may not refuse to provide an inventory list.

If attorney-client privileged materials are within the search area (*i.e.*, documents going to and from attorneys), inform the lead agent and ask for a procedure that allows the company to review the material you suspect is privileged and to retain such documents until privilege issues can be resolved. The search team often has members who may review privileged materials. These agents— sometimes called a "taint team"—should be separate from agents with substantive knowledge of the investigation.

Post-search interviews with employees. Ask employees to refrain from speaking with one another about the search until they've spoken with company counsel. Explain that doing so will protect them from allegations of collusion or obstruction and will prevent the waiver of attorney-client privilege. Interview employees separately in a privileged setting, taking thorough notes on each's knowledge of the subject of the search and the search procedure.

Also ask employees to identify anything that was seized by the government, so you can later have the property returned.

III. ROLE OF THE BOARD

Although some situations, such as the execution of a search warrant, will trigger a crisis-type response that is too immediate to involve the board, other circumstances may allow for earlier involvement. At a time appropriate under the circumstances, a presentation should be made to the board concerning the investigation with a recommendation that the board convene a special committee to oversee internal processes and responses to the investigation.[420] If an internal investigation occurs as part of the company's response, consult with outside counsel to determine whether the findings should be reported to the board, and if that report should be oral or written.

When an investigation—internal or external—concludes, the board is frequently prompted to take corrective action to remediate whatever issues gave rise to the investigation. At times, this self-examination of the company by the board may be a condition of leniency or an agreement not to prosecute. Depending on the nature of the company, an investigation may also require notice to shareholders or trigger separate reporting requirements.

IV.   SPECIAL CONSIDERATIONS WITH WHISTLEBLOWERS

Some investigations will be triggered by a whistle-blower. If this is the case, whistle-blower protections put the company at greater risk of wrongdoing in the course of responding to the investigation. Outside counsel can help ensure compliance with anti-retaliation provisions by protecting the whistle blower's identity from inadvertent disclosure within the organization, and can also protect against unnecessarily disclosing further information to that whistle-blower.

---

[420] Continue to maintain privilege and be aware that disclosures to the board may constitute waiver. *SEC v. Roberts*, 254 F.R.D. 371 (N.D. Cal. 2008).

Analyze internal policies and procedures, including anti-retaliation provisions. A whistle-blower can be a person involved in the wrongdoing; he or she still retains all the whistle-blower protections. Therefore, it is prudent to have incentives for internal reporting that allow for remediation before a government investigation can be triggered. If the company does not already have an effective compliance program in place, its ability to self-report to the government is hampered and it risks greater legal penalties, including the imposition of a corporate compliance monitor.

Where a whistle-blower is anonymous, a company might seek to identify that whistle-blower for the sole purpose of protecting him or her from retaliation. Remind managers and supervisors of the company's anti-retaliation policy and encourage all to avoid even the perception of retaliation when dealing with the whistle-blower. Do not disclose the whistle-blower's identity when it is not necessary.

Manage communications with a whistle-blower. Consult with outside counsel to manage communications with the whistle-blower, ensuring that any interviews and assessments of credibility cannot be construed as retaliatory. Be concerned with privilege when communicating with the whistle-blower; the whistle-blower may be continually disclosing information to the government about the internal response to the investigation. Do attempt to interview the whistle-blower and request that he or she provide any evidence that supports the claims, but recognize that the whistle-blower may already have outside counsel who will be present. Do not subject the whistle-blower to discipline, even if it preceded the claim or is unrelated to the claim, without first contacting employment counsel.

V.   CONCLUSION

Corporate behavior in the context of a criminal investigation or prosecution is often evaluated under a standard of good faith. Whether in the context of compliance, cooperation, internal investigation, or disclosure, it is critical that a company's actions indicate good faith efforts. Preventive measures, a robust and

211

effective compliance program, curative efforts, and proactive responses to government go a long way toward minimizing the risk of facing a criminal penalty. These same considerations are true when a government investigation is civil in nature or, even if criminal, may give rise to a future civil action. The corporate response to the initiation of an investigation can mitigate or aggravate the effect any wrongdoing may have on subsequent criminal or regulatory penalties.

VI.   REFERENCES

18 U.S.C. § 3486.

31 U.S.C. § 3733.

Fed. R. Crim. P. 6.

Fed. R. Crim. P. 41.

Gray B. Broughton, Responding to Government Investigations in the New Era of Enforcement, 38 VBA News J. 17 (2011).

Samuel W. Cooper, *Guideposts for Handling Corporate Investigations*, 41 Litigation 30 (2014-2015).

George B. Curtis, *Is There Any Good in a Government Investigation?*, 38 Litigation 6 (2011-2012).

Nicholas S. Goldin, Jonathan K. Youngwood, and Yafit Cohn, *Should You Waive Privilege in Government Investigations?* Law360 (May 11, 2015), *available at* http://www.law360.com/articles/651446/should-you-waive-privilege-in-government-investigations-.

Investigations and Police Practices, 43 Geo. L. J. Ann. Rev. Crim. Proc. 3 (2014).

Joseph M. McLaughlin, *Corporate Litigation: Privilege and Work Product in Internal Investigations* (April 10, 2014), *available at* http://www.stblaw.com/docs/default-source/cold-fusion-existing-content/publications/pub1737.pdf.

Evaluation of Corporate Compliance Programs, U.S. Dep't of Justice Criminal Division (June 2020), *available at* https://www.justice.gov/criminal-fraud/page/file/937501/download.

Memorandum from Deputy Attorney General Paul J. McNulty to Heads of Department Components and United States Attorneys, "Principles of Federal Prosecution of Business Organizations" (Dec. 12, 2006), *available at* http://www.justice.gov/sites/default/files/dag/legacy/2007/07/05/mcnulty_memo.pdf.

Memorandum from Deputy Attorney General Mark R. Filip to Heads of Department Components and United States Attorneys, "Principles of Federal Prosecution of Business Organizations" (Aug. 28, 2008), *available at* http://www.justice.gov/sites/default/files/dag/legacy/2008/11/03/dag-memo-08282008.pdf.

Memorandum from Deputy Attorney General Lisa O. Monaco to Head of Department Components and United States Attorneys, "Further Revisions to Corporate Criminal Enforcement Policies Following Discussions with Corporate Crime Advisory Group" (September 15, 2022) *available at* https://www.justice.gov/opa/speech/file/1535301/download.

Lisa Noller, *Ten Tips if you are Facing a Government Investigation*, Association of Corporate Counsel Legal Resources (Apr. 23, 2013), *available at* http://www.acc.com/legalresources/publications/topten/ttfgi.cfm.

O'Melveny & Myers L.L.P., In-House Counsel's Guide to Conducting Internal Investigations.

Taylor J. Phillips, *Responding to Government Investigations: Pitfalls and Procedures*, 48 Tenn. B. J. 23 (2012).

213

U.S. Dep't. of Justice, Criminal Resource Manual § 163 (2005).

Justice Manual [JM] 9-28.010 et seq.

United States v. BDO Seidman, L.L.P., 492 F.3d 806, 815-816 (7th Cir. 2007).

Upjohn Co. v. United States, 449 U.S. 383, 389-90 (1981).

Attorney General Merrick B. Garland Delivers Remarks to the ABA Institute on White Collar Crime, (March 3, 2022), *available at* https://www.justice.gov/opa/speech/attorney-general-merrick-b-garland-delivers-remarks-aba-institute-white-collar-crime.

Deputy Attorney General Lisa O. Monaco Gives Keynote Address at ABA's 36th National Institute on White Collar Crime (October 28, 2021) *available at* https://www.justice.gov/opa/speech/deputy-attorney-general-lisa-o-monaco-gives-keynote-address-abas-36th-national-institute.

Deputy Attorney General Lisa O. Monaco Delivers Remarks on Corporate Criminal Enforcement (September 15, 2022) *available at* https://www.justice.gov/opa/speech/deputy-attorney-general-lisa-o-monaco-gives-keynote-address-abas-36th-national-institute.

Chapter 9

Securities and Exchange Commission Investigations

By: Amy Jane Longo[421]

I.   INTRODUCTION

When facing an inquiry by the United States Securities & Exchange Commission ("SEC"), many questions or concerns may come to mind. This chapter explores issues that commonly arise in SEC investigations, and provides resources for counsel advising clients in this area.

II.   HOW DOES AN SEC INVESTIGATION BEGIN?

A.   Overview

The SEC conducts confidential, non-public investigations of suspected securities law violations, conducted by staff in the SEC's Enforcement Division. During an investigation, the SEC develops facts through its administrative subpoena power, and via "informal inquiry, interviewing witnesses, examining brokerage records, reviewing trading data, and other methods."[422]

The SEC's authority to investigate and prosecute suspected securities law violations originates from four primary statutes: the Securities Exchange Act of 1934 (the "Exchange Act"), the Securities Act of 1933 (the "Securities Act"), the Investment

---

[421] Ms. Longo is a Litigation and Enforcement partner in the Los Angeles office of Ropes & Gray LLP. She previously served as Regional Trial Counsel for the SEC's Los Angeles Regional Office in the Division of Enforcement. This chapter was drafted with the assistance of Ropes & Gray associates Stephanie K. Dowd and Sean Adessky and summer associate Dillon Yang.

[422] SEC, How Investigations Work (Jan. 27, 2017), https://www.sec.gov/enforce/how-investigations-work.html.

Company Act of 1940 (the "Investment Company Act"), and the Investment Advisers Act of 1940 (the "Advisers Act").[423]

SEC investigations must comply with the federal regulations set forth in 17 C.F.R. § 203. These address SEC subpoenas, the non-public nature of the investigation, and rights of witnesses. Pursuant to 17 C.F.R. § 203.2, "unless made a matter of public record, [investigations are] non-public."[424] Investigations can become public if the SEC files an enforcement action once the investigation concludes, or if the SEC, during an investigation, seeks to enforce one of its subpoenas in federal court. While there are rare circumstances where the SEC will make an inquiry public, inquiries typically become public because the target entity or individual will disclose it. For example, a company may disclose the inquiry to its investors.

B. How SEC Inquiries Are Opened

An SEC inquiry can be opened in one of two ways: (1) when a Matters Under Inquiry ("MUI") converts to an investigation, or (2) independently of a MUI.[425] In both instances, the assigned staff (at the Assistant Director level and below) evaluates the facts to determine the investigation's potential to address conduct that violates the federal securities laws.[426] A MUI can be opened on the basis of very limited information, but an investigation is generally opened only "after the assigned staff has done some additional information-gathering and analysis."[427]

To open a MUI, the staff first conducts an analysis to determine: "(1) whether the facts underlying the MUI show that there is

[423] See 15 U.S.C. §§ 78u, 78u-3 (Exch. Act. §§ 21, 21C); 15 U.S.C. §§ 77h-1 77t (Sec. Act. §§ 8A, 20); 15 U.S.C. §§ 80a-35, 80a-41 (Inv. Co. Act §§ 36, 42); 15 U.S.C. § 80b-9 (Inv. Adv. Act § 209).

[424] 17 C.F.R. § 203.2.

[425] See SEC, Div. Enf't, Enforcement Manual, § 2.3.2 (2017) (hereinafter "Enf't Manual"), https://www.sec.gov/divisions/enforce/enforcementmanual.pdf.

[426] Id.

[427] Id.

potential to address conduct that violates the federal securities laws; and (2) whether the assignment of a MUI to a particular office will be the best use of resources for the Division as a whole."[428] If the analysis weighs in favor of opening a MUI, staff will then seek approval from the assigned Associate Director or Regional Director.[429] Generally, a MUI is either converted to a formal investigation or closed within sixty days.[430]

To determine whether to close a MUI or convert it to an investigation, staff, in consultation with an assigned senior officer in the relevant office as necessary, evaluates the facts and determines whether and to what extent the investigation has the potential to address violative conduct.[431] The staff considers various threshold issues, including whether the facts "suggest a possible violation of the federal securities laws involving fraud or other serious misconduct[,]" if an investment of resources is warranted by factors that include the "magnitude or nature of the violation" and the "size of the victim group," and whether the conduct is ongoing or within the statute of limitations period.[432]

If the staff determines that it is appropriate to proceed with the investigation, then they request approval to convert the MUI to an investigation.[433] If the Associate Director/Regional Director/Unit Chief agrees, they will approve the conversion of the MUI to an investigation.[434] If the staff and the assigned Associate Director/Regional Director/Unit Chief determine that the investigation does not have the potential to address violative conduct, or would be an inappropriate use of resources, then the

---

[428] *Id.* § 2.3.1.

[429] *Id.*

[430] *Id.*

[431] *Id.* § 2.3.2.

[432] *Id.*

[433] *Id.*

[434] *Id.*

MUI is closed.[435] Unlike an investigation, a MUI can be closed at the local level, rather through SEC headquarters. In limited circumstances, an investigation is opened without a MUI—for example, on certain occasions when the staff seeks to pursue an emergency action.[436]

C. Primary Sources that Prompt an Investigation

Typically, SEC investigations originate from one of three sources: (1) tips, complaints, or referrals ("TCRs") from external parties, including "whistleblowers"; (2) internal referrals from the SEC's Division of Examinations (formerly the Office of Compliance Inspections and Examinations, or "OCIE") following an examination of a registrant; or (3) SEC surveillance.

1. Tips, Complaints, Referrals, and Whistleblowers

The Enforcement Division receives many external referrals in the form of TCRs.[437] According to recent estimates, the SEC receives 46,000 TCRs per year, has approximately 1,500 ongoing investigations at any given time, and in 2021, had 2,000 pending litigations and 1,200 pending administrative proceedings agency-wide.[438]

The SEC's whistleblower program has grown in recent years. Since the start of the program in 2011, enforcement matters

---

[435] *Id.*

[436] *Id.*

[437] *See* SEC, Report Suspected Securities Fraud or Wrongdoing (Aug. 26, 2022), https://www.sec.gov/tcr.

[438] *See* Gurbir S. Grewal, Testimony on "Oversight of the SEC's Division of Enforcement" Before the United States House of Representatives Committee on Financial Services Subcommittee on Investor Protection, Entrepreneurship, and Capital Markets (Jul. 21, 2022), https://www.sec.gov/news/statement/grewal-statement-house-testimony-071922.

brought based on information from whistleblowers have resulted in orders for almost $5 billion dollars in monetary sanctions.[439]

Under the whistleblower program, the SEC can give monetary awards to individuals who provide original information that leads to a successful enforcement action with a sanction of over $1 million.[440] Generally, the SEC shall not disclose any information "which could reasonably be expected to reveal the identity of a whistleblower . . . unless and until required to be disclosed to a defendant or respondent in connection with [certain] public proceeding[s]."[441] No person can interfere with any individual attempting to communicate with the SEC about a potential securities law violation, and employers are prohibited from retaliating against whistleblowers. As of August 2022, the SEC has awarded more than $1.3 billion to over 280 individuals.[442]

In February 2022, the SEC proposed two amendments to Rule 21F.[443] The first would allow the Commission to pay awards for certain actions brought by other entities, including designated federal agencies. The second would affirm the Commission's authority to consider the dollar amount of a potential award for the purpose of increasing the award amount and eliminate its authority to consider the dollar amount of a potential award for the purpose of decreasing the amount.[444]

---

[439] SEC, 2021 ANNUAL REPORT TO CONGRESS: WHISTLEBLOWER PROGRAM (2021), https://www.sec.gov/files/owb-2021-annual-report.pdf.

[440] *Id.* at 5.

[441] 15 U.S.C. § 78u-6(h)(2).

[442] *See* Press Release, SEC, SEC Awards More Than $16 Million to Two Whistleblowers (Aug. 9, 2022), https://www.sec.gov/news/press-release/2022-139.

[443] 17 C.F.R. § 240.21F *et seq.*

[444] *See* SEC, The Commission's Whistleblower Program Rules, Exchange Act Release No. 34-94212, 2022 WL 3703833 (Feb. 10, 2022).

2. Enforcement Referrals from Inside and Outside the SEC

In addition to TCRs and whistleblowers, the SEC receives referrals from civil and criminal government agencies, and non-government bodies such as self-regulatory organizations. The Financial Industry Regulatory Authority ("FINRA") frequently refers matters to the SEC, particularly in the areas of insider trading, market manipulation, and broker-dealer conduct.[445] The SEC also receives referrals from state and local law enforcement bodies, licensing regulators such as the Public Company Accounting Oversight Board,[446] and foreign securities authorities.

The SEC's Division of Examinations commonly refers matters to the Division of Enforcement for investigation. The Examinations Division reviews "certain practices, products, and services that it believes present potentially heightened risks to investors or the integrity of the U.S. Capital Markets."[447] The Division of Examinations has many offices and program areas that help support its mission, including the Investment Adviser/Investment Company Examination Program, the Broker-Dealer and Exchange Examination Program, the Clearance and Settlement Examination Program, the FINRA and Securities Industry Oversight Examination Program, the Technology Controls Program, the Office of Risk and Strategy, and the newly created Event and Emerging Risks Examination Team.[448]

---

[445] *See, e.g.*, FINRA, Actions Resulting from Referrals to Federal and State Authorities, https://www.finra.org/media-center/actions-resulting-referrals-federal-and-state-authorities (last visited Sept. 8, 2022) (listing actions resulting from FINRA referrals to the SEC and other regulators).

[446] *See* PCAOB, Rule 5112, https://pcaobus.org/about/rules-rulemaking/rules/section_5.

[447] SEC, 2022 Examination Priorities, Division of Examinations 11 (2022), https://www.sec.gov/files/2022-exam-priorities.pdf.

[448] SEC, Statement on the Renaming of the Office of Compliance Inspections and Examinations to the Division of Examinations (Dec. 20, 2020), https://www.sec.gov/news/public-statement/joint-statement-division-examinations.

When the Examinations Division staff closes an examination, a registrant sometimes receives a "deficiency letter," notifying it of issues the staff discovered during the exam. The registrant then has the opportunity to respond in writing. Issues identified in the deficiency letter or otherwise discovered by examiners can be referred to the Enforcement Division for further investigation. Accordingly, how a registrant responds to questions and requests during an exam is crucial.

3.   <u>Research and Surveillance</u>

A third primary source of SEC investigations is the work of Enforcement staff to research and uncover matters to investigate. SEC attorneys and accountants regularly surveil the markets for potential securities law violations. This can range from ad hoc news reports to sophisticated electronic monitoring. For example, the Division of Enforcement's Market Abuse Unit's ("MAU") Analysis and Detection Center uses data analytics tools to detect suspicious trading patterns.

Data analytics are credited in many of the SEC's recent enforcement actions. For example, in 2021, the SEC announced charges against eight companies for failing to disclose that requests to belatedly file quarterly or annual reports were caused by anticipated restatements or corrections to prior financials.[449] The announcement noted that "[t]he violations were uncovered by an initiative focused on Form 12b-25 filings by companies that quickly thereafter announced financial restatements or corrections."[450] Another similar effort, the Division's EPS initiative, uses risk-based data analytics to uncover potential

---

[449] *See* Press Release, SEC, SEC Charges Eight Companies for Failure to Disclose Complete Information on Form NT (Apr. 29, 2021), https://www.sec.gov/news/press-release/2021-76.

[450] *Id.*

accounting and disclosure violations caused by earnings management practices.[451]

D.   Who Conducts SEC Investigations

The initial outreach from the SEC to a company or individual under investigation generally comes from the assigned staff attorney. Over the course of an investigation, most contact will be through the staff attorney and assigned staff accountant, where applicable, with supervisors at various levels frequently attending meetings of special importance, such as proffer sessions, significant testimonies, and preliminary settlement negotiations. Staff attorneys are supervised by Assistant Directors, who in turn report to Associate Directors, with a similar structure on the staff accountant side.

E.   Formal Order of Investigation

Generally, SEC investigations start with the issuance of a nonpublic Formal Order of Investigation. The Formal Order identifies who is being investigated and under what statutory provisions they are being investigated, and designates the staff members conducting the investigation.[452] A Formal Order does not set forth the facts and circumstances that led the staff to suspect the potential statutory violation, but merely identifies the jurisdictional bases for the investigation. It is not uncommon for an SEC inquiry to shift from an informal inquiry to a formal investigation.

After the issuance of the Formal Order, the staff has the power to issue subpoenas for documents and testimony, as well as to request the voluntary production of documents or other information. Upon receiving a subpoena, counsel should contact the SEC to request a copy of the Formal Order pursuant to 17 C.F.R. § 203.7(a).[453] After receiving a copy of a Formal Order, counsel should

---

[451] *See, e.g.*, *In re Healthcare Servs. Grp., Inc.*, Exchange Act Release No. 92735, 2021 WL 3742091 (Aug. 24, 2021).

[452] *See* Enf't Manual, *supra* note 5, § 2.3.4.

[453] *See id.* § 2.3.4.2.

determine the elements that are required for the SEC to prove a violation under the cited statutes or rules.

In addition, after receiving a subpoena, counsel should promptly send a preservation or hold notice to employees who may have documents or communications responsive to the subpoena. The hold notice should describe the content of the subpoena and instruct employees to preserve potentially relevant information. Counsel should also consider third parties who may be in possession of potentially relevant information that could be deemed to be in the company's custody, possession, or control.

When a party receives an SEC subpoena, it is important to make an initial outreach to the SEC confirming that the subpoena has been received and counsel is working through it. Typically, SEC subpoenas will contain short deadlines, and counsel will negotiate deadlines for responding as well as potentially utilize rolling productions. SEC subpoenas are often broad in nature, and counsel should communicate with the staff to clarify the scope and any areas of priority in the response, and potentially negotiate to narrow the scope of the subpoena.

F. Potential for Parallel Investigation by Other Regulators

Other regulators—like the Department of Justice, the IRS, the CFTC, state securities regulators, and even foreign securities regulators—can conduct parallel investigations into potentially violative conduct. DOJ involvement is especially true in two scenarios – insider trading, and Foreign Corrupt Practices Act ("FCPA") cases. While these investigations are distinct, Enforcement staff can share information with other agencies and regulators through an "access request."[454] The SEC's Form 1662, provided to recipients of SEC voluntary information requests and/or subpoenas, sets forth the SEC's routine uses of information it receives, including the ability to share information with other

---

[454] *See* 17 C.F.R. § 240.24c-1.

regulators.[455] Therefore, counsel should be mindful that information they share with the SEC could be shared with criminal or other enforcement authorities.

III. WHAT CLAIMS CAN THE SEC ASSERT AND AGAINST WHOM?

The SEC can assert claims for violations of federal securities laws against individuals or entities. Claims can be brought against those who are registered with the SEC in any capacity (for example, public companies, investment advisers, investment companies, broker-dealers, and transfer agents), as well as against those who are not registered, but are still subject to securities laws claims (for example, private companies, unregistered individuals, and unregistered firms). Certain of the SEC's most common claims are highlighted here.

A.   The Exchange Act[456]

The Exchange Act regulates securities trading on the secondary market. Key provisions include Section 10(b) and Rule 10b-5, which prohibit fraud in connection with the purchase or sale of a security.[457] Rule 10b-5(a) and (c) specifically forbid, in connection with the purchase or sale of securities, employment of "any device, scheme, or artifice to defraud" and any "act, practice, or course of business" that operates as a fraud.[458] Rule 10b-5(b) prohibits making false or misleading statements, such as in SEC filings or during earnings calls.[459] The Supreme Court has observed that

---

[455] *See* SEC, Supplemental Information for Persons Requested to Supply Information Voluntarily or Directed to Supply Information Pursuant to a Commission Subpoena (2021), https://www.sec.gov/files/sec1662.pdf ("The Commission often makes its files available to other governmental agencies, particularly United States Attorneys and state prosecutors.").

[456] 15 U.S.C. §§ 78u, 78u-3 (Exch. Act. §§ 21, 21C).

[457] *See* 15 U.S.C. § 78j(b), 17 C.F.R. § 240.10b-5.

[458] 17 C.F.R. § 240.10b-5.

[459] *Id.*

Rule 10b-5 "capture[s] a wide range of conduct."[460] Rule 10b-5 is also the securities statute that prohibits insider trading.[461] Claims under Rule 10b-5 require a showing of scienter, *i.e.*, fraudulent intent or at least recklessness.

Under Exchange Act Section 13, public companies are required to file periodic and annual reports with the SEC.[462] The SEC can bring enforcement claims against officers of public companies under Rule 13a-14, which requires officers to certify to the accuracy of the company's financial statements.[463] In addition, the SEC can bring claims for violations of Section 13(b)(2), which requires issuers to "make and keep books [with] 'reasonable detail' [to] fairly reflect . . . transactions" and to "devise and maintain" a system of internal accounting.[464] Notably, to prove a Section 13(b)(2) violation, the SEC only needs to prove that books were materially misstated or that internal controls were not reasonably sufficient.[465] Under Section 13(b)(5), the SEC can also bring claims against officers who "knowingly falsify any book, record or account," or who "knowingly circumvent . . . or fail to implement . . . internal accounting controls."[466]

On February 10, 2022, the SEC proposed significant amendments governing beneficial ownership reporting under Section 13(d) and Section 13(g).[467] The amendments would shorten filing deadlines

---

[460] *Lorenzo v. SEC*, 139 S. Ct. 1094, 1101 (2019).

[461] *See, e.g., Salman v. United States*, 580 U.S. 39 (2016).

[462] 15 U.S.C. § 78m(b)(2)(A) & (B).

[463] *See* 17 C.F.R. § 240.13a-14; *SEC v. Jensen*, 835 F.3d 1100, 1112-13 (9th Cir. 2016).

[464] 15 U.S.C. § 78m(b)(2)(A) & (B).

[465] *Id.* § 78m(b)(5).

[466] *Id.*; *see, e.g., United States v. Reyes*, 577 F.3d 1069, 1079, 1080-81 (9th Cir. 2009).

[467] Press Release, SEC, SEC Proposes Rule Amendment to Modernize Beneficial Reporting (Feb. 10, 2022), https://www.sec.gov/news/press-release/2022-22.

for Schedule 13D and 13G beneficial ownership reports.[468] In addition, they would "expand the application of Regulation 13D-G to certain derivative securities" and "clarify the circumstances under which two or more persons have formed a 'group' that would be subject to beneficial ownership reporting obligations."[469]

Exchange Act Section 15(a) regulates broker-dealers. Any party acting as a broker or dealer must register with the SEC.[470] The conduct of registered broker-dealers is subject to examination by SEC staff, and registered broker-dealers must provide information to SEC staff when requested. The SEC can also bring claims under Section 15(a) against individuals who act as brokers or dealers without first registering with the SEC.

Exchange Act Section 20(a) permits the SEC to charge "control persons" who may not have been directly involved in the fraud itself.[471] Section 20(a) states that every person who "directly or indirectly, controls any person liable under any provision of this chapter or any rule or regulation thereunder shall also be liable jointly" for the controlled person's violation(s).[472] Likewise, Section 20(e) permits the SEC to charge aiders and abettors of securities violations, provided they acted with scienter.[473]

B.   The Securities Act[474]

The Securities Act regulates the offer and sale of securities, and requires companies to disclose certain information through securities registration. The Securities Act regulates IPOs and secondary offerings of public company stock and debt.

---

[468] *Id.*

[469] *Id.*

[470] 15 U.S.C. § 78o(a).

[471] 15 U.S.C. § 78t(a).

[472] *Id.*

[473] *See id.* § 78t(e).

[474] 15 U.S.C. §§ 77h-1 77t (Sec. Act. §§ 8A, 20).

Securities Act Section 17(a) is similar to Rule 10b-5. In the "offer and sale of any securities," Section 17(a)(1)-(3) prohibits false statements and omissions and fraudulent schemes.[475] Unlike Rule 10b-5(b), the SEC is not required under Section 17(a)(2) to show that a company officer or employee actually *made* a misstatement.[476] Instead, it is enough that the SEC show that the officer or employee "obtain[ed] money or property by means of" an untrue statement.[477] Unlike Section 10(b) and Rule 10b-5 claims, which can be brought by any party with standing, only the SEC can bring claims under Section 17(a). Further, Sections 17(a)(2) and (3) do not require proof of scienter, but can be satisfied by a showing of negligence.[478]

Section 17(b) prohibits stock "touting"—or recommending a stock without disclosing the nature and substance of any consideration received from an issuer, underwriter, or dealer.[479] In other words, an individual cannot promote a security without disclosing that they received consideration for doing so. Like Section 17(a), Section 17(b) is only enforceable by the SEC.

The registration requirements of Securities Act Section 5, which are strict liability provisions, are among the Act's most important aspects. Section 5 requires issuers to file a registration statement when publicly offering securities, subject to certain exemptions.[480] Once the SEC approves the registration statement, an issuer may offer and sell its securities.

The Securities Act does not have a provision that the SEC can use to hold "control persons" secondarily liable for the Act's

---

[475] 15 U.S.C. § 77q(a)(1), (2), (3).

[476] *SEC v. Big Apple Consulting USA, Inc.*, 783 F.3d 786, 796 (11th Cir. 2015)

[477] 15 U.S.C. § 77q(a)(2); *SEC v. Genovese*, 553 F. Supp. 3d 24, 40 (S.D.N.Y. 2021); *SEC v. Complete Bus. Sols. Grp., Inc.*, 538 F. Supp. 3d 1309, 1328 (S.D. Fla. 2021); *Big Apple Consulting USA, Inc.*, 783 F.3d at 796.

[478] *SEC v. Dain Rauscher, Inc.*, 254 F.3d 852 (9th Cir. 2001).

[479] *See* 15 U.S.C. § 77q.

[480] *See* 15 U.S.C. § 77e.

violations—control persons can only be liable for other violations of the Act that private parties may bring.[481] It does, however, provide for the SEC to sue aiders and abettors of Securities Act violations who act "knowingly or recklessly."[482]

C. The Advisers' Act[483]

The Advisers Act regulates investment advisers and "imposes on them a broad fiduciary duty to act in the best interest of their clients."[484] With some exceptions, the Act requires that "firms or sole practitioners compensated for advising others about securities investments must register with the SEC and conform to regulations designed to protect investors."[485] Generally, advisers with at least $100 million in assets under management or who advise a registered investment company must register with the SEC.[486] Other advisers may register under state law with state securities authorities.[487]

Section 206 of the Advisers Act prohibits advisers from making false and misleading statements to investors.[488] Under the Act, an adviser has "an affirmative obligation of utmost good faith and full and fair disclosure of all facts material to the client's engagement of the adviser to its clients."[489]

---

[481] *See* 15 U.S.C. § 77o(a).

[482] *See id.* § 77o(b).

[483] 15 U.S.C. § 80b-9 (Inv. Adv. Act § 209).

[484] *See* SEC, Regulation of Investment Advisers, § VI (2013), https://www.sec.gov/about/offices/oia/oia_investman/rplaze-042012.pdf.

[485] SEC, Laws and Rules (May 13, 2020), https://www.sec.gov/investment/laws-and-rules.

[486] *Id.*

[487] *Id.*

[488] Prohibition of Fraud by Advisers to Certain Pooled Investment Vehicles, Release No. IA – 2628, 91 S.E.C. Docket 938, 2007 WL 2239114, at *1 n.4 (Aug. 3, 2007).

[489] *See* SEC, Regulation of Investment Advisers, *supra* note 64, § V.A.

Section 204 of the Advisers Act and Rule 204-2 thereunder require that SEC-registered investment advisers maintain and preserve specified books and records.[490] These records are subject to examination by SEC staff.[491] Required records include advertisements sent to 10 or more persons and documents "substantiating any performance advertised."[492] Section 204A of the Advisers Act requires advisers to "establish, maintain, and enforce written policies and procedures reasonably designed, taking into consideration the nature of such investment adviser's business, to prevent the misuse" of material nonpublic information, while Rule 204A sets forth requirements for registered advisers' codes of ethics.[493] Only the SEC can enforce violations of the Advisers Act.

D.   The Investment Company Act[494]

The Investment Company Act regulates companies, including mutual funds, that "engage primarily in investing, reinvesting, and trading in securities, and whose own securities are offered to the investing public."[495] Under the Act, companies are required to disclose their financial condition and investment policies to investors when stock is initially sold and on a regular basis thereafter.[496] The goal of the Act is to require companies to disclose to the investing public information about the fund and its investment objectives.[497]

Generally, the provisions of the Investment Company Act are enforced by the SEC, save for a statutory claim for excessive

---

[490] *Id.* § VI.D.

[491] *Id.* § VI.F.

[492] *Id.* § VI.D.2.m.

[493] *See* 15 U.S.C. § 80b-4a; 17 C.F.R. § 275.204A-1.

[494] 15 U.S.C. §§ 80a-35, 80a-41 (Inv. Co. Act §§ 36, 42).

[495] SEC, Laws and Rules, *supra* note 65.

[496] *Id.*

[497] *Id.*

advisory fees, which can be brought by mutual fund shareholders under Section 36(b), for breaches of fiduciary duty by the investment adviser to an investment company.[498] Investment Company Act Section 47(b) provides that contracts made, or whose performance violates, the Act's registration requirements, are unenforceable and subject to rescission.[499] Currently, there is a circuit split as to whether this provision creates an implied right of action for private parties.[500]

IV.   WHERE CAN THE SEC CAN ASSERT ITS CLAIMS?

The SEC brings enforcement actions in either federal district court or in administrative proceedings before its administrative law judges ("ALJs"). The Sarbanes-Oxley Act of 2002 and the Dodd-Frank Act of 2010 give the SEC the power in administrative proceedings to seek the full range of relief available in district court.[501]

Recent litigation has, however, conscribed the Commission's use of ALJs. In *Lucia v. SEC*, the Supreme Court held that SEC ALJs are officers of the United States subject to the constitution's Appointments Clause, which requires that they be appointed by the President, a court of law, or a department head.[502] Accordingly, the Supreme Court ruled that the appointment of an ALJ, who presided over an enforcement proceeding against an investment company

---

[498] *See* 15 U.S.C. § 80a-35; *Gartenberg v. Merrill Lynch Asset Mgmt., Inc.*, 694 F.2d 923, 928 (2d Cir. 1982).

[499] *See* 15 U.S.C. § 80a-46(b).

[500] *Compare Oxford Univ. Bank v. Lansuppe Feeder, LLC*, 933 F.3d 99 (2019), *with* S*antomenno ex rel. John Hancock Tr. v. John Hancock Life Ins.*, 677 F.3d 178 (3d Cir. 2012).

[501] *See* 15 U.S.C. §§ 78u-2, 78u-3(f) (Exch. Act. §§ 21B, 21C(f)); *see also* Sarbanes-Oxley Act of 2002, Pub. L. No. 107-204 § 1105, 116 Stat. 745, 809; Dodd-Frank Wall Street Reform & Consumer Protection Act, Pub. L. No. 111-203 § 929P, 124 Stat. 1376, 1862.

[502] 138 S. Ct. 2044, 2051, 2055 (2018).

and its owner, was unconstitutional.[503] In response to *Lucia*, the SEC "remanded all pending administrative cases for new proceedings before constitutionally appointed ALJs."[504]

The SEC is now contending with a similar issue based on the constitution's Removal Clause—namely, whether SEC ALJ's have multiple layers of tenure protection that impede the President's removal authority. In May 2022, the Supreme Court granted certiorari in the Fifth Circuit case of *SEC v. Cochran*[505] to determine "[w]hether a federal district court has jurisdiction to hear a suit in which the respondent in an ongoing [SEC] administrative proceeding seeks to enjoin that proceeding, based on an alleged constitutional defect in the statutory provisions that govern the removal of the [ALJ] who will conduct the proceeding."[506] The case will be heard in the Supreme Court's Fall 2022 term.

The Fifth Circuit further explored the constitutionality of SEC administrative proceedings in *Jarkesy v. SEC*.[507] In *Jarkesy*, the Fifth Circuit concluded that certain SEC enforcement proceedings "suffered from three independent constitutional defects: (1) Petitioners were deprived of their constitutional right to a jury trial; (2) Congress unconstitutionally delegated legislative power to the SEC by failing to provide it with an intelligible principle by which to exercise the delegated power; and (3) statutory removal restrictions on SEC ALJs violate Article II."[508] As of September 2022, the SEC's petition for *en banc review* remains pending.[509]

---

[503] *Id.* at 2051, 2055.

[504] *Cochran v. SEC*, 20 F.4th 194, 198 (5th Cir. 2021).

[505] 142 S. Ct. 2707 (2022).

[506] *Petition for Certiorari Granted, Cochran v. SEC*, 20 F.4th 194 (5th Cir. 2021), *cert. granted*, 142 S. Ct. 2707 (2022) (No. 19-10396) at 2.s.

[507] 34 F.4th 446 (5th Cir. 2022).

[508] *Id.* at 450-51.

[509] *Jarkesy v. SEC*, No. 20-61007 (5th Cir.).

V. WHAT REMEDIES CAN THE SEC SEEK?

The SEC has a range of available remedies pursuant to both its statutory authority as well as in equity. Counsel should familiarize themselves with the most commonly sought remedies—and any limitations to these remedies—so they can assess risk as an investigation progresses.

A. Permanent Injunctions, Cease-and-Desist Orders, and Undertakings

In nearly all cases, the SEC will seek an order barring the violative conduct from continuing—either via a court-ordered permanent injunction or an administrative cease-and-desist order. The SEC's power to pursue these remedies derives from Sections 8A(a) and 20(b) of the Securities Act, and Sections 21C(a) and 21(d)(1) of the Exchange Act.[510] Permanent injunctions and cease-and-desist orders, at a minimum, prohibit a party from engaging in ongoing or future violations of the securities laws provisions that it has been charged with violating. These are known as "obey the law" injunctions.[511] Another form of permanent injunctive relief can also prohibit a party from engaging in specific activities—these are known as "conduct-based," Relatedly, under Rule 102(e), the Commission can censure, suspend or bar professionals who appear or practice before it, when professionals have engaged in "improper professional conduct."[512]

Undertakings are an additional form of relief in SEC enforcement actions. They "require a defendant to take affirmative steps . . . in order to come into and remain in compliance with the specific

---

[510] *See* 15 U.S.C. §§ 77h-1(a), 77t(b) (Sec. Act §§ 8A(a), 20(b)); 15 U.S.C. §§ 78u(d)(1), 78u-3(a) (Exch. Act §§ 21(d)(1), 21C(a)). The Investment Companies Act § 9(f)(1), 15 U.S.C. § 80a-9(f)(1)) and the Advisers Act § 203(k)(2), 15 U.S.C. § 80b-3(k)(2)) have similar provisions.

[511] Currently, two circuits have criticized the use of obey-the-law injunctions, finding them insufficiently tailored to satisfy Fed. R. Civ. P. Rule 65. *See SEC v. Russell Goulding*, 40 F.4th 558, 562 (7th Cir. 2022); *SEC v. Goble*, 682 F.3d 934, 952-53 (11th Cir. 2012).

[512] 17 C.F.R. §201.102(e)

terms of the court's order."[513] Undertakings can require the settling party to retain a compliance consultant or monitor that makes recommendations to the issuer and reports to the SEC.[514] Through undertakings, an SEC action can "seed change in a corporation's processes in a way that serves the long-term interests of investors."[515] The SEC can tailor undertakings to address the specific conduct as issue. For example, undertakings have been utilized in digital asset settlements, where issuers have undertaken to register cryptocurrency tokens with the SEC.[516]

SEC injunctions or cease-and-desist orders may have several collateral consequences. Under Rule 506(d) of the Exchange Act, also known as the bad actor disqualification, an offering is disqualified from relying on 506(b) and 506(c) if the issuer or any other person covered by 506(d) has a relevant criminal conviction, regulatory or court order, or other disqualifying.[517] Furthermore, Item 401 under Regulation S-K requires proxy disclosures that identify Director and Officer involvement in certain legal proceedings.[518] The requirement of these disclosures can effectively bar individuals from serving as Officers and Directors of public companies even if they are not barred under the Securities or Exchange Acts, as public companies typically do not wish to make such proxy disclosures. The Investment Company Act provides for similar penalties, only permitting the individual to serve in their present capacity if they are eligible for waiver under subsection (c).[519] Additionally, companies with injunctions or

---

[513] *See* Steven Peikin, SEC Co-Dir., Div. Enf't, Address at SEC's PLI White Collar Crime 2018: Prosecutors and Regulators Speak, Remedies and Relief in SEC Enforcement Actions (Oct. 3, 2018), https://www.sec.gov/news/speech/speech-peikin-100318.

[514] *Id.*

[515] *Id.*

[516] *See In re Blockfi Lending LLC*, Exchange Act Release No. 34503, 2022 WL 462445 (Feb. 14, 2022).

[517] 17 C.F.R. 15 U.S.C. § 330.506(d).

[518] 17 CFR § 229.401

[519] 15 U.S.C. § 80a-9(c).

cease-and-desist orders cannot use the "safe harbor" protections for forward-looking statements under Securities Act Section 27A(c) and Exchange Act Section 21E(c).[520] A cease-and-desist order can also strip companies of their eligibility to be deemed a "well-known seasoned issuer" ("WKSI").[521] The SEC can grant waivers of ineligible issuer status "upon a showing of good cause, that it is not necessary under the circumstances that the issuer be considered an ineligible issuer."[522]

B.   Monetary Relief

The SEC frequently seeks monetary relief through disgorgement awards and civil penalties. In fiscal year 2021, the SEC ordered parties to pay nearly $2.4 billion in disgorgement and more than $1.4 billion in penalties.[523]

Such monetary relief can be, and often is, distributed to investors through the SEC's use of "Fair Funds." In a fair fund, disgorgement and civil penalty monies paid by defendants are used for the benefit of investors harmed by the securities law violation.[524] Any funds not returned to investors are sent to the U.S. Treasury or the Investor Protection Fund.[525] Neither disgorgement nor penalties are used for the SEC's own expenses.[526]

---

[520] 15 U.S.C. §§ 77z-2(c), 78u-5(c).

[521] *See* 17 C.F.R. § 230.405 (Sec. Act Rule 405).

[522] *Id.* (quoting 17 C.F.R. § 200.30-1(a)(10).

[523] *See* SEC, Addendum to Division of Enforcement Press Release 2 (2021), https://www.sec.gov/files/2021-238-addendum.pdf.

[524] 17 C.F.R. § 201.1100.

[525] SEC, Fiscal Year 2023 Congressional Budget Justification Annual Performance Plan & Fiscal Year 2021 Annual Performance Report 120 (2022), https://www.sec.gov/files/FY%202023%20Congressional%20Budget%20Justification%20Annual%20Performance%20Plan_FINAL.pdf.

[526] *Id.*

1. Disgorgement

The function of disgorgement is to deprive wrongdoers the "fruits of their ill-gotten gains."[527] Individuals charged with insider trading violations, for example, can be required to disgorge their profits from the illicit trades. Advisers found to have charged excessive fees can be required to disgorge the fees; persons involved in an offering fraud can be required to disgorge the monies raised under false pretenses; and brokers can be ordered to disgorge ill-gained commissions.

Several recent Supreme Court cases have addressed the SEC's disgorgement remedy. First, in *Kokesh v. SEC*, the Supreme Court held that disgorgement was a "penalty" under 28 U.S.C. § 2462, and was therefore subject to a five-year statute of limitations.[528] Next, in *Liu v. SEC*, the Supreme Court held that the SEC may seek and obtain disgorgement from a court as "equitable relief" for a securities law violation.[529] But the Supreme Court held that disgorged funds must be for the benefit of investors and reflect only net profits with legitimate business expenses deducted.[530]

In 2021, Congress passed legislation codifying the SEC's ability to seek disgorgement in federal court actions and establishing separate statutes of limitations for different claims brought by the SEC.[531] For cases involving scienter-based fraud, Congress set the statute of limitations as ten years, instead of the five-year period prescribed under *Kokesh*.[532] The statute potentially opens the door for the SEC to seek larger disgorgement relief and open investigations for scienter-based fraud that apply to conduct farther back in time. Additionally, this legislation may expand the

---

[527] *Liu v. SEC*, 140 S. Ct. 1936, 1948 (2020).

[528] *Kokesh v. SEC*, 137 S. Ct. 1635, 1643-44 (2017).

[529] *Id.* at 1943-48.

[530] *Id.* at 1949-50.

[531] 15 U.S.C. § 78u.

[532] *Id.* § 78u(d)(8).

availability of disgorgement in actions where funds cannot be feasibly distributed to harmed investors.[533]

Where the SEC seeks disgorgement, it typically seeks post-judgment interest on the disgorgement amount, calculated in accordance with a statutory prejudgment interest calculator.[534]

2. Penalties

Civil penalties are designed to deter misconduct.[535] The amount of the penalty sought depends on the conduct and impact on others.[536] Each of the acts under which the SEC has authority to bring claims has a corresponding penalties provision. For example, under Section 20(d) of the Securities Act, adjusting for inflation, the ceiling for the first tier of penalties is set at the greater of $9,753 for a natural person or $97,523 for any other person, or the gross amount of pecuniary gain to the wrongdoer.[537] The second tier dictates penalties for violations involving "fraud, deceit, manipulation or deliberate or reckless disregard of a regulatory requirement."[538] Penalties that fall within the second tier shall not exceed the greater of $97,523 for a natural person or $487,616 for any other person, or the gross amount of pecuniary gain to the

---

[533] *See, e.g., SEC v. Spartan Sec. Grp., Ltd.*, No. 19-cv-448, 2022 WL 3224008, at *9 (M.D. Fla. Aug. 10, 2022) (stating that "15 U.S.C. § 78u(d)(7) explicitly provides this Court the ability to order disgorgement and does not require that such disgorgement be 'for the benefit of investors,' [and] [t]he Court holds that it may order disgorgement and direct that disgorged funds be sent to the Treasury under Section 78u(d)(7)").

[534] *See In re Eagle Bancorp, Inc.*, Exchange Act Release No. 95505, 2022 WL 3368230 (Aug. 16, 2022).

[535] *See* Caroline A. Crenshaw, SEC Comm'r, Address Before the Council of Institutional Investors, Moving Forward Together – Enforcement for Everyone (Mar. 9, 2021), https://www.sec.gov/news/speech/crenshaw-moving-forward-together.

[536] 15 U.S.C. § 77t(d)(2).

[537] *Id.* § 77t(d)(2)(A).

[538] *Id.* § 77t(d)(2)(B).

wrongdoer.[539] The third tier prescribes penalties for violations that involved "fraud, deceit, manipulation, or deliberate or reckless disregard of a regulatory requirement" and "directly or indirectly resulted in substantial losses or created a significant risk of substantial losses to other persons."[540] Penalties that fall within the third tier shall not exceed the greater of $195,047 for a natural person or $975,230 for any other person, or the gross amount of pecuniary gain to the wrongdoer.[541] The statutory tiers under the Exchange Act, the Advisers Act, and the Investment Company Act operate similarly.[542] Under a special statute that applies to insider trading violations, civil penalties in those cases can be up to three times the profit gained or the loss avoided.[543]

C. Bars and Suspensions

Bars are among the SEC's most utilized remedies. Because they target people's continued ability to operate in the securities industry, and because they are a remedy unique to the SEC, they are viewed by the Commission as an important deterrence measure.

- **Public company officer and director bars:** The SEC can seek a court order or can impose through an administrative order a bar precluding an individual from serving as a public company officer or director for a limited time or permanently.[544]

---

[539] *Id.*

[540] *Id.* § 77t(d)(2)(C).

[541] *Id.*

[542] 15 U.S.C. § 78(b) (Exchange Act); 15 U.S.C. §80b-3 (Investment Advisors Act); 15 U.S.C §80a (Investment Company Act).

[543] 15 U.S. Code § 78u–1(a)(2).

[544] *See* 15 U.S.C. § 77h-1(f); *see also SEC v. Bentley*, No. 22-cv-02772, 2022 WL 3500133 (S.D. Tex. Aug. 17, 2022*).*

- **Attorney and accountant bars:** Under 102(e) of the SEC Rules of Practice, the SEC can bar individuals, including accountants, auditors, and lawyers, from appearing or practicing before the SEC.[545] Individuals can be barred from representing issuers who file reports or register offerings with the SEC.[546] Any professional found to have "engaged in unethical or improper professional conduct," or to have willfully violated the securities laws, can be barred from practicing before the SEC.[547]

- **Investment adviser bars:** The SEC can bar securities laws violators from acting as or associating with an investment adviser.[548]

- **Broker-dealer bars:** The SEC can bar securities laws violators from acting as or associating with broker-dealers.[549]

- **Investment company bars:** The SEC can disqualify the affected entity and its affiliates from serving as an investment advisor, depositor, or principle underwriter of certain registered public companies.[550]

---

[545] *See* SEC, Rules of Practice (2003), https://www.sec.gov/rulesprac072003htm#102.

[546] 15 U.S.C. § 78d-3; 17 C.F.R. § 201.102(e).

[547] 17 C.F.R. § 201.102(e)(1).

[548] 15 U.S.C. § 80b-3(e) (Adv. Act § 203(e)); *see also In re Lattanzio*, Exchange Act Release No. 5367, 2019 WL 4693572 (Sept. 26, 2019).

[549] *See* 15 U.S.C. § 78o(b)(4) (Exch. Act § 15(b)(4); *see also Lattanzio*, 2019 WL 4693572.

[550] 15 U.S.C. § 80a-9(a).

- **Penny stock bars:** The SEC can bar individuals or entities from participating in penny stock offerings.[551]

The SEC can also suspend public companies from trading and offering securities. As the SEC's reporting rules are designed to "help ensure that investors are provided timely access to reliable interim financial information," the SEC will typically suspend public companies when they fail to file quarterly or annual reports.[552] Section 12(j) of the Exchange Act allows the SEC to suspend or revoke the registration of a company's securities through a noticed administrative proceeding.[553]

Alternatively, through Section 12(k)(1)(A) of the Exchange Act, the SEC can suspend the trading of a company's securities for a period not exceeding ten business days.[554] Unlike Section 12(j) proceedings, the SEC can issue this relief without notice. The SEC will suspend trading when it determines that a trading suspension "is required in the public interest and for the protection of investors."[555]

D.　　Forfeitures

Under Section 304 of the Sarbanes-Oxley Act of 2002, if an issuer is required to prepare an accounting restatement due to

---

[551] *See* 15 U.S.C. § 78o(b)(4) (Exch. Act § 15(b)(4); Press Release, SEC, SEC Files Settled Charges Against Kansas Man for Violating Penny Stock Suspension (Dec. 16, 2021), https://www.sec.gov/litigation/litreleases/2021/lr25290.htm#:~:text=Alexander%20Kon%20(Release%20No.,16%2C%202021).

[552] *See* Press Release, SEC, Public Companies Charged With Failing to Comply With Quarterly Reporting Obligations (Sept. 21, 2018), https://www.sec.gov/news/press-release/2018-207; *see In re Gateway Int'l Holdings, Inc.*, Exchange Act Release No. 53907, 2006 WL 1506286, at *5 n.28 (May 31, 2006).

[553] 15 U.S.C. § 78l.

[554] *Id.* § 78l(k)(1)(A).

[555] *See* SEC, Trading Suspensions (Aug. 1, 2022), https://www.sec.gov/litigation/suspensions.htm.

noncompliance as a result of misconduct with any financial
reporting requirement, the SEC can seek disgorgement of bonuses
or other incentive-based or equity-based compensation, or profits
from the sales of company stock, that a CEO or CFO received
during the 12-month period following the issuance of misstated
financial results.[556] Notably, the CEO or CFO need not have been
involved in the misconduct—provided that it happened on their
watch.[557]

E.   Emergency Relief

At times, the SEC pursues various forms of emergency relief
where, for example, the SEC seeks to halt an ongoing fraud. The
SEC can seek a temporary restraining order or a preliminary
injunction that enjoins a defendant from violating the securities
laws or from participating in the issuance, purchase, offer, or sale
of any security.[558] The SEC can ask a court to freeze a defendant's
assets to ensure that if the SEC obtains a judgment, money will be
available to satisfy it.[559] The court will consider whether the
defendant could dissipate their assets or transfer them beyond the
jurisdiction of the U.S.[560] In addition, the SEC can seek
repatriation of assets.[561] The SEC can seek appointment of

---

[556] 15 U.S.C. § 7243.

[557] *Jensen*, 835 F.3d at 1116 (holding that "disgorgement [was] merited [under
Section 304] to prevent corporate officers from profiting from the proceeds of
misconduct, whether it [was] their own misconduct or the misconduct of the
companies they are paid to run"); *see also SEC v. Life Partners Holdings, Inc.*,
854 F.3d 765, 786-89 (5th Cir. 2017) (remanding to determine appropriate
reimbursement amounts by CEO given company's misconduct).

[558] *See, e.g.*, Press Release, SEC, SEC Obtains Preliminary Injunctions Against
Frack Master and Four Others in Purported House Flipping Scheme (Nov. 3,
2017), https://www.sec.gov/sec-obtains-preliminary-injunctions-against-frack-
master-and-four-others-purported-house.

[559] *SEC v. Collector's Coffee Inc.*, No. 19 Civ. 04355, 2022 WL 1448432, at *11
(S.D.N.Y. May 8, 2022).

[560] *Id.* at *2.

[561] *See, e.g.*, Press Release, SEC, SEC Uncovers $194 Million Penny Stock
Schemes that Spanned Three Continents (Apr. 18, 2022),
https://www.sec.gov/news/press-release/2022-62.

temporary and permanent receivers to take control of or distribute assets,[562] or of a corporate monitor to oversee the company's affairs.[563]

VI.   WHAT TOOLS DOES THE SEC USE TO GATHER EVIDENCE?

The SEC strives to push the pace of investigations and develop the tools to do so.[564] As described recently by Gurbir S. Grewal, Director of the Division of Enforcement: "The public needs to know when they read a news story about corporate malfeasance that [the SEC] will move quickly to investigate what happened and hold wrongdoers accountable, even in the most complex cases."[565] To this end, the SEC has a variety of tools in its arsenal to investigate potential wrongdoing. For example, the SEC relies on algorithms, prime brokerage records, cooperating witnesses, incentivizing individuals to tip, telephone records, wiretaps, search warrants, screen captures, IP addresses, and reviewing emails and instant messages.

A.   Interviews and Testimony

The SEC gathers evidence by interviewing individuals. For example, the SEC may conduct voluntary telephone interviews.[566] The staff may also request voluntary transcribed ("on the record")

---

[562] SEC, Receiverships, https://www.sec.gov/files/2019%20OMWI%20Receiverships%20Card_FINAL.pdf.

[563] *See, e.g.*, Press Release, SEC, The Honorable Jed Rakoff Approves Settlement of SEC's Claim for a Civil Penalty Against Worldcom (July 7, 2003), https://www.sec.gov/news/press/2003-81.htm.

[564] *See* Gurbir S. Grewal, SEC Dir., Div. Enf't, Remarks at Securities Enforcement Forum West 2022 (May 12, 2022), https://www.sec.gov/news/speech/grewal-remarks-securities-enforcement-forum-west-051222.

[565] *Id.*

[566] *See* Enf't Manual, *supra* note 5, § 3.3.3.1.

testimony from witnesses.[567] The staff cannot require and administer oaths or affirmations without a Formal Order of Investigation, but can conduct voluntary testimony with a court reporter who will produce a verbatim transcript.[568] If a witness is voluntarily willing to testify under oath, a court reporter will place the witness under oath.[569] If a witness is under oath, they are subject to federal perjury laws.[570] Regardless of whether a witness is under oath, 18 U.S.C. § 1001, which prohibits false statements to government officials, applies.[571] A witness may have counsel present at voluntary on-the-record testimony.[572] The SEC can also require a person to provide testimony under oath through the issuance of a subpoena.[573]

B.   Documents

Documents are still the "lifeblood" of many investigations.[574] Documents "provide investigative leads, help refresh witness recollections of distant events, and supply powerful, contemporaneous evidence of those same events."[575] Whether the staff's request for documents comes in the form of an official subpoena or an informal ask for the voluntary production of documents, counsel should be cognizant of the importance of complying with document production obligations. The SEC accepts production of documents in accordance with its Data Delivery Standards; producing materials as called for by these

---

[567] *See id.* § 3.3.4.

[568] *See id.*

[569] *Id.*

[570] *Id.*

[571] *Id.*

[572] *Id.*

[573] *See id.* § 3.3.5.1.

[574] Grewal, Remarks at Securities Enforcement Forum West 2022, *supra* note 144.

[575] *Id.*

Standards is an important aspect of compliance with a document request or subpoena.[576]

C.   Data Analytics

In certain kinds of investigations, such as insider trading and market manipulation, the SEC uses sophisticated programs like the Advanced Relational Trading Enforcement Metrics Investigation System, or "ARTEMIS," which "analyzes patterns and relationships among multiple traders using the Division's electronic database of over six billion electronic equities and options trading records."[577] ARTEMIS combines "historical trading and account holder data with other data sources to enable longitudinal, multi-issuer, and multi-trader data analyses."[578]

The Palantir Enterprise Data Analytics Program ("EDAP") is an "enterprise wide single-platform analytic software tool that provides the SEC the capability of integrating structured, unstructured, and semi-structured data."[579] The SEC uses EDAP to "find, analyze, and visualize connections between disparate sets of data" in order to generate leads, identify schemes, and uncover fraud.[580] Through EDAP, the SEC can run queries to find data uniquely relevant to an investigation or examination, and can

---

[576] *Id.*; *see also* SEC, Data Delivery Standards (2021), https://www.sec.gov/divisions/enforce/datadeliverystandards.pdf.

[577] May Jo White, SEC Chair, Remarks at the International Institute for Securities Market Growth and Development (Apr. 8, 2016), https://www.sec.gov/news/statement/statement-mjw-040816.html.

[578] Michael S. Piwowar, SEC Comm'r, Remarks at the 2018 RegTech Data Summit – Old Fields, New Corn: Innovation in Technology and Law (Mar. 7, 2018), https://www.sec.gov/news/speech/piwowar-old-fields-new-corn-innovation-technology-law.

[579] SEC, Div. Enf't, Privacy Impact Assessment (PIA), Palantir Enterprise Data Analytics Platform (EDAP) (2021), https://www.sec.gov/about/privacy/pia/pia-palantir.pdf.

[580] *Id.*

uncover previously unknown relationships and links between entities and individuals.[581]

VII.   HOW DOES THE SEC DECIDE WHAT INVESTIGATIONS TO PRIORITIZE?

A.   SEC Enforcement Division Priorities

The SEC seeks to identify and prioritize certain investigations having "potential programmatic significance, which are deemed 'National Priority Matters.'"[582] In ranking investigations and determining whether an investigation qualifies as a National Priority Matter, the SEC considers a variety of factors including "[w]hether the matter presents an opportunity to send a particularly strong and effective message of deterrence"; "[w]hether the matter involves particularly egregious or extensive misconduct"; "[w]hether the matter involves potentially widespread and extensive harm to investors"; and "[w]hether the matter involves misconduct by persons occupying positions of substantial authority or responsibility, or who owe fiduciary or other enhanced duties and obligations to a broad group of investors or others"; and "[w]hether the matter involves products, markets, transactions or practices that the Division has identified as priority areas."[583] A key criteria—considered in connection with whether the matter presents an opportunity to send a particularly strong and effective message of deterrence—is whether the matter is tied to "newly developing" markets, products, and transactions.[584] When allocating resources among investigations, the SEC considers, in addition to the potential significance of the investigation, "[w]hether there is an urgent need to file an enforcement action, such as an investigation into ongoing fraud or conduct that poses a threat of imminent harm to investors"; "[t]he volume of evidence that the staff must collect and review, such as trading records,

---

[581] Id.

[582] Enf't Manual, supra note 5, § 2.1.1.

[583] See id.

[584] See id.

corporate documents, and e-mail correspondence"; and "[t]he level of analysis required for complex data and evidence, such as auditor workpapers, bluesheets, or financial data."[585]

B.   SEC Examinations Division Priorities

Unlike the Enforcement Division, the Examinations Division publishes annual examination priorities that identify areas of potential risk to investors and the integrity of U.S. capital markets that the SEC is focused on. In turn, the Enforcement Division may be more willing to pursue claims that implicate these priorities.

On March 30, 2022, the SEC Division of Examinations announced that it was focusing on five areas in particular in 2022: private funds; environmental, social, and governance ("ESG") investing; retail investors and working families; information security and operational resiliency; and emerging technologies and crypto-assets.[586] When designing and enhancing compliance programs, counsel should keep the SEC's examination priorities in mind and pay particular attention to ensure there are robust policies and procedures that address the SEC's focus areas.

VIII.   HOW DOES THE SEC DECIDE WHETHER TO BRING A CLAIM AND WHAT CLAIMS TO PURSUE?

A.   The Wells Notice Process

The Wells process commences towards the end of the investigation, when the staff believes it has gathered sufficient evidence to warrant recommending to the Commissioners that a case be brought. The staff provides a Wells Notice to the party, informing them that the Division has made a preliminary determination that the SEC should bring an enforcement action,

---

[585] *See id.*

[586] Press Release, SEC, SEC Division of Examinations Announces 2022 Examination Priorities (Mar. 30, 2022), https://www.sec.gov/news/press-release/2022-57.

and providing the statutory grounds for the suspected violations.[587] Provision of the Wells notice starts a 180-day clock, for staff to either recommend the SEC file an action/proceeding or provide notice to the Director of Enforcement of their intent not to file.[588]

The Wells notice permits the party to provide a response explaining why the SEC should not pursue the identified claims, or why the relief being sought is not appropriate. An effective response may persuade the staff to cease certain avenues of investigation or drop the case in its entirety. A party may be permitted to examine certain portions of the investigative file that are not privileged, and if desired, a party receiving a Wells notice may request a meeting with Commission staff to discuss the substance of the staff's proposed recommendation to the Commission.[589] The meeting request may be granted or denied— and if granted, it may be held with SEC staff, supervisors, and/or the Division of Enforcement Director or Deputy Director, depending on the circumstances.[590] In particular, the Director or Deputy Director may not join Wells meetings that do not "present novel legal or factual questions, or raise significant programmatic issues."[591]

Parties should be mindful that Wells notices and submissions may have collateral consequences. Public companies may decide that

---

[587] See Enf't Manual, supra note 5, § 2.4. Providing a Wells notice is not a requirement, however, and involves the exercise of discretion by the staff. For example, if the Commission determines that providing a Wells notice and waiting for a responsive submission would delay its ability to halt ongoing fraud, staff may determine that a Wells notice is not appropriate.

[588] See 15 U.S.C. § 78d-5 (Exch. Act. § 4E). The 180-day deadline is only internal, and cannot be used as a basis to dismiss an enforcement action that was not filed within the deadline. See, e.g., Montford & Co., Inc. v. SEC, 793 F.3d 76, 85 (D.C. Cir. 2015).

[589] See Enf't Manual, supra note 5, § 2.4.

[590] See Gurbir S. Grewal, SEC Dir., Div. Enf't, Remarks at SEC Speaks 2021 (Oct 13, 2021), https://www.sec.gov/news/speech/grewal-sec-speaks-101321.

[591] See id.

receipt of a Wells notice should be disclosed,[592] and receipt of a Wells notice may adversely affect company plans.[593] Wells submissions can be evidence in SEC enforcement actions as admissions and may be discoverable in private litigation.[594]

B.   Instituting Enforcement Actions

Although investigations may begin informally, an enforcement action may only begin after formal approval by a majority of the Commissioners. This process begins with the submission of an "action memorandum" by staff conducting the investigation that provides the basis for the staff's recommendation, including a "comprehensive" analysis of the facts and legal bases for the recommendation.[595] Staff circulate the action memo to relevant Divisions and Offices such as the Office of the Chief Counsel ("OCC") and Office of the General Counsel ("OGC"), who can offer their input. The action memo is then presented to the Commissioners for review and formal vote among the Commissioners.[596] This process applies whether the action is instituted on a settled basis or as a litigated matter.

Before a vote is conducted, parties must be given an opportunity to provide their own view of the case to the staff and the Commissioners through the Wells process described above. If the

---

[592] *See* Michelle Leder, *What Was Coinbase Thinking When It Dissed the SEC?*, WASH. POST (Sept. 15, 2021), https://www.washingtonpost.com/business/what-was-coinbase-thinking-when-it-dissed-the-sec/2021/09/15/07c1ff1e-162e-11ec-a019-cb193b28aa73_story.html.

[593] *See* Parker Doyle, *Coinbase Will Not Launch "Lend" Product, Weeks After Receiving Wells Notice From the SEC*, VETTAFI (Sept. 22, 2021), https://www.etftrends.com/crypto-channel/coinbase-will-not-launch-lend-product-weeks-after-receiving-wells-notice-from-the-sec (Coinbase announced its decision to not launch "Lend" product, weeks after receiving a Wells notice from the SEC stating the SEC's intent to sue Coinbase should they launch "Lend.").

[594] *See* Enf't Manual, *supra* note 5, § 2.4 (noting that "any Wells submission may be used by the Commission in any action or proceeding that it brings and may be discoverable by third parties in accordance with applicable law").

[595] *See id.* § 2.5.1.

[596] *See id.*

Commissioners vote to approve an enforcement action, a case will be instituted in federal district court or as an administrative proceeding. The Commission institutes a press release or a litigation release notifying the public that it has initiated an enforcement action.

IX. HOW DOES THE SEC ASSESS PARTIES' COOPERATION?

In considering the appropriate relief against a party, the SEC will consider the party's cooperation with the staff's investigation. The SEC may pursue less extreme sanctions when parties cooperate and assist the SEC by providing relevant and timely information; additionally, to the extent a party frustrates or hampers the staff's investigation, this lack of cooperation may result in the SEC seeking consequences of greater significance.

A. The Cooperation Program

In October 2001, the SEC issued the "Seaboard Report," a settled administrative order which identified four primary factors that the SEC analyzes in determining whether an entity provided sufficient cooperation.[597]

- **Self-policing:** The SEC will evaluate the level of self-policing engaged in by the company prior to any misconduct being uncovered.[598] The SEC will focus on the company's compliance program and whether there was an appropriate "tone at the top."[599]

---

[597] *See* Report of Investigation Pursuant to Section 21(a) of the Securities Exchange Act of 1934 and Commission Statement on the Relationship of Cooperation to Agency Enforcement Decisions, Exchange Act Release No. 34-44969 (Oct. 23, 2001), www.sec.gov/litigation/investreport/34-44969.htm.

[598] *See* Enf't Manual, *supra* note 5, § 6.1.2.

[599] *See id.*

- **Self-reporting:** The SEC will consider whether the company self-reported the misconduct to the SEC and the extent to which the company promptly and thoroughly reported the misconduct to the public and to the SEC.[600]

- **Remediation:** The SEC will consider the steps, if any, a company took to remediate the problem, including by appropriately disciplining or terminating any wrongdoers, improving the internal controls that contributed to the misconduct, and compensating those adversely affected by the misconduct.[601]

- **Cooperation:** The SEC will examine the extent to which the company cooperated with relevant law enforcement authorities, including by providing prompt and relevant information to the SEC regarding the underlying violations and remedial efforts.[602]

In 2010, the SEC expanded the cooperation program to individuals.[603] Similar to its evaluation of companies, the SEC identified four primary factors to assess an individual's cooperation:

- **Assistance provided:** The SEC will consider the value of the individual's cooperation, including the timeliness of it, the time and resources conserved as a result of the cooperation, and

---

[600] *See id.*

[601] *See id.*

[602] *See id.*

[603] *See* Policy Statement of the Securities and Exchange Commission Concerning Cooperation by Individuals in its Investigations and Related Enforcement Actions, Exchange Act Release No. 34-61340 (Jan. 13, 2010), www.sec.gov/rules/policy/2010/34-61340.pdf.

whether the cooperation provided substantial assistance to the Commission.[604]

- **Importance of the underlying matter:** The SEC will consider the importance of the underlying matter, and cooperation in investigations that "involve priority matters or serious, ongoing, or widespread violations will be viewed most favorably."[605]

- **Interest in holding the individual accountable:** The SEC will consider the severity of the individual's misconduct, the degree to which the individual tolerated illegal activity, and the extent to which the individual was a driving force in the improper actions.[606]

- **Profile of the individual:** The SEC will assess whether the individual accepts responsibility for their action, whether they have a history of compliance issues, and the degree to which they will have an opportunity to commit future violations by virtue of their occupation.[607]

The ultimate question in the SEC's analysis is whether the cooperation truly assisted the SEC in holding the wrongdoers accountable and whether the company provided the SEC all relevant information. Timely and complete compliance with subpoenas, for example, is likely not enough. If the SEC finds that the cooperation was substantial, the company may benefit from

---

[604] *See id.*

[605] *See id.*

[606] *See id.*

[607] *See id.*

reduced charges or a deferred prosecution agreement, or it may avoid an enforcement action entirely.[608]

B. Current Views on Cooperation

Recent public commentary by senior SEC officials suggests that the staff has heightened expectations for parties' cooperation.[609] For example, Director Grewal has stated publicly that: "As we've seen in a number of recent cases, when clients take steps to self-report potential violations, or to proactively cooperate with our investigations and remediate violations, the Commission is often willing to credit that cooperation, including through reduced penalties, or even no penalties at all."[610] He explained that "cooperation is more than the absence of obstruction; it's an affirmative behavior."[611] Director Grewal also provided examples of "good cooperation" that included making documents or witnesses available to the SEC on an "expedited basis," highlighting "hot" documents, providing translations of documents, and flagging documents that the party knows will be helpful to the SEC, even if technically outside the scope of a subpoena.[612] Conversely, cooperation credit will not be given to entities or individuals who delay the SEC's investigative process "by slow-walking document productions, trying to put off witness testimony for an excessive time, or being obstructive during testimony."[613]

A recent settlement by the SEC reinforces the above guidance. In July 2022, the SEC settled with voxeljet AG, a Foreign Private Issuer headquartered in Germany ("voxeljet") and Rudolf Franz,

---

[608] *See id.* § 6.2.

[609] *See* Grewal, Remarks at SEC Speaks 2021, *supra* note 170.

[610] Grewal, Remarks at Securities Enforcement Forum West 2022, *supra* note 144.

[611] *Id.*

[612] *Id.*

[613] *See id.*

its Chief Financial Officer.[614] The action concerned voxeljet's reporting during two quarters of its compliance with a contract and the state of its internal accounting controls.[615] In the settlement order, the SEC emphasized the considerable cooperation that voxeljet demonstrated throughout the investigation. Voxeljet self-reported the violation and shared with the SEC facts that it had developed in its internal investigation;[616] provided regular updates, identified key documents, and facilitated interviews and testimony with witnesses;[617] and undertook considerable remedial efforts, including developing and implementing new controls regarding the documentation, review, and reporting of the company's compliance with its debt covenants.[618]

Considerable cooperation by a party, including by self-reporting, prompt and thorough assistance to the SEC's investigative efforts, and strong remedial efforts, can serve a party well in reaching a more favorable settlement.

X. HOW DOES THE SEC DECIDE WHETHER TO RESOLVE A CLAIM AND ON WHAT TERMS?

A. Settlements

The SEC settles a significant majority of the investigations it conducts,[619] and the processes for resolving an investigation are generally consistent across SEC proceedings. When a settlement is filed in district court, the settling defendant signs a consent to

---

[614] *In re voxeljet AG*, Exchange Act Release No. 95193, 2022 WL 2390014 (July 1, 2022).

[615] Press Release, SEC, SEC Files Settled Charges Against voxeljet AG and Its CFO Rudolf Franz; Notes Self-Reporting, Cooperation, and Remediation (July 1, 2022), https://www.sec.gov/enforce/34-95193-s.

[616] *voxeljet AG*, 2022 WL 2390014, at *5-6.

[617] *Id.*

[618] *Id.* at *5.

[619] Jay Clayton, SEC Chairman, Statement Regarding Offers of Settlement (July 3, 2019), https://www.sec.gov/news/public-statement/clayton-statement-regarding-offers-settlement.

judgment, which typically includes the party's agreement to a permanent injunction, any other injunctive or equitable relief, and any corresponding monetary relief. A proposed form of the final judgment is attached to the consent, and, if approved by a federal judge, is entered by the court. In administrative proceedings, the settling party signs an offer of settlement, and the SEC issues an order instituting proceedings ("OIP")—similar to a final judgment—which contains the agreed-upon relief. Where an investigation is settled at the matter's outset, the settlement documents include an underlying charging document—for district court cases, the complaint; in administrative proceedings, the OIP.[620]

Factors that the SEC considers when deciding whether to settle a case vary. One driver of settlements is avoiding the cost of litigation.[621] Other factors include the willingness of the SEC to litigate zealously and the importance of promptly remedying harm to investors.[622] If the SEC determines that an appropriate settlement offer has been made—one that provides appropriate remedial relief (sometimes including a return of funds to the injured party) and that would provide such relief faster than litigation—the SEC may lean towards settling a case.[623] As previously discussed, the SEC may take into account an individual or company's cooperation when determining whether a settlement is appropriate, and what the terms of that settlement should be.

---

[620] When in district court, the SEC files the complaint, laying out the factual allegations and basis for its case, and serves as the plaintiff. But in administrative proceedings, the charging document is an order by the SEC that officially begins the proceedings. If the proceedings are not settled, the facts recited in the charging document are considered allegations asserted by the Division of Enforcement. If a case is settled when it is filed, the factual allegations in the charging document are considered findings of the SEC.

[621] *See* Clayton, Statement Regarding Offers of Settlement, *supra* note 199.

[622] *See id.*

[623] *See id.*

B.   Closing Investigations

Generally, the following factors are considered when determining whether to close an investigation: the seriousness of the conduct and potential violations; the staff resources available to pursue the investigation; the sufficiency and strength of the evidence; the extent of potential investor harm if an action is not commenced; and the age of the conduct underlying the potential violations.[624]

The procedures for closing an investigation vary depending on whether there has been an enforcement action. If there has been an enforcement action, closing an investigation is a relatively simple process, and simply requires that staff follow through on every step authorized by the SEC.[625] Importantly, an investigation cannot be closed until all enforcement actions are complete.[626] This requires a final judgment or SEC order, and confirmation that all ordered monetary relief is accounted for.[627] In other words, all disgorgement and civil penalties have to be paid in full, all funds collected have to be distributed to investors or paid into the Treasury, and all money has to be properly recorded.[628]

If no enforcement action will be recommended, closing an investigation can be a "harder judgment call."[629] Staff are encouraged to close an investigation as soon as it becomes apparent that no enforcement action will be recommended.[630] If the SEC has not uncovered any actionable violations of the securities laws, it will provide a termination letter to the investigated parties informing them that no enforcement action will be recommended

---

[624] *See* Enf't Manual, *supra* note 5, § 2.6.1.

[625] *See id.*

[626] *See id.*

[627] *See id.*

[628] *See id.*

[629] *See id.*

[630] *See id.*

against them.[631] A termination letter must be sent to anyone who was identified in the caption of the Formal Order, submitted or was invited to submit a Wells submission, asks for a termination notice, or to the staff's knowledge, reasonably believes that the staff was considering recommending charges against them.[632]

XI.   WHAT FORMS DO SEC SETTLEMENTS TAKE?

A.   No-Admit-No-Deny

Historically, most SEC cases have settled on a "no-admit-no-deny" basis—whether before or during litigation—meaning that the settling defendant in a district court case or the settling respondent in an administrative proceeding neither admits nor denies the factual allegations in the charging document.[633] While that individual or entity may disagree with how the SEC presented or characterized certain facts, the standard district court consent judgment forms and administrative proceeding offer and order templates contain provisions stating that the settling party cannot make any public statements denying the allegations and cannot otherwise indicate that the allegations have no factual basis.[634] Notably, the SEC has long maintained that indemnification for penalties for violations of securities laws is against public policy and unenforceable; the standard SEC consent judgments reflect this prohibition.[635]

---

[631] *See id.* § 2.6.2.

[632] *See id.*

[633] Only about 2% of all SEC cases filed between 2014 and 2017 involved admissions. *See* Dave Michaels, *Wall Street, Companies May have to Give Up More to Settle with SEC*, WALL ST. J. (Oct. 13, 2021), https://www.wsj.com/articles/sec-to-seek-admissions-of-wrongdoing-in-some-enforcement-actions-11634139229.

[634] *See* 17 C.F.R. § 202.5(e).

[635] 17 CFR § 229.510 - (Item 510) Disclosure of Commission position on indemnification for Securities Act liabilities (The required disclosure provides: "Insofar as indemnification for liabilities arising under the Securities Act of 1933 may be permitted to directors, officers or persons controlling the registrant pursuant to the foregoing provisions, the registrant has been informed that in the

B.   **Admission-Based Settlements**

In some instances, the SEC pursues what are known as "admissions" settlements. This may occur in cases where the defendant has pled guilty to related charges in a parallel criminal case. Additionally, the SEC sometimes seeks admissions in other cases deemed appropriate for this remedy. Based on criteria first announced in 2016 by then-SEC chair Mary Jo White[636] and recently reiterated by Director Grewal,[637] examples include (i) cases where a large number of investors have been harmed or the conduct was otherwise egregious; (ii) cases where the conduct posed a significant risk to the market or investors; (iii) cases where admissions would aid investors deciding whether to deal with a particular party in the future; and (iv) cases where reciting unambiguous facts would send an important message to the market about a particular case.[638]

A recent SEC settlement illuminates the application of these criteria. In June 2022, the SEC charged Ernst & Young L.L.P. ("EY") in connection with a significant number of EY audit professionals cheating on the ethics components of the Certified Public Accountant ("CPA") exam, primarily by using answer keys that had been shared with them by colleagues.[639] EY admitted the facts underlying the SEC's charges and agreed to pay a $100

---

opinion of the Securities and Exchange Commission such indemnification is against public policy as expressed in the Act and is therefore unenforceable.").

[636] *See* Mary Jo White, SEC Chair, Address at the Council of Institutional Investors Fall Conference in Chicago, Ill, Deploying the Full Enforcement Arsenal (Sept. 26, 2013), www.sec.gov/news/speech/spch092613mjw.

[637] *See* Grewal, Remarks at SEC Speaks 2021, *supra* note 170.

[638] *See* White, Deploying the Full Enforcement Arsenal, *supra* note 216; *see also* Grewal, Remarks at SEC Speaks 2021, *supra* note 170 (noting that "in appropriate circumstances, [the SEC will] be requiring admissions in cases where heightened accountability and acceptance of responsibility are in the public interest" and that "[a]dmissions, given their attention-getting nature, also serve as a clarion call to other market participants to stamp out and self-report the misconduct to the extent it is occurring in their firm").

[639] *In re Ernst & Young LLP*, Exchange Act Release No. 95167, 2022 WL 2339592, at *1-2 (June 28, 2022).

million penalty and implement extensive remedial measures.[640] In the order, the SEC demonstrated the application of the factors described above. First, the SEC highlighted that EY's misconduct was significant, and stretched out over two separate periods—separated by a supposed implementation of new audit controls.[641] Second, the SEC found that EY consistently misled the SEC throughout their investigation, including by providing numerous false submissions.[642] Third, the SEC noted that EY did not self-police, self-report, or cooperate in the SEC's investigation.[643] EY never engaged in a thorough review of the nature, extent, origins, and consequences of the misconduct and continued to withhold information about the misconduct that EY knew the SEC was investigating. [644] As a result, the Commission concluded that EY significantly hindered the SEC's ability to take action that would protect investors from audit professionals who did not understand their ethical obligations.[645]

XII.   CONCLUSION

The SEC has a wide-ranging mandate to pursue claims and seek remedies across every aspect of the securities laws. Interactions with the staff—around responses to subpoenas, interviews or testimony, cooperation, and advocacy of a party's defenses—can have tremendous impact on the course of an investigation and the ultimate claims and relief the Commission pursues. Counsel's knowledge of the SEC's areas of focus and how it operates, as well as an understanding of the staff's expectations in any given matter,

---

[640] Press Release, SEC, Ernst & Young to Pay $100 Million Penalty for Employees Cheating on CPA Ethics Exams and Misleading Investigation (June 28, 2022), https://www.sec.gov/news/press-release/2022-114.

[641] *Ernst & Young LLP*, 2022 WL 2339592, at *1.

[642] *Id.* at *3-4.

[643] *Id.* at *5.

[644] *Id.*

[645] *Id.*

can greatly benefit clients who become the subject of interest by the SEC.

Chapter 10

Federal Trade Commission Investigations

By:

David C. Shonka
Tara Emory
Nick Snavely[646]

The Federal Trade Commission ("FTC") educates consumers, issues reports and guidance to consumers and businesses, and studies industries and business practices. It is also, and primarily, a law enforcement agency. Like every other U.S. government agency, its authority is limited by three factors: (1) the scope of the jurisdiction Congress has given it; (2) the statutes Congress has empowered it to enforce; and (3) the tools Congress has given it to exercise its jurisdiction.

Paradoxically, very little has changed formally at the FTC since this Chapter was last revised in 2018, but everything is somehow different. On the one hand, the governing statutes, 15 U.S.C. §§ 41 (*West*), *et seq.* and the FTC's Rules of Practice governing investigations, 16 C.F.R. Part 2, are virtually unchanged. On the other hand, a unanimous Supreme Court has struck down the Agency's decades-old practice of routinely seeking monetary remedies under Section 13(b) of the FTC Act, which authorizes the Commission to seek permanent injunctions,[647] and the Biden Administration has appointed a majority of Commissioners whose

---

[646] Mr. Shonka is a Partner at Redgrave LLP, where his practice focuses on privacy and data security issues and government investigations. He also serves as the Firm's General Counsel. Mr. Shonka previously served in various roles at the FTC, including three terms as the Agency's Acting General Counsel and ten years as Principal Deputy General Counsel. Ms. Emory is the Senior Vice President of Strategic Operations and Consulting at Redgrave Data, where she assists clients in identifying and leveraging technology and processes to complement legal strategies and improve project success. Mr. Snavely is an experienced litigator and a Partner at Redgrave LLP, where he focuses his practice on complex issues related to data privacy, eDiscovery, and information governance.

[647] *AMG Cap. Mgmt., LLC v. Fed. Trade Comm'n*, 141 S. Ct. 1341 (2021).

agenda relies on the FTC increasing and broadening both the scope of its enforcement of the antitrust laws and its consumer privacy and security jurisdiction.[648] Whether the Commission's new approach to law enforcement is insightful and correct, folly—or something in between—is not the subject of this Chapter. What matters here is that the Agency's new approach to enforcement also translates into a different way of conducting its investigations. This Chapter discusses the FTC's current approach to investigations in the context of its binding statutes and rules, and the ways parties can productively respond to those investigations.

I.   FTC'S JURISDICTIONAL REACH

The FTC essentially has regulatory jurisdiction over most entities that are engaged in commerce and not regulated exclusively by somebody else. More precisely, the Agency has law enforcement jurisdiction in most sectors of the economy over all natural persons and entities in commerce that conduct business for their own profit

---

[648] *See* Statement of Chair Lina M. Khan, Joined by Commissioner Rebecca Kelly Slaughter and Commissioner Alvaro M. Bedoya Regarding the Strategic Plan for Fiscal Years 2022-2026 (Aug. 26, 2022); *available at* https://www.ftc.gov/system/files/ftc_gov/pdf/Majority%20Statement.2022-2026%20Strategic%20Plan.pdf ("During the agency's review of present challenges, it became clear that the Commission's goals, objectives, and metrics needed to be re-evaluated and refined to ensure that the Commission is continuing to learn from past experiences and adapt to present realities so that we can successfully navigate the road ahead"); See also, e.g., Statement of the Commission on the Use of Prior Approval Provisions in Merger Orders (Oct. 25, 2021), https://www.ftc.gov/system/files/documents/public_statements/1597894/p859900 priorapprovalstatement.pdf (discussing withdrawal of 1995 policy so that merging parties subject to Commission orders to seek approval for future transactions); Statement of Chair Lina M. Khan Joined by Commissioner Rebecca Kelly Slaughter In the Matter of Napleton Automotive Group Commission File No. 2023195 (March 31, 2022), *available at* https://www.ftc.gov/system/files/ftc_gov/pdf/Statement%20of%20Chair%20Lina%20M.%20Khan%20Joined%20by%20RKS%20in%20re%20Napleton_Finalize d.pdf (taking position that discrimination is actionable by the FTC as an unfair trade practice). *See generally,* Federal Trade Commission Strategic Plan for Fiscal Years 2022-2026, *available at* https://www.ftc.gov/system/files/ftc_gov/pdf/fy-2022-2026-ftc-strategic-plan.pdf (last visited, August 31, 2022).

or that of their members. For example, the FTC generally has jurisdiction over non-profit trade associations, but not over non-profit charities and public universities.[649] Sections 5 and 6 of the FTC Act define the FTC's jurisdiction, exempting, in whole or in part: depository institutions (*e.g.*, banks, federal credit unions, and savings and loan institutions), communications and transportation common carriers subject to regulation under certain other laws,[650] air carriers subject to regulation by the Department of Transportation, and packers and stockyards to the extent they are regulated by the Packers and Stockyards Act.[651] Although exempt from the FTC's regulatory jurisdiction, these entities are still required to provide evidence and testimony in FTC investigations and other proceedings.[652]

II.   FTC STATUTES

The Commission administers or enforces more than 70 statutes.[653] The FTC Act itself is the principal statute and many of the other 70—with the most notable exception being the Clayton Act, discussed below—simply provide that a violation of that statute is

---

[649] These limitations are derived from the definitions found in Section 4 of the Federal Trade Commission Act (the "FTC Act").15 U.S.C.A. § 44 (West). Also, the Clayton Act gives the FTC jurisdiction over non-profit entities in cases involving violations of that Act.

[650] The FTC Act exempts from the FTC's jurisdiction, "common carriers subject to the Acts to regulate commerce . . . ." 15 U.S.C.A. § 45(a)(2) (West). This language means that common carriers are exempt from the FTC Act only when they are engaged in regulated common carrier activities. *Fed. Trade Comm'n v. AT&T Mobility LLC*, 883 F.3d 848 (9th Cir. 2018)(*en banc*).

[651] *See*15 U.S.C.A. § 45(a)(2), 46(a).

[652] *See, e.g., F.T.C. v. Citicorp*, No. M 18-304, 1979 WL 1633, at *2 (S.D.N.Y. Apr. 19, 1979).

[653] Such statutes range from the Dolphin Protection Consumer Information Act and the Muhammed Ali Boxing Reform Act to the Telemarketing and Consumer Fraud and Abuse Prevention Act. A brief description and link to each of these 70 statutes may be found at https://www.ftc.gov/enforcement/statutes (last visited September 2, 2022).

also a violation of the FTC Act. Section 5(a) of the FTC Act itself is straightforward:

> Unfair methods of competition in or affecting commerce, and unfair or deceptive acts or practices in or affecting commerce, are hereby declared unlawful.[654]

This language points to the FTC's two distinct programs that define its single statutory mission, which involves protecting consumers by protecting both competition itself and the consumer marketplace.

A.   Competition

On the competition side, Section 5's prohibition against unfair methods of competition has been held to subsume Sections 1 and 2 of the Sherman Act; and in that sense, the FTC is sometimes said to enforce the Sherman Act's prohibitions on unreasonable restraints of trade, such as monopolization and collusion. In addition to enforcing the Sherman Act antitrust standards under Section 5, the Commission may sometimes bring "stand alone" Section 5 cases to challenge anticompetitive conduct that is not expressly covered by the Sherman Act. Examples of such conduct-related matters would include "invitations to collude" and certain patent abuse cases.

Besides Section 5, the FTC's principal competition statute is Section 7 of the Clayton Act, which prohibits mergers and acquisitions that may substantially lessen competition.[655] Relatedly, the Commission is charged with administering and enforcing the Hart-Scott-Rodino ("HSR") Antitrust Improvements Act (also variously known as the HSR Act, the premerger notification statute, or Section 7A of the Clayton Act), which requires notification to the Commission about large mergers before they occur. Notably, while the HSR Act provides an opportunity

---

[654] 15 U.S.C.A. § 45(a)(1).

[655] 15 U.S.C.A. § 18 (West).

for FTC review of potentially anticompetitive mergers by requiring merging parties who meet certain threshold requirements[656] to provide notice and wait to close the merger while an investigation takes place, Section 7 challenges can still be raised for parties who do not file the notice and/or have already closed the transaction.[657]

With respect to the HSR Act, the Commission, along with the Department of Justice, promulgates the rules governing premerger notification requirements. In addition, the Commission may itself enforce compliance with the HSR Act's waiting period requirements or, through the Department of Justice, seek civil penalties for non-compliance.

In this way, the FTC and DOJ share responsibilities for investigating and challenging potentially anticompetitive mergers, albeit through different administrative processes and rules, which may affect the course of such investigations. While parties' filing of an HSR notification typically begins a 30-day waiting period, the agencies may issue a "Second Request," which imposes an additional waiting period until 30 days after the merging parties provide the additional requested information and discovery to the

---

[656] The thresholds that trigger an obligation for merging parties to file under the HSR Act are adjusted annually. See, e.g., FTC, HSR threshold adjustments and reportability for 2022 (Feb. 11, 2022), *available at* https://www.ftc.gov/enforcement/competition-matters/2022/02/hsr-threshold-adjustments-reportability-2022.

[657] *See* FTC, Adjusting merger review to deal with the surge in merger filings (Aug. 3, 2021), *available at* https://www.ftc.gov/enforcement/competition-matters/2021/08/adjusting-merger-review-deal-surge-merger-filings; see also R. Bell and A. Butler, Institutional Factors Contributing to the Under-Enforcement of Merger Law, The Antitrust Source (October 2020) at 13 (contains Unreported Mergers Challenged), *available at* https://www.americanbar.org/content/dam/aba/publishing/antitrust-magazine-online/2020/oct-2020/oct2020-bell-2.pdf.

requesting agency.[658] The agencies and parties may extend the statutory waiting period to close the transaction by agreement.[659]

Many, though not all, Second Requests are broad in scope and involve large productions of data and documents. In addition, not only are merging parties often incentivized to comply quickly with a Second Request, but because the requests are "continuing in nature," parties generally try to comply relatively quickly to avoid continuing burdens of continually collecting, reviewing, and producing new documents.[660] Therefore, parties' compliance with Second Requests can often be burdensome, fast, and furious.

Beyond Second Requests issued to merging parties, the FTC may also issue civil investigative demands ("CIDs"), further discussed below, to third parties as part of merger investigations.

B.   Consumer Protection

On the consumer protection side, the Commission principally enforces Section 5's prohibitions against unfair or deceptive acts or practices.[661] Section 5(n) of the FTC Act codifies the unfairness standard and provides that an act or practice is unfair if it "causes

---

[658] In the case of cash tender offers or bankruptcy sales, the waiting period after an HSR filing is 15 days and a Second Request can extend the waiting period through ten days after the acquiring person complies. *Id.*

[659] *See* Bruce Hoffman, Timing is Everything: The Model Timing Agreement, Bureau of Competition, Federal Trade Commission (Aug. 7, 2018), *available at* https://www.ftc.gov/enforcement/competition-matters/2018/08/timing-everything-model-timing-agreement.

[660] See FTC Model Second Request (Oct. 2021) at 16, Instruction I.2. (productions must be current to within 45 days of compliance and within 21 days for certain specifications). The length of the actual permitted period can vary from the Model Second Request, *available at* https://www.ftc.gov/system/files/attachments/hsr-resources/model_second_request_-_final_-_october_2021.pdf.

[661] *See LabMD, Inc. v. Fed. Trade Comm'n*, 894 F.3d 1221 (11th Cir. 2018)(setting aside a Commission Final Order on the grounds it was too vague to be enforced, but not questioning the Commission's ability to exercise its power under Section; *In re Equifax, Inc., Customer Data Sec. Breach Litig.*, 362 F. Supp. 3d 1295, 1328 (N.D. Ga. 2019).

or is likely to cause substantial injury to consumers which is not reasonably avoidable by consumers themselves and not outweighed by countervailing benefits to consumers or competition."[662] Recent FTC enforcement initiatives show that consumer injury under the unfairness doctrine does not need to have a monetary component to be actionable.[663] Generally, deception cases concern practices that involve material misrepresentations, which are those that a consumer may reasonably be expected to rely upon. A material misrepresentation may be direct or indirect, express or implied, and it need not be misleading to all people. It need only be misleading to a significant minority of reasonable consumers.

As noted above, the FTC administers or enforces more than 70 statutes, and many (if not most) of those relating to consumers point back to Section 5, providing that a violation of the relevant statute is a violation of Section 5. For the most part, these consumer protection statutes fit into three subject areas: (1) financial practices (*e.g.*, Fair Credit Reporting Act, the Fair Debt Collection Practices Act); (2) marketing practices (*e.g.*, the Telemarketing and Consumer Fraud and Abuse Prevention Act, the Fair Packaging and Labeling Act); and (3) privacy (*e.g.*, the Children's Online Privacy Protection Act, the Gramm-Leach-Bliley Act). In addition to enforcement in these subject areas under specific statutes, the FTC also brings enforcement actions based on deceptive conduct relating to these areas. For example, with respect to privacy protections, the FTC has enforced violations directly under Section 5 against parties who misled consumers by

---

[662] 15 U.S.C.A. § 45(n).

[663] *See, e.g., FTC v. Kochava, Inc.,* No. 2:22-cv-377 (D. Idaho) filed August 29, 2022 (alleging that sale of geolocation data improperly allows "entities to track consumers movements to and from sensitive locations."); *see also,* Cohen, Kristin, "Location, health, and other sensitive information: FTC committed to fully enforcing the law against illegal use and sharing of highly sensitive data", *available at* https://www.ftc.gov/business-guidance/blog/2022/07/location-health-other-sensitive-information-ftc-committed-fully-enforcing-law-against-illegal-use (last visited, August 31, 2022) (collecting and summarizing recent cases).

promising to protect consumer data that was not actually
adequately protected.[664]

The FTC Act also allows the Commission to challenge violations
of its orders and rules. And in this regard, the FTC has recently
sought to reinvigorate its rulemaking process by, for example,
seeking public comment relating to harms caused by commercial
surveillance and lax data security practices.[665]

III. CONFIDENTIALITY AND FTC INVESTIGATIVE TOOLS

Information the FTC receives in investigations is exempt from
disclosure under the Freedom of Information Act ("FOIA"), and
the FTC's right to disclose or use the information is limited by
statute. The protections are set out in Sections 6(f) and 21 of the
FTC Act, in Section 7A(h) of the Clayton Act in the case of
premerger materials, and in Commission Rules of Practice 4.10
and 4.11. Thus, Section 21 exempts from disclosure under FOIA
all materials the Commission receives in any investigation
pursuant to compulsory process, or that are provided voluntarily in
lieu thereof. Together with the Commission's Rules of Practice,
this prohibits the Commission from disclosing the material except
in the following circumstances: (a) in response to formal requests
from Congress (with notification to the producing party); (b) in
cases where the Commission is a party; and (c) to other law
enforcement agencies, provided the requesting agency certifies that
it will maintain confidentiality and use the material only for law
enforcement purposes.[666] However, this authority to disclose
information to other law enforcement agencies does not extend, to

---

[664] FTC, Privacy and Security Enforcement, *available at*
https://www.ftc.gov/news-events/topics/protecting-consumer-privacy-
security/privacy-security-enforcement (last viewed September 2, 2022).

[665] *See,* https://www.ftc.gov/news-events/news/press-releases/2022/08/ftc-
explores-rules-cracking-down-commercial-surveillance-lax-data-security-
practices (last viewed August 31, 2022). In this last instance, the materials may
not be used in any proceeding without prior authorization from the Commission
and notice to the producing party.

[666] 15 U.S.C.A. § 57b-2 (West).

foreign law enforcement authorities, except in very limited circumstances. Similarly, Section 6(f) provides that the Commission, with limited exceptions, "shall not have any authority to make public any trade secret or any commercial or financial information which is obtained from any person and which is privileged or confidential...."[667] Finally, if a party who voluntarily discloses information to the Commission designates the information as confidential and the Commission disagrees with that designation, it may disclose the information, but only after giving the producing party at least 10 days' notice,[668] during which time the interested party may seek a protective order or other relief. Of course, if a party gives its express consent, the Commission may disclose any information the party is willing to have disclosed.

The FTC has a wide range of resources for gathering information in a pre-complaint investigation. At one end of the spectrum, the FTC's statutes allow it to—and in practice, the Agency does— encourage voluntary cooperation by issuing access letters,[669] which are unenforceable requests for information.[670] As already noted, the FTC Act protects such information by affording it the same level of confidential treatment that it provides to information it receives through the compulsory process.[671]

On the other end of the spectrum, the FTC may compel parties to give information. For example, in competition conduct investigations, but generally not in consumer protection investigations, the FTC may issue orders directing persons to submit "special reports" providing detailed information about their

---

[667] 15 U.S.C.A. § 46(f) (West).

[668] 16 C.F.R. § 4.10(e).

[669] 15 U.S.C.A. § 46(a), 49; *see also* FTC Rule 2.4, 16 C.F.R. § 2.4.

[670] *See Fed. Trade Comm'n v. Am. Tobacco Co.*, 264 U.S. 298, 44 S. Ct. 336, 68 L. Ed. 696 (1924).

[671] *See* 15 U.S.C.A. § 57b-2(f), FTC Rule 4.10(a)(8)(ii), 16 C.F.R. § 4.10(a)(8)(ii).

conduct and other matters.[672] Such orders are judicially enforceable,[673] and failure to comply with a court order of enforcement may result in the imposition of civil penalties, which accrue daily.[674] In its competition investigations, the FTC additionally has the power to issue administrative subpoenas for documents or live testimony almost anywhere in the country.[675] Finally, in all its investigations, the FTC has the authority to issue civil investigative demands ("CIDs") that may compel the recipient to provide information through interrogatory-style questions, produce documentary materials, or appear and give testimony at investigational hearings.[676] FTC CIDs and subpoenas are both judicially enforceable, and those who do not comply with a court's enforcement order may face contempt charges,[677] or even adverse inference or curative sanctions under Federal Rule 37(e)[678]

The premerger notification statute, the HSR Act,[679] lies somewhere between "voluntary" and "compulsory." On the one hand, that Act authorizes the FTC (or DOJ) to request detailed information relating to covered transactions. On the other hand, the parties are not required to respond to the requests – although they are forbidden to consummate their transaction unless they observe a

---

[672] 15 U.S.C.A. § 46(b). The Commission's authority to order such reports is limited to investigations that do not involve unfair or deceptive acts or practices. 15 U.S.C.A. § 57b-1(b) (West).

[673] 15 U.S.C.A. § 49 (West).

[674] 15 U.S.C.A. § 50 (West).

[675] 15 U.S.C.A. § 49.

[676] 15 U.S.C.A. § 57b-1.

[677] 15 U.S.C.A. § 49, 57b-1(h). *See, e.g.*, Stipulation for Entry of Order, *FTC v. W. Union Co.,* No. 13-mc-00131 AKH (S.D.N.Y. Dec. 9, 2013), ECF No. 67. Other agencies have also successfully sought civil contempt against parties who disobeyed court orders. *See, e.g.*, Contempt Order, *SEC v. Coronati,* No. 13-mc-00372-P1 (S.D.N.Y. Jan. 17, 2014), ECF No. 19.

[678] *See, FTC v. Nolan,* No. 20-cv-00047 DWL (D. Ariz. August 30, 2021) (adverse inference for destruction of documents); *FTC v. Vyera Pharms., LLC,* 2021 U.A. Dist. LEXIS 102689 (S.D.N.Y. June 1, 2021 (prohibiting testimony by a witness and barring introduction of documents prepared by same person).

[679] 15 U.S.C.A. § 18a (West).

statutory waiting period after providing either all the requested information or a detailed statement of reasons why they cannot provide it.[680] Failure to comply with the HSR reporting and waiting period requirements may trigger a court action to enjoin the transaction until there has been compliance,[681] an action to rescind the transaction if it has been consummated,[682] or a suit for substantial civil penalties which accrue daily.[683]

While the FTC's investigative tools have remained constant since 1994,[684] FTC antitrust investigations have grown in size and complexity. While the expansion of electronic data has contributed mightily to the complexity of such investigations and cases, the Commission's recently expanded inquiry into these matters has further enlarged the demand for information and the volume of materials that must be produced by parties and reviewed and analyzed by Commission staff.

The quantity of data responsive to FTC demands is at times vast. As in other matters involving discovery, this is compounded by the complexities of modern data storage and types. Every major business uses an array of computer systems, applications, networks, electronic devices, and social media tools to administer its operations, transact business, and communicate both internally and externally. The vast post-2019 increase in remote working has exacerbated the problem. Email, voicemail, instant messages, text messages, tweets, word processing, spreadsheets, presentations, and data compilations move freely and quickly through (and often outside) an enterprise's systems, and in various forms may be modified, preserved, replicated, and archived in the process.

---

[680] *See* 18 U.S.C. § 18a(a), (e); 16 C.F.R. § 803.3.

[681] 15 U.S.C.A. § 18a(g)(2).

[682] *See, e.g., F.T.C. v. Elders Grain, Inc.*, 868 F.2d 901 (7th Cir. 1989) (granting rescission on the merits).

[683] 15 U.S.C.A. § 18a(g)(1).

[684] The U.S. SAFE Web Act expanded the Commission's ability to provide investigative assistance to foreign governments, but did not enlarge the set of investigative tools at the FTC's disposal. *See* 15 U.S.C.A. § 46(j).

Despite restrictions imposed by employers, employees often work around the information structure of the enterprise and generate, carry, or transmit data and information off-site or into impermissible places. In addition, cloud-based applications, as well as social networking sites, are hosted by third parties. Further, organizations increasingly allow employees to conduct business on any device they choose, rather than restricting them to company-owned equipment. Thus, important information can be widely dispersed across corporate networks, third-party servers, company-owned and privately-owned devices, electronic media storage (*e.g.*, thumb drives and CD-ROMS), and Internet websites.

In order to retrieve all the relevant electronic evidence and identify those with knowledge of it, the government must cast a broad net; this need often results in substantial demands on investigative targets and others. Indeed, discovery burdens on the target become even more pronounced when responsive information is located outside the United States and in countries with data protection, privacy or localization laws, or blocking statutes that impede the transfer of information to the United States.

IV. HOW FTC INVESTIGATIONS BEGIN

Except in merger cases, where the parties have usually planned their transactions with an eye on the antitrust laws, parties often have little opportunity to shape an FTC investigation at its nascent stages. Information that triggers an investigation may come from many different sources, ranging from news reports to consumer complaints, leaked information, Congressional inquiries, or referrals from other agencies—state, federal, or foreign. No matter the origin, the FTC Commissioners and Bureau Directors control the process, and the Commission opens a formal investigation if a majority of voting Commissioners approve it—at which time the Commission will issue a Resolution Authorizing Compulsory Process (the "Resolution"). The Resolution identifies the target or potential targets of the investigation, the conduct being investigated, and the legal basis for the inquiry.

Notably, the Resolution is not the Commissioners' last contact with the matter. Although the actual investigators – meaning the staff working on the matter directly -- is responsible for drawing up the specifications for each subpoena and CID, they have no authority to issue compulsory process. By law, all compulsory process issued by the FTC must be signed by an individual Commissioner. This means that staff must prepare the papers and submit them to the Commissioner assigned to the matter, who in turn must review and sign them before the FTC's Secretary may serve them.

No matter how FTC investigations begin, they typically fall into two categories: (1) those that the parties cannot anticipate because they are not aware of the FTC's concerns about a matter or business practice; and (2) those that they can anticipate because they are engaging in activities that are likely to trigger an inquiry or are related to other active, already known, inquiries. In the former situation, the parties usually have little or no opportunity to shape the FTC's inquiry because the groundwork for the inquiry is laid before the investigation officially begins. However, parties who can anticipate an investigation and who are willing to engage the FTC proactively—sometimes even before any event can trigger an inquiry—have some opportunity to shape the investigation by discussing matters that they believe may raise particular concerns. Parties who are candid and cooperative in this early engagement have a unique potential to focus and limit the scope of an inquiry (or at least better understand it). For example, parties planning a merger or acquisition may find it useful to meet with Commission staff early if they are aware of potential competitive concerns that might be raised by the transaction.

V.   RESPONDING TO FTC INVESTIGATIONS

Companies employ one or a combination of three methods in responding to FTC inquiries. First, some believe in "making the government work for it." At least one corporate counsel has said that the best approach is to deploy litigation counsel to deal with every government inquiry because there is no reason not to consider each matter to be an adversarial one in which counsel should "push back" at every opportunity. Second, some take an approach of cooperating but communicating at a bare minimum with the FTC. They volunteer nothing, leave FTC staff to figure out what it needs, and surrender only precisely what is requested either on the date that it is due or when threatened with enforcement. They engage in dialogue with staff only when, and if, the staff starts the conversation. Third, others cooperate by engaging early and often with the FTC to determine what the Agency seeks and what it needs, providing the requested materials on time, and proactively working with staff to find the best way to focus the inquiry narrowly while addressing the Agency's concerns.

It is generally impossible for FTC staff to distinguish between those who have something to hide, those who have nothing to hide but are clueless about the process, and those who are merely taking a "make-them-work-for-it" approach. Practitioners who take either of the first two approaches may well be seeking to advocate a strongly held view of the merits from the outset. However, the approach entails a bet that the FTC will back off, either from exhaustion or intimidation, and not pursue an investigation thoroughly if the company plays hardball. It could be a risky bet that may cost the company dearly in the long run,[685] as it depletes human and capital resources while the investigation methodically grinds through each new lead the investigators uncover.[686] Once the FTC authorizes compulsory process, it should be assumed that the inquiry will continue until the Commission determines whether an enforcement action may be warranted.

---

[685] See, nn.32, 33, supra.

[686] Note too, that, while courts may employ proportionality factors to require the requesting party in litigation to bear part of the cost of discovery (see Fed. R. Civ. P. 26(c)(1)(B)), cost-shifting mechanisms are rarely available to those subject to an FTC investigation, or even to third parties. See, e.g., F.T.C. v. Texaco, Inc., 555 F.2d 862, 882 (D.C. Cir. 1977)(enforcement of compulsory process will not be denied on grounds of burdensomeness and breadth, absent a showing that "compliance threatens to unduly disrupt or seriously hinder normal operations of a business"), cert. denied, 431 U.S. 974 (1977). The one exception to this is a rarely invoked Section of the FTC Act, which allows a party responding to a CID to reduce its costs by making copies of the requested materials available at its business location for FTC staff to inspect and copy or reproduce. 15 U.S.C.A. § 57b-2(b)(2)(B).

The third option, cooperation, does not preclude a practitioner from maintaining an arms-length relationship with the Agency and from fully and vigorously representing a client's interests. To be clear, cooperation requires only honesty, candor, and a willingness to work with the Agency to address the issues. Admittedly, the approach all but guarantees that the FTC will find the relevant information it seeks, and will deal with any law violation that it uncovers, but it can also offer distinct advantages. Although it usually does not lead to leniency *per se*, it at least gives the company an opportunity to focus and narrow the inquiry, with a consequently more speedy and relatively less expensive resolution of the matter.

Whatever the approach, counsel must ensure it has enough information to make accurate representations regarding the matter. The FTC has reminded counsel that intentionally misleading the Commission could lead to "public reprimands, sanctions and even disbarment" from practicing before the Commission.[687]

VI. PRACTICAL WAYS TO APPROACH FTC DOCUMENT REQUESTS

There are two practical pieces of advice for dealing with FTC investigations that are so obvious that they can be overlooked. First, a person receiving an FTC investigation request should read Part 2 of the Commission's Rules of Practice, 16 C.F.R. § 2.1 *et seq.* These Rules tell practitioners everything they must know about the FTC's investigative processes and procedures involved. Second, after reading the Rules carefully, the person should read the request and any attachments that accompany it. These documents identify the people to contact at the FTC, the purpose and scope of the inquiry, the type and categories of information the FTC is seeking, and the manner in which the FTC would like to receive it.

---

[687] *Joining the Issues on the High Road*, FED. TRADE COMM'N, *available at* https://www.ftc.gov/news-events/blogs/competition-matters/2019/05/joining-issues-high-road (last visited August 31, 2022).

Regarding the specific requests, the recipient should keep two overarching facts in mind when reading them:

First,

The FTC staff rarely knows anything about the organizational structure of any specific corporation; or the manner in which it creates, distributes, analyzes, uses, retains, and destroys records.

Second,

The FTC staff is frequently under pressure to complete investigations promptly and without making repeated demands for information.

FTC staff keep these facts in mind when shaping requests for documents and information. Therefore, their instructions regarding the definition of the "target," and the scope of the expected search for responsive information, is often very broad, with their instructions telling a party that to comply fully, it must search every desk and file drawer, even in its affiliates' offices, as well as every computer, server, cloud-based source, notebook, smartphone, phone mail system, tablet, and other device that may hold responsive information.[688]

The instructions for producing electronic files are similarly comprehensive: providing instructions on producing personal information;[689] and specifying whether files must be submitted in native format, in image format with extracted text and metadata, in image format accompanied by optical character recognition

---

[688] *See* Fed. Trade Comm'n. *Model Request for Additional Information and Documentary Material (Second Request)*, FED. TRADE COMM'N, 13 (October 2021) [hereinafter "Model Second Request"], *available at* https://www.ftc.gov/system/files/attachments/hsr-resources/model_second_request_-_final_-_october_2021.pdf (last visited September 1, 2022).

[689] *Id.* at 16 ¶ 13

("OCR"), or some combination thereof.[690] The instructions may address the metadata fields that must be submitted; the use of de-duplication or email threading software; the criteria for submitting data, such as data in Excel spreadsheets; and the media to be used in submitted productions.[691] The instructions also include interrogatory questions regarding the use of electronic production tools or software packages, including Technology Assisted Review ("TAR").[692]

Unless the recipient of an investigative demand is prepared to face the consequences of conducting an inadequate search or of having important evidence obliterated, its lawyers should discuss search and preservation with the investigators before committing to a discovery plan. That conversation should generally address, at minimum, the following six subjects: (1) the scope of the search, both as to time periods and as to custodians; (2) data preservation and retrieval issues, if any problems are anticipated, including email, voicemail, tweets and instant messages, social media, and cloud sources; (3) privilege logs; (4) materials located outside the United States and whether the parties expect delays or difficulty in getting them (and if so, how they will address the issues); and (5) the timing and staging of production.

A.   Implementing a Litigation Hold / Directing Preservation

At common law, the duty to preserve evidence attaches when a person with possession, custody, or control over the evidence reasonably anticipates litigation in which that evidence may be relevant. Under Rule 37 of the Federal Rules of Civil Procedure, a party who fails to produce relevant evidence may face substantial sanctions.[693] The FTC does not have immediate access to Rule 37 sanctions—at least not until after it files a case—but it can enforce

---

[690] *Id.* at 17-21 ¶ 14.

[691] *Id.*

[692] *Id.* at 22 ¶ 15.

[693] Fed. R. Civ. P. 37.

its pre-complaint discovery demands and, in some instances, exact penalties for non-compliance. For the FTC, the most significant tools are the ability to seek judicial enforcement of its compulsory process, and then civil contempt against those who do not obey court orders enforcing such process. In addition, the FTC has the option of referring obstruction of justice cases to the Department of Justice for prosecution.[694]

The potential for civil and criminal liability shows the importance of a party taking immediate steps to preserve information when it has notice of an actual or contemplated government inquiry. Because every law enforcement investigation, by definition, suggests the possibility of a follow-on enforcement action, even when the party does not expect a government inquiry to result in litigation, the party should always consider preserving relevant information until it knows the investigation is concluded.[695] This is so because the FTC has the right to conduct investigations, even if it is only "seeking assurance" that the law is not being violated. Also, in many situations, it has the authority to "investigate" matters, for the purpose of preparing a study or a report.[696] In short, lawsuits and sanctions are not always the object of investigations. Parties who ignore or, worse yet, "dispose" of information responsive to even an "informal" inquiry do so at their peril.

The principles that govern retention in investigations are the same principles that govern retention in civil litigation: parties are to take prompt and reasonable—not Herculean—steps to preserve and stop the routine destruction and disposition of relevant materials. This requires identifying the custodians of relevant

---

[694] 18 U.S.C.A. §§ 1505, 1506, 1509, 1519, 1520 (West); *See,* "Former Health Care Staffing Executive Convicted of Obstructing FTC Investigation into Wage-Fixing Allegation" , Department of Justice, Office of Public Affairs (April 14, 2022), *available at* https://www.justice.gov/opa/pr/former-health-care-staffing-executive-convicted-obstructing-ftc-investigation-wage-fixing (last visited, September 1, 2022). In addition, civil contempt can sometimes result in imprisonment. *See, e.g., Coronati, supra* note 20.

[695] See 16 C.F.R. § 2.14(c).

[696] 15 U.S.C.A. § 46(b).

information, informing them of their obligation to preserve relevant information and materials, and following up to ensure that they are complying. It also means identifying non-custodial sources of potentially relevant electronic or non-electronic information and implementing procedures to ensure that such information will not be destroyed. To the extent information is located outside the United States, it may also mean that parties may need to take additional steps to retain the information the government seeks. Finally, parties must always remember to document what they are doing to preserve information in order to have a contemporaneous and accurate record of what they did and the reasons they did it.

Parties also need to consider when they can remove a litigation hold, which can be difficult as they may not know when an investigation has closed. The FTC's preservation requirements cease for parties twelve months after the last written communication by the FTC with a party or its counsel.[697]

B.   Preparation: Assessing the Landscape / Developing a Plan

Those who have regular interactions with the FTC or who plan mergers or acquisitions know that advance preparation can pay big dividends. In those situations, best practices—in addition to retaining experts and meeting with Agency staff in advance— include establishing internal procedures that anticipate the inquiries and assembling a "SWAT team" of personnel both inside and outside of the company who are prepared to assist in responding to an investigation.

The first step in dealing with an FTC inquiry is to develop a discovery and disclosure plan. Records and information generally fit into two categories. Either they are "corporate" files found in centralized storage places (such as shared network folders or workspaces, or databases which may or may not be in cloud-based storage applications), or they are "custodian-based" files that are

---

[697] *See,* n.50, *supra.*

either (1) network-based files that are readily associated with particular custodians (such as email or voicemail); or (2) files maintained off-network in localized sources (such as file drawers, personal computers, corporate-owned or "bring your own device" smartphones or tablets, or portable media such as CDs and flash drives). These groups, and the type and volume of accessible data within each group, shape negotiations about the scope of the search and ultimate production. Although information located outside the United States will largely fit into the same two categories, the responding company will need a plan for dealing with any applicable data protection, privacy or localization laws, or blocking statutes that may affect the company's ability to respond in a timely manner.

The Commission's Resolution (which is attached to every subpoena and CID) defines the scope of each formal Commission investigation — it identifies the subject matter and time periods of interest and sets the potential boundaries of the search. Accordingly, the best way to understand the scope of the search for corporate files is often to talk to Commission staff about the issues that are of concern and the time periods and sources of relevant information that need to be produced. To do this, counsel will want to know the structure and content of corporate data systems and any special costs or burdens associated with retrieving data from those systems or have someone who does know these things join the meeting with staff. Once counsel defines and understands the scope of what may be relevant, he or she can draw distinctions between the corporate sources that are essential, those that are marginal and might not need to be searched or reviewed if the essential files are sufficient to satisfy the FTC's needs, and those that are irrelevant or only arguably relevant.

Custodian-based files present a different problem. Production of information from those sources often requires an interview of the custodians and a search of each custodian's files to separate the relevant from the irrelevant and the privileged relevant from the non-privileged relevant. Even with the use of TAR and other efficiency-enhancing technologies and processes, this is often a very expensive and labor-intensive effort. Thus, one important key to minimizing cost and burden is to limit the number of custodians. This requires a thorough understanding of both the formal and informal organizational structure, the allocation of job responsibilities, and the way people and offices communicate and interact. With that knowledge, counsel can identify the personnel who have direct, unique knowledge of the relevant issues, those who have no knowledge (even though to an outsider it may appear otherwise) or whose information will be wholly duplicative of other custodians, and those who are somewhere in the middle. After making these determinations, counsel may propose a list of custodians and undertake some sample searches to see how the search plan will work and may wish to share the results of those sample searches with the FTC. He or she might also be able to propose a staged production, where key custodian files are produced first and files from other "relevant but not critical" custodians are deferred. Note that departed employees may still be relevant custodians based on the relevant time period, and the FTC frequently requires including predecessor custodians who have held a current custodian employee's role.

In addition to limiting the number of custodians, counsel may also seek to limit the type and volume of data files that must be searched for each custodian. After counsel determines which data sets are relevant to the investigation, he or she should then learn how the company collects, maintains, and uses that data as well as any software used to maintain and analyze it. Email, short message chats, and other digital communications are the primary means of communication today. They also enable wide input into final written materials. As a result, digital messages, their attachments, and draft documents all have an uncanny ability to show up at unexpected times and in unexpected places. They can be expensive to deal with because of their enormous volume. If the FTC's demand for them is not limited, they and their associated files and emails must all be located, collected, processed, analyzed, and reviewed for responsiveness and privilege and, if privileged, logged. In developing the response plan, counsel should consider preparing data samples to demonstrate the types of information the company has and the capabilities of its systems and software to sort and analyze electronic information.

Besides limiting the number of custodians whose files must be searched and the types of files that must be searched, another key to minimizing the cost and burden of an investigation—one that works not only for email and word processing documents, but for other electronic information as well—is to use one or more advanced technology options that use computer software to assist in determining "relevance" based on user-selected criteria, which may include "seed sets." In this regard, TAR applications or artificial intelligence ("AI"), can be especially effective and efficient when properly used and verified. And indeed, the FTC's Model Second Request specifies the means for validating the use of such technologies.[698] Other techniques, such as the use of search terms, concept clustering, de-duplication, near de-duplication, and email threading, can yield efficiencies. Each variation of each technology is different; and the results are greatly influenced by the particular program and protocols employed in the process, as well as the skill and knowledge of the humans doing the work. Thus, early in the planning stage counsel should design his or her project management workflow, including which specific TAR or AI applications will be used. Always assume the FTC will ask for all the details of a party's search and review processes and technologies. As mentioned previously, the Commission routinely asks for detailed information about electronic searches and reviews in merger investigations. Ultimately, in presenting any technological approach to FTC staff, candor and transparency will be critical to acceptance of the final production.

Finally, counsel should assess the time periods that may be relevant for each set of relevant documents and data. A reduction in the time period across which data must be searched will usually result in substantial savings in search, review, and production costs. However, counsel should be mindful that a one-size-fits-all approach might not be appropriate for all searches, even within the same investigation. For example, some data sets may make sense only when viewed over several seasonal cycles. Similarly, it may be appropriate to take a longer look back into the individual emails

---

[698] *See,* n.43 *supra.*

of some employees, while a shorter period may be appropriate for others. Counsel should draw rational lines when seeking to limit discovery periods and be prepared to be transparent and candid with the FTC about the reasoning underlying those choices.

After counsel has identified the appropriate files and custodians, and the appropriate periods for searching each, he or she can develop a systematic plan and methodology for searching and producing relevant information from those files. Depending on the case and circumstances, that plan might include a suggestion that the investigation proceeds in a layered fashion, whereby the company first produces "core" files, and the FTC agrees to give those files at least a preliminary look before determining whether to require additional information (including especially information that may not be readily available due to foreign laws).

C.   Presenting the Plan

The next step in dealing with the FTC is to convince the staff to accept the discovery plan or something close to it. Here it is especially important to know the Commission's Rules of Practice. A careful reading of the Rules and the available proactive guides show several steps that a party may consider taking, should they wish to take a cooperative approach with the FTC:

- Meet with staff as soon as possible. When the parties anticipate an investigation, this may mean meeting before the investigation is formally opened.

- Provide staff with organization charts or equivalent materials so they can identify the parties' employees and their positions.

- Provide staff with brief written descriptions of the responsibilities of each person the investigators identify as a person whose files might be searched.

- Present the discovery plan and ideally provide sample search results so the staff can assess the plan and methodology.

- Make one or more knowledgeable people readily (and repeatedly) available to staff. These people should be knowledgeable about the issues and be able to assist staff in identifying people whose files must be searched.

- Discuss with staff the types and forms of electronic data the parties maintain and provide data samples to assist them in determining what data and data compilations are available.

- Discuss documents and information that is not located in the United States and explore the potential for staggered productions, for culling and de-duplicating to eliminate redundant materials, and explore the use of other data-minimization tools.

- Make available to staff one or more people thoroughly knowledgeable about the parties' computer systems and software and the way in which the parties collect, store, maintain, analyze, and use the data and other electronic information that is relevant to the investigation. Note that these people are not necessarily the same people mentioned in the fifth bullet in this paragraph.

- Where appropriate to the investigation, discuss the parties' own economic or financial analyses with (and suggest appropriate analyses to) staff. In doing so, the parties should provide backup data and information to enable staff to test the parties' data, programs, and results.

- Consider submitting "white papers" that address the issues and provide a sound analysis of the issues from the parties' perspectives.

The goal is to provide the FTC with the relevant information it needs to finish its investigation while limiting the cost and burden for the parties, particularly with respect to the production of information that may be unnecessary, duplicative, or only tangentially relevant. Phased or prioritized discovery can often achieve these goals, particularly when combined with a good faith effort to address the FTC's concerns through voluntary submissions on the merits.

D. Privilege Issues

To avoid confusion, parties should discuss two privilege-related issues with staff: waivers and privilege logs. In some limited situations, parties are willing to knowingly waive privilege claims and allow staff to review at least some of their privileged materials.[699] The FTC's policy is to return privileged documents that are produced unintentionally.[700] If parties intend to waive any privilege claims, they should make this clear at the outset so the FTC is able to distinguish between the documents staff may review

---

[699] This paper does not discuss the scope or implications of such intentional waivers and does not consider whether they result in waivers as to third parties.

[700] *See, e.g.*, Fed. R. Evid. 502(a); Commission Rule 2.11(d)(1)(ii), 16 C.F.R. § 2.11(d)(1)(ii). Similarly, in the merger context the FTC's Bureau of Competition has said: "By 'inadvertent production' [the Bureau of Competition] refer[s] to the established body of case law that defines truly inadvertent production as a mistake that occurs despite the existence and use of reasonable procedures to screen out privileged materials. This situation differs from production that occurs because of negligence so significant that — taking into account the totality of the circumstances, including the extent and timing of production—it may still constitute a waiver." Statement of the Federal Trade Commission's Bureau of Competition on Guidelines for Merger Investigations, ¶ 3 (footnote omitted), *available at* www.ftc.gov/system/files/documents/public_events/114015/ftc_statement_on_gui delines_for_merger_investigations_12-22-02_2.pdf ("Bureau of Competition Guidelines) (last viewed September 1, 2022).

and those documents they must set aside to determine if they should be returned.

Complete privilege logs are usually time-consuming and expensive to produce, but the information in such logs is essential for determining whether documents are being withheld improperly. An agreement with the FTC concerning the preparation of a partial log can save time and money while meeting the investigative needs of the staff.

With respect to both waiver and the potential for reducing the privilege review/logging burden, civil litigants can rely on the protections of Federal Rule of Evidence 502.[701] That Rule governs the disclosure of privileged information in court proceedings or "to a federal office or agency," and may offer some prospect for relief from detailed privilege review in investigations. In brief, the Rule applies to work product materials and attorney-client communications. It provides that the intentional disclosure of such information usually results only in a waiver of the information disclosed (Rule 502(a)) and, if certain criteria are met, the inadvertent disclosure of such information results in no waiver (Rule 502(b)). The Rule further provides that agreements relating to the disclosure of privileged information (often referred to as "claw back" or "quick peek" agreements) are binding only on the parties to the agreement (Rule 502(e)). Such agreements will bind non-parties if the agreements are incorporated into court orders (Rule 502(d)).

Although Rule 502 leaves a gap with respect to pre-litigation agreements, such as those reached in a government investigation, subsections 502(d) and (e) suggest there is room for the government and private parties to negotiate claw back or quick peek agreements to facilitate privilege review during investigations. Such agreements would necessarily be reached before any court complaint is filed, but courts in any subsequent proceedings—either in law enforcement actions or in unrelated actions seeking access to the information provided to the

---

[701] Fed. R. Evid. 502.

government—may be willing to give effect to the purpose of Rule 502 and hold that such agreements do not constitute broad subject matter waivers. Alternatively, in appropriate cases, the FTC could, at least in principle, file a subpoena enforcement action and simultaneously ask the court to "So Order" a settlement that incorporates a claw back or quick peek agreement under its Rule 502(d) authority. Here, the FTC's Rule 2.11(d) closely tracks Rule 502 and signals the Commission's willingness to work with parties on these issues.

E. Legacy Systems, Archives, and Backup Tapes

If a party has recently deleted or lost relevant electronic information, staff will often be interested in obtaining the same or equivalent information from alternative sources. As the FTC's Bureau of Competition has stated, "in our experience, in some cases the search of even a small portion of the parties' archive and backup systems produces valuable information that is helpful to the staff's investigation."[702] However, the FTC also recognizes that backup tapes are not always configured for routine document collection when they are intended solely for disaster recovery or archiving purposes and that review of backup tapes "is expensive and may be duplicative."[703]

To balance the potential cost to companies of reviewing disaster recovery tapes or other sources that are very difficult to access against the potential benefit to the government (and the public) in securing relevant evidence, the FTC's policy in merger cases is to "require a party to produce documents contained on backup tapes only when responsive documents are not available through other more accessible sources."[704] However, if a company uses backup

---

[702] Bureau of Competition Guidelines, *supra* n.55, ¶ 6(c).

[703] *Id.*

[704] *See* Deborah Platt Majoras, Chairman, Fed. Trade Comm'n, *Reforms to the Merger Review Process*, FED. TRADE COMM'N, 24 (Feb. 16, 2006) [hereinafter "Reforms to Merger Review"], *available at* http://www.ftc.gov/sites/default/files/attachments/mergers/mergerreviewprocess.pdf (last visited September 1, 2022).

tapes as its sole means of preserving material subject to a litigation hold or relevant to the investigation, it should expect the FTC in both merger and consumer protection cases to demand that the backup tapes be searched for relevant information. Thus, the question, at least initially, is not whether documents contained on backup tapes must be produced. Rather, the question is whether and how documents relevant to an investigation must be preserved, pending a determination of whether any or all of the backup tapes must be searched.

Here, too, the FTC's merger review policy statement offers a solution that might be applied in its other investigations:

> [A] party may elect to preserve backup tapes for only two calendar days identified by staff, and.... [i]f a party's document storage system does not permit designation of backup tapes for two specific calendar days, staff will work with the party to designate a comparable set of backup tapes that the party must preserve.[705]

FTC staff might not demand that a company preserve all backup tapes, but only a small subset, which may need to be reviewed if there are significant gaps in the materials obtained from other sources. However, the company puts itself at risk if it unilaterally decides which backup tapes to preserve and which to recycle. That determination should be made by the FTC after the counsel and staff have met "to discuss information about the archives and backup systems."[706] This is yet another topic for discussion between staff and counsel. There can be significant benefits in resolving questions about the preservation of backup tapes and other less accessible sources, particularly with respect to reducing costs and future litigation risks.

---

[705] *Id.*

[706] Bureau of Competition Guidelines, *supra* n.55, ¶ 6(c).

F. Parallel Investigations: Foreign and Domestic

Private conduct will sometimes interest more than one federal agency, raise concerns with various state agencies, and frequently get the attention of foreign authorities as well. In other words, multiple law enforcement agencies and jurisdictions may conduct parallel investigations. Not surprisingly, the FTC generally recognizes the advantages of cooperating with other agencies, foreign and domestic,[707] and that cooperation may take the form of sharing information and granting other foreign and domestic agencies access to FTC files. The FTC has also entered into several agreements and memoranda of understanding with various domestic agencies and foreign law enforcement authorities.[708] These agreements have the potential for facilitating the transfer and exchange of information across domestic agencies as well as across international borders, and the resulting sharing of information has the potential to benefit everyone. On the one hand, the agencies have "an interest in reaching, insofar as possible, consistent, or at least non-conflicting, outcomes."[709] On the other hand, the parties also benefit from speedier resolution of all matters, reduced discovery costs resulting from agency sharing,

---

[707] *See, e.g., Antitrust Guidelines for International Enforcement and Cooperation,* U.S. DEPT. OF JUSTICE & FED. TRADE COMM'N, ¶ 5 (Jan. 13, 2017), *available at* https://www.justice.gov/atr/internationalguidelines/download (last visited September 1, 2022).

[708] *See, e.g., International Competition and Consumer Protection Cooperation Agreements,* FED. TRADE COMM'N, *available at* http://www.ftc.gov/policy/international/international-cooperation-agreements (last September 1, 2022). An interesting example of international cooperation is the U.S. SAFE Web Act, which allows the FTC to assist foreign law enforcement agencies under certain conditions. *See In re FTC,* No. 13-mc-524-MJG, 2014 U.S. Dist. LEXIS 106214 (D. Md. Aug. 4, 2014) (enforcing an FTC Application under 28 U.S.C.A. § 1782 (West) to obtain information on behalf of the Canadian Competition Bureau).

[709] US-EU Merger Working Group, *Best Practices on Cooperation in Merger Investigations,* FED. TRADE COMM'N, ¶ 1 (Oct. 2011), *available at* http://www.ftc.gov/system/files/documents/public_statements/310481/111014eu merger.pdf (last visited September 1, 2022).

and less risk of facing conflicting (*i.e.,* mutually exclusive) regulatory requirements.

Notably, the benefits of international cooperation depend largely on the willingness of the investigative target to cooperate in the investigation. Such cooperation may include the granting of waivers to allow the jurisdictions to share information they might otherwise be barred from sharing. [710] It may also require the parties to engage in multilateral negotiations to coordinate the production of responsive materials and synchronize the investigations, so all jurisdictions conclude their investigations at more or less the same time.

VII.   CONCLUSION

The key to successfully navigating an FTC investigation lies in understanding the Commission's Rules of Practice, its law enforcement concerns, and its objectives; devising a comprehensive plan for efficiently getting the relevant non-privileged information to staff; and meeting with staff frequently throughout the process. It is an understatement to say the FTC is not anxious to spend time and resources reviewing irrelevant documents and data compilations. It is a rare civil investigation in which staff absolutely must have unlimited access to all the materials conceivably responsive to the original request. FTC staff is generally willing to talk meaningfully with counsel who demonstrate candor, transparency, and honesty. If a company knows that its conduct will likely result in an order to take corrective action, its best course is likely to "come clean," get all the facts out, and resolve the issue as quickly as possible. Conversely, if it honestly thinks the FTC's investigation is misdirected and unnecessary, the best way to address that is to lay

---

[710] *Id.* at ¶¶ 3-7. In this regard, the antitrust agencies have jointly published a Model Waiver of Confidentiality for international civil matters, along with a set of Frequently Asked Questions, to assist parties in determining how and when to waive confidentiality with the enforcement agencies. *See International Waivers of Confidentiality in FTC Antitrust Investigations*, Fed. Trade Comm'n, *available at* https://www.ftc.gov/policy/international/international-competition/international-waivers-confidentiality-ftc-antitrust (last visited September 1, 2022).

out the facts and let the FTC satisfy itself that the investigation can be closed. In either circumstance, cooperation generally works best.

Chapter 11

Consumer Financial Protection Bureau (CFPB) Investigations

By:

Alexandra Megaris
Ellen Berge
Jonathan Pompan
Brandon Wong[711]

I. INITIATION OF CFPB INVESTIGATIONS

The Dodd-Frank Wall Street Reform and Consumer Financial
Protection Act of 2010 (CFPA) gives the Consumer Financial
Protection Bureau (CFPB or "the Bureau") "significant discretion
to determine whether and when to open an investigation." The [712]
CFPB has the authority to investigate any potential violation of
federal consumer financial law within its jurisdiction, which
includes a prohibition against unfair, deceptive, and abusive acts or
practices, as well as 19 enumerated consumer protection
statutes.[713] The CFPB has concluded that "the public benefits from
a process whereby the Bureau can open and close investigations
efficiently."[714] That said, the CFPB regulations limit the ability to
open and close investigations to senior staff, namely the Assistant

---

[711] Alexandra Megaris, Ellen Berge, and Jonathan Pompan are Partners at
Venable LLP. Brandon Wong is an Associate at the firm.

[712] Final Rule, Docket No. CFPB-2011-0007, Rules Relating to Investigations
(June 6, 2012), https://files.consumerfinance.gov/f/201206_cfpb_final-rule_rules-
relating-to-investigations.pdf.

[713] 12 C.F.R. § 1080.3; Final Rule, Docket No. CFPB-2011-0007, Rules Relating
to Investigations (June 6, 2012),
https://files.consumerfinance.gov/f/201206_cfpb_final-rule_rules-relating-to-
investigations.pdf; 12 U.S.C. § 5511(c). For listing of all enumerated consumer
protection laws, see Appendix A.

[714] Final Rule, Docket No. CFPB-2011-0007, Rules Relating to Investigations
(June 6, 2012), https://files.consumerfinance.gov/f/201206_cfpb_final-rule_rules-
relating-to-investigations.pdf.

Director and Deputy Assistant Directors of the Office of Enforcement.[715]

The primary statute covering investigations is 12 U.S.C. § 5562, which, among other provisions, permits the CFPB to open investigations and issue civil investigative demands and subpoenas. More specific requirements and procedures are found in the implementing regulations, beginning at 12 C.F.R. § 1080. The CFPB Office of Enforcement has also published a manual of policies and procedures outlining the Bureau's investigative protocols.[716] Investigations are generally kept confidential, though the Bureau "may disclose the existence of an investigation to potential witnesses or third parties to the extent necessary to advance the investigation."[717] Of course, to the extent that any person under investigation files a petition to set aside or modify a civil investigative demand, that information may become public.[718]

The threshold for the Bureau to open an investigation is relatively low. According to the Bureau, "The Bureau is authorized to

---

[715] 12 C.F.R. § 1080.4; Final Rule, Docket No. CFPB-2011-0007, Rules Relating to Investigations (June 6, 2012), https://files.consumerfinance.gov/f/201206_cfpb_final-rule_rules-relating-to-investigations.pdf.

[716] CONSUMER FIN. PROT. BUREAU, POLICIES AND PROCEDURES MANUAL 34–95 (2021), https://files.consumerfinance.gov/f/documents/cfpb_enforcement-policies-and-procedures-memo_version-3.2_2022-02.pdf (hereinafter "CFPB Enforcement Manual").

[717] 12 C.F.R. § 1080.14(b); *see also* John *Doe Co. No 1 v. Consumer Fin. Prot. Bureau*, 195 F. Supp. 3d 9, at *19 (D.D.C. June 15, 2016) (noting the importance of identifying circumstances in which an investigation is disclosed); *Consumer Fin. Prot. Bureau v. Education Credit Management Corporation*, 2022 WL 102275, at *4 (D. Minn. Jan. 11, 2022) (noting that "the CFPB has authority to file a petition in federal district court when a party 'fails to comply with any civil investigative demand'" and that "[n]othing prohibits the CFPB from disclosing the existence of the investigation when it files said petition") (internal citation omitted); *John Doe v. Consumer Fin. Prot. Bureau*, 2015 WL 6317031, at *3 (D.D.C. Oct. 16, 2015) (determining that here "Plaintiffs have identified no statutory language or purpose that creates a confidentiality interest of the sort that compelled secrecy").

[718] 12 C.F.R. § 1080.6(g).

investigate merely on suspicion that any person has violated any provision of federal consumer financial law, or to seek assurance that a violation has not occurred."[719] Per the manual, the Bureau considers several factors when determining whether to open an investigation:

- The potential subject(s);

- The market in general;

- Bureau and Enforcement resources;

- The Enforcement Strategic Plan;

- Other Bureau divisions; and

- Law enforcement partners.[720]

These factors are quite broad, which allows for significant discretion and flexibility in how or when the Bureau opens or closes investigations. Some sources used by the Bureau to open an investigation include, but are not limited to, the following: publicly available research, a whistle-blower or other tip, any consumer complaint, and referrals from state attorneys general or another federal agency.[721] Sometimes the basis for opening an investigation may stem from non-public information or be a combination of non-public and public information. Regardless of how an investigation is opened, it is important to remember that

---

[719] CFPB Enforcement Manual, *supra* note 6, at 37; *see also Consumer Fin. Prot. Bureau v. Accrediting Council for Indep. Colls. & Schs.*, 854 F.3d 683, 688 (D.C. Cir. 2017) (internal citations omitted) (citing *United States v. Morton Salt Co.*, 338 U.S. 632, 642–43 (1950)) ("Pursuant to their 'power of inquisition,' agencies may use subpoenas to "investigate merely on suspicion that the law is being violated, or even just because [they] want[ ] assurance that it is not.").

[720] CFPB Enforcement Manual, *supra* note 6, at 37–39.

[721] For more on the beginnings of the CFPB's investigatory process, see *Life Cycle of an Enforcement Action*, CONSUMER FIN. PROT. BUREAU, https://www.consumerfinance.gov/enforcement/life-cycle-of-enforcement-action/ (last visited June 22, 2022).

because the Bureau can open an investigation on mere suspicion of a violation, the existence of an investigation does not indicate that the CFPB has evidence of any wrongdoing.[722]

II. WHAT IS THE SIGNIFICANCE OF RECEIVING A CIVIL INVESTIGATIVE DEMAND?

The CFPA authorizes the CFPB to issue civil investigative demands (CIDs) to persons or entities to investigate potential violations of federal consumer financial protection laws.[723] Generally, a CID will require the production of documentary material or tangible things, a written report, answers to questions, or oral testimony. Sometimes CIDs have a short deadline requiring immediate action. A Deputy Enforcement Director may authorize the response period to be negotiated and extended. At a minimum, receipt of a CID means that the CFPB's Office of Enforcement has opened an investigation related to some activity of a business. It also means that certain legal obligations have been imposed upon the recipient. Although CIDs are not self-executing documents, the CFPB can, and does, move to compel compliance through a United States District Court proceeding.[724]

Upon receipt of the CID, it is imperative that the recipient promptly (i) assess the scope of and the potentially responsive material required by the CID and (ii) determine whether the CID deadline can be met and/or if it should be necessary to file a petition to set aside or modify the CID. It can be challenging for a recipient to assess the CID and develop a response strategy within the Bureau's short meet and confer deadline (discussed further, below). Outside counsel frequently is engaged at the inception of a

---

[722] CFPB Enforcement Manual, *supra* note 6, at 37.

[723] 12 U.S.C. § 5562(c).

[724] *Id.* at § 5562(e); *see Consumer Fin. Prot. Bureau v. Educ. Credit Mgmt. Corp.*, 2022 WL 102275, at *4 (D. Minn. Jan. 11, 2022) (demonstrating that the CFPB filed a motion to compel for allegedly withheld email documents); *see also Consumer Fin. Prot. Bureau v. Accrediting Council for Indep. Colls. & Schs.*, 854 F.3d 683, 688 (D.C. Cir. 2017); *Morgan Drexen, Inc. v. Consumer Fin. Prot. Bureau*, 785 F.3d 684, 694, 698 (D.C. Cir. 2015).

CFPB investigation to help a recipient efficiently and effectively navigate this critical early stage and then provide guidance throughout the process. Experienced outside counsel can direct an appropriate response to the CID, which will help to insulate the CID recipient from making unnecessary mistakes and stave off accusations of unlawful behavior in responding to the CID.

Assessing the CID's notification of purpose from the outset is important. This assessment indicates whether the company is the subject of the investigation, or merely a third party with relevant information, which may influence a CID recipient's response to the CID. The CFPB historically has interpreted the notification of purpose requirement broadly, resulting in high-profile court challenges.[725] The CFPB announced changes to its policies in 2019,[726] which benefitted CID recipients significantly in terms of

---

[725] For example, the D.C. Circuit's decision in *CFPB v. Accrediting Council for Independent Colleges and Schools (ACICS)*, where the D.C. Circuit unanimously upheld a decision by the district court ruling that a CID issued by the Bureau was unenforceable because the CFPB failed to provide ACICS "with sufficient notice as to the nature of the conduct and the alleged violation under investigation." 854 F.3d 683, 690 (D.C. Cir. 2017). The Fifth Circuit issued a similar ruling in *CFPB v. Source for Pub. Data, L.P.*, where the CFPB failed to advise the recipient of "the nature of the conduct constituting the alleged violation which is under investigation and the provision of law applicable to such violation." 903 F.3d 456, 458 (5th Cir. 2018) (internal citation omitted). This prevented the court from reviewing whether the information sought was "reasonably relevant to the inquiry." *Id.* at 459.

[726] On April 23, 2019, the CFPB announced changes to its policies, explaining that, under the new policy:

> CIDs will provide more information about the potentially applicable provisions of law that may have been violated. CIDs will also typically specify the business activities subject to the Bureau's authority. In investigations where determining the extent of the Bureau's authority over the relevant activity is one of the significant purposes of the investigation, staff may specifically include that issue in the CID in the interests of further transparency.

See CFPB Announces Policy Change Regarding Bureau Civil Investigative Demands, CONSUMER FIN. PROT. BUREAU (Apr. 23, 2019), https://www.consumerfinance.gov/about-us/newsroom/cfpb-announces-policy-change-regarding-bureau-civil-investigative-demands/; *see also* CFPB Enforcement Manual, *supra* note 6, at 68.

time and cost in responding, as well as the scope of the response. and scope.[727]

III.   WHAT LEGAL OBLIGATIONS DO RECIPIENTS HAVE ONCE THEY RECEIVE A CID?

The recipient has a duty to preserve responsive information necessary to respond to the CID,[728] attend a meet and confer in good faith,[729] and respond fully and completely to the CID.[730]

Upon engagement, outside counsel will work with the CID recipient to identify how best to comply with the CID and whether a petition to set aside or modify is appropriate. The first step in responding to a CID is identifying possible custodians of responsive documents and other responsive material. It is important to consider which custodians are likely to have privileged, confidential, or private information (such as trade secrets, private health information, or social security numbers), and whether it makes sense to request confidential treatment, including under the Freedom of Information Act (FOIA) exemption (b)(4)[731] for any material produced to the CFPB.

After relevant custodians are identified, the near-simultaneous and second step entails the issuance of a document preservation notice to ensure that all potentially responsive material is safeguarded. This notice usually takes the form of a written directive instructing custodians (*i.e.*, employees, directors, officers, contractors, and IT personnel) to preserve any and all types of information (hard copy

---

[727] These recent changes benefit recipients of CIDs significantly, as they may make it easier to identify what conduct is under investigation and the potential liabilities, make it less burdensome and costly for the recipient to respond, allow the recipient to narrow the scope of the response, and may provide additional opportunities for the recipients to object to specific requests that fall outside the stated purpose of the investigation.

[728] 12 C.F.R. § 1080.6(a).

[729] 12 C.F.R. § 1080.6(c).

[730] *See, e.g.*, 12 C.F.R. § 1080.6(a).

[731] 5 U.S.C. § 552(b)(4).

and electronic[732]) in the custodian's possession that may be relevant to the CID response. In addition, the notice should trigger a freeze of routine record destruction procedures. Recipients should err on the side of broad preservation in case additional information related to the ongoing investigation is requested.

IV. MEET AND CONFER

The recipient must meet and confer in good faith with the CFPB, typically either with or through outside counsel.[733] The CID will contain contact details and instructions for initiating the meet and confer, which must take place within 10 days after receipt of the CID or before the deadline to file a petition to set aside the CID, whichever is earlier.[734] Outside counsel or a representative of the business should be present who is knowledgeable about the business's organizational structure, information or records management system(s), and methods of retrieval. The purpose of the meet and confer is to discuss with the CFPB how the recipient will comply with the CID. This discussion includes explaining any issues with compliance and seeking clarification of any necessary components of the CID.

While not the norm, this meeting may result in some modifications to the CID that satisfy the recipient's concerns. For example, such modifications could entail the use of search terms versus a manual review of all potentially responsive documents, limitation of custodians to be searched, rolling productions on an ongoing timeline, extension of compliance deadlines, or confidentiality agreements. The meet and confer is also an opportunity to clarify or narrow the scope of the CID. Sometimes it is as simple as informing the CFPB that some of the requested information or materials do not exist. In other cases, narrowing the scope of the CID requires negotiation by counsel. The meet and confer also provides an opportunity for the CID recipient to engage the CFPB

---

[732] "Electronically stored information" (ESI) includes emails, databases, and audio or other recordings. *See* 12 C.F.R. § 1080.6(c)(1)–(2).

[733] 12 C.F.R. § 1080.6(c).

[734] *Id.*

regarding its initial understanding of the facts surrounding the investigation and clarify any misconceptions.

If any modification is necessary or agreed to during the meet and confer, the Bureau will ask that the recipient formally request the modification in writing, including the reasons for such modification.[735] Upon receipt of a formal modification request, the Enforcement Attorneys will seek approval for the modification from their management or Litigation Deputy, which will memorialize the modification in writing.[736]

V.   PETITION TO SET ASIDE OR MODIFY CID

The CFPA provides a mechanism whereby the recipient of a CID may challenge CID by filing a Petition to Modify or Set Aside the CID ("Petition") with the Bureau Director seeking modifications to the CID or that it be set aside completely.

When deciding whether to file a petition, the recipient of a CID must balance many factors. For instance, while the investigation itself is nonpublic, a petition to modify or set aside the CID is made public by the Bureau. On the other hand, the failure to file a petition could result in the waiver of any objections to the CID. If a recipient is unable to reach an agreement with the CFPB during the meet and confer, it should consider whether it is necessary to file a Petition.

Petitions must be filed with the CFPB's Executive Secretary and a copy sent to the Assistant Director of the Office of Enforcement within 20 calendar days of receipt of the CID, or before the return date if the return date is less than 20 days after service.[737] While not required, it is recommended that Enforcement Attorneys be copied on the submission to the Executive Secretary. Extensions of

---

[735] CFPB Enforcement Manual, *supra* note 6, at 64.

[736] *Id.* at 64.

[737] 12 C.F.R. § 1080.6(e).

time to file a Petition are possible, but disfavored.[738] The time to comply with the challenged portion of the CID is stayed while the Petition is pending, and a new return date will be specified if it is denied.[739]

The Petition must set forth "all factual and legal objections to the [CID], including all appropriate arguments, affidavits, and other supporting documentation."[740] There may be many reasons to file a Petition. For example, a CID can be challenged because the CID seeks information outside the CFPB's authority or jurisdiction or is unduly burdensome. Objections must be signed by counsel.[741] The Petition also must include a signed statement from counsel that she attempted in good faith to resolve the issues raised by the Petition through the meet and confer but was unable to reach agreement.[742] This statement should specify any matters that were successfully resolved through meeting and conferring, and those that remain. It also should include the date, time, place, and attendees of each meet and confer.[743]

The CID process and responses are stayed during the pendency of the Petition. Petitions are reviewed by the CFPB Director,[744] who, historically, has rarely ruled in favor of the challenging recipient.[745] The current Bureau policies mandate that unless good cause is shown, the Petition and the Director's decision become

---

[738] 12 C.F.R. § 1080.6(e)(2).

[739] 12 C.F.R. § 1080.6(f).

[740] 12 C.F.R. § 1080.6(e).

[741] Id.

[742] 12 C.F.R. § 1080.6(e)(1).

[743] Id.

[744] 12 C.F.R. § 1080.6(e)(3).

[745] As of August 5, 2022, the CFPB has granted 2 of 55 petitions, and even those only granted partial, not complete, relief. *See generally Petitions to Modify or Set Aside*, CONSUMER FIN. PROT. BUREAU, https://www.consumerfinance.gov/enforcement/petitions/ (last visited Aug. 5, 2022).

public.[746] The petitioner may request confidential treatment of the Petition or that the CFPB provide advance notice before publishing the materials. The CFPB, however, does not always provide notice to Petitioners before making the Petition and Director's decision public. Before filing a Petition, therefore, it is important to consider the business impact public disclosure of a CFPB investigation may have.

VI.   RESPONDING TO CID FOR INVESTIGATIONAL HEARING

The CFPB can issue CIDs for investigational hearings to obtain oral testimony to uncover and make a record of facts relevant to an investigation. Typically, individuals sought for investigational hearings include current owners, officers, directors, managers, or other employees, past employees, and even consumers. Often the CFPB will issue CIDs for investigational hearings in conjunction with CIDs seeking answers to interrogatories, document requests, and/or requests for a written report. It would be rare for the CFPB to conduct an investigational hearing without having obtained some information from a prior production or other source. Thus, to the extent interrogatories, documents, or written reports have been produced, these must be considered when preparing for any investigational hearing.

The general requirements relating to responding, holding a meet and confer, and filing a petition to set aside or modify are the same as noted above. Although the CID will always specify a date, time, and location for the investigational hearing, these terms can be negotiated with CFPB Enforcement Attorneys. If the CID seeks oral testimony from an entity, the business will need to designate one or more officers, directors, managing agents, or other persons

---

[746] *See Petitions to Modify or Set Aide*, CONSUMER FIN. PROT. BUREAU, https://www.consumerfinance.gov/policy-compliance/enforcement/petitions/ (last visited June 19, 2022).

to respond to the matters for examination, and specify the topics that each will address.[747]

A.   Testimony

Investigational hearings are taken under oath or affirmation, under penalty of perjury.[748] As with courtroom or deposition testimony, witnesses are obligated to give truthful responses.

B.   Practical Considerations

Thorough preparation is essential when going into an investigational hearing. The witness should understand the legal framework that the CFPB is seeking to enforce, the allegations or practices underpinning its investigation, and the documents and written responses already produced, if applicable. Counsel should prepare the witness, typically by reviewing relevant documents and information and subjecting the witness to practice questions— much like preparing for a deposition.

One of the biggest differences between investigational hearings and depositions, however, is the extremely limited ability of counsel to lodge objections. Objections are limited to "grounds of any constitutional or other legal right or privilege, including the privilege against self-incrimination [.]"[749] In layman's terms, that means counsel can object to questions that could result in a breach of the attorney-client privilege or the attorney work product doctrine or would result in self-incrimination, and little else.

Because counsel will not be able to lodge standard evidentiary objections, such as objecting to the form of the question, it is imperative that the witness listen to the questions carefully and answer only the questions asked. The classic example, "Do you know what time it is?" is properly answered yes or no, *not* by volunteering the current time. If a question contains an incorrect or

---

[747] 12 C.F.R. § 1080.6(a)(4)(ii).

[748] 12 C.F.R. § 1080.7(b).

[749] 12 U.S.C. § 5562(c)(13)(D)(iii); 12 C.F.R. § 1080.9(b)(2).

misleading premise, the witness should point out the flaw when answering or otherwise qualify her answer. If the witness is shown exhibits that are incomplete or have been created by the CFPB, the witness should state these facts clearly on the record and base any answer upon this factual predicate. If the witness is asked to speculate or asked about hypothetical scenarios, her answers should be equally clear that she is merely speculating or responding hypothetically—if she responds at all.

Even with thorough preparation, witnesses are likely to be shown documents that they did not specifically review during their prep session or asked questions not previously posed. The witness should take the time to review the document carefully and ask the questioner to repeat the question or provide additional context if necessary.

After the questioner has concluded the examination, counsel may request that the witness be permitted to clarify his or her answers. This request may or may not be granted, solely within the discretion of the questioner.[750] Each person compelled to testify has the right to request a transcript of her testimony.[751] However, the CFPB can deny such a request for good cause.[752] It is recommended to make such a request on the record and then follow up with a written request to the Enforcement Attorneys.

VII. NORA PROCESS

A. Legal Basis and Obligations

Once the CFPB Enforcement Attorneys have concluded their investigation, they may utilize the Notice and Opportunity to Respond and Advise (NORA) process to notify a company under investigation that the Office of Enforcement is considering recommending that the CFPB take legal action against the company or individual under investigation. The Bureau has

---

[750] 12 C.F.R. § 1080.9(b)(4).

[751] 12 C.F.R. § 1080.9(a).

[752] 12 C.F.R. § 1080.9.

explained that the "objective of the notice is to ensure that the potential subjects of enforcement actions have the opportunity to present their positions to the Bureau before an enforcement action is recommended or commenced."[753]

However, the Bureau's use of the NORA process is discretionary—that is, the Bureau is not required to issue a NORA before authorizing legal action.[754] That said, it has become a customary practice for Enforcement Attorneys to conduct a NORA prior to seeking authority to settle or sue. In addition, Bureau policy recommends that the Office of Enforcement use the NORA process in most cases where they expect to recommend a lawsuit.[755] But if the Bureau believes that any delay will result in undue harm to consumers, it may bypass the NORA process and proceed directly to litigation.[756]

If the Office of Enforcement decides to use the NORA process, Enforcement Attorneys will contact the attorney representing the company under investigation by telephone to schedule a NORA call. During the NORA call, the Enforcement Attorneys will state the potential allegations they will seek to assert and describe some facts that substantiate their case. The NORA call will be followed by a letter memorializing, generally, the Enforcement Attorneys advised counsel that they are going to recommend the Director authorize an enforcement action for alleged law violations. A publicly available sample NORA letter depicts the limited detail the Bureau provides about the substance of the claims that it may

---

[753] CONSUMER FIN. PROT. BUREAU, CFPB BULLETIN 2011-04 (ENFORCEMENT) 1 (2012), https://files.consumerfinance.gov/f/2012/01/Bulletin10.pdf (hereinafter "NORA Bulletin").

[754] See id.; CFPB Enforcement Manual, supra note 6, at 89–90; Life Cycle of an Enforcement Action, CONSUMER FIN. PROT. BUREAU, https://www.consumerfinance.gov/enforcement/life-cycle-of-enforcement-action/ (last visited June 22, 2022).

[755] CFPB Enforcement Manual, supra note 6, at 90.

[756] Id. at 89.

pursue.[757] However, Bureau policy requires the NORA letter to identify the charges that the Enforcement Attorney is considering recommending, the specific laws alleged to be violated, a general description of the allegedly violative conduct, and a general description of the types of relief, remedies, and penalties that may be sought.[758]

B.   Considerations in Responding to a NORA Letter

Any recipient of a NORA must determine whether preparing a written response is necessary. The cost, including attorneys' fees, and the diversion of resources from business operations to respond to the NORA—all within a relatively short time—may outweigh the benefits of responding. Another consideration that should factor into whether to file a NORA response is that any materials provided in response to a NORA letter may not be protected by any settlement privilege (and attempting to designate a NORA response as inadmissible under Federal Rule of Evidence 408 may cause the Bureau to reject the response as noncompliant).[759] If the Bureau ultimately decides to file an enforcement action, it may use the materials or written statement in the litigation. In addition, any materials provided in a NORA response may be discoverable by a third party.[760] But if no response is filed with the Office of Enforcement, then the Director will read only one side of the argument for bringing a lawsuit or settling.

For businesses that decide to respond, the deadline to do so is generally 14 calendar days from receipt of the NORA letter.[761] The Bureau will review written requests for an extension, but any such extensions are usually brief. Unless the NORA letter states

---

[757] CONSUMER FIN. PROT. BUREAU, SAMPLE NORA LETTER, https://files.consumerfinance.gov/f/2012/01/NORA-Letter1.pdf.

[758] CFPB Enforcement Manual, *supra* note 6, at 91–92.
[759] *Id.* at 93.

[760] NORA Bulletin, *supra* note 52.

[761] CFPB Enforcement Manual, *supra* note 6, at 92.

303

otherwise, a NORA response may be no longer than 40 pages, double spaced.[762] The Bureau has explained that the "primary focus of the written statement in response [to a NORA] should be legal and policy matters relevant to the potential enforcement proceedings."[763] If the submission contains any factual statements, such statements must be supported by an accompanying affidavit sworn under oath by someone with personal knowledge.[764]

The recipient may request an in-person meeting with the Bureau in connection with its NORA response. The Bureau often grants such requests, although it is not required to do so. The recipient also may request to view the Bureau's investigative file, although requests are generally denied.[765]

Although the Bureau will accept unsolicited settlement offers, the enforcement attorneys are generally unwilling to undertake an informal process to allow for a discussion to reach a settlement until after the NORA process. The Bureau diverges from other enforcement agencies, including the Federal Trade Commission, the prudential banking regulations, and the Department of Justice, all of which will engage in settlement discussions before making a recommendation to senior management, provided the terms of the settlement are contingent upon management or Commission approval. As a result, the subject or target of a CFPB investigation may be forced to spend significant resources responding to a NORA before even beginning settlement discussions.

VIII.   SPECIAL CONSIDERATIONS FOR A SUPERVISED ENTITY

Any company that is subject to the CFPB's supervisory authority should understand the interplay between supervision and the enforcement authorities of the Bureau. The CFPB's Office of

[762] NORA Bulletin, *supra* note 52.

[763] *Id.*

[764] *Id.*

[765] CFPB Enforcement Manual, *supra* note 6, at 93.

Enforcement can receive a referral from the Office of Supervision after a supervisory examination. The CFPB's internal policy dictates that the Office of Enforcement may decline to proceed on a matter through enforcement and return to the matter to supervision to resolve through the supervisory process.

The CFPB supervisory process is non-public. Companies subject to the Bureau's supervisory authority can resolve matters through a non-public memorandum of understanding (MOU) or corrective action (matter requiring attention) mandated by a final report of examination.

When facing an investigation or supervisory examination, companies have a period of time in which to advocate their preferable manner of resolution. The argument that an issue is best resolved confidentially through the Office of Supervision may be available, given the proper circumstances.

A.   CFPB Supervisory Authority

The CFPA provides the CFPB with supervisory authority over certain institutions, including (1) large banks (with assets equal to or greater than $10 billion) concerning the offering or provision of a consumer financial service or product, and these banks' affiliates; (2) nonbank mortgage originators and servicers; (3) small-dollar lenders; (4) private student lenders; (5) "larger participants" in defined markets (*e.g.*, credit reporting and debt collection); and (6) service providers of any of the above-mentioned entities.[766] In addition to limiting the scope of the CFPB's supervisory authority to these "supervised entities," examinations are also limited to the "enumerated consumer laws" and the implementing regulations of those laws.[767] While the

---

[766] 12 U.S.C. §§ 5514(a); 5515.

[767] *Id.* § 5481(12). Additionally, the Bureau has asserted it has enforcement authority in some areas where the foundation is actually unclear. Notably, the Bureau had previously claimed that it does not have supervisory authority over the Military Lending Act. *See Consumer Financial Protection Bureau Asks Congress for Clear Authority to Supervise for Compliance with the Military Lending Act*, CONSUMER FIN. PROT. BUREAU (Jan 17, 2019), https://www.consumerfinance.gov/about-us/newsroom/consumer-financial-

CFPB has broad supervisory authority, that authority is limited by the CFPA and is narrower than the Bureau's enforcement authority.

Although enforcement and supervision administratively are in the same division within the Bureau, these two offices follow different policies and procedures to carry out their consumer protection mandates. Supervisory examinations are not investigations per se, meaning that examiners are not searching for evidence of specific violations of law. Rather, examinations are periodic reviews of a company's practices and compliance management systems that ensure adherence with the law.[768]

Historically, supervisory examinations were the purview of the prudential banking regulators and were focused primarily on banks' "safety and soundness"—ensuring that banks were not engaging in activities that would put customers' deposits, the bank

---

protection-bureau-asks-congress-clear-authority-supervise-compliance-military-lending-act/; Arbitration Agreements, CFPB No. 2016-CFPB-0020 (July 19, 2017); SUPERVISORY HIGHLIGHTS, CONSUMER FIN. PROT. BUREAU 27, 27 n.56 (2015), https://files.consumerfinance.gov/f/201506_cfpb_supervisory-highlights.pdf. However, under new leadership, the CFPB has argued that the Military Lending Act falls under its jurisdiction. See Seth Frotman & Jim Rice, *Protecting Servicemembers from Predatory Lending*, CONSUMER FIN. PROT. BUREAU (Jan. 7, 2022), https://www.consumerfinance.gov/about-us/blog/protecting-servicemembers-from-predatory-lending/; *What is the Military Lending Act and What are My Rights?*, CONSUMER FIN. PROT. BUREAU, https://www.consumerfinance.gov/consumer-tools/educator-tools/servicemembers/military-lending-act-mla/ (last visited June 22, 2022); Examinations for Risk to Active-Duty Servicemembers and Their Covered Dependents, 86 Fed. Reg. 32,723, 32,723 (June 23, 2021).

[768] Like the federal bank regulators, the CFPB has published and periodically updates a Supervision and Examination Manual that provides instructions and guidance to CFPB examiners. See generally CONSUMER FIN. PROT. BUREAU, CFPB SUPERVISION AND EXAMINATION MANUAL (Mar. 2022), https://files.consumerfinance.gov/f/documents/cfpb_supervision-and-examination-manual.pdf. The CFPB also periodically publishes a compendium of recent issues and findings that have occurred during examinations, while maintaining the confidentiality of the entities being supervised, called Supervisory Highlights. *Supervisory Highlights*, CONSUMER FIN. PROT. BUREAU, https://www.consumerfinance.gov/policy-compliance/guidance/supervisory-highlights/ (last visited June 20, 2022).

and its reputation, or the overall market at risk. Unlike traditional "safety and soundness" examinations, the CFPB's primary focus is on consumer protection. To this end, the Bureau will often focus on specific product lines during an examination instead of undertaking a comprehensive examination of all products and services offered by a large bank.[769] The Bureau states this focus succinctly when describing the purpose of its supervision of covered entities and the examination process as follows:

- To assess compliance with federal consumer financial laws,

- To obtain information about activities and compliance systems or procedures, and

- To detect and assess risks to consumers and to markets for consumer financial products and services.[770]

B. Confidentiality of the Supervisory Process

The process and results of examinations of banks have traditionally been highly confidential. Similarly, in the CFPB context, "supervisory information," including examination reports, ratings, and corrective actions, is confidential (termed in CFPB regulations "confidential supervisory information" or "CSI").[771] CSI includes the reports, communications, and other documents obtained through CFPB exams, inspections, and other forms of inquiry conducted under the CFPB's supervisory authority; supervisory letters and similar documents; and information derived from such documents that are provided to the supervised entity for its

---

[769] CONSUMER FIN. PROT. BUREAU, CFPB SUPERVISION AND EXAMINATION MANUAL 11 (2022), http://files.consumerfinance.gov/f/documents/cfpb_supervision-and-examination-manual.pdf.

[770] Id. at 3.

[771] See, e.g., Amendments Relating to Disclosure of Records and Information, 85 Fed. Reg. 75,194, 75,194 (Nov. 24, 2020).

confidential use only. CSI is essentially considered the property of the regulator and may be disclosed only by the supervised entity, or by the Bureau, in limited circumstances.[772]

C. Resolution Through Referrals to Office of Supervision

If examiners find violations of laws or regulations, they will typically issue a Potential Action and Request for Response Letter (PARR Letter) that alerts the company and provides a chance to respond to the findings.[773] The Bureau does not intend for this process to be a surprise, but rather an ongoing dialogue between the examination staff and the supervised entity. Potential violations discovered during an examination can be addressed through non-public means as part of the supervisory process—such as entering into an MOU with the supervised entity,[774] or identifying Matters Requiring Attention (MRAs) in the Examination Report[775]—or referred to the Office of Enforcement for a public enforcement action.[776]

The CFPB's Action Review Committee (ARC) reviews potential violations discovered during an examination.[777] The ARC represents a formal process for determining whether a potential violation of the consumer financial protection laws should be resolved within the confidential confines of the Office of Supervision or referred to the Office of Enforcement for further

---

[772] *Id.* at 75,198.

[773] CONSUMER FIN. PROT. BUREAU, SUPERVISORY HIGHLIGHTS 27 (2015), https://files.consumerfinance.gov/f/201506_cfpb_supervisory-highlights.pdf.

[774] *See* CFPB Enforcement Manual, *supra* note 6, at 169.

[775] *See* CONSUMER FIN. PROT. BUREAU, CFPB SUPERVISION AND EXAMINATION MANUAL 6 (2022), https://files.consumerfinance.gov/f/documents/cfpb_supervision-and-examination-manual.pdf.

[776] *See id.* at 2.

[777] *See generally* CONSUMER FIN. PROT. BUREAU, SUPERVISORY HIGHLIGHTS 27 (2015), https://files.consumerfinance.gov/f/201506_cfpb_supervisory-highlights.pdf.

investigation and a public resolution.[778] According to the Bureau's ARC Memo,[779] the committee evaluates several factors[780] regarding both the potential violation and the supervised entity when determining how to direct a potential violation, including:

- Violation-Focused Factors[781]

    o Severity of each violation;

    o Whether the violation(s) has ceased or is ongoing and the likelihood that it will be repeated;

    o Whether the identified violations indicate targeting of protected classes or classes for which the CFPB has a special mandate;

---

[778] *Id.*

[779] *Action Review Committee (ARC) Memo*, CONSUMER FIN. PROT. BUREAU, https://tinyurl.com/mrx3bj7h (last accessed Aug. 5, 2022).

[780] *See* Supervisory Highlights: Mortgage Servicing Special Edition 2016, 81 Fed. Reg. 46,063, 46,064 (July 15, 2016); Responsible Business Conduct: Self-Assessing, Self-Reporting, Remediating, and Cooperating (CFPB Bulletin 2020–01), 85 Fed. Reg. 15,917, 15,917 (Mar. 20, 2020); Supervisory Highlights: Summer 2017, 82 Fed. Reg. 48,703, 48,712 (Oct. 19, 2017). *See also* CONSUMER FIN. PROT. BUREAU, CFPB BULLETIN 2020-01 (GUIDANCE AND INTERPRETATION ON RESPONSIBLE BUSINESS CONDUCT: SELF-ASSESSING, SELF-REPORTING, REMEDIATING, AND COOPERATING) 2 (Mar. 6, 2020) ("For entities within the Bureau's supervisory authority, the Bureau's Division of Supervision, Enforcement, and Fair Lending makes determinations of whether violations should be resolved through non-public supervisory action or a possible public enforcement action through its Action Review Committee (ARC) process. The ARC process includes factors that are closely aligned with the elements of responsible conduct. Thus, for entities under the Bureau's supervisory authority, responsible conduct could result in resolving violations non-publicly through the supervisory process.").

[781] *See generally* Responsible Business Conduct: Self-Assessing, Self-Reporting, Remediating, and Cooperating (CFPB Bulletin 2020–01), 85 Fed. Reg. 15,917, 15,917 n.1 (Mar. 20, 2020).

309

- The importance of deterrence, considering the significance and pervasiveness of the practice; and

- The variety of violations and number of products affected by the violations.

- Institution-Focused Factors[782]

  o Size, complexity, and financial health of the institution;

  o Extent of the institution's cooperation to date and its willingness and ability to comply in the future;

  o Whether the institution knew or should have known of the violation (*e.g.*, through the volume of consumer complaints relating to the violations); and

  o Prior regulatory action.

It has been reported that the Bureau may allow supervised entities to shift potential violations discovered by the Office of Enforcement or those referred to it back through this same ARC process to the Office of Supervision for non-public supervisory resolution (the so-called "reverse" ARC).[783] However, these steps do not appear to be governed by formal processes. Supervisory resolutions, largely because of their non-public nature, are often more palatable for the supervised entity, and can result in more immediate corrective action and cessation of problematic

---

[782] *See generally id.* at 15,917–18.

[783] *See* Jean Veta & Eitan Levisohn, *A Fresh Look at CFPB's Enforcement Process*, LAW360 (Feb. 12, 2018, 11:51 AM), https://www.law360.com/articles/1011249/a-fresh-look-at-cfpb-s-enforcement-process.

activities, at a far lower expenditure of Bureau resources when compared to litigation or administrative adjudication.

IX. CONCLUSION

Following the 2020 election, the Bureau has broadened in focus and scope. The Bureau rescinded several policy statements and internal practices, including Director Kathy Kraninger's January 2020 policy statement that made it more challenging for enforcement staff to bring abusiveness claims.[784] Under Director Rohit Chopra the Bureau's scope has expanded to include major technology companies[785] and areas of law not officially covered under consumer finance laws such as antitrust,[786] discrimination in

---

[784] *See* Evan Weinberger, *CFPB Lifts Limits on Penalizing Banks for Abusive Conduct*, BLOOMBERG L. (Mar. 11, 2021, 3:15 PM), https://news.bloomberglaw.com/banking-law/cfpb-reverses-trump-era-limits-on-going-after-abusive-conduct; *Consumer Financial Protection Bureau Rescinds Abusiveness Policy Statement to Better Protect Consumers*, CONSUMER FIN. PROT. BUREAU (Mar. 11, 2021), https://www.consumerfinance.gov/about-us/newsroom/consumer-financial-protection-bureau-rescinds-abusiveness-policy-statement-to-better-protect-consumers/.

[785] *See CFPB Orders Tech Giants to Turn Over Information on their Payment System Plans*, CONSUMER FIN. PROT. BUREAU (Oct. 21, 2021), https://www.consumerfinance.gov/about-us/newsroom/cfpb-orders-tech-giants-to-turn-over-information-on-their-payment-system-plans/; *cf.* Jon Hill, *With Chopra Poised to Take Over, What's Next for the CFPB?*, LAW 360 (Oct. 1, 2021, 11:28 PM), https://www.law360.com/articles/1427434; *Kraninger Marks Second Year as Director of the Consumer Financial Protection Bureau*, CONSUMER FIN. PROT. BUREAU (Dec. 11, 2020), https://www.consumerfinance.gov/about-us/newsroom/kraninger-marks-second-year-director-consumer-financial-protection-bureau/.

[786] *See CFPB Launches New Effort to Promote Competition and Innovation in Consumer Finance*, CONSUMER FIN. PROT. BUREAU (MAY 24, 2022), https://www.consumerfinance.gov/about-us/newsroom/cfpb-lauches-new-effort-to-promote-competition-and-innovation-in-consumer-finance/; Promoting Competition in Our Financial Markets, CONSUMER FIN. PROT. BUREAU (July 11, 2022), https://www.consumerfinance.gov/about-us/blog/promoting-competition-in-our-financial-markets/.

non-credit products,[787] employment arrangements.[788] This further increases the importance of understanding enforcement procedures related to the CFPB.

---

[787] *See CFPB Targets Unfair Discrimination in Consumer Finance*, CONSUMER FIN. PROT. BUREAU (Mar. 16, 2022), https://www.consumerfinance.gov/about-us/newsroom/cfpb-targets-unfair-discrimination-in-consumer-finance/; Evan Weinberger, *CFPB Will Look to Fill Gaps in Fair Lending Laws, Chopra Says*, BLOOMBERG L. (Mar. 16, 2022, 5:29 PM), https://news.bloomberglaw.com/banking-law/cfpb-will-look-to-fill-gaps-in-fair-lending-laws-chopra-says (noting how "[t]he CFPB plans to expand its enforcement against discrimination into consumer finance areas where fair lending laws don't officially apply").

[788] *See CFPB Launched Inquiry into Practices that Leave Workers Indebted to Employers*, CONSUMER FIN. PROT. BUREAU (Jun. 9, 2022), https://www.consumerfinance.gov/about-us/newsroom/cfpb-launches-inquiry-into-practices-that-leave-workers-indebted-to-employers/.

Chapter 12

Government Investigations Under the Civil False Claims Act and FIRREA

By:

Douglas W. Baruch
Jennifer M. Wollenberg
Kayla Stachniak Kaplan[789]

I.   INTRODUCTION

For almost 40 years, the government has relied on the civil False Claims Act ("FCA") as its primary weapon for seeking to recover its monetary losses from alleged fraud. The "success" of federal FCA enforcement has spread to the states, as well, with more than 30 states with false claims laws – mostly patterned on the FCA, and State Attorneys General and relators' counsel taking advantage of those enforcement tools. Companies and individuals across the business and industry spectrum – well beyond traditional government contractors – have found themselves defending against FCA allegations. In addition, more recently, the Justice Department has dusted off the civil monetary penalty provision of the Financial Institutions Reform, Recovery and Enforcement Act of 1989 ("FIRREA") and used it to pursue substantial recoveries for allegedly fraudulent activity principally involving financial institutions. These statutes generally are "plaintiff friendly" due to the relative ease with which cases can be filed and the powerful (and, in some instances, draconian) damages, penalties, and collateral consequences they can impose upon companies and individuals. Indeed, in many FCA and FIRREA cases, the magnitude of the allegations and potential consequences present an existential threat to the company's ability to remain in business.

---

[789] Douglas W. Baruch, Jennifer M. Wollenberg, and Kayla Stachniak Kaplan are leaders of the False Claims Act practice group within the White Collar and Government Investigations practice area at Morgan, Lewis & Bockius LLP. The views expressed by the authors are their own and do not necessarily represent the views of Morgan Lewis or any of its clients.

Therefore, company counsel must be attentive to the first hints of any government FCA or FIRREA investigation.

Proper handling of these civil fraud enforcement matters at the investigation stage increases the odds of a successful outcome, including narrowing the allegations or even resolving the matter in its entirety and avoiding risks associated with preserving, gathering, and producing information in response to government investigations. Active counsel involvement from the outset also maximizes the company's flexibility to respond to and defend against the allegations and avoid pitfalls (such as the failure to properly protect legal privileges) that can undermine the company's defenses and result in collateral harm with respect to other litigation or administrative action arising from the matters under investigation.

FCA and FIRREA investigations arise in a variety of scenarios. This chapter does not attempt to predict and address each one. Moreover, because this chapter is focused on the investigation stage of these matters, strategies for litigation and settlement once suit has been filed (or unsealed in certain FCA cases) are not addressed here. Instead, this chapter provides overarching considerations and best practices for in-house counsel who are confronted with FCA and FIRREA investigations.

II. OVERVIEW OF THE FCA AND FIRREA

A. The FCA (31 U.S.C. §§ 3729-3733)

The FCA is intended to protect the U.S. Treasury from fraud. Basically, the FCA is violated when a person knowingly submits a materially false or fraudulent claim for money or property to the government or fails to remit money to the government despite an obligation to do so. Potential FCA liability also extends to false records or statements made or used in support of a false claim or in avoidance of a payment obligation.

Federal FCA cases can be initiated in two ways. First, the Justice Department, including U.S. Attorney's Offices, can bring an affirmative FCA claim on behalf of allegedly defrauded federal agencies or entities. Information prompting these investigations can come from a variety of sources, including agency inspector general referrals and even mandatory and voluntary disclosures (discussed below). Often, where the alleged victim is a program funded by both the United States and individual states – such as Medicaid – the FCA matter is handled jointly by federal and state enforcement entities.[790] Second, the FCA permits private parties (known as "*qui tam* relators") to file FCA suits (known as *qui tam* actions) on behalf of the government. The *qui tam* provision is discussed in more detail in Subsection B below.

With only limited exceptions,[791] any individual or corporation is a "person" subject to suit under the FCA.[792] Thus, while government contractors and companies in the healthcare industry are most frequently in the crosshairs of FCA enforcement, commercial businesses with no obvious ties to the government – such as importers subject to customs duties and oil and gas companies extracting minerals from federal land – often are FCA defendants as well.

In addition to relatively straightforward allegations premised on "factually" false misconduct such as mischarging, overbilling, embezzling, and/or providing non-conforming parts, products, or services, FCA claims have expanded to alleged "legally" false conduct. For example, under the "implied false certification"

---

[790] Because approximately 30 states plus the District of Columbia (as well as a number of city and municipal governments) have enacted false claims laws with *qui tam* enforcement, state and local government agencies as well as *qui tam* relators may enforce violations of these state and local false claims laws. Notably, while the failure to pay (or the underpayment of) state/local taxes due is a basis for liability under some of these false claims laws, the FCA specifically bars FCA claims based on violations of the Internal Revenue Code. 31 U.S.C. § 3729(d).

[791] For example, a current or former military service member may not bring an action against another member of the armed forces if the alleged violation arises out of the second member's service. *See* 31 U.S.C. § 3730(e)(1).

[792] *See Vermont Agency of Natural Res. v. United States ex rel. Stevens*, 529 U.S. 765, 782 (2000) (citing the Dictionary Act, 1 U.S.C. § 1, which defines "person" to include "corporations, companies, associations, firms, partnerships, societies, and joint stock companies, as well as individuals").

theory, FCA liability can be premised on a company's misrepresentation of its compliance with an ancillary (but material) statutory, regulatory, or contractual requirement. Importantly, the misrepresentation (or false certification) can be made *by implication or omission* – no false statement is required. In 2016, the Supreme Court validated the implied false certification theory as a basis for FCA liability,[793] ensuring that the FCA will continue to be used to enforce other regulatory regimes, including those covering defense, procurement, healthcare (pharmaceutical, medical devices, doctors, hospice, and nursing homes), federal insurance programs (flood, mortgage, agriculture), education and research funding, and wherever else government-controlled funds are involved. With respect to any company importing goods into the United States, the alleged avoidance of customs duties frequently has been the basis for FCA liability theories brought under the "reverse false claim" provision.[794]

The potential adverse consequences of FCA liability can be tremendous. The statute provides for treble damages, plus civil penalties per false claim.[795] The FCA's statute of limitations extends to claims for payment within six years of suit and, in some limited instances, reaches back ten years.[796] FCA recoveries have increased more than 50-fold since the 1986 amendments to the statute increased the damages multiplier, loosened restrictions on *qui tam* enforcement, lowered the intent standard, and reduced the

---

[793] *See Universal Health Servs., Inc. v. United States ex rel. Escobar*, 579 U.S. 176 (2016).

[794] *See* 31 U.S.C. § 3729(a)(1)(G).

[795] The range for FCA penalties, which doubled in 2016 due to a budget law inflation "catch-up" provision, is subject to adjustment upward annually, and as of January 30, 2023, was $13,508 to $27,018 per false claim. 31 U.S.C. § 3729(a) (as adjusted by the Federal Civil Penalties Inflation Adjustment Act of 1990, 28 U.S.C. § 2461 note). *See* Civil Monetary Penalties Inflation Adjustments for 2023, 88 Fed. Reg. 5776, 5778 (Jan. 30, 2023) (FCA penalties are codified at 28 C.F.R. § 85.3(a)(9)).

[796] *See* 31 U.S.C. § 3731(b). In 2019, the Supreme Court held that *qui tam* relators can take advantage of the extended limitations period in § 3237(b)(2) even in cases where the government does not intervene in the action. *See Cochise Consultancy, Inc. v. United States ex rel. Hunt.*, 139 S. Ct. 1507 (2019).

burden of proof (at least for actions brought by the United States) to a preponderance of the evidence. According to the Justice Department, FCA recoveries since 1986 are over $72.5 billion and in government fiscal years 2021 and 2022 alone were over $5.7 billion and $2.2 billion, respectively. In addition, companies (and their personnel) confronting FCA investigations face the prospect of criminal prosecution as well as suspension, debarment, or exclusion from government programs. Rather than "bet the company" and litigate cases through trial, FCA defendants – particularly publicly-traded companies and their boards of directors – often feel they have little choice but to attempt to settle these matters. And government attorneys and relators' counsel alike are fully aware of and seek to exploit this reality.

B.   The FCA's *Qui Tam* Provision

The FCA has a rare enforcement mechanism that warrants special attention. In particular, the FCA empowers *qui tam* relators (or "whistleblowers") to pursue potential FCA violations on the government's behalf. While the government is considered the real party in interest, the relator has standing to bring the *qui tam* suit based on a partial assignment of the government's damages claim.[797] The original purpose of this enforcement mechanism included "setting a rogue to catch a rogue."[798] Today, relators include not only company insiders, but also business competitors, special purpose entities formed for the purpose of bringing suits, and professional relators, who have no inside knowledge but rely instead on data mining from public sources to compile claims based on billing or other behavior patterns gleaned from such sources.

Qui tam relators are eligible to receive a substantial bounty – generally between 15% and 30% of the government's recovery

---

[797] *See Stevens*, 529 U.S. at 773–74. While the Supreme Court in *Stevens* resolved the constitutionality of the FCA's *qui tam* provisions in terms of standing, other constitutional challenges remain. *See United States ex rel. Polansky v. Exec. Health Res., Inc.*, 143 S. Ct. 1720, 1737 (2023) (Thomas, J. dissenting) (describing "serious constitutional questions").

[798] Cong. Globe, 37th Cong., 3d Sess. 955–56 (1863) (remarks of Sen. Howard).

through judgment, settlement, or an alternate remedy. As a result, the Justice Department's FCA docket largely is comprised of *qui tam* complaints (rather than affirmative Justice Department suits), with 600-700 new *qui tam* suits filed on average in recent years. *Qui tam* suits raise a host of unique issues not present in other litigation, including potential misappropriation of company documents by relators, unusual conflicts and complications at settlement, and the potential for "personal" retaliation claims, as the FCA protects confirmed or suspected whistleblowers from retaliation or discrimination by their employer and others.[799]

FCA *qui tam* complaints must be filed in federal court under seal, and they must remain sealed for at least 60 days.[800] During this seal period, which the court often extends multiple times at the Justice Department's request, the government investigates and decides whether to intervene and take over the case.[801]

In the majority of cases, after investigation, the government declines to intervene in the *qui tam* case and so notifies the court. Even in instances in which the Justice Department learns through investigation that the *qui tam* claims have no merit, it rarely takes action to dismiss the case, with a few recent exceptions.[802] In

---

[799] *See* 31 U.S.C. § 3730(h).

[800] *See* 31 U.S.C. § 3730(b).

[801] The Justice Department may obtain court approval to partially unseal a *qui tam* complaint for the purpose of discussing the matter with the defendant and facilitating settlement discussions.

[802] In early 2018, the Justice Department – through a January 10, 2018 memorandum from the Director of the Commercial Litigation Branch – issued internal guidance that signaled a willingness by the Justice Department to seek dismissal of *qui tam* cases. *See* Memorandum from Michael D. Granston to U.S. Attorneys, *Factors for Evaluating Dismissal Pursuant to 31 U.S.C. § 3730(c)(2)(A)* (Jan. 10, 2018). The dismissal factors listed in the "Granston Memo" are incorporated in the Department's Justice Manual, § 4-4.111, *available at* www.justice.gov/jm/jm-4-4000-commercial-litigation#4-4.111. In 2023, the Supreme Court confirmed the Justice Department's ability to obtain dismissal, even over a relator's objection and even after an initial decision not to intervene. In order to exercise this authority, the Justice Department must intervene but then need only satisfy the relatively low bar of Federal Rule of Civil Procedure 41 to

declined *qui tam* cases, the relator may proceed with the suit. Although the government does not actively participate in the litigation of declined cases, Justice Department lawyers almost always are copied on all pleadings and otherwise monitor the proceedings and often seek to weigh in on legal issues by filing "Statements of Interest" or *amicus* briefs. Pursuant to 31 U.S.C. § 3730(b) (1), a relator cannot dismiss or settle a declined action without notice to and consent by the government and the court.

If the government intervenes and proceeds with the action, relators may remain involved in the litigation, as they retain an interest in the outcome of the case. In intervened cases, relators retain the right to proceed with any personal claims, such as retaliation claims, and may also seek to pursue non-intervened claims. In such cases, relators are afforded an opportunity to register their objection to any settlement,[803] but have little power to prevent the government from using its statutory authority to dismiss an action under 31 U.S.C. § 3730(c) (2) (A).[804]

Whether or not the government intervenes, the FCA also provides that, in the event of a recovery with respect to the substantive claims, the relator is entitled to an award of reasonable attorney's fees and costs from the defendant, separate and apart from the relator's bounty or share of the recovery.[805]

---

demonstrate that dismissal should be permitted. *United States ex rel. Polansky v. Exec. Health Res., Inc.*, 143 S. Ct. 1720 (2023).

[803] *See* 31 U.S.C. § 3730(c)(1) (relator's right to continue as a party to the action after government's intervention); 31 U.S.C. § 3730(c)(2)(B) (hearing on relator's objections to settlement).

[804] *See also Polansky*, 143 S. Ct. 1720 (establishing relative ease with which Justice Department can meet both "good cause" for intervention and the Rule 41 standard for voluntary dismissal, which is all that is needed for exercise of (c)(2)(A) dismissal authority in non-intervened cases).

[805] *See* 31 U.S.C. § 3730(d)(4).

C.   FIRREA (12 U.S.C. § 1833a)

Congress enacted FIRREA in the aftermath of the savings and loan crisis of the 1980s. While FIRREA enforcement was relatively dormant for almost two decades, FIRREA emerged as an important Justice Department enforcement tool, in part due to its generous ten-year statute of limitations, the ability to bring cases even where the government itself did not suffer harm, and the potential for substantial monetary penalties.

The Justice Department's initial FIRREA enforcement efforts largely targeted financial institutions involved with residential mortgage lending. However, companies that do business with financial entities, ratings agencies, companies that provide financing (including in the auto loan industry), and – most recently – companies that received COVID-19 relief benefits, along with the individuals who work for the above-described entities also have been the subjects of FIRREA investigations. FIRREA even was employed with respect to the Volkswagen "emissions scandal."[806]

FIRREA creates civil liability for fourteen criminal predicate offenses, including the so-called "catch-all" mail and wire fraud crimes:

- 18 U.S.C. § 215 (receipt of commissions or gifts for procuring loans),

- 18 U.S.C. § 656 (theft, embezzlement, or misapplication by bank officer or employee),

---

[806] *See Volkswagen Says Agrees to Pay $4.3 Billion to Resolve U.S. Emissions Troubles,* REUTERS (Berlin), Jan. 11, 2017, *available at* www.reuters.com/article/us-volkswagen-emissions/volkswagen-says-agrees-to-pay-4-3-billion-to-resolve-u-s-emissions-troubles-idUSKBN14V2E8?il=0; Devlin Barrett & Aruna Viswanatha, *U.S. Pursues New Tack in VW Emissions Probe,* WALL ST. J., Mar. 8, 2016.

- 18 U.S.C. § 657 (embezzling, abstracting, purloining, or wilfully misapplying property of lending, credit, and insurance institutions),

- 18 U.S.C. § 1005 (false bank entries, reports, and transactions),

- 18 U.S.C. § 1006 (federal credit institution entries, reports, and transactions),

- 18 U.S.C. § 1007 (Federal Deposit Insurance Corporation transactions),

- 18 U.S.C. § 1014 (loan and credit applications generally; renewals and discounts; crop insurance),

- 18 U.S.C. § 1344 (bank fraud),

- 18 U.S.C. § 287 (false claims),

- 18 U.S.C. § 1001 (false statements),

- 18 U.S.C. § 1032 (concealment of assets from conservator, receiver, or liquidating agent),

- 18 U.S.C. § 1341 (mail fraud),

- 18 U.S.C. § 1343 (wire fraud), and

- 15 U.S.C. § 645(a) (fraud in connection with Small Business Administration transactions).[807]

While FIRREA liability arises from these criminal predicates, proof of these offenses can be established on a mere

---

[807] 12 U.S.C. § 1833a(c).

321

preponderance of the evidence, greatly easing the government's trial burden.[808]

For the predicate offenses of false claims, false statements, mail fraud, and wire fraud, FIRREA liability can be imposed only if the underlying conduct "affect[s] a federally insured financial institution."[809] However, FIRREA's text does not itself define the term "affect." The federal courts that have confronted this question have defined the term so broadly as to suggest that the resulting effect does not have to be a negative one and that a financial institution can be liable under FIRREA for misconduct that affects itself (even for "effects," such as litigation costs and reputational damage, caused by having the Justice Department bring a FIRREA suit).[810] Although the validity of the rather circular "self-affecting" interpretation remains a contested issue, the Second Circuit has authored a *per curiam* opinion that endorses an expansive reading of FIRREA's "affect" provision.[811]

FIRREA provides for three alternative civil penalty possibilities, allowing for (1) a more than $2.3 million per violation penalty; (2) up to a nearly $12 million penalty for continuing violations; or (3) these penalty "caps" to be exceeded if they are less than the defendant's "pecuniary gain" or the victim's "pecuniary loss."[812]

---

[808] 12 U.S.C. § 1833a(f).

[809] 12 U.S.C. § 1833a(c)(2).

[810] *See United States v. Bogucki,* No. 18-cr-00021-CRB-1, 316 F. Supp. 3d 1177 (N.D. Cal. 2018); *United States v. Bank of N.Y. Mellon,* 941 F. Supp. 2d 438, 456–60 (S.D.N.Y. 2013); *United States v. Wells Fargo Bank, N.A.,* 972 F. Supp. 2d 593, 629–31 (S.D.N.Y. 2013); *United States ex rel. O'Donnell v. Countrywide Fin. Corp.,* 961 F. Supp. 598, 604–05 (S.D.N.Y. 2013), *rev'd,* 822 F.3d 650 (2d Cir. 2016) (reversing jury verdict in plaintiff's favor on ground that Justice Department failed to adduce evidence sufficient to establish predicate offenses of mail and wire fraud, while bypassing ruling on Justice Department's controversial "self-affecting" theory under FIRREA).

[811] *United States v. Heinz,* 790 F.3d 365 (2d Cir. 2015) (per curiam).

[812] 12 U.S.C. § 1833a(b). As with FCA penalties, FIRREA penalties are subject to annual upward adjustments. The penalties described above are as of the 2023 annual adjustment. *See* Civil Monetary Penalties Inflation Adjustments for 2023,

However, FIRREA does not specify the criteria to be used in assessing penalties within the permissible ranges nor does it provide guidance with respect to the terms "gain" or "loss," and those issues have only briefly been touched on by the courts.[813] While very few FIRREA cases have gone to trial, FIRREA settlement amounts have been extremely high – particularly in cases involving residential mortgage backed securities (RMBS) – demonstrating the threat that companies face from this statute. In 2017 alone, announced RMBS settlements of FIRREA claims exceeded $13.4 billion, far surpassing total FCA recoveries during the same period.[814]

---

88 Fed. Reg. 5776, 5778 (Jan. 30, 2023) (as of January 30, 2023, the per violation penalty is $2,372,677, and the penalty for continuing violations is $11,863,393).

[813] *See, e.g., United States v. Luce,* 2019 WL 3003300 (N.D. Ill. July 10, 2019) (granting summary judgment in favor of defendant on FCA claims but awarding FIRREA penalties even though there was no accompanying loss proximately caused by defendant); *United States ex rel. O'Donnell v. Countrywide Home Loans, Inc.*, 33 F. Supp. 3d 494 (S.D.N.Y. 2014) (reasoning that a $1.3 billion civil penalty was appropriate because, unlike FCA damages which are meant to compensate for losses, FIRREA penalties are designed to deter and punish, and thus should be measured by gross (rather than net) gains or losses), *rev'd on other grounds*, 822 F.3d 650 (2d Cir. 2016); *United States v. Menendez,* No. 11-cv-6313 MMM (JCGx), 2013 WL 828926 (C.D. Cal. Mar. 6, 2013) (setting forth criteria to consider when imposing a FIRREA penalty, including the good/bad faith of the defendant, injury to the public, the egregiousness of violation, and the defendant's ability to pay).

[814] In February 2020, the Justice Department announced a $3 billion settlement with Wells Fargo & Co. to resolve both potential criminal and civil FIRREA liability. Press Release, Dep't of Justice, *Wells Fargo Agrees to Pay $3 Billion to Resolve Criminal and Civil Investigations into Sales Practices Involving the Opening of Millions of Accounts without Customer Authorization* (Feb. 21, 2020), *available at* www.justice.gov/opa/pr/wells-fargo-agrees-pay-3-billion-resolve-criminal-and-civil-investigations-sales-practices. In April 2019, the Justice Department announced a $1.5 billion settlement with General Electric to resolve potential FIRREA liability. Press Release, Dep't of Justice, *General Electric Agrees to Pay $1.5 Billion Penalty for Alleged Misrepresentations Concerning Subprime Loans Included in Residential Mortgage-Backed Securities* (Apr. 12, 2019), *available at* www.justice.gov/opa/pr/general-electric-agrees-pay-15-billion-penalty-alleged-misrepresentations-concerning-subprime. In August 2018, the Justice Department announced a $4.9 billion settlement with The Royal Bank of Scotland Group plc to resolve potential FIRREA liability. Press Release, Dep't of Justice, *Royal Bank of Scotland Agrees to Pay $4.9 Billion for Financial*

D. Comparing the Two Statutes

Certain key differences between the FCA and FIRREA dictate that the FCA will remain the favored statute of "whistleblowers" and their counsel. While the FCA provides for *qui tam* actions and the related bounty, Congress did not include any comparable provision in FIRREA.[815] Moreover, unlike the FCA, there is no anti-retaliation provision or provision for whistleblower counsel to recover their fees and costs under FIRREA.

On the other hand, FIRREA has a standard ten-year statute of limitations, as opposed to the FCA's default six-year limitations period. And, unlike the FCA, FIRREA liability does not require proof of any government involvement at all, let alone any losses sustained by the government.[816] These factors, along with the proven record of hefty recoveries under both FIRREA and the FCA, mean that companies can expect the Justice Department to investigate and advance claims under both statutes, wherever possible, for the same underlying conduct.[817]

Crisis-Era Misconduct (Aug. 14, 2018), *available at* www.justice.gov/opa/pr/royal-bank-scotland-agrees-pay-49-billion-financial-crisis-era-misconduct. And in March 2018, the Justice Department announced a $2 billion settlement with Barclays Capital Inc. and various affiliates to end a civil action in the United States District Court for the Eastern District of New York. Press Release, Dep't of Justice, *Barclays Agrees to Pay $2 Billion in Civil Penalties to Resolve Claims for Fraud in the Sale of Residential Mortgage-Backed Securities* (March 29, 2018), *available at* www.justice.gov/opa/pr/barclays-agrees-pay-2-billion-civil-penalties-resolve-claims-fraud-sale-residential-mortgage.

[815] FIRREA allows for whistleblower reports and recovery through the Financial Institutions Anti-Fraud Enforcement Act of 1990, 12 U.S.C. § 4201, but the recovery often is just a small percentage of what a relator would receive as a "bounty" under the FCA.

[816] The government abandoned its FCA claims in the *O'Donnell* case because the alleged false claims submitted to Fannie Mae and Freddie Mac were not actionable under the FCA before a 2009 amendment expanded the definition of "claim" beyond government entities to government programs or interests. *See O'Donnell*, 961 F. Supp. 2d at 608–09 (S.D.N.Y. 2013).

[817] Although the statute FIRREA most commonly is paired and compared with is the FCA, the Justice Department also has boosted FIRREA's breadth by including

III. RECOGNIZING THE BEGINNING OF A GOVERNMENT INVESTIGATION

A. Notice through Civil Investigative Demands and Subpoenas

The FCA authorizes the Justice Department to investigate possible FCA violations by using an administrative tool called a Civil Investigative Demand ("CID").[818] The Attorney General, senior enforcement officials in the Civil Division, and U.S. Attorneys are authorized to issue and serve CIDs on companies and individuals who may possess information relevant to a FCA investigation, and a CID recipient is required to produce documents, give sworn testimony, answer written interrogatories, or any combination of the above. There is no right to reciprocal discovery by a CID recipient or the target of the investigation during the pre-suit or pre-intervention stage of a FCA investigation.

Prior to recent FCA amendments that made it easier to authorize the issuance of CIDs, the Justice Department often relied on federal agency subpoena authority – available through agency inspectors general ("IG") – to compel the production of documents for purposes of FCA investigations.[819] Even with the increased usage of CIDs, however, service of an IG subpoena remains one of the first indicators a company may have that it is facing a FCA investigation.

The investigative tools available to the Justice Department under FIRREA include the authority to issue subpoenas compelling testimony and document productions, all in mere "contemplation" of filing suit and with no prior judicial review.[820] The Justice Department has capitalized on this authority in several cases. For instance, the Justice Department itself announced that prior to

---

FIRREA claims alongside traditional Securities and Exchange Commission lawsuits.

[818] 31 U.S.C. § 3733.

[819] 5a U.S.C. § 6(a)(4).

[820] 12 U.S.C. § 1833a(g).

filing a FIRREA complaint against Standard & Poor's it had conducted a multi-year investigation which included the issuance of *hundreds* of subpoenas, the production of millions of pages of documents, and interviews of dozens of current and former Standard & Poor's employees.[821]

Under the FCA, the information the government obtains can be shared with a *qui tam* relator if the government believes it may be useful to the investigation, and the information may be used by other government agencies for an "official use." Production of the material is not required if it would be protected from disclosure in a grand jury investigation or in discovery under the Federal Rules of Civil Procedure. However, unlike evidence gathered in the course of a federal grand jury investigation, where grand jury secrecy rules place strict limitations on the government's use of material subpoenaed by the grand jury, no such restrictions limit the Justice Department's ability to disseminate evidence compelled pursuant to FIRREA subpoenas. Nor is there any reason to believe that courts will, in any meaningful way (in response to a motion to quash or a Justice Department motion to enforce), curtail the Justice Department's ability to gather information in the course of a pre-suit FIRREA investigation.

Many companies routinely receive subpoenas seeking information for use in litigation, and they have well-established procedures for ensuring timely review of and compliance with such subpoenas. However, CIDs, IG subpoenas, and FIRREA subpoenas are anything but routine and require special attention. These information demands are indicators that the company or its personnel are in some manner enmeshed in a FCA or FIRREA investigation, and it is essential that company counsel assemble the appropriate personnel and resources to handle and respond to these demands.

---

[821] Press Release, Dep't of Justice, *Principal Deputy Assistant Attorney General for the Civil Division Stuart F. Delery Speaks at the Press Conference Announcing Lawsuit against S&P* (Feb. 5, 2013), *available at* www.justice.gov/opa/speech/principal-deputy-assistant-attorney-general-civil-division-stuart-f-delery-speaks-press.

B.   Other Indicia of a Government Investigation

There are more subtle indicia of a government investigation that in-house counsel should keep in mind.

First, internal reporting may indicate a pending or forthcoming government investigation. Internal reporting comes in many forms and descriptions, not all of which immediately suggest potential FIRREA or FCA allegations. In-house counsel often have the difficult task of making sure such reports come to the legal department's attention and then sorting through complaints to decide whether a looming FCA or FIRREA enforcement issue needs to be addressed. But it is key for in-house counsel to handle such reports correctly in order to minimize the risk or ramifications of a related government investigation.

Second, news that company personnel, associates, and counter-parties – including current or former employees, subcontractors, and suppliers – have received a CID or subpoena should trigger an analysis as to whether the company itself is at risk.

Third, claims leveled against other industry players (particularly where the allegation is that the misconduct is widespread) likewise should place company counsel on alert that it may be vulnerable to similar claims.

Finally, a FCA or FIRREA investigation can be propelled by other actions, including criminal matters, administrative audits, and civil suits.[822]

---

[822] *See, e.g., United States ex rel. Moore & Co. v. Majestic Blue Fisheries, LLC,* 812 F.3d 294 (3d Cir. 2016) (noting discovery in wrongful death action revealed defendants' alleged false certifications to the U.S. Coast Guard).

IV. EARLY CONSIDERATIONS FOR IN-HOUSE COUNSEL

A. Document Preservation

Once a company receives a subpoena, CID, or some other indicator of a FCA or FIRREA investigation, such as a government request that a company "voluntarily" produce documents or make its personnel available for interviews, prompt action must be taken to preserve any responsive documents. In most companies, this action will include issuance of a "legal hold" memorandum or similar document preservation instruction. Counsel, outside and in-house, must be knowledgeable about the issues, relevant employees, and the company's information storage locations and protocols in order to ensure that preservation efforts are appropriate. And counsel should consider suspension of company-wide document destruction policies, at least for key employees or groups relevant to the subject matter of the potential claims.

With a subpoena or CID in hand, in-house or outside counsel (as appropriate) should contact the government attorney(s) handling the matter to understand what types of information the government is seeking, to begin to explain any burdens associated with compliance, and to try to narrow the scope of the subpoena as much as possible. All such communications – and particularly any agreements to modify the scope, production date, or preservation obligations – should be memorialized.

Counsel should re-visit a hold memorandum whenever additional information about the potential claims is gained, and updates or reminders should be issued at appropriate times. Beyond that, legal departments should work with human resources departments and information technology departments to ensure the ongoing preservation of documents (and potentially devices), including as individuals leave the company's employment.

The proper preservation of documents (and written recordation of the same) is key to avoiding spoliation claims and adverse inferences in litigation. Moreover, a company that can demonstrate full compliance with its preservation obligations may gain a litigation advantage in cases where the affected agency and/or relators have failed to comply with their preservation obligations.

B.   An Internal Investigation

In addition to complying with the government's investigative demands, the company should consider conducting its own internal investigation in order to determine the facts,[823] brief management and board members, make any disclosures, and take necessary action to stop any ongoing misconduct. The internal investigation will enable company counsel to engage with the government at the earliest opportunity. It is often the case that government FCA investigations – particularly ones prompted by *qui tam* filings – are the product of misunderstandings, lack of knowledge about government procurement or programs, gross exaggerations, and otherwise spurious claims of wrongdoing. Armed with the actual facts gained through an internal investigation, company counsel often are able to demonstrate to the government attorneys that the allegations lack merit or are blown out of proportion. The ability to have those types of discussions with the government early in the investigation, before the government invests significant time and effort, and certainly before a FCA intervention decision, is invaluable.

C.   Preserving Privileges

The company's ability to assert attorney-client privilege and work product protection in litigation often depends on the steps taken to protect the privileges during the investigation stage. And the failure to protect privileged material or communications can have implications for the company well beyond just one investigation or litigation. However, since the preservation of the attorney-client and work product privileges are treated extensively in other chapters, only a few key considerations are highlighted here.

---

[823] In appropriate circumstances, this may include retention of an expert to evaluate the information gathered, particularly where the government has indicated that it is engaged in expert analysis.

Counsel should consider marking the legal hold memorandum as privileged in order to protect any applicable privilege.

With respect to an internal investigation, it is important to have written policies, procedures, and other documentation to indicate the privileged nature and purpose of the investigation. Also key to preserving privilege over investigation materials is having an attorney play a principal role in – and certainly direct – the investigation.[824]

During internal investigation interviews, counsel should provide *Upjohn* warnings,[825] *i.e.,* they should tell the employees that they are gathering facts in order to provide legal advice to the company, that the interviewer is counsel for the company and not the employee, that the interview is confidential and protected by the company's attorney-client privilege, and that the company expects the employee to preserve the company's privilege with respect to the interview.[826]

Communications regarding and materials generated for the investigation should contain appropriate legends to preserve any applicable privilege.[827] In investigations involving multiple potential defendants, such as a company and its subcontractor or supplier, joint defense and common interest agreements should be considered in order to avoid the waiver of any privilege.

---

[824] *See In re Kellogg Brown & Root, Inc.*, 756 F.3d. 754 (D.C. Cir. 2014).

[825] *See Upjohn Co. v. United States*, 449 U.S. 383 (1981).

[826] Of course, counsel may not instruct a witness to avoid government investigators or provide other instructions that would obstruct justice. And in-house counsel should be aware of the relevant ethical rules for their locale, as many provide guidance regarding instructions to current and former employees when the company is facing litigation.

[827] Counsel should take particular care if company employees use a shared server or government-controlled email system, as the government or a relator later could argue that there was no expectation of confidentiality when using that system.

D.   Separate Counsel for Individuals (and the Importance of the *Upjohn* Warning)

Individuals may need independent counsel, and this issue needs to be considered early in the investigation.[828] Obviously, subpoena or CID requests that appear to focus on an individual are indicators that separate counsel for that individual may be warranted. Any hint of a criminal investigation of an individual is another indicator and should be thoroughly assessed.

Justice Department focus on individuals and individual accountability serves to reinforce the importance of the *Upjohn* warning during internal investigations. Interviewers should make clear to any individuals being interviewed that the interviewer is counsel for the company only and is not representing the individual being interviewed or any other individuals at the company.

E.   Avoiding Retaliation Liability

In addition to the issue noted above, the process of interviewing employees and addressing any issues learned through an internal investigation is delicate for another reason: the need to avoid retaliation (and the appearance of retaliation) for any employee internal reporting or external whistleblowing activity. As mentioned above, § 3730(h) of the FCA protects a relator

---

[828] In 2015, the Justice Department adopted a policy – applicable to both the FCA and FIRREA – requiring that civil and criminal corporate investigations focus on individuals from the beginning of the investigation through resolution and ensuring that the resolution of the matter includes "accountability from the individuals who perpetrated the wrongdoing." *See* Memorandum from Sally Quillian Yates, Deputy Attorney Gen., Dep't of Justice, *Individual Accountability for Corporate Wrongdoing* (Sept. 9, 2015) ("Yates Memo"), *available at* www.justice.gov/dag/file/769036/download; Dep't of Justice, Justice Manual § 4-4.000 *et seq.*, *available at* www.justice.gov/jm/jm-4-4000-commercial-litigation; Justice Manual § 9-28.000 *et seq.*, *available at* www.justice.gov/jm/jm-9-28000-principles-federal-prosecution-business-organizations. In 2019, the Justice Department updated and relaxed its policies on the pursuit of claims against individuals and on cooperation credit for corporations. *See* Justice Manual § 4-3.100, *available at* /www.justice.gov/jm/jm-4-3000-compromising-and-closing#4-3.100.

"employee, contractor, or agent" from retaliation for lawful acts in furtherance of a FCA action and "other efforts to stop" a FCA violation, which can include an internal complaint to management about a false claim. In addition, a "whistleblowing" employee may have state or local law employment or tort claims that could be pursued against the company. Thus, counsel should reinforce the message that the company will not tolerate any retaliation against relators or persons engaged in whistleblowing activities.

V. MANDATORY AND VOLUNTARY DISCLOSURES TO THE GOVERNMENT

Another important consideration for counsel when dealing with a pending or possibly forthcoming FCA and/or FIRREA investigation is whether disclosures to the government are required or, if not required, nevertheless prudent.

Within every industry there are regulating bodies, and in-house counsel needs to be aware of any rules regarding reporting requirements. For example, companies that contract with the Department of Defense have counterfeit parts reporting requirements,[829] while banks and other mortgage lenders providing government-insured loans to borrowers have to meet the reporting requirements of the Federal Housing Administration and the U.S. Department of Veterans Affairs. As another example, the Centers for Medicare & Medicaid Services' regulations state that an "overpayment" retained from a government healthcare program must be reported (and/or returned) within a specified time.[830]

More broadly, the Federal Acquisition Regulation ("FAR") mandatory disclosure rule requires reporting to the government whenever there is "credible evidence" of any violation of the FCA

---

[829] See FAR 46.317; FAR 52.246-26.

[830] See Medicare Program: Reporting and Returning of Overpayments, 81 Fed. Reg. 7654-7684 (Feb. 12, 2016) (codified at 42 C.F.R. pts. 401 and 405) (establishing rules for reporting and returning overpayments).

or certain criminal statutes.[831] The disclosure must be "timely," and there is an obligation to take reasonable steps to determine that the evidence is credible, taking into account the facts and legal issues involved.

Beyond any mandatory reporting requirements that may apply, in-house counsel also should consider the potential benefit of a voluntary disclosure when facing potential FCA and/or FIRREA violations. Voluntary disclosure could allow for one or more of the following: demonstration of a robust and effective compliance program, resulting in fewer or no corporate integrity agreement obligations when resolving the matter with the government; potential cooperation credit or the application of a lower multiplier or smaller penalty amount; mitigation of other potential exposure; and/or the strengthening of the company's relationship with the government (as the company's partner, client, and/or regulator).

While the FCA itself has a voluntary disclosure provision, it rarely is used because of the timing strictures in place and the uncertainty of gaining any benefit from that reporting.[832] The Department of Health and Human Services also has established voluntary disclosure programs for providers, contractors, and grantees, including a separate self-referral disclosure protocol for Stark Law violations, but the program has its own subjective requirements that provide no immediate guarantee of a benefit for the reporting company. The Department of Defense replaced its voluntary disclosure program with the FAR mandatory disclosure rule outlined above. Beyond any defined programs, companies also can make voluntary disclosures to a governing agency's office of inspector general or through a number of other avenues, but those

---

[831] Contractor Business Ethics Compliance Program and Disclosure Requirements, 48 C.F.R. pts. 2, 3, 9, 42, and 52 (FAR mandatory disclosure rule).

[832] 31 U.S.C. § 3729(a)(2) (stating a company will be assessed double rather than treble damages where the company: (1) discloses "all information" about the FCA violation within 30 days of obtaining the information, (2) fully cooperates with the government investigation, and (3) had no actual knowledge of any pending government investigation of the violation – and no investigation had commenced – at the time of the disclosure).

avenues often offer even less certainty with respect to any benefit that will be received for reporting.

Obviously, each disclosure decision will be dependent on a number of factors unique to the situation. However, when making a disclosure – mandatory or voluntary – counsel should take care to protect company privileges,[833] as well as confidential/proprietary information (such as through a FOIA exemption request).

VI.   OTHER CONSIDERATIONS AND BEST PRACTICES

Other items to keep in mind when facing a government FCA and/or FIRREA investigation include:

- Establishing a separate internal "billing" code for efforts related to the investigation;

- Instructing employees regarding ongoing, day-to-day communications with their government counterparts;

- Establishing a reserve for any potential liability (and/or litigation costs);

- Providing information (without violating a FCA seal) to the company's board, outside auditors, the company's shareholders, and/or the public;

---

[833] Justice Department attorneys are not supposed to require a company to waive attorney-client privilege or to disclose attorney work product in order to be viewed as cooperative. *See* Dep't of Justice, Justice Manual §§ 9-28.710, 9-28.720 (Principles of Federal Prosecution of Business Organizations), *available at* www.justice.gov/jm/jm-9-28000-principles-federal-prosecution-business-organizations#9-28.710. However, the defense bar generally has a concern that companies choosing not to waive privilege bear the risk that their voluntary disclosure will not be deemed a "full" disclosure for purposes of cooperation credit.

- Considering any related administrative actions, including suspension, debarment, and program exclusion, and reaching out to the relevant administrative officials as appropriate;

- Monitoring public filings in the event a whistleblower complaint is unsealed without advance warning from the Justice Department; and

- Drafting (and updating) a press release/media response so that the company is not caught unaware by a media inquiry.

Chapter 13

The Foreign Corrupt Practices Act – An Overview

By: Robert J. McCully[834]

Congress enacted The Foreign Corrupt Practices Act ("FCPA") in 1977. Congress did so in response to a series of Watergate-sparked investigations that revealed widespread and substantial corporate payments to foreign governments and foreign officials to secure and retain business. Once enacted, the FCPA was only rarely used as a basis for civil or criminal charges;   it turned out to be legislation that was simply ahead of its time in terms of an appetite by the Department of Justice (DOJ) and the Securities and Exchange Commission (SEC) to use it, perhaps out of a concern of placing U.S. companies at a competitive disadvantage in a global economy where bribery was a routine (and expected) practice.

Now, more than forty years later, those concerns are gone (for the most part) as the FCPA, and the discussions it spawned, have resulted in global anti-corruption efforts and laws. Enforcement actions continue to increase year after year. In 2020, FCPA had their biggest enforcement actions with $3.3 billion resolution. In 2021, the biggest case in 2021 the settlement amount was just $122.9 million, and in 2015 the biggest case was $25 million. Even in the case where a monetary settlement is not as significant, company costs of investigating alleged violations continue to increase, often because of the requests made to companies by the government to demonstrate cooperation.

Any company doing business abroad must be aware of the FCPA and its civil and criminal strictures, and must further be aware of the agencies' predilections in bringing enforcement actions and seeking penalties. The purpose of this chapter is to act as a starting

---

[834] Robert ("Rob") McCully is a litigation Partner in the Kansas City, Missouri offices of Shook, Hardy & Bacon, LLP. Rob heads Shook's Government Enforcement and Investigations Practice Group. Tory Martin is a Summer Associate in the Houston office of Shook, Hardy & Bacon LLP, and provided research assistance.

point for that awareness, and to be a guide to the FCPA's requirements, the consequences of violating those requirements, and the benefits of establishing and maintaining a robust compliance program.

I. BRIEF HISTORY OF THE PASSAGE OF THE FCPA

The FCPA has its genesis in a botched break-in at the Watergate Hotel in 1972. The break-in resulted in the appointment of a Special Prosecutor and, as is often the case, one investigation begets another as records and information are turned over, and previously unknown and unforeseen facts and issues become apparent. In this case, the Watergate Special Prosecutor found evidence of several corporations and executive officers using corporate funds for illegal domestic political contributions.

The SEC opened its own investigation, recognizing that these uses of corporate funds potentially involved matters of possible significance to public investors, and that the nondisclosure of such payments could involve violations of federal securities laws. The SEC's Final Report states:

> The Commission's inquiry into the circumstances surrounding alleged illegal political campaign contributions revealed that violations of the federal securities laws had indeed occurred. The staff discovered falsification of corporate financial records, designed to disguise or conceal the source and application of corporate funds misused for illegal purposes, as well as the existence of secret "slush-funds" disbursed outside the normal financial accountability system. These secret funds were used for a number of purposes, including in

some instances, questionable or illegal foreign payments.[835]

The SEC findings resulted in further government scrutiny, this time by the Senate Subcommittee on Multinational Corporations. The Subcommittee Chair, Senator Frank Church, D-Idaho, opened the 1975 subcommittee hearings by recognizing that the SEC's concerns were with the disclosure requirements of U.S. securities laws, whereas the subcommittee's concerns were with the "foreign policy consequences of these payments by U.S. based multinational corporations."[836]

The Subcommittee held hearings involving four separate multinational corporations, each of which were the subject of allegations of payments made directly or indirectly to foreign governments or foreign government officials for business purposes. At the close of those hearings, there was little doubt that at least some U.S. based multinational corporations were making payments to foreign governments and foreign government officials for commercial purposes, and that such payments were likely not being properly disclosed.

In debates that foreshadowed the use of the FCPA as an enforcement tool for the first twenty years of its existence, government officials were divided over the severity of the issue, the pervasiveness of the issue, the fairness to U.S. companies in being singled out for conduct occurring as a part of normal business transactions, and the need for legislation beyond that already found in U.S. securities laws.

Ultimately, the Congress in 1977 took what had initially been an effort to ensure that publicly held companies were accurately recording and disclosing all payments to foreign governments and

---

[835] U.S. Sec. & Exch. Comm'n, Report of the Securities and Exchange Commission on Questionable and Illegal Corporate Payments and Practices (1976).

[836] Multinational Corporations and United States Foreign Policy: Hearings before the Subcommittee on Multinational Corps. of the S. Comm. On Foreign Relations, 94th Cong. 1 (1975).

338

foreign government officials, and determined that the very payment itself should be criminalized. And thus was born the first aggressive anti-bribery statute among the developed nations of the world.[837]

The accompanying House Report stated that the payment of bribes to influence foreign officials is unethical, counter to the moral expectations and values of the American public, and is "just bad business in a free market system."[838] The accompanying Senate Report said much the same – "in our free market system, it is basic that the sale of products should take place on the basis of price, quality, and service" and "[a] strong anti-bribery law is urgently needed to bring these corrupt practices to a halt and to restore public confidence in the integrity of the American business system."[839]

The same debates that marked the legislative response to the issue of payments to foreign governments seemed to influence the use of the FCPA as an enforcement tool in its first 10 years. In those 10 years, there were just 8 criminal actions brought. Concerns continued over the fact that the FCPA, with its focus on U.S. companies, put these companies at a competitive disadvantage in international markets, since foreign competitors were not similarly constrained by laws prohibiting bribery.

In 1988, Congress added two affirmative defenses to the FCPA.[840] Just as significantly, Congress directed the executive branch to

---

[837] For a comprehensive and historically-entertaining description of the passage of the FCPA, *see* M. Koehler, *The Story of the Foreign Corrupt Practices Act*, 73 Ohio State L.J. 929 (2012).

[838] H. REPT. 95-640 (1977).

[839] S. REPT. 95-114, at 4 (1977).

[840] The first of these defenses is that the payment, gift, offer, or promise to anything of value made was lawful under the written laws and regulations of the foreign official's country. The second was that the payment, gift, offer, or promise of anything of value made was a reasonable and bona fide expenditure, such as travel and lodging expenses, directly related to the promotion of products or the performance of a contract with a foreign government. 15 U.S.C. §§78dd-1(c), 78dd-2(c), 78dd-3(c). The FCPA continues to exclude a "facilitating or

commence negotiations in the Organization of Economic Cooperation and Development ("OECD") to try to reach an agreement binding upon other countries to enact legislation similar to the FCPA so that U.S. companies were no longer disadvantaged in international markets. Those negotiations came to fruition in the 1997 OECD Convention on Combating Bribery of Foreign Public Officials in International Business Transactions, ratified by the U.S. and 33 other countries at that time. There are now 43 signatories to the Convention, which establishes legally binding standards to criminalize bribery of foreign government officials in international business transactions and requires each signatory country to put into place the necessary measures to establish the criminal liability of legal persons for the bribery of a foreign public official.

Congress amended the FCPA in 1998 to ratify the 1997 OECD Convention and to enact implementing legislation. Congress expanded the scope of the FCPA by broadening its jurisdictional reach to cover non-U.S. persons acting within the U.S. as well as U.S. persons acting outside the United States. The 1998 amendments also expanded the types of business activities covered, and broadened the definition of a "foreign government official" to include employees of public international organizations such as the World Bank and the International Monetary Fund. The amendments also broadened the purpose of the bribe to mean more than just securing business – it now included the securing of "any improper advantage" from the foreign government or its officials.

More recently, the Senate introduced a bill, entitled Countering Corporate Corruption in China Act of 2023, in January 2023. S. 151, 118th Cong. (2023). This bill proposes amendments to the FCPA due to difficulties in enforcing the FCPA against certain practices of the Chinese Communist Party, the Government of the People's Republic of China, and instrumentalities thereof. *Id.* at § 2(2). These amendments are specifically tailored to only apply to individuals in connection with the Chinese Communist Party, the

---

expediting payment" to a foreign office to expedite or secure a routine governmental action (such as processing visas or providing utilities). 15 U.S.C. §§78dd-1(b), 78dd-2(b), 78dd-3(b).

Government of the People's Republic of China, and instrumentalities thereof. *Id.*

II.   THE FCPA – ANTI-BRIBERY PROVISIONS[841]

The anti-bribery provisions of the FCPA are found in 15 U.S.C. §§78dd-1 (Issuers), 78-dd-2 (Domestic Concerns), 78dd-3 (Persons Other Than Issuers or Domestic Concerns) and 78ff (Penalties). The elements of the anti-bribery provisions can be categorized as: (a) The Covered Payor; (b) The Covered Recipient; (c) The Impermissible Action; (d) The Impermissible Purpose; and (e) The Impermissible Intent.

A.   The Covered Payor

The FCPA has three separate sections addressing each of three different categories of Covered Payor: Issuers, Domestic Concerns, and Persons Other Than Issuers and Domestic Concerns.

15 U.S.C. 78dd-1 addresses Issuers and states that "any issuer which has a class of securities registered pursuant to [Section 12 of the Exchange Act] or which is required to file reports under [Section 15(d) of the Exchange Act] or "any officer, employee, or agent of such issuer or any stockholder thereof acting on behalf of such issuer" is subject to the FCPA's anti-bribery provisions. This means that any company with a class of securities listed on a U.S. national securities exchange, or any company with a class of

---

[841] The FCPA has been the subject of very few judicial decisions. Much of the interpretation and analysis of its language has come only in the form of DOJ and SEC interpretations and their exercise of enforcement authority, as detailed in settlement agreements. In November 2012, the DOJ and SEC published *A Resource Guide to the U.S. Foreign Corrupt Practices Act*, partially in response to increasing uncertainty about the reach of the FCPA, in light of the lack of judicial interpretation. In their Foreword, the agencies stated that the Resource Guide "endeavors to provide helpful information to enterprises of all shapes and sizes – from small businesses doing their first transactions abroad to multinational corporations with subsidiaries around the world." The Resource Guide provides "insight into DOJ and SEC enforcement practices...." While certainly authored from a government perspective, the Resource Guide is a required publication for the bookshelf of any practitioner in this substantive area of practice.

securities quoted in the U.S. over-the-counter market and required to file periodic reports with the SEC, is an Issuer and subject to the FCPA. There is no requirement that the Issuer be a U.S. company, so long as the above Exchange Act requirements are satisfied.

15 U.S.C. 78-dd2 addresses Domestic Concerns. Like Issuers, Domestic Concerns and their officers, directors, employees, or agents, or shareholders thereof acting on behalf of the Domestic Concern are deemed to be subject to the FCPA's anti-bribery provisions. The statute defines Domestic Concern as any individual who is a citizen, national, or resident of the U.S., and any business entity which either has its principal place of business in the U.S. or is organized under the laws of a State of the U.S. [842]

Finally, 15 U.S.C. 78dd-3 addresses Persons Other Than Issuers or Domestic Concerns. These "Persons" are defined as any person, and their officers, directors, employees, or agents, or any shareholder acting on behalf of such person, who take any act in furtherance of an Impermissible Action while in the territory of the United States. This section covers non-US citizens or residents acting on U.S. soil. [843]

---

[842] Domestic Concerns that also fit the definition of Issuers are treated in accordance with the Issuers section, 15 U.S.C. §78dd-1.

[843] The U.S. Government has consistently looked to extend the FCPA's jurisdictional reach. In a recent Second Circuit ruling (*U.S. v. Hoskins,* Case No. 16-1010-cr (2d. Cir. Aug. 24, 2018), the Court found that there are indeed limits to the FCPA's reach, with the FCPA clearly setting forth the categories of persons that can be found to be in violation of the FCPA. Hoskins was charged with conspiracy to violate the FCPA, both in an individual capacity and as an agent of a U.S. company. The Court dismissed the government's charges, to the extent they were brought against Hoskins in an individual capacity, because the FCPA's language is clear that foreign nationals, not acting as agents of an issuer or domestic concern, can only be charged with an FCPA violation if that foreign national engaged in Impermissible Actions while on U.S. soil.

The practical and precedential effect of the Court's decision may be minimal because of the unique factual circumstances presented in Hoskins. Still, the Court's ruling does stand for the proposition that there are limits to the FCPA's reach, and those limits are found in the statutory language. As an additional note, the Court's detailed opinion is another good resource to consult in researching

B.   The Covered Recipient

Each of the three anti-bribery sections defines the element of Covered Recipient in the same way. The categories of Covered Recipient are:

- Foreign Official

- Foreign Political Party or Official Thereof

- Candidate for Foreign Political Office

- Any Person Knowing That All or Some of Money or Thing of Value will be Offered to Any of the Above

The sections further define "Foreign Official" as:

> Any officer or employee of a foreign government or any department, agency, or instrumentality thereof, or of a public international organization, or any person acting in an official capacity for or on behalf of any [of the foregoing].

The FCPA prohibits payments to foreign officials, not to foreign governments. However, any company considering a payment or provision of anything of value to a foreign government should take care that the transaction is not for an Impermissible Purpose, as it

---

Congressional intent in the 1977 passage of, and subsequent 1998 amendments to, the FCPA.

This argument may not work in every jurisdiction. For example, in *U.S. v. Firtash* the Northern District of Illinois distinguished *Hoskins* by comparing two cases— *U.S. v. Amen*, 831 F.2d 373 (2nd Cir. 1987) and *U.S. v. Pino-Perez*, 870 F.2d 1230 (7th Cir. 1989). 392 F. Supp. 3d 872, 889–92. In doing so, the *Firtash* court refused to apply *Hoskins* to the defendants' motion to dismiss FCPA claims. *Id.* at 889. The *Firtash* court reasoned that there was no basis to infer an affirmative legislative policy to constrain the statute's extraterritorial application because the Seventh Circuit has determined that legislative history—on which *Hoskins* relied—is unreliable in this type of inquiry. *Id.* at 892.

could be relatively simple to find evidence of individual foreign officials receiving some benefit/value from the transaction.

C. The Impermissible Action

Each of the three anti-bribery sections define the element of The Impermissible Action in the same way. Specifically, the FCPA makes it unlawful for any Covered Payor to make use of the mails or any means or instrumentality of interstate commerce in furtherance of an offer, payment, promise to pay, or authorization of the payment of any money, or offer, or gift, promise to give, or authorization of the giving of anything of value to a Covered Recipient if done with an Impermissible Intent for an Impermissible Purpose.

The scope of this Impermissible Action, when one considers that it encompasses offers as well as payments of money, and offers as well as actual gifts "of anything of value" is substantial. The DOJ has routinely prosecuted cases involving payments of cash; it has also prosecuted cases involving travel expenses, household maintenance expenses, payment of cell phone bills, country club memberships, job or internship offers, and entertainment expenses. Even charitable contributions can come under the scrutiny of the DOJ if viewed as a pretense to direct bribes to foreign government officials.

D. The Impermissible Purpose

Again, each of the three anti-bribery sections define the element of The Impermissible Purpose similarly. The FCPA makes it unlawful for a Covered Payor to engage in The Impermissible Action with a Covered Recipient for the purpose of:

- Influencing any act or decision of a Covered Recipient in his or her official capacity,

- Inducing a Covered Recipient to do or omit to do any act in violation of the lawful duty of that official,

- Securing any improper advantage, or

- Inducing a Covered Recipient to use his or her influence with a foreign government or instrumentality to affect or influence any act or decision of such government or instrumentality, in order to assist such Covered Payor in obtaining or retaining business.

This element is often referred to as the "business purpose" test. At the time the FCPA was first amended in 1988, Congress stated its "wish to make clear that the reference to corrupting payments for 'retaining business' in present law is not limited to the renewal of contracts or other business, but also includes a prohibition against corrupt payments related to the execution or performance of contracts or the carrying out of existing business...." Congress gave "favorable tax treatment" as an example. The DOJ and SEC have pursued charges related to bribes to obtain favorable tax assessments, expedited importing of goods and equipment, and the avoidance of applicable customs duties on imported goods. Courts have typically supported this broad interpretation of the "business purpose" test. In _United States v. Kay_, 359 F. 3d 738 (5th Cir. 2004), the Court reviewed Congress' intent and concluded that "Congress meant to prohibit a range of payments wider than only those that directly influence the acquisition or retention of government contracts...The congressional target was bribery paid to engender assistance in improving the business opportunities of the payor or his beneficiary,...irrespective of whether it be related to administering the law, awarding, extending, or renewing a contract, or executing or preserving an agreement." 359 F. 3d at 749-50.

E.   The Impermissible Intent

Finally, each of the three anti-bribery sections use a single word, otherwise undefined in the FCPA, to set the necessary standard of intent for criminal liability to attach – the word is "corruptly." To violate the FCPA, the offer or payment of money, or the offer or gift of anything of value must be done "corruptly." "Corruptly" is the same standard of intent found in the domestic bribery statutes (12 U.S.C. §201(b)). The accompanying Senate and House reports to the FCPA both state that "corruptly" connotes an evil purpose or motive, an intent to wrongfully influence the recipient. Both reports further state that an intent to wrongfully influence the recipient is the key; it makes no difference that the act be fully consummated or succeed in producing the desired outcome.

A related concept to intent relates to the willfulness of any individual criminal defendant, which is a further prerequisite to individual criminal liability under the FCPA. As with "corruptly," there is no further definition of the term "wilfully," as used in the FCPA, and there is very little FCPA case law directly on point. That which does exist looks to case law examining "wilfully" under other criminal statutes. Those courts have held generally that it is sufficient that the government establish that the defendant acted with knowledge that his conduct was unlawful, that it was undertaken with a bad purpose. It is not necessary that the government prove a specific awareness of the FCPA or its specific requirements; it is enough to prove that the defendant knew generally that his conduct was unlawful.

III.   BOOKS AND RECORDS PROVISIONS

In addition to the more-publicized anti-bribery provisions, the FCPA also requires companies to maintain accurate financial books and records, as well as a system of internal controls. These accounting provisions are found at 15 U.S.C. §78m (b) (2) and (b) (5).

A.   Covered Parties

The entities covered by the FCPA's accounting provisions is a much smaller group. Generally, the accounting provisions apply to the group of Covered Entities deemed Issuers under the anti-bribery provisions (i.e., those companies that have securities registered on a national stock exchange under Section 12 of the Exchange Act or those required to file reports under Section 15(d) of the Exchange Act). The provisions apply to all dealings by the

Issuer, regardless of whether the transaction has any aspects of a bribe or even involves foreign operations.

B.   Two Primary Requirements

1.   Record Keeping

The FCPA accounting provisions require that the Issuer "make and keep books, records, and accounts which, in reasonable detail, accurately and fairly reflect the transactions and dispositions of the assets of the Issuer." 15 U.S.C. §78m (b) (2) (A). The statute defines "reasonable detail" as "such level of detail...as would satisfy prudent officials in the conduct of their own affairs." 15 U.S.C. §78m (b) (7).

The accompanying Senate Report noted that, in the past, "corporate bribery has been concealed by the falsification of corporate books and records" and these accounting provisions "remove [] this avenue of cover-up." Senate Report No. 95-114, at 3 (1977). These provisions are intended to address both (a) the complete failure to record illegal transactions; and (b) the falsification of records, usually through mischaracterization of transactions, to conceal illegal transactions.

2.   Internal Controls

The FCPA accounting provisions also require that the Issuer "devise and maintain a system of internal accounting controls sufficient to provide reasonable assurances that:"

- Transactions are properly authorized by management;

- Transactions are recorded as necessary to permit preparation of financial statements in accordance with generally accepted accounting principles;

- Access to assets is only permitted in accordance with management's authorization; and

- The recorded accountability for assets is compared with existing assets at reasonable intervals and appropriate action is taken with respect to any discrepancies.

15 U.S.C. §78m (b) (2) (B). The statute defines "Reasonable Assurances" as "such…degree of assurance as would satisfy prudent officials in the conduct of their own affairs." 15 U.S.C. §78m (b) (7).

C.   Criminal Liability for Violation of Accounting Provisions

The FCPA imposes an intent requirement of "Knowing" before criminal liability attaches for violation of either the "books or records" or internal controls accounting provisions. Specifically, the statute states:

> No person shall knowingly circumvent or knowingly fail to implement a system of internal accounting controls or knowingly falsify any book, record, or account described in [15 U.S.C. §78m (b) (2)].

Additionally, and consistently with the anti-bribery provisions, individuals must act "wilfully" in order to be subject to criminal liability for accounting violations. 15 U.S.C. §78ff (a).

Commonplace accounting deficiencies do not violate the accounting provisions. *See* 15 U.S.C. §78m (b)(4) (no criminal liability attaches unless there is a knowing circumvention of internal accounting controls, a knowing failure to implement internal accounting controls, or a knowing falsification of books, records, and accounts). Further, the Act contains a good faith exception to issuers who own 50 percent or less of a business entity. *See* 15 U.S.C. §78m (b)(6) (such issuer only required by the accounting provisions to show that it "proceed[ed] in good faith to use its influence, to the greatest extent reasonable under the issuer's circumstances, to cause such domestic or foreign firm to devise and maintain a system of internal accounting controls consistent with [15 U.S.C. §78m (b)(2)]...An issuer which demonstrates good faith efforts to use such influence shall be conclusively presumed to have complied with the requirements of [15 U.S.C. §78m (b)(12)].")

D.   The Enforcement Agencies

The DOJ and SEC share enforcement authority for the FCPA. Specifically, DOJ has criminal enforcement authority over Issuers and their officers, directors, employees, agents, or stockholders acting on the Issuer's behalf. The SEC has civil enforcement authority over those Issuers and persons acting on the Issuer's behalf. The DOJ has both criminal and civil enforcement authority over Domestic Concerns (U.S. citizens and residents, and U.S. businesses not registered on a national stock exchange) and persons acting on their behalf; the DOJ has the same dual enforcement authority over foreign persons and businesses that violate the FCPA while on U.S. territory.

For the DOJ, the FCPA Unit within the Fraud Section of the Criminal Division has primary responsibility for all FCPA matters, often in coordination with U.S. Attorneys' offices across the United States. For the SEC, the FCPA Unit (comprised of attorneys in both Washington, D.C., and SEC Regional Offices) within the Enforcement Division has primary responsibility for all FCPA-related matters.

Especially on the criminal side, a number of other federal agencies have significant and substantial involvement in the investigation of FCPA-related matters. These agencies include the Federal Bureau of Investigation (with its International Corruption Unit and specialized FCPA Unit), the Department of Homeland Security, the Internal Revenue Service's Criminal Investigations Division, and the Treasury Department's Office of Foreign Assets Control. Further, there is an ever-increasing level of cooperation and coordination with other countries' anti-corruption and criminal investigation agencies.

IV. PENALTIES FOR VIOLATIONS OF THE FCPA

A. Criminal Penalties

Anti-Bribery	Corporations/Businesses	Fine up to $2 Million[844]	
	Individuals	Fine up to $250,000[845]	Imprisonment up to 5 years[846]
Accounting Provisions	Corporations/Businesses	Fine up to $25 Million[847]	
	Individuals	Fine up to $5 Million[848]	Imprisonment up to 20 years[849]

[844] 15 U.S.C. §§78dd-2(g)(1)(A), 78dd-3(e)(1)(A), 78ff(c)(1)(A).

[845] 15 U.S.C. §§78dd-2(g)(2)(A), 78dd-3(e)(2)(A), 78ff(c)(2)(A), 18 U.S.C. §3571(b)(3), (e). The FCPA sections provide a fine of only up to $100,000. 18 U.S.C. §3571(b)(3) ("Sentence of Fine") supersedes these provisions by stating that "an individual who has been found guilty of an offense may be fined not more than the greatest of – (1) the amount specified in the law setting forth the offense;…(3) for a felony, not more than $250,000…

[846] 15 U.S.C. §§78dd-2(g)(2)(A), 78dd-3(e)(2)(A), 78ff(c)(2)(A).

[847] 15 U.S.C. §78ff (a).

[848] *Id.*

[849] *Id.*

B.   Civil Penalties[850]

Anti-Bribery	Corporations/Businesses	Civil Penalty up to $16,000/violation[851]
	Individuals	Civil Penalty up to $16,000/violation[852]
Accounting Provisions	Corporations/Businesses	Civil Penalty from $75,000 to $725,000/violation[853]
	Individuals	Civil Penalty from $7,500 to $150,000/violation[854]

C.   Collateral Consequences

1.   Debarment

Individuals and companies that violate the FCPA may be barred from doing business with the federal government. Debarment from

---

[850] The Gabriella Miller Kids First Research Act 2.0 proposes an amendment to 15 U.S.C. 78dd-1. S. 1624, 118th Cong. (2023). The amendment would add a provision mandating the Secretary of the Treasury to transfer civil monetary sanctions, including penalties, disgorgement, and interest, to the Pediatric Research Initiative Fund if the defendant (1) registered under the FDA to manufacture, prepare, propagate, compound, or process a drug or medical device in the United States or in a foreign country but imported the drug or device into the United States, (2) produced, manufactured, sold, transported or distributed dietary supplements, or (3) produced, manufactured, sold, transported, or distributed cosmetics. *Id.* The amendment provides an exception for funds to be paid to harmed investors when the Sarbanes-Oxley Act of 2002 is implicated. *Id.*

[851] 15 U.S.C. §§78dd-2(g)(1)(B); 78dd-3(e)(1)(B), 78ff(c)(1)(B); *see also* 17 C.F.R. §201.1004 (adjustments for inflation).

[852] 15 U.S.C. §§78dd-2(g)(2)(B); 78dd-3(e)(2)(B), 78ff(c)(2)(B); *see also* 17 C.F.R. §201.1004 (adjustments for inflation).

[853] 15 U.S.C. §78u(d)(3); *see also* 17 C.F.R. §201.1004 (adjustments for inflation). The amounts provided by the statute are the permitted range of civil penalties for violations of the accounting provisions. The exact amount of the penalty is not to exceed the greater of (a) the gross amount of the pecuniary gain to the defendant as a result of the violations or (b) a specified dollar limitation. The specified dollar limitations are ultimately based on the egregiousness of the offense.

[854] *Id.*

government contracting is not automatic, but is left to the discretion of debarment authorities within each specific government agency, such as the Department of Defense or the Department of Health and Human Services. The Federal Acquisition Regulation (FAR) provides for these debarment decisions, which are triggered upon conviction or civil judgment for bribery, falsification of records, or "[c]ommission of any other offense indicating a lack of business integrity or business honesty that seriously and directly affects the present responsibility of a Government contractor or subcontractor." 48 C.F.R.§§9.402(b).

The independent debarment authorities are to consider such factors as (a) the presence of effective internal control systems in place (either at the time of the activity or prior to any Government Investigation); (b) the extent to which the contractor self-reported the activity to the Government; (c) the extent to which the contractor fully investigated the circumstances, and then shared that investigation with the Government; (d) the level of cooperation by the contractor in the Government investigation of the activity; (e) the extent to which proper remedial measures, including employee disciplinary actions and restitution, have been implemented; and (f) the extent to which the contractor's management recognizes and understands the seriousness of the misconduct and has implemented programs to prevent recurrences. 48 C.F.R. §9.406-1. The contractor bears the burden of demonstrating that debarment is not necessary. 48 C.F.R. §9.406-1(a). A decision by one agency to debar or suspend will be concurrently applied by all Executive Branch agencies, unless a department or agency shows compelling reasons not to adopt the debarment or suspension decision. Exec. Order No. 12,549, 51 Fed. Reg. 6,370 (Feb. 18, 1986); Exec. Order No. 12,689, 54 Fed. Reg. 34131 (Aug. 18, 1989).

2.   Disgorgement

Disgorgement is an equitable remedy authorized by the Securities Exchange Act of 1934 that is intended as a tool to deprive wrongdoers of their ill-gotten gains and to deter violations of federal securities laws. Specifically, the Act gives the SEC authority to enter an order requiring "accounting and disgorgement," including reasonable interest, as part of administrative or cease and desist proceedings.[855] Disgorgement is not to be punitive in nature; accordingly, the SEC is only permitted to recover the approximate amount earned from the alleged violations. Because disgorgement is remedial, rather than punitive, companies may be able to claim disgorged amounts, with any interest assessed, as a tax-deductible expense.

The SEC first used disgorgement in the civil settlement of a FCPA action in 2004. Since that time, the SEC has sought disgorgement in the vast majority of FCPA enforcement actions that it has brought and it is virtually a given today that disgorgement will be on the table. Disgorgement, at $2.245 billion, decreased by 6 percent from the prior fiscal year 2021.[856] In prior years, the disgorgements amounts have reached $350 million. The largest disgorgement in history.

In calculating disgorgement, the SEC is required to distinguish between legally and illegally obtained profits. To do so, the SEC must identify the causal link between the unlawful activity and the profit to be disgorged. Courts tend to give the SEC considerable discretion in determining the amount of this ill-gotten profit by requiring only "a reasonable approximation of profits which are causally connected to the violation."[857] Once the SEC satisfies this threshold, the burden shifts to the defendant to rebut the causal connection and the amount of profits sought.

In the FCPA context, the burden of rebutting can be extremely difficult. The violation involved will typically be the payment of money or anything of value to secure a contract, which may have then led to additional contracts. The SEC will almost always take

---

[855] Securities Exchange Act of 1934, §§78u-2(e) and 78u-3(e).

[856] U.S. Securities and Exchange Commission, *SEC Announces Enforcement Results for FY22* https://www.sec.gov/news/press-release/2022-206 (Nov. 15, 2022)

[857] *See, e.g., SEC v. First City Financial Corp.* 890 F.2d 1215, 1231 (D.D.C. 1989).

the approach that those subsequent contracts or business deals are a result of the first procurement of business, and that the profits from all of the contracts or business deals can be the subject of a disgorgement order. The defendant is left with attempting to prove a break in the causal chain, often by establishing a change in the contract bidding or award process.

In the past couple of years, the DOJ has begun to use the disgorgement tool as well in resolving its investigations into alleged violations of the FCPA by non-Issuers. Disgorgement significantly increases the financial exposure faced by companies in FCPA enforcement matters, and the trend is towards an ever-increasing use of the tool in addition to civil and criminal penalties.

D.   Third Party Issues

The FCPA expressly prohibits improper payments made through third parties. Each of the three anti-bribery provisions contains language covering payments made to "any person, while knowing that all or a portion of such money or thing of value will be offered, given, or promised, directly or indirectly" to a foreign official. 15 U.S.C. §78dd-1(a)(3), 15 U.S.C. §§78dd-2(a)(3), 15 U.S.C. §78dd-3(a)(3). Accordingly, the fact that a bribe is paid by a third party does not eliminate the possibility of liability for an FCPA violation.

The linchpin to liability for payments made through third parties is whether the company "knew" that all or a portion of the thing of value was being offered or paid to a foreign official. "Knowing" under the FCPA is not constrained to "actual knowledge;" it's broader than that. Congress defined "knowing" as that state of mind where the person:

- Is aware that a third party is engaging in improper conduct, or

- That such a result is substantially certain to occur, or

- Has a firm belief that the third party is engaging in improper conduct, or

- Has a firm belief that such a result is substantially certain to occur, or

- Is aware of a high probability of the existence of such conduct, unless the person actually believes that such conduct is not occurring.

15 U.S.C. §§78dd-1(f)(2), 78dd-2(h)(3), 78dd-3(f)(3). In the accompanying House Report, Congress stated:

> [T]he so-called "head-in-the-sand" problem – variously described in the pertinent authorities as "conscious disregard," "willful blindness," or "deliberate ignorance" – should be covered so that management officials could not take refuge from the Act's prohibitions by their unwarranted obliviousness to any action (or inaction), language or other "signaling device" that should reasonably alert them of the "high probability" of an FCPA violation.

H.R. Rep. No. 100-576, at 920 (1988).

What Congress called a "signalling device," the DOJ calls "red flags," and it has identified the following "red flags" as commonly associated with violating payments made to third parties:

- Excessive commissions to third-party agents or Consultants;

- Unreasonably large discounts to third-party distributors;

- Third-party "consulting agreements" that only vaguely describe services to be performed;

- The third-party consultant is in a different line of business than that for which it has been engaged;

- The third party is related to or closely associated with a foreign official;

- The third party became part of the transaction at the request of a foreign official;

- The third party is a shell company, especially if incorporated in an offshore jurisdiction; or

- The third party requests payments to offshore bank requests.

In the DOJ's opinion, each of these "red flags" is sufficient to put the company into a "knowing" state of mind, especially in the absence of an effective compliance program, which includes as one of its key components a process to effectively vet and train third-party agents regarding FCPA requirements and expectations.

E.   Corporate Compliance Programs

The DOJ and SEC consider the adequacy of a company's compliance program when making decisions regarding charging of offenses and the appropriate resolution of such charges. Four of the eleven factors in the DOJ's *Principles of Federal Prosecution of Business Organizations*[858] relate to the design and execution of a corporate compliance program:

- The pervasiveness of wrongdoing within the corporation, including the complicity in, or the condoning of, the wrongdoing by Corporate Management (Factor 2)

---

[858] U.S. Dep't of Just., Just. Manual § 9.28.300 (2023).

- The existence and effectiveness of the corporation's pre-existing compliance program (Factor 5)

- The corporation's timely and voluntary self-disclosure of wrongdoing (ostensibly discovered as part of a compliance program) (Factor 6)

- The corporation's remedial actions, including any efforts to implement an effective corporate compliance program or improve an existing one (Factor 7).

Similarly, the SEC's *Seaboard Report*[859] identified the fact that a company had effective compliance procedures with "tone at the top" that provided for (a) self-policing, (b) self-reporting of misconduct upon discovery, and (c) implementation of appropriate remedial steps (including employee discipline, restitution, and improvement of internal controls) as factors that would cause the SEC to grant credit to a company for cooperation and good corporate citizenship when making decisions regarding enforcement actions.

Finally, the agencies consult the United States Sentencing Guidelines in determining appropriate resolution. Chapter Eight of the Guidelines apply to corporations – under that chapter, an effective compliance program will reduce the culpability score. *See generally* U.S.S.G. Manual §8C2.5 (2005).

The Resource Guide to the FCPA describes what DOJ and SEC have deemed the "Hallmarks of Effective Compliance Programs." The agencies have identified these "hallmarks" while simultaneously stating that there are "no formulaic requirements" regarding compliance programs. Resource Guide, at 57. The

---

[859] SEC Report of Investigation Pursuant to Section 21(a) of the Securities Exchange Act of 1934 and Commission Statement on the Relationship of Cooperation to Agency Enforcement Decisions (2001).

"hallmarks" do stand, however, as signposts to determining the answer to the agencies' three basic questions:

- Is the company's compliance program well designed?

- Is it being applied in good faith?

- Does it work?

USAM §9-28.800. B.

The "hallmarks" include:

1. Commitment from Senior Management and a Clearly Articulated Policy Against Corruption: Has senior management, including the Board of Directors, clearly articulated and communicated company standards, and adhered to them scrupulously, thereby creating a culture of compliance?

2. Code of Conduct and Compliance Policies and Procedures: Are there clear and concise policies designed to address the specific risks associated with the business, and have those policies been made accessible to all employees (in their native language), and have the policies been periodically reviewed to ensure that necessary updates are made to keep the policies current and effective?

3. Oversight, Autonomy, and Resources: Has the company assigned compliance responsibility to appropriate senior management, and do such senior management have requisite authority, autonomy from management, and sufficient resources to ensure effective implementation of the compliance program?

4. <u>Risk Assessment</u>: Does the company's compliance program comprehensively assess and analyze the particular risks faced by the company, so that appropriate resources are brought to bear on economically significant, high-risk transactions (even if it means that some low-risk transactions might result in infractions)?

5. <u>Training and Continuing Advice</u>: Has the company taken steps to ensure that relevant policies and procedures are communicated (including through periodic training and certification) to all affected personnel (including, where appropriate, agents and business partners), and has the company created and made available a means to provide guidance and advice on complying with the company's ethics and compliance program?

6. <u>Incentives and Disciplinary Measures</u>: Does the company consistently enforce its compliance program across all levels of the organization, including the use of disciplinary measures commensurate with the violation, as well as the use of positive incentives (such as positive personnel evaluations, promotions, monetary rewards for compliance leadership, bonuses conditioned on compliance performance) to drive compliant behavior?

7. <u>Third-Party Due Diligence and Payments</u>: If called for by the company's business model, does the compliance program provide adequately for the vetting, training, and ongoing monitoring of third parties, including agents, distributors, and consultants?

8. <u>Confidential Reporting and Internal Investigation</u>: Does the program include a means by which employees (and others) can report actual or

suspected misconduct or policy violations on a confidential basis without fear of retaliation, and does a reliable and properly funded process exist to investigate such reports and document the company's response?

9. <u>Continuous Improvement – Periodic Testing and Review</u>: Does the company regularly review and test its compliance program and policies to determine whether improvements should be made as the company's business and business environments change?

10. <u>Mergers and Acquisitions – Pre-Acquisition Due Diligence and Post-Acquisition Integration</u>: Does the company perform adequate FCPA due diligence prior to a merger or acquisition?

11. <u>Investigation, Analysis, and Remediation of Misconduct</u>: Does the company have a well-functioning and appropriately funded mechanism for the timely and thorough investigations with a well-established means of documenting the company's response and integrating lessons learned from any misconduct?

In February 2017, the DOJ's Criminal Division (Fraud Section) published an eight-page document entitled "Evaluation of Corporate Compliance Programs," which it updated in March 2023. While the document repeats the agencies' statement that there is no checklist or formula to determine whether a compliance program is effective, it recognizes that there are common questions that may be asked in making the individualized determination specific to any particular company.

F.   **DOJ's FCPA Corporate Enforcement Policy – Self-Disclosure, Cooperation, and Remediation**

In November 2017, the DOJ announced a formal policy guiding when business entities can avoid criminal charges for FCPA violations. The policy, found at United States Attorney's Manual (USAM) Insert § 9-47.120, is most significant for its presumption that the government will decline to prosecute companies based on their corporate behavior, if that company has voluntarily self-disclosed its misconduct, fully cooperated in the government's investigation of the same, and timely and appropriately remediated for the FCPA violations (*i.e.*, root cause analysis, implementation of effective compliance program, discipline of individuals involved, disgorgement and restitution).

The DOJ policy does provide that the presumption will be overcome if "aggravating circumstances" exist involving the seriousness of the offense or the nature of the offender. The DOJ provides the examples of "involvement by executive management of the company in the misconduct," "a significant profit to the company from the misconduct," "pervasiveness of the misconduct within the company," and "criminal recidivism." Even in those instances, if the DOJ determines that aggravating circumstances do exist, the policy (a) requires the government to recommend to the sentencing court a 50 percent reduction off the low-end of the U.S. Sentencing Guidelines fine range (except in the case of a criminal recidivist) and (b) generally will not require the appointment of a monitor if the company has implemented an effective compliance program. The policy further provides that if a company did not voluntarily disclose its misconduct to the DOJ, but later fully cooperated and timely and appropriately remediated the misconduct, the government will recommend to the sentencing court a 25 percent reduction off the low-end of the Guidelines fine range.

V. CONCLUSION

The FCPA will continue to be a very significant tool in the government's efforts to deter corrupt business behaviour as it relates to doing business abroad. As more countries around the world adopt (and take steps to enforce) similar anti-corruption regimes, the requirements for multi-national companies will increase and evolve. For "U.S. based" companies, it is critical to remain aware of the FCPA's requirements, and of the agencies' current policies and practices regarding their enforcement of FCPA requirements. Importantly, it is vital that the "U.S. based" company remain aware of its own compliance policies and procedures, ensuring that they are monitored, tested, and modified as needed to meet the needs of the ever-evolving global marketplace.

Chapter 14

Attorney General Civil Investigations and Litigation

By: Gregg W. Mackuse and Nicholas Alford[860]

What was once a relatively rare occurrence has been transformed into constant litigation with virtually every major industry under scrutiny. Historically, class action litigation was at the forefront of a company's greatest litigation exposure and that concern still remains. Now, Attorney General investigations and civil litigation—with the threat of massive civil penalties for what seems like ordinary (if not innocuous) business practices and conduct—have added to a company's exposure and the anxiety of its general counsel. *See, e.g.*, Conn. Unfair Trade Practices Act, Conn. Gen. Stat. § 42-110o (civil penalty of $5,000 per violation; no cap on penalties); Tex. Bus. & Com. Code § 17.47 (authorizing civil penalty of $10,000 per violation; no cap on penalties).

In recent years, state attorneys general have broadened the scope of industries that may be the target of investigations. Pharmaceutical and medical device manufacturers remain a primary target. Other targets include automobile and consumer goods manufacturers, food and beverage providers, and for-profit colleges. State attorneys general have also increased the types of claims in their arsenal, such that a company may face one or more of claims under consumer protection, false claims, antitrust, or environmental statutes, as well as common law claims such as public nuisance, unjust enrichment, or fraud.

Companies must methodically approach every single aspect of an attorney general action. For example, at the investigative stage, companies should engage in discussions with attorney general staff about the precise conduct at issue, and the types of claims—common law and/or statutory—that the attorney general seeks to

---

[860] Gregg W. Mackuse is a Partner, and Nicholas Alford is an Associate, in the law firm of Faegre Drinker Biddle & Reath LLP. The views expressed in this chapter are their own, do not necessarily represent the views of the firm, and should not be considered legal advice.

pursue. If the matter proceeds to litigation, companies should (1) consider changing the forum, (2) challenge the oft-employed practice of a state's use of private contingency counsel to pursue the action, (3) focus on narrowing the scope and number of claims by challenging the availability of the claims in the first instance and the lack of evidence as to the essential elements of the claims, and (4) vigorously attack a state's calculation of damages and civil penalties.

I.   THRESHOLD ISSUES

State attorneys general that opt to pursue a corporate investigation may proceed independently, relying on internal staff, or as part of a multi-state group, under the umbrella of the National Association of Attorneys General ("NAAG"). A company that is the target of either type of investigation will want to coordinate early on with the investigative staff on a host of procedural issues. For instance, it is important to determine if the parties will enter into a tolling agreement. The company will also want to execute a comprehensive confidentiality agreement before it produces any information or documents. Another important procedural issue is the type and scope of information that the attorney(s) general will seek, typically by means of a civil investigative demand or subpoena. If a large multi-state group is involved, they will often designate certain members to comprise an executive committee that will take the lead on the investigation and any ensuing settlement.

Single or multi-state attorney general investigations often result in settlements involving monetary payment and a consent decree. Sometimes, though, an investigation may proceed to litigation because, for example, the parties in a single attorney general matter are not able to resolve the issues. Another not infrequent scenario is for an individual attorney general to peel away from a multi-state group to institute its own litigation. An attorney general may also forego an investigation and proceed directly to litigation.

The unvarnished reality is that once litigation ensues, a company is faced with defending against an adversary who claims to be imbued with the public interest in his or her home forum. An additional reality is that it is highly unlikely that a court will dismiss completely an action brought by a state attorney general. Rather, a state will be given every opportunity to remedy any deficiencies in its claims and to prove its case.

With that in mind, the initial task is to identify those issues that may allow a company to at least narrow the case and, where possible, even change the forum. To that end, the initial analysis should focus on the following threshold issues.

A.   Removal to Federal Court

If a state pursues a claim that implicates a federal statutory scheme, the company may be able to invoke federal question subject matter jurisdiction even if a state is not directly pursuing a federal claim. *E.g.*, *Grable & Sons Metal Prods., Inc. v. Darue Eng'g & Mfg.*, 545 U.S. 308, 314 (2005) ("[A]rising under" jurisdiction exists not only over federal-law claims, but also over state-law claims that "necessarily raise a stated federal issue, actually disputed and substantial, which a federal forum may entertain without disturbing any congressionally approved balance of federal and state judicial responsibilities"); *In re Zyprexa Prod. Liab. Litig.*, No. 04-MD-1596, 2008 WL 398378, at *5 (E.D.N.Y. Feb. 12, 2008) ("Here Lilly's alleged submission of a claim for non-medically accepted indication and promotion of Zyprexa for an off-label use is central and disputed in this case. The extensive use of these terms in the complaint establishes that Montana regards Lilly's alleged violations of federal law as essential to its case."). *But see Nessel ex rel. Michigan v. AmeriGas Partners, L.P.*, 954 F.3d 831, 836-37 (6th Cir. 2020) (holding that where a consumer protection statute does not require the state attorney general to satisfy the core requirements of a federal class action, the statute is not similar to Rule 23 for purposes of CAFA and cannot therefore be removed to federal court pursuant to CAFA).

B.   Use of Outside Counsel on a Contingency Basis

It remains a common practice for states to use private counsel retained on a contingency basis to pursue this type of litigation. This practice has constitutional considerations and has been the subject of court challenges. *See, e.g., Merck Sharp & Dohme Corp. v. Conway*, 947 F. Supp. 2d 733, 739 (E.D. Ky. 2013) ("[A]s long as the required safeguards are in place, a government entity may engage contingency-fee counsel to assist in a civil prosecution without infringing on the defendant's due process rights."); *State v. Lead Indus., Ass'n, Inc.*, 951 A.2d 428, 477 (R.I. 2008) ("[T]he following limitations should be expressly set forth in any contingent fee agreement between that office and private counsel: (1) that the Office of the Attorney General will retain complete control over the course and conduct of the case; (2) that, in a similar vein, the Office of the Attorney General retains a veto power over any decisions made by outside counsel; and (3) that a senior member of the Attorney General's staff must be personally involved in all stages of the litigation." (footnote omitted)). Where a state legislature has not enacted legislation addressing the issue, or a court has not had an opportunity to judge the propriety of the retention, it may be an issue worthy of challenge. Moreover, although formal "control" has been deemed sufficient by a handful of courts, a company should still consider pursuing the argument that "control" by a state attorney general should not excuse the otherwise unconstitutional use of contingent fee counsel in penalty cases any more than "control" by a disinterested district attorney would excuse the prosecution of a case by a subordinate with a financial interest in the outcome.

II. SUBSTANTIVE CLAIMS

In addition to the analysis as to the proper forum and the use of private counsel, another important step is to assess the viability of the claims asserted as well as possible defenses to the claims as the litigation proceeds. The preferred claims in attorney general civil litigation range from traditional common law claims to state-specific statutory claims. Each type of claim carries both opportunities and pitfalls for a corporate defendant.

A. Common Law Claims

Three common law claims often pursued in attorney general litigation are claims of (1) fraud, (2) unjust enrichment, and (3) public nuisance.[861] The former is often asserted to support sweeping allegations that taxpayers were defrauded by corporate misconduct. The second is often asserted due to the broad elements that typically define an unjust enrichment claim, which allow a state to attack virtually any corporate conduct as unjust. *See, e.g., Com. ex rel. Pappert v. TAP Pharm. Prods., Inc.*, 885 A.2d 1127, 1137 (Pa. Cmwlth. 2005) ("A party alleging that a defendant has been unjustly enriched must establish the following: (1) plaintiff conferred a benefit on the defendant; (2) the defendant appreciated the benefit; and (3) acceptance and retention by the defendant of the benefits, under the circumstances, would make it inequitable for the defendant to retain the benefit without paying for the value of the benefit."). And the third has most recently been asserted by state attorneys general and other political subdivisions of a state through novel attempts to address large-scale social problems— such as climate change, the opioid epidemic, tobacco use, gun violence, and lead paint toxicity. *See, e.g., People v. ConAgra Grocery Prods. Co.*, 17 Cal. App. 5th 51, 163-164 (2017) (finding plaintiffs satisfied all the elements of a public nuisance claim in a lead-based paint action).

Fraud claims often can be defended on the basis that a state has no evidence as to the essential element of causation. *E.g., Commonwealth v. Ortho-McNeil-Janssen Pharm., Inc.*, 52 A.3d 498, 511 (Pa. Cmwlth. 2012) ("[O]n the common law element of causation, the Commonwealth did not offer proof that it would have acted differently with knowledge of the 'true' facts. After a week of trial, none of the Commonwealth witnesses stated that they would have acted differently....").

An additional area of inquiry (for both common law claims as well as any statutory claims) should be the extent of a state's knowledge as to the claimed fraudulent conduct. Where the evidence establishes that a state was aware of the conduct later claimed to be

---

[861] Although many states have codified their public nuisance laws, because public nuisance has its origins in common law, we treat it as a common law claim here. Note, however, that when defending a public nuisance claim, counsel should evaluate whether a state has a public nuisance statute, including any statutory defenses that may apply.

fraudulent, an argument can be made that any fraud claim fails. *Sandoz, Inc. v. State*, 100 So.3d 514, 532 (Ala. 2012) ("The evidence in the instant case demonstrates that the State knew, or should have known, that the WACs and AWPs did not represent fully discounted net prices."); *AstraZeneca LP v. State*, 41 So.3d 15, 33 (Ala. 2009) ("[G]iven the State's particularized knowledge of the challenged reporting practices, a claim of common-law fraud—with its element of reasonable reliance—is, like the proverbial 'square peg in a round hole,' particularly ill-suited for the task to which it was put in this dispute.").

For unjust enrichment claims, the defense is often simply that a state received precisely what it paid for and, as a result, it was not "unjust" for the corporate defendant to receive payment for a product. Stated another way, if the product "worked," there is no unjust enrichment because the company provided exactly what was paid for by a state. Also, if a state continues to pay for the product at issue even after litigation is brought, that may also preclude a claim of unjust enrichment. *See, e.g., Prohias v. Pfizer*, 485 F. Supp. 2d 1329, 1335 (S.D. Fla. 2007) (applying Florida and New York law) (holding that plaintiffs failed to state claim for unjust enrichment where plaintiffs "still pay for the drug even though they now know the 'truth'").

Public nuisance claims are often be defended on multiple grounds. First, in many states, public nuisance has historically been limited to facts involving misuse of interference with public property or resources and courts have refused to extend it to circumstances involving the distribution or sale of a product. *See City of Huntington v. AmerisourceBergen Drug Corp.*, 2022 WL 2399876, at *57-59 (S.D. W. Va. July 4, 2022) (declining to extend public nuisance law beyond its historic use) *appeal filed sub nom., Cabell Cnty. Comm. V. AmerisourceBergen Drug Corp.* (4th Cir. Aug. 4, 2022). As various courts have explained, "'[t]o permit otherwise would risk letting everyone sue almost everyone else about pretty much everything that harms us.'" *City of New Haven v. Purdue Pharma, L.P.*, 2019 WL 423990, at *2 (Conn. Super. Ct. Jan. 8, 2019); *see also State ex rel. Attorney General of Oklahoma v. Johnson & Johnson*, 499 P.3d 719, 730 (Okla. 2021) (declining to extend Oklahoma public nuisance law to the manufacturing, marketing, and selling of prescription opioids, noting that such an expansion of public nuisance law would convert nearly every products liability action into a public nuisance claim); *State ex rel. Stenehjem v. Purdue Pharma L.P.*, 2019 WL 2245743, at *13 (D.N.D. May 10, 2019) (declining to extend public nuisances statutes to cases involving the sale of goods); *Tioga Public School Dist. No. 15 of Williams County, State of N.D. v. U.S. Gypsum Co.*, 984 F.2d 915, 920-921 (8th Cir. 1993) (holding nuisance law does not afford a remedy against a manufacturer of a product containing asbestos).

Second, public nuisance laws often require a plaintiff to show an unreasonable interference with a right common to the public. This often requires the court to balance the alleged harm with the social utility of the defendant's conduct to determine its reasonableness. *City of Huntington* 2022 WL 2399876, at *60. In many cases, the alleged harm will be offset by the social utility of defendant's conduct. *Id.* (finding that "the distribution of medicine to support the legitimate medical needs of patients as determined by doctors exercising their medical judgment in good faith cannot be deemed an unreasonable interference with a right common to the general public"); *see also State v. Lead Indus. Ass'n, Inc.*, 951 A.2d 428, 455 (R.I. 2008) (finding plaintiffs failed to identify a public right that was infringed on).

And third, the plaintiff's theory of causation in public nuisance cases is often too attenuated and remote to be plausible because the causal chain between the alleged conduct and the complained of harm is often long and tenuous at best. *See City of Huntington* 2022 WL 2399876, at *60 ("The core of plaintiffs' case is the assertion that the alleged nuisance within their borders was caused by oversupply and diversion of opioids from their legitimate channels, resulting in overuse, addiction and the 'gateway' to malicious illegal substances such as heroin and fentanyl. Such oversupply and diversion were made possible, beyond the supply of opioids by defendants, by overprescribing by doctors, dispensing by pharmacists of excessive prescriptions, and diversion of the drugs to illegal usage—all effective intervening causes beyond the control of defendants. Accordingly, the court concludes that plaintiffs have failed to meet their burden to prove that defendants' conduct was the proximate cause of their injuries.").

B. Consumer Fraud/Deceptive Trade Practices Act Claims

Faced with problems of proof associated with common law claims, states often retreat to the comfort of statutory claims under consumer fraud or deceptive trade practices statutes ("consumer fraud claims"). The reason for that strategy is self-interest—in addition to limited statutory requirements, courts often impose minimal evidentiary requirements (or, in some cases, remove typical evidentiary requirements) on state attorneys general in the context of state consumer fraud claims.

First, the liability standard is exceedingly broad—an act or practice need only have a "tendency to deceive" or be "unfair." *See, e.g., Health Promotion Specialists, LLC v. S.C. Bd. of Dentistry*, 743 S.E.2d 808, 816 (S.C. 2013).

Second, the traditional element of reliance is often eliminated. *See, e.g., Duran v. Leslie Oldsmobile, Inc.*, 594 N.E.2d 1355, 1362 (Ill. App. 1992) ("[R]eliance remains an element of a private cause of action although it has been eliminated as a requirement for actions brought by the Attorney General."); *Nuttall v. Dowell*, 639 P.2d 832, 840 (Wash. App. 1982) ("We agree in general with amicus that consumer reliance need not be shown to establish that a misrepresentation is unfair or deceptive so long as it has a capacity or tendency to deceive. This principle would and should apply to any action which seeks to enjoin or otherwise deter CPA misconduct, *e.g.*, where the Attorney General sues to enforce the CPA on behalf of the public generally." (citation omitted)).

Finally, a state attorney general may be given enhanced rights not available to private litigants. *See, e.g., People ex rel. Madigan v. United Const. of Am., Inc.*, 981 N.E.2d 404, 411 (Ill. App. 2012) ("Private individuals have standing to litigate a violation only if they have actual damages, but the Attorney General may litigate a violation and seek injunctive and other relief without that same requirement.") (citation omitted); *Knapp v. Potamkin Motors Corp.*, 602 A.2d 302, 303 (N.J. Super. 1991) ("[T]he Attorney General has the authority to seek to redress and enjoin violations of the act whether or not any person has been misled, damaged or deceived thereby . . . ."); *Reed v. Allison & Perrone*, 376 So.2d 1067, 1069 (La. Ct. App. 1979) (granting Attorney General the right to injunctive relief without burden of proving irreparable injury or that he has no adequate remedy at law); *State v. Ledwith*, 281 N.W.2d 729, 736 (Neb. 1979) ("Whether the Attorney General has 'cause to believe' is irrelevant to whether deceptive trade practices actually exist. The only reasonable basis for its existence in the statutes is to prevent random investigations by the Attorney General's office."); *Charlie's Dodge, Inc. v. Celebrezze*, 596 N.E.2d 486, 487–88 (Ohio App. 1991) (noting that state consumer protection act affords state attorneys general broad authority to issue subpoenas on "sufficient reasonable cause to believe" that violations had occurred; no definitive proof of deceptive and unconscionable sales practices are required).

Several defenses nevertheless are available to consumer fraud claims. Specifically, because state consumer fraud statutes are typically modeled after the Federal Trade Commission ("FTC") Act, federal policy statements should be applicable in defining the proper scope of liability. *See, e.g.*, N.M. Stat. Ann. § 57-12-4 ("It is the intent of the legislature that in construing Section 3 of the Unfair Practices Act the courts to the extent possible will be guided by the interpretations given by the federal trade commission and the federal courts."); *State v. Nelson*, 2001 Me. Super. LEXIS 202 at *14-15 (June 18, 2001) (observing that UTPA requires courts to be guided by the interpretations given by the FTC; defining a "deceptive" practice by citing the Policy Statement on Deception).

The FTC's substantive policy statements are essential because they allow for viable defenses against consumer fraud claims. For example, the FTC's Policy Statement on Deception recognizes essential elements for a deceptive trade practices claim that are often absent in a state consumer fraud statute. *F.T.C. v. Tashman*,

318 F.3d 1273, 1277 (11th Cir. 2003) (citations omitted) ("[T]he FTC must establish that (1) there was a representation; (2) the representation was likely to mislead customers acting reasonably under the circumstances; and (3) the representation was material.").

Similarly, the FTC also adopted a Policy Statement on Unfairness (later codified as part of the FTC Act), which again provides for specific evidentiary requirements beyond vague assertions of violations of public policy or unscrupulous conduct. 15 U.S.C. § 45(n) (act or practice is not unfair "unless the act or practice causes or is likely to cause substantial injury to consumers which is not reasonably avoidable by consumers themselves and not outweighed by countervailing benefits to consumers or to competition."). The key is to convince courts that these specific policy pronouncements are part and parcel of a state's consumer fraud statute, an argument that has had some success. *See, e.g., Suminski v. Me. Appliance Warehouse, Inc.*, 602 A.2d 1173, 1174 n.1 (Me. 1992).

In addition, many state consumer fraud statutes have statutory "safe harbor" provisions that may prevent application of the statute to an entity that is subject to regulation by a federal or state agency. *See, e.g., Arloe Designs, LLC v. Arkansas Capital Corp.*, 431 S.W.3d 277, 281 (Ark. 2014) (actions and transactions of individuals or entities "regulated by a regulatory body acting under statutory authority of Arkansas or of the United States... are not subject to claims that can be brought under the ADTPA [Arkansas Deceptive Trade Practices Act] unless a specific request has been made to the Attorney General."); Mich. Comp. Laws Ann. § 445.904(1)(a) (Michigan Consumer Protection Act does not apply to "[a] transaction or conduct specifically authorized under laws administered by a regulatory board or officer acting under statutory authority of this state or the United States"). Such safe harbor provisions are critical as they represent one of the few possibilities to have a claim dismissed at the outset of a case.

C.   State False Claims Act Claims

Many states have enacted their own state false claims act claims based on the federal false claims act, ("FCA"), 31 U.S.C. §§ 3729, *et seq.* Careful review of the state-specific false claims act needs to be undertaken as the particular state statute may not mirror the federal statute in all respects.

As a result of the lack of uniformity, there is an opportunity for statutory construction arguments, which may allow a company to defend itself against a claim under a false claims act or Medicaid fraud act on the grounds that the statute should be narrowly applied. *See, e.g., Ortho-McNeil-Janssen Pharm., Inc. v. State*, 432 S.W.3d 563, 574 (Ark. 2014) (dismissing state's Medicaid fraud claim; "Janssen is indisputably not a healthcare facility and applying for certification or re-certification as described in the statute. Hence, the statutory provision is not applicable."); *State ex rel. King v. Behavioral Home Care, Inc.*, 346 P.3d 377, 388 (N.M. App. 2014) ("[T]here is no evidence that Medicaid provider payments were conditioned upon compliance with CCHSA regulations. We conclude that BHC's practice of failing to comply with CCHSA was not in violation of the MFA as a condition for payment of Medicaid services."); *Commonwealth v. Ortho-McNeil-Janssen Pharm., Inc.*, 52 A.3d 498, 506 (Pa. Cmwlth. 2012) ("We are bound by the statutory definition of 'provider.' Contrary to the Commonwealth's assertions, a drug manufacturer does not qualify."). *See generally In re Miss. Medicaid Pharm. Average Wholesale Price Litig.*, 2015 WL 6533344, at *14 (Miss. Oct. 29, 2015) ("We affirm the trial court's dismissal of the MFCA claims on the ground that the civil liability provision does not provide for recovery beyond the amount the defendant has improperly received. The parties do not dispute that Sandoz never received any direct payment from the State, and under the language of this statute the parties are too far removed to permit recovery.").

Another major line of defense for false claims act cases is the argument that the alleged fraudulent conduct did not impact any reimbursement decision and, as a result, there is no liability due to a lack of materiality. Recently, the United States Supreme Court clarified the definition of materiality under the federal false claims act. *Universal Health Servs., Inc. v. United States*, 136 S. Ct. 1989, 2003–04 (2016). Although the Court acknowledged that a lack of materiality may be resolved in the context of a motion to dismiss (based on the pleading requirement of particularity), *id.* at 2004 n.6, the broad contours of the Court's materiality holding reflect that a defense of a lack of materiality will likely be fact-intensive:

> In sum, when evaluating materiality under the False Claims Act, the Government's decision to expressly identify a provision as a condition of payment is relevant, but not automatically dispositive. Likewise, proof of materiality can include, but is not necessarily limited to, evidence that the defendant knows that the Government consistently refuses to pay claims in the mine run of cases based on noncompliance with the particular statutory, regulatory, or contractual requirement. Conversely, if the Government pays a particular claim in full despite its actual knowledge that certain requirements were violated, that is very strong evidence that those requirements are not material. Or, if the Government regularly pays a particular type of claim in full despite actual knowledge that certain requirements were violated, and has signaled no change in position, that is strong evidence that the requirements are not material.

Id. at 2003–04. Given that state false claims statutes are modeled on a federal counterpart, it is likely that the Supreme Court's decision as to materiality will find favor at a state court level.

Additional defenses might also be available, particularly in the context of pharmaceutical products. For example, many false claims act cases are based on the allegation that alleged fraudulent conduct constitutes Medicaid fraud. However, given that a state is required to pay for "covered outpatient drugs" subject to limited statutory exceptions, unless a state can show that it would have limited reimbursement of the medicine if it knew the "truth," (*e.g.,* it would have subjected the medicine to a prior authorization requirement), there is no Medicaid fraud. *See, e.g., In re Vioxx Prods. Liab. Litig.,* MDL No. 1657, 2010 WL 2649513, at *18 (E.D. La. June 29, 2010) ("[T]he FDA required manufacturers of all NSAIDs—including COX-2 inhibitors—to place a 'black box' warning on the drugs' labeling about such potential cardiovascular risks.... LDHH did not institute an exclusive formulary in response to this development. Instead, it continued to keep these drugs on its preferred drug list." (citations omitted)). In a similar vein, absent evidence that the alleged fraudulent conduct did not affect any reimbursement decision, false claims act liability should not exist. *Caldwell, ex rel. State v. Janssen Pharm., Inc.,* 144 So.3d 898, 910 (La. 2014) ("There is no evidence in this record that the defendants' improper marketing statements caused any health care provider or his billing agent to submit a claim for payment the provider or his agent knew was false or misleading or that violated a federal or state law or rule.").

III.   OTHER MAJOR DEFENSES/ISSUES

A.   Statutes of Limitation

It is important to undertake an analysis of statute of limitations issues. Certain states still cling to the past in finding that a state is not subject to a statute of limitations at all. *See, e.g., State v. LG Elecs., Inc.,* 340 P.3d 915, 928 (Wash. App. 2014) ("As in England, where it was said, 'no time runs against the king,' it is apparent that in Washington—given our legislature's adoption of a slightly modified version of '*nullum tempus occurrit regi*'—no time runs against the Attorney General when he brings an action as parens patriae pursuant to the CPA."), *aff'd,* 375 P.3d 636 (Wash. 2016).

Courts, however, have begun to recognize that an attorney general's claims should be subject to a statute of limitations defense. *See, e.g., State ex. rel. Brady v. Pettinaro Enters.,* 870 A.2d 513, 532 (Del. Ch. 2005) (rejecting Attorney General's argument that statute of limitations tolled until consumer complaint filed with the Attorney General's office; "[T]he Attorney General's theory, that a state agency is not on inquiry notice of statutory violations because those violations are inherently unknowable to the agency until it receives actual notice in the form of complaints from aggrieved citizens, is intuitively implausible"); *see also State ex rel. Wilson v. Ortho-McNeil-Janssen Pharm., Inc.*, 777 S.E.2d 176, 199 (S.C. 2015) ("We find that the only reasonable conclusion supported by the evidence is that the Attorney General knew, or most assuredly should have known, of potential SCUTPA violations regarding the Risperdal label prior to January 24, 2004. Thus, the labeling violations occurring prior to January 24, 2004, were therefore barred by the statute of limitations."), *reh'g granted*, (July 8, 2015), *cert. denied sub nom. Ortho-McNeil-Janssen Pharm., Inc. v. S. Carolina ex rel. Wilson*, 136 S. Ct. 824 (2016).

The importance of a statute of limitations defense cannot be understated. At a minimum, it may allow a defendant to substantially limit the period of exposure.

B.   Preemption / Lack of Standing

While cast as state law claims, the foundation of claims brought by state attorneys general are often, in fact, alleged violations of federal law. In those instances, analysis should be undertaken as to whether enforcement of such violations is reserved exclusively to the federal government. *See, e.g., Buckman Co. v. Pls.' Legal Comm.*, 531 U.S. 341, 352 (2001) (21 § 337(a) provides "clear evidence here that Congress intended that the" FDCA and regulations enacted under it "be enforced exclusively by the Federal Government"); *People ex rel. Harris v. Delta Air Lines, Inc.*, 247 Cal. App. 4th 884, 906, 202 Cal. Rptr. 3d 395, 412 (2016) ("We therefore hold that state enforcement of the OPPA's [Online Privacy Protection Act of 2003's] privacy policy requirements as applied to Delta's Fly Delta mobile application is expressly preempted by the ADA [Airline Deregulation Act].").

C.   Discovery

In the context of state attorney general litigation, parties should be prepared to expect that the State will be given wide latitude in the scope of discovery that will be permissible. For example, one court found that a state was entitled to the discovery of materials governed by confidentiality agreements, concluding that the public policy considerations underlying the state's unfair practices act rendered any confidentiality agreement unenforceable. *State ex rel. Balderas v. ITT Educ. Servs., Inc.*, No. A-1-CA-35204, 2018 WL 1940990, at *5 (N.M. Ct. App. Apr. 24, 2018) ("[W]e conclude that, under the circumstances of this case, it would be contrary to public policy to allow ITT to use the confidentiality clause with its students to shield itself from the State's investigation and litigation authorized under the [New Mexico] UPA [Unfair Practices Act].").

IV.   DAMAGES/PENALTIES

Last but certainly not least are challenges to any demand for damages or civil penalties. In the haste to institute litigation, little thought is given to whether a state will be able to actually prove the typically grandiose allegations that a state has been defrauded on a massive scale. As a result, defense challenges to claimed damages and penalties often may be the most successful area of litigation.

Often, as litigation proceeds, a state recognizes that it has no evidence to support a claim that a state actually lost any money. The result is that a state then retreats to the position of seeking only civil penalties. This position raises constitutional issues. In particular, when a state seeks penalties disproportionate to any actual harm (which is typically non-existent), the Excessive Fines Clause of the United States Constitution comes into play. *United States v. Bajakajian*, 524 U.S. 321, 337, 339–40 (1998) ("There was no fraud on the United States, and respondent caused no loss to the public..." and the forfeiture "bears no articulable correlation to any injury suffered by the Government."). The penalty theory of a state attorney general has been found to implicate excessive fines issues. *In re Zyprexa Prods. Liab. Litig.*, 671 F. Supp. 2d 397, 463

(E.D.N.Y. 2009) (excessive fine consideration where state requested civil penalties on a "per prescription" basis).

Apart from the constitutional issues, potential substantive attacks on the likely damage and penalty theories remain as well. In short, in many cases, to enhance a damages or civil penalties amount, a state may engage in overreaching.

At the outset, a damages theory may be found to be impermissibly speculative and not properly supported by expert testimony. *See, e.g., Commonwealth v. TAP Pharm. Prods., Inc.,* 94 A.3d 350, 363 (Pa. 2014) ("By the Commonwealth's abject failure to account responsibly for rebates taken from the defendants it sued, it has proved no harm as a result of pharmaceutical-company pricing practices, and we decline to sustain any judgment in the circumstances as they have come before us here." (footnote omitted)); *Commonwealth v. Ortho-McNeil-Janssen Pharm. Inc.,* 13 Pa. D. & C.5th 187, 208 (Pa. Ct. Com. Pl., Phila. Cty. June 25, 2010) ("[T]here was no foundation testimony presented to permit the lay jurors to comprehend the genesis of the damage numbers—initially, a quarter of a billion dollars."), *aff'd, Com. v. Ortho-McNeil-Janssen Pharm., Inc.,* 52 A.3d 498, 511 n.9 (Pa. Cmwlth. 2012) ("[G]iven the complexity of this type of case, expert damage testimony is usually needed.")

Further, a penalty theory may impermissibly be based on double counting. *See, e.g., People v. Toomey,* 203 Cal. Rptr. 642, 656 (Cal. Ct. App. 1984) ("[W]e believe the Legislature intended that the number of violations is to be determined by the number of persons to whom the misrepresentations were made, and not the number of separately identifiable misrepresentations involved."); *People v. Bestline Prods., Inc.,* 61 Cal, App. 3d 879, 923, 132 Cal. Rptr. 767, 794–95 (Cal. Ct. App. 1976) ("While the intent of [the statute] was to strengthen the hand of the Attorney General in seeking redress for violations of [the statute], it is unreasonable to assume that the Legislature intended to impose a penalty of this magnitude for the solicitation of one potential customer.").

Finally, a state may pursue a penalty theory unrelated to the conduct that purportedly constitutes the fraud, thereby allowing for an opportunity to substantially eliminate or reduce large swaths of claimed damages or penalties. *See, e.g., Cooper Indus., Inc. v. Leatherman Tool Grp., Inc.*, 532 U.S. 424, 441 (2001) ("[Plaintiff] calculated that 'potential harm' by referring to the fact that [defendant] had anticipated 'gross profits of approximately $3 million during the first five years of sales. Even if that estimate were correct, however, it would be unrealistic to assume that all of [defendant's] sales of the [product] would have been attributable to its misconduct . . . in its initial advertising materials.'" (internal citation omitted)); *In re Mississippi Medicaid Pharm. Average Wholesale Price Litig.*, 190 So.3d 829, 847 (Miss. 2015) (upholding trial court decision to impose penalty for each instance of improper reporting rather than the state's request for a penalty for each instance that Medicaid reimbursed a claim); *State v. Abbott Labs.*, 816 N.W.2d 145, 173–74 (Wis. 2012) ("[W]hatever legal significance one chooses to place upon the number of times Medicaid overpaid for Pharmacia drugs, that number cannot represent the number of times Pharmacia 'made or caused to be made' any representations. By the time of overpayment, Pharmacia had already reported its AWP, and FDB had already published it to Medicaid. Any fraudulent 'statements' had already been communicated and the alleged fraud was complete. The number of times pharmacies were overpaid is merely a consequence of the alleged fraud, not the fraudulent conduct itself.") (reducing amount of alleged violations from 1,440,000, as found by a jury, to 4,578).

V.   SETTLEMENTS

Whether an attorney general action proceeds as an investigation or litigation, it often resolves in a settlement. This is typically the result in attorney general matters for the same reason it is the result in matters involving private parties: the parties want to avoid the significant time and expense associated with litigation. Just because the parties' focus shifts to settlement negotiations does not necessarily mean that a resolution is soon in sight. It may take several months for the parties to agree on a settlement. The process may be aided by a private mediator who may be able to get the parties to an agreement in principle in a day-long session.

An agreement on a monetary amount is typically only one half of the settlement. The other half manifests in the form of a consent decree terms. Companies willing to enter into a consent decree must pay close attention to various terms, particularly as to the scope of conduct at issue and which entities are subject to the decree. Another key aspect of a consent decree is the scope of the release. An attorney general may be reluctant to agree to a release that it perceives to be overly broad; yet, the company wants assurance that the attorney general will not be back in a matter of months pursuing an alternative theory involving the same conduct.

A company that does enter into a consent decree should be mindful of its duties under the terms of the agreement. Attorneys general have been known to open post-settlement inquiries into whether a company has violated the terms of a consent decree. It may take months to convince the attorney general that no violation has occurred. If the company is unable to persuade the attorney general of the company's compliance with the consent decree, the attorney general may pursue penalties against the company for failure to comply with the consent decree.

Another potential hurdle to settlement in state attorney general litigation is the rise of political subdivisions as plaintiffs in the mass tort context. As recent experience in the opioid litigation has illustrated, the large number of potential political subdivisions with competing interests can make it extremely difficult to resolve a matter in anyway that provides sufficient closure for a corporate defendant. *See* U.S. Chamber Institute for Legal Reform, Mitigating Municipality Litigation: Scope and Solutions, at 14 (March 2019). Although there is growing recognition that this is a problem that may require a legislative solution, *see id.*, at 19-44, until such legislative change is enacted, corporate defendants negotiating settlements with state attorneys general should seek creative solutions, such as a minimum participation rate, to ensure that any settlement with the state will sufficiently foreclose additional litigation from the state's political subdivisions for the same alleged conduct.

VI.   CONCLUSION

In sum, attorney general investigations and related civil litigation are facts of life in corporate America, with potentially significant financial consequences. Further, there is no shortage of imagination as to the corporate acts or practices that may become the subject of investigations or litigation. Faced with this reality, the targets of such actions have little choice but to face such actions directly. While the exposure is real, equally real are the viable defenses to such actions.

Chapter 15

Maximizing The Protections Provided By The Attorney-Client Privilege And The Work Product Doctrine

By: David M. Greenwald[862]

Corporations conduct investigations. Not all investigations are privileged. The purpose of this chapter is to provide practical observations regarding how corporations and other organizations may decide which investigations to treat as privileged, and what steps they may take to maximize the protections of the attorney-client privilege and the work product doctrine.[863]

I.   TWO SOURCES OF PROTECTION

It is imprecise to say that an investigation is privileged. It is more accurate to say that the attorney-client privilege and the work product doctrine may protect certain investigatory materials from compelled disclosure in civil and criminal proceedings. Nevertheless, for ease of reference, this chapter uses "legal investigation" or "privileged investigation" to refer to an investigation that is intended to address primarily legal issues, even where there is a dual business purpose. "Business investigation" or "business review" refers to an investigation that is conducted primarily for a business purpose. As discussed in this chapter, the difference between the two is not always clear.

Although the attorney-client privilege and the work product protection may both protect investigation materials from discovery, it is important to consider the two doctrines separately for each category of information that may be withheld. The

---

[862] David Greenwald is a Partner of Jenner & Block LLP. The views expressed by the author are his own and do not necessarily represent the views of the firm or any of its clients.

[863] Many aspects of the law relating to the attorney-client privilege and the work product doctrine may be relevant to an internal investigation. For detailed discussion of these issues, please refer to DAVID M. GREENWALD, MICHELE L. SLACHETKA, TESTIMONIAL PRIVILEGES (Thomson Reuters 2021).

doctrines further different policy interests, provide different scopes of protection, and have distinct elements for establishing and for waiving the protections. It is often the case in investigations that, where the attorney-client privilege may be deemed waived, the information at issue may still be protected as work product.

The attorney-client privilege is the oldest of the common law privileges. [864] The privilege promotes full and frank communication between attorneys and their clients, thus enabling attorneys to provide informed legal advice by removing the fear of compelled disclosure of their communications. The privilege is absolute if established and not waived and, in the case of individual clients, survives the client's death.[865] Although absolute, the privilege is also fragile. Disclosure to a third party who is not within the protected attorney-client circle may waive the privilege and, under the common law, such a disclosure may result in waiver not just of the privileged material disclosed, but of the entire subject matter of the disclosed communications.[866]

The work product doctrine provides a qualified immunity from disclosure. Articulated by the United States Supreme Court in *Hickman v. Taylor*, 329 U.S. 495 (1947), the doctrine is designed to provide a "zone of privacy" within which attorneys may prepare a client's case and plan strategy without fear of undue interference by a litigation adversary.[867] Fed. R. Civ. P. 26(b)(3) partially codifies the doctrine, protecting from discovery documents and

---

[864] Although there are many articulations of the privilege, the common elements are: (1) a communication, between (2) a client and (3) a lawyer, acting as a lawyer, (4) made for a legal purpose that is (5) made in confidence and kept in confidence. *See generally*, TESTIMONIAL PRIVILEGES § 1:5 ("The Privilege Defined – Common Law Definitions").

[865] TESTIMONIAL PRIVILEGES § 1:74 ("Duration of the Privilege").

[866] TESTIMONIAL PRIVILEGES § 1:76 n.1.

[867] *See generally* TESTIMONIAL PRIVILEGES § 2:2 and ff (discussing the origins and rationales of the work product doctrine).

tangible things[868] that are prepared in anticipation of litigation or for trial by or for a party or its representative, including a party's attorney.[869] Work product falls into two categories: ordinary work product and opinion work product. Ordinary work product may be discovered where a party demonstrates a substantial need for the materials to prepare its case and that it cannot, without undue hardship, obtain the substantial equivalent by other means.[870] Fed. R. Civ. P. 26(b)(3)(B) provides heightened protection for opinion work product by directing courts to protect against disclosure of the mental impressions, conclusions, opinions, or legal theories of a party's attorney or other representative concerning the litigation. Opinion work product is afforded near absolute protection in many jurisdictions and is discoverable, if at all, only upon a showing of extraordinary need.[871] The work product protection is not waived merely by disclosure to a third party. Waiver occurs where work product is disclosed to an adversary or to someone who substantially increases the opportunities for potential adversaries to obtain the information ("conduits").[872]

The attorney-client privilege is broader than the work product doctrine, in that it applies to any type of legal communication. The work product doctrine is narrower, in that it applies only in the context of anticipated litigation or trial. The attorney-client privilege is easily waived; the work product protection is more robust. As discussed in some detail here, investigatory materials may be protected by one or both doctrines. Where one protection

---

[868] Although Fed. R. Civ. P. 26(b)(3)(A) addresses only documents and tangible things, the "intangible work product doctrine" may protect oral communications made in anticipation of litigation or for trial. TESTIMONIAL PRIVILEGES § 2:2 n.14.

[869] Although often referred to as "attorney work product", Fed. R. Civ. P. 26(b)(3) and many state analogues protect materials prepared by non-lawyers as well as by lawyers. TESTIMONIAL PRIVILEGES § 2:2 n.15.

[870] Fed. R. Civ. P. 26(b)(3)(A)(ii).

[871] TESTIMONIAL PRIVILEGES at §§ 2:4, 2:22.

[872] TESTIMONIAL PRIVILEGES at § 2:28.

does not apply or has been waived, the other may protect against discovery.

II. INVESTIGATION MATERIALS

Investigations generate several categories of information that may be protected from discovery, including: witness interviews and related outlines, notes and summary memoranda; team notes, outlines, legal analyses and communications among team members; reports to the client and drafts of those reports; communications between the investigation team and the client; and documents and other factual information collected, selected, and organized by the investigation team. At the outset of an investigation, it is helpful to establish rules for creating and maintaining documents in a way that establishes and maintains confidentiality, including labeling documents as privileged.[873] In addition, the team may want to establish document management rules, for example, segregating investigation materials from business materials, allowing access only to individuals who are directly working on the investigation, and requiring that work product be encrypted and password protected when sent to team members or to the client.

III. TRIAGE AND INVESTIGATION PROTOCOLS

The impetus for a legal investigation may arise in a number of ways, some of which are more obviously legal in nature than others. Where a company or a senior officer receives a grand jury subpoena or a civil investigative demand, the matter will likely find its way quickly to the General Counsel, who will be able to take steps to initiate a privileged investigation. Other matters requiring legal attention may arise less directly. The Human Resources Department may receive what appears to be a routine employment complaint that develops into something more serious

---

[873] An investigation team may decide to have all team members use a standard format for labeling the team's work product. For example, use of a header on all pages of a document with language similar to: "Privileged and Confidential: Protected by the Attorney-Client Privilege and as [Attorney] Work Product, DRAFT: [DATE]".

during an investigation undertaken by non-legal HR personnel. The Ethics and Compliance Office may receive a vague report about seemingly minor alleged employee misconduct through a call to the company's ethics hotline. Follow-up review by compliance personnel may reveal that the matter is significant enough to justify undertaking a legal investigation.

In order to enable the company to decide whether to conduct a non-privileged business review or instead to initiate a privileged internal investigation, it is helpful to have policies and procedures in place that identify a process for triaging matters when they first come to the attention of the company, and for escalating matters for legal review when potentially significant legal issues arise during the course of routine business reviews ("Investigation Protocol"). An Investigation Protocol may be tailored to a company's specific business needs and its organizational structure. One size does not fit all. For a publicly traded company, it will be important to channel for legal review issues potentially relevant to Sarbanes-Oxley reporting requirements. Similarly, for government contractors, it will be important to obtain legal review of reported conduct that may violate the False Claims Act or relevant acquisition regulations. For any company, it will be important to obtain legal review of potentially serious violations of the law and of the company's code of business conduct.

An Investigation Protocol may establish a specific process for requesting review by the legal department to determine whether a matter should be investigated at the direction of counsel as a privileged investigation, and the steps that the company will take when it decides to conduct a privileged investigation.[874] The Investigation Protocol may describe specific steps, including who may authorize a legal investigation and how the decision will be documented, who will conduct and supervise fact-finding, and how to conduct employee interviews and engage third party consultants in ways that will maximize protection by the attorney-client

---

[874] An Investigation Protocol may address circumstances in which a matter should be brought directly to the attention of the Chair of the Board of Directors, or to the Chair of the Audit Committee.

privilege and the work product doctrine.[875] An Investigation Protocol may also describe when non-legal investigations should be escalated to the attention of the legal department. Having an Investigation Protocol in place, coupled with effective training of key departments and personnel regarding the protocol, will make it more likely that complaints raising legal issues will find their way to counsel promptly. In addition, if a company follows its own established procedures for identifying and conducting a privileged investigation, it is evidence that the company, from the outset, intended to conduct the investigation for a legal purpose.

IV.   ESTABLISHING A LEGAL PURPOSE

In order to be privileged, an internal investigation must be undertaken primarily for a legal purpose.[876] It is helpful to articulate the legal purpose of an investigation, and where applicable that the company anticipates litigation, at the outset of an investigation, for example, in the memorandum from the General Counsel to in-house attorneys authorizing an investigation, or in an engagement letter with outside counsel.

Where there are dual legal and business purposes for an investigation, as there often are, the question is what investigation-related communications are made "primarily" for a legal purpose. Some courts may apply a narrow standard, asking whether communications were made "because of" a legal purpose, or whether a business purpose would have served as a sufficient cause for the communications independent of a request for legal advice.[877] A broader standard, more in keeping with the United

---

[875] An Investigation Protocol may include templates and materials commonly used by the company for legal investigations, for example, standard language that may be used in consultants' engagement letters, or language that may be used by non-lawyer investigators to provide *Upjohn* warnings to employees.

[876] *See generally* TESTIMONIAL PRIVILEGES § 1:49.

[877] *See, e.g., Phillips v. C.R. Bard, Inc.*, 290 F.R.D. 615, 628-30 (D. Nev. 2013) (applying "because of" test); *Visa U.S.A., Inc. v. First Data Corp.*, 2004 WL 1878209, *4 (N.D. Cal. 2004) (applying "because of" test; documents prepared for dual purposes not privileged if documents had a "clear, readily separable business purpose"); *U.S. v. Chevron*, 1996 WL 264769, *3 (N.D. Cal. 1996) ("No

States Supreme Court's decision in *Upjohn Co. v. United States*, 449 U.S. 383 (1981), was articulated by the U.S. Court of Appeals for the District of Columbia Circuit in *In re Kellogg Brown & Root, Inc.*, 756 F.3d 754, 760 (D.C. Cir. 2014) ("*KBR I*"). The court in *KBR I* articulated the test as: "Was obtaining or providing legal advice *a* primary purpose of the communication, meaning *one* of the significant purposes of the communication?"[878]

In *KBR I*, KBR had undertaken an internal investigation at the direction of the legal department in response to a *qui tam* action in which the Relator alleged violations of the False Claims Act. The Relator argued that investigation-related documents were not privileged because the investigation was undertaken for the business purpose of complying with the company's Code of Business Conduct and with federal acquisition regulations, and not primarily for a legal purpose.[879] The district court agreed, finding that KBR had not shown that the investigation would not have been conducted "but for" the fact that legal advice was sought.[880]

The appellate court disagreed, rejected the "but for" test, and granted KBR's petition for a writ of mandamus. The appellate court explained that KBR's assertion of privilege was indistinguishable from the assertion of privilege in *Upjohn*, where the U.S. Supreme Court made it clear that the attorney-client privilege exists to protect not only the giving of professional advice to a client, but also the giving of information to the lawyer to enable the lawyer to provide sound and informed legal

---

privilege can attach to a communication as to which a business purpose would have served as a sufficient cause"); *see also* TESTIMONIAL PRIVILEGES § 1:50 n.8.

[878] *See also Federal Trade Comm'n v. Boehringer Ingelheim Pharma., Inc.*, 892 F.3d 1264, 1266 (D.C. Cir. 2018) (applying *KBR I*); *In re General Motors LLC Ignition Switch Litigation*, 80 F.Supp.3d 521, 529-31 (S.D. N.Y. 2015) (applying test articulated in *KBR I*); *see also In re Grand* Jury, 23 F.4th 1088, 1094-95 (9th Cir. 2022) (court noted the *KBR I* "a primary purpose" test, but did not rule on its applicability as the "predominant purpose" test was sufficient to decide the case before it); TESTIMONIAL PRIVILEGES § 1:50 fn.7.

[879] KBR I, 756 F.3d at 756.

[880] *Id.*

advice.[881] The court found that the primary purpose test "sensibly and properly applied" does not draw a rigid distinction between a legal purpose on the one hand and a business purpose on the other.[882] "[T]rying to find *the* primary purpose for a communication motivated by two sometimes overlapping purposes (one legal and one business, for example) can be an inherently impossible task."[883] "In the context of an organization's internal investigation, if one of the significant purposes... was to obtain or provide legal advice, the privilege will apply."[884]

V.   INDICIA OF A LEGAL PURPOSE

When a company conducts an investigation, it cannot predict with certainty where the privilege will be tested: In which state? In state or federal court? If in federal court, pursuant to diversity or federal question jurisdiction? If federal question jurisdiction, in what Circuit and before which judge?[885] Where federal common law applies, although there are some rules that have been established by the U.S. Supreme Court and the Circuit Courts of Appeal, the majority of federal decisions addressing the law of privilege are made at the trial court level by United States District Judges and United States Magistrate Judges. Although these opinions are often detailed and well-reasoned, and are therefore persuasive, and

---

[881] *KBR I*, 756 F.3d at 757.

[882] *KBR I*, 756 F.3d at 759.

[883] *Id.*

[884] *KBR I*, 756 F.3d at 760. In *In re Kellogg Brown & Root, Inc.*, 796 F.3d 137, 149 (D.C. Cir. 2015) (*KBR II*), a subsequent decision in which the D.C. Circuit granted a second petition for a writ of mandamus filed by KBR, the court held that the work product doctrine protected many of the investigation-related documents.

[885] The attorney-client privilege is substantive law, governed by the common law or statutory law of each State or Territory, and by federal common law. Although there are significant similarities from jurisdiction to jurisdiction, there can also be significant differences. In federal court, Federal Rule of Evidence 501 generally provides that state privilege law will apply in matters where jurisdiction is based on diversity, and federal common law will apply where jurisdiction is based on a federal question, including with respect to pendant state claims. *See* TESTIMONIAL PRIVILEGES §§ 1:7 – 1:11.

although courts within a district or a Circuit may gravitate to a common approach, these decisions are not binding precedents, leaving a great deal of discretion to a court to select a legal approach to apply to the particular set of facts presented in a particular case. The outcome often depends both on what steps a company took at the time of the investigation, and how well the company marshals that evidence to meet its burden of demonstrating that a privilege or protection applies.[886]

As a result, the practical questions are: What steps may a company take to maximize the chance that a court will deem an investigation to be protected from discovery? And what steps may a company avoid that would either decrease that chance, or create risk that a court may find that a company has waived otherwise applicable privileges and protections?

VI. LAWYER INVOLVEMENT AND DIRECTION

First and foremost, for the attorney-client privilege to apply to communications relating to an investigation, there must be a lawyer, acting in a legal capacity, involved in the investigation.[887] Depending on the circumstances, a company may choose to have either in-house counsel or outside counsel conduct an investigation. For more sensitive and significant investigations, a company may choose to engage outside counsel to conduct an investigation.[888] Where outside counsel conducts an investigation,

---

[886] The party asserting the attorney-client privilege or the work product protection has the burden of establishing the elements of the privilege or protection. TESTIMONIAL PRIVILEGES § 1:62 n.5; § 2:9 n.2.

[887] *See, e.g., Koumoulis v. Independent Financial Marketing Group, Inc.,* 295 F.R.D. 28, 45-46 (E.D. N.Y. 2013) (communications with outside counsel who supervised and directed an internal investigation as an adjunct member of the human resources team were prepared predominantly for a business purpose and were not privileged legal communications); *U.S. v. ISS Marine Services, Inc.,* 905 F.Supp.2d 121, 130 (D.D.C. 2012) (audit report prepared by non-lawyer employees was not privileged because counsel did not oversee the audit or the creation of the report).

[888] Although a lawyer's status as in-house counsel "does not dilute the privilege", where an in-house lawyer has both legal and business duties, it may be more difficult to establish that communications were made for a legal purpose. Courts

some courts consider it significant that an engagement letter specifies that, in addition to gathering facts, outside counsel will provide legal advice to the company.[889]

In order to be protected by the work product doctrine, an investigation must be conducted at a time when the company anticipates or is engaged in litigation.[890] To establish anticipation of litigation, a party must demonstrate that the threat of litigation was imminent.[891] A general fear of ever-present litigation in the future will not meet the anticipation requirement; there must be some particularized suspicion that litigation is likely.[892]

VII.   BUILDING THE INVESTIGATION TEAM

Choosing who will conduct the actual fact-finding and which third parties, if any, will be involved in an investigation may have

---

may presume that communications with outside counsel are privileged, but they may not apply the same assumption to in-house counsel. Instead, courts often require in-house counsel to make a "clear showing" that counsel was acting in a legal capacity as to each category of withheld information. TESTIMONIAL PRIVILEGES §§ 1:26, 1:51. In addition, there are situations in which a company decides it needs someone outside the company to conduct an investigation, for example, where senior officers or legal department personnel may be implicated, or where independent directors of the Board of Directors want to have comfort that an investigation is objective and is allowed to go wherever the facts take it.

[889] See Sandra T.E. v. South Berwyn School Dist. 100, 600 F.3d 612, 619-20 (7th Cir. 2010) (reversing order to disclose privileged communications where engagement letter stated that the firm was retained to investigate and to provide legal advice); Sullivan v. Warminster Tp., 274 F.R.D. 147, 151-52 (E.D. Pa. 2011) (internal investigation report privileged where engagement letter stated counsel had been retained to provide legal services and to represent client in future claims, and where the report discussed legal strategy).

[890] Courts interpret "litigation" broadly to include criminal and civil trials, as well as other adversarial proceedings such as administrative proceedings, arbitration or other alternative dispute resolution proceedings, grand jury proceedings and investigative legislative hearings. TESTIMONIAL PRIVILEGES § 2:14 n.9.

[891] TESTIMONIAL PRIVILEGES § 2:15 n.1.

[892] Courts conduct case-by-case analysis and apply a variety of tests to determine whether litigation was anticipated. See generally TESTIMONIAL PRIVILEGES § 2:15 ("Required Imminence of Litigation").

significant ramifications for a company's ability to assert privilege successfully.

VIII.   WHO MAY CONDUCT FACT-FINDING?

Using attorneys, either in-house lawyers or outside counsel, to conduct all witness interviews and other fact-finding involved in an investigation requires significant resources that a company may be reluctant to devote to all but the most significant investigations. May in-house counsel deputize non-lawyers to conduct interviews and other fact-finding? As a general matter, non-lawyers who conduct employee interviews at the direction of counsel may be deemed to be agents of counsel and their communications with employees will be within the attorney-client privilege.[893] As a practical matter, delegating all or most of an investigation to non-lawyers may make it more difficult to persuade a court that the investigation was primarily for a legal purpose. This may be

---

[893] Many courts have applied the attorney-client privilege to communications between company employees and non-lawyer investigators who are working at the direction of counsel. *KBR I,* 756 F.3d at 758 (privilege applied to communications between company employees and non-attorney investigators acting at the direction of counsel; "[C]ommunications made by and to non-attorneys serving as agents of attorneys in internal investigations are routinely protected by the attorney-client privilege."); *Farzan v. Wells Fargo Bank,* 2012 WL 6763570, *1-2 (S.D. N.Y. 2012) (where investigation was conducted by non-attorney "EEO Consultant" under the supervision of the bank's legal department, conversations with bank employees were "plainly protected by the attorney-client privilege"); *Geller v. North Shore Long Island Jewish Health System,* 2011 WL 5507572, *3 (E.D.N.Y. 2011) (where Corporate Compliance Officer conducted internal investigation both before and after defense counsel was engaged and began supervising the investigation, communications occurring *after* counsel began supervision were privileged); *Gucci America, Inc. v. Guess?, Inc.,* 271 F.R.D. 58, 71 (S.D. N.Y. 2010) (communications with non-lawyer conducting investigation at the direction of in-house counsel and in coordination with outside counsel were privileged); *Carter v. Cornell University,* 173 F.R.D. 92, 94 (S.D. N.Y. 1997) (where Associate Dean conducted an investigation "at the request of counsel and for the exclusive use of counsel in rendering legal representation", communications with persons she interviewed were privileged). *But see Wierciszewski v. Granite City Illinois Hospital Co.,* 2011 WL 5374114, *1 (S.D. Ill. 2011) (where investigation by non-attorney was supervised by his non-attorney supervisor and the company's general counsel was merely copied on emails providing updates on the investigation, the investigation was not directed by counsel and interviews conducted by the non-attorney were not privileged).

particularly true where the non-lawyer investigators also conduct non-privileged business investigations for the company. The more that counsel is directly involved in the investigation, the more likely the legal purpose of the investigation will be evident to a court. Direct involvement by counsel could include: conducting at least some interviews personally; meeting regularly with non-lawyer investigators to discuss status and strategy; and communicating directly with company personnel who have relevant documents or other data, to inform them that the investigators who will be contacting them with requests for information are doing so at the direction of counsel for a legal purpose. It is also advisable for non-lawyer investigators to provide written reports or findings directly to counsel and not to distribute those materials to business personnel.[894] Counsel will then be able to assess who in the company should receive information developed during the investigation.

IX. PROVIDING *UPJOHN* WARNINGS TO EMPLOYEE WITNESSES

When the company's lawyer interviews an employee in the course of an investigation, at the beginning of the interview, before anything substantive has been discussed, the lawyer should provide "*Upjohn* warnings" to the employee, and the notes of the interview should reflect that the employee received these warnings. No particular wording is required, as long as the following elements are communicated to the employee: (1) at the direction of the company, the lawyer is conducting the interview for the purpose of

---

[894] *In re Vioxx Products Liability Litigation,* 501 F.Supp.2d 789, 805 (E.D. La. 2007) (when a business "simultaneously sends communications to both lawyers and non-lawyers, it usually cannot claim that the primary purpose of the communication was for legal advice or assistance because the communication served both business and legal purposes"); *U.S. v. Chevron Corp.,* 1996 WL 264769 (N.D. Cal. 1996) (same); *MediaTek,Inc. v. Freescale Semiconductor, Inc.,* 2013 WL 5594474, at *4-5 (N.D. Cal. 2003) (technical consultant's report and drafts of the report that were never reviewed by counsel relating to purchase of patents were found to have been prepared for a business purpose). *See also Roth v. Aon Corp.,* 254 F.R.D. 538 (N.D. Ill. 2009) (simultaneous disclosure of draft 10K report to legal and non-legal personnel did not waive privilege where all recipients were directly involved in the preparation of the document).

obtaining factual information to enable counsel to provide legal advice to the company; (2) the lawyer represents the company and does not represent the employee individually; (3) the interview is privileged, but it is the company's privilege, not the employee's, and the company may decide whether to assert or to waive the privilege in its sole discretion; and (4) the employee should keep the substance of the interview confidential and should not discuss it with others unless a company lawyer directs them otherwise.

The purpose for giving these warnings to employee witnesses is at least three-fold. First, the United States Supreme Court in *Upjohn* recognized that, in an organizational setting, employees at all levels of the company may have information that a company lawyer needs to know in order to provide informed legal advice to the company. To summarize the five factors articulated in *Upjohn*: The attorney-client privilege applies to communications between company counsel and a company employee at any level within the company who has information obtained by the employee within the scope of their duties that the lawyer needs to understand in order to provide legal advice to the company, and where the communications are made by the employee at the direction of more senior company personnel, and where the employee is informed that the communications are confidential and need to be maintained in confidence.[895] Providing *Upjohn* warnings may be instrumental in establishing that employee interviews are

---

[895] The Court in *Upjohn* set out five factors to guide courts in determining whether the attorney-client privilege applies to communications between company counsel and lower-echelon (that is, not control group) employees. TESTIMONIAL PRIVILEGES § 1:40 nn.11-15. *Upjohn* is controlling in federal courts applying federal substantive law. In matters in federal court applying state substantive law, and in state proceedings, state law will apply. Several states have followed the *Upjohn* approach. TESTIMONIAL PRIVILEGES § 1:40 n.32. Many states apply some form of the "subject matter" test first articulated in *Harper & Row Publishers, Inc. v. Decker*, 423 F.2d 487 (7th Cir. 1970) and adopted by the Restatement Third, The Law Governing Lawyers § 73, which extends the privilege to agents or employees of the corporation so long as the communication relates to the subject matter for which the organization is seeking legal representation. TESTIMONIAL PRIVILEGES § 1:40 nn.22-23. Eight states continue to apply the narrower "control group" test. TESTIMONIAL PRIVILEGES § 1:40 n.33.

privileged communications by providing employees with the knowledge required to satisfy the *Upjohn* factors.[896]

Second, if an employee is able to show that he or she reasonably believed that the lawyer represented the employee individually, the employee may be able to prevent the company from waiving privilege or otherwise disclosing the information discussed during the interview, for example, to cooperate with the government or to sue the employee. This is a very real concern during an internal investigation, when employees may be facing personal liability and their interests may not align with those of the company. Providing *Upjohn* warnings will defeat an employee's later assertion of a reasonable belief that company counsel represented them individually during the interview.

Third, if in the absence of *Upjohn* warnings an employee does reasonably believe that company counsel represented the employee personally in an interview, and counsel later discloses the substance of the interview without the employee's consent, the lawyer could run afoul of state ethics rules.[897]

Where a non-lawyer investigator conducts interviews of employees, it is advisable that the investigator provide *Upjohn* warnings after first explaining that the investigator, although not a lawyer, is conducting the interview at the direction of company counsel to assist counsel in providing legal advice to the company.

---

[896] *See Sandra T.E. v. South Berwyn School Dist. 100*, 600 F.3d 612, 620 (7th Cir. 2010) (citing *Upjohn* warnings given during employee interviews as evidence supporting that investigators were acting as attorneys); *Davine v. Golub Corp.*, 2017 WL 517749, *8 (D. Mass. 2017) (finding that failure to provide an *Upjohn* warning to employees precluded defendant from withholding non-lawyer consultant's interview notes).

[897] *See* discussion of *United States v. Ruehle,* 583 F.3d 600 (9th Cir. 2009), and *U.S. v. Nicholas*, 606 F. Supp. 2d 1109, 1116-17 (C.D. Cal. 2009), order rev'd, 583 F.3d 600 (9th Cir. 2009) (finding that investigative counsel failed to give *Upjohn* warnings to company employee, despite representing employee personally in a related case, and referring matter to state disciplinary committee) at Testimonial Privileges § 1:41 nn.14-17.

X.   INCLUDING NON-LAWYER AGENTS ON THE INVESTIGATION TEAM

The definition of privileged persons includes agents of the client and of the lawyer who assist in the legal representation.[898] The participation of these third party agents in communications does not waive the privilege if their presence was to permit the client and lawyer to communicate effectively or otherwise to facilitate the attorney to provide legal advice, if the attorney supervises the agent's work.[899]

Pursuant to what is referred to as the "*Kovel* doctrine", a consulting expert retained by the attorney or client to assist the attorney in providing legal advice to the client qualifies as a privileged agent if consulted for the purpose of improving the attorney's comprehension of relevant factual information or the client's comprehension of legal advice rendered by the attorney.[900] Privilege may apply where an agent is necessary to "translate" or "interpret" complicated factual information for the attorney.[901] Courts extend the privilege to such agents where the agent is "necessary, or at least highly useful for the effective consultation

---

[898] TESTIMONIAL PRIVILEGES §§1:28-1:29.

[899] Wigmore on Evidence §2301 (2011 Supp.) ("The assistance of these agents being indispensable to his work and the communications of the client being often necessarily committed to them by the attorney or by the client himself, the privilege must include all the persons who act as the attorney's agents); *see, e.g., In re Grand Jury Investigation*, 918 F.2d 374, 386 n.20 (3d Cir. 1990) (presence of agent does not abrogate privilege)*; See also* RESTATEMENT THIRD, THE LAW GOVERNING LAWYERS § 70, cmt. g.

[900] *U.S. v. Kovel*, 296 F.2d 918, 922 (accountant hired by tax firm to assist in interpreting client conversations was a privileged agent). *See* TESTIMONIAL PRIVILEGES § 1:29 n.7.

[901] *U.S. v. Kovel*, 296 F.2d at 922; *U.S. v. Ackert*, 169 F.3d 136, 139-40 (2d Cir. 1999). *See also Jenkins v. Bartlett*, 487 F.3d 482, 490-91 (7th Cir. 2007) (presence of police liaison officer during meeting between police officer and his attorney did not destroy privilege where liaison officer interpreted information from attorney to client).

between the client and the lawyer".[902] Some courts interpret this language narrowly to require that the agent be "nearly indispensable or serve some specialized purpose in facilitating the attorney-client communications".[903]

Depending on the nature of the investigation, it may be necessary to engage third-party consultants to assist counsel in an investigation. Certain types of consultants, for example, forensic accountants in matters involving allegations of bribery or other financial misconduct, fit easily within the definition of "agents of counsel", that is, agents who are needed to assist counsel to provide informed legal advice.[904] However, courts may be reluctant to extend privilege to certain categories of consultants, whose advice may be vital to the business interests of a company, but who may not facilitate providing legal advice to the company.

A.   Public Relations Consultants

A significant majority of the courts that have considered the issue have determined that public relations consultants are not privileged agents of counsel, because their services are provided for a business purpose and not to assist counsel to provide legal advice to the company.[905]

---

[902] *Cavallaro v. U.S.*, 284 F.3d at 24748 (1st Cir. 2002); *Heriot v. Byrne*, 257 F.R.D. 645, 666-67 (N.D. Ill. 2009).

[903] TESTIMONIAL PRIVILEGES § 1:29 n.7.

[904] *See, e.g., Graff v. Haverhill North Cake Co.*, 2012 WL 5495514, at *5 (S.D. Ohio 2012) (communications with accountant were privileged where outside counsel hired accountant for help in rendering legal advice); *Lawrence E. Jaffe Pension Plan v. Household Int'l, Inc.*, 244 F.R.D. 412, 420 (N.D. Ill. 2006) (accounting firm was necessary and indispensable to counsel's ability to render legal advice given the "complex quantitative analyses and extensive information-gathering that was beyond . . . counsel's resources and abilities, but was uniquely within [accountant's] qualifications.").

[905] TESTIMONIAL PRIVILEGES § 1:30 (collecting cases).

B.   Financial Advisors

There is a risk that a court may not consider financial consultants, such as investment bankers, to be privileged agents.[906] However, at least one jurisdiction has expressed an interest in protecting attorney-client communications involving financial advisors.[907]

Where public relations consultants, financial advisors, or other consultants who may not be considered within the privilege will interact with the investigation team, it is advisable to take steps to maximize the chance that privilege will apply, while also being circumspect regarding what is shared with the consultant to minimize potential harm in the event that a court finds that privilege does not apply.

XI.   ENGAGING CONSULTANTS

A party asserting attorney-client privilege must demonstrate that privileged persons, including agents of counsel, communicated in confidence and that they maintained confidentiality thereafter. In

---

[906] *Crane Security Techs., Inc. v. Rolling Optics, AB,* 2017 WL 470890, *5 (D. Mass. 2017) (communications between patent purchaser and its investment bankers were privileged where the financial advisor was indispensable in facilitating counsel to provide legal advice to purchaser); *Dahl v. Bain Capital Partners, LLC,* 714 F. Supp. 2d 225, 229 (D. Mass. 2010) (communications between client's investment bankers and counsel not privileged where investment bankers acted in business capacity and were not necessary or indispensable for counsel to provide legal advice); *Green v. Beer,* 2010 WL 2653650, *3 (S.D. N.Y. 2010), aff'd in part, rev'd in part on other grounds, 2010 WL 3422723 (S.D. N.Y. 2010) (communications between counsel and clients' financial advisors not privileged because communications not demonstrated to be necessary, let alone "nearly indispensable" to the provision of legal advice to the clients); *Louisiana Mun. Police Employees Retirement System v. Sealed Air Corp.,* 253 F.R.D. 300, 313-14 (D.N.J. 2008) (communications between defendant and defendant's investment bankers were not protected by attorney-client privilege because defendant failed to show that they were retained to provide or facilitate legal advice, as opposed to provide business and tax advice). *See also* TESTIMONIAL PRIVILEGES § 1:29 n.7.

[907] *3Com Corp. v. Diamond II Holdings, Inc.,* 2010 WL 2280734, at *4 (Del. Ch. 2010) (Delaware has a "broad [ ] rule" protecting attorney-client communications that include investment bankers, particularly for corporate transactions).

order to ensure that a third party consultant understands the consultant's role as a privileged person, and in order to be able to demonstrate with contemporaneous evidence that the consultant was intended to serve a legal function, it is helpful to include language in a consultant's engagement letter conveying the following: (1) The consultant is being engaged, by the attorney, or by the client, to assist counsel in providing legal advice to the company; (2) The consultant acknowledges that counsel and the client consider communications with the consultant to be privileged and, where applicable, that the consultant's work is protected by the work product doctrine; and (3) The consultant agrees to take steps to maintain confidentiality and to preserve applicable privileges and protections.[908]

XII.   AVOIDING WAIVER

Having taken steps to establish the attorney-client privilege and work product protections, a company and its counsel need to take steps to maintain confidentiality. Waiver can occur in myriad ways. The three general categories of waiver are: (1) intentional disregard for confidentiality through intended disclosures; (2) inadvertent disclosure in the course of a proceeding or otherwise; and (3) implied waiver through putting privileged information "at issue". Detailed discussion of waiver is beyond the scope of this chapter. The following are general comments regarding waiver.

---

[908] These points can be made briefly, or the engagement letter can include additional, related provisions. For example, engagement letters may include one or more of the following types of provisions: a commitment by the consultant to contact the company and counsel promptly if the consultant receives a discovery request or a subpoena; a commitment to cooperate with the company's and counsels' efforts to maintain applicable privileges and protections in the event the consultant receives a discovery request or a subpoena; or procedures for maintaining confidentiality during and after contract performance.

XIII. CONSIDER BOTH THE ATTORNEY-CLIENT PRIVILEGE AND THE WORK PRODUCT PROTECTION

It seems that most decisions addressing waiver address waiver of the attorney-client privilege rather than the work product protection. Frequently, following a court's detailed analysis of why a company has waived the attorney-client privilege over certain documents, there is a briefer section in which the court concludes that many of those same documents are protected by the work product doctrine. This is particularly true with respect to investigations, where documents like counsel's notes of employee interviews and draft investigation reports are at issue. These notes and draft reports are clearly protected by both doctrines where the company anticipates or is in the midst of litigation. Even in the rare instances in which courts order production of these types of investigation materials, the court will allow redaction of opinion work product prior to production pursuant to Fed. R. Civ. P. 26(b)(3)(B).

XIV. MAINTAIN STEPS TO KEEP INVESTIGATION MATERIALS CONFIDENTIAL

Where a company has established reasonable measures during an investigation to keep investigation materials confidential, the company should maintain those measures after the investigation has concluded. The materials should remain segregated from normal business documents and data; only those with a need-to-know legal advice should have access to privileged material; and the company should not provide the material to third parties without first consulting with company counsel.[909]

---

[909] One area where a company should make sure that the business people and the company's lawyers are on the same page is with respect to disclosures to the company's auditors. Although more than a dozen states provide some level of protection for accountant-client communications, under federal common law there is no accountant-client privilege. *Couch v. U.S.*, 409 U.S. 322, 335 (1973). Disclosure of attorney-client privileged material to an auditor, acting as an auditor, waives privilege under federal common law. However, a majority of federal courts have held that disclosure of work product to an auditor does not

XV.   DISCLOSURE OF FACTS

It is black-letter law that the attorney-client privilege protects communications, but it does not protect underlying facts.[910] Similarly, the work product doctrine protects the actual document prepared, not the underlying facts reflected in the document.[911]

A company may wish to disclose facts learned during an investigation, while avoiding waiver of any privileges or protections. For example, a company may be required or may choose voluntarily to make a disclosure to the government about a potential violation of law, or it may want to cooperate fully with government investigators to qualify for cooperation credit by providing all relevant facts to the government.[912] What steps can a company take to avoid waiver or at least to minimize the scope of waiver during the course of the government investigation?

Although facts are not privileged, it is sometimes difficult to disclose facts in a way that does not risk waiver of privilege. For

---

waive work product protections. *See, e.g., United States v. Deloitte*, 610 F.3d 129, 140 (D.C. Cir. 2010). *See also* TESTIMONIAL PRIVILEGES § 3:5.

[910] *Upjohn*, 449 U.S. at 395 ("[T]he protection of the privilege extends only to communications and not to facts. A fact is one thing and a communication concerning that fact is an entirely different thing. The client cannot be compelled to answer the question, 'What did you say or write to the attorney?' but may not refuse to disclose any relevant fact within his knowledge merely because he incorporated a statement of such fact into his communication to his attorney."). *See also* TESTIMONIAL PRIVILEGES § 1:13.

[911] TESTIMONIAL PRIVILEGES § 2.6 n.4.

[912] The U.S. Justice Manual ("JM") provides: "Eligibility for cooperation is not predicated upon waiver of the attorney-client privilege or work product protection. Instead, the sort of cooperation that is most valuable to resolving allegations of misconduct by a corporation and its officers, directors, employees, or agents is disclosure of the relevant *facts* concerning such misconduct... If a corporation wishes to receive credit for such cooperation, which then can be considered with all other cooperative efforts and circumstances in evaluating how fairly to proceed, then the corporation, like any person, must disclose the relevant facts of which it has knowledge." JM § 9-28.720 (Nov. 2017) (emphasis in original). The SEC Enforcement Manual provides: "[I]f a party seeks cooperation credit for timely disclosure of relevant facts, the party must disclose all such facts within the party's knowledge." SEC Enf. Manual (Nov. 2017) § 4.3.

example, where a fact learned during the investigation is based on oral statements made during privileged interviews, and no pre-existing document provides the same information. How can a company provide that factual information without waiving privilege?[913]

Where a company does not wish to waive privilege, the following steps may minimize the risk of waiver:

1. Provide underlying, non-privileged information that forms the basis for a privileged report, rather than the report itself.[914]

2. Prepare a report specifically for the government that discloses facts, but does not disclose the substance of individual privileged communications or any protected work product. When submitting the report to the government, state in the body of the report or in a cover letter that the company does not intend to waive any privilege or protection, and that it is the company's position that the report reflects only non-privileged facts.

Where a company decides that it wants to disclose privileged information to the government, the following steps may minimize the scope of waiver:

a. Where the disclosure will be to a federal office or agency:

1. Invoke the protections of Federal Rule of Evidence 502(a), discussed below.

---

[913] The cases addressing this issue are fact-specific and involve nuances beyond the scope of this chapter.

[914] TESTIMONIAL PRIVILEGES § 1:39 ("Recommendations: Disclosures to Government Agencies").

2. If there is a pending proceeding, have the court enter a FRE 502(d) order.[915]

3. Where there is no pending proceeding, seek the government's agreement to obtain a FRE 502(d) order from a court with jurisdiction over the investigation,[916] or at a minimum, reach agreement that the government will allow the company to claw back privileged documents, and that the government will seek to have a FRE 502(d) order entered if there is a subsequent federal proceeding.

b. Where possible, enter into a confidentiality agreement with the government. Although a majority of courts have rejected the selective waiver doctrine, a few courts, particularly in the Southern District of New York, may find that a confidentiality agreement prevents waiver as to third party litigants.[917]

XVI. FEDERAL RULE OF EVIDENCE 502

Federal Rule of Evidence 502 is designed to reduce the cost of discovery by limiting the scope of waiver and by eliminating the fear of subject matter waiver where disclosure is made in a federal proceeding or to a federal office or agency.[918]

Federal Rule of Evidence 502(a) provides:

---

[915] For discussion of FRE 502(d), *see* THE FEDERAL JUDGES' GUIDE TO DISCOVERY (Electronic Discovery Institute 2015) Ch. 7 at 61-62; TESTIMONIAL PRIVILEGES § 1:76 ("The Scope of Waiver – Federal Rule of Evidence 502").

[916] If the disclosure is pursuant to a subpoena, consider filing a motion to modify the subpoena pursuant to Fed. R. Civ. P. 45(d)(3) and seek entry of a FRE 502(d) order. Among other things, a FRE 502(d) order will enable the court to provide protection of privileged or other protected information pursuant to Fed. R. Civ. P. 45(d)(3)(A)(iii).

[917] *See* TESTIMONIAL PRIVILEGES § 1:102 nn.9-10, § 1:139.

[918] THE FEDERAL JUDGES' GUIDE TO DISCOVERY (Electronic Discovery Institute) Ch. 7 at 60. *See also* TESTIMONIAL PRIVILEGES § 1:76.

a. **Disclosure Made in a Federal Proceeding or to a Federal Office or Agency; Scope of Waiver.** When the disclosure is made in a federal proceeding or to a federal office or agency and waives the attorney-client privilege or the work product protection, the waiver extends to an undisclosed communication or information in a federal or state proceeding only if:

1. the waiver is intentional;

2. the disclosed and undisclosed communications or information concern the same subject matter; and

3. they ought in fairness to be considered together.

The Advisory Committee Notes make it clear that subject matter waiver is reserved for those unusual and rare circumstances in which fairness requires further disclosure of related material to prevent a selective and misleading presentation of evidence to the disadvantage of the adversary.[919] Note: An increasing number of states have adopted analogues to FRE 502.

At least with regard to disclosures to federal offices or agencies, the scope of waiver resulting from disclosure will be limited to the actual information disclosed and will not result in any further waiver, unless the company intentionally discloses protected information in a "selective, misleading and unfair manner".[920]

---

[919] Judicial Conference Committee Note on FRE 502(a). *Accord In re General Motors LLC Ignition Switch Litigation,* 80 F.Supp.3d 521, 533-34 (S.D. N.Y. 2015) (case did not present the "unusual and rare circumstances in which fairness requires a judicial finding of waiver with respect to related, protected information").

[920] Judicial Conference Committee Note on FRE 502(a).

Chapter 16

The Role of Compliance and Compliance Monitoring in Corporate Enterprise

By: Rachel Lewis[921]

I.   INTRODUCTION AND BACKGROUND

I would like to start by apologizing for the acts that have brought us here. The nation has a right to expect its rules and laws to be obeyed.

My job is to deal with both the past and the future. The past actions of Salomon are presently causing our 8,000 employees and their families to bear a stain. Virtually all of these employees are hardworking, able and honest. I want to find out exactly what happened in the past so that this stain is borne by the guilty few and removed from the innocent. To help do this, I promise to you, Mr. Chairman, and to the American people, Salomon's wholehearted cooperation with all authorities. These authorities have the power of subpoena, the ability to immunize witnesses, and the power to prosecute for perjury. Our internal investigation has not had these tools. We welcome their use.

But in the end, the spirit about compliance is as important or more so than words about compliance. I want the right words and I want the full range of internal controls. But I also have asked every Salomon employee to be his or her own compliance officer. After they first obey all rules, I then want employees to ask themselves whether they are willing to have any contemplated act appear the next day on the front page of their local paper, to be read by their spouses, children, and friends, with the reporting done by an informed and critical reporter. If they follow this test, they need

---

[921] Rachel Lewis is Senior Counsel at Shook, Hardy, and Bacon L.L.P. in Chicago, where she counsels clients on complex discovery, data management, and regulatory compliance. This chapter was derived from a combination of two chapters from our prior editions previously edited by Michael Simmon, Thomas Zingale, Wayne Matus, and Brandon Daniels. t

not fear my other message to them: Lose money for the firm, and I will be understanding; lose a shred of reputation for the firm, and I will be ruthless[922].

- Warren Buffett, CEO of Berkshire Hathaway, chairman of Salmon Brothers, Inc.

In today's global economy, companies face a complex and evolving regulatory compliance environment. The alphabet soup of federal agencies and regulations – FCPA, HIPAA, OSHA, FIRREA, GAAP, AML/BSA, et cetera – create a compliance minefield for the unwary, with potentially significant consequences for running afoul of prescribed guidelines for acceptable corporate conduct.

"Compliance" can be simply defined as "[a]dherence to the laws and regulations passed by official regulating bodies as well as general principles of ethical conduct."[923] Brooklyn Law School Professor Miriam Baer defines "compliance" as "a system of policies and controls that organizations adopt to deter violations of law and to assure external authorities that they are taking steps to deter violations of law."[924] As a practical matter, corporate compliance and ethics ("C&E") programs are, at their core, concerned with managing risk – risk to the corporation's reputation, risk to financial performance, and some instances, risk of personal liability for corporate boards or officers of the company.

Though the financial crisis of 2008 brought governance, risk management, and compliance ("GRC") principles to the forefront of public scrutiny, C&E programs have become increasingly integral facets of corporate operational structures over the last four

---

[922] Opening statement of Warren Buffett before the Subcommittee on Telecommunications and Finance of Energy and Commerce Committee, (May 1, 2010)

[923] Society of Corporate Compliance and Ethics' *Compliance Dictionary.*

[924] Miriam Hechler Baer, *Governing Corporate Compliance*, 50 B.C. L. Rev. 949, 958 (2009).

decades. The need for formalized, documented C&E programs began to gain prominence in 1977 with the passage of the Foreign Corrupt Practices Act ("FCPA") and its mandate that companies maintain internal controls to guard against bribery of foreign officials. The movement to consistently demonstrate GRC principles as a single unified concept and not discreet, isolated functions, is at the forefront of this effort. Underlying these efforts, members of an interdependent framework exist in an effective corporate risk management strategy, with mechanisms for managing threats to the lawful and ethical operation of a business.

The incarnation of corporate governance most familiar to western corporate citizens was largely sculpted by committees of industry, regulatory and professional bodies coming together to establish standards for listed companies. Progressive, and in some instances aspirational, initiatives such as the Cadbury Report (1992), the Greenbury Report (1995), the Combined Code (1998), Turnbull Report (1999) and the Organization of Economic Cooperation and Development ("OECD") Principles (1999) were a response to a crisis in investor confidence and a demand for transparency, honesty and accountability in risk versus benefit decisions, financial performance and the accurate reporting of results.

One critical landmark in the development of modern C&E programs was the coalescence of the Committee of Sponsoring Organizations of the Treadway Commission ("COSO") in 1985. Still in existence, the conglomerate is jointly sponsored by five private-sector industry groups: the American Accounting Association; the American Institute of Certified Public Accountants; Financial Executives International; the Institute of Internal Auditors; and the Institute of Management Accountants. COSO's work has transformed and guided the nature of compliance development and management. Most notably, the 1992 "Internal Controls – Integrated Framework" paper has set the tone for thirty years of GRC controls management by proposing a method for designing, implementing and executing a system of internal controls.[925]

In the "Internal Controls" paper, COSO set forth five critical and integrated components for establishing an internal controls system. First is the control environment, a defined set of standards, processes and structures that provide the basis for carrying out internal controls across an organization. Second is a business's risk assessment process. A risk assessment involves a dynamic and iterative process for identifying and assessing risks to the achievement of objectives.[926] Third, control activities are established through policies and procedures that help ensure management's duty to mitigate risks to the achievement of the entity's objectives.[927] Fourth, the evaluation of information and communication supporting controls in an organization.[928] Information is necessary for an entity to carry out internal control responsibilities to support the achievement of its objectives.[929] And communication is the continual and iterative process of providing, sharing and obtaining necessary information.[930] The fifth and final component is monitoring. In the COSO components, monitoring is both a separate and ongoing evaluation of the internal controls system overall and of the functional efficacy of the components of each control.[931] Monitoring is not only a component, it is the thread that holds together the remaining components integral to an effective control. Today, the COSO guidance is firmly rooted in the way corporations and financial institutions manage and monitor risk.

---

[925] Guidance on Internal Control, Internal Control Guidance and Thought Papers; refreshed in 2013 (2013), https://www.coso.org/Pages/ic.aspx.

[926] Id.

[927] Id.

[928] Id.

[929] Id.

[930] Id.

[931] Id.

Also in the mid-1980's, a group of 32 defense contractors created the Defense Industry Initiative ("DII") in response to public disclosure of waste, fraud and abuse in defense procurement contracts. The DII's principal purpose was to encourage self-regulation among defense contractors by "promulgat[ing] and vigilantly enforc[ing] codes of ethics."[932]

The work of COSO and DII found legal authority in the November 1991 watershed legislation of the Federal Sentencing Commission's Federal Sentencing Guidelines for Organizations ("FSGO"). Broadly stated, the FSGO seeks to punish and deter corporate wrongdoing.[933] Under the FSGO, one of the four factors that can increase punishment of an organization is "the involvement in or tolerance of criminal activity," and one of the two mitigating factors on punishment is "the existence of an effective compliance and ethics program."[934]

In 2003, the Introductory Commentary to the FSGO was amended to add the following language:

These guidelines offer incentives to organizations to reduce and ultimately eliminate criminal conduct by providing a structural foundation from which an organization may self-police its own conduct through an effective compliance and ethics program. The prevention and detection of criminal conduct, as facilitated by an effective compliance and ethics program, will assist an organization in encouraging ethical conduct and in complying fully with all applicable laws.[935]

---

[932] The Packard Commission's February 1986 Interim Report

[933] Diana E. Murphy, The Federal Sentencing Guidelines for Organizations: A Decade of Promoting Compliance and Ethics, 87 Iowa L. Rev. 697, 703 (2002).

[934] United States Sentencing Commission's *Guideline Manual,* Introductory Commentary, Chapter 8, Sentencing of Organizations (Nov. 1, 2016).

[935] Information in Table 54 of the U. S. Sentencing Commission's annual *Sourcebook of Federal Sentencing Statistics* shows that of the 245 organizations sentenced under the FSGO between 2012 and 2015, 242 had no compliance program.

In the 30 years since FSGO was enacted, government and private sector stakeholders have worked to overhaul and redefine corporate compliance programs to integrate the FSGO guidelines, balancing the fear of over-regulation against the risk of another potentially destabilizing event rooted in weak or ineffective C&E programs. The result is that organizations of all sizes now dedicate substantial efforts and resources to effectively monitor and implement guidelines to mitigate financial, reputational, and regulatory risk.

II.   THE EFFECTIVE C&E PROGRAM[936]

A C&E program's credibility and value to its organization and to regulators, is for the most part, measured by its ability to prevent, detect and correct criminal and unethical conduct. As no C&E program is capable of preventing, identifying, or eradicating all instances of potentially criminal or unethical conduct, such programs must be considered organic, with frequent updates to protocols for policy, process, training, and monitoring.

The topic of compliance monitoring in a global and heterogeneous universe of industries, market demands, and public interests conjures a different image in every sector. The size and complexity of the company's operations, the risks unique to its operations and industry, its corporate structure, the extent to which it is regulated, whether it is privately-held or publicly traded, and many other factors influence and in some instances dictate the content of its C&E program. Companies should tailor C&E programs to their individual needs, while avoiding the temptation to "boil the ocean" with the program's structure, remembering that the C&E program should be easy to follow, implement, monitor, and enforce.

C&E demands a level of accountability and awareness that has shifted compliance from passive to active and has turned investigations from episodic to business-as-usual ("BAU") activities in the form of continuous compliance monitoring, with cautionary tales for compliance officers that fail to build effective

---

[936] There are volumes detailing C&E programs; this section is a primer only.

programs – a prime example being the 2017 settlement between Thomas Haider, former Chief Compliance Officer of MoneyGram International, Inc., and United States Attorney's Office for the Southern District of New York ("SDNY") and the Financial Crimes Enforcement Network ("FinCEN") for claims brought under the Bank Secrecy Act/Anti-Money Laundering laws and regulations ("BSA/AML")[937].

Development of an effective C&E program should be a product of collaboration among the C&E officer ("C&EO"), corporate and/or counsel, finance, risk management, audit, HR, IT, and operational personnel. For all industries, monitoring is a key component of an effective GRC strategy. Monitoring can take two primary forms: monitoring for the underlying risk in a given business activity; or monitoring the execution and efficacy of the controls performed to mitigate the underlying risk.

At a minimum, an effective C&E program has three front lines of defense. First, there must be a risk assessment. The risk assessment will consider the particular industry's risks in addition to the company's general and specific risks. This includes the sales, operations and executive staff responsible for generating revenue. For example, in the banking industry, the Office of the Comptroller of the Currency ("OCC") defines this as any organizational unit that: "(i) engages in activities designed to generate revenue for the parent company or Bank; (ii) provides services, such as administration, finance, treasury, legal, or human resources, to the Bank; or (iii) provides information technology, operations, servicing, processing, or other support to any organizational unit covered by these Guidelines."[938] The inclusion of the business's front-line operations in compliance monitoring is

---

[937] https://www.reuters.com/article/us-moneygram-intl-moneylaundering/former-moneygram-executive-settles-closely-watched-u-s-money-laundering-case-idUSKBN1802P3

[938] 12 C.F.R. Parts 30 and 170. OCC Guidelines Establishing Heightened Standards for Certain Large Insured National Banks, Insured Federal Savings Associations, and Insured Federal Branches; Integration of 12 CFR Parts 30 and 170. https://www.occ.gov/news-issuances/news-releases/2014/nr-occ-2014-4a.pdf.

an essential part of a successful risk management program. It provides both accountability and awareness to the people most influential and familiar with the culture and practices of an organization. It also provides an immediate first-hand assessment of the underlying risk that the business is attempting to mitigate.

Once understood, the risks must be prioritized according to the likelihood of occurrence and severity of consequences. This might involve surveying regulatory and enforcement actions across the particular industry to determine where regulators and law enforcement personnel are focusing. In addition, the company should consider the severity of the consequences from a violation. For example, in the healthcare industry, certain violations can result in exclusion from federal healthcare programs. An antitrust violation can result in treble damages and irreparable damage to business reputation. Prioritization allows companies to focus limited resources on critical risks and the risks with the gravest consequences.

The second line is typically defined as the risk management or compliance function of an organization. Although these functions are part of the organization, they are considered independent "check and balance" functions for the business. Again, the OCC defines this as, "any organizational unit within the Bank that has responsibility for identifying, measuring, monitoring, or controlling aggregate risks."[939] The second line is typically responsible for ensuring the conclusions of the first line, assessing any gaps, monitoring ongoing activity and assisting in the remediation of weaknesses. This is a proactive and integrated function in the organization and, in many cases, it is the center of excellence of compliance monitoring and improvement.

The third line of defense in a C&E program is the role of independent internal audit. What is most remarkable about the third line of defense is its independence. In not only OCC definitions, but in common practice, this form of independence is not duplicated elsewhere in the business organization. Reporting

---

[939] *Id.*

lines, incentives, budgets and procedures are commonly all separate from the functions they monitor. Internal audit's remit is to assess the efficacy of GRC practices of the organization, including the abilities of the first and second lines of defense to monitor risk management and control objectives. Together, these three components lay the foundation for effective C&E programs.

Additionally, regulators and the law provide the general and specific contours of an effective C&E program. By way of example, Section 8B2.1 of the FSGO outlines the minimum requirements of an effective compliance program:[940]

> (a) To have an effective compliance and ethics program... an organization shall:
>
>> (1) exercise due diligence to prevent and detect criminal conduct; and
>>
>> (2) otherwise promote an organizational culture that encourages ethical conduct and a commitment to compliance with the law.

Such compliance and ethics program shall be reasonably designed, implemented, and enforced so that the program is generally effective in preventing and detecting criminal conduct. The failure to prevent or detect the instant offense does not necessarily mean that the program is not generally effective in preventing and detecting criminal conduct.

Promotion of a "culture of compliance" is the hallmark of an effective C&E program. In both policy and practice, the company must communicate a commitment to conducting business in an ethical, legal manner. However, the standard for determining the program's effectiveness is not perfect adherence nor detections of a failure, but rather creating a corporate framework that encourages compliance.

---

[940] The authors' commentary appears following some italicized section of Section 8B2.1.

(b) Due diligence and the promotion of an organizational culture that encourages ethical conduct and a commitment to compliance with the law within the meaning of subsection (a) minimally require the following:

(1) The organization shall establish standards and procedures to prevent and detect criminal conduct.

(2)(A)The organization's governing authority shall be knowledgeable about the content and operation of the compliance and ethics program and shall exercise reasonable oversight with respect to the implementation and effectiveness of the compliance and ethics program.

(B) High-level personnel of the organization shall ensure that the organization has an effective compliance and ethics program, as described in this guideline. Specific individual(s) within high-level personnel shall be assigned overall responsibility for the compliance and ethics program.

(C) Specific individual(s) within the organization shall be delegated day-to-day operational responsibility for the compliance and ethics program. Individual(s) with operational responsibility shall report periodically to high-level personnel and, as appropriate, to the governing authority, or an appropriate subgroup of the governing authority, on the effectiveness of the compliance and ethics program.[941] To carry out such operational responsibility, such individual(s) shall be given adequate resources, appropriate authority, and direct access to the

---

[941] See *In re Caremark Int'l Derivative Litigation,* 698 A.2d 959 (Del. Ch. 1996), board members should be informed and ensure an effective C&E program is implemented and operational within their organization. In *Caremark,* the Delaware Chancery Court held that board members are obligated to ensure their company has an effective "information and reporting system . . . ." The court further held that "failure to do so under some circumstances may, in theory, render a director liable for losses caused by non-compliance with applicable legal standards."

governing authority or an appropriate subgroup of the governing authority.

Section (2) emphasizes the importance of internal, high level responsibility for the care and oversight of the C&E program. Senior management must take an active role in designing and implementing the C&E program. In addition, the company must assign specific members of senior management to implement and manage the C&E program. This may be a C&E manager or officer, in-house counsel or another senior member of management. The take-away is that there must be a captain of the C&E ship, and that captain should reside in the C-suite of the company.

Regardless of who is at the head of the C&E program, that person cannot do it alone. The C&EO must have sufficient human resources to implement, manage and monitor the C&E program. Such personnel may be drawn from or reside in a C&E, risk management, audit, or legal department. These personnel must in turn report to the C&EO or other high-level officer or, as appropriate, the board of directors or a committee appointed by the board of directors to oversee the C&E program. These operational C&E managers must also have adequate resources and authority to implement and manage the C&E program and access to the board or a committee of the board.

> (3) The organization shall use reasonable efforts not to include within the substantial authority personnel of the organization any individual whom the organization knew, or should have known through the exercise of due diligence, has engaged in illegal activities or other conduct inconsistent with an effective compliance and ethics program.

The requirement that a known offender not participate in managing the C&E program is self-evident. However, companies should do their due diligence when vetting personnel responsible for implementing and managing a C&E program to ensure that such personnel have not been found -- by an internal investigation, a professional organization or in a civil proceeding -- to have committed ethics violations or engaged in questionable business practices.

> (4)(A) The organization shall take reasonable steps to communicate periodically and in a practical manner its standards and procedures, and other aspects of the compliance and ethics program, to the individuals referred to in subparagraph (B) by conducting effective training programs and otherwise disseminating information appropriate to such individuals' respective roles and responsibilities.

(B) The individuals referred to in subparagraph (A) are the members of the governing authority, high-level personnel, substantial authority personnel, the organization's employees, and, as appropriate, the organization's agents.

Regulators expect companies to provide training and disseminate communications on the requirements and expectations of the C&E program more than once; in practice many companies choose annual Compliance & Ethics training programs, either in person or through online learning systems and when changes are made to the content of the C&E program, ensuring that those changes are effectively communicated to employees (via email with a read receipt requested and posting the notice in public places if appropriate). Section (4)(A) also requires C&E training to be practical, meaning that it should be appropriate to the business sector the company serves. For example, addressing vendor relations and contract negotiations may be appropriate for personnel engaged in procurement, while such training may not be necessary for production line workers. In addition, the company's written C&E program should be available to employees electronically, either on an intranet or on a shared drive available to all employees. In certain instances, a CE&O may post the company's C&E program on the internet, making it available the general public. Section 4(B) makes clear that C&E is the responsibility of everyone within the business, even agents of the company appropriate. While it would be unlikely that a vendor's illegal or unethical conduct could be legally imputed to the company, such conduct can certainly damage a company's reputation.

(5) The organization shall take reasonable steps—

> (A) to ensure that the organization's compliance and ethics program is followed, including monitoring and auditing to detect criminal conduct;

> (B) to evaluate periodically the effectiveness of the organization's compliance and ethics program; and

> (C) to have and publicize a system, which may include mechanisms that allow for anonymity or confidentiality, whereby the organization's employees and agents may report or seek guidance regarding potential or actual criminal conduct without fear of retaliation.

The key takeaway from this requirement is that a company's C&E program must include active, mindful monitoring of employee activity and communications and internal audits to detect wrongdoing. This may require engaging external auditors and relying on internal audit and IT departments to detect wrongdoing. For some organizations, it may mean leveraging available technologies to improve the prevention and detection of criminal or unethical conduct. In addition to regularly scheduled audits, which may allow wrongdoers to cover their tracks and conceal bad conduct or illegal transactions, companies should also conduct random and surprise audits as a best practice for uncovering illegal or unethical conduct.

Companies are expected to engage in self-critical analysis of the effectiveness of their C&E program. Without such evaluations, it is not possible to make needed changes to the C&E program. These evaluations should consider many factors, including without limitation, the number and frequency of (1) violations detected, (2) civil lawsuits alleging bad behavior by company personnel, and (3) whistle-blower complaints. Additionally, the findings of internal and government investigations are highly relevant to periodic C&E program review. In addition, C&E officers should stay abreast of government findings of illegal conduct in other companies and consider whether such conduct may be occurring in their own company. These and other metrics allow the C&EO to adequately evaluate the effectiveness of a C&E program.

The import of 5(C) is that employees are less likely to report unethical or illegal conduct if they fear retaliation or are not guaranteed confidentiality. Consequently, companies should maintain a system whereby employees can anonymously report actual or suspected unethical conduct or criminal wrongdoing or request guidance on whether a particular action or event might be unethical or illegal. Such a system could be in the form of an anonymous tip telephone line. The reporting system should include the assurance of confidentiality in both policy and practice.

> (6) The organization's compliance and ethics program shall be promoted and enforced consistently throughout the organization through (A) appropriate incentives to perform in accordance with the compliance and ethics program; and (B) appropriate disciplinary measures for engaging in criminal conduct and for failing to take reasonable steps to prevent or detect criminal conduct.

Companies should use the proverbial "carrot and stick" to incentivize its personnel to follow and abide by its C&E program. Companies can offer bonuses for compliant departments and individual employees. Conversely, companies should appropriately discipline employees for non-compliant behavior, up to and including termination. Employee discipline should be administered in an even-handed, non-discriminatory manner.

> (7) After criminal conduct has been detected, the organization shall take reasonable steps to respond appropriately to the criminal conduct and to prevent further similar criminal conduct, including making any necessary modifications to the organization's compliance and ethics program.

Responding appropriately to criminal or unethical conduct might include employee discipline, self-reporting to regulators, the board of directors, and other stakeholders but should always include review of the C&E program to determine if modifications are needed to deter and detect similar conduct in the future.

(c) In implementing subsection (b), the organization shall periodically assess the risk of criminal conduct and shall take appropriate steps to design, implement, or modify each requirement set forth in subsection (b) to reduce the risk of criminal conduct identified through this process.

It is axiomatic, but companies must stay abreast of changes in the law in order to know what previously legal conduct might have become illegal. Bad actors are notoriously adept at finding and exploiting loopholes in the law, which is why the law is usually reactionary to bad conduct. Sarbanes-Oxley and Dodd-Frank are examples of the law's reaction conduct that was either unregulated or fell into a legal gray area. Part of this process requires the company to modify its C&E program to reflect changes in the law, changes in the business climate and the actual business of the company and to follow any such modifications with appropriate training and monitoring.

The Commentary to the FSGO states that companies should "incorporate and follow applicable industry practice or the standards called for by any applicable government regulation" and failure to do so "weighs against a finding of an effective compliance and ethics program."[942] Most regulated industries – such as healthcare, pharmaceutical, financial and insurance – have industry-specific requirements or best practices. For example, in 1997, the Office of Inspector General of the Department of Health and Human Services published "OIG Compliance Program for Individual and Small Group Physician Practices" which sets forth seven best practices for compliance.[943]

In addition, when evaluating C&E programs, regulators consider the size of the organization. Larger companies are expected to

---

[942] https://www.ussc.gov/guidelines/2016-guidelines-manual/2016-chapter-8

[943] 65 Fed. Reg. 59434-59552 (Oct. 5, 2000).

devote greater human and financial resources to its C&E program. However, the Commentary provides that smaller companies are expected to "demonstrate the same degree of commitment to ethical conduct and compliance with the law as large organizations."[944] As a cost-saving measure, companies, in particular smaller companies, may consider using outside experts and consultants to assist in their C&E programs, particularly in the areas of audits and training.

Finally, the Commentary provides that recurrence of the same or similar bad conduct casts doubt on a company's commitment to its C&E program. When designing a C&E program, a company should carefully consider each facet of its operations and the industry within which it operates to intuit the ways in which employees might knowingly or unwittingly violate the law or ethical business morays. The business should consider the requirements of the company's operations and tailor the C&E program so as not to unduly impede legitimate business operations, while still providing firm standards for compliance and ethics for personnel to follow.

III. THE C&E OFFICER STRUCTURE

"There is no standard regulatory metric, nor is there any prescription. Is culture about the right 'vibe'? If so, that's not very satisfactory. One way of knowing when culture has failed is when things go wrong and get worse or just go wrong again. This may be worth some thought. How quickly does it take for problems to escalate to the right person or group of persons for effective decision making or action? How many problems linger in the inbox or the bottom drawer beyond their easily fixable date? How difficult is it to fix things once they are detected? How long? How soon? How hard? These questions beg qualitative or numerative answers that may be capable of measuring and, in a proxy sense,

---

[944] https://www.ussc.gov/guidelines/2016-guidelines-manual/2016-chapter-8

*giving us a metric for how well an organisation is able to deal with
things that don't go well or don't go according to plan."*[945]

- Mark Steward, Director of Enforcement and Market Oversight

Companies should think about the C&EO position not as an
expense but a value add. C&EOs help protect the company's good
will and reputation, often the company's most valuable assets. In
addition, the C&EO can assist in strategic planning in order to
avoid regulatory delays and investigations which drain valuable
corporate resources and derail business plans.

There is a great deal of ongoing academic and practical debate
concerning whether the general counsel ("GC") may also serve as
C&EO, and if the positions are filled by different persons, whether
the C&EO should report to the GC. In the late-1980's, the role and
position of Compliance & Ethics Officer ("C&EO") began to
emerge as a distinct position within companies. Generally, the
C&EO is tasked with overseeing and managing a company's C&E
program so that the company's business is conducted in a legal,
ethical manner. The C&EO role is dynamic in light of the complex
and evolving ethical, economic, and social environments within
which business is conducted. Increased regulatory activity and
enforcement activity over the last decade make the position even
more complex and critical. To be effective at managing C&E risks,
the C&EO must have adequate human and financial resources,
access to all company books and records, and the ability to
effectively collaborate with senior management and/or the board of
directors or a committee of the board regarding C&E risks. The
C&EO should manage C&E risks both in day-to-day operations
and in the company's strategic planning.

There are no federal regulations mandating that the C&EO and GC
positions be split or dictating reporting chains for a stand-alone
C&EO. GCs in many companies successfully wear two hats, also
serving as C&EO. However, the Department of Health and Human

---

[945] Mark Steward, Culture and governance Financial Conduct Authority (2015),
https://www.fca.org.uk/news/speeches/culture-and-governance.

Services' Office of Inspector General has issued non-binding guidance that the roles of C&EO and GC should be separate when feasible.[946] By separating the roles, the OIG reasons that "a system of checks and balances is established to more effectively achieve the goals of the compliance program."

The American Bar Association's Task Force on Corporate Responsibility concluded that "[t]he general counsel of a public corporation should have primary responsibility for assuring the implementation of an effective legal compliance system under the oversight of the board of directors."[947] Companies with sufficient resources to separate the positions should consider the roles, duties and objectives of GC and C&EO and reconcile any differences before deciding to have the same person wear both hats. In a landmark settlement with Pfizer, Chief OIG counsel stated that "lawyers tell you whether you can do something, and compliance tells you whether you should."[948]

In companies in which the GC and C&EO positions are separate, the C&EO's reporting chain may go through the GC or be directly to the board of directors or a committee of the board. For companies in which the GC also serves as the C&EO, there is a risk that the attorney-client privilege and work product immunity may be difficult to assert if there is ambiguity as to which hat the attorney was wearing. In such companies, the attorney should make clear that communications intended to be privileged are given for purposes of rendering legal advice. Ultimately, whether a company separates the GC and C&EO functions may be dictated by cost, however, as the Commentary to the FSGO makes clear, financial considerations cannot drive compliance.

---

[946] OIG Compliance Program Guidance for Pharmaceutical Manufacturers, 68 Fed. Reg. 23731 (May 2003).

[947] Report of the American Bar Association Task Force on Corporate Responsibility (2003).

[948] Pfizer Inc., Office of Inspector General of the Department of Health and Human Services Corporate Integrity Agreement (Aug. 31. 2009).

IV.   PRACTICAL DATA MANAGEMENT

"In [one] sense, 'big data' is a continuation of an old theme. In another sense, the developments in data over the last 10 to 15 years represent a wholly new phenomenon, in the same way that satellite imaging is completely different from surveying a landscape from the top of a hill. At that scale, patterns become evident that would have been impossible to piece together by considering one plot at a time. This means that both market participants and regulators have new opportunities for developing knowledge. Moreover, this is a qualitatively different kind of knowledge, encompassing entire data sets in one pass rather than slowly accumulating insight from individual experiences."[949]

- Commissioner Kara Stein, Securities and Exchange Commission ("SEC")

With exponentially developing technology advances in the way businesses operate and manage data, the intersection between the amorphous and qualitative measures of compliance and the increasingly complex and voluminous quantitative variables upon which it may be measured create a hurdle for many organizations when defining and monitoring compliance standards.

On March 20th 2017, Ravi Menon, Managing Director of the Monetary Authority of Singapore ("MAS"), delivered keynote remarks at the Australian Securities and Investments Commission Annual Forum, where he stated that culture is a defining element for the future state of compliance. Menon stressed that MAS would look beyond the question of "Is this legal?" to the larger question of "Is this right?"[950] He also proposed that the rapid advancement of technology would be the sands upon which compliance risk

---

[949] Kara Stein, A Vision for Data at the SEC. Securities and Exchange Commission (2016), https://www.sec.gov/news/speech/speech-stein-10-28-2016.html.

[950] Reading Room, Financial Regulation – The Forward Agenda Monetary Authority of Singapore (2017), http://www.mas.gov.sg/News-and-Publications/Speeches-and-Monetary-Policy-Statements/Speeches/2017/Financial-Regulation.aspx.

would shift. Menon highlighted the double-edged sword presented by emerging technologies, pointing out both the challenges and benefits of algorithmic decision-making and vast sums of enriched data points generated by financial institutions about people, places and things.

Policies, or the procedures and controls that represent or reinforce those policies, should be characterized by a systematic, documented and process-driven set of rules that are increasingly reinforced by technology. These controls and procedures may be take the form of process documentation, checklists, disclosures, or risk evaluation procedures applied to situations identified as integral to the performance of a policy or points in time where policy assessment indicators, in some form of data, are available for review.

For example, in retail mortgage lending, a control may be the requirement to evidence the completion of a certain set of disclosures when underwriting a mortgage for a US military veteran under the guidelines of the Servicemembers Civil Relief Act. This control could go through multiple checks, where different groups require reaffirmation and evidence of the control, such as credit risk. Legal and compliance groups maintain independent controls as they usher the mortgage application through an approval process. Similarly, in pharmaceutical sales, pharmaceutical companies must evidence that all requests from healthcare professionals for educational materials describing off-label use of a product are referred to an independent medical affairs function.

Although polices allow a company or institution to establish a set of desired standard operating procedures ("SOPs"), a lack of adherence to these policies and the haphazard completion of controls can still open the organization to risk. Or, on the other end of the spectrum, the purposeful evasion of these controls can create even more substantial risk for an organization if the activity is systemic. The ability to prioritize and emphasize these SOPs and ensure that shortcuts are not taken on checks and balances, even in strained circumstances, is the second layer of compliance monitoring. This is an element of compliance defined by organizational values or "culture" and is often demonstrated by employee conduct, with personnel in leadership positions setting good examples. Culture is not only a matter of adhering to policy, it encompasses how an organization addresses and escalates risk that has been identified and, more importantly, sensitizes employees to conduct risk that is outside of a policy or control framework.

V.   COMPLIANCE MONITORING IN STRUCTURED DATA

"Successful BSA/AML compliance is a company-wide endeavor, dependent on the actions of employees throughout the organization, including frontline personnel responsible for customer identification program compliance, business line employees that feed data into the transaction monitoring and filtering programs, technology experts that build and manage the monitoring and screening systems, and BSA/AML compliance employees who investigate suspicious activity, file required reports, and oversee the entire BSA/AML program."[951]

- American Bankers Association

Compliance programs designed to monitor and mitigate the risk of violating BSA/AML and Office of Foreign Assets Control of the Treasury Department ("OFAC") requirements have become a central focus for regulatory and enforcement bodies over the last fifteen years. As the control of funding has manifested as one of the most effective weapons in the fight against terror, crime and states that jeopardize human rights and global stability, the organizations that police this activity have become more rigid in their application of compliance monitoring standards. Since its enactment in 1970, the Bank Secrecy Act has stood apart from other laws because of its prescriptive outline of an acceptable

---

[951] Comment Letters, NYDFS Transaction Monitoring, American Bankers Association, 2016,
https://www.aba.com/Advocacy/commentletters/Documents/cl-NYDFS-TransactionMonitoring2016.pdf.

money laundering compliance program. The four pillars of the compliance program described in BSA are: internal policies, procedures, and controls; a designated compliance officer; an employee training program; and, an audit function to test the program. To this day, these four pillars remain the recognized minimum standards for a compliance program and are echoed in many other laws and regulations.

Transaction monitoring systems require three operative components to function effectively: transaction and customer data; policies or rules; and the ability to present flagged transactions per those rules. However, each of these requirements is rife with impediments and challenges to operational consistency. Take, for example, the data element of transaction monitoring systems. Often drawing from diverse data sources in multiple formats, the unexpected mutations of data can render programs useless. In transaction monitoring and filtering, information from different transaction types (wires, credit cards, ATMs, debit card purchases, securities clearing, checks, etc.), platforms (core banking systems, SWIFT messaging, Credit Card Networks, CHIPS, etc.), and processes (Know Your Customer ("KYC"), Lending Application, Suitability, etc.) are all drawn into one environment.

Systems like SWIFT, created to facilitate the interbank flow of funds, are not geared toward the transparent and complete presentation of transaction details. For instance, in the case of trade records, the MT 700 series dealing with letters of credit and other trade related messages is often sparse in terms of detail and forces any system to revert to a manual review of any transaction of interest. In other instances, where data source complexity is not the issue, accuracy is. KYC records languish in disrepair, disabling institutions from picking up on high-risk customers that could jeopardize the organization's financial crime posture. Or, the translation of data from source systems, like the truncation of an address removing a sanctioned country or the incorrect mapping of a transaction code, to a compliance surveillance system can cause substantial harm to a bank's ability to monitor suspicious transactions or sanctioned entities.

The uptick in regulatory actions highlights the need for key stakeholders to truly understand the triggering mechanisms underpinning legacy BSA/AML and OFAC monitoring systems, as well as the next generation systems that will ultimately replace them. Organizations must adopt a purpose driven approach that embeds their risk mitigation strategies within their technology platforms. No longer can system opaqueness be used as reasonable grounds for compliance gaps. Regulatory expectations mandate that companies understand and ultimately adopt technological and analytics based solutions to mitigate risk. Corporate transaction monitoring as an archetype of compliance monitoring in structured content, such as monitoring gifts and entertainment expenses for potential Foreign Corrupt Practices Act ("FCPA") violations, or analyzing inventory to detect washed assets, teaches two core lessons. First, the unproductivity of modern transaction monitoring systems creates the need for some form of AI-driven solution, as a monitoring system is only as good as the policy driven rules used to currently detect problematic activity. Second, the underlying quality of data is integral to the function of monitoring systems – accurate data is the foundation of a well-functioning program.

Data quality is just one component of a broader data governance framework that in the coming years must incorporate significantly more data attributes to support future, AI-based transactional monitoring systems. Many current monitoring systems rely on just a handful of data points that are internally stored and periodically updated at fixed intervals, lacking the breadth of data and open source information needed to truly drive AI-based solutions. An effective AI-based transaction compliance initiative will identify and assess critical data sources and elements to facilitate the monitoring and filtering systems to operate.

The first of its kind, the New York Department of Financial Services ("NYDFS"), a notoriously stringent regulator, issued its final regulation on banking transaction monitoring and filtering program requirements, Part 504. An extremely comprehensive and prescriptive regulation, NYDFS calls for banks to clearly establish, document, harden and potentially automate BAU monitoring programs, from payment data to investigation findings. In this regulation NYDFS communicates three objectives, to clarify requirements, demand accountability, and emphasize a firm's need for robust transaction monitoring controls. However, the regulator does not stop there. NYDFS specifies the need for precise items such as, "protocols setting forth how alerts generated by the Transaction Monitoring Program will be investigated, the process for deciding which alerts will result in a filing or other action, the operating areas and individuals responsible for making such a decision, and how the investigative and decision-making process will be documented."[952] For filtering solutions, NYDFS specifies, "The technology used in this area may be based on automated tools that develop matching algorithms, such as those that use various forms of so-called 'fuzzy logic' and culture-based name conventions to match names. This regulation does not mandate the use of any particular technology, only that the system or technology used must be reasonably designed to identify prohibited transactions." In effect, the regulator, demands each regulated institution adopt and adhere to a COSO compliant AML and OFAC set of internal controls to ensure there is "governance, oversight, and accountability at senior levels." The NYDFS first defines the controls in the three overarching definitions for the control environment:

1) "Each Regulated Institution shall maintain a Transaction Monitoring Program reasonably designed for the purpose of monitoring transactions after their execution for potential BSA/AML violations and Suspicious Activity Reporting, which system may be manual or automated..."

2) "Each Regulated Institution shall maintain a Filtering Program, which may be manual or automated, reasonably designed for the purpose of interdicting transactions that are prohibited by OFAC..."

---

[952] New York, Department of Financial Services, Sec. § 504, Banking Division Transaction Monitoring and Filtering Program Requirements and Certifications. www.dfs.ny.gov/legal/regulations/adoptions/dfsp504t.pdf.

3) And, "Each Transaction Monitoring and Filtering Program shall require...identification of all data sources that contain relevant data...validation of the integrity, accuracy and quality of data to ensure that accurate and complete data flows through the Transaction Monitoring and Filtering Program...data extraction and loading processes to ensure a complete and accurate transfer of data...governance and management oversight, including policies and procedures governing changes to the Transaction Monitoring and Filtering Program to ensure that changes are defined, managed, controlled, reported, and audited...vendor selection process if a third party vendor is used to acquire, install, implement, or test the Transaction Monitoring and Filtering Program or any aspect of it...funding to design, implement and maintain a Transaction Monitoring and Filtering Program that complies...qualified personnel or outside consultant(s) responsible for the design, planning, implementation, operation, testing, validation, and on-going analysis of the Transaction Monitoring and Filtering Program."

Second, NYDFS mandates that controls, "be based on the Risk Assessment of the institution." Third, as part of the control environment definition, NYDFS requires senior management oversight, information sharing and communication, including "governance and management oversight, including policies and procedures governing changes to the Transaction Monitoring and Filtering Program to ensure that changes are defined, managed, controlled, reported, and audited." This is reinforced by Section 504.1 of 504, which states that NYDFS has "identified shortcomings in the Transaction Monitoring and Sanctions Filtering programs of these institutions attributable to a lack of robust governance oversight, and accountability at senior levels." Finally, the NYDFS instructs firms to harden the monitoring control environment by constantly monitoring the efficacy of the control utilizing "protocols setting forth how alerts generated by the Transaction Monitoring Program will be investigated, the process for deciding which alerts will result in a filing or other action, the operating areas and individuals responsible for making such a decision, and how the investigative and decision-making process will be documented; and... be subject to an on-going analysis to assess the continued relevancy of the detection scenarios, the underlying rules, threshold values, parameters, and assumptions."

The key to transitioning to next generation, AI-driven monitoring systems is the pairing of unstructured data with structured content to drive more targeted scrutiny of client and counterparty behavior. Next generation, automated due diligence systems are at the forefront of this evolution. These systems deemphasize legacy data frameworks that rely solely on customer provided data stored in large mainframe-intensive IT infrastructures in favor of open-source, unsupervised methods. No longer will it be necessary for organizations to constantly monitor and update customer data using manually intensive, operationally focused processes. AI-based solutions will replace these legacy KYC/CDD mechanisms with automated, real-time, and technology focused processes that extract key customer and counter-party information from open sources, and, just as importantly, utilize machine learning techniques to identify hidden patterns and relationships that ultimately help inform more accurate risk measures. The byproduct will be far less labor-intensive transaction monitoring programs that are adaptable to changes in transaction behavior and thus produce far fewer yet more productive alerts. These systems will leverage advances in behavioral analytics, automated pattern analysis, and machine learning.

VI. COMPLIANCE MONITORING OF UNSTRUCTURED DATA AND METHODS FOR MANAGING MISCONDUCT

"There are understandable, human tendencies that can cause each of us to avoid rocking the boat. People want to be team players. Those behavioral traits can be amplified through a firm's culture, which can weigh on one's willingness to do the right thing. This is, unfortunately, what seems to have occurred [at] one of the largest retail banks in the United States. Whether to obtain a bonus or

*simply to keep a job, employees felt they had to keep quiet and
meet sales targets despite the cost to customers.* "[953]

- William Dudley, President and CEO, Federal Reserve Bank of
New York

Culture and conduct have been hot topics with nearly every major
financial regulator in recent years, but the industry initially pushed
back against perceived gray areas and vague definitions. Without
suffering set-backs in compliance controls or creating a messy
patchwork of disparate approaches to risk management, financial
institutions and multinational corporations are turning to
surveillance in communications and operational systems to find
ways of standardizing the measures and metrics of culture. Also,
taking a page from transaction surveillance, keywords, known as
lexicons, have become poor substitutes for typologies and
scenarios. Oftentimes, these lexicons are both over and under
inclusive and are not fit for purpose when determining the nature
and severity of risk in an organization.

Recent advances in cognitive computing may hold the key to
moving discreet culture indicators out of gray areas and into black
and white clarity, as Dudley suggests. The use of cognitive
computing in conduct surveillance, for example, can identify early-
indicators and patterns of misconduct, negative sentiment, and
systemic pressure across various internal data streams, including
email, chat, calls, and HR systems to create a set of metrics around
controls violations or misconduct found. Andrew Bailey, Chief
Executive Officer of the FCA, confirmed that regulators examine
these early indicators and smaller behaviors as the best markers for
culture, saying, "culture is characterized by a pattern of
behaviors."

Despite not knowing exactly what they are looking for, regulators
still expect organizations to meet the standard of good culture. And
courts are not shy to condemn behavior which is detrimental to a

[953] William C Dudley, Panel Remarks at Worthy of Trust? Law, Ethics and
Culture in Banking New York Federal Reserve (2017),
https://www.newyorkfed.org/newsevents/speeches/2017/dud170321a.

fair and transparent market. As Menon stated in his keynote remarks at the Australian Securities and Investments Commission Annual Forum, "Ultimately, it is the financial institution itself that must bear the responsibility for getting the culture right."[954] Dudley went further to caution that organizations using existing regulations and law as the guide for good behavior will not go far enough. In the absence of regulatory or legal measures of culture, organizations will have to carefully craft, document and monitor their own interpretation of culture. This is why it is so important right now for corporations to start adopting a harmonized approach to developing, enforcing and policing metrics that denote a culture of compliance.

If illegal or unethical conduct has been reported, the company needs to understand exactly what happened so that the company can appropriately respond to a government investigation and take remedial action to prevent similar conduct in the future. In most minor events, the C&E department can work with supervisors and related managers to determine what occurred. For more serious cases, an internal investigation should be launched, led by in-house or outside counsel. The C&EO should participate in the investigation. The investigation should be conducted pursuant to the company's investigation plan. The plan should be written and at minimum should consider the following non-exhaustive elements:

- The method of detecting the non-compliance:

  o Audit (internal or external)

  o Risk management

  o Suspicious transaction report

---

[954] Reading Room, Financial Regulation – The Forward Agenda Monetary Authority of Singapore (2017), http://www.mas.gov.sg/News-and-Publications/Speeches-and-Monetary-Policy-Statements/Speeches/2017/Financial-Regulation.aspx.

- o Corporate security

- o Rotation of personnel

- o Whistleblower (internal or external tip)

- o Accident

- o Law enforcement

- Consideration of the initial scope and other preliminary matters:

  - o Specificity and scope of the allegations, including the severity of alleged misfeasance

  - o Whether government investigation commenced, either through a subpoena, civil investigative demand or law enforcement raid

  - o Whether civil litigation is threatened or filed

  - o Credibility of source or detection method

  - o Identification of critical decision points

  - o Self-reporting to regulators

  - o Other reporting requirements

  - o Cooperation with regulators and regulatory expectations

  - o Anticipated questions

  - o Data privacy requirements

  - o Urgency

  - o Investigation budget

- o Establishment of timelines

- Composition of the investigation team:

  - o Counsel (in-house / outside)

  - o C&EO

  - o Human resources

  - o Finance

  - o IT

  - o Outside experts and consultants

- Determining the investigation format:

  - o Communications among members of investigation team

  - o Reporting chains

  - o Assertion of applicable privilege protections, including attorney-client, work product, joint defense, common interest, accountant-client privilege, peer review privilege, and other qualified privileges

  - o Separate counsel for officers and employees

  - o Identification of key custodians and custodian interviews

  - o Implementation of document preservation and collection

  - o Managed document review

  - o IT and forensic review of data

- ○ Written report of investigation findings
- Disclosure obligations
  - ○ Investors
  - ○ Shareholders
  - ○ Public
  - ○ Regulators
  - ○ Insurance carriers
  - ○ Other stakeholders
  - ○ Post-Investigation outcomes
- ○ Appropriate disciplinary actions
- ○ Risk management resolutions
- ○ Restitution and penalties
- ○ C&E program changes
- ○ Employee training
- ○ Public image repair

The foregoing list of considerations is by no means exclusive or applicable to every company or investigation. In an April 2015 speech to New York University Law School's Program on Corporate Compliance and Enforcement, Assistant Attorney General Leslie R. Caldwell stated: "[T]here is no 'off the rack' internal investigation that can be applied to every situation at every company. Effective investigations must be tailored to the unique misconduct at issue and the circumstances of each company." Regardless of the size, scope, or severity of an investigation, the C&EO should participate in developing the investigations plan and in conducting investigations unless their participation would somehow compromise its integrity.

VII. C&E DURING AND AFTER A GOVERNMENT INVESTIGATION

"The financial crisis can be traced back to failures of corporate governance and risk management systems. At some institutions boards of directors and senior managers did not sufficiently comprehend aggregate risk within their firms and lacked a sufficiently robust risk framework—that is, the people, systems, and processes for monitoring a complex set of risks. In some cases, bank compensation programs were structured to share upside benefits but not the downside risks. Inadequate and fragmented technology infrastructures hindered efforts to identify, measure, monitor, and control risk. And some of these institutions' risk cultures lacked effective credible challenge from independent risk managers, audit, and control personnel. While these problems existed to some extent at banks of all sizes, it was in the largest, most complex banking institutions that the problems were most pronounced and where they created the greatest potential threat to the stability of the financial system."[955]

-Thomas Curry, Comptroller of the Currency

A company can receive notice of an actual or possible government investigation through several means: a Civil Investigative Demand, subpoena or other government request for information, a regulator or government law enforcement agent's request to interview an officer or employee, receipt of a whistle-blower complaint, or a law enforcement raid. Whatever the means by which notice is received, immediately upon receipt of notice, a company should swiftly initiate its investigation action plan.

At the outset of an internal investigation and any parallel government investigation, the investigation team should be

---

[955] Thomas Curry, Remarks Before the ABA Risk Management Forum (2014), https://www.occ.treas.gov/news-issuances/speeches/2014/pub-speech-2014-58.pdf.

assembled. Because of privilege issues and other considerations, the C&EO should seldom lead the investigation or be the primary contact with regulators. However, the C&EO should be an integral member of the investigation team[956] as their familiarity with the C&E program places them in the best position to assess which written C&E policies, procedures and guidelines may have been violated by the alleged illegal or unethical conduct. The C&EO can provide critical guidance and assistance to in-house or outside counsel in sorting through raw data to identify possible illegal or unethical conduct. Likewise, with the C&E program as a guide, the C&EO can often assist in unraveling the means and methods a wrongdoer may have used to conceal illegal or unethical conduct.

The C&EO's chief functions in an investigation should be to assist in (a) identifying specific C&E policies, procedures and guidelines that may have been violated, (b) determining how such violations occurred, and (c) determining why such violations were undetected, or if detected, why they were not adequately remedied. Of course, the C&EO can also assist with witness interviews, document reviews, and other critical tasks during the investigation to most efficiently facilitate the ultimate objective of determining if and how illegal conduct occurred. In most instances, the C&EO will need to demonstrate the reasonableness of the company's C&E program to regulators and law enforcement.[957] In addition, involvement of the C&EO in an investigation assists that officer in formulating necessary changes or additions to the company's C&E program, conducting training to avoid future violations, and audits to ensure compliance with changes to the C&E program.

Once the scope of the failure or misconduct is understood, the compliance department should examine the incident to determine whether it was an isolated occurrence or if it points to a systemic weakness in the company's C&E program that needs to be remediated. In general, the C&EO should work with the GC to

---

[956] The obvious exception to this general rule is if the C&E officer is suspected of participating in the alleged unethical or illegal conduct.

[957] As noted above, an effective C&E program is a mitigating factor in sentencing under the FSGO.

review the causes of the incident and develop a post-mortem action plan and associated procedures. The following are general questions that may be considered:

1.	Does the incident demonstrate insufficiencies in the C&E program that need changing?

2.	Did the employee(s) involved understand the written policies and procedures that prohibited their conduct or are there ambiguities that led to the violation?

3.	Why did the wrongful conduct go undetected and are changes to the C&E monitoring mechanisms needed?

4.	Is additional C&E program training needed?

5.	What reporting should be made to the board of directors or other corporate stakeholders?

After a government investigation is closed, the C&EO should ask these and other questions in light of the government's findings, as well as the conclusions of any internal investigation.

Though changes to the C&E program are not always necessary following an investigation, they should always be considered. The C&EO should also consider whether training is needed to avoid similar misconduct in the future. Training should be tailored to the particular constituency – employees, officers, directors – within the company so that it meaningfully informs company personnel of changes to the C&E program, needed behavioral modifications, and the compliance message generally. These supplemental trainings should be documented, whether web-based or in-person and may need to be phased in order to be effective. Using an outside provider to conduct training may increase its effectiveness and credibility.

With respect to employee disciplinary actions flowing from an investigation, the CE&O can be involved in deciding who should be disciplined and the level of discipline of each person found to have either participated the wrongdoing or failed to detect the wrongdoing.

Following an investigation, surprise audits should be conducted in order to ensure compliance with existing C&E program and any changes to the program. Changes to compliance monitoring mechanisms should also be considered.

Finally, the C&EO may be required to report to the board of directors or a committee of the board any findings and remedial action specifically related to the C&E program.

Chapter 17

Corporate Internal Investigations

By: Robert Keeling[958]

No company wants to plan for investigating misconduct within its ranks. Yet, when confronted with misconduct, conducting a proper internal investigation is critical to protecting the company, whether the allegations involve entry-level employees or senior leadership. From the moment an allegation of potential wrongdoing is reported, prompt action is vital to understanding the conduct at issue, preventing future misconduct, and promoting a culture of transparency and compliance within the company. This chapter outlines insights into conducting internal investigations, which seek to minimize risk and disruption to the business while observing the need for thoroughness and consistency with guidance from the U.S. Department of Justice ("DOJ").

I. DOJ'S EXPECTATIONS FOR CORPORATE INTERNAL INVESTIGATIONS

Recognizing that not every investigation involves criminal misconduct, DOJ has established expectations for companies conducting internal investigations, which remain instructive regardless of DOJ's enforcement priorities. For one, it is DOJ's longstanding position that companies have an affirmative duty both to respond to potential wrongdoing and to implement policies and procedures designed to deter and detect potential misconduct.[959] A company's policies and procedures should be

---

[958] Robert Keeling is a Partner in the Washington, D.C. office of Sidley Austin LLP. Robert has substantial experience conducting investigations in the U.S. and abroad. Robert regularly represents clients in internal investigations and other enforcement matters involving healthcare fraud and abuse, embezzlement, accounting irregularities, and violations of securities and banking regulations. He has represented numerous client in international Foreign Corrupt Practices Act investigations and advises companies on implementing effective FCPA compliance programs.

[959] *See* Leslie R. Caldwell, Ass't Att'y Gen., U.S. Dep't of Justice, Address at SIFMA Compliance and Legal Soc'y N.Y. Reg'l Seminar (Nov. 2, 2015),

tailored to fit the specific needs of the company in light of relevant
factors, such as its size, industry, management structure,
geographic locations, and relationships with vendors. In so doing,
a company better positions itself to identify and remediate
misconduct and signals its intention to stand against wrongful
behavior.

When it comes time to conduct an investigation, a company is not
expected to "boil the ocean," but the company is expected to carry
out a thorough and diligent review. And although many
companies do not have an affirmative legal obligation to report to
or cooperate with DOJ concerning the results of an internal
investigation, if a company chooses to cooperate, DOJ expects that
cooperation to be candid, complete, and timely.[960] In this context,
credit for cooperation will be conditioned on the company
providing DOJ with "all non-privileged information about
individuals involved in or responsible for the misconduct at issue,"
including identifying *all* individuals involved in the misconduct
"regardless of their position, status or seniority" within the
company.[961] This policy position, which was first announced

---

available at https://www.justice.gov/opa/speech/assistant-attorney-general-leslie-r-caldwell-speaks-sifma-compliance-and-legal-society.

[960] *See* Caldwell, Address at New York City Bar Ass'n Fourth Annual White Collar Crime Inst. (May 12, 2015), *available at* https://www.justice.gov/opa/speech/assistant-attorney-general-leslie-r-caldwell-delivers-remarks-new-york-city-bar-0; *see also* Caldwell, Address at Compliance Week Conference (May 19, 2015), *available at* https://www.justice.gov/opa/speech/assistant-attorney-general-leslie-r-caldwell-delivers-remarks-compliance-week-conference; *see also* Monaco, Remarks on Corporate Criminal Enforcement, New York University (Sept. 15, 2022), *available at* https://www.justice.gov/opa/speech/deputy-attorney-general-lisa-o-monaco-delivers-remarks-corporate-criminal-enforcement; Polite, Remarks at the University of Texas Law School (Sept. 16, 2022), *available at* https://www.justice.gov/opa/speech/assistant-attorney-general-kenneth-polite-delivers-remarks-university-texas-law-school.

[961] *See* Monaco, Address at ABA's 36th Nat'l Inst. on White Collar Crime (Oct. 28, 2021), *available at* https://www.justice.gov/opa/speech/deputy-attorney-general-lisa-o-monaco-gives-keynote-address-abas-36th-national-institute; Memorandum from Lisa O. Monaco, Deputy Att'y Gen., U.S. Dep't of Justice, Corporate Crime Advisory Group and Initial Revisions to Corp. Crim. Enf't Policies (Oct. 28, 2021), *available at*

during the latter years of the Obama administration in what is known as the Yates Memo, was relaxed in a number of ways during the Trump administration but has been expressly reinstated during the Biden administration. Specifically, DOJ's public statements in 2021 and 2022 appear to have restored the policy first outlined in the Yates Memo that, in order to receive any cooperation credit, a company must provide all non-privileged information uncovered during its investigation regarding *all* individuals involved in the misconduct, rather than only for individuals who the company determines, in its discretion, were substantially involved in the misconduct.[962] In addition to the increased focus on individual accountability, the DOJ suggests that companies act quickly in disclosing documents or information to DOJ. According to the DOJ, companies that delay or engage in

---

https://www.justice.gov/dag/page/file/1445106/download; Memorandum from Sally Quinlan Yates, Deputy Att'y Gen., U.S. Dep't of Justice, Individual Accountability for Corp. Wrongdoing (Sept. 9, 2015), *available at* http://www.justice.gov/dag/file/769036/download; *see also* Polite, Remarks at the University of Texas Law School, *supra* note 2 (noting that, as part of its efforts to prioritize individual accountability, DOJ will be examining whether to shift the corporate financial burden for misconduct away from shareholders and onto the responsible individuals, in appropriate cases); Monaco, Remarks on Corporate Criminal Enforcement, New York University, *supra* note 2 (reiterating that DOJ's top priority in enforcement is individual accountability regardless of the individual's position, status, or seniority); Garland, Address at ABA Inst. on White Collar Crime (Mar. 3, 2022), *available at* https://www.justice.gov/opa/speech/attorney-general-merrick-b-garland-delivers-remarks-aba-institute-white-collar-crime (reiterating that the Department's first priority is to prosecute individual wrongdoers); Polite, Address at ABA Inst. on White Collar Crime (Mar. 3, 2022), *available at* https://www.justice.gov/opa/speech/assistant-attorney-general-kenneth-polite-jr-delivers-justice-department-keynote-aba (emphasizing the importance of individual accountability in the DOJ's enforcement efforts). Chapter __ of this treatise provides a detailed explanation of the Yates memorandum.

[962] *See* Monaco, Address at ABA's 36th Nat'l Inst. on White Collar Crime, *supra* note 3; Memorandum from Lisa O. Monaco, *supra* note 3; Memorandum from Sally Quinlan Yates, *supra* note 3; Rosenstein, Address at the Am. Conf. Inst.'s 35th Ann. Int'l Conf. on the Foreign Corrupt Practices Act (Nov. 29, 2018), *available at* https://www.justice.gov/opa/speech/deputy-attorney-general-rod-j-rosenstein-delivers-remarks-american-conference-institute-0 (announcing a "substantially involved" standard implemented during the Trump administration). Chapter __ offers further insights on DOJ's enforcement priorities under Attorney General Garland.

strategic gamesmanship related to the disclosure of critical documents risk losing some or all of their cooperation credit.[963]

II. CORPORATE INTERNAL INVESTIGATIONS: STEP-BY-STEP CONSIDERATIONS

At a high level, an investigation should be structured to enable a company to capture and preserve relevant documents and evidence, as well as identify and interview the knowledgeable actors in an effort to root out the relevant facts.[964] If the initial fact-gathering unearths misconduct, then the inquiry should broaden as needed to fully understand the evidence and address the misconduct, and company leadership should determine what compliance shortcomings allowed the problem to arise in the first place.[965] Consistent with DOJ's statements on internal investigations, the following chart sets forth a basic, high-level approach for organizing an investigation with these ends in mind.

---

[963] Monaco, Address at New York University, Remarks on Corporate Criminal Enforcement, *supra* note 2 ("Going forward, undue or intentional delay in producing information or documents—particularly those that show individual culpability—will result in the reduction or denial of cooperation credit.").

[964] *See* Caldwell, Address at Compliance Week Conference, *supra* note 2.

[965] *See id.*

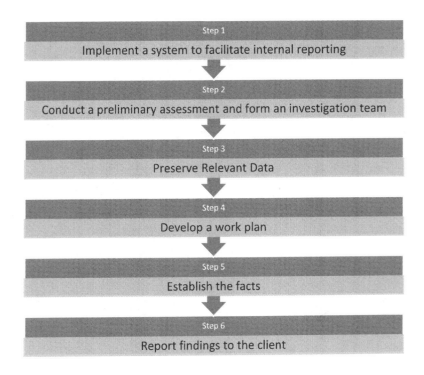

A. **Step 1: Implement a system to facilitate internal reporting**

A company should be in a position to learn of allegations of wrongdoing in order to determine whether an internal investigation is warranted. To this end, companies should consider establishing a first line of defense, such as an anonymous whistleblower hotline or an Internet-based reporting system, to receive allegations of misconduct. These reporting programs encourage employees to be candid about potential misconduct and enable the company to learn of potential misconduct as soon as possible.[966] Of course, a company should consider implementing procedures for evaluating

---

[966] *See* U.S. Dep't of Justice, Criminal Division, "Evaluation of Corporate Compliance Programs" at 6-7 (June 1, 2020), *available at* https://www.justice.gov/criminal-fraud/page/file/937501/download (explaining the importance and features of a confidential reporting system in the context of evaluating corporate compliance programs). Chapter __ covers recommendations for companies seeking to put in place or improve their reporting programs.

complaints as they are received, as many complaints will not merit an investigation. In some cases, a brief interview with the employee who submitted the complaint can help confirm that an internal investigation is unnecessary.[967]

B. Step 2: Conduct a preliminary assessment and form an investigation team

If allegations of misconduct may potentially warrant an investigation, a company's general counsel or the general counsel's designee should consider drafting a memorandum, conforming to the requirements of the attorney-client privilege, which sets forth the allegations that have been made, the potential legal issues involved, and, as appropriate, the need to obtain legal advice.[968] Note that this preliminary assessment may indicate that further investigation is not necessary, a decision that also should be documented.[969] Where further investigation is needed, a company must determine who should conduct the investigation, in light of the nature of the allegations and the company's internal policies and procedures.

At this point, it may be wise to engage outside counsel, as investigations led by outside counsel tend to be favored by courts and regulators, as compared to those conducted "in house."[970] Outside counsel frequently has more experience and greater resources to conduct an investigation, and outside counsel's

---

[967] *See* Assoc. of Corporate Counsel & Philip W. Turner, *Top Ten Tips for Conducting Effective Internal Investigations*, ASS'N OF CORPORATE COUNSEL, Nov. 9, 2010,
http://www.acc.com/legalresources/publications/topten/internalinvestigations.cfm
.

[968] DAN WEBB, ROBERT TARUN & STEVEN MOLO, CORPORATE INTERNAL INVESTIGATIONS § 4.03[1] (2016).

[969] *Id.*; *see also* Nicole Di Schino, *Audit Comm. Responsibilities Before, During and After an Anti-Corruption Investigation: Determining When and How to Proceed (Part Three of Four)*, *in* THE FCPA REPORT (Mar. 19, 2014), at 8.

[970] NAVIGANT CONSULTING, INC., *Effectively Managing an Indep. Investigation*, 2011, at 1, http://www.coblentzlaw.com/images/uploads/content/effectively-managing-independent-investigations.pdf (hereinafter "Navigant").

independence from company leadership affords greater credibility both with the government and company employees. This independence allows internal counsel, the board of directors, and senior management to rely more fully on the findings of the investigation. In addition, involving outside counsel helps to establish a clear demarcation between legal advice and business advice and thereby preserves the company's protections under the attorney-client privilege and work product doctrine.[971] For example, engaging outside counsel tends to insulate the company from risk that the investigation could be deemed "business" advice in any subsequent civil dispute, which could arise when plaintiffs' attorneys seek information about the investigation or when the findings of the investigation prompt a company to discipline or terminate an employee. Finally, outside counsel's experience is often useful at the close of the investigation, whether when making recommendations to close the investigation, to address the misconduct at issue, or to enhance the company's internal controls, as needed. A company should be mindful, however, that where outside counsel is engaged to conduct an internal investigation, the company's chief compliance officer typically should continue to play a role in the investigation and in making any recommendations to improve upon the company's compliance program.[972]

Even if outside counsel is engaged, a preliminary question a company should consider is who within the company should be responsible for overseeing the investigation. Whether conducted internally or by outside counsel, when circumstances present heightened risk or otherwise dictate that the investigation be conducted without management's involvement, the board of

---

[971] Chapter __ provides further details on the application of the attorney-client privilege and work product doctrine in the context of internal investigations.

[972] *See* Polite, Address at NYU Law's Program on Corporate Compliance and Enforcement (PCCE) (Mar. 25, 2022), *available at* https://www.justice.gov/opa/speech/assistant-attorney-general-kenneth-polite-jr-delivers-remarks-nyu-law-s-program-corporate (emphasizing that the chief compliance officer and other senior management should be directly involved in and knowledgeable about a company's compliance efforts and that "check-the-box" presentations from outside counsel are disfavored).

directors often directs the investigation. The Board is permitted, however, to delegate the investigative process to a committee and/or rely on the work of internal or external personnel.[973] Considerations such as the level of financial risk, the nature or extent of the misconduct (including potential criminal acts), and who within the company was involved in the supposed misconduct will dictate the role the board of directors or audit committee play in the investigation.[974] Notably, in such cases the Board will remain the ultimate finder of fact; the investigation "belongs" to the Board, and its delegation does not relieve Board members of their fiduciary duties to oversee the investigation.[975] By contrast, if the allegations do not suggest wrongdoing on the part of senior management, the investigation likely can be overseen by the company's general counsel, the chief compliance officer, or the internal audit and legal teams.[976] In these situations, the company's board of directors (or the audit committee) would not be actively involved in leading the investigation and, at most, would serve only in an advisory capacity.

C.   Step 3: Preserve relevant data

Preserving potentially relevant information is of first priority when instituting an investigation. To that end, the investigative team should take steps to identify document custodians and issue a litigation hold to these custodians as quickly as possible.[977] Where potential custodians are expected to depart the company—or, worse, where concerns exist about possible intentional or unintentional destruction of evidence in violation of a hold notice—the investigative team, in consultation with counsel,

---

[973] Chapter __ outlines the special considerations and precautions that must be taken when an investigation is undertaken by a company's board of directors.

[974] See Nicole Di Schino, *Audit Comm. Responsibilities Before, During and After an Anti-Corruption Investigation: Determining When and How to Proceed (Part Two of Four)*, in THE FCPA REPORT (March 5, 2014), at 3-5.

[975] See Navigant, *supra* note 12, at 2-3.

[976] See Navigant, *supra* note 12, at 1-2.

[977] See Di Schino, *supra* note 11, at 6-7.

should establish a plan to secure this evidence without delay.[978]
The DOJ has asserted that companies should take steps to preserve
data from employees' personal devices and from any third-party
messaging systems or collaboration tools, "including those
offering ephemeral (or disappearing) messaging," that are used for
business purposes.[979]

D.   Step 4: Develop a work plan

The investigative team's next step is to develop a work plan that
sets forth the purpose and objectives of the investigation and is
broad enough to address the problems at issue while remaining
sufficiently well-tailored to avoid an aimless and expensive
search.[980] This approach is consistent with and complementary of
the duties of company leadership to oversee the business by
ensuring that misconduct is evaluated and appropriate remedial
action, including adjustments to processes and internal controls,
are given due consideration.[981] In planning the scope of the
investigation, investigators should understand the relevant
company policies, familiarize themselves with the information
from the complainant, identify the key facts to be discovered, and
raise any legal questions that should be considered. The work plan
may also outline potential data sources and witnesses and establish
a timeline for interviewing these witnesses.[982] In certain cases, the
work plan should avoid disclosing certain high-value confidential

---

[978] Chapter __ gives recommendations for successfully directing complex
document collection efforts.

[979] Polite, Remarks at the University of Texas Law School, *supra* note 2 (noting
that DOJ will examine whether to provide guidance on preservation of data from
personal devices and third-party messaging applications, and stating that
"companies must ensure that they can monitor and retain these communications
as appropriate").

[980] *See* Di Schino, *supra* note 11, at 2; *see also* Caldwell, *supra* note 2.

[981] *See* Navigant, *supra* note 12, at 3 (citing In re Caremark Int'l Inc. Derivative
Litig., 698 A.2d 959 (Del. Ch. 1996)).

facts, such as the name of a whistleblower, that could compromise the investigation if revealed outside the investigative team.

E.   Step 5: Establish the facts

The fact-finding mission of the investigation continues by reviewing the relevant documents and conducting witness interviews to gather more information about the alleged misconduct. To the extent practicable, a careful document review should be completed prior to key witness interviews in order to ensure that the interviewer is in the best position to examine relevant documents with the witness, to avert diversions or obfuscation by the witness, and to separate fact from fiction. It is also important that interviewers observe the formalities that protect the company and the witness: the witness typically should be provided an *Upjohn* warning when questioned by an attorney,[983] and the investigator should advise the witness of his or her obligation to preserve the confidentiality of the interview. Moreover, while the interview typically is not recorded, it is usually advisable to prepare a non-verbatim summary of the interview to document the information learned, which is generally protected under the work product doctrine.[984]

Decisions about the order of interviews tend to be dictated by the availability of witnesses and circumstance. Some investigators prioritize interviews of lower-level personnel,[985] while others first interview the source of the allegations in order to establish trust or facilitate continued dialogue with that employee. Note that, whatever the order of interviews, the investigative team should attempt to ensure that any departing employees with relevant

---

[983] *See Upjohn Co. v. United States*, 449 U.S. 383 (1981) (requiring that a witness be advised of the attorney's representation of the company, in order to avoid conflicts of interest by the attorney and confusion on the part of the witness); *see also* WEBB ET AL., *supra* note 10.

[984] Chapter __ provides further information on conducting effective witness interviews.

[985] Juan Castaneda, *4 Keys to Witness Interviews in Internal Investigation*, LAW360, Mar. 12, 2015, http://www.law360.com/articles/629255/4-keys-to-witness-interviews-in-internal-investigations.

information be interviewed prior to departing the company. Likewise, while the ideal meeting place to conduct the interviews will be different in every case, experienced investigators tend to hold interviews in locations that offer privacy and minimal distraction and where the witness feels comfortable, in order to promote candor on the part of the witness.[986]

Following witness interviews, the investigative team should consider what additional legal or fact issues require further review. Depending on the importance of these matters to closing the current investigation, they may be added to the work plan, presented as part of the investigation's findings for further discussion, or investigated separately.

F. Step 6: Report findings to the client

When preparing to issue the investigation's findings, companies should consider whether counsel should compose a comprehensive, written report. Note that preparing a written investigation report may increase risk and may not be in the client's best interests.[987] Such reports may present unwanted complications for a company seeking to cooperate with the government and when responding to subsequent discovery requests. For example, disclosure of a written report to the government to secure a favorable resolution for the company— even if the disclosure is subject to a confidentiality agreement with the government—will likely be deemed a waiver of privilege in subsequent civil litigation.[988] Moreover, even a well-written report may omit facts or issues that prove harmful when the company is faced with civil litigation years later.

Considering the risks associated with preparing a written report, an oral presentation by counsel to company management may be an

---

[986] See WEBB ET AL., *supra* note 10, at § 4.03[2][b].

[987] See Di Schino, *supra* note 11, at 9-10.

[988] *Accord* WEBB ET AL., *supra* note 10, at § 4.03[4][a]. Chapter __ provides discussion of "selective waiver" and associated risks.

appropriate alternative.[989] The oral presentation may include visual aids, such as PowerPoint slides, but generally these written materials should not be released to company management. This approach allows the investigation's findings to be communicated efficiently to the decision makers within the company and forecloses an opportunity for civil litigants to misuse the report.

Whether a written report is issued or the investigation's findings are presented verbally, the investigative team should recommend remedial measures based upon those findings. Of paramount concern, both during and at the close of the investigation, is whether any of the potential wrongdoers are still in a position to continue their harmful conduct. If so, company leadership, in consultation with counsel, should intervene accordingly. Additional remedial measures—including disciplining or terminating an employee who engaged in misconduct, requiring additional ethics or compliance training for relevant personnel, revising the company's policies and procedures, and so forth— should be implemented swiftly, in order to promote compliance within the company and to prevent similar misconduct from reoccurring. If the investigation concludes that a crime was committed, or the investigation's findings present substantial regulatory risks, company leadership should consult with counsel to determine if a voluntary disclosure to the government is appropriate.[990]

III. CONCLUSION

When faced with credible allegations of misconduct, a company should conduct a careful investigation to understand the nature of the problem so that it can be addressed appropriately. This chapter has highlighted several steps a company can take to lay the foundation for a successful internal investigation: implementing a

---

[989] See id.; Di Schino, *supra* note 11, at 9-10.

[990] See Monaco, Address at New York University, Remarks on Corporate Criminal Enforcement, *supra* note 2 (noting the benefits to companies of voluntary self-disclosure). Chapter __ presents further insights on the circumstances in which a voluntary disclosure may be appropriate.

system to facilitate internal reporting, carefully assigning oversight responsibility, developing a work plan, preserving documents and conducting a fact investigation, and reporting on the investigation's findings. The following chapters expand on these subjects so that companies can maximize their ability to successfully investigate misconduct and take strides toward preventing similar misconduct in the future.

Chapter 18

Forensic Accounting

By: Vincenzo Toppi[991]

I. FORENSICS ISN'T JUST FOR CSI

Years ago, my young son asked, "Dad, what do you do at work?"

How do you explain to a six-year-old what a forensic accountant does at work? I started to describe the cases I was working on and the services that we were providing.

My son kept asking, "But what do you do? Do you make something? Do you sell something?"

I wasn't getting through to him.

At that point, my wife came to the rescue. She asked my son, "Do you know all those "CSI" shows we watch together? What do the officers on that show do?"

"They try to figure out what happened to the dead body," my son responded. He turned to me with wide eyes. "Do you work with dead bodies?"

---

[991] Vincenzo ("Vinni") Toppi is a Partner with CohnReznick Advisory. He conducts special investigations and fraud examinations on behalf of CohnReznick clients in matters that involve misappropriation of funds or assets, asset tracing and recovery, insider and third-party transfers, and insolvency analysis. Vinni investigates financial crimes such as misrepresentation of financial facts, bankruptcy fraud, and computer fraud. He leads the computer forensic and eDiscovery service teams, providing eDiscovery and litigation support services that include electronic data acquisitions, forensic data examinations, data mining and analysis, and document management and review. Vinni also provides workout and insolvency accounting and consulting services to financially troubled companies, creditors, and secured creditors during workout or turnaround situations, and to constituencies in bankruptcy proceedings that include court-appointed trustees, receivers and examiners. He is a Certified Computer Forensics Examiner (CCFE).

His conclusion was a little short of the mark, but to this day, I still use the CSI dead body example as a set up for the question, "what is forensic accounting?"

A. Defining Forensic Accounting

According to Oxford Dictionaries Online, forensic accounting is defined as the use of accounting skills to investigate fraud or embezzlement and to analyze financial information for use in legal proceedings. "Forensic" means "suitable for use in a court of law." Often, these situations involve litigation that revolves around uncovering and presenting financial data to substantiate the claims in a case. Accounting in an adversarial context requires specialized knowledge and a range of technological and forensic tools. That is why financial stakeholders, counsel, senior management, and others turn to forensic accountants for assistance and advice. Forensic accountants generally conduct an investigation and analysis, assisting with the discovery, analysis, and presentation of information to be used in trial. Through comprehensive evidence gathering and sophisticated investigative techniques, forensic accountants are able to extract and reconstruct accounting and business records to reveal discrepancies often undetected by others.

Forensic accountants are often engaged by law firms, insurance companies, financial institutions, law enforcement, and government agencies to serve in a variety of situations as advisers to defendants, plaintiffs, and/or other stakeholders in civil and criminal matters, including embezzlement, professional malpractice, mergers and acquisitions, business interruption, and contract termination. Companies turn to forensic accountants to trace and recover misappropriated funds, uncover and quantify damages and losses, analyze collateral for bankers and lenders, provide due-diligence investigations, investigate white-collar crimes, determine royalty compliance, and provide business valuation and solvency analyses.

Forensic accountants can also assist with critical business issues, including analyzing joint venture operations, verifying amounts due under revenue sharing agreements, and navigating litigation or other matters in a court setting.

Most often, forensic accounting is used when fraud is suspected. For this reason, forensic accountants are often referred to as fraud investigators or fraud examiners. Fraud takes many forms, and as business environments or practices continue to evolve, more opportunity for the theft of funds, information, or the use of someone's assets without permission is created. Situations relating to management fraud, money laundering, tax fraud, bankruptcy fraud, and securities fraud remain rampant and are occurring at an increasing rate.

Fraud, corruption, and ethical misconduct have become commonplace across the public and private sectors. Governments, private companies, and not-for-profit organizations have felt the widespread repercussions. This impact can extend well beyond lost revenue. Fraud, corruption, and other acts of malfeasance can destroy a company's reputation, financial stability, stakeholder confidence, and employee morale.

Enterprises with multinational operations face broader fraud and corruption risks when conducting business in countries with differing standards of regulatory compliance. Contrasting cultural norms, regulations, and government interaction further complicate compliance requirements and pose a unique set of risks and obligations. Heightened enforcement of the United States Foreign Corrupt Practices Act (FCPA) and foreign anti-bribery/anti-corruption legislation have made the need for a robust anti-corruption compliance program not merely a best practice, but a cost-effective necessity.

The Association of Certified Fraud Examiners' (ACFE) 2016 Report to the Nations on Occupational Fraud and Abuse provides an analysis of 2,410 cases of occupational fraud that occurred in 114 countries throughout the world.[992] The ACFE's study concludes that the typical organization loses 5% of revenue in a

---

[992] http://www.acfe.com/rttn2016.aspx

given year as a result of fraud. The study demonstrates that the average loss per case amounts to approximately $2.7 million, with 23.2% of cases causing losses of $1 million or more. Asset misappropriation occurred in 83% of the cases with a median loss of $125,000. Financial statement fraud occurred in less than 10% of the cases in the study and had a median loss of $975,000.

In this chapter, we will explore how forensic accountants can help in detecting and preventing fraud. In addition, we will discuss other areas in which forensic accountants can assist an organization.

B.   A Combination of Many Disciplines

Forensic accountants combine many disciplines in order to complete their analysis. Trained to look beyond the numbers, forensic accountants rely upon an understanding of accounting and auditing standards, business information and financial reporting systems, economic theories, data management, electronic discovery, data analytics, and litigation processes and procedures in order to complete their investigation and present their findings. Forensic accountants must be able to describe the underlying financial information clearly to their client, counsel, or in a courtroom setting.

Forensic accountants are highly trained and have an understanding of many different areas, including:

Accounting and auditing: The combination of financial and advanced accounting skills with auditing skills form a solid foundation for a forensic accountant. The suspect commits fraud in order to gain some sort of economic advantage, and fraud typically involves financial information. As such, an individual with an accounting and auditing background makes a logical choice to conduct a forensic investigation.

Financial reporting systems: The financial reporting system of an organization may hold valuable evidence that needs to be analyzed during the investigation. In addition, the forensic accountant must understand how the financial reporting systems operate in order to develop a series of tests that will identify anomalies or fraudulent transactions.

Data analytics: Forensic accountants need to be able to extract information from financial reporting systems in order to conduct their analysis. Forensic accountants must understand the transaction data within the systems, and in many situations, they must be able to analyze large quantities of data. They may need to use specialized data analytic or mining software in order to analyze the data.

Computer applications: A forensic accountant must be proficient with common computer applications and data files such as Word, Excel, and Access. This is because the target of the investigation may use these applications, and the associated data files may hold evidence that must be analyzed. In addition, the forensic accountant may use many of the applications to conduct the analysis and to present the findings in the form of reports, charts, or exhibits.

The legal process: Forensic accountants frequently operate in court environments. The court may request a forensic accountant to work in the capacity as a court-appointed examiner, forensic accountant or independent party to investigate certain transactions that may be at the center of a dispute. In these cases, the forensic accountant must complete the required analysis and report the findings directly back to the court. The reporting most often includes a written report to the court accompanied with trial testimony.

Outside of a court-appointed role, forensic accountants may be hired directly by companies involved in a dispute and requiring specialized investigation and analysis. In these situations, a written report to the client and counsel are prepared. In addition, the forensic accountant's report may be submitted to the court, with depositions and trial testimony frequently following in the legal process.

It is important to understand that forensic accounting and fraud investigation methodologies are different than internal auditing.

Forensic accounting investigations should be conducted by individuals trained in forensic accounting disciplines as outlined above. A forensic accountant is focused on translating complex financial transactions and financial data into terms that the court and ordinary persons can understand. That is necessary because if the fraud comes to trial, the forensic accountant may be required to explain their procedures and findings to a judge and jury.

C. Certifications

Certain traits are common among forensic accountants, including strong analytic skills, and an intuitive, inquisitive, and investigative nature. Some of the core skills of effective forensic accountants include the ability to identify the key issues and simplify the information by determining what is most relevant to the case. Being able to communicate complex financial and business matters in a clear, concise, well-supported manner is critical to success. It is also important to take an "open-minded" approach to the investigative process by allowing the evidence to build the case on its own without bias or prejudice. Furthermore, forensic accountants need to pay attention to and scrutinize the smallest of details, while also keeping an eye on the "big picture" of the case.

There is no specific license or requirement to become a forensic accountant, however, there are certain certifications related to forensic accounting and fraud investigation that are issued by several professional associations.

Certified Public Accountant (CPA): The CPA designation is very valuable to a forensic accountant. The CPA designation indicates that the individual is an accountant who has had a rigorous education and passed one of the toughest licensing examinations in the United States. This provides a sound foundation for the forensic accountant. In addition, the Association of Certified Public Accountants issues a Certified in Financial Forensics (CFF) credential for forensic accountants. The CFF designation is granted to professional accountants who demonstrate considerable expertise in forensic accounting through their knowledge, skills, and experience. The CFF encompasses fundamental and specialized forensic accounting skills that practitioners apply in a variety of service areas, including bankruptcy and insolvency; computer forensic analysis; family law; valuations; fraud prevention, detection, and response; financial statement misrepresentation; and economic damages calculations.[993]

Certified Forensic Examiner (CFE): The CFE is a credential specifically related to forensic accounting and fraud. The Association of Certified Fraud Examiners (ACFE) issues the CFE designation. CFEs have a unique skillset that combines an understanding of complex financial transactions and the methods, law, and techniques to investigate allegations of fraud. CFEs are trained to understand how and why instances of fraud occur.

When looking to retain a forensic accountant, it isn't necessary to restrict your search to individuals who possess these designations. It is important to understand that individuals with these credentials have the knowledge and skillsets to conduct the analyses required and are familiar with the reporting requirements that will be discussed in the following sections.

II.   SITUATIONS REQUIRING FORENSIC ACCOUNTANTS

When one hears the term forensic accounting, fraud quickly comes to mind. When fraud is suspected, one must be able to investigate what happened, what facts and circumstances allowed the transactions to take place, and how similar transactions can be avoided going forward. Forensic accountants must rely upon the various skillsets discussed above in order to answer these questions for their client and to describe the results of their investigation to the court.

We've all heard that there are two sides to every story, and somewhere in the middle, the truth can be found. A forensic accountant must diligently gather the facts, analyze the

---

[993] http://www.aicpa.org/Membership/Join/Pages/CFF-Credential-Canada.aspx

information, and present the results in an impartial and comprehensive manner in order to determine the truth.

An organization, or individual, may be the victim of the fraud. On the other hand, the organization may be suspected of conducting fraudulent transactions. In either case, someone with specialized knowledge and skills is needed to conduct the investigation, analyze the transactions, and reach a conclusion on the transactions in question. Some examples of fraudulent situations include:

Financial statement fraud: An organization may deliberately misstate components of its financial statements in order to overcome operating shortfalls or to mask the organization's financial weakness. Generally speaking, financial statement fraud may include improper revenue recognition, understatement of liabilities or expenses, improper or missing financial statements disclosures, and overstating assets. For example, a company might understate liabilities in an effort to meet debt covenants within a loan agreement. Financial statement fraud is typically committed by one or more individuals in top management of an organization. Financial statement fraud impacts lenders, shareholders, vendors, and employees of an organization. A forensic accountant will combine traditional financial analyses, such as financial ratio analysis and trending analysis, with forensic accounting procedures, including advanced journal entry and general ledger testing. This includes transaction time stamp analysis and user ID testing to determine transactions posted by unauthorized users.

Accounting malpractice: The investigation of alleged accounting malpractice incidents requires specific knowledge of technical issues relating to the application of and compliance with Generally Accepted Accounting Principles (GAAP) and Generally Accepted Auditing Standards (GAAS). Forensic accountants combine in-depth accounting knowledge with deep expertise in the assessment of loss causation and damages. Their investigations are focused on whether the auditors failed to exercise reasonable care, whether they were negligent or reckless in performing an audit, or if they failed to identify material errors or irregularities in the client's financial statement.

Vendor fraud: Vendor fraud occurs when an organization's accounts payable or disbursement system is manipulated in order to generate disbursements to the target vendor. Vendor fraud may be conducted solely by a vendor, or the vendor may collude with an organization's employee in order to conduct the fraud. Vendor fraud may include overbilling, duplicate billing, or billing for services that were never performed. Vendor fraud may also include manipulating the bidding process and new vendor approval in order for contracts to be awarded to unqualified vendors. A forensic accountant might be called to analyze vendor data in order to identify suspect transactions. The forensic accountant may conduct analyses including check number gap detection, duplicate invoice testing, and invoice approval testing to uncover fraudulent vendor transactions.

Employee fraud: Employee fraud may occur in payroll, expense reimbursement or unauthorized purchases for personal use. Although employee fraud is conducted with the goal of personal enrichment, depending on the complexity of the fraud and the magnitude of the fraud, employee fraud may also impact financial statement results or be connected to vendor fraud. Forensic accounting procedures to detect employee fraud include testing for ghost employees, address matching, purchase order entry/approval testing, and testing for split purchase orders or invoices under set approval limits.

Theft of corporate data: Employees, either former or active, may access unauthorized data, copy or move sensitive data files, or provide critical corporate data to external parties. This data may include customer data, product data, or employee data. Access to such data may prove to be detrimental to an organization. Individuals with specialized skillsets are needed to identify these transactions and to quantify the impact on the affected organization. Further detail of the impact of these actions can be found in the section discussing lost profit analysis and economic damages.

It is important to understand that forensic accounting requires specialized knowledge and expertise beyond traditional accounting and audit skills. It is equally important to understand that financial statement audit procedures may not detect the items described above. In many cases, it may be beneficial for an organization to conduct a forensic analysis from time to time in order to test for the transactions discussed above. Not only may policies and procedures be ignored or circumvented by employees, controls may not be perfectly effective. In addition, the ACFE's 2016 Report to the Nations concluded that in 94.5% of the cases where fraud was identified, the perpetrator took some efforts to conceal the fraud. The most common concealment methods were creating and altering physical documents.

Performing the testing procedures outlined above may help identify fraudulent transactions. Another result of the forensic analysis may be somewhat less tangible, but may have great positive impact on an organization: employees will be aware of the procedures and the additional oversight may deter employees from attempting to initiate fraudulent transactions.

It is important to realize that forensic accounting is useful in different situations, not only when fraud is suspected. Forensic accounting may help answer many different business questions in very diverse situations. Forensic accountants combine the various disciplines discussed above, along with a deep sense of scepticism in order to conduct these services.

Examples of these situations include:

Royalty audits, joint ventures and profit sharing agreements:
These agreements will typically include certain rights that allow the licensing party the ability to verify the accuracy of the amounts reported by the licensee. The rights may have limitations in regard to periods that can be analyzed or the procedures that can be performed. In addition, the parties may interpret the language of the agreement differently. Differences may include timing of transactions to be included in the royalty period, allowance of certain deductions or reductions to reported sales amounts, or geographic limitations of the covered products. A forensic accountant that specializes in these types of engagements will be

able to work with the parties and perform the procedures required to complete the analysis.

Post-acquisition disputes: Disputes that arise out of merger and acquisition agreements may include post-closing purchase price adjustments and earnout disputes. Under the terms of an earnout provision, a portion of the purchase price is set aside and will be paid out only if or when certain milestones are met. The milestones are typically financial benchmarks that must be achieved within a certain time frame after closing. Earnout disputes arise as to whether the milestones were met or the measurement of the company's post-closing performance related to the earnout agreement. Earnout agreements may be complex, and the ultimate language negotiated and documented by legal teams may be open to different interpretations by the buyer and seller. These factors commonly lead to post-acquisition disputes that require the skills of a forensic accountant to investigate and analyze.

Economic damages calculations: Organizations can fall prey to events or actions that impact their normal operations. These events may have been caused by a natural disaster or they may be the result of the actions of a third party. In either case, these events create economic losses representing the difference between what an organization would have accomplished, and the level of profitability they were able to perform under the conditions caused by the event. These events can be items such as business interruption due to a natural disaster, the termination of a contract, or the breach of certain contract provisions. In these situations, a forensic accountant will be able to navigate the adversarial environment and calculate the damages incurred as a result of the event.

Bankruptcy, insolvency, and reorganization: These situations are very different and require specialized knowledge in order to manage the operational, financial, and legal process. Not only are bankruptcy laws unique, but accounting and reporting requirements also differ in bankruptcy situations. In addition, the focus of a company or entity that has filed for bankruptcy may be different than the focus of the businesses and employees that are owed outstanding amounts from the bankrupt entity. It is important to understand that a bankruptcy is a legal proceeding, and that almost everything related to the entity filing for bankruptcy will be reviewed and may require court approval. It is critical that the entity seeking bankruptcy court protection take the proper steps and perform the analysis required to support the legal proceedings in the bankruptcy court. On the other side of the courtroom, the creditors must also make sure that they navigate the bankruptcy process successfully. Typically, creditors have two main concerns when their customers file for bankruptcy: 1) the amounts that are owed to the creditor at the time of the bankruptcy filing, and 2) how to transact with the bankrupt customer moving forward. The bankruptcy process has a mechanism to deal with these issues. As such, creditors must hire advisors that are knowledgeable of the process and understand the timing and requirements of what the creditor must file with the bankruptcy court to support their claim for unpaid amounts.

One item that often surprises creditors in a bankruptcy is the fact that the bankrupt entity may demand repayment of amounts that were remitted by the bankrupt entity to the creditor within a certain timeframe preceding the bankruptcy. These demands are commonly referred to as preference demands or claw back suits. The bankruptcy laws include various defenses available to the creditor in these situations. A forensic accountant familiar with the bankruptcy rules and defenses will be able to prepare an analysis that not only reduces the total exposure to the creditor, but also an analysis that meets the requirements of the bankruptcy court.

Business valuation: In some situations, it is important to analyze the tangible and intangible aspects of a business in order to determine the value of a business. This exercise may be necessary when new business partners are admitted, when divisions are divested, or to support buyout calculations. In these engagements, it is important to gather pertinent data, piece it together, and consider all of the variables so as to determine a realistic value. A valuation report requires the blend of strong fundamentals, detailed operational knowledge, and the consideration of competitive data. The expert conducting the valuation should have the proper experience, industry knowledge, and access to the proper tools and data in order to complete the analysis.

The various situations described above require the same specialized knowledge and skillsets as utilized in the cases of fraud. These situations require someone with a strong financial foundation, a sense of scepticism, and the experience to conduct the investigation in order to complete the analysis and present the findings.

A.   Other Litigation Support Activities

A forensic accountant operates within an environment that is the combination of specialized accounting skills and a legal atmosphere. As such, forensic accountants are able to assist an organization and counsel in many litigation support areas including:

- Reviewing documentation to form an initial case assessment, explain the financial issues of the case, and identify areas requiring additional financial analysis

- Assisting with preparing depositions outlines and questions to be asked

- Analyzing the opposition's expert damages report to identify strengths and weaknesses of the analysis completed or the positions taken

- Assisting with settlement discussions and negotiations

- Attending trial to hear testimony of opposing experts to provide assistance with cross-examination

In these situations, the forensic accountant may not be required to prepare an independent analysis of the financial facts, but the forensic accountant's skills and experience will assist with the critique of the adverse party's position or arguments.

B.   Stages of a Typical Forensic Accounting Assignment

Forensic accounting professionals can assist with evidence discovery – and in reconstructing accounting and business records – to uncover the critical facts of an investigation. They can identify discrepancies undetected by others by employing comprehensive evidence gathering, eDiscovery, and investigative techniques. Every case or investigation is different, and the specific scope and approach employed or the procedures and techniques performed will be dependent on the nature of each assignment. Generally, a forensic accounting engagement will involve the following stages:

- **Developing an Action Plan**: Includes gaining an understanding of the case through discussions with the client and counsel; the execution of an initial investigation; and establishing the objectives and techniques to be applied.

- **Gathering the Relevant Evidence**: May include tracking down documents or financial data, performing eDiscovery or data analytics; tracing assets, or identifying individuals or entities.

- **Conducting the Analysis**: May include calculating economic damages, summarizing a large number of transactions, performing a tracing of assets, etc.

- **Preparing the Report**: May include a summary of the case, the scope of the investigation, the approach and techniques employed, and a summary of the conclusions reached by the forensic accountant. It will properly support and effectively provide explanation of the findings.

C.   The Work Product of a Forensic Accountant

A forensic accountant's investigation usually concludes with a report and related exhibits summarizing the procedures performed and the result of those procedures. As previously discussed, in many situations, the forensic accountant's report will be used in litigation and may be shared with the opposing party and a court of law. The report will serve as a means for the forensic accountant to educate the judge and jury as to the bases and opinions that the forensic accountant will speak to if called to testify. The forensic accountant will not be permitted to testify beyond the scope of their report. As such, the report must be direct, clear, and concise.

In many of these situations, the forensic accountant will be retained as an expert with the objective of testifying in court. The forensic accountant must understand the rules under which the expert is required to operate. These rules may vary from one jurisdiction to another. Federal rules may apply, or some other rules may impact communications with counsel and what must be disclosed to the adversary in discovery. The forensic accountant must be aware of these rules, as a mistake may cost the organization greatly. A misstep or misunderstanding of the rules may result in negative publicity, sanctions, or fines from the court. In the worst-case scenario, the expert's report and opinion may be excluded. As such, it is important that an organization find an expert that not only has experience testifying, but has the ability to quickly build a rapport with counsel and the court when taking the stand.

D.   Preventative Measures

The challenging realities of today's enforcement environment places even more importance on preventing wrongdoing. Investing in prevention programs not only enhances long-term competitiveness and decreases the likelihood of improper or fraudulent activities, but also enables companies to demonstrate their best compliance efforts and assert that a violation is an anomaly that should not trigger significant punitive action.

To help prevent violations, investigations and compliance teams should evaluate compliance programs, assess the risks of improper activities, and develop robust control frameworks and integrity monitoring activities designed to enhance compliance and minimize risk and damages.

A forensic accountant may assist an organization in developing policies and procedures that will prevent many of the items described above. They may also assist by reviewing existing policies and procedures, combined with the results of testing conducted by the forensic accountant, to identify improvements that can be made to combat fraud. The preventative measures may include fundamental testing or analysis the organization can conduct during month-end closing procedures, or more sophisticated procedures conducted on a recurring basis by a dedicated team of internal investigators.

In addition, the forensic accountant may conduct a fraud prevention check-up for an organization. During this process, the forensic accountant works with an organization to determine if the organization is vulnerable to fraud and if the organization has adequate controls in place to prevent fraud. A strong fraud prevention program will increase the confidence investors, regulators, and the general public have in the integrity of an organization.

The ACFE's 2016 Report to the Nations highlighted that the presence of anti-fraud controls correlated with both lower fraud losses and quicker detection. The study concluded that organizations having specific anti-fraud controls in place compared to organizations lacking those controls experience 14.3%–54% less fraud losses, and frauds were detected 33.3%–50% more quickly.

E.   Managing Government Investigation

Today's enforcement environment presents major challenges for unprepared, ill-equipped companies. Federal and state investigations are conducted using more invasive methods, such as corporate whistle-blowers and far-reaching subpoenas. The higher frequency of multi-regulator investigations is creating increased complexity, and the presence of foreign regulators is also on the rise. These more robust investigative methods are occurring in a political climate where business wrongdoing is increasingly regarded as a criminal issue. Behavior that was previously not prosecuted or handled through civil enforcement is now investigated by criminal authorities.

Not only are the risks of a government investigation increasing, but enforcement investigations are becoming more and more costly. Settlements have become more severe with lasting consequences. A settlement may now include an admission of wrongdoing that creates reputational and brand risk, business restrictions that limit future growth and operating agility, and long-term post-settlement integrity monitoring and reporting that can increase operating costs significantly. The risk of post-settlement class action law suits must also be taken into account. Direct costs in the form of fines and penalties can reach or exceed the billion-dollar threshold.

If a government investigation is forthcoming, companies must work to limit exposure, protect assets, and enhance compliance efforts by fortifying internal investigative efforts, enhancing transparency, and enacting measures to strengthen compliance with government investigative procedures.

Forensic accountants play a critical role in managing government investigations and should be a member of an organization's response team, working together with company insiders, counsel, and other professionals to keep control of the investigation for an organization. They can help fine-tune risk mitigation efforts and develop control environments that help prevent violations, which ultimately mitigates litigation exposure.

Forensic accounting professionals assist internal and government investigations with evidence discovery and in reconstructing accounting and business records to uncover critical facts. They reveal discrepancies undetected by others by employing comprehensive evidence gathering, discovery, and investigative procedures. Representative services may include data extraction, analysis, and reconstruction; expert reports and witness testimony;

tracing and recovery of misappropriated funds; and uncovering and quantifying damages.

Forensic accountants can perform an initial assessment of the situation and help the organization identify risk areas or gauge exposure for the organization. An organization may undertake the initial assessment in order to develop a response plan to the investigation, including identifying individuals familiar with the underlying facts, determining supporting information that must be shared in the investigation, and formulating defense strategies.

Absent an initial assessment, the organization may wish to conduct a parallel analysis and review the information gathered by the government organization in an effort to keep pace with the external investigation. This will help the organization avoid any surprise in the results of the investigation. Finally, the analysis may identify faults in the investigation or conclusions reached by the investigation. This may prove critical in defusing the investigation and related exposure.

When your organization is faced with a government investigation, forensic accountants will prove an invaluable asset to your organization.

Chapter 19

The Forensic Accounting Reference Model (FARM) Overview

By: Vincenzo Toppi[994] and Jon Scherr[995]

The FARM takes a deeper dive into the investigative phase described within the Government Investigation Reference Model (GIRM). The FARM provides a description of the processes and procedures to be utilized when the investigation focuses on financial transactions or events. The FARM will provide guidance and an outline for performing a forensic accounting investigation.

I.   INTRODUCTION

As described in the "Forensic Accounting" chapter in this Guide, forensic accounting is a specialized discipline that uses accounting skills to perform analysis that can be used in legal proceedings. As that chapter discusses further, the individuals who perform these procedures are trained in multiple disciplines including accounting

---

[994] Vincenzo ("Vinni") Toppi is a Partner with CohnReznick LLP. He conducts forensic accounting and fraud examinations, conducts internal investigations, he leads the computer forensic and eDiscovery service team and he provides litigation support services including electronic data acquisitions, forensic data examinations, data mining and analysis and dispute resolution services. Vinni is a Certified Public Accountant, Certified in Financial Forensics, is a Certified Computer Forensic Examiner and is a member of The Government Investigations and Civil Litigation Institute Advisory Board.

[995] Jon Scherr is an Associate Director – Forensic Accounting & Investigations at KHA. At the time this chapter was written, he was a Senior Manager with CohnReznick LLP. He has a wide range of experience providing forensic investigations, anti-money laundering, anti-bribery and corruption, and litigation support services to clients in both domestic and international engagements. His services include forensic financial investigations; risk assessments (including fraud, anti-bribery and corruption, and AML risk assessments); assessment of fraud risk management programs; assessment of anti-money laundering processes, procedures, and controls; financial and operational internal control assessments; process improvements; compliance services (e.g. Sarbanes Oxley); and developing Standard Operating Procedures (SOP) for various business functions. Jon is a Certified Fraud Examiner and is a Licensed Investigator.

and auditing standards, financial analyses, data analytics and investigation techniques. In many cases, government investigations focus on areas that require the skillset of forensic accountants.

II.   TERMS

The GIRM identifies and defines many of the relevant terms that will be referenced in this chapter, the FARM incorporates those terms into this discussion. In addition, the following terms are important to understand:

A **forensic accountant** is an individual who blends financial analysis, data analytics, investigative techniques and storytelling skills to examine a set of transactions, gather evidence and report the findings in a formalized report, usually to be used in a legal setting. A forensic accountant's report presents a detailed description of the procedures performed, the information analyzed and the results of the investigation. Please see the "Forensics Accounting" chapter herein for further discussion on the role and capabilities of a forensic accountant.

When an audit is not an **Audit**: the term 'audit' is typically included in contracts as a means for one party to check or verify the accuracy of the financial information that is provided by the counter-party under the terms of the agreement. Unfortunately, to the reader, the term audit may have a different meaning than what the author of the contract intended it to have. As outlined in the "Forensic Accounting" chapter herein, forensic accountants have a set of professional standards and rules that must be followed. For forensic accountants who are also Certified Public Accountants ("CPA"), the term audit is a term that is well defined.

It represents a level of service that is conducted under certain rules governed by the American Institute of Certified Public Accountants ("AICPA")[996]. While many agreements include an

---

[996] "An audit is the highest level of assurance service that a CPA performs and is intended to provide a user comfort on the accuracy of financial statements. The CPA performs procedures in order to obtain "reasonable assurance" (defined as a high but not absolute level of assurance) about whether the financial statements are free from material misstatement." aicpa.org : Guide to Financial Statement

audit right, the intent of the contractual clause is not to trigger a financial statement audit under the AICPA rules. Rather, the goal is to provide a mechanism for the parties to determine if financial information is accurate and supports the transactions reported.

The **forensic audit**, or investigation, may be triggered by a contractual clause, as mentioned above, it may be initiated under a directive from an organization's Board of Directors or it may be required to satisfy information requests related to an investigation initiated by external parties. A forensic audit is focused on inspecting a set of circumstances or transactions, gathering evidence and determining if the transactions were recorded in accordance with the presiding rules. When the transactions do not follow the rules, a forensic investigation is structured to raise red flags for transactions that require additional review and analysis. As such, the forensic audit focuses on identifying transactions, gathering evidentiary support, and presenting the items in a manner to be used in legal proceedings.

As discussed further in the "Forensics Accounting" chapter herein, there are many situations that may trigger a forensic audit. A forensic audit can be used as a defensive tool once an investigation has been initiated, it may be required to uncover the dealings of a rogue employee or it may be used to enforce contractual rights within a contract. It is important to note, as discussed in the "Forensics Accounting" chapter herein, a company that is the target of an investigation may also initiate a forensic accounting investigation to perform an initial assessment, stay ahead of the investigating parties and to gauge exposure related to the investigation.

Services: Compilation, Review, and Audit. AICPA. 2015 AU-C 200: Overall Objectives of the Independent Auditor. AICPA. 2015. AU-C 240: Consideration of Fraud in a Financial Statement Audit. AICPA. 2015.

III.   THE INVESTIGATION TEAM

A.   Government

Government agencies that are tasked with pursuing these types of investigations are well prepared, have a long track record of running the investigations and experience with the various schemes used by **targets**. Depending on the agency structure, and the ability to work across agencies, once an investigation has started, resources with forensic accounting, data analytics and investigation skills are available to the agency.

B.   Company

A company may not be as well equipped to handle the forensic accounting investigation. A company may not have experience with investigations, may not have the proper internal resources, and may have limited financial wherewithal to support the investigation efforts. These are all factors that a company must consider, and in some cases, may dictate the strategy and response that a company employs in the investigation.

After a company has been made aware of an issue, or an investigation, it needs to start pulling together the appropriate team to respond to the investigation. Timing of the investigation, areas covered by the investigation and overall exposure will all need to be considered to determine the team that the company will assemble. The team may be comprised of many different resources, both internal and external, as described below.

> Internal resources: A company needs to evaluate if it possesses the correct resources, with the skillsets and capabilities required, to provide the support required during an investigation. Certain roles, depending on the type of investigation, such as general counsel, the chief financial officer or internal audit resources may be called upon to support the company's efforts during the investigation. Other areas, including compliance, technology or human resources are typically involved in the investigations as well.

The company must evaluate if internal resources possess the qualifications and subject matter expertise to perform the investigation. While there are certain organizations and industries where regulatory oversight or government investigations are more common than others, in many organizations, the internal resources are focused on duties such as servicing clients, not on conducting investigations or responding to government inquiries. In addition, the internal resources might not have the expertise to conduct the forensic procedures required for the investigation.

The forensic accountant may need to testify in court, interact with regulatory agencies conducting an investigation, or the focus of the investigation may be on an area that requires very specialized knowledge. A company must determine if its internal resources are well equipped to meet these needs.

A final item to consider is the government agency's perception, or public's perception depending on the issue being investigated, that the internal resources may appear to not be truly independent from the company or the situation. It is important for a company to have a well-documented set of **compliance** policies and procedures in order to overcome this perception.

In many cases, a company determines that internal resources will not be sufficient to handle the investigation and will retain external resources to fill the roles required.

External resources: Once a company determines that external resources are required to assist with an investigation, there are a couple more items to consider.

First, the company must identify the external resources to be retained as part of the investigation team. The resources may include external counsel, private investigators, eDiscovery providers, public relations firms and forensic accountants.

Retention: A company must not only determine what external resources will be hired, but must also determine who will hire those resources. While that sounds like an easy answer-the company is hiring them...the question is really, who is directing the forensic accountant's work and who will receive the findings of the work performed. Depending on the organization, the forensic accountant may report to the chief financial officer, internal audit, the Board of Directors or a special committee. In many cases, the forensic accountant is a member of a team of professionals that the company has assembled to handle an investigation. Typically, external counsel is also part of the investigation team and it is common to have the forensic accountant retained by external counsel. The forensic accountant is directed by counsel on the procedures they will perform, and they report the results of those procedures to counsel. This retention structure allows the forensic accountant the ability to conduct the forensic procedures on an autonomous basis, free of internal company silos or obstacles. In addition, the reporting structure ensures that the forensic accountant's findings are presented to someone not involved with the transactions under investigation and free from any internal management roles.

Once the retention structure has been determined, the specific procedures and activities of the external resources need to be defined.

Scope: As discussed earlier, a forensic accountant performs very specific procedures during an investigation. The forensic accountant will evaluate the issue, develop a defined scope of procedures, identify relevant data sources and determine the applicable time frame to analyze. The forensic accountant and counsel, or the applicable party that retained the forensic accountant, will execute an engagement letter that captures these components. In addition, the engagement letter will identify who will be the recipient of the forensic accountant's findings and report. A detailed outline of the forensic accounting procedures is discussed below.

IV.   FRAUD THEORY

Fraud Theory: Donald Cressey, a notable sociologist and criminologist was the first to propose the theory of the fraud triangle. Cressey theorized that three (3) factors must be present at the same time to drive someone to commit fraud.

Generally, the first factor to present itself is ***pressure***. The perpetrator may have a financial problem that they feel they cannot solve through legitimate means. This may be a personal financial problem such as gambling debt or living above their means. These financial problems could also be professional, causing a person's business to be in jeopardy. Financial problems may present themselves in any number of ways, however when the pressure mounts to a point where the perpetrator believes that they cannot solve the issue through legitimate means, the pressure continues to build until there is some type of relief.

With the pressure building, the perpetrator then begins to evaluate how they may take advantage of their position and ***opportunity*** to alleviate the financial pressure. In this leg of the fraud triangle, the perpetrator will formulate their methodology to maintain secrecy to attempt to ensure that the crime is not detected. The perpetrator generally perceives a low risk of being caught and now has a plan to move forward with the fraud.

The third and final leg of the fraud triangle is *rationalization.* As research has shown that most fraudsters are first-time offenders, they generally do not view themselves as criminals. Rather, they may feel that they are owed something by their employer, or that their criminal actions were justified because of some perceived wrongdoing. Additionally, many of those who commit fraud may originally intend on repaying the money or replacing it, however, get in too deep and ultimately just continue to steal more until they get caught.

For each leg of the fraud triangle, there is a counter approach that can assist companies in combatting occupational fraud. When it comes to pressure, company *culture* can be used as a great prevention technique. Many times, the financial pressure that may come about to drive someone to commit fraud may be driven by corporate culture. Ensuring that financial goals are met without forcing undue pressure onto employees is a key to combatting the *pressure* leg of the fraud triangle. Additionally, promotion of an ethical culture in which employees are driven to behave in a moral and principled way, serves to combat fraud.

When it comes to methodologies that companies can use to combat fraud, the easiest and most straightforward of these combats *opportunity*. To combat this leg of the fraud triangle, companies should ensure that proper internal *controls* are in place. Ensuring proper controls are in place is not only paramount to combatting occupational fraud, but is the cornerstone of corporate compliance. Internal controls allow for the checks and balances necessary to mitigate the risk of fraud. Controls do not have to be complex to achieve a high level of risk mitigation. Approaches as simplistic as segregation of duties contribute to a reduction of the ability of a single person to commit fraud on their own.

To combat the *rationalization* leg of the fraud triangle, it is important for companies to build a system of shared *values*. These shared values create an internal thought process for the would-be perpetrator to battle against their attempt to rationalize committing a fraud. Creating shared values amongst employees is paramount to battling rationalization.

Fraud Prevention: Companies can employ a variety of fraud prevention programs, but no matter what types of fraud prevention measures are employed, the success of those programs is predicated on the company embracing fraud prevention as part of their culture. When we consider fraud prevention, a great place to start is with Human Resources. Something that is often overlooked is the scrutiny that we place on candidates before we make the decision to hire them as an employee. Considering a person's background beyond their professional experience through a thorough background check can easily prevent someone who may have a questionable past from being placed in a position in which they may have opportunity to commit occupational fraud. What is most often overlooked when it comes to background checks is ongoing monitoring of those who are in key positions. Most view background checks as a step in the initial hiring process, however in most companies, once an initial background check is completed, another background check is not completed during the person's employment. This means that once someone is in the door, an employer may not know if the employee has been arrested for example. Implementation of periodic background checks for those in key positions is a best practice that few execute on, however, can play a key role in ensuring those in key positions continue to live up to the character that was assessed at the time they were hired.

Internal Audit / Internal Controls: The role of the internal audit department in preventing fraud is paramount. Internal audit departments take on the responsibility of ensuring that the controls in place are operating effectively day-to-day in the context of the business. By conducting a risk assessment annually, Internal Audit Departments are able to determine the areas of the business that present the highest risk to the company. Internal audits throughout the year can then be targeted towards those higher-risk areas to ensure that the most critical of internal controls are operating effectively. During the course of internal investigations, issues may be identified that may require more detailed investigation and review. The appropriate personnel and resources can then be assigned to complete an investigation and report on their findings.

One of the features of Internal Audit departments that makes them an invaluable asset to organizations is that they do not report to anyone in the corporate structure. Rather, they operate under an internal audit charter and generally report to the Board of Directors or may report to the General Counsel's Office in certain circumstances. This is done to ensure that the personnel who are part of the Internal Audit Department can be impartial and do not have the risk of undue pressure from others within the organization to diminish findings or results of audits or investigations conducted.

V.   FORENSIC ACCOUNTING PROCEDURES

Each forensic accounting investigation is unique and, as such, a tailored approach and plan to the specific facts, circumstances, and objectives is required. As a framework and point of reference, a typical project plan includes the phases listed below:

1. Evaluate investigation objectives: Discuss the investigation with the company and its investigation team to determine the background, scope and focus of the investigation. In addition, gain an understanding of the investigation procedures performed to date and any limitations faced by the company.

2. Conduct management interviews: Conduct management interviews to determine data sources and custodians, data format and internal resources required to gather the supporting information. During this phase, it is critical to identify other investigation team members, such as data discovery experts or private investigators that will be required to assist with data gathering. At this stage, international data sources and **data privacy**

concerns should be considered in order to eliminate any issues or limitations that need to be addressed.

3. Submit data request: Prepare and submit an initial data request to the company. Data requests may include the following:

    i. Financial reports and supporting data.
    ii. Operational data such as time clock reports, ERP system reports or manufacturing database information.
    iii. Internal reports or findings.
    iv. Email or other electronic communications.
    v. Copies of statements from financial institutions.
    vi. Vendor, customer or employee data.

4. Prepare project plans and detailed work scope: Prepare a detailed work scope, including rules and testing procedures intended to flag items requiring additional research and investigation. The testing procedures should be designed and discussed with the company and counsel to ensure that it meets the investigation objectives. The forensic accountant, the company and the investigation team should be prepared to reevaluate and adjust the scope as information is analyzed and findings point to additional areas to investigate.

5. Perform detailed testing and analysis: Perform testing of data set to identify items meeting the testing criteria. During this stage, the forensic accountant must determine the tools needed, based upon the information available and the data sources, to complete the analysis. The tools may include data mining software, investigative databases and computer forensic or artificial

intelligence tools. The testing may include the following procedures:

    i.   Data mining and analytics.
    ii.   eDiscovery and keyword searches.
    iii. Tracing of assets.
    iv. Interviewing **subjects** and **witnesses**.
    v.   Perform background investigations.
    vi. Performing financial calculations and analysis such as quantifying financial statement fraud, lost profits, damage calculations, enterprise valuations and royalties owed.

6. Discuss findings: Summarize findings for discussion with the company's investigation team. At this stage, a detailed listing of the flagged items, along with the testing parameters should be shared with the investigation team.

7. It is important to mention that the company may conduct a parallel forensic investigation and analyze the information gathered by the government agency in an effort to keep pace with the external investigation. This will help the organization avoid any surprise findings and may prove to be critical in defusing the investigation and related exposure.

VI.   REPORTING

Once the forensic accounting procedures have been concluded, the forensics accountant must communicate the findings to the investigation team. Reporting the findings of a forensic accounting investigation raises other areas that must be addressed.

Report format: Typically, the forensic accountant's report will be a written report that outlines the procedures performed, the data analyzed and the testing results. The forensic accountant's initial reporting will most likely be to the other members of the investigation team. As we discussed earlier, this team may include internal and external resources with various backgrounds. It is important that the forensic accountant keeps in mind the audience's financial literacy or familiarity with some of the financial records that were analyzed. As such, the forensic accountant's report should focus on the facts and be written in simple language to convey the findings of the procedures performed. Also, the forensic accountant should work with the investigation team to determine dissemination of the report. This will not only provide an understanding of the audience, but this will also highlight any privilege issues or restrictions that need to be addressed prior to issuance of the report.

Testimony: In some cases, the forensic accountant may find themselves testifying in court as an expert witness. The forensic accountant will provide an opinion and conclusion regarding the transactions analyzed. The forensic accountant will be called upon to summarize the findings of the investigation and to convey the highly specialized area of expertise that the forensic accountant possesses to the court in a concise manner and in user-friendly terms. As such, it is important that counsel, as part of the investigation team, prepare the forensic accountant for deposition and testimony.

VII.   MONITORING AND PREVENTATIVE MEASURES

Once the investigation has concluded, the forensic accountant's role may include fraud prevention, fraud detection or monitoring services. In many instances, the forensic accountant assists with developing compliance programs, or more likely, they are involved with developing testing procedures to monitor an organizations transaction and to flag items that may require additional analysis to verify compliance with corporate policies. As such, the forensic accountant may play a critical role within an organization's internal detection program. In other cases, the forensic accountant may be a member of a federal monitor's team that is put in place to oversee an organization's compliance with settlement or deferred prosecution agreements.

Forensic accountants may also be involved with an organization's training program. The insight obtained during the investigation phase, such as internal control shortcomings, risk areas and data warehouse sources, must be addressed in training programs to ensure an organization develops robust programs and trains employees to combat fraud.

VIII.   CONCLUSION

Forensic accounting services may be a critical component of the investigation. The FARM provides a high-level framework and provides a description of the processes and procedures to be utilized. It is important to note that procedures and analyses will need to evolve as the business environment changes, as data sources advance or grow more complex and as laws and regulations change.

Chapter 20

Electronic Discovery Issues

By:

Rishi Chhatwal
Robert Keeling
Ashish Prasad
Todd Haley[997]

I.   WHAT IS E-DISCOVERY? WHY DOES IT MATTER?

The costs and burdens of discovery in litigation and investigations have increased dramatically over the past decade as a result of the growth of electronically stored information, or ESI. Boxes of documents copied and physically delivered to opposing counsel or agencies are largely a thing of the past. In their place, millions of electronic documents and a myriad of formats for electronic data have emerged, forcing a sea change in the way the legal system approaches information technology and data.

Routine discovery requests and investigations now require searches of a multitude of storage devices for ESI, including "servers, networked workstations, desktops and laptops, home computers, removable media (such as CDs, DVDs, and USB flash drives), and handheld devices (such as PDAs, cell phones, and iPods)."[998] In addition, the emergence of text messaging, social media, blogs, wikis, ephemeral messaging applications, and

---

[997] Rishi Chhatwal is Managing Director at Alvarez & Marsal Disputes and Investigations, LLC. Robert Keeling is Partner at Sidley Austin LLP. Ashish Prasad is Vice President and General Counsel at HaystackID. Todd Haley is Executive Vice President of Operations at HaystackID. Views expressed herein are in the authors' personal capacities and do not reflect the views of their employers or related entities.

[998] *The SEDONA CONFerence Best Practices Commentary on the Use of Search and Information Retrieval Methods in E-Discovery*, 8 SEDONA CONF. J. 189, 196 (Fall 2007).

productivity sharing tools (*e.g.*, Slack, Teams, and Yammer) in organizations has further fueled the growth of discoverable ESI.[999] Put succinctly, "technology has impacted legal discovery more than any other area of the law, and the growth of the volume of ESI has changed the way technology is used in legal practice."[1000]

Due to the ever-increasing amount and variety of ESI that organizations and individuals now generate and store, the eDiscovery industry has emerged over the past 25 years, to help parties to litigation and investigations comply with discovery obligations. The industry is wide-ranging and includes personnel in law firms, in-house legal departments, electronic discovery and document review companies, and consulting firms, and provides services across the Electronic Discovery Review Model, or EDRM, which is the established process model for an eDiscovery project lifecycle.[1001] The EDRM outlines the stages of the eDiscovery process, including data preservation and collection, processing and search, document review, and production. Each stage of the process is addressed in Section 2 of this chapter.

Moreover, the Federal Rules of Civil Procedure, which established specific rules for eDiscovery in 2006, were amended in 2015 to include significant changes, particularly regarding eDiscovery, with new rules about scope, timing, and preservation of ESI. Many states adopted electronic discovery rules as well, and while most states have followed the current federal rules, there are important

---

[999] *See* Collin Hite, Heather Simpson & Susan Dent, *Discovery Considerations Presented by Group Collaboration Tools*, 51 FALL BRIEF 51 (2021); *The SEDONA CONFerence Commentary on Ephemeral Messaging*, 22 SEDONA CONF. J. 435, 441-45 (2021); *The SEDONA CONFerence Primer on Social Media, Second Edition*, 20 SEDONA CONF. J. 1, 10-20 (2019); 2016 Mid-Year Discovery Update, Gibson Dunn (Aug. 2016).

[1000] Michael I. Quartararo, *Project Management in Electronic Discovery* 23 (2016). According to one study, there was about 470 times more data in the world in 2020 than in 2005, and that is expected to nearly quadruple again by 2025, equaling nearly 20 terabytes for every human on the planet. *See* https://statinvestor.com/data/35219/data-created-worldwide/.

[1001] http://www.edrm.net/frameworks-and-standards/edrm-model/.

differences in some states, which must be investigated by counsel engaging in discovery in state court proceedings.

The failure to adequately preserve and produce ESI, cooperate with other parties in the discovery process, or follow discovery orders or rules can have severe consequences, including unpredictable and high costs for collection, processing, hosting, review and production of information, likelihood of errors in the discovery process, risk of sanctions, or inadvertent production of privileged documents. In addition, the increasingly strict data privacy requirements under the EU General Data Protection Regulation ("GDPR") and state privacy laws are but one prominent example of the legal requirements surrounding data in corporations, especially personal data, and the legal risks of mishandling corporate data during the discovery process.

With this reality as background, the demand for eDiscovery services is expanding at a rapid pace, with the global eDiscovery market expected to grow substantially in the coming years..[1002] Increased litigation and investigation activity in the US, expanding acceptance from corporate legal departments and law firms of outsourcing certain legal functions, and rising electronic discovery activity in Europe and Asia have all contributed to the rapid growth of the eDiscovery market.

Facing such rapid expansion, corporate organizations, government agencies, and law firms continue to seek ways to manage increasing amounts of data efficiently and effectively, thereby lowering the cost of litigation, streamlining project management, and ensuring adherence to regulatory compliance requirements.[1003]

Accordingly, there is little doubt that familiarity with eDiscovery processes and procedures is becoming essential for counsel working in a variety of practice areas, especially litigation and investigation areas. To that end, this chapter will aim to provide an

---

[1002] FMI, eDiscovery Market Analysis, Global Industry Analysis and Opportunity Assessment, June 2016.

[1003] Id.

overview of the eDiscovery process, including data collection, processing, managed review, and production, as well as project management best practices for eDiscovery. We will conclude with a look toward 2023 and expectations for technology in the eDiscovery industry going forward.

II.   THE E-DISCOVERY PROCESS

This Section will provide a brief overview of the eDiscovery process.

A.   Data Preservation and Collection

The preservation and collection of electronic data has become an important responsibility for parties facing litigation or subject to a government investigation. Under Rule 26(g), for example, a party or that party's attorney must attest that "to the best of the person's knowledge, information and belief formed after a reasonable inquiry," a document production is "complete and correct as of the time it is made."[1004] Should a party fail to undertake diligent and reasonable preservation and collection efforts under the Rules, a court has wide discretion to impose appropriate sanctions, which in some instances may include instructing a jury to draw an adverse inference.[1005] It is important, therefore, for a party to be able to show that it made a reasonable effort to preserve and collect any and all relevant and responsive documents in the matter.

The preservation obligation commences when there is "reasonable anticipation" of a litigation or regulatory action, at which time regular records and information management policies must be suspended to ensure that relevant information is not lost or

---

[1004] FED. R. CIV. P. 26(g).

[1005] *See* FED. R. CIV. P. 37(e) (authorizing sanctions for failure to preserve ESI); *see also Membreno v. Atlanta Rest. Partners, LLC*, 338 F.R.D. 66, 76-79 (D. Md. 2021) (adverse inference instruction warranted as a sanction for spoliation of ESI); Neel Guha, Peter Henderson, & Diego A. Zambrano, *Vulnerabilities in Discovery Tech*, 35 HARV. J.L. & TECH. 581, 591-92 (2022); Jason Fliegel & Robert Entwisle, *Electronic Discovery In Large Organizations*, 15 RICH. J.L. & TECH. 7, Note 1 at 12 - 23 (2010).

destroyed.[1006] Typically, upon receiving a complaint or information that reasonably suggests future litigation or regulatory action, a company will issue a legal hold notice to employees and other necessary third parties, and will then put a hold monitoring protocol into place.[1007] With this type of notice in place, custodians will be alerted to preserve any relevant ESI where it resides, and to ensure that it is not destroyed, altered, or deleted.[1008]

Other data, such as data stored on the hard drives of key custodians, may be simultaneously preserved and collected through forensic imaging, full file collection, or other methods.[1009] Preservation and collection are often parallel processes, occurring simultaneously, and the choice to preserve-in-place versus the choice to preserve and collect at the same time will ultimately depend on the requirements of the litigation or investigation, the potential relevance of the data, and the potential importance of the custodians.[1010]

Parties must be cautious in how they proceed with data collection, taking steps to ensure that the collection is carried out in a reasonable and legally defensible manner, whether conducted by internal corporate personnel or outside forensic companies. With respect to the scope of collection, generally it is important to

---

[1006] *See In re Abilify (Aripiprazole) Prods. Liab. Litig.*, No. 3:16-md-2734, at *2-3 (N.D. Fla. Oct. 5, 2018); *see also The SEDONA CONFerence Commentary on Legal Holds, Second Edition: The Trigger & The Process*, 20 SEDONA CONF. J. 341, 354-55 (2019); Fleigel & Entwisle, *supra* n. 921 at 29-31.

[1007] Ann Marie Gibbs, Sheila Mackay & Doug Stewart, *The Data Preservation Data Collection Continuum*, ELECTRONIC DISCOVERY & RECORDS MANAGEMENT QUARTERLY, 6 (Winter 2007); *see also The SEDONA CONFerence Commentary on Legal Holds, Second Edition: The Trigger & The Process*, 20 SEDONA CONF. J. at 354-57.

[1008] *See* Gibbs *et al., supra* n. 923; *The SEDONA CONFerence Commentary on Legal Holds, Second Edition: The Trigger & The Process*, 20 SEDONA CONF. J. at 357.

[1009] *See* Gibbs *et al., supra* n. 923; *The SEDONA CONFerence Commentary on Legal Holds, Second Edition: The Trigger & The Process*, 20 SEDONA CONF. J. at 397-98

[1010] *Id.*

review the network topology of the system (*e.g.*, servers, workstations, and printers), determine all locations of the relevant data (*e.g.*, onsite, offsite, and archive), and identify the key timeframes of the data required for collection. Consideration must be given to whether all files will be collected from a device, with filtering to be done later, or whether only targeted files will be collected, based on file type, date range, key words or other parameters. Special provisions must be made for collection of data from mobile devices, social media, text messaging applications, ephemeral messaging applications, productivity sharing tools, and other "non-traditional" data sources, beyond laptops, desktops, and servers.

With respect to maintaining the proper chain of custody, it is important to prohibit unauthorized access to the data, track all data access, and establish authentication and identification requirements for the data. It is especially important to have procedures in place for tracking and documenting what documents have been collected and when, to make sure that all of the pertinent data and metadata have been collected, as well as to prevent collecting duplicate data during subsequent collections as the litigation continues.[1011] This will allow counsel to accurately convey the actions that were taken and will allow, where necessary, eDiscovery experts to attest to the validity of the collection process.[1012]

B. Data Processing and Search

The data processing and search phase of an eDiscovery project centers on preparing the electronic documents that have been collected so that they can be reviewed, with a subset produced to

---

[1011] Ashish Prasad, Effective Project Management in Discovery, The Practical Litigator 15, 20 (2009); see also Jay E. Grenig & William C. Gleisner, III, 1 eDiscovery & Digital Evidence § 14:32 (Nov. 2021); The SEDONA CONFerence Commentary on ESI Evidence and Admissibility, Second Edition, 22 SEDONA CONF. J. 83, 156-58, 173-74 (2021).

[1012] The SEDONA CONFerence Best Practices, Commentary on the Use of Search and Information Retrieval Methods in E-Discovery, 8 SEDONA CONF. J. at 212; see also The SEDONA CONFerence Commentary on ESI Evidence and Admissibility, Second Edition, 22 SEDONA CONF. J. at 156-58, 173-74.

the opposing party, as required. This preparation involves converting the collected ESI to a format suitable for attorney review and analysis.[1013] In brief, data processing requires inputting the universe of collected ESI, which is often in a wide variety of file formats, into a software tool that extracts and indexes the metadata of each file, creating data and image load files.[1014]

The essential goal of the processing and search phase is to reduce or cull down the universe of documents that will need to be reviewed by attorneys (or paralegals when appropriate). This can be done by employing tools such as filtering, de-NISTing (removing certain computer system files and file extensions according to National Institute of Standards and Technology ("NIST") standards), keyword searches, de-duplication, and certain types of analytics processes such as near de-duplication, email threading, and clustering.[1015] eDiscovery industry benchmarks suggest that using these techniques during processing leads to a substantial decrease, *e.g.*, 80% or more, in the number of documents that will have to be reviewed during the review phase of an eDiscovery project.

An important aspect of data processing and search is the identification of the original source of data at each stage of processing, such as the file location, directory and drive mappings (on hard drives), as well as the contents and file counts, all of which should be meticulously maintained and well documented.[1016] This will ensure data accountability through what is essentially a chain-of-custody process, with clear documentation at each step of the processing phase of an eDiscovery project.[1017] For example, "if Internet email is not processed for review, that should be documented. If a party uses forensic tools to recover

---

[1013] Quartararo, *supra*, at 145.

[1014] *Id.*

[1015] Quartararo, *supra*, at 147–53.

[1016] *The SEDONA CONFerence, Commentary on Achieving Quality in the E-Discovery Process*, 15 SEDONA CONF. J. 265, 288 (2014).

[1017] *Id.*

deleted emails from a custodian's mailbox, that use should be documented (including the specific tool and the results)."[1018]

At the conclusion of the processing and search phase, the ESI that has been earmarked for review is loaded onto a document review platform for review by attorneys or other legal professionals.

C.   Document Review

Whether the document review team is at a law firm, corporate legal department, or document review provider, the review team selection is one of the most important aspects of the document review phase of an eDiscovery project. Creating a methodology for recruiting, staffing, and evaluating contract reviewers and adhering to that methodology in every matter will result in the creation of excellent review teams on a consistent basis.

A standardized and well-planned training process for contract reviewers also is a key element in ensuring a successful document review project. Virtual review (with appropriate security protocols and workflows for remote reviewers) has become the standard practice since the COVID-19 pandemic began. Counsel in the matter should train the contract reviewer team by providing background information on the matter and instructions to help reviewers correctly analyze and code the documents. In explaining the nuances of the coding, it is particularly helpful for counsel to use sample documents from the review, whenever possible. Special attention should be paid to privilege training. Counsel should outline privilege fundamentals and provide details regarding any specific privilege situations the reviewers are likely to encounter in the documents.

Once training has been completed, the review team will proceed to actual review. Reviewers should be split into teams of manageable size with a Quality Control ("QC") reviewer monitoring the quality and productivity of each team. Generally, review attorneys may commit two types of errors: (1) analytical defects (*i.e.*, incorrect

---

[1018] *Id.*

analysis of a document); and (2) coding defects (*i.e.*, properly analyzing a document, but then incorrectly filling out the database coding template). The QC process should check for both of these potential defects. For analytical defects, the QC process will often entail (after any initial heavy QC process) a daily review of up to 10% of the work generated by each reviewer the previous day.

QC review should generally be performed while the review is taking place to ensure that any errors are caught before they become systemic, which will reduce the possibility of having to re-review documents later if errors occur. Daily reports should be generated and reviewed by the project manager and provided to counsel managing the review, and appropriate follow-up action, including any necessary retraining, should be taken based on the results of that review. Often, the review project manager will provide counsel with a set of coded documents on a regular basis so that counsel can conduct a secondary review of these documents and provide the project manager with timely feedback that can help improve the overall quality of the review. The percentage of documents for which counsel will conduct a secondary review will vary based on client-specific and matter-specific factors, such as the amount of total documents and the cost to the client of counsel's secondary review.

Integration among the client, outside counsel, and project manager at the review provider is critical to the overall success of the document review project. Ongoing collaboration during the actual review period between the client, outside counsel, and the project manager, including regularly scheduled conference calls to discuss the progress of the review project, is essential.

1. Technology Assisted Review

It has become "black letter law" that courts will permit the producing party to use technology-assisted review ("TAR") for document review and, in fact, many judicial decisions have encouraged attorneys to consider the benefits of TAR, which can improve the efficiency and accuracy of the document review phase of an eDiscovery project. TAR, at its core, uses the knowledge of a specialized group of reviewers to train a computer program to analyze data.[1019]

There are a variety of views in the legal community on the effects of TAR. According to some sources, TAR lowers costs and may offer more accurate results, but other observers have suggested that large numbers of human reviewers should still play a major role in document review, including in TAR projects.[1020] The experience of corporate organizations, government agencies, law firms and electronic discovery service providers over the past five years has

---

[1019] *See, e.g., Youngevity Int'l Corp. v. Smith*, No. 16-cv-00704-BTM, 2019 WL 1542300, at *8, 15 (S.D. Cal. Apr. 9, 2019); *Entrata, Inc. v. Yardi Systems, Inc.*, No. 2:15-CV-00102, 2018 WL 5470454 (D. Utah Oct. 29, 2018); *Story v. Fiat Chrysler Automotive*, No. 4:17-CV-12, 2018 WL 5307230 (N.D. Ind. Oct. 26, 2018); *Rio Tinto PLC v. Vale S.A.*, 306 F.R.D. 125, 126-27 (S.D.N.Y. 2015); *DaSilva Moore v. Publicis Groupe & MSL Grp.*, 28 F.R.D. 182, 183 (S.D.N.Y. 2012). *See also The SEDONA CONFERENCE TAR Case Law Primer*, 18 SEDONA CONF. J. 1, 7, 24 (2017). The SEDONA CONFERENCE defines TAR as "[a] process for prioritizing or coding a collection of Electronically Stored Information using a computerized system that harnesses human judgments of subject matter expert(s) on a smaller set of documents and then extrapolates those judgments to the remaining documents in the collection." *The SEDONA CONFERENCE Glossary E-Discovery & Digital Information Management*, 4th Ed at 48 (July 2014).

[1020] *See*, for benefits, Maura R. Grossman & Gordon V. Cormack, *'Reaffirming the Superiority of Human Attorneys in Legal Document Review and Examining the Limitations of Algorithmic Approaches to Discovery': Not So Fast*, 27 RICH. J.L. & TECH. 3 (Summer 2021); Maura R. Grossman & Gordon V. Cormack, *Technology-Assisted Review in E-Discovery Can Be More Effective and More Efficient Than Exhaustive Manual Review*, 17 RICH. J.L. & TECH. 11, (Spring 2011). *See*, for pitfalls, Robert Keeling, Rishi Chhatwal, Peter Gronvall & Nathaniel Huber-Fliflet, *Humans Against the Machines: Still Reaffirming the Superiority of Human Attorneys in Legal Document Review*, 27 RICH. J.L. & TECH. 4 (Summer 2021); Robert Keeling, Rishi Chhatwal, Peter Gronvall & Nathaniel Huber-Fliflet, *Humans Against the Machines: Reaffirming the Superiority of Human Attorneys in Legal Document Review and Examining the Limitations of Algorithmic Approaches to Discovery*, 26 RICH. J.L. & TECH. 5 (Summer 2020); Guha *et al., supra* n. 921; Bay, *Law Technology News: EDI Oracle Study: Humans Are Still Essential in E Discovery*, Law Tech. News (Nov. 20, 2013). http://www.lawtechnologynews.com/id=1202628778400/EDIOracle-Study-Humans-Are-Still-Essential-in-EDiscovery (looking at the results of the EDI-Oracle Study on predictive coding); Andrew Strickler, *E-Discovery Tool Relieves But Doesn't End Doc Review Burden*, Law360 (Apr. 16, 2014), http://www.law360.com/articles/527585/e-discovery-tool-relieves-but-doesn-t-end-doc-review-burden.

generally been that, while TAR has resulted in a smaller percentage of documents requiring human review than was the case before TAR was common, the large growth of document volumes during that time has offset the effect of TAR, leading to a growth in the volume of documents requiring human review.

TAR is often most useful in high-volume data cases with short discovery periods and mostly textual electronic data. In such cases, using TAR can allow for a quicker analysis of large data sets than manual review. Moreover, any upfront software costs of TAR can be defrayed by having less manual review in the later stages of the review project.

The TAR workflow differs significantly from the traditional linear review model. In a typical linear review, reviewers are given groups of documents, generally batched by custodian, and they review them one by one until all documents are coded. In contrast, in a standard TAR workflow, a group of specialized, highly knowledgeable attorneys will code groups of documents (seed sets), which will then be used to train the software to code the remaining documents. This will continue in successive iterations until confidence in the software's coding results reaches a certain threshold.

There are typically four main roles in a TAR workflow: (1) lead attorney; (2) subject matter expert (SME); (3) contract attorneys; and (4) project manager.[1021] The lead attorney ultimately is responsible for guiding the TAR process and making executive decisions, such as when to end the seed set review and how to provide additional training to the machine. The SME is an attorney who has a deep knowledge of the case and the relevant issues, and is knowledgeable enough to make high-level, substantive coding decisions. The contract attorneys are trained to have knowledge of a specific issue or issues, but they generally do not have the expansive knowledge and decision-making ability of the SME. Finally, the project manager, who has specialized knowledge of the

---

[1021] *See* http://www.theediscoveryblog.com/tag/technology-assisted-review/.

tool and the TAR process, must design the workflow and validate and track the results.

Predictive coding is perhaps the most recognized version of TAR. It allows for systemic coding of large data sets based on human analysis of a more limited set of exemplar documents, which is then used to code the rest of the data set. The initial stages of a predictive coding review are of paramount importance. If an incorrect coding regime is put into place, the knowledge on which the software bases its decisions will be flawed. This can potentially result in incorrect coding decisions being applied to the entire data set. Having a well-defined methodology is essential to producing accurate predictive coding results.

Although, as noted above, there may be different views among observers as to the utility of predictive coding versus manual review, over time more litigators have concluded that predictive coding provides time and cost savings over manual review, at least in the appropriate circumstances.

Continuous active learning ("CAL"), which is also known as TAR 2.0, is a more recent advancement in TAR. While it has the same differences from linear review as predictive coding, CAL provides a scalable, continuous review solution for large data sizes, while not requiring the same amount of burden on SMEs.[1022] With CAL, reviewers can begin reviewing the documents at the beginning of the review without requiring the need for a separate seed set. Additionally, the reviewers can be trained by an experienced SME to understand the types of documents that they need to identify (*e.g.*, as responsive), and to begin immediately to identify those documents within the total document population. As the reviewers are coding the documents, the algorithm is working behind the scenes to update the document population, using the coded documents as "like" documents and coding them appropriately.

[1022] *Gordon V. Cormack and Maura R. Grossman, Scalability of Continuous Active Learning for Reliable High-Recall Text Classification* at 1039-1048 (Oct. 24, 2016), *available at* https://doi.org/10.1145/2983323.2983776; *see also In re Diisocyanates Antitrust Litig.*, No. 18-md-1001, 2021 WL 4295729, at *2 (W.D. Pa. Aug. 23, 2021) (explaining the differences between TAR 1.0 and TAR 2.0).

Additionally, CAL allows the documents to be batched to the reviewers with more and more certainty as to the proper grouping of the documents, allowing the reviewers to review the documents in a more streamlined manner.

The workflows of CAL provide significant enhancements over predictive coding workflows. Because CAL is constantly re-looking at the document population, it is constantly updating and improving the algorithm to allow reviewers to get through more documents with less manual review. As already discussed, predictive coding requires that a select set of highly experienced lawyers review the documents to create the sample set; with CAL, the requirement for an SME is minimized and the SME can focus on training the contract reviewers. Another major benefit to the CAL workflow is its ability to take more and more documents into the document population without affecting the overall success of the workflow, which allows for rolling uploads of data over an extended period. Finally, the richness of the documents that are identified in CAL increases as the algorithm continually updates to account for the information it is gathering from the new documents that are reviewed.

D.   Production

In litigation matters, production formats for ESI are typically the subject of agreements between opposing counsel, which specify whether ESI will be produced as native files, as electronic images (*i.e.*, TIFF or PDF format), or as native files with accompanying metadata (electronic information about the document).[1023]

Production of documents to government agencies raises special issues.

At the outset, it is important to recognize that government investigations are conducted pursuant to statutory grants of

---

[1023] *The Sedona Principles, Third Edition: Best Practices, Recommendations & Principles for Addressing Electronic Document Production*, 19 SEDONA CONF. J. 1, 171-74 (2018) (noting that parties are encouraged to reach agreement on the form of production).

authority before a court complaint is filed. The scope of discovery is not limited to information relevant to a claim or defense of a party, and extends to any information reasonably related to the investigation; the government's request for information will receive deference from, and almost always be upheld by, the courts if challenged. Government requests for information are often very broad, and preservation steps implemented in response to government requests should follow the same best practices as those described above for litigation requests for information.

One such government request for information that can be tremendously burdensome for companies is what is known as a "Second Request." Under the Hart-Scott-Rodino Antitrust Improvements Act of 1976, in some circumstances, a company must provide the government with advance notice of a planned merger or acquisition, and it may then receive a Request for Additional Information and Documentary Materials, which is commonly referred to as a Second Request, from the Department of Justice ("DOJ") or Federal Trade Commission ("FTC"). A Second Request requires the company to respond to a significant number of requests for information and documents to allow the government to investigate possible antitrust concerns raised by the proposed deal.[1024]

The issuance of a Second Request brings unique eDiscovery challenges due to the size and scope of information that must be produced and the unusual posture in which it places the underlying transaction. Responding to a Second Request typically involves massive amounts of data, along the lines of several million documents, and the data sources involved are numerous and varied. Moreover, Second Requests are fundamentally different from traditional litigation or even other government investigations. A merger or acquisition that receives Second Request scrutiny is likely to be large and complex with significant business and

---

[1024] The DOJ and FTC have issued a model Second Request, which is publicly available online. *See* https://www.justice.gov/atr/file/706636/download (DOJ model Second Request); https://www.ftc.gov/system/files/attachments/hsr-resources/model_second_request_-_final_-_october_2021.pdf (FTC model Second Request).

financial consequences. However, the parties cannot close the transaction until they have substantially complied with the Second Request and endured the additional 30-day waiting period for agency review. This places tremendous pressure on counsel to complete the review and production as quickly as possible. To address these challenges, counsel should consider leveraging eDiscovery solutions, such as TAR, to increase the efficiency and accuracy of what is typically a complex document review.

In an information technology industry that often lacks reliable uniformity on data formatting, electronic documents can pose challenges for an agency requesting data from multiple sources with dozens of different formats.[1025] For this reason, agencies have developed their own unique, internal discovery format requirements in an attempt to make the electronic document production process more efficient for investigators, more predictable for the investigated party, and less burdensome and expensive for both.

The public nature of agency guidelines makes compliance by counsel relatively straightforward, so long as due care is exercised, but non-compliance can bring with it significant consequences for a company that is producing data to a government agency.

The DOJ has taken steps over the years to establish electronic document submission standards, but has recently done so on an internal, division-by-division approach.[1026] This practice allows the agency to cater its document production protocols to the industries that it most commonly investigates. The DOJ's Antitrust Division, in particular, has published a prominent example of agency

---

[1025] *The Sedona Principles, Third Edition: Best Practices, Recommendations & Principles for Addressing Electronic Document Production*, 19 SEDONA CONF. J. at 171-74 (explaining the different forms of production).

[1026] Allison C. Stanton, *DOJ Director Talks About Investigations and E-Discovery Technology*, Corporate Counsel Business Journal (Feb. 25, 2013), *available at* https://ccbjournal.com/articles/doj-director-talks-about-investigations-and-e-discovery-technology (explaining DOJ's approach to providing public guidance relating to eDiscovery).

production standards.[1027] The standards require that data be presented in an image-based format and that a number of relevant metadata fields accompany each submission to the agency.[1028] The standards are comprehensive in the formats covered by their requirements, including categories for "(1) email and other electronic messages (*e.g.*, instant messaging), (2) other electronic documents, (3) hard copy documents, (4) shared resources, (5) databases, (6) audio and video data, and (7) foreign-language materials."[1029] Each format is then provided its own section, complete with supplementary information to be submitted with each document provided by the various methods.[1030]

One of the most common recommendations for dealing with a DOJ investigation (and other agency action) is proactive cooperation and compliance on the part of the investigated party.[1031] Not only does such an approach enhance the company's ability to advocate for its positions over the course of the investigation generally, but it can also significantly decrease the amount of time and money spent by the company to comply with document production obligations.[1032]

In many respects, the DOJ and Securities and Exchange Commission ("SEC") production guidelines are similar. The SEC guidelines have resulted from the tremendous complexity and cost associated with transferring, storing, and reviewing digital

---

[1027] DOJ Standard Specifications for Production of ESI, Attachment B to Joint Case Management Statement and [Proposed] Order: DOJ Standard Specifications for Production of ESI, *United States v. eBay Inc.*, No. 12-CV-05869-EJD (N.D. Cal. May 31, 2013); *see also Electronic Production Letter Using Load Files*, The United States Dep't of Justice, Antitrust Division, Electronic Discovery (Sept. 25, 2018), *available at* https://www.justice.gov/sites/default/files/atr/legacy/2014/10/27/237704.pdf

[1028] *Electronic Production Letter Using Load Files, supra.*

[1029] *Id.* at 1.

[1030] *Id.* at 1-4.

[1031] Stanton, *supra* n. 941.

[1032] *Id.*

evidence.[1033] The SEC standards are similar to the DOJ's in that they delineate unique, preferred methods of conveyance for each type of data being produced, along with requirements for the maintenance of all requested documents on the company's side.[1034] For all stages of document production, the SEC guidelines repeatedly suggest that the subject of an investigation should be in regular contact with SEC staff throughout the process.[1035] A precise and thorough reading of the guidelines is critical in order to maximize the chances of a company getting the production right the first time, while also maintaining cordial relations with the agency.

Considering other agency standards, the Federal Trade Commission ("FTC") echoes a number of the requirements we have seen from the SEC and DOJ. The FTC production requirements, however, come with a few caveats. Among them, the FTC requires a meeting with agency staff and the investigated party within fourteen days of the initial request for documents.[1036]

[1033] U.S. Securities and Exchange Commission, Division of Enforcement, Enforcement Manual at 43-49 (Nov. 28, 2017), *available at* https://www.sec.gov/divisions/enforce/enforcementmanual.pdf; *see generally* Thomas O. Gorman, Defending SEC Investigations: The Basics, Program #1883, CELESQ, INC (Oct. 2, 2008).

[1034] SEC, Enforcement Manual *supra* n. 948, at 43-48; U.S. Securities and Exchange Commission, Division of Enforcement, Data Delivery Standards (Aug. 2021), *available at* https://www.sec.gov/divisions/enforce/datadeliverystandards.pdf.

[1035] SEC, Enforcement Manual *supra* n. ¬948, at 45, 48.

[1036] Fed. Trade Comm'n, *Model Request for Additional Information and Documentary Material (Second Request)* (revised Oct. 2021), *available at* https://www.ftc.gov/system/files/attachments/hsr-resources/model_second_request_-_final_-_october_2021.pdf; Fed. Trade Comm'n, Holly Vedova, *Making the Second Request Process Both More Streamlined and More Rigorous During this Unprecedented Merger Wave* (Sept. 28, 2021), *available at* https://www.ftc.gov/news-events/blogs/competition-matters/2021/09/making-second-request-process-both-more-streamlined; Fed. Trade Comm'n, *Business Blog* (Jan. 19, 2018), *available at* https://www.ftc.gov/business-guidance/blog/2018/01/so-you-received-cid-faqs-small-businesses. Katie W. Johnson, *FTC Privacy, Data Security Investigations Require Cooperation, Honesty, Speakers Say*, BLOOMBERG BNA (Dec. 5,

This meeting is generally an opportunity to set the schedule for responding to the Second Request and to address preliminary issues, including potentially narrowing the scope of impending discovery and lowering the cost and complexity for both sides.[1037] Production standards for the Commodity Futures Trading Commission ("CFTC") and Consumer Financial Protection Bureau ("CFPB") are substantially similar to other agency standards, though they do carry some unique submission and transmission requirements.

In sum, compliance with production requirements has many benefits, not the least of which is the promotion of good will on the part of the investigating agency toward the company under investigation. As many commentators have noted, credibility in the eyes of the agency conducting the investigation can be one of the most valuable currencies to have as a company progresses through an active investigation.[1038]

III.   E-DISCOVERY PROJECT MANAGEMENT

Lawyers on litigation and investigation teams often do not appreciate the importance of bringing sound project management processes to an eDiscovery project. In most cases, lawyers do not seek to be project managers, and implementing high-level processes and procedures with respect to case management can be difficult, both in a law firm and a corporate legal department context. Increasingly, however, corporate legal departments expect their own lawyers and law firms to be more efficient and adept at applying the latest technologies. In view of this, the benefits of bringing legal project management best practices to the discovery process can be substantial, including a reduction in potential risks

---

2014), *available at* https://news.bloomberglaw.com/tech-and-telecom-law/ftc-privacy-data-security-investigations-require-cooperation-honesty-speakers-say.

[1037] FTC, *Business Blog, supra*; Johnson, *supra* n. 951.

[1038] William C. Athanas & Jennifer L. Weaver, What to do When the Government Asks for Everything: Strategies for Healthcare companies to Negotiate the Scope of Civil Investigative Demands in False Claims Act Investigations, 10 A.B.A. HEALTH L. SEC. 5 (Jan. 2013).

and errors, increased efficiencies, streamlined oversight of technical and professional support staff, greater defensibility, and lower overall costs.[1039]

Generally speaking, the key aspects of eDiscovery project management include the coordinated management of scope, time, and costs throughout the lifecycle of the project. Defining these key project aspects requires a full understanding of the scope of discovery and applicable discovery rules, any time constraints (particularly around production deadlines), and cost expectations, especially those related to data processing volumes and attorney document review time.[1040] A fully developed Project Management Plan, or PMP, will address not only the scope, time constraints, and budget for the eDiscovery project, but will also establish reporting mechanisms, quality controls, workflow structure, and potential risks as to project success.[1041]

Assembling a team of professionals for all the required roles in an eDiscovery project is essential. The project manager is the cornerstone of effective project management in eDiscovery and has responsibility for planning and organizing the entirety of the matter, including keeping each stage of the process on track.[1042] The project manager is expected to guide the high-level aspects, including the processes for training, workflows, quality controls, and reporting, but also must be familiar with industry best practices related to the collection, processing, review, and production of ESI.[1043]

Creating standardized processes and workflows for each phase of eDiscovery, from initial discovery management planning to preservation, collection, processing, review, and production, will

---

[1039] Michael I. Quartararo, *supra* n. _ at 14.

[1040] Id. at 91.

[1041] *Id.* at 48.

[1042] *The Sedona Conference, Commentary on Achieving Quality in the E-Discovery Process*, 15 SEDONA CONF. J. at 288.

[1043] Michael I. Quartararo, *supra* n. _ at 30 – 31.

ensure that the steps taken are repeatable, defensible, and in line with project objectives.[1044] A company's information governance and standard operating procedures, or "playbooks," for discovery across a company's litigation and investigation portfolio can help prepare for document preservation, and can create a roadmap for knowing what information the company has and where it is located. The playbooks should take into account specific data types and sources, procedures for handling specific requirements, document requests and exceptions, and triggers or factors that will lead to use of eDiscovery service providers for assistance in the various stages of the EDRM lifecycle.[1045] The roles, responsibilities, and standardized processes and workflows should all be integrated as part of the PMP at the outset of the eDiscovery project, along with identification of the project manager and project team.

IV.   EDISCOVERY TECHNOLOGY IN THE COMING YEARS

The intersection of technology and eDiscovery is here and has brought with it many changes to eDiscovery practice in recent years. Further, there will continue to be cutting-edge developments in eDiscovery in the years to come, as emerging and shifting technologies are likely to lead to niche eDiscovery solutions that become more and more mainstream. This will likely result in greater acceptance and use of analytics, as well as the further proliferation of cloud-based data management and new eDiscovery services.

According to the Coalition of Technology Resources for Lawyers' ("CTRL") annual Advanced Analytics Research survey, analytics support professionals serving legal departments widely confirm that data analytics were indispensable and in wide use in their

---

[1044] *The Sedona Conference, Commentary on Achieving Quality in the E-Discovery Process*, 15 SEDONA CONF. J. at 275.

[1045] Michael I. Quartararo, *supra* n. _ at 92.

departments in 2016.[1046] Indeed, 71% of legal departments predict increased spending for analytics services in 2017, while twice as many legal departments say they are going to start using analytics for matter management.[1047] While analytics, such as email threading and clustering, were once a niche solution geared for TAR, they are now being used for culling data, early case assessment, and "fact-finding," reflecting a sea change with respect to these technologies.[1048] With the continuing and rapid expansion of ESI across the corporate landscape, analytics are now being used to achieve advantages early on in the discovery process, generating insights in early case assessment that can enhance litigation strategies and compliance efforts.

In addition, cloud-based data management solutions continue to contribute to a shifting eDiscovery landscape. Many organizations are utilizing cloud-based enterprise content management through services such as Microsoft Office 365.[1049] Moreover, many of these services offer native eDiscovery functionality and tools, including data retention, archiving, and other tools to assist in the management of ESI.[1050] Knowing whether such tools are right for an organization, or whether another third-party eDiscovery tool or service provider is best, requires a thorough understanding of the organization's data sources, requirements, capabilities and processes for ESI management. The more data sources the organization wants and needs to search, the more sophisticated and more expensive the tool that is likely needed to do the broad range of searching.[1051]

[1046] Use of Analytics in Corporate Legal Departments 2016–2017, Coalition of Technology Resources for Lawyers, Feb. 2017.

[1047] Id.

[1048] Id.

[1049] Gartner's Magic Quadrant for eDiscovery Software, May 2015.

[1050] Rand Morimoto, *Handling Electronically Stored Information in the Era of the Cloud* 86 (2015).

[1051] Id.

V.   CONCLUSION

The intent of this chapter has been to serve as a primer and brief summary of eDiscovery in litigation and government investigations, touching upon the key aspects of the eDiscovery process, project management in eDiscovery, and future considerations for the industry. With the rapid growth of ESI across organizations everywhere, most corporate legal departments would be well served to evaluate their established eDiscovery process and technology applications and make recommendations for any necessary changes or updates to those systems, thereby ensuring a leg up in this rapidly shifting and essential area of the law.

Chapter 21

Board of Director and Audit Committee Issues

By:

Christopher G. Oprison
Maia Sevilla-Sharon
Brian Young[1052]

I. INTRODUCTION

Following our first edition in 2017, we continue to witness an enforcement age of intense scrutiny on corporate governance issues, as well as financial transparency, as evidenced by passage of Dodd-Frank.[1053] In May 2018, a decade after the 2008 financial crisis, Congress approved and President Trump signed the Economic Growth, Regulatory Relief, and Consumer Protection Act (the "Reform Law"), the first major reform bill since the passage of Dodd Frank. The Reform Law signaled a regulatory rollback and significant dilution of Obama-era rules. As indicated in the 2017 edition of this chapter, it is unlikely that we will be headed back to pre-2008 recession practices. Increased attention toward these issues from lawmakers and regulators alike have amplified the need for public companies to be prepared to initiate prompt, timely, accurate and objective investigations of allegations of wrongdoing by the company, its officers, senior management or employees.

[1052] Christopher G. Oprison is a litigation Partner with DLA Piper LLP (US) in its Miami and Washington, DC offices, and is a former Special Assistant and Associate Counsel to President George W. Bush. Mr. Oprison focuses his practice on white-collar criminal defense, government investigations and complex civil litigation matters. Special thanks go to Maia Sevilla-Sharon, Of Counsel in DLA Piper's Miami Office, and Brian Young, a litigation Associate in DLA Piper's Washington, DC office, for their assistance. The views expressed by the authors are their own and do not necessarily represent the views of the Firm or any of its clients.

[1053] Dodd-Frank Wall Street Reform and Consumer Protection Act, July 21, 2010, 124 Stat 1376.

In this 2019 edition, we discuss issues confronting Boards of Directors ("Boards") and Audit Committees in connection with mitigating and minimizing risk exposure. Such measures should be one of the top agenda items at any Board or Audit Committee because discussion leads to self-awareness which, in turn, facilitates self-improvement.

Despite best efforts by Boards and management, misconduct persists. Boards and Audit Committees must respond appropriately including determining how to best structure and conduct an investigation, and specific best practices considerations for executing any investigation. Because investigations do not occur in a vacuum, we also discuss considerations for Boards and Audit Committees regarding what, if anything, should be done with respect to reporting on an investigation's findings and recommendations (mandatory or voluntary disclosure, for instance), and the central driving force behind such considerations – cooperation credit.

As discussed herein, while management-directed investigations may suffice for low-grade or isolated allegations of wrongdoing, allegations involving potential wrongdoing by officers, senior management or issues having or potentially having a material impact on a company's financials or posing risk of harm to consumers and/or the general public, militate in favor of entrusting the investigation to Boards or outside advisors. Board- or Audit Committee-initiated and managed investigations, particularly those led by outside counsel, while typically costlier and more time-intensive, are more likely to be viewed favorably as objective and independent and afforded greater weight by courts, government regulators, auditors and other third parties when assessing the effectiveness of remedial action and contemplating enforcement, litigation or punitive measures.[1054]

[1054] *See* American College of Trial Lawyers, Recommended Practices for Companies and Their Counsel in Conducting Internal Investigations, 46 Am. Crim. L. Rev. 73, 84 (2009) ("choosing independent counsel with few, if any, prior ties to the Company . . . has become commonplace and is generally regarded as the first step in convincing governmental authorities of the 'authenticity' of its cooperation."); Brian & McNeil, Internal Corporate

II. MITIGATING RISK: CORPORATE BOARD AND AUDIT COMMITTEE RESPONSIBILITIES

As the adage goes, "[a]n ounce of prevention is worth a pound of cure."[1055] There is no adequate substitute for routine, proactive planning, preparation and training to avoid situations in which a company must embark on an internal investigation to sort out allegations of misconduct.

Boards must regularly examine internal controls, assess the effectiveness and relevance of compliance programs and identify prophylactic measures to mitigate the risk of compliance failings. Such assessments would include the hiring of an in-house compliance officer that is independent and has a direct reporting relationship to the Board, CEO, or President, or conducting a thorough review and upgrade of the current compliance policy and training manuals at regular intervals and as needed following changes or deviation in corporate business model and relationships.

A. Corporate Board Responsibilities

Board responsibilities with respect to proactive action designed to mitigate risk and exposure for a corporate entity include, among other things, strengthening and tightening internal controls, and

---

Investigations at 12 (3d ed. 2007) ("Although the government will not perceive outside counsel as totally independent, outside counsel is presumptively more independent than inside counsel. Inside counsel, after all, has only one client— the company"); Richmond, Law Firm Internal Investigations: Principles and Perils, 54 Syracuse L. Rev. 69, 106 (2004) (noting that the hiring of outside counsel to conduct an internal investigation best insulates a firm against all claims of conflict of interest or common interest); Gideon Mark, The Yates Memorandum, 51 U.C. Davis L. Rev. 1589, 1611–12 (2018). *See also, e.g.*, *Madvig v. Gaither*, 461 F. Supp. 2d 398, 410 (W.D.N.C. 2006), which shows the benefits of using independent counsel hired by either independent Board members or by an independent committee – a company's decision to deny a demand or request to pursue a derivative lawsuit is more easily justified when any investigation into the allegations at issue are conducted by independent counsel hired by independent directors or an independent committee.

[1055] Benjamin Franklin, circa 1736.

ensuring and overseeing management's efforts regarding compliance and ethics programs. Regarding internal controls, Boards must understand and oversee internal controls and procedures that management has implemented to assure accuracy of financial reporting. Boards must also take "ownership" for the relevance and efficacy of the company's compliance policies and programs, including: (1) overseeing management's efforts to educate personnel about the corporate code of conduct and ethical standards, fraud or abuse reporting (including but not limited to whistleblower reporting), and identifying pitfalls and problem areas; (2) exercising reasonable care to ensure the company is managed in compliance with law, regulations and corporate policies; (3) working to foster and encourage a corporate culture that values ethical behavior, fair dealing and integrity; (4) knowing and/or taking reasonable steps to learn how to identify related party transactions and conflicts of interests, especially those involving board members or senior management; and (5) depending on its size and scope of operations, considering establishing a corporate compliance department.

In attending to the foregoing responsibilities, the Board must necessarily assess whether the company has a robust compliance program that would pass muster under the U.S. Sentencing Guidelines ("USSG" or the "Sentencing Guidelines"), § 8B2.1 (Effective Compliance/Ethics Program).[1056] USSG § 8B2.1, typically viewed as the benchmark by which the efficacy of compliance programs are measured,[1057] provides detailed guidance to rely on in the design and implementation of "effective"

[1056] U.S.S.G. 8B2.1 and Application Note 2 ("Each of the requirements set forth in this guideline shall be met by an organization; however, in determining what specific actions are necessary to meet those requirements, factors that shall be considered include: (i) Applicable industry practice or the standards called for by any applicable governmental regulation; (ii) the size of the organization; and (iii) similar misconduct.").

[1057] See In re Caremark Int'l Inc. Deriv. Litig., 698 A.2d 959, 970 (Del. Ch. 1996) ("Caremark") ("[a]ny rational person attempting in good faith to meet an organizational governance responsibility would be bound to take into account [the framework of the Sentencing Guidelines and guidance derived from prosecutorial activity] and the enhanced penalties and the opportunities for reduced sanctions that it offers.").

compliance programs, and is also used by the government to evaluate the efficacy of compliance programs. Other industry specific guidance may also be found. For organizations falling under supervision of the Consumer Financial Protection Bureau ("CFPB" or "the Bureau"), for example, resources also include the CFPB examination manuals designed to guide CFPB supervision of the design and effectiveness of compliance management systems as well as supervisory highlights.[1058] To be sure, there are no formulaic requirements and no "one size fits all" solution for a compliance program. An effective program must be tailored to the particular company, which should engage in periodic risk assessments to determine what sorts of criminal conduct pose the greatest exposure, and then implement controls to prevent, detect and address such misconduct.

An assessment of what constitutes an "effective" compliance program is centered on three "fundamental questions: (1) is the program well-designed?; (2) is the program being applied earnestly and in good faith? In other words, is the program being implemented effectively; and (3) does the corporation's compliance program work in practice?[1059] Implementation of such programs should be designed to deter, identify and remediate violations of laws and regulations, coupled with equally robust employee training and issue reporting mechanisms. The Board should examine the company's decision-making approach to self-report or cooperate, and ensure the company maintains documentation and records that will allow company executives to demonstrate they are working in good faith to operate the company in an ethical and compliant fashion. Boards should therefore be proactive participants in formulating, updating, upgrading, and ensuring proper testing of corporate compliance programs.[1060] In

---

[1058] See CFPB Supervision and Examination Manual (V.2), at: https://files.consumerfinance.gov/f/201210_cfpb_supervision-and-examination-manual-v2.pdf (last accessed (last accessed Aug. 5, 2019).

[1059] DOJ, "Evaluation of Corporate Compliance Programs," Guidance Document, Updated April 2019, available at https://www.justice.gov/criminal-fraud/page/file/937501/download (last accessed Aug. 4, 2019).

[1060] Dep't. of Justice, Assistant Attorney General Leslie R. Caldwell Delivers Remarks at the Second Annual Global Investigations Review Conference,

other words, Boards must heed the framework of the Sentencing Guidelines when assessing whether the compliance program is designed to address the particularized issues confronting that company.

The Criminal Division, Fraud Section of the U.S. Department of Justice ("DOJ") recently updated its *Evaluation of Corporate Compliance Programs* (April 2019) ("Compliance Program Guidance"). The Compliance Program Guidance is but the latest by the Fraud Section setting out DOJ's expectations for effective compliance programs. Part I of the Compliance Program Guidance addresses various hallmarks of a well-designed compliance program relating to risk assessment, company policies and procedures, training and communications, confidential reporting structure and investigation process, third-party management, and mergers and acquisitions. Part II describes features of effective implementation of a compliance program, including commitment by senior and middle management, autonomy and resources, and incentives and disciplinary measures. Part III, in turn, discusses metrics of whether a compliance program is in fact operating effectively, exploring a program's capacity for continuous improvement, periodic testing, and review, investigation of misconduct, and analysis and remediation of underlying misconduct. These are not novel topics, but rather an encapsulation of considerations appearing in other DOJ guidance, including the US Attorney's Manual, the U.S. Sentencing guidelines, DOJ's and the Securities and Exchange's ("SEC") Foreign Corrupt Practices Act ("FCPA") Guide,[1061] among others. The "questions" posed in the Compliance Program Guidance also make clear that a prominent piece of that exercise is robust data compilation, retention and accessibility. For instance, important data metrics useful for persuading DOJ that a company has an effective and appropriate compliance program include, but are not limited to: (1) the number of transactions halted or more closely scrutinized due to compliance concerns, (2) the number of internal audits performed related to allegations of misconduct, (3)

---

https://www.justice.gov/opa/speech/assistant-attorney-general-leslie-r-caldwell-delivers-remarks-second-annual-global-0 (last visited Aug. 4, 2019).

[1061] *A Resource Guide to the U.S. Foreign Corrupt Practices Act* (Nov. 2012). The Compliance Program Guidance also supplements portions of the FCPA Pilot Program.

the number of "red flags" identified during an audit or investigation, and (4) what types of audit findings and remediation progress were reported to management and the Board.[1062] In short, issuance of the Compliance Program Guidance provides visibility into DOJ's views on compliance best practices. It also creates a valuable opportunity for a Board to examine, assess and, as necessary, revamp a company's compliance program to be responsive to changing business models and expansions in operations.

In sum, the foregoing provides only a general overview of issues Boards must be mindful of. Audit Committees, too, are held to a heightened standard, as discussed below.

B.   Audit Committee Responsibilities

For 17 years, the Sarbanes-Oxley Act of 2002 ("SOX" or "the Act")[1063] has directed that Audit Committees are responsible for (1) obtaining and reviewing independent auditor reports on internal controls and procedures, (2) meeting and discussing quarterly and annual audited financial statements with management and the independent auditor, (3) reviewing, assessing and discussing a company's earnings and press releases, (4) evaluating a company's risk assessment and risk management policies, (5) periodically meeting with a company's management, and internal and independent auditors and discussing, among other things, potential problems encountered during the audit or management's response thereto, and (6) reporting regularly to the company's Board.

Audit Committees must also maintain required independence under Section 301 of the Act. In particular, committee members must not be affiliated with the company or any affiliated entities and, other than compensation for serving as Board members, must not receive any direct or indirect compensation from the company.

[1062] For further information about the Compliance Program Guidance, Boards should consult the Guidance itself, which can be found at https://www.justice.gov/criminal-fraud/page/file/937501/download.

[1063] *See* Sarbanes-Oxley Act of 2002, PL 107–204, July 30, 2002, 116 Stat 745 (current version at 15 U.S.C. § 78j–1).

Section 301 of the Act also makes Audit Committees responsible for appointment and compensation of the company's independent auditors and for overseeing the independent auditor's work. Audit Committees cannot be passive bystanders in this process: They must require the independent auditors to report regularly on the company's accounting principles, policies and practices, alternative treatment of financial information within generally accepted accounting principles ("GAAP") that have been previously discussed with management and other issues materially impacting the company's financial statements or auditor reports.

Such communications are themselves regulated and must comply with standards established by the Public Company Accounting Oversight Board (PCAOB),[1064] including Ethics and Independence Rule 3526 ("Communication with Audit Committees Concerning Independence") (April 2008) which governs pre-engagement communications, the PCAOB's *Information for Audit Committees about the PCAOB Inspection Process*, and the PCAOB's Accounting Standard No. 16 ("*Communications with Audit Committees*") ("AS 16"). AS 16 requires, among other things, the independent auditor must annually acknowledge the terms of the audit, inquire about and gather from Audit Committees information that would be relevant to the audit, provide details about the audit strategy, comment on the company's specific accounting policies and practices, unusual transactions, and financial reporting.

Audit Committees also fulfill a critical oversight role.[1065] While Boards are generally charged with overseeing operational risks, Audit Committees focus on risks that affect a company's financial

---

[1064] According to its own website, the PCAOB "is a nonprofit corporation established by Congress to oversee the audits of public companies in order to protect investors and the public interest by promoting informative, accurate, and independent audit reports. The PCAOB also oversees the audits of brokers and dealers, including compliance reports filed pursuant to federal securities laws, to promote investor protection." https://pcaobus.org/About.

[1065] Peter Ferola, The Role of Audit Committees in the Wake of Corporate Federalism, 7 J. Bus. & Sec. L. 143, 151 (2007); Michael Klausner, Fact and Fiction in Corporate Law and Governance, 65 Stan. L. Rev. 1325, 1360 (2013).

statements, including the strength of internal controls over financial reporting and those designed to prevent and detect fraud. Audit Committees are often called upon to assist Boards in monitoring legal or regulatory compliance including, for instance, the "books and records" provisions under the FCPA.

Finally, SOX calls upon audit committees to receive and investigate complaints of wrongdoing, including financial fraud involving auditing, accounting or internal controls issues,[1066] discussed more extensively below.

C.   Board and Audit Committee Oversight and Investigative Responsibilities

All of the foregoing are key proactive steps to mitigate and control against the proliferation of misconduct that so often gives rise to the need for internal investigations. When such proactive measures are ineffective in preventing or mitigating misconduct, Boards must then be prepared and equipped to identify and appropriately respond to complaints or concerns about corporate misconduct or statutory or regulatory violations. This would include initiating, managing and/or overseeing internal investigations.

When a Board becomes aware of potential misconduct, companies and their Boards must take immediate steps to determine whether any employees may have violated federal or state laws or regulations and impose appropriate sanctions on any offending employees. At that time, the Board must determine **whether** an internal investigation should be conducted in any event – that is, do circumstances warrant or require the company to commence an internal investigation? If it is decided that circumstances do require or warrant an internal investigation, then the company must decide who conducts or directs and oversees the investigation – that is, management, the Board, a special committee created by the Board, or an independent committee? Finally, once it is decided who the

---

[1066] 15 U.S.C. § 78j-1(m)(4) (2006) (also requiring that audit committees be empowered to retain independent counsel or experts to fulfill such duties).

most appropriate party is to conduct the investigation, how to best structure and conduct the investigation is of paramount importance.

III.   *WHETHER* TO CONDUCT AN INVESTIGATION?

If the company learns of improper or illegal conduct by an officer, employee, board member, or other person acting on behalf of the company, the company must act promptly to investigate the allegations. For instance, Boards should consider conducting an internal investigation in the event of whistleblower allegations of wrongdoing, which has become more commonplace given the increased incentives for and protection of whistleblowers under Section 301 of the Act, and Dodd-Frank. Complaints of wrongdoing involving financial fraud involving auditing, accounting or internal controls issues are precisely the types of issues within the province of an audit committee for investigation.[1067]

Additionally, pending and ongoing government or regulatory investigations, such as an SEC, DOJ, or congressional investigation, may trigger the need for an internal investigation. Once a company is aware of a government investigation, it should take prompt steps to understand the scope of the investigation and seriously consider conducting its own internal investigation to determine potential exposure. Finally, shareholder allegations of wrongdoing, including written demands by shareholders to investigate wrongdoing of Board or management, trigger an obligation to investigate.

IV.   *WHO* SHOULD CONDUCT AN INVESTIGATION

Internal investigations and more informal inquiries have, traditionally, been conducted by in-house counsel. Allegations of widespread misconduct, however militate in favor of an independent investigation, *i.e.* one that cannot or should not be conducted or overseen by in-house counsel or even the company's

---

[1067] *See id.*

usual outside counsel.[1068] Categories of misconduct warranting an independent investigation may include repeat conduct, conduct that implicates senior or executive officers, directors, or senior management, or implicates issues having or potentially having a material impact on a company's financials, suggests potential illegal conduct, or which is currently under investigation by a government regulator. It must also separately be considered, even absent any strong factor above, whether the optics, perception, and credibility of the investigation will improve in the eyes of prosecutors or government regulators by having the Board direct the investigation, thereby creating an air of independence and objectivity.

If an investigation is indeed warranted, it must be "independent." Independent investigations are led by or overseen by the Board (or an independent committee or special committee of the disinterested Board members). Board driven investigations can be delegated to an existing or special committee with specific oversight responsibilities (for example, allegations of improper revenue recognition practices, or other accounting irregularities). If no such special committee exists at the time of the alleged misconduct to be investigated, it may become necessary to establish a special committee of independent directors to oversee and direct the investigation. Special committees are typically formed if no existing committee structure would support such an obligation or if vesting responsibility in an existing committee could create an actual or apparent conflict. Establishing the independence of members of a special committee charged with conducting the investigation is absolutely critical, particularly when a company must demonstrate not only that the conclusions reached by the committee were supportable and sound, but also that the committee itself was independent.

[1068] One exception to this may be if the company has regular investigation counsel whose scope of work would be limited to conducting investigations. The touchstone is "independence" – the counsel called in to conduct the investigation must be genuinely viewed as independent and capable of objectively conducting an investigation.

Additionally, selection of counsel in board-driven investigations reflects on the degree of independence (and, thus, credibility and ultimate success) of an investigation. In cases of isolated and low-grade misconduct allegations, in-house counsel may appropriately conduct the investigation. It makes sense in some cases to do so, given the generally steep knowledge in-house counsel would have about the company's business, operations, controls and organization. Such a move also has implications for protection of privilege and work product.

Courts have, on many occasions, permitted the discovery of sensitive corporate files related to internal investigations where in-house counsel does not follow best practices for such investigations. When conducting internal investigations, it is important for in-house counsel to clearly act in the capacity as legal counsel for the company rather than offering business advice or management advice. The reason is simple: the attorney-client privilege only attaches to communications made for the purpose of obtaining legal advice or assistance.[1069] Therefore, for example,

---

[1069] *See, e.g., Owens v. Stifel, Nicolaus & Co., Inc.*, No. 7:12-CV-144 HL, 2013 WL 6389035, at *7 (M.D. Ga. Dec. 6, 2013) (ruling email with in-house counsel not privileged because "it does not seek or contain legal advice."); *Lindley v. Life Investors Ins. Co. of Am.*, 267 F.R.D. 382, 390 (N.D. Okla. 2010), *aff'd in part as modified*, No. 08-CV-0379-CVE-PJC, 2010 WL 1741407 (N.D. Okla. Apr. 28, 2010) ("the unstated operating presumption in situations involving outside retained counsel with limited responsibilities to the client (*e.g.*, strictly legal capacity as opposed to business responsibilities because of a corporate position that he holds), is that the consultations were held for the purpose of obtaining legal advice or assistance. The same presumption does not apply to in-house counsel because of the many non-legal responsibilities in-house counsel assumes (whether given a separate position and title or not)."); *AIU Ins. Co. v. TIG Ins. Co.*, No. 07CIV.7052SHSHBP, 2008 WL 4067437, at *6 (S.D.N.Y. Aug. 28, 2008), *modified on reconsideration*, No. 07 CIV. 7052 SHSHBP, 2009 WL 1953039 (S.D.N.Y. July 8, 2009) ("However, where in-house counsel also serves as a business advisor within the corporation, only those communications related to legal, as contrasted with business, advice are protected.") (internal quotations omitted); *UMG Recordings, Inc. v. Global Eagle Entm't, Inc.*, No. CV14-3466-MMM, 2015 WL 12914328, at *1 (C.D. Cal. May 22, 2015) (noting that communications made by in-house counsel in non-legal business capacity are not privileged)(citations omitted);*Am. Nat. Bank & Trust Co. of Chicago v. AXA Client Solutions*, LLC., No. 00 C 6786, 2002 WL 1058776, at *2 (N.D. Ill. Mar. 22, 2002) (ruling that a draft letter and notes written by in-house counsel were not

the company's in-house counsel should refrain from combining its communications about internal investigations with other business advice, and the company should not use lawyers who have a significant business or management role for internal investigations. It is also important for documents related to any internal investigation to be kept strictly confidential. This means documents collected or prepared during an investigation by an in-house counsel performing the investigations should only be shared with persons within the company, and only on a "need-to-know" basis.[1070] Absent some recognized privilege – including joint

---

privileged when letter was not sent to any other party and notes were not disclosed to anyone for the purpose of obtaining legal advice);; *Anderson Energy Grp. (Ohio), LLC v. Endeavor Ohio, LLC*, No. 3:13-CV-1784-P-BK, 2014 WL 12580471, at *1 (N.D. Tex. Sept. 4, 2014) (observing that "the line between legal and non-legal communications of in-house counsel can sometimes be blurred.")

[1070] *See, e.g., In re Allen*, 106 F.3d 582, 606 (4th Cir. 1997) ("the attorney-client privilege exists to protect not only the giving of professional advice to those who can act on it but also the giving of information to the lawyer to enable him to give sound and informed advice.") (internal quotations omitted) (citing *Upjohn Co. v. United States*, 449 U.S. 383, 391 (1981)); *Norton v. Town of Islip*, No. CV 04-3079 PKC SIL, 2015 WL 5542543, at *4 (E.D.N.Y. Sept. 18, 2015) ("Defendants have presented no reason, however, why all or even most Building Department personnel have a need to know confidential legal communications in order to perform their jobs. As Defendants have failed to carry their burden, the Court finds that they have waived attorney-client privilege as to the Memos."); *In re N.Y. Renu with Moistureloc Prod. Liab. Litig.*, No. CA 2:06-MN-77777-DCN, 2008 WL 2338552, at *1 (D.S.C. May 8, 2008) ("Intra-corporate communications to and from counsel can retain a privilege if disclosure is limited to those who have a 'need to know' the advice of counsel") (citations omitted); *Carolina Elec. Membership Corp. v. Carolina Power & Light Co.*, 110 F.R.D. 511, 516 (M.D.N.C. 1986) (ruling that documents were not privileged because, among other reasons, they were sent to in-house counsel that also held important management positions and the documents also constituted updates on ongoing business developments).800 *Cavallaro v. United States*, 284 F.3d 236, 246–47 (1st Cir. 2002) ("Generally, disclosing attorney-client communications to a third party undermines the privilege."); *Shah v. Dep't of Justice*, 714 Fed. Appx. 657, 659 (9th Cir. 2017) (noting that in the attorney-client privilege context, voluntarily disclosing privileged documents to third parties will generally destroy the privilege."); *Roe v. Catholic Health Initiatives Colorado*, 281 F.R.D. 632, 636 (D. Colo. 2012) ("disclosing attorney-client communications to a third-party results in a waiver of the attorney-client privilege.").In a recent case, *SEC v. Herrera*, 324 F.R.D. 258, 260 (S.D. Fla. 2017), the court addressed the legal consequences of a firm's "oral downloads" of witness interviews memoranda to the regulatory agency investigating its client. The firm contended that no waiver

defense or common interest privilege – privileged information should not be shared outside of the company.[1071] Accordingly, as any seasoned attorney well knows, and any junior attorney quickly learns, at the outset of employee interviews, document collection, or other activities related to an internal investigation, in-house counsel must clearly communicate to subjects of the investigation or company employees that are assisting in the investigation that such activities are in aid of an internal investigation and for the purposes of assisting the company in obtaining legal advice or assistance. Additionally, such employees being interviewed or assisting with an internal investigation should be made aware of the company's attorney-client privilege, that all communications and documents relating to the internal investigation are not to be disclosed to third parties or those within the company lacking any need to know about the investigation in order to render legal advice to the company. The foregoing raise issues of profound importance when determining the critical involvement of Boards in determining who should be responsible for directing the conduct and course of an internal investigation.

Where there are allegations of material or widespread misconduct, outside counsel should be engaged to conduct the investigation. Even if a Board makes the right decision to engage outside counsel to conduct an investigation rather than entrust its course and conduct to in-house counsel, there are also considerations about

---

occurred, because it never actually produced attorney notes and memoranda. The court disagreed, finding that a waiver occurred because the firm provided not only general impressions, but substantive downloads of 12 witness interview notes. *See id.* The case highlights the risks associated with voluntary disclosure of privileged material in the context of a government investigation, where targets are frequently called upon to cooperate and provide potentially incriminating information gleaned in the course of their own internal investigations.

[1071] *Cavallaro v. United States*, 284 F.3d 236, 246–47 (1st Cir. 2002) ("Generally, disclosing attorney-client communications to a third party undermines the privilege."); *Roe v. Catholic Health Initiatives Colorado*, 281 F.R.D. 632, 636 (D. Colo. 2012) ("disclosing attorney-client communications to a third-party results in a waiver of the attorney-client privilege."); *Allied Irish Banks v. Bank of Am., N.A.*, 240 F.R.D. 96, 104 (S.D.N.Y. 2007) ("Courts routinely find waiver where otherwise attorney-client privileged materials are shared with outsiders to whom privileged materials were shown unnecessarily.").

which outside counsel should be engaged. "Regular" outside counsel, that is, counsel that handles corporate and compliance matters for the company, may be appropriate in certain circumstances. Except in cases where the company has regular investigation counsel that is deemed to be independent and capable of objectively conducting an appropriately scoped investigation, regular counsel may not be appropriate for a particular investigation whether because counsel lacks expertise or has potential conflicts (for instance, the investigation centers on or touches on matters outside counsel may have been involved with), and might not be viewed as sufficiently independent to lead a more significant or sensitive investigation. In such cases, the company must engage truly independent counsel. When allegations involve fraud or other misconduct by senior management, employees or officers, or board members, fully independent outside counsel should be engaged, even if doing so is more costly or onerous. Likewise, in relation to pending shareholder or derivative litigation, or if the company is subject of a government investigation, lawyers conducting the investigation must be truly independent and unbiased. At a minimum, a Board's investigation will naturally stand a greater chance of being successful, and will likely be afforded greater weight by government regulators, if outside counsel is not only independent,[1072] but is experienced in conducting internal investigations, well-versed in spotting criminal behavior or telltale signs of private misconduct, and knowledgeable in the particular area being investigated.

Ultimately, the Board must be independent when conducting, or directing the conduct of, an internal investigation – free from divided loyalties or conflicts of interest, real or perceived. The Board also has a duty conduct the investigation with the level of care that a reasonable person would exercise in like circumstances.[1073]

[1072] .

[1073] See In re Lemington Home for Aged, 659 F.3d 282, 290 (3d Cir. 2011). See also Higgins v. N.Y. Stock Exch., Inc., 10 Misc. 3d 257, 285, 806 N.Y.S.2d 339, 362 (N.Y. Sup. Ct. 2005) ("[D]irectors may be liable to shareholders for failing reasonably to obtain material information or to make a reasonable inquiry into

V. *HOW* TO STRUCTURE AND CONDUCT A "CREDIBLE" INVESTIGATION

A Board-directed investigation, including its scope, proposed methodology (including selection of counsel), and execution, must be credible. Otherwise, a company will have wasted precious time and resources on an evaluation of limited utility. The investigation must inspire confidence and mitigate skepticism (principally among third parties such as government regulators, courts or potential private litigants) about the manner in which the investigation was conducted and factual findings formulated. Because there is no script, each investigation will differ based on its particular facts and circumstances. When structuring and conducting an investigation, Boards and Audit Committees alike should ensure that it is: (i) independent and objective; (ii) prompt and timely; (iii) prudent and careful; (iv) appropriately scoped, yet always flexible; and (v) thorough, comprehensive and accurate.

A. Independent and Objective

To ensure independence and objectivity, an investigation must be conducted by an individual or body that is not constrained in the search for truth. The investigation must be viewed as unencumbered so that potentially unfavorable facts are scrutinized. Board-driven or -directed investigations have an air of objectivity. But, the Board itself should typically not *conduct* the investigation. Appropriate outside counsel should be selected to conduct the investigation. Whether selected counsel is the company's usual outside counsel or an entirely new firm will depend on the facts of each case.

What the company's law firm of first resort offers in terms of economic benefit by virtue of its ability to leverage institutional knowledge and avoid the costs or expense attendant with bringing in new counsel may be outweighed by optics that the investigation

---

material matters.") (internal quotation marks and citation omitted); *Stockbridge v. Gemini Air Cargo, Inc.*, 269 Va. 609, 620, 611 S.E. 2d 600, 606 (2005) ("A failure to make reasonable inquiry or inadequate monitoring by a director may constitute a breach of duty." (citation omitted))

lacks the requisite independence and objectivity. The reality is a
law firm that has been engaged previously or on an ongoing basis
with the company may have the same types of affinity and
closeness to the company and its officers that would militate
against entrusting the investigation to such counsel. On the other
hand, the benefits of using a new firm are the immediate air of
objectivity that comes from not having the trappings of prior
business relationships with the company and senior executives of
the company.

B.   Prompt and Timely

The company's initial response will also affect the integrity of the
investigation. The investigation must commence promptly after a
credible allegation of potential wrongdoing to avoid any
appearance that the company failed to appreciate the gravity of the
allegations.

C.   Prudent and Careful

Boards directing investigations that are short-fused and involve
matters of substantial sensitivity should be wary of developing
impaired "vision," that is, a myopic mentality focused on prompt
"conclusion" rather than the thoughtful and prudent conduct of the
investigation. Missteps during the investigation can have far-
reaching implications. The Board, as well as counsel conducting
the investigation, should be ever vigilant in protecting privileged
information and work product. Steps must be taken at the outset to
protect information not only from spoliation but from waiver of a
privilege, confidentiality, or protection through inadvertent
disclosure. There must be a clear plan for preserving relevant
documents – both hard copy and electronically stored information
("ESI") – and protecting against spoliation, as courts and
enforcement agencies may impose steep fines or other
consequences for a failure to preserve evidence.[1074] Care should be

---

[1074] *See, e.g., Zubulake v. UBS Warburg LLC*, 220 F.R.D. 212, 217 (S.D.N.Y.
2003) (ruling, with respect to back up tapes with computer files and deleted emails
"[w]hile a litigant is under no duty to keep or retain every document in its
possession . . . it is under a duty to preserve what it knows, or reasonably should

taken to promptly preserve all potentially relevant records by, first, issuance of a litigation hold directive to all custodians of such records. Additionally, the Board should ensure that the company's IT point of contact is notified promptly of the need to preserve all ESI from being purged, either intentionally through the company's auto-delete functionality or inadvertently by an unsuspecting or absentminded custodian.

There must also be clear steps communicated to and understood by all involved directed to protecting the confidentiality and privileged nature of any communications or work product. At the outset of any witness interview, for instance, *Upjohn* warnings[1075] should be given.

This involves warning any employees of the company that counsel represents the company or organization only, and that counsel does not represent the employee or other party subject to the interview.[1076] Such a warning not only clarifies the nature of

---

know, is relevant in the action, is reasonably calculated to lead to the discovery of admissible evidence, is reasonably likely to be requested during discovery and/or is the subject of a pending discovery request.") (citation omitted); *see also Genger v. TR Inv'rs, LLC*, 26 A.3d 180, 192 (Del. 2011) (affirming trial court's imposition of sanctions of $3.2 million in fees when "trial court rested its spoliation and contempt findings on more specific and narrow factual grounds— that Genger, despite knowing he had a duty to preserve documents, intentionally took affirmative actions to destroy several relevant documents on his work computer."); In the Matter of Fresenius Medical Care AG & Co. KGaA, Exchange Act Release No. 85468, ¶ 12 (March 29, 2019) (explaining that numerous documents were falsified and destroyed, and that it intensified once the company's internal investigation into bribery allegations began).

[1075] *Upjohn Co. v. United States*, 449 U.S. 383, 394 (1981). Despite being a rote staple of any internal investigation, the *Upjohn* warning remains a critical component of any witness interview to ensure the witness being interviewed fully understands counsel's role at the interview, who (or what) is the client (in this scenario, either the Board, or the special committee, or audit committee) and who (or what) owns the privilege attaching to the communications during that interview.

[1076] *See, e.g., United States v. Connolly*, No. 1:16-CR-00370 (CM), 2018 WL 2411216, at *9 n.4 (S.D.N.Y. May 15, 2018) (describing the *Upjohn* warning as "[t]he notice an attorney (in-house or outside counsel) provides a company

counsel's representation, but also solidifies and creates a record to establish privilege, namely, it establishes that any witness interviews are for the purpose of and in furtherance of providing legal advice to the company.[1077] In order to ensure the broadest possible work product protection,[1078] witness interview memos should not be a verbatim recitation of the interview, but rather a summary with attorney notes, perceptions, and opinions interspersed throughout.[1079] And, there must be concerted efforts made in conjunction with the human resources and other corporate departments to ensure any known or suspected whistleblower does not become the subject of any actual or perceived retaliation.[1080]

---

employee to inform her that the attorney represents only the company and not the employee individually").

[1077] See *Sandra T.E. v. S. Berwyn Sch. Dist. 100*, 600 F.3d 612, 622 (7th Cir. 2010); *Buck v. Indian Mountain Sch.*, No. 3:15-CV-00123 (JBA), 2017 WL 421648, at *7 (D. Conn. Jan. 31, 2017); *Lerman v. Turner*, No. 1:10-CV-02169, 2011 WL 62124, at *7 (N.D. Ill. Jan. 6, 2011), *objections overruled*, 2011 WL 494623 (N.D. Ill. Feb. 4, 2011)..

[1078] There are necessarily two types of work product entitled to protection: (1) fact work product, and (2) opinion work product. "Fact" work product refers to documents containing factual information and, while protected, can be discoverable upon a showing of "substantial need." *See* Fed. R. Civ. P. 26(b)(3). "Opinion" work product is that which contains an attorney's opinions, legal analysis, and mental impressions and, for that reason, enjoys near absolute protection from disclosure.

[1079] Indeed, any written interview memo that is prepared should conspicuously note that it is not a verbatim recitation but rather a summary that contains attorney mental impressions and opinions. *See United States ex rel. Landis v. Tailwind Sports Corp.*, 303 F.R.D. 419, 425 (D.D.C. 2014) ("Other courts in this district have held substantially verbatim witness statements contained in interview memoranda that have not been 'sharply focused or weeded' by an attorney to be 'fact' rather than 'opinion' work-product." (citations omitted)).

[1080] This is due to the several federal and state statutory provisions that give rise to liability against companies that take adverse employment action against a whistleblower. *See, e.g.*, 31 U.S.C. § 3730(h) (False Claims Act protection and remedy for whistleblower experiencing retaliation by company); 18 U.S.C. § 1514A (anti-retaliation provisions of Sarbanes-Oxley Act); 15 U.S.C. § 78u-6 (same but for Dodd-Frank Act); 29 U.S.C. § 218c (same but for Affordable Care Act); 10 U.S.C. § 2409 (providing whistleblower protections to employees of Department of Defense contractors and subcontractors); N.Y. Lab. Law § 740

D.   Appropriately Scoped and Flexible

At the outset, the investigation work plan must also be appropriately scoped based on the circumstances of the alleged wrongdoing, but remain flexible throughout in order to adjust, adapt and address new information and allegations that may come to light during the course of the investigation. The Board should anticipate and embrace that its work plan, in execution, will not be static, but rather dynamic in order to account for new or unanticipated facts and information. "Scope" as defined for each investigation necessarily considers the nature and severity of the allegations at issue. Therefore, the Board must define the scope and subject matter of the investigation but not define it too narrowly (in which case, facts or information germane to the investigation may be overlooked), nor too broadly (in which case, the investigation may become obtrusive or cost prohibitive).

Where the Board delegates authority to an independent Board committee or the Audit Committee, it should do so by formal resolution or other formal writing. The written delegation becomes the charter from which the investigating body's authority flows. It must be crystal clear during the course of any investigation that the body conducting the investigation has the full authority of the Board, which would include the power to exact some punitive measures (such as suspension or termination, or at least the power to make the recommendation for such action). Note, however, that the Board, or the Board committee acting on a proper and formal delegation of authority, should retain flexibility to redefine the contours of the scope of work as facts develop and the Board's or committee's understanding of the facts crystallizes. In addition to formalizing in writing the authority or delegation of authority to act, a detailed **work plan** which provides a road map for the investigation should be prepared by counsel for the Board's consideration and approval.

(McKinney) (providing whistleblower protection to employees who make disclosures to a public body regarding dangers to public health and safety).

E.   Thorough, Comprehensive and Accurate

The investigation must obviously be sufficiently thorough to either substantiate or refute the actual allegations of wrongdoing. It must be sufficiently comprehensive to address all potential allegations and not be viewed as artificially limited. Thus, as stated above, the work plan should serve as a road map, at least initially, defining the alleged misconduct or wrongdoing that serves as the trigger for the investigation, the context in which that allegation arose, and the scope of the proposed investigation including but not limited to what documents or document categories will be gathered and what individuals will need to be interviewed. If wrongdoing is discovered, the investigation must identify what went wrong, that is, any failures of internal controls or the compliance program. The investigation must lend itself to identifying appropriate remedial and/or disciplinary action, thereby providing the company an opportunity to strengthen its internal controls and compliance program. The findings and recommendations will need to be internally reported, either through oral presentation or by written report.

Consideration must also be given to whether any findings are the subject of SEC public disclosure (a question on which each company should seek guidance from its own disclosure counsel). Finally, the Board will need to examine any self-reporting to government regulators which, if constructed and executed correctly, will go far as a show of good faith cooperation and will serve as a basis to mitigate civil liability or criminal punishment.[1081] Any report should be based on sound and supportable factual findings. Any dissonance between information

---

[1081] Further below, we discuss –the DOJ Memorandum of September 2015 by then-Deputy Attorney General Sally Quillian Yates, *Individual Accountability for Corporate Wrongdoing* (the "Yates Memo"). The Yates Memo was said to echo and reaffirm DOJ's best practices guidance memorialized in the U.S. Attorney's Manual that governs criminal and civil corporate investigations, but in reality it went beyond longstanding practice by seeking to "up the ante" on corporate entities as set forth in "six key steps" or guiding principles. In November 2018, DOJ updated some of the principles reflected in the Yates Memo, particularly the policy on cooperation credit in criminal and civil enforcement matters.

and factual findings will call into question the credibility of an investigation, thereby undermining its success.

VI.   AUDIT COMMITTEE OVERSIGHT AND INVESTIGATIVE RESPONSIBILITIES

Audit Committees also have a critical role where investigations involve financial or other matters within the audit committee's province. Audit Committees are typically responsible for, among other things, receiving and investigating complaints (including whistle-blower complaints) of wrongdoing, including financial fraud involving auditing, accounting or internal controls issues.[1082] Section 301 of the Act, and now Dodd-Frank[1083] increased incentives for and protection of whistle-blowers to report potential financial misconduct.

In the wake of Dodd-Frank,[1084] Audit Committees find themselves tasked with oversight and management of an increasing number of internal investigations.[1085] Audit committee investigations may be directed to examining suspected financial or accounting improprieties, FCPA bribery or other improper payment issues, financial crimes (embezzlement or theft), practices related to certain products or services offered by the company, or conflict or

---

[1082] 15 U.S.C. § 78j-1(m)(4) (2006) (also requiring that audit committees be empowered to retain independent counsel or experts to fulfill such duties).

[1083] *See* 15 U.S.C. §§ 78u-6, 78u-7.

[1084] 15 U.S.C. § 78u-6.

[1085] *See* 17 C.F.R. §§ 240.21F-1-240.21F-17, regulations promulgated under Dodd-Frank which greatly enhance incentives for whistleblowers to uncover a company's violation of federal securities laws and report such wrongdoing to the SEC. *See also* 15 U.S.C. § 78u-6 (same). On July 20, 2018, the SEC proposed for public comment several amendments to the Dodd-Frank whistleblower regulations. Whistleblower Program Rules, 83 Fed. Reg. 34702-01 (proposed July 20, 2018) (to be codified at 17 C.F.R, pts. 240 and 249). Among other things, the amendments would clarify that the SEC may pay whistleblower awards when a company enters into a deferred-prosecution agreement or non-prosecution agreement. The amendments would also provide the SEC additional flexibility to adjust upward or downward exceedingly large or small whistleblower awards. *See id.* at 34703-05. As of the date of publication of this chapter, the public comment period had closed but the final rule had not been published

related party transactions. Like Board-directed investigations, Audit Committee directed investigations must be prompt and timely and have all other indicia of a credible and comprehensive investigation in order to be successful. And, as with Boards, questions about who conducts the investigation (usual outside counsel or independent counsel), measures to preserve data, ensuring the investigation is appropriately scoped, protection of privileged communications and work product, recommending appropriate remedial or corrective action and making a recommendation on self-reporting to the government drive Audit Committee considerations as well.

At the conclusion of an investigation, typically a report (or reporting) of the findings is made. The Board will then need to determine whether to disclose the findings, or the report itself, outside the company. That assessment necessarily turns, at least in part, on whether disclosure is mandatory or voluntary and, if voluntary, the benefit to the company from disclosure.

Disclosure may be mandatory in cases where, for instance, a publicly held company must disclose information that is deemed "material," that is, information the disclosure of which would make the company's public filings with the SEC not misleading.[1086] Whether such disclosure is mandatory is a question that is not resolved here, but which should be raised with the Company's SEC disclosure counsel.

Even if not mandatory, disclosure of a report and its findings may be beneficial and advisable under certain circumstances. Aside from enabling the company to control the timing and placement of the information contained in the report, the Board may decide that it is beneficial to disclose a report and its findings to government authorities as a demonstration of good faith in order to obtain credit for this cooperation. Government agencies, whether the SEC, DOJ, the Commodity Futures Trading Commission ("CFTC"), CFPB, or others, encourage voluntary disclosures of

---

[1086] See generally 15 U.S.C. § 78j(b); 17 C.F.R. § 240.10b-5.

misconduct.[1087] Deputy Attorney General Rod Rosenstein, on May 9, 2018, announced a new policy to encourage cooperation among DOJ components and other enforcement agencies when imposing multiple penalties for the same conduct. When assessing whether multiple penalties are necessary to achieve justice, DOJ will, among other factors, consider the timeliness and adequacy of a company's disclosures to DOJ.[1088] The question then becomes what must be disclosed in order to be eligible for cooperation credit.

The Yates Memo, as modestly modified by the Trump Administration, remains DOJ's standing written guidance on investigating and prosecuting individuals involved in alleged corporate wrongdoing. It set forth six guiding principles.[1089] Of those, the first principle is the most relevant and significant to this analysis. It states:

*"To be eligible for **any** cooperation credit, corporations must provide the Department all relevant facts about the individuals involved in corporate misconduct."* (Emphasis in original).[1090]

A corporation that fails to disclose all relevant facts, or "declines" to learn of all relevant facts, would not be eligible for cooperation

---

[1087] *See, e.g.*, Dep't. of Justice, U.S. Attorney's Manual, § 9-47.120 (FCPA Corporate Enforcement Policy) (updated March 2019), *available at* https://www.justice.gov/usam/usam-9-47000-foreign-corrupt-practices-act-1977#9-47.120. The DOJ now applies a presumption that, absent aggravating circumstances such as executive management involvement or the accrual of significant profit from the wrongdoing, it will resolve a company's FCPA case by declining to prosecute if the company voluntarily discloses misconduct, fully cooperates, and timely and appropriately remediates. *Id.*

[1088] Deputy Attorney General Rod J. Rosenstein, Remarks to the New York City Bar White-collar Crime Institute (May 9, 2018), *available at* https://www.justice.gov/opa/speech/deputy-attorney-general-rod-rosenstein-delivers-remarks-new-york-city-bar-white-collar.

[1089] Memorandum from Deputy Attorney General Sally Quillian Yates to all United States Attorneys (Sept. 9, 2015), *available at* https://www.justice.gov/dag/file/769036/download.

[1090] *Id.* at 3.

credit.[1091] The guidance has impacted the manner in which internal investigations are conducted, from defining the scope of an investigation, to prioritizing and approaching witnesses and fact-gathering efforts, to preparing self-disclosures.

Assistant Attorney General Caldwell, speaking at the Global Investigations Review Conference in New York shortly after the Yates Memo, sought to provide clarification on disclosing corporate misconduct to the government: "Companies cannot just disclose facts relating to general corporate misconduct and withhold facts about the responsible individuals. And internal investigations cannot end with a conclusion of corporate liability, while stopping short of identifying those who committed the criminal conduct."[1092]

Questions remain regarding how far must an entity go in its effort to collect "all relevant facts" and whether certain actions taken by an entity (provision of separate counsel for certain employees, for instance) which may hamper the government's collection of facts and testimony, will negatively affect an entity's ability to obtain cooperation credit under the DOJ's internal guidelines. Further, DOJ's revised FCPA Corporate Enforcement Policy announced November 29, 2017, also adds some helpful gloss to the meaning of "full cooperation":

- "[D]isclosure on a timely basis of all facts relevant to the wrongdoing at issue, including: all relevant facts gathered during a company's independent investigation; attribution of facts to specific sources where such attribution does not violate the attorney-client privilege, rather than a general narrative of the facts; timely updates on a company's internal investigation, including but not limited to rolling

---

[1091] *Id.*

[1092] Dept. of Justice, Assistant Attorney General Leslie R. Caldwell Delivers Remarks at the Second Annual Global Investigations Review Conference, https://www.justice.gov/opa/speech/assistant-attorney-general-leslie-r-caldwell-delivers-remarks-second-annual-global-0 (last visited Feb. 28, 2017).

disclosures of information; all facts related to involvement in the criminal activity by the company's officers, employees, or agents; and all facts known or that become known to the company regarding potential criminal conduct by all third-party companies (including their officers, employees, or agents);

- Proactive cooperation, rather than reactive; that is, the company must timely disclose facts that are relevant to the investigation, even when not specifically asked to do so, and, where the company is or should be aware of opportunities for the Department to obtain relevant evidence not in the company's possession and not otherwise known to the Department, it must identify those opportunities to the Department;

- Timely preservation, collection, and disclosure of relevant documents and information relating to their provenance, including (a) disclosure of overseas documents, the locations in which such documents were found, and who found the documents, (b) facilitation of third-party production of documents, and (c) where requested and appropriate, provision of translations of relevant documents in foreign languages;

- Where requested, de-confliction of witness interviews and other investigative steps that a company intends to take as part of its internal investigation with steps that the Department intends to take as part of its investigation; and

- Where requested, making available for interviews by the Department those company officers and employees who possess relevant information; this includes, where appropriate and possible, officers, employees, and agents located overseas as well as former officers and employees (subject to the individuals' Fifth

Amendment rights), and, where possible, the facilitation of third-party production of witnesses."[1093]

More recently, in November 2018, DOJ announced revisions to its policy on cooperation credit by requiring a company to identify every individual who was "substantially involved in or responsible for the criminal misconduct," as opposed to every individual involved in the misconduct.[1094] According to then Deputy Attorney General Rosenstein, this change responded to "concerns raised about the inefficiency of requiring companies to identify every employee involved regardless of relative culpability," and the need to clarify that "investigations should not be delayed merely to collect information about individuals whose involvement was not substantial, and who are not likely to be prosecuted."[1095]

Furthermore, DOJ announced that it would depart from an "all or nothing" approach to cooperation credit in civil cases, noting that its experience had found that approach to be counterproductive and DOJ attorneys need flexibility to accept settlements that remedy the harm and deter future harm in order to move on to other matters.[1096] As a preliminary matter, "a company must identify all wrongdoing by senior officials, including members of senior management or the board of directors, if it wants to earn any credit

---

[1093] Dep't. of Justice, U.S. Attorney's Manual, § 9-47.120 (FCPA Corporate Enforcement Policy) (updated November 2017), *available at* https://www.justice.gov/usam/usam-9-47000-foreign-corrupt-practices-act-1977#9-47.120.

[1094] *See* Deputy Attorney General Rod J. Rosenstein, Remarks at the American Conference Institute's 35th International Conference on the Foreign Corrupt Practices Act (Nov. 29, 2018), *available at* https://www.justice.gov/opa/speech/deputy-attorney-general-rod-j-rosenstein-delivers-remarks-american-conference-institute-0.

[1095] *Id. See also* U.S. Attorney's Manual, § 4-3.100(2) (updated Nov. 2018).

[1096] Deputy Attorney General Rod J. Rosenstein, Remarks at the American Conference Institute's 35th International Conference on the Foreign Corrupt Practices Act (Nov. 29, 2018), *available at* https://www.justice.gov/opa/speech/deputy-attorney-general-rod-j-rosenstein-delivers-remarks-american-conference-institute-0.

for cooperating in a civil case."[1097] But when a company honestly and meaningfully assist's a government's investigation, civil attorneys now have the discretion to offer some cooperation credit even if the company does not qualify for maximum credit.[1098] This situation might arise, for example, if a company made voluntary disclosures that provide valuable assistance yet is unwilling to stipulate about the culpability of non-executive employees.[1099]

Although DOJ policy proclaims, and DOJ officials have repeatedly affirmed, that DOJ will not seek a waiver of the attorney-client privilege or work product protections as a condition of obtaining cooperation credit,[1100] such a position would appear to be at odds with the notion that all relevant facts regarding individual accountability and culpability must be disclosed and is a flashback to the Thompson Memo[1101] before relevant portions were rejected

---

[1097] *Id.*

[1098] *Id.*

[1099] *Id.*

[1100] *See, e.g.* Dep't of Justice, U.S. Attorney's Manual, § 9-28.710 (updated August 2008); Richard Smith, Caldwell Remarks Clarify Yates Memo's Purpose, https://www.law360.com/corporate/articles/708596/caldwell-remarks-clarify-yates-memo-s-purpose (last visited February 28, 2017) ("It is important to note that Caldwell said the memo did not change the DOJ's policy on attorney-client privilege or work product protection and the DOJ would not ask companies to waive privilege to receive cooperation credit, consistent with existing DOJ policy.")

[1101] *See* Memorandum from Larry D. Thompson, Deputy Attorney General, on Principles of Federal Prosecution of Business Organizations to Heads of Department Components and United States Attorneys (Jan. 20, 2003). The Thompson Memo's aggressive pursuit of privilege disclosures was tempered with the McNulty Memorandum and the Filip Memorandum, both of which made clear that cooperation credit would be based on disclosure of "relevant facts" and not on waiver of any privilege or work product protection. *See also* Stewart Bishop, 'Yates Memo' Author Defends Policy, Says Shift is in Effect, Law360 (May 10, 2016), https://www.law360.com/articles/794679/yates-memo-author-defends-policy-says-shift-is-in-effect ("'I think we may see, although the Yates Memo says you are not actually required to waive the attorney-client privilege to satisfy the Yates Memo, the practical impact of how you give information to the government is really, at the end of the day, going to require in many instances that you waive privilege," said Cole, a former deputy attorney general.'").

as an unconstitutional overreach by prosecutors.[1102] The risk of disclosing the report, beyond merely communicating the factual findings themselves is that such voluntary disclosure of arguably privileged information may be deemed to be a complete, subject matter waiver privilege, that is, a waiver of privilege as to any documents concerning the same subject matter of the report.[1103] Indeed, the selective waiver theory has been rejected by a majority of federal circuits.[1104]

All this to say that Boards will need to weigh the benefits of disclosure and obtaining cooperation credit against the drawbacks associated with a potential subject matter waiver, not to mention public airing of potentially criminal misconduct or, at a minimum, embarrassing facts.

A company's calculus, however, must constantly evolve. In addition to the new DOJ policies discussed above, the Trump Administration has also scaled back enforcement activity at the CFPB and pursued a more collaborative approach, seeking to negotiate with companies to settle disputes and only pursuing

---

[1102] See U.S. v. Stein, et al, 435 F. Supp. 2d 330 (S.D.N.Y. 2006) (holding portion of Thompson Memo unconstitutional insofar as it compelled prosecutors to violate individuals' constitutional right to counsel; KPMG's decision to stop advancing legal fees for its "uncooperative" employees who had been indicted was the direct result of unconstitutional government pressure), aff'd U.S. v. Stein, 541 F.3d 130 (2d Cir. 2008).

[1103] See, e.g., In re Grand Jury Proceedings, 219 F.3d 175, 183 (2d Cir. 2000) ("This type of waiver is also known as subject-matter waiver. As explained in Wigmore, '[t]he client's offer of his own or the attorney's testimony as to a specific communication to the attorney is a waiver as to all other communications to the attorney on the same matter.' 8 J. Wigmore, Evidence § 2327, at 638 (McNaughton ed., 1961).").

[1104] See, e.g., Permian Corp. v. U.S., 665 F.2d 1214, 1219-22 (D.C. Cir. 1981); U.S. v. Massachusetts Institute of Technology, 129 F.3d 681, 685-86 (1st Cir. 1997); Westinghouse Elec. Corp. v. Republic of Philippines, 951 F.2d 1414, 1424-27 (3d Cir. 1991); In re Martin Marietta Corp., 856 F.2d 619, 623 (4th Cir. 1988); Columbia/HCA Healthcare Corp. Billing Practices Litigation, 293 F.3d 289, 294– 310 (6th Cir. 2002); In re Pacific Pictures Corp., 679 F.3d 1121, 112728 (9th Cir. 2012); In re Qwest Communications Intern. Inc., 450 F.3d 1179, 1194 (10th Cir. 2006).

litigation as a last resort.[1105] This approach followed the implementation of a months-long pause in enforcement activity, and it is consistent with the views of longtime critics of the CFPB who have argued it is overly bureaucratic, too powerful, not subject to appropriate oversight and outside the bounds of constitutional checks and balances.[1106] Indeed, on April, 2, 2018, Acting Director Mick Mulvaney recommended in the CFPB's Semi-Annual Report that Congress adopt statutory changes to Dodd-Frank that would further circumscribe the CFPB's authority and make it more accountable to Congress.[1107] The current director of the CFPB has described enforcement as a "more deliberate tool in the [CFPB's] toolkit" that she hopes will be utilized less frequently.[1108]

[1105] *See, e.g.*, Yuka Hayashi, "CFPB Enforcement Is Back—With a Softer Touch," Wall Street Journal (July 26, 2018); Mick Mulvaney, "The CFPB Has Pushed its Last Envelope," Wall Street Journal (Jan. 23, 2018).

[1106] Unlike other regulatory bodies, for instance, Congress does not set the Bureau's budget, which is instead funded through transfers from the Federal Reserve. In October 2016, in *PHH Corp. v. CFPB*, the D.C. Circuit Court of Appeals ruled that the Bureau's structure was unconstitutional - that it was a violation of Article II for the Bureau to lack the "critical check" of presidential control or the "substitute check" of a multi-member governance structure necessary to protect individual liberty against "arbitrary decision-making and abuse of power." The court remedied this constitutional defect by severing the removal-only-for-cause provision from the Dodd-Frank Act. *See PHH Corporation v. CFPB*, No. 15-1177, (D.C. Cir. Oct. 11, 2016). The CFPB petitioned for an en banc rehearing of the decision and the court had invited the DOJ to state its position. In a filing made prior to President Trump taking office, DOJ supported the CFPB's petition. After President Trump's inauguration, however, DOJ indicated it planned to file an amicus brief, which the DC Circuit permitted to be filed on or before March 17, 2017.

[1107] Press Release, "CFPB Issues Semi-Annual Report: Acting Director Mulvaney Recommends Statutory Changes in His First Report to Congress" (April, 2, 2018), *available at* https://www.consumerfinance.gov/about-us/newsroom/cfpb-issues-semi-annual-report/ (recommending that Congress (1) fund CFPB through annual appropriations; (2) require Congress to approve significant regulations; (3) reduce the independence of the Director of the CFPB by making him answer to the President; (4) create an inspector general for the CFPB).

[1108] Kathleen L. Kraninger, Director, Consumer Financial Protection Bureau, Speech at the Bipartisan Policy Center (Apr. 17, 2019), available at

The takeaway, then, is that while certain policy initiatives may be shifting, and certain agencies may be more lenient and cooperative than under the prior Administration, the Trump Administration's overall enforcement posture is likely to remain aggressive. Recent policy announcements from the Department of Justice confirm as much. And, compliance and investigative best practices transcend politics and political agendas because they have (or are intended to have) an altruistic focus of striving for what truly serves the company's best interests in being a lawful, compliant corporate citizen. Regardless of what the future may hold, Boards and Audit Committees should remain vigilant and diligent in regularly examining and assessing internal controls and the efficacy of compliance programs and, when credible allegations are raised, identifying, investigating and promptly addressing potential misconduct within a company.

VII.   CONCLUSION

Best practices for Board and Audit Committees are not likely to become more forgiving. Boards and Audit Committees will continue to have heightened responsibilities to proactively identify ways for companies to navigate the perils and pitfalls of conducting business in a global economy. While merely scratching the surface in this chapter, the issues – both proactive and reactive – are profound for companies. Adhering to the guidance in this chapter provides a starting point for any company... but *only* a starting point. What risk mitigation efforts are appropriate, and what investigative contours should be followed, are entirely dependent on the particular dynamic and need of each company.

---

https://www.consumerfinance.gov/about-us/newsroom/kathleen-kraninger-director-consumer-financial-protection-bureau-bipartisan-policy-center-speech/.

Chapter 22

Public Relations and Media:
Media Relations is the Court of Public Opinion

By David Beck and Michelle Metzger[1109]

*"A lie gets halfway around the world before the truth has a chance
to get its pants on" - Winston Churchill*

So – you've gotten a civil investigative demand, or an actual
subpoena, or in some less formal way, you have been alerted that
the government is investigating your company. You have acted
quickly to put a legal hold in place; to identify the internal and
external investigative resources you need to respond, including
experienced defense counsel, and set that process in motion.
You've briefed the key executives and (if warranted) the
appropriate members of the Board on the existence of the
investigation and the company's plans for a response.

Then you get the call from a reporter. She also has learned of the
investigation, or at least knows that something is going on and
wants your response to several rather unflattering questions for the
story that is slated for tonight's evening news.

Reporters are not like you and me. Very few of them went to law
school and almost none of them studied the very detailed laws and
rules that apply to the industry you represent. They typically are
not doctors, nurses, engineers or technical gurus. They tell stories
for a living. And the more sensational, the story the more it garners
rewards for the teller from readers, viewers and followers.

[1109] David Beck, principal at the Law Offices of David Beck, PLLC, is a
healthcare lawyer and mediator who has served as Chief Legal Officer and as
Chief Ethics and Compliance Officer for several large healthcare providers, and
Michelle Metzger serves as the Senior Director of Communications for Reliant
Rehabilitation and has over 25 years in crisis and traditional public relations
including qui tam, class action and false claims litigation.

Today, many reporters have not even gone to journalism school, much less earned a degree in the field, so time-honored journalistic traditions - embargoed news, objectivity, having at least two sources for a story, and even basic fact checking - have gone by the wayside. Independent bloggers and literally anyone with a camera on their smartphone or an itchy Twitter finger can post stories with their own spin on the facts. Or, things can get really strange, and your company can be enmeshed in completely false stories, popularly known as "fake news," that are created for profit, for political gain - or specifically to harm your company - and circulated on social media where they convince many, regardless of their (at best) remote relationship to the truth.

For those of us still laboring under the illusion that the truth is a powerful shield, research suggesting that the public puts more credibility in fake news than it does in accurate, curated stories comes as an unwelcome wake up call.[1110] In today's newsrooms, in small third world towns where making up stories to attract viewers and "clicks" on the web is seen as a good employment option, and among the mass of people "doing their own research" and sharing it loudly with others, there is tremendous pressure to get a story first versus getting a story right. – or simply in casting a story in the worst and therefore most "click attractive" light. These hard truths do not work in your favor.

There is, of course, nothing bad about telling a good story, and telling it well. Indeed, one trait of a great trial lawyer is the ability to tell the most compelling, believable story that fits the evidence. As general counsel of a company facing a government investigation, that is precisely the story you need to tell to the government investigators – and if you do not convince them, to the judge or the jury. When a reporter is calling, or a Twitter storm is

---

[1110] See Interview with Craig Silverman of Buzzfeed News, http://www.npr.org/2016/12/14/505547295/fake-news-expert-on-how-false-stories-spread-and-why-people-believe-them. More recently, research has determined that inaccurate information diffuses more rapidly and has a deeper impact than the truth. *Vosoughi, S., Roy, D., & Aral, S. (2018)* The spread of true and false news online. *Science, 359(6380),* 1146-1151. https://doi.org/10.1126/science.aap9559.

brewing with alleged unlawful acts by your client at its heart, try to see it as an opportunity to start getting at least the theme of that story out there. But keep in mind that the reporter may not feel the same need you do to tell a story that is consistent with the facts and evidence. Even worse, those pushing the unfavorable narrative may be intentionally seeking to harm your client.

It is important to keep in mind that what you say in response to an investigation, as well as how you say it, can also end up as evidence in its own right. And, of course, your defense counsel should weigh in on the risks of various possible responses to media inquiries, so that your efforts to tell your story do not destroy any needed privileges or otherwise help that story progress to an unhappy ending for you and your company.

It is equally important to keep an open mind about all crisis communications advice. Simply put, it has a short shelf life these days. The sheer amount of information that is available is staggering – indeed, more than 90% of the data in the world as of 2018 was generated since 2016, and more than 2.5 quintillion (that is, 2.5 followed by 17 zeroes) bytes of data are created every day.[1111] Developments in public expectations around corporate social responsibility and the myriad ways in which crisis communication may evolve to embrace artificial intelligence and virtual reality are moving at a similar pace, so General Counsel would be wise to devote time and energy to implementing proactive strategies and to building up reserve accounts of trust for their clients to draw upon when needed,

I.   WHAT MAKES A GREAT STORY?

Great storytellers understand that all stories fall within the parameters of seven basic plots - Overcoming the Monster, Rags to Riches, The Quest, Voyage and Return, Comedy, Tragedy, and Rebirth. Becoming aware of the arc of these seven basic storylines will help you understand how a journalist – trained or citizen –

[1111] https://www.forbes.com/sites/bernardmarr/2018/05/21/how-much-data-do-we-create-every-day-the-mind-blowing-stats-everyone-should-read/#4d83f60f60ba.

crafts the elements of their story and how some stories can take off like wildfire, often with similar scorching results.

The "Overcoming a Monster" storyline has retained its uncanny ability to attract a large audience from *Beowulf* through the 1970s thriller *Jaws* to modern stories of suddenly accelerating cars, widespread outbreaks of exotic and deadly disease, or catastrophic oil leaks at the bottom of the Gulf of Mexico. Journalists know this and use it to attract viewers with catchphrases such as "reporting for you" and "on your side" that evoke the feeling that there is some "monster" out there from which only the righteous journalist can defend the unwitting victim, er, citizen. While a moment's reflection may lead one to suspect other motives that could include higher ratings, awards and fulfillment of career ambitions, journalists can and do claim that they are simply speaking out in the public's interests, and filling a key role as the alert watchdog to ensure that big, bad companies (like yours) are not taking advantage of the citizenry.

Remarkably, even those who generally are highly skeptical of the role of government and the accuracy or reliability of information from government bureaucrats tend to accept, at least initially, the idea that the government would not be investigating someone if there was not a serious problem. So when your company faces a government investigation, you automatically are assumed to be that big, bad monster doing harm to the average citizen, while the government is almost universally viewed as simply doing the essential job of protecting the taxpayers by investigating you. When the fact of a government investigation becomes the fodder for a tale of Overcoming the Monster, you need to decide quickly what counter narratives may be available to you based on the facts as you know them. Which story you choose to tell depend on many factors.

A. Who is the Audience for This Story?

Effective communication requires knowing your audience, so that you have the best chance of making "what they hear" bear as close a relationship as possible to "what you say." A moment's reflection makes it plain that the audience for a story about a government investigation of your company is quite broad, and includes:

- Members of your Board of Directors or other governing body

- Management

- Employees

- Shareholders

- The agenc(ies) investigating you

- Other state and federal enforcement agencies

- Private plaintiffs and plaintiffs' attorneys generally

- Auditors

- Insurers

- Lenders

- Competitors

- Customers and suppliers

Disclosure of the fact of the investigation, and perhaps details about the underlying facts, may be mandatory to some of these groups, even in the absence of media attention to an investigation. But if the story gets legs and is widely disseminated, it likely will attract at least some attention from each of these groups. Because investigations often are prelude to litigation, what you say and how and to whom you say it should be informed by a thoughtful analysis of what is and should remain privileged and how to best preserve that privilege. Your response to media inquiries also must be shaped based on the impact you want your communications to have on each of the audience groups listed above. That, in turn, will depend to a great extent on how you plan to respond to the underlying investigation.

B.   Court of Public Opinion

Right, wrong or indifferent, "monster" is the initial role in the storyline that will be assigned to you by the court of public opinion. It will be a nearly impossible challenge to be seen as anything other than the monster in this narrative.

Conventional wisdom urges companies in this position to "get ahead of the story" by laying out the facts, as if "transparency" will wash away any taint. To be sure, when it is clear that "mistakes were made,"[1112] and that the results of those mistakes either have been or will shortly be laid out in public detail, it may be that admission of error, sincere apology, and announcement of prompt, effective corrective action is your best option. But such an approach implicitly assumes that you have decided to settle litigation that may arise from the matter under investigation. And it may not achieve the goal of quieting the storm – your adversaries (who may include the investigating agency, a private citizen and his attorneys looking for a payday, a competitor, or simply someone with a different political agenda) may not be looking for the truth and an apology. They may be looking for your downfall, and not in the least deterred in that aim by your heartfelt *mea culpa.*[1113] Experts on social media have noted that modern social media attack campaigns draw inspiration from Saul Alinsky's 1971 Rules for Radicals – in which, among other things, he suggests withholding some damaging information to be released

---

[1112] A classical allusion to avoid expressing any responsibility for error, from President Ulysses S. Grant to modern bureaucrats and politicians. *See* http://www.npr.org/sections/thetwo-way/2013/05/14/183924858/its-true-mistakes-were-made-is-the-king-of-non-apologies.

[1113] For an excellent discussion of this reality and detailed ideas on how to respond, see Damage Control: The Essential Lessons of Crisis Management by Eric Dezenhall and John Weber, Prospecta, 2008.

after the target has made a public apology, with predictable impact on the effectiveness of the apology.

What if your internal review of the situation being investigated leads you to conclude that your company is not at fault, or at least committed no intentional wrongdoing? It still may be a prudent decision to seek a settlement of whatever is being investigated – assuming that, despite your firm conviction of innocence, you cannot convince the investigating agency to agree with you and let the matter drop. Perhaps settlement makes economic sense because it would cost a fraction of projected discovery, defense and distraction costs. Or you have decided that the reputational hit of the fact of the investigation on your customers and other vital constituencies is so great that you are willing to pay just to limit the pain from the matter. After all, while the investigation continues to be a matter of interest in the public sphere, even long-time supporters, such as institutional shareholders, may express their happiness at your reassurances that you have strong defenses and will vigorously challenge the allegations against you – but, at the same time, they also may tell you that they have sold their position and will invest in your company again after this all blows over.

If you choose to settle, be aware that it is standard operating procedure for many government agencies to issue a press release trumpeting the success of their efforts to protect the public – and, after several paragraphs restating in the worst possible light the allegations being settled and the unflagging determination of the government to crack down on all who would inflict such injuries on the public, there may even be a glancing reference in that press release to the effect that none of these claims were ever proven and that your company denies them all. Even with a settlement that includes no admission of wrongdoing, the public mind is likely to view any settlement, particularly if the dollar amount involved is high, as some type of admission of guilt.

Some investigation targets decide instead to go on offense and fight back against not only the investigating agency, but also against any resulting enforcement action, as well as carrying the fight to those seeking to condemn you in the court of public opinion. This is no doubt the road less traveled – for example, Department of Justice officials will tell you that very few of the hundreds of civil False Claims Act cases brought each year actually go to trial. If your company has the intestinal fortitude to choose this path, part of your strategy – consistent of course with your legal defense strategy – should be to create risk for your adversary by introducing new themes into the public discussion. For example, Dan Gilbert, founder and Chairman of the Board of Quicken Loans, which was sued by the government along with many others for allegedly making bad loans, recently said: "it would lack integrity and ring hollow to our 17,000 employees to pay some large, unwarranted settlement and admit things we did not do just because a young lawyer walks in with a business card that says 'DOJ' on it."[1114]

Another recent example of a company and an individual choosing to fight back with everything available while under government investigation involves billionaire businessman Mark Cuban. After successfully winning a court battle when he was accused of insider trading, Cuban has continued to carry the fight to the Securities and Exchange Commission, filing amicus briefs in at least three different Supreme Court cases involving the SEC. In these briefs, Cuban's attorneys have summarized succinctly the story he has consistently told in response to this investigation: "Mark Cuban is a successful businessman and investor who defeated an attempt by the [SEC] to sanction him as an 'insider trader' based on an incorrect legal theory and defective facts."[1115] This is not a subtle message. Nor is it one that audiences would have a hard time understanding.

Whichever course the facts and the inclinations of owners and management lead you to steer when an investigation makes the

---

[1114] http://www.wsj.com/articles/the-quicken-loans-signal-1482193421; this WSJ editorial also discusses some of the tangible points in its favor that Quicken is putting out into the public debate based on facts about its loan portfolio.

[1115] https://www.washingtonpost.com/news/business/wp/2016/03/16/mark-cuban-takes-his-grudge-against-the-sec-to-the-supreme-court/?utm_term=.b542afeb72b6.

news, the tools in this chapter can help you mitigate the damage done to your reputation - or at least help shed light on the great work your company actually does - to help offset the perceived injustice. Unlike a court of law, the court of public opinion does not require evidence, facts or expert witnesses. Instead of a judge or jury of your peers, how your company fares will most likely be determined by a ratings-hungry journalist who knows very little about your industry or, worse, by a mob of angry anonymous sources who have decided you are guilty for no reason at all, or for their own private reasons, and who have active social media accounts.

The first rule is that there are no universally applicable rules – our goal here is to provide food for thought and to suggest some general best practices that can help guide you in selecting the course of action for your particular situation. Realistic expectations are crucial. Some situations simply cannot be made better, and the goal there should be simply to contain the damage.

C.   To Respond or Not to Respond

"Randy lay there like a slug ... it was his only defense" – Ralphie, A Christmas Story

It wouldn't be wise to respond publicly to every negative news story or disgruntled customer or employee's public grievances – sometimes a private, individually tailored response, or no response at all, is the best way to make a situation blow over.[1116] But, when confronting a reporter on a mission, or an enemy bent on making you pay, the best response to publicity about a government investigation may call for taking and plainly expressing a substantive position that at least gives you a fighting chance in the court of public opinion.

Even if you decide not to comment substantively, or perhaps not to comment at all, you should not use the phrase "no comment" to do

---

[1116] Or perhaps just make a bad situation time-limited, or slightly less bad. Your goals should be realistic, and it may well prove impossible to do more than limit the damage when your company is attacked in the media.

so. Like taking the Fifth Amendment, the words "no comment" are often perceived as a passive admission of guilt. If you have decided that you are better served by not responding to a request from a reporter, strive to find an articulable reason that will make sense to the average viewer; a phrase that follows the word "because." For example, we are not going to get into that topic "because we take seriously our obligation to protect the privacy of our patients" or "because the Court has asked us not to discuss this matter outside of the courtroom."

Of course, even a "no comment" expressed using different verbiage is still functionally no comment. And if you don't take the time to respond to inquiries about an investigation with a thoughtful position, it could appear – or be made to appear - that your company thinks the investigation is not significant enough to warrant your attention. This sends potentially very negative signals to your employees, your customers, your stockholders, as well as the government officials investigating you, and each of the other potential audiences identified above. It also completely misses your opportunity to show your company's heart or concern for your mission.

Here is one way to craft a media statement:

First phrase: Address the investigation to clarify why you are making the statement.

Example: "We have been made aware of this investigation…" or "Regarding the [agency] investigation of our company…"

Second phrase: Extend a bear hug to the opposing side. Sincerity optional, but it makes the statement read better (and may come easier if you can identify goals you share with the agency in question).

Example: "We appreciate the role of this [insert agency name] and all they do to protect the taxpayer…"

Third phrase: Take the opposing side's hand – they may well also be your company's regulators, and part of your job is making them comfortable with who you are and how you do things so they will not assume the worst.

Example: "We are cooperating fully with [insert agency name] and will work collaboratively with them to help ensure [insert issue of concern]…"

Fourth phrase: Drive home your defensive position to the greatest extent you feel you can.

Example: "We stand behind our team and will vigorously defend our reputation" or "We disagree with the allegations and will vigorously defend our case in court." If your constituents, including your defense team, will permit it, this could also be the place to start reframing the topic – *e.g.*, "given that our ratio of loan defaults is by far the lowest of any major lender during the years at issue, we have every confidence that we will prevail."

Fifth phrase: Affirm your company's mission and commitment to your customers.

Example: "We believe in our [mission statement] and will keep our focus on providing [company value proposition] to our customers. They are our highest priority."

Once you have your plan for a response, and have used that to understand the story you want to tell about the investigation and how to express that story briefly and clearly, it is time to get that message out. Don't fall into the trap of having a "response only strategy," unless that approach is based on a strategic decision (for example, you have decided that many potential audience members may not engage with or be impacted by the story, so you will only give your statement reactively). Instead, think about short, clear and appropriate ways to reframe the situation, and tell your story. Don't limit your thinking to traditional approaches like a press release or a statement on your corporate webpage. Is there a friendly reporter that you can work with to get your part of the dialogue out there? And do not, under any circumstances, neglect to include social media in your thinking. The Pew Research Center has found that over 72% of American adults are active users of social media.[1117] Twitter messages, which are limited to 140 characters, now have unprecedented impacts on our public discourse, driving the focus of traditional media and directly impacting our political process. Companies under attack must be sure that their point of view is represented in this vital arena. Have no doubt – investigators will be looking through social media for evidence against you, as well.[1118]

D.   The Messenger

"The art of communication is the language of leadership." – James Humes

To the general public and consumer audience, the natural choice of messenger for a corporation is the CEO or President, as long as that person also has been the public face of the company in other situations and has been thoroughly media trained. Train cautiously, however – research suggests that authenticity may be the most critical factor in how the public evaluates a corporate response.[1119]Generally the public will expect to hear from the CEO if the matter is important.

While the CEO may be an essential spokesperson, and a team should be designated to handle the major media questions, every employee will become a de facto spokesperson for your company to your customers and employees, and to their own network of social media followers, friends and counterparts. While you will hold a hand-to-hand combat style media training for the main corporate spokesperson, conducting media training for field leaders, store managers, agency leaders, and as many key employees as you can will help ensure everyone is speaking with the same set of talking points. Local news outlets will want to

---

[1117] http://www.pewinternet.org/fact-sheet/social-media/.

[1118] http://jolt.richmond.edu/index.php/social-media-evidence-in-government-investigations-and-criminal-proceedings-a-frontier-of-new-legal-issues/.

[1119] *Claeys, A., & De Waele, A.,* The Importance of Authenticity in Organizational Crisis Communication Via Social Media, *collected in* Social Media and Crisis Communication, edited by Yan Jin and Lucinda Austin, 2d Edition 2022.

localize the story for their viewers and readers, so the local team leaders may get their share of media calls, too. Of course, if you have the ability to get this learning distributed before the crisis hits, so much the better.

And do not neglect to ensure that everyone who interacts with any members of the audiences identified earlier is equipped with simple, plain and accurate talking points for use when a customer or someone else asks about the investigation. As surely as sparks fly upwards, everyone is interested when it looks like someone is in trouble – do all you can to be sure that this natural human interest is met with points that reflect your view of the situation, and not left hanging to be answered by imagination or with intentionally derogatory comments from adversaries.

E.   Media Protocol

Review your corporate policy about media protocol. While your onboarding of new employees may have included the process for employees to follow if they are approached by a reporter, take the opportunity to revisit how media inquiries are handled across the company. To ensure a consistent message, designating one point of contact to process all requests will be necessary. This could be an unmanageable burden for a single individual, so be sure there are backup resources and other team members that can help respond quickly. If it becomes overwhelming, the corporate response statement can be posted to your website or social media outlets and dropped on a wire service.

If you choose to have local company leaders regularly respond directly to media inquiries, they should have gone through rigorous media training to be prepared for that role. Generally, allowing all calls to come through a central corporate representative presents the least risk and ensures consistency of messaging to the greatest degree.

F.   Media Training

Regardless of any previous media training your executive team or local leaders have been through, you will need to conduct a media and message training session with them that is specific to this news. While the corporate media statement can be issued broadly, when and if one of your company representatives is ambushed by a reporter, they will need to be prepared with quick (and hopefully effective and at least well thought-out) sound bites and a calm authentic demeanor that is consistent with your corporate brand and with their own prior public expressions. This consistency of values, modes of expression, and even body language is a major part of what drives a sense of whether your spokesperson is or is not being truthful.[1120]

G. Understanding "Day 2" Stories

"Things are never so bad they can't be made worse." – Humphrey Bogart

The first day the investigation is made public will be ground zero for your media strategy, and indeed may trigger the main onslaught of media coverage about it. But if the first news was well followed, or if you are in an industry where the investigation could be sensationalized easily, or if adversaries see an advantage to be pressed, you can expect a wave of "Day 2" stories to follow the initial announcement. These stories typically involve a disgruntled customer, employee or another regular man-on-the-street who has a story for the camera about how the investigation is justified. And, not coincidentally, how the reporter is actively working to protect the viewing public from also being victimized by this corporate ogre.

Be aware that these sources are often given to the reporters by the team pushing the case against you. However, they are real people with real stories to tell, so there will be little you can do to combat this onslaught of additional coverage except having a thoughtful media response ready to distribute when your company is given the opportunity to comment. Refuting misinformation via an on camera interview may be tempting, but be very careful how you do this. To the general public, your company needs to stay focused on

---

[1120] Id.

your mission and commitment to take care of your customers and employees. And your defense attorneys may not want you to comment substantively on an active investigation, particularly in an environment like a live on-camera interview where your spokesperson might make commitments that are hard to keep, or could otherwise go down unfavorable pathways. Given that there always will be competing priorities here, it will be crucial to balance the potential harm that could come from specific messages and responses against your best judgment of the harm that would follow from not making those replies.

H.   Ongoing Media Relations

"The best defense is a good offense." – Proverb

While the news cycle about the case will come and go eventually, implementing an ongoing proactive media relations program will help shore up the corporate reputation with key reporters and the general public. If all the media hear about your company is negative or driven by other parties who do not have your best interests at heart, that negative sentiment will linger far longer than it should – and will color the perceptions of your company virtually every time you are involved in a newsworthy event. If your team can make it a priority on those days without a crisis to work to secure positive news stories – regardless of the reach, scope or impact – it will help balance the negative news coverage that may surround an investigation.

Ensure your company recruits and provides sufficient resources to a strong communications team, or at least has a positive and comfortable relationship with an external agency that can generate positive news coverage for the company. Instead of simply profiling executives or talking strictly about business operations, regularly seek to profile the human interest stories of non-executive employees or customers and highlight the things that make you a good corporate citizen and neighbor, such as employee assistance or charitable giving programs. To be successful, this functional team must also have the commitment from executives and from the Board to ensure the access and support needed for proactive media relations, and for defanging the monstrous stories that an investigation may bring with it. As General Counsel, make it your business to think about how communications can and should be one of the tools you use to manage these realities of modern business, before the reporter calls or the tweet hits the fan.

Chapter 23

International Investigations

By: Lamia R. Matta[1121]

I.   INTRODUCTION

On December 15, 2008, the German engineering company Siemens AG entered into a settlement agreement with the United States ("U.S.") Department of Justice ("DOJ") and the U.S. Securities and Exchange Commission ("SEC") for violations of the U.S. Foreign Corrupt Practices Act ("FCPA"). On the same day, Siemens settled charges in a related investigation brought by German authorities. The company also announced that it faced related charges in Greece, Italy, and Norway, and that it was under investigation in a number of other jurisdictions. In the fifteen years since that settlement, the number of cross-border investigations, settlements and prosecutions has increased significantly. For example, in the last two years, at least six companies have entered into settlements with the U.S. and another country in the anti-corruption arena alone.[1122]

These settlements are but limited examples of the increased cooperation over the last decade and a half between the United States and foreign governments around the world in the

---

[1121] Lamia R. Matta is Senior Investigations Counsel at Ericsson. Lauren E. Briggerman and Ann Sultan, members in the Litigation and International departments, respectively, of Miller & Chevalier Chtd. in Washington, D.C., were co-authors of this Chapter for Editions 2 and 3 of the General Counsel's Guide to Government Investigations. The views expressed by the author are her own and do not necessarily represent the views of the Company.

[1122] These settlements are: Glencore International A.G. (settled with U.S., U.K., and Swiss authorities in May 2022), Stericycle Inc. (settled with U.S. and Brazilian authorities in April 2022), Credit Suisse Group AG (settled with U.S. and U.K. authorities in October 2021), Amec Foster Wheeler Energy Limited (settled with U.S., Brazilian, and U.K. authorities in June 2021), The Goldman Sachs Group, Inc. (settled with U.S., U.K., Hong Kong, and Singapore authorities in October 2020), Airbus SE (settled with U.S., U.K. and French authorities in January 2020).

investigation and prosecution of regulated activities. It is more and more common that the U.S. is only one among a number of countries pursuing prosecutions of the same corporate entities for the same or related conduct. Indeed, in May 2018, the DOJ revised the U.S. Attorneys' Manual[1123] to reflect a so-called "No Piling On" policy aimed at protecting companies from redundant fines and penalties in multiple jurisdictions. The policy directs U.S. prosecutors to (1) not threaten criminal prosecution "solely" as a negotiation tactic to increase the value of a civil settlement, (2) to coordinate with U.S. and foreign enforcement agencies, including on the apportionment of fines, and to (3) "consider all relevant factors" in determining the appropriateness of coordinated enforcement and apportionment of penalties.

In this chapter, we examine what a corporate counsel needs to consider when multiple regulatory and enforcement agencies come calling.

For a company being investigated for activity that has taken place in multiple countries, the likelihood is that all governments that have jurisdiction will seek to get their share of the investigative action. There is often coordination between multiple governments, even at the information-gathering stage. Governments will often share information among themselves, both before an investigation is launched and as it progresses. This may occur informally between individuals working with relevant enforcement agencies, or through more formal mechanisms such as mutual legal assistance ("MLA") requests, either pursuant to a treaty (a mutual legal assistance treaty, or "MLAT"), on the basis of reciprocity, or through letters rogatory if charges have been brought. Once the agencies collect the initial information they require, there are many ways they can draw a company into their investigation. An agency may decide to conduct a raid of a corporation's office, it may issue a subpoena (or other formal legal process) requiring the company to produce documents and witnesses relating to particular topics, or it may simply request that a company voluntarily provide certain categories of information to the agency. Once an agency

---

[1123] U.S. Attorneys' Manual §1-12.100.

detects wrongdoing in a company, it may make requests of similarly situated companies to determine if the detected wrongdoing is systemic across an industry.

Immediately after being contacted by an investigating government agency, company counsel should quickly determine the scope of the investigation and which jurisdictions and agencies are involved. When a government agency comes knocking, it is almost always advisable to engage outside counsel. This is particularly the case if the conduct implicates the company's senior officers (the "C-suite"), members of the Board of Directors or the activity of the legal or compliance functions. The company will want to identify dedicated outside counsel in each jurisdiction implicated. Because the company will need to have a coordinated strategy, it is critical that the company designate one of the outside counsels to manage the work being conducted by the lawyers and consultants across jurisdictions to ensure the company has a harmonized and consistent response. If the company can identify the main regulatory or enforcement agency leading the investigation, it may be most helpful to have the chosen outside counsel in that country serve as the coordinating counsel for all outside counsel. Another benefit of having a coordinating counsel is that it can help to prevent duplication of efforts and spiraling of costs. Local outside counsel can provide valuable insight into local dynamics and relationships in a supporting role to the primary outside counsel.

Often, the breadth of the investigation will not be immediately evident, so strategy will have to adjust as information about the investigation becomes available and as new jurisdictions become involved. As we will discuss below, outside counsel will have to work with differing countries' agencies to ensure a coordinated response to each. Counsel will have to deal with competing demands from different agencies and seek to harmonize those demands to minimize disruption and cost to the company. That will require coordinating, among other things, communication with the governments, investigation priorities, document preservation and production, witness interviews, privilege issues, and data privacy rules.

Depending on the structure of the company, the company's leadership may have to alert its subsidiaries to the fact that the company is under investigation. The company should have a coordinated strategy for keeping all senior management, both in headquarters and in relevant subsidiaries, apprised of relevant developments of the investigation, balancing that need against the risk of being perceived by enforcement authorities to be "tipping off" wrongdoers within the company. The company will also need to form a core internal team to handle communications with outside counsel and facilitate relationships when outside counsel needs access to company employees. Most companies under investigation opt to create an internal investigation management team that consists of representatives from the legal department, finance function, internal audit, and often compliance. If there is a separate forensic fraud investigation function, it should also be included in the core investigation team.

Finally, the company will need to develop a media strategy for handling communications about the investigation. Companies often include internal communications specialists in the core investigation team and ask them to head the media strategy. If the investigation is high-profile, it may be valuable to engage a public relations firm to help manage the communication strategy (though communications with such firms must be carefully calibrated to ensure the preservation of any applicable legal privileges).

One important issue to address at the beginning of the investigation is how the laws of each country with jurisdiction over the company will overlap. As we discuss below, for example, the European Union ("E.U.") has significantly stricter data privacy rules than does the United States,[1124] in particular since the entry

---

[1124] The legislative landscape, however, is changing in the United States where in recent years a number of state legislatures have passed data privacy laws. California, for instance, enacted the California Consumer Privacy Act and the California Privacy Rights Act. The former, which went into effect in January 2020, gives Californians the right to opt out of having their data sold. The California Privacy Rights Act, which went into force in January 2023, affords, among other provisions, greater protection for "sensitive data" of California citizens and establishes a Privacy Protection Agency that enforces the Act's privacy protections.

into force of the European General Data Protection Regulation 2016/679 ("EU GDPR" or "GDPR") in May 2018. The outside counsel coordinating communications with the investigative authorities will have to reach agreement about such issues early in the process. It will be especially important to arrive at an arrangement for the disclosure of information that ensures that the company does not violate any laws of the relevant jurisdictions.

The company also must understand the basis on which each country asserts jurisdiction. Countries will usually assert jurisdiction because at least part of the wrongful conduct took place in that country's territory or had an effect on that country, or because there is involvement of a particular country's national. In the U.S. and the United Kingdom, the presence of a subsidiary in the respective country or the listing of the company's shares on a public exchange may create jurisdiction for conduct that takes place on foreign soil. At times, the assertion of jurisdiction may be tenuous, and the company will want to consider whether a particular enforcement agency has adopted an overly aggressive view of its jurisdictional reach such that the company should challenge it. In addition, the company will want to pay close attention to the double jeopardy protections in the various jurisdictions involved. In some jurisdictions enforcement action may not be taken against a company for conduct regarding which the company has already faced civil or criminal liability outside of the country. Accordingly, it will be important for outside counsel from the various jurisdictions to coordinate closely, and at the outset, on defense strategies.

II. INVESTIGATION PLAN – INFORMATION GATHERING

Whether or not a company has previously investigated the alleged misconduct, a company's own fact gathering will be an important part of any international investigation. Knowledge of the facts relevant to an investigation is critical in the company's assessment of its posture vis-à-vis the government(s) involved and will guide decision-making whether, or when, the time comes to consider possible settlement or litigation in the U.S. and abroad (further discussed in Section V, below). Companies must consider the varying legal regimes in each of the countries at issue in the investigation and must keep apprised of any changes to those legal regimes. For example, in November 2017, the Department of Justice revised section 9-47.120 of the U.S. Attorneys' Manual,[1125] codifying in connection with its prosecution of FCPA violations its emphasis on the importance of a company's disclosure of all relevant facts as part of a company's cooperation and listing other steps companies can take to mitigate their potential exposure and penalties. In September 2022, the DOJ further emphasized the importance of self-disclosure by announcing changes to is Corporate Criminal Enforcement Policy that provide specific incentives to companies for voluntary self-disclosures, cooperation and remediation.[1126] In this section, we discuss managing each of the main sources of information—documents and witnesses.

A. Managing Documents

A government request or demand[1127] for documents presents an early opportunity for the company to constrain the costs of the investigation by narrowing the scope of the document universe. This can be done by negotiating custodians, search terms, and time-frames of responsive documents to the company's advantage so as to limit the company's disclosure obligations.

Because a request for documents can become a very costly exercise for a company, it must be managed carefully. Costs associated with efforts to collect, process, review, translate, redact, and produce documents can easily escalate. Companies should, as a general rule, presume that "everything is negotiable" with regards to initial document requests or demands. Negotiating a document request can be an opportunity, early in an investigation,

---

[1125] U.S. Attorneys' Manual § 9-47.120

[1126] https://www.justice.gov/opa/speech/deputy-attorney-general-lisa-o-monaco-delivers-remarks-corporate-criminal-enforcement

[1127] For purposes of this section, we will consider so-called voluntary document requests and compulsory demands, such as subpoenas, collectively and refer to them as "document requests."

to engage with a government agency to limit the scope of the information sought, minimize potential expenditures, and set an early tone for the investigation.

In addition, while a document request identifies what a government is looking for, it also provides insight into what a government already knows. As the company evaluates a document request, it can think about whether there are other more cost-effective and advantageous ways to provide a government with what it needs. And, if the company finds it is in its interest to assume a very cooperative posture, it might also consider how it can provide additional information that a government might not have known to ask about.

1.   Document Preservation Notice

One of the first steps to take after receiving a document request or demand is to issue an internal document preservation notice (also commonly referred to as a "document hold" or "litigation hold"). This notice should encompass the scope of a government's request and be sensitive to how various documents and communications may be stored. It should be distributed, at a minimum, to employees who may have relevant information. The company should also consider whether it will distribute the document preservation notice to non-employees who may have relevant data, such as board members, former employees, and various potentially relevant third parties, such as agents or vendors. Company counsel should keep in mind, however, that, depending on contractual relationships and local legal regimes, these recipients may not have any obligation to follow a document preservation notice and communications with them may not be protected under the attorney-client privilege. Depending on the nature of the company's operations and the focus of the investigation, the company may wish to distribute the document preservation notice in various languages. The company should also consider, with the advice of counsel, whether to first issue a document preservation notice, preserve potentially relevant data, or do these things simultaneously.

2.   <u>Scope of the Document Request and Production of Documents</u>

After issuing a document preservation notice and evaluating the scope of the document request received, the company should engage with the government to try to narrow the scope of the document request. Different governments may be more or less receptive to such efforts, but the company should work to ensure that any progress achieved with one government is reflected in its obligations to other governments as well. If possible, the company should request that there be coordinated discussions and responses on document production scope and specifications.

The company should consider the following in discussions with a government on the scope of a document request:

- Are the governments coordinating among themselves?

- Will the company be producing the same materials to all involved governments?

- Will the company be translating documents in connection with productions?

In collecting, analyzing, and eventually producing documents, the company will need to look at applicable data privacy, national security, and other legal regimes with jurisdiction over where the data is located and where it might be transferred. Some countries also have strict regimes regarding who may look at certain types of data. This may be a more sensitive area if the company is in a highly regulated industry, such as defense manufacturing, telecommunications, or healthcare. Local laws may also require a company to secure consent from existing and former employees in order to look at or transfer their data.

Since the passage of the EU GDPR in May 2018, many jurisdictions have followed suit and developed similar frameworks for the protection of their citizens' data rights. China, for instance, passed in 2021 the Data Security Law and the Personal

Information Protection Law, which focus respectively on data security in a national security context as well as personal privacy. Companies should be aware of the responsibilities of data "controllers" and data "processors" and ensure that they have established a program that complies with the data privacy obligations of the various jurisdictions in play. In addition, the company should involve the local data protection officer as well as local counsel and, if EU countries are involved, conduct a data protection impact assessment in order to determine whether supplementary safeguards will be required.

In meeting production obligations, the company will want to ensure that it can produce documents at the required technical specifications. This may necessitate retaining a vendor to host and process data. Depending on the location of the data and local law, the company may be able to assert that certain data located abroad is outside the scope of an investigating government's jurisdiction. Company counsel should consult with local outside counsel when determining where to host the data. While many sophisticated multi-national companies now have in-house forensic IT capabilities and may be capable of processing and hosting company data (and may prefer to do so to conserve costs), in some cases it is advisable to nonetheless engage an outside vendor to avoid any allegation the company manipulated or spoliated the data during the course of the processing and review. Depending on the volume of data to be reviewed and produced, the company may also need to retain additional personnel or contract out the review of the data. Regardless of whether data is reviewed in-house or outside, consistency in the process of identifying, reviewing, translating, redacting, and producing documents will decrease costs and increase efficiency. If the company can make identical productions to multiple authorities, that will be of great benefit.

B.   Interviewing Witnesses

Conducting witness interviews is a critical component of the company's investigation, both for developing facts and for building defenses. Witness interviews in international investigations pose legal and practical challenges that may not exist in exclusively U.S.-based investigations. Where witness interviews take place abroad, it is important to work with local outside counsel in those jurisdictions to identify and properly address those issues.

1. Practical Issues Regarding Interviewing Witnesses Abroad

As the company identifies witnesses to interview and makes plans for such interviews, certain practical issues arise. For example, some jurisdictions have laws governing interview procedures and logistics, such as where the interviews may take place, how they must be conducted, who can be present, and what documents may be shown to a witness. It is important to consult with local counsel to identify these rules before contacting witnesses to set-up interviews.

The company should also take into account language and cultural barriers that arise with witness interviews. If company counsel does not speak the same language as the interviewee, the company should consider whether to retain a third-party interpreter for the interview. If the company chooses to use an outside party, company counsel or coordinating outside counsel should require the interpreter to clear conflicts and enter into a confidentiality agreement. The company should be aware that, to the extent employees have their own outside counsel, those lawyers may request different translators if they fear a potential conflict of interest between the employee(s) and the company. To expedite the interview, company counsel should also ensure that documents to be used during the interview are translated ahead of time and have local outside counsel verify that the translations are complete and accurate. Company counsel should factor in the additional time translation takes during an interview when scheduling the interview.

When conducting an interview of a foreign national, cultural conventions should be recognized to put the witness at ease, so long as they do not impede the purpose of the interview. For example, bowing and formally presenting business cards at the beginning of an interview is conventional in Japan. In the Middle

East and Southeast Asia, interviewers should be conscious of not showing the soles of their shoes to interviewees. In India, common Western non-verbal cues may have a different meaning than intended. Local outside counsel is a good source of information regarding cultural norms.

It is always preferable to interview witnesses in person rather than over the phone or by video conference. In-person interviews allow for a personal connection that puts an interviewee at ease while simultaneously conveying the seriousness of the matter. As a result, an in-person interview will typically result in more information and will allow the interviewer to better assess the witness's credibility and truthfulness. These interviews are also more efficient, particularly when dealing with a language barrier or when using multiple documents. However, given the near global trend of remote work and even remote litigation, video interviews may slowly become more and more common and even necessary. When conducting an interview with a witness that is not physically in the room, the examining counsel should ask the witness whether there is anyone else in the room in which the witness is located. Counsel may even want to ask the witness to scan the room with their camera in order to ensure that there are no others in the room who could be coaching the witness or somehow impacting the attorney-client privilege.

As company counsel schedules the location of interviews abroad, they should factor in logistical hurdles such as the need for passports, visas, vaccinations, or permission from government authorities to conduct interviews in their jurisdictions.

2.   <u>U.S. Laws and Conventions Governing
Interviews of Company Employees</u>

Even though an investigation may be international in scope, the company should still uphold U.S. conventions when conducting interviews of company employees in order to protect legal privilege in the U.S.

At the beginning of the interview, the interviewer should give a so-called "Upjohn" warning[1128] so that the witness understands the context of the interview and U.S. rules that apply to legal privilege and confidentiality. That warning should include at least the following elements:

1. that the interview is being conducted by counsel for the purpose of providing legal advice;

2. that the attorney conducting the interview represents the company, and not the witness individually;

3. that the attorney-client privilege protects the substance of the communication and that the privilege belongs to the company and not the witness;

4. that the company, and not the witness, may choose to waive privilege in the future and share information with other parties, including if appropriate in the circumstance, enforcement authorities;

5. that, in order to protect the legal privilege, the witness should keep the interview confidential and not discuss it with anyone, except as may be required by U.S. or local law; and

6. that the witness should cooperate and tell the truth.

The exact details of the required Upjohn warning may be affected by the circumstances surrounding the investigation. If, for example, the company has committed to cooperating, and counsel knows the results of the investigation will be shared with

---

[1128] *See Upjohn Co. v. United States*, 449 U.S. 383 (1981) and it progeny. In *Upjohn,* the Supreme Court held that a company could invoke the attorney–client privilege to protect communications between company lawyers and non-management employees.

enforcement authorities, local ethics rules and basic considerations of fair dealing may require disclosure of that fact to the interviewee. Moreover, if the company is already in the posture of sharing information learned from interviews with enforcement authorities, it should advise the interviewee of this fact.

At the end of the interview, counsel should remind the witness to keep the substance of the interview confidential. Finally, counsel should inform the witness that he or she should contact counsel at any time if the witness remembers additional information or wishes to correct a statement.

3.   <u>Foreign Laws and Conventions Governing Company Interviews of Employees</u>

Company counsel and coordinating outside counsel should also work with local outside counsel to identify and address any local laws that may apply to witness interviews. For example, some jurisdictions have labor and employment or privacy laws that permit employees to refuse to submit to an interview in a corporate internal investigation. Foreign jurisdictions may have laws that permit witnesses to refuse to answer certain types of questions, even where the witness agrees to submit to the interview. In addition, for interviews conducted by government agencies, many jurisdictions have protections comparable to the Fifth Amendment Constitutional right against self-incrimination recognized in the United States that allows witnesses to refuse to answer questions that may subject them to criminal liability. However, employees generally do not have a right to remain silent in interviews by their employers; choosing not to answer questions can be grounds for termination. Foreign jurisdictions may also have privilege laws comparable to the U.S. that protect spousal or attorney-client communications.

To the extent that other jurisdictions have conventions regarding admonitions that should be given to witnesses at the beginning of an interview, company counsel and coordinating outside counsel should work with local outside counsel to ensure those are properly addressed.

It is important to comply with local laws not only for the sake of compliance, but also because running afoul of them could have implications for the company's ability to introduce witness testimony—or any documents authenticated by those witnesses—as evidence at trial, either in the U.S. or abroad.

4.   Recording and Memorializing Interviews

Company counsel and coordinating outside counsel should consult with local outside counsel regarding who may be present for an interview and what rules and laws govern the recording and memorializing of witness interviews. Ideally, two attorneys are present for the interview—one to conduct the interview, and the other to take notes. As discussed above, the company may also need to provide an interpreter.

The person charged with taking notes should take a detailed account of the interview to ensure an accurate record. However, in keeping with U.S. law regarding the work product doctrine, the attorney should consider whether the notes should not be verbatim and whether they should capture in some manner the attorney's mental impressions. To the degree they are not verbatim and contain such impressions, the memorandum may be easier to protect under the work product doctrine. However, the strongest protection for memoranda related to interviews of company personnel will be the attorney-client privilege, not attorney work product, so counsel should not let concerns about work product protection result in a less thorough memorandum.

It is almost never advisable to create a video or audio recording of the interview for a variety of reasons, including because doing so may create a statement that must be turned over to third parties. Local outside counsel should advise company counsel and coordinating outside counsel regarding any rules or laws related to recording or note-taking that may require the company to deviate from these conventions.

5.   Treatment of Former Employees

As early as possible in the investigation, the company should determine what position it will take with respect to former employees, including whether it will seek to interview former employees and whether local law may permit the attorney-client privilege to attach to such interviews (for instance if the subject of the interview relates entirely to the individuals' former job functions). If the company chooses to conduct such interviews, company counsel and coordinating outside counsel should consult local outside counsel regarding any laws or ethical rules that may apply to communications with former employees, particularly if they are unrepresented.

The company should also assess whether it will indemnify former employees who are involved in a government investigation and obtain counsel, either voluntarily or because company policies or bylaws require it to do so. In addition, the company should consult its director and officer insurance policy to determine whether current or former executives may seek insurance coverage for their legal fees. Former employees are likely to need separate local counsel in multiple jurisdictions, depending on the investigation and their posture vis-à-vis the company.

6.   Government Interviews of Company Employees

The U.S. government may seek to interview company employees located abroad. Local law will dictate whether employees can be required to cooperate and submit to such interviews. If an employee presents certain specific reasons for not agreeing to be interviewed by a foreign government, depending on those reasons and the company's cooperation posture, the company could undertake steps to allay the employee's concerns. For example, if an employee is hesitant about traveling to a particular location for an interview, the company should negotiate an alternative location for the interview. Similarly, if the employee is concerned about representation, the company may secure the employee independent outside counsel in order to facilitate the interview.

While the expectation of U.S. enforcement authorities will be that current employees can be "required" to submit to interviews if requested by their employer, if local laws do not comport with this expectation, local counsel will have to educate U.S. enforcement authorities in the case of a non-cooperating employee. Notably, however, if a U.S. person located abroad does not wish to appear voluntarily for an interview, the U.S. government can seek to compel testimony by asking a U.S. court to issue a subpoena pursuant to 28 U.S.C. § 1783. For non-U.S. persons, the U.S. government may seek to utilize local legal processes (via an MLAT) to compel an interview.

In most jurisdictions (including the United States), the MLAT is not public or transparent. Requests are made through diplomatic or judicial channels and can take months to be approved, if not longer. Furthermore, there is no obligation on the U.S. government to notify company counsel or the witnesses they wish to interview that they have sought a foreign government's cooperation through an MLAT request. It may be the case, therefore, that a government has already sought and even secured an MLAT request prior to making a similar request through the company.

If the foreign jurisdiction does grant the U.S. government's request for assistance in facilitating an interview, the laws and procedures of that jurisdiction generally dictate the terms of the interview, including where and when it occurs, who can attend, and substantive protections for the witness. Oftentimes, local law enforcement agencies will be present at such interviews and may even lead the questioning. Prior to this point, local counsel should be engaged to advise regarding the company's, and company employees', rights under local law. It is also important that the company consider what rights and protections exist under U.S. law, as well as the extent to which employee interviews by the U.S. government are admissible in other jurisdictions' investigations.

C. Privilege Issues

It is important to understand the privilege laws of the jurisdictions in which an investigation is being conducted. This is so not only because the laws of a foreign jurisdiction may apply to any disputes arising over an investigation in that jurisdiction, but also because some U.S. courts may apply the privilege law of that foreign jurisdiction to communications in a foreign country.

While many countries recognize some form of the attorney-client privilege, the scope varies widely across the globe. The U.S. generally applies the attorney-client privilege broadly to communications made in confidence between a client and attorney for the purpose of giving or receiving legal (not business) advice. The privilege attaches to applicable communications with an attorney, regardless of whether the attorney is located in-house or at an outside firm.

However, unlike the U.S., many countries do not recognize the attorney-client privilege for communications involving in-house counsel. According to a 2007 survey, fewer than 40% of all European countries recognize the attorney-client privilege for in-house counsel.[1129] The European Union followed this trend when, in 2010, the European Court of Justice ruled that the attorney-client privilege does not apply to communications between a company and its in-house counsel in antitrust investigations conducted by the European Commission.[1130] To date, the European Court of Justice has failed to clarify whether its ruling is narrowly tailored to antitrust inquiries or should be interpreted more broadly. Clients and their lawyers have thus far taken the cautious view that only advice provided by outside counsel is likely to meet the European Court's narrow definition of privilege.

Jurisdictions may also differ over whether they attach an expiration date to the privilege; whether it covers solely the communications with an attorney or also the underlying facts; and the exceptions to the privilege (such as the "crime-fraud" exception in the U.S.).

[1129] *See Attorney-Client Privilege in Europe: Understanding How the Relationship Works*, Eversheds (Apr. 2007).

[1130] *See Akzo Nobel Chems. Ltd. & Akcros Chems. Ltd. v. Comm'n*, Case C-550/07P (E.C.J. 2010).

There are practical steps a company can take to maximize coverage of the attorney-client privilege in jurisdictions that do not protect communications with in-house counsel. Most obviously, they can retain outside counsel to lead the investigation rather than rely on in-house counsel. The company, including in-house counsel, should also limit written communications with the outside legal team, and instead communicate via phone or in-person meetings on sensitive issues. Furthermore, the company may wish to avoid having in-house counsel present during witness interviews. Depending on local law as to privilege, it may be advisable to retain local counsel through the company's external U.S. counsel, rather than for the company to engage local counsel directly.

Finally, company counsel should determine to what extent investigating jurisdictions recognize the attorney work product doctrine or similar litigation privilege. For example, in the U.S., the work product doctrine generally protects from disclosure materials prepared "in anticipation of litigation" (though what constitutes "anticipation of litigation" varies widely amongst jurisdictions, even within the U.S.). While many other common law countries recognize some form of attorney "work product" protections, the scope of such protections may differ across borders. Indeed, many countries do not recognize any "work product" or "litigation materials" doctrine at all. It is imperative that company counsel have a firm understanding of these rules as it moves forward with internal investigation into the alleged misconduct.

III.   TRAVEL CONCERNS FOR EXECUTIVES AND WITNESSES

Company employees involved in a government investigation must be made aware of travel concerns that may arise once an investigation has been triggered.

Government agencies like the DOJ use border watches to detect foreign nationals deemed witnesses, subjects, or targets of an investigation who enter the U.S. If a foreign national is stopped at the border, the government may detain the individual at the border for questioning, serve that individual with a formal subpoena for documents or testimony, or even an arrest warrant. In addition, government agencies may issue a so-called "Red Notice" through the International Criminal Police Organization (INTERPOL), the world's largest international police organization, requesting member countries to arrest or detain specified individuals entering their territory. Where active government investigations are known to be underway that may be targeting individual employees or officers, company counsel should be consulted regarding potential international travel, especially any involving key personnel and senior management.

Company employees who travel abroad voluntarily for witness interviews, whether conducted by the company or a government agency, may also face travel hurdles. Traveling abroad requires a passport and possibly visas or other permits. The party conducting the interview should factor these issues into the scheduling of the interview.

If a government agency such as the DOJ requests that a witness voluntarily travel to the U.S. for an interview, the individual (through company or individual counsel) should request a "safe passage" letter from the relevant government agencies conducting the interviews. Such letters typically provide that the individual will be permitted to enter the U.S. without arrest, detention, or service of process, or prevented from leaving the country based on any information provided during the course of the interview. Additionally, in the U.S., law enforcement agencies can often intervene with the State Department to procure expedited visas (or visa waivers) for individuals to be interviewed.

Individuals to be interviewed in the U.S. may also request a so-called "Queen for a Day" or proffer letter prior to any interview. Such letters generally prevent the U.S. from directly using information provided in the interview as evidence against the individual in subsequent criminal proceedings, except that such statements may be used against the individual to prosecute perjury or false statement crimes, or to impeach the individual if he or she provides testimony contrary to statements during the interview.

Moreover, the government is generally not precluded from investigating leads uncovered during an interview conducted under a proffer letter. Accordingly, counsel should consider carefully whether such proffer letters can actually provide meaningful protection.

With respect to the location of a government-conducted interview, some witnesses may have concerns about traveling to certain locations for political or safety reasons. If the company is cooperating in a U.S. investigation, it should try to strike a balance between appearing helpful to the government and honoring its employees' preferences for location. Oftentimes, negotiating a politically neutral country may be the best compromise.

IV.   Interacting with foreign governments

A.   Coordination

Coordinating an investigation process with multiple governments is a daunting task. The company may need to contend with a variety of complicating factors, from time zone differences that make scheduling calls more difficult, to potential language barriers, cultural differences, and idiosyncrasies in the laws through which governments view the investigation.

As noted, one government often takes the lead in cross-border investigations, and it is important to identify which government is taking that lead. However, there may be multiple agencies within the jurisdiction competing for their piece of the investigation. In such cases, the company or its outside counsel should discuss with the lead government or agency, depending on the situation, how best to manage communication and coordination with the other involved governments and agencies. No matter what is agreed, it is important to keep the various governments involved abreast of the situation so that no government feels that it is being shut out of the process. This can be done through simultaneous or individual communications with the involved governments; some governments may have a preference for one or the other.

B.   Confidentiality

Jurisdictions may have different regulations regarding not just privilege (discussed in greater detail in section C, above), but also business confidential information. The company should be mindful of these differences in interacting with local governments. Even when a government has specific regulations in place for protecting business confidential information, it may share certain information obtained from an investigation with those who do not have such protections, including other governments. This can be done through an MLAT, discussed in the introduction and II.B.6, above.

If the company knows about an information-sharing agreement between the recipient of confidential information and another body without desired confidentiality protections, it should discuss the precise parameters of information-sharing prior to any disclosure. It is possible that the potential recipient of information will be open to a creative approach to information-sharing so that it cannot be passed along further, such as through an in-person or electronic "view only" session. Even in cases where a company may not ultimately be able to avoid disclosure and further distribution of certain information, having an understanding of the scope of the same may help the company manage potential fallout.

V.   CONCLUDING AN INVESTIGATION

If violations or potential violations are uncovered during the course of an investigation, the company will reach a point when it needs to decide whether or not to engage in settlement negotiations. Whether to negotiate or litigate is a complicated and nuanced decision that can only be made on a case-by-case basis, considering the individual details of each particular case and the risk tolerance of the company.

A.   Decision-Making Processes

As it nears this decision point, the company should ensure that it has strong processes in place for making and acting upon the decision. For example, will management be making a recommendation to the Board of Directors or shareholders? Will the full Board or only a committee of the Board make the decision? Does a decision require more than a majority vote? Company by-laws and local corporate governance laws may ultimately require a specific process.

If the company decides to move forward with settlement negotiations, a clear chain of decision-making should be established for planning strategy and making key decisions (including the ultimate decision of whether to accept or propose any settlement or plea offers from prosecuting agencies). Increasingly, government agencies are incentivizing rapid resolutions of corporate criminal matters and, if a company is positioned to move quickly and aggressively in its settlement negotiations, it may be able to achieve a more favorable result. In this regard, the company may want to disclose its decision-making process to the government so that timing expectations can be managed.

If the company decides to move forward with litigation, it will similarly want a clear chain of command established for making strategic and other decisions. The company should also consider whether special litigation counsel should be appointed.

Finally, as high-profile cases move to resolution—whether through settlement or litigation—it will become increasingly difficult to contain any leaks to the news media. As noted previously, a coordinated media strategy may have already been instituted during the investigation phase. As the company moves toward resolution, any media strategy will require revisiting and updating. Moreover, depending on the company's reporting obligations or the terms of any resolution, it may be necessary to clear any press release or public statements with relevant regulatory or law enforcement agencies.

B.   Considerations - Collateral Consequences

In addition to financial, reputational, and other consequences, the company should be sure to consider collateral consequences unique to international investigations. Depending on the language of any settlement, or information that comes to light in the litigation process, a company may find itself subject to civil litigation by disgruntled shareholders, terminated employees, customers, or others. Similarly, following a resolution with a company, enforcement agencies may pivot to pursue charges against individual wrongdoers, including current and former employees or officers. Depending on the circumstances of any resolution, the company may be obligated to cooperate and assist with the prosecution of such individuals. There may also be additional governments or agencies which were not previously involved in the investigative process, but who discover a jurisdictional or other hook from information that comes to light in resolving the matter in another jurisdiction.

VI.   CONCLUSION

As government investigations become increasingly global, companies are more likely to be swept up in investigations involving multiple jurisdictions. Such cross-border investigations are complicated and require thoughtful planning, ongoing coordination, and almost always the advice of outside legal experts. It is imperative that any company finding itself in investigative cross-hairs develop a bespoke response anticipating and accommodating the unique laws and practices of each investigating jurisdiction. Coordinating counsel experienced in managing the moving pieces of a cross-border investigation will be critical to ensuring that all of the company's advisors and consultants are working in tandem to achieve a favorable outcome for the company.

Chapter 24

Representing Individuals

By: Joseph De Simone and Matthew A. Rossi[1131]

I. INTRODUCTION

Over the last fifteen years, there has been a significant increase in the number and scope of government investigations focused on alleged corporate wrongdoing. The Sarbanes-Oxley Act,[1132] which was enacted in 2002, imposed reporting obligations concerning internal controls and the accuracy of financial statements upon corporations and their management. Corporate officers and directors responded to Sarbanes-Oxley by becoming more vigilant about preventing and detecting misconduct. Corporations now pay closer attention to their compliance procedures and increasingly conduct internal investigations to ferret out potential wrongdoing on their own before it comes to the government's attention. Moreover, the government has made it clear that law enforcement will be focused on individual accountability, not just the corporation's liability.

For example, on September 9, 2015, former Deputy Attorney General Sally Quillian Yates issued a policy memorandum to all Department of Justice attorneys concerning "Individual Accountability for Corporate Wrongdoing" (the "Yates Memo").[1133] The Yates Memo stated that "[o]ne of the most effective ways to combat corporate misconduct is by seeking

---

[1131] Joseph De Simone is a Partner at Mayer Brown LLP. Matthew A. Rossi is a Shareholder at Vedder Price LLP; this chapter was written while he was a Partner at Mayer Brown. The views expressed in this chapter are their own, do not necessarily represent the views of either law firm, and should not be considered legal advice.

[1132] Sarbanes-Oxley Act of 2002, Pub. L. No. 107-204, 116 Stat. 745 (codified at 15 U.S.C. §§ 7201 *et seq.*).

[1133] Memorandum from Sally Quillian Yates, Deputy Attorney General, Dep't of Justice, Individual Accountability for Corporate Wrongdoing (Sept. 9, 2015) (the "Yates Memo"), *available at* https://www.justice.gov/dag/file/769036/download.

accountability from the individuals who perpetrated the wrongdoing."[1134] Before the issuance of this memorandum, corporations were already under pressure to cooperate with government investigations. Now, the Yates Memo requires corporations to reveal all relevant facts related to an individual's misconduct in order to receive cooperation credit. According to the Yates memo, prosecutors are now directed to bring cases against culpable individuals, even if those individuals cannot afford to pay the likely monetary penalties. The new policy also states that no corporate resolution will protect an individual from criminal or civil liability.

Eight months after issuing the Yates Memo, former Deputy Attorney General Yates discussed the shift she had seen in how cases are approached within the Department of Justice ("DOJ"). DOJ prosecutors now consider the culpability of individuals from the beginning of an investigation and DOJ civil attorneys no longer solely focus on recovering the most money, but also on deterring misconduct and holding those culpable for their misconduct.[1135] U.S. Securities Exchange Commission ("SEC") officials have also publicized statements emphasizing that the agency is focused on holding individuals accountable for corporate wrongdoing while at the same time encouraging individuals to cooperate with SEC investigations in exchange for their own cooperation credit.[1136]

Thus, corporations now have a powerful incentive to conduct internal investigations and disclose possible evidence of wrongdoing by corporate employees, officers, and directors to the

---

[1134] *Id.* at 1.

[1135] Former Deputy Attorney General Sally Quillian Yates Delivers Remarks at the New York City Bar Association White-collar Crime Conference (May 10, 2016), *available at* https://www.justice.gov/opa/speech/deputy-attorney-general-sally-q-yates-delivers-remarks-new-york-city-bar-association.

[1136] *See, e.g.,* Speech by Mary Jo White, SEC Chair, Three Key Pressure Points in the Current Enforcement Environment (May 19, 2014), *available at* https://www.sec.gov/news/speech/2014-spch051914mjw.html; Speech by Andrew Ceresney, Director of Enforcement Division, The SEC's Cooperation Program: Reflections on Five Years of Experience (May 13, 2015), *available at* https://www.sec.gov/news/speech/sec-cooperation-program.html.

government. Individuals, in turn, face a greater threat of civil and criminal liability than ever before.

This chapter highlights the important issues that counsel should be aware of when representing an individual in a government investigation.

II.   INITIAL CONSIDERATIONS

This increase in government investigations means new challenges and considerations for both the lawyers representing individuals in government investigations as well as for corporate counsel. Often the first decision to be made is whether an individual corporate officer, director, or employee needs separate representation at all. When considering separate representation, it is critical to understand the focus of the government's investigation and the individual's likely role in the events under investigation— including whether government lawyers view the individual as a witness or potential target of the investigation. This will assist not only in ascertaining whether separate representation is advisable, but also with evaluating the likelihood and scope of potential conflicts and making strategic decisions throughout the representation.

It may be difficult to determine the nature of the government's interest in a particular individual or even whether the investigation relates to a civil enforcement matter or to both civil and criminal matters. It is SEC policy in most cases not to disclose during an investigation whether an individual is a target or a witness.[1137] The SEC also typically will not disclose the existence of a parallel criminal investigation.[1138] Therefore, in a parallel investigation

---

[1137] In fact, the SEC claims that its investigative process does not have targets and thus, it is "not required to provide any type of target notification when it issues subpoenas to third parties or witnesses for testimony or documents...."SEC Enforcement Manual §3.3.2, *available at* https://www.sec.gov/divisions/enforce/enforcementmanual.pdf. *See also SEC v. Jerry T. O'Brien, Inc.*, 467 U.S. 735, 751 (1984) (SEC is not required to provide notice to individuals that it is investigating).

[1138] The SEC Enforcement Manual instructs that if asked by counsel whether there is a parallel criminal investigation, the SEC staff's response should include

there may be a time when counsel is only aware of the investigation by a civil enforcement agency such as the SEC if the criminal authorities have not yet surfaced. However, it is frequently possible to learn at least the general subject of an investigation and ascertain the nature of the government's interest in an individual through discussions with government counsel and a careful evaluation of the information sought in the investigation.

There are sometimes significant advantages to both the individual and the corporation if a corporate director, officer or employee retains separate counsel in a government investigation. It may, therefore, be in the corporation's interest to encourage individuals to retain separate counsel. Perhaps the most significant advantage is that it reduces the likelihood that the corporation's outside counsel will face an ethical conflict that disqualifies counsel from representing the corporation. The avoidance of conflicts is obviously also advantageous to individual corporate employees. Separate counsel may afford an individual an additional measure of assurance that counsel is acting in the individual's best interests and is not influenced by loyalty to a corporate client. Another important advantage of separate representation for individuals is that it can reduce the appearance of impropriety, collusion or coercion by the corporation over its employees. Thus, the government may have greater confidence that is it receiving information that is true, accurate, and untainted by possible collusion between witnesses. Of course, as explained below, counsel for the corporation and separate counsel for individual officers, directors, and employees may still share appropriate information pursuant to a joint defense agreement.

These advantages should be weighed against the disadvantages of separate representation. Separate representation typically costs the corporation more than joint representation if the corporation is indemnifying its employees for defense costs. It may also result in delay and thus protract the government's investigation. Perhaps

---

a statement that "it is the general policy of the Commission not to comment on investigations conducted by law enforcement authorities responsible for enforcing criminal laws." SEC Enforcement Manual §5.2.1, *available at* https://www.sec.gov/divisions/enforce/enforcementmanual.pdf.

most significantly, it may also decrease information sharing between the corporation and the individuals with separate counsel and lessen the corporation's control over and knowledge of the information being obtained by the government.

Depending on these factors, as well as the role and status of the individuals within the corporation, the corporation may encourage—if not facilitate—the process of individuals engaging individual counsel. In fact, many corporations offer—or, according to corporate charter, are required—to indemnify employees for money spent on legal fees in connection with an investigation. In some situations, certain states even require indemnification or advancement of legal fees. Finally, in a criminal investigation where an individual employee is facing criminal penalties, including possible prison time, the individual should always consult an attorney separate from the corporation's attorney.

Once the decision is made that an individual should retain separate counsel, the myriad of questions and considerations that any attorney or general counsel should be asking themselves when it comes to individuals include: Does the individual have possible civil or criminal liability? What is the status of the individual employee within the corporation at large? What type of investigation is the corporation responding to? What knowledge does the individual employee have? How is it relevant to the investigation? How does it impact the liability of the corporation? Are the individual's interests aligned with or counter to the interests of the corporations?

A.   Criminal vs. Civil Investigations

Government investigations can begin in a multitude of ways, such as through audits, complaints, tips, news coverage, criminal investigations, referrals from state and federal regulators, or referrals from civil investigative agencies. As covered in other chapters, investigations may be civil or criminal and may involve multiple government agencies across several jurisdictions. Parallel civil and criminal investigations may also occur at the same time. The type of demand a corporation or individual receives can provide information about whether an investigation is civil or criminal. For example, a grand jury subpoena means that a criminal investigation has already begun, whereas an administrative subpoena or civil investigative demand means a case is civil—at least until more information is gathered on whether a crime was committed.

For an individual, the stakes are much greater when the investigation is criminal, rather than civil, in nature. The SEC does not have the authority to initiate criminal proceedings. However, the SEC may—and often does—refer matters to the DOJ for criminal prosecution. Furthermore, criminal enforcement authorities often initiate their own criminal investigations. In a civil investigation, individual's counsel should always evaluate the possibility that the investigation will lead to a criminal investigation or vice versa. Strategic decisions in a civil or criminal investigation can have significant impact on a parallel investigation.[1139] One must consider how the resolution in a civil or criminal investigation may affect the parallel investigation. Of course, the existence of a civil investigation does not guarantee the absence of a parallel criminal investigation that has not yet surfaced.

III.   EFFECTS OF GOVERNMENT FOCUS ON HOLDING INDIVIDUALS ACCOUNTABLE

Many have said that the Yates Memo marks a significant, even revolutionary, change in how the DOJ will prosecute individuals, but it remains unclear whether the Yates Memo will, in fact, materially change government prosecutions and investigations. What is clear is that the Yates Memo puts a laser focus on individual culpability through provisions such as the directive that companies turn over "all relevant facts" related to individuals "responsible for" the misconduct at issue, along with the directive that DOJ investigators focus on individuals from the outset of a criminal or civil probe.

[1139] For a discussion on evaluating the impact of an individual's decision to waive his or her Fifth Amendment privilege, *see infra* section VI.

A.   Policy Changes Outlined in the Yates Memo

The Yates Memo outlines six policy changes or clarifications that are intended to strengthen existing DOJ policies concerning corporate executives and individuals.[1140] These policies include:

1. Companies must "identify all individuals involved in or responsible for the misconduct at issue, regardless of their position, status, or seniority and provide to the Department all facts relating to that misconduct" in order to be eligible for a cooperation credit.[1141]

2. The memorandum directs DOJ attorneys to focus on individuals at the outset of the corporate investigation.[1142]

3. The DOJ's criminal and civil attorneys should maintain "[e]arly and regular communication" with each other to ensure that parallel proceedings are coordinated.[1143]

4. The DOJ will not release executives from criminal liability except in "extraordinary circumstances"

[1140] Yates Memo at 2.

[1141] *Id* at 3.

[1142] *Id.* at 2.

[1143] *Id.* at 4; *see also* DEP'T OF JUSTICE, U.S. ATTORNEYS' MANUAL, tit. 1, §12.000, *available at* https://www.justice.gov/usam/united-states-attorneys-manual ("early and regular communication between civil attorneys and criminal prosecutors handling corporate investigations can be crucial to our ability to effectively pursue individuals in these matters. Consultation between the Department's civil and criminal attorneys, together with agency attorneys, permits consideration of the fullest range of the government's potential remedies and promotes the most thorough and appropriate resolution in each case.").

or as a part of DOJ's Corporate Leniency program.[1144]

5. DOJ attorneys must have a "clear plan" to resolve criminal cases against executives in order to seek resolution of the corporate investigation, and any releases of executives must be approved by the relevant U.S. attorney or assistant attorney general.[1145]

6. The DOJ's civil attorneys should "consistently focus on individuals as well as the company," and "[p]ursuit of civil actions against culpable individuals should not be governed solely by those individuals' ability to pay."[1146]

B. Impact on Individual Representation

While it is too early to determine the full effects of the Yates Memo, employees are asking their firm and its corporate counsel whether they should be represented by individual counsel (1) earlier in investigations, and (2) more frequently than ever. It is

---

[1144] Yates Memo at 5 ("Because of the importance of holding responsible individuals to account, absent extraordinary circumstances or approved departmental policy such as the Antitrust Division's Corporate Leniency Policy, Department lawyers should not agree to a corporate resolution that includes an agreement to dismiss charges against, or provide immunity for, individual officers or employees.").

[1145] Id. at 6 ("If a decision is made at the conclusion of the investigation not to bring civil claims or criminal charges against the individuals who committed the misconduct, the reasons for that determination must be memorialized and approved by the United States Attorney or Assistant Attorney General whose office handled the investigation, or their designees.").

[1146] Id.; see also Daniel Wilson, DOJ Official Says Civil Side of Yates Memo Wrongly Ignored, LAW360 (Nov. 12, 2015) (Assistant U.S. Attorney General Bill Baer remarking that "We will be looking, going forward, at whether there ought to be individual accountability. . . . It doesn't mean we're going to do it, but it is I think a fair thing for the deputy attorney general to ask all components [of the DOJ] to look at [whether] there is an additional deterrent effect that comes with holding responsible the individuals who adopt a policy that is in violation of the antitrust laws or some other federal standard.").

incumbent on corporate counsel to inform the employee that they represent the firm and remind the employee of their obligation to cooperate in internal investigations. The last thing corporate counsel wants is to realize six months into an internal investigation after a conflict has already arisen that an employee needs individual representation and that the corporation may need new counsel. Thus, corporate counsel should consider factors regarding individual counsel early in an investigation. Factors to consider at the outset of a government or internal investigation include:

1. If an employee has apparent "exposure" – especially exposure to the DOJ – the firm should provide individual counsel at the outset of the investigation.

2. If an employee has no apparent chance of exposure, joint representation is more likely to be appropriate. However, if the circumstances change with respect to the individual, the individual should be informed immediately of their need for separate counsel.

3. If an employee has no apparent exposure, but it is reasonable to believe that individual counsel may eventually be needed (due to the nature of the investigation), a firm should consider retaining "shadow counsel." Shadow counsel would stay apprised of the investigation but would not appear on behalf of the employee. Thus, shadow counsel would accrue lower legal fees than if appearing as counsel, but if needed, could relatively easily step in and provide an employee with meaningful advice and representation.

C.   Company Counsel May Need to Provide More Robust *Upjohn* Warnings

Given the increased focus on individuals, companies should consider making more robust "*Upjohn* Warnings"[1147] and memorializing them to ensure that employees understand the scope of the attorney-client relationship, and that the company can disclose facts learned during the interview at its sole discretion. These *Upjohn* warnings should be made early in the company's internal investigation because executives may choose to retain their own counsel at a much earlier stage of the investigation. It is unclear as a practical matter whether corporate counsel must now advise that the company will provide the details of any interview to the government to ensure employees fully understand their rights. Certainly, such a warning would likely chill an employee from speaking freely or without counsel.

IV.   IDENTIFYING CONFLICTS OF INTEREST

In the wake of the Yates Memo, addressing potential conflicts of interest has become increasingly important in government investigations. These conflicts of interest arise between the individual employees and the corporation itself and many argue that the DOJ policy set forth in the Yates Memo makes these conflicts more frequent. It is critical then that counsel for the individual be mindful of these potential pitfalls and secure conflict of interest waivers early on. Rule 1.13(a) of the Model Rules of Professional Conduct provides: "A lawyer employed or retained by an organization represents the organization acting through its duly authorized constituents." Furthermore, Rule 1.13(g) states: "A lawyer representing an organization may also represent any of its directors, officers, employees, members, shareholders or other constituents, subject to the provisions of Rule 1.7."[1148] Since the

---

[1147] *See Upjohn Co. v. United States*, 449 U.S. 383 (1981); *see also infra* Section VI. Witness Interviews.

[1148] Rule 1.7 of the Model Rules of Professional Conduct governs conflicts of interest. Under certain circumstances, Rule 1.7 dictates where a conflict of interest is present, an attorney may continue to represent both clients if both

Yates Memo, corporations are under more pressure to identify culpable employees to the government and to force employees to fully cooperate with the government. Corporations may become more aggressive in their investigations, focusing on finding the culpable individuals rather than defending against the government's claims. The likelihood that the interests of the corporation differ from the interests of the individual are much higher and individual's counsel should beware of the corporation cooperating with the government, against the individual's interest. In addition, government initiatives encouraging individual employees to cooperate in investigations, such as the SEC's cooperation program, encourage individuals to act against the corporation's interests in some cases. Furthermore, if an individual decides not to cooperate or asserts a privilege, the government may think corporate counsel influenced the individual's testimony. Corporations can minimize many of these conflicts of interest by encouraging employees to retain their own attorneys.

Counsel should also consider the advantages and disadvantages of representing multiple parties. There can be benefits in having counsel represent multiple parties, such as effectiveness and an increased understanding of the investigation. In contrast, the risks are that individuals or corporations could become adverse to each other and counsel would be unable to adequately advocate for either the individual or the corporation. Failure to adequately address potential conflicts can force counsel to be disqualified from providing representation for anyone in the government investigation. If counsel decides to represent both the corporation and an employee, counsel should obtain agreement from the individual at the outset, so that if a conflict arises where counsel cannot represent the individual anymore, counsel can continue to represent the corporation. If counsel represents multiple individuals, designate one as the "first client" and have each individual agree beforehand that if a conflict of interest arises requiring withdrawal, counsel can continue to represent the "first client." Before deciding to represent multiple individuals, counsel

---

affected parties provide "informed consent, confirmed in writing." MODEL CODE OF PROF'L RESPONSIBILITY R. 1.7(b)(4).

should assess each individual's scope and level of culpability, the relationship between the individuals, and whether it is necessary to obtain waivers of potential conflict.

A.   Cooperating with the Government

When engaged in the representation of an individual, it is important to consider whether the individual should cooperate with the government against the corporation. This decision involves an assessment of the individual's level of culpability. If the individual is solely a witness perhaps the individual should cooperate with the government. On the other hand, if the individual may face criminal charges then full cooperation with the government may be impossible. The decision should be made early on because, if not, the value of cooperating will diminish. Deciding to cooperate is extremely difficult to take back and the decision should not be made lightly. One consequence of cooperating with the government against the corporation is that the corporation will likely stop paying the individual's legal fees if the payments are not required by contract, corporate by-laws or otherwise. The individual could also face termination and lose access to the company's information and resources. The individual should also be aware that he or she may have to testify against friends, colleagues and co-workers. The government could require the individual to participate in multiple interviews, testify in grand jury and trial proceedings, and make written statements. If an individual decides to cooperate with the government, ensure that a cooperation agreement is negotiated.

With the implementation of numerous government cooperation programs, individuals are under more pressure to cooperate with the government. For instance, the SEC Whistle-blower Program allows a whistle-blower to be eligible for 10% to 30% of monetary sanctions that total more than $ 1milllion, so long as the whistle-blower voluntarily provides the SEC with original information leading to a successful enforcement action.[1149] Every year since 2011, the SEC has obtained more tips from whistle-blowers and

---

[1149] Dodd-Frank Section 922(a)-(b); Exchange Act Final Rule 21F.

the program has resulted in more than $904 million in sanctions.[1150] Other programs, such as the False Claims Act Whistle-blower Program, the Commodity Futures Trading Commission ("CFTC") Whistle-blower Program and the SEC Enforcement Division's Cooperation Program all incentivize employees to cooperate with government investigations for leniency and financial award. The programs even protect the whistle-blowers from retaliation by bringing actions against the corporations for retaliating against employees. Government agencies are focused on targeting individuals in an effort to more effectively handle larger scale enforcement actions. Agencies can leverage individuals and whistle-blowers against corporations and use an individual's information to their advantage. In response, counsel for the individual should consider the implications of such cooperation and reward programs carefully.

B.   Joint Defense Agreements

In an effort to aid in communication between the corporation's counsel and the employee's counsel, many attorneys enter into joint defense agreements. Joint defense agreements allow attorneys for all parties involved in the litigation or investigation whose interests are aligned – including corporate counsel – to exchange information about the matter and to coordinate legal defenses without waiving privileges. The joint defense privilege, also known as the common-interest doctrine, is not a separate privilege: it flows from the attorney client privilege and the work product doctrine. It is an exception to the rule that communications made to third parties are not subject to those protections. To assert the joint defense privilege, it must be shown that: (1) the communications were made in the course of a joint defense effort, (2) the statements were designed to further the effort, and (3) the privilege was not waived.[1151] The joint defense privilege covers all

---

[1150] Whistleblower Awards, SEC, (January 19, 2017) *available at* https://www.sec.gov/page/whistleblower-100million.

[1151] *In re Bevill, Bresler & Schulman Asset Mgmgt. Corp.*, 805 F.2d 120, 126 (3d Cir. 1986) (citing *In re Grand Jury Subpoena Duces Tecum*, 406 F. Supp. 381, 385 (S.D.N.Y. 1975)).

communications that are made by any attorney within the scope of the common interest, not just an individual's own attorney.

For many years, joint defense agreements were entered into as a matter of course because it aided the investigation and established a rapport between counsel for all parties involved. At a certain point, the trend toward joint defense agreements ebbed because corporations became increasingly concerned that these types of agreements created an appearance of bias or collusion between the corporation and its employees. As a consequence of the Yates Memo, joint defense agreements between corporate counsel and employee counsel are likely to become even less common because the corporation's interest may be at odds with the employee's interest. Also, the existence of a common interest between the corporation and an employee may not be found if those parties' interests are adverse. Consequently, counsel for the employee should consider entering into a joint defense agreement solely with other attorneys representing employees, excluding corporate counsel.

Counsel should also weigh the benefits and costs of entering into a joint defense agreement rather than entering into them reflexively as a matter of course. Before entering into an agreement, counsel should have an understanding of the case and the possible liability of each member of the joint defense group. Counsel should assess the likelihood that members of the group will eventually become adverse to each other. If there is a high risk, entering into a joint defense agreement may not be the right choice since the joint defense privilege is waived as soon as one of the participants becomes adverse to the other joint defense members. Information shared under the agreement remains confidential after the joint defense agreement is terminated, unless the information is held to have been communicated when there was no common interest. Although cooperating with the government generally does not rise to becoming adverse with the other members, there is a still a slight risk that the joint defense information will not remain privileged. In most cases, the joint defense agreement prevents the individual from revealing the information he or she learned from participating in the joint defense group. However, some courts have allowed waiver of privilege for statements made by an individual's own attorney, but not for the statements made by other attorneys.

One pitfall of a joint defense agreement is that the joint defense privilege does not allow any member to reveal the privileged information without consent from the entire group. Corporate counsel are often wary of entering into joint defense agreements with individual employees for fear of being unable to fully cooperate with the government. Counsel for individuals should also be wary of entering into joint defense agreements with the corporation. In *United States v. Leroy,* the court ruled that even though employees and corporations had entered into a joint defense agreement before the interview, the joint defense privilege was waived because the employees were aware that the corporation would waive privilege if the government pushed.[1152] Another drawback is that if a member withdraws from the joint defense agreement, counsel could face potential ethical conflicts. For instance, if counsel is aware of information obtained in confidence from a joint defense agreement, but because of a conflict of interest is unable to cross examine the cooperator, counsel may be disqualified from continuing to represent his or her current client.[1153] A joint defense agreement may create an implied attorney-client relationship between counsel for one individual and the other individuals. If such an implied attorney client relationship were found, counsel would have an ethical obligation to all participants in the joint defense agreement.

If counsel decides to enter into a joint defense agreement, consider whether the agreement should be oral or in writing. Some attorneys prefer oral joint defense agreements because they are less formal and restricting. But oral agreements are more common among attorneys who have an established good working relationship. As a general rule, a written agreement can address many of the

---

[1152] *See United States v. Leroy,* 348 F. Supp. 2d 375 (E.D. Pa. 2004).

[1153] *United States v. Henke,* 222 F.3d 633, 638 (9th Cir. 2000) (stating the joint defense privilege created "a disqualifying conflict where information gained in confidence by an attorney [became] an issue").

problems associated with joint defense agreements. A written agreement can memorialize the obligations of each member and can also be used as evidence if a dispute arises among the joint defense group. Be aware of the fact that the existence of a joint defense agreement is likely discoverable by the government. The discoverability of a joint defense agreement itself is unclear, but some courts have stated that parts of the agreement may not be privileged.[1154]

Joint defense agreements can be tailored to the circumstances of each case. As a practical tip, a written joint defense agreement should generally include the following points:

- Each member is being represented by the individual's attorney and that each member understands the obligations under the joint defense agreement. There is no attorney client relationship between the members and the other attorneys;

- The extent to which each member will share information, including the type of information to be shared but no obligation exists to share information;

- A confidentiality statement, that the information shared will not be disclosed to parties outside of the joint defense group and should remain confidential even after the joint defense agreement terminates;

- Each party agrees to respond to discovery requests with an assertion of the joint defense privilege;

[1154] *Warren Distrib. Co. v. InBev USA L.L.C.,* No. CIV. 07-1053, 2008 WL 4371763, at *3 (D.N.J. Sept. 18, 2008) (stating that "a party's mere characterization of a document as a joint defense agreement is not controlling as to whether the document is relevant and therefore subject to discovery...some portions of the document may be irrelevant or privileged, and another part may be relevant and discoverable").

- Members should not be allowed to use the shared information adversely against other members;

- In the event that members become adverse, each member waives its right to claim a conflict of interest again the other attorneys;

- Describe a process for terminating participation in the joint defense group;

- All modifications must be made in writing.

C.   Indemnification of Legal Fees

In the past, in assessing cooperation credit, the government considered whether the corporation was paying legal fees for employees. However, the U.S. Attorneys' Manual currently states that "prosecutors should not take into account whether a corporation is advancing or reimbursing attorneys' fees or providing counsel to employees, officers, or directors under investigation or indictment. Likewise, prosecutors may not request that a corporation refrain from taking such action."[1155] Accordingly, with the higher likelihood that individual employees may retain separate counsel for government investigations, corporations should review their directors and officers ("D&O") insurance policies for sufficient coverage. Some individuals may not be covered under D&O insurance, but such policies should always be immediately reviewed for applicability and limitations. Counsel for individuals should also be mindful that some indemnification agreements impose conditions upon the employee in exchange for payment of legal fees and require cooperation with the corporation's internal investigations or sometimes even the government's investigations. Counsel should ensure that the individual employee fully understands the obligations under any indemnification agreement.

[1155] DEP'T OF JUSTICE, U.S. ATTORNEYS' MANUAL, tit. 9, §28.730, *available at* https://www.justice.gov/usam/united-states-attorneys-manual.

V.   DOCUMENT PRESERVATION

One of the first steps that counsel must take after learning that the company and/or its officers and employees are under investigation is to suspend automatic document destruction practices and issue a legal hold notice. Additionally, in the age of smart phones, instant messaging, and social media it is important for individuals to understand their document preservation obligations and the consequences even of inadvertent destruction.

Destruction of relevant documents, even if inadvertent, can have dire ramifications for the company and the individual. The government undoubtedly will investigate the circumstances of any destruction to determine whether criminal obstruction charges are warranted.[1156] Federal law provides severe criminal penalties for anyone who "knowingly alters, destroys, mutilates, conceals, covers up, falsifies, or makes a false entry in any record, document, or tangible object with the intent to impede, obstruct, or influence the investigation... within any matter within the jurisdiction of any department or agency of the United States...." [1157] The DOJ is "very serious about prosecuting cases where there is destruction of evidence," according to John Haried, e-discovery

---

[1156] One of the criminal obstruction statutes that the government may consider (among others) is section 802 of the Sarbanes-Oxley Act of 2002 (18 U.S.C. § 1519), which provides: "[w]hoever knowingly alters, destroys, mutilates, conceals, covers up, falsifies, or makes a false entry in any record, document, or tangible object with the intent to impede, obstruct, or influence the investigation or proper administration of any matter within the jurisdiction of any department or agency of the United States or any case filed under title 11, or in relation to or in contemplation of any such matter or case, shall be fined under this title, imprisoned not more than 20 years, or both." To date, this language, although referenced, has not been interpreted by a court. It appears, however, to eliminate the nexus between the destruction of documents and an official proceeding. The statute also does not appear to require a willful or corrupt state of mind, although it is unclear, after the Supreme Court's decision in *Arthur Andersen v. United States*, 544 U.S. 696 (2005), whether one can be convicted of criminal obstruction without such intent.

[1157] 18 U.S.C. § 1519.

working group chair for the DOJ,[1158] so it is vital that attorneys take extra precaution to have clients maintain electronically stored information ("ESI") as soon as there is reason to believe the government will seek information from them in an investigation. Even if the government determines that there is insufficient evidence to bring obstruction charges, the government may well view the company with suspicion in future dealings and question the sincerity of the company's stated desire to cooperate. The government may also be less likely to agree, at least preliminarily, to limit the scope of any subpoena and to grant additional time to gather documents. The government might even consider seeking a search warrant.

For these reasons, counsel should work with the individual to acquire an understanding of the individual's personal computer habits. Where is data stored? Do they instant message or text other employees? Do they e-mail corporate documents or e-mails to a personal e-mail account? Do they use social media and, if so, what apps?

Document preservation can also be a weapon for the individual and counsel may wish to advise individuals of the circumstances when document preservation is to the individual's benefit. In many instances the retention of corporate information by an individual, even after leaving the company, is not a criminal or ethical violation. For instance, the Defend Trade Secrets Act provides that an individual shall not be held criminally or civilly liable under any federal or state trade secret law for the disclosure of a trade secret that – (A) is made (i) in confidence to a federal, state, or local government official, either directly or indirectly, or to an attorney; and (ii) solely for the purpose of reporting or investigating a suspected violation of law; or (B) is made in a complaint or other document filed in a lawsuit or other proceeding, if such filing is made under seal.[1159]

[1158] Gavin Broady, *DOJ Chiefs Share The Wrong Way To Respond To A Subpoena*, LAW360 (Feb. 5, 2015).

[1159] 18 U.S.C. § 1833 (b)(2)(A)-(B).

VI.   WITNESS INTERVIEWS

In the course of a government investigation, the documents and electronic data frequently do not provide a complete picture of events. As another means of gathering information, government investigators may conduct witness interviews of employees who have knowledge of the subject matter being investigated. Employee witness interviews generally take place once background information for the investigation has been developed. In order to effectively represent an individual, it is important for counsel to review documents prior to conducting witness interviews. Valuable information concerning an individual's role and conduct may be obtained through interviews based on the documents authored, sent, or received by the individual.

Counsel should exercise caution when taking notes during interviews. The attorney work product doctrine protects an attorney's mental impressions, conclusions, opinions or legal theories.[1160] Attorney notes are typically considered work product,[1161] but the privilege is not absolute. The notes could be discoverable if a substantial need for the information was shown and the requesting party could not obtain the same information elsewhere without undue hardship. Therefore, interviews should not be recorded and notes should not be taken verbatim. If counsel drafts a memorandum of the interview, counsel should summarize the interview in a way that separates the facts from the attorney's subjective thoughts. In the end, the decision about whether to formally memorialize interviews should weigh the risk of discovery against the benefits of having summarized interviews.

Counsel should interview the client immediately after being retained. A client interview should cover relevant background information about the individual, as well as specific about the government investigation. It is important to fully understand the individual's perspective early on and to know both the good and

---

[1160] FED. R. CIV. P. 26(b)(3)(B).

[1161] *See In re General Motors LLC Ignition Switch Litigation*, 2015 WL 221057 (S.D.N.Y. January 15, 2015).

bad facts. If counsel has a full picture of the individual's role in the government investigation, counsel can better represent the individual.

If an individual agrees to being interviewed by the government, counsel should come up with a plan to prepare the individual. Counsel must understand the facts, prepare a chronology of the key events, and be aware of the key issues of the case. If counsel is prepared before a preparation session, the session will go more efficiently and in a more logical manner. During a preparation session, review with the individual the witness's background, work history, and ask the witness about key documents. Take note of the witness's personality and demeanor; if the witness is too talkative, coach the witness to focus on answering only the specific questions asked. If the witness is anxious or confrontational, address those issues before the government interview. Ask open-ended questions, but also anticipate difficult questions that the government investigator may ask the individual. Consider the risks of allowing corporate counsel to participate in preparation sessions. Typically, the corporation is the holder of the privilege concerning conversations involving the employee and corporate counsel. Therefore, the corporation can decide to waive the privilege and disclose the conversation to the government.

Before a government interview, counsel should contact the government agent and ask why the individual is being interviewed. Attempt to ascertain the nature, scope, and age of the investigation. Whether an individual is a witness, subject, or target can affect counsel's defense strategy and any other information obtained can provide more insight into the government's investigation. Some government agents are more forthcoming than others. If the government agent classifies the client as a witness, ask for a "Non-Subject" letter. A "Non-Subject" letter provides assurance that the individual is a witness, rather than a subject or target, though the letter is likely to be qualified. Obtaining a "Non-Subject" letter can give counsel support to advise the client to cooperate with the government agents. Though the SEC generally will not indicate whether the individual is a subject or target, counsel may still be able to gather useful information from the SEC about the individual's conduct and the SEC lawyer's viewpoint of the client. An SEC lawyer's unwillingness or willingness to speak about the client can also indicate the level of culpability they have ascribed to the individual. The SEC lawyer is more likely to be tight lipped if he or she believes the client is culpable.

Individuals should also be aware that, if they do decide to participate in an interview with the government, they have the right to have an attorney present and to speak to their attorney before, during, and after the interview. Most importantly, employees should know that any statements made during the interview are legal admissions that could later be used against the corporation or the individual. Of course, counsel should advise clients to tell the truth in interviews. False statements made to any government investigator could lead to criminal charges.

A.   Risk of Making False Statements

During government interviews, there is always a risk that an individual will make a false statement or commit perjury.[1162] Counsel should warn clients about these risks. Often, clients do not understand that a civil investigation could result in a criminal perjury charge and thus need to be advised accordingly. The government could later charge an individual with making a false statement "knowingly and wilfully" under 18 U.S.C. § 1001, even if the statement is not made while under oath. A defendant could face a maximum of five years in prison and up to $250,000 in criminal fines.[1163] For instance, high profile defendants, such as Martha Stewart[1164] and John Schulte,[1165] were charged and found guilty for making false statements to a government agency.

[1162] 18 U.S.C. §§ 1621 & 1623.

[1163] See 18 U.S.C. § 1001; 18 U.S.C. § 3571(b)(3).

[1164] See United States v. Stewart, 433 F.3d 273 (2nd Cir. 2006) (Jury found Stewart made false statements to the SEC, the FBI and federal prosecutors regarding the sale of stock).

[1165] See United States v. Schulte, 741 F.3d 1141 (10th Cir. 2014) (Schulte was convicted of making material false statements to federal investigators during a

In the past, some courts held that prosecutors only needed to show that the individual made the statement while aware of the fact that it was false. However, in 2014, the DOJ adopted a more defendant-friendly definition of "wilfully."[1166] Now, federal prosecutors must also show that the defendant knew making his or her statement was unlawful, requiring a higher burden. Before the individual makes a statement, consult with the prosecutor to gauge whether the prosecutor believes any information from the individual is false or inaccurate. If the differences cannot be reconciled, then an interview should be refused, unless immunity can be provided.

B. Fifth Amendment Privilege

Counsel should advise individual clients of their Fifth Amendment rights. Unlike corporations, individuals have a Fifth Amendment right against self-incrimination, which guarantees an individual's right to remain silent without the silence being used against the individual in a criminal case.[1167] The Supreme Court stated that the protection of the Fifth Amendment "must be confined to instances where the witness has reasonable cause to apprehend danger from a direct answer."[1168] If an individual wants to assert his or her Fifth Amendment privilege, that decision must be made with care. In civil cases, the Fifth Amendment protection does not apply. Instead, if an individual asserts their Fifth Amendment privilege in a civil case, the government may seek to have an adverse inference drawn from the individual's refusal to answer. Also, if an individual testifies in a civil proceeding, it may result in the waiver of the individual's Fifth Amendment privilege in other proceedings.

---

voluntary interview and was found guilty even though the defendant tried to correct his statements later).

[1166] Joel M. Athey, *DOJ "Willfully" Corrects Its Stance on False Statement Prosecutions: Change Could Have Major impact on Future White-collar Investigations and Prosecutions*, ABA (Fall 2014).

[1167] U.S. CONST. amend. V.

[1168] *Hoffman v. United States*, 341 U.S. 479, 486 (1951).

An individual cannot be compelled to testify in a criminal proceeding—even if he or she has testified in a parallel civil proceeding. But, investigators may still be able to use the evidence from the civil proceeding against the individual in criminal proceedings. Note, in some cases, federal courts have suggested that the SEC may have violated an individual's Fifth Amendment right against self-incrimination by knowingly interviewing an individual who was also a target of a criminal investigation by the DOJ.[1169] However, there is still a serious risk that criminal investigators may use evidence from civil investigations against the individual or vice versa. If an individual has a pending parallel criminal investigation, counsel should consider requesting a stay of the civil proceeding. Individuals should also be mindful of participating in corporate internal investigations because information learned by the corporation can be turned over to the government. If an individual may have criminal liability, counsel may want to suggest that the individual assert his or her Fifth Amendment right during the corporate internal investigation or else refuse to submit to an interview during that investigation. However, employees may be terminated if they refuse to participate in the corporate internal investigation. It is not a clear violation of an individual's Fifth Amendment right to be asked to cooperate in an internal investigation.[1170] In order to assert Fifth Amendment privilege in an internal investigation, the court must find that the corporation's actions rose to the level of state action.[1171]

Counsel must weigh the benefits and risks of disclosing information to the government and how such disclosures may amount to waiver of privilege for other parties. Selective waiver is the attempt to disclose privileged material but still claim privilege over the material with other third parties. Most courts do not

---

[1169] *See United States v. Scrushy,* 366 F. Supp. 2d 1134, 1139-40 (N.D. Ala. 2005) (holding that the SEC civil investigator may have violated the target's constitutional right by taking a deposition of the target without notifying the target that a parallel criminal investigation had begun).

[1170] *See Gilman v. Marsh & McLennan Cos.,* No. 15-0603-cv (2d Cir. 2016).

[1171] *Id.*

recognize selective waiver. Be wary of disclosing privileged material to the government and arguing later that the disclosure was not a waiver of privilege for other third parties. Selective waiver remains uncertain and should not be relied upon.

C.   *Upjohn* Warnings

Before the start of an interview, corporate counsel will likely ensure that an employee is advised of his or her right to retain separate counsel. This is especially important if corporate counsel is aware that an employee's interests are or likely will be adverse to the corporation's. Beyond advising the employee of his right to retain separate counsel, corporate counsel cannot ethically provide any other legal advice.[1172] Once an individual is represented by counsel, the corporation's counsel may not interview the individual unless the employee's attorney is present or the attorney consents to the interview.[1173] Of course, the attorney for the individual should always be present at the witness interview, but corporate counsel should still provide the employee with an "*Upjohn* warning."

Pursuant to the Court's holding in *Upjohn v. United States*, 449 U.S. 383 (1981), this warning requires that the corporation's counsel explain to company employees that counsel is representing the company and not the individual witness. Counsel must warn the employee that the attorney-client privilege belongs to the

---

[1172] MODEL CODE OF PROF'L RESPONSIBILITY R. 4.3 ("In communicating on behalf of a client with a person who is not represented by counsel, a lawyer shall not state or imply that the lawyer is disinterested. When the lawyer knows or reasonably should know that the unrepresented person misunderstands the lawyer's role in the matter, the lawyer shall make reasonable efforts to correct the misunderstanding. The lawyer shall not give legal advice to an unrepresented person other than the advice to secure counsel if the lawyer knows or reasonably should know that the interests of such person are or have a reasonable possibility of being in conflict with the interests of the client.").

[1173] MODEL CODE OF PROF'L RESPONSIBILITY R. 4.2(a) ("In representing a client, a lawyer shall not communicate about the subject of the representation with a person the lawyer knows to be represented by another lawyer in the matter, unless the lawyer has the consent of the other lawyer or is authorized to do so by law or a court order.").

company and not the individual. As a matter of best practices, an *Upjohn* warning should convey to the employee the following points: (i) counsel for the corporation represents the corporate entity and does not represent the individual employee; (ii) the interview is being conducted to gather information to assist in counsel's representation of the corporation and not the individual; (iii) the interview is subject to attorney-client privilege, but the privilege belongs to the corporation and not the individual; (iv) the corporation may decide to waive privilege in the future and disclose the contents of the interview to the government or other third parties; and (v) the interview is confidential and should be treated as such. Corporations may require employees to acknowledge in writing that they understood the *Upjohn* warning. By doing so, misunderstandings regarding whether *Upjohn* warnings were given or understood will be avoided. Before an employee agrees to be interviewed, counsel for the individual should advise the employee about possible waivers of privilege and that any information discussed with corporate counsel may be turned over to the government.

VII.   FREQUENT MISTAKES TO AVOID

A.   Avoid Retaining a Single Law Firm Without Considering Potential Conflicts of Interest

One common mistake to avoid in handling the representation of individuals in a government investigation is using one lawyer to represent everyone without considering the potential ethical conflicts that may arise. If a corporation is responsible for handling the representation of an individual, it is important to consider whether to hire separate counsel for the individual. There can be pitfalls in having a single law firm act as counsel for both the corporation and its employees. The interests of culpable individuals are likely to become adverse to the corporation's interest and a conflict of interest may arise. Therefore, it is important to weigh the costs and benefits of retaining a single law firm. If a single law firm is retained, conflict of interest waivers should be obtained.

B. Avoid Failing to Communicate With Other Counsel

In situations where there is separate counsel for multiple parties, counsel's failure to communicate with other counsel in the matter can lead to unintended consequences. For instance, when counsel for an individual is not notified of or consulted about a corporation's plan to fire the culpable individual, the individual may possess documents detrimental to the corporation and firing the individual can lead to the individual taking revenge on the corporation. This does not mean employees should not be fired, only that corporate counsel must consider the possible consequences. It is also important for an individual's counsel to try to work alongside corporate counsel because helpful information can be traded between the two. However, separate counsel should operate with the mindset that such conversations can be discoverable and are not protected by attorney-client privilege, unless there is a joint defense privilege.

C. Avoid Voluntary Disclosure Without Fully Understanding the Requirements

Another common mistake can be electing to voluntarily disclose information to the government investigators without fully understanding the requirements behind voluntary disclosure. Individuals and corporations should not disclose information to the government without considering waiver of privilege. The Yates Memo has made it clear that a corporation's eligibility for cooperation credit is based upon an all or nothing policy. Corporations cannot cherry pick what to disclose or not to disclose. Before disclosure, counsel for the corporation and the individual must critically assess the appropriateness of voluntary disclosure. Disclosure decisions should be made on a case by case basis. It is much worse for an individual or corporation to decide to cooperate with the government without knowledge of all the facts and then later fail to disclose relevant information. Rather than benefiting from disclosure, the corporation or individual may be instead punished.

D.   Avoid Giving Insufficient *Upjohn* Warnings

Failure to give clear *Upjohn* warnings[1174] during witness interviews can have severe consequences and should be avoided. Now, the stakes are even higher because to receive cooperation credit the corporation must be able to disclose all information learned during the interview. Retaining control of attorney client privilege is crucial for a corporation hoping to receive cooperation credit from the government. If a culpable individual does not want the information revealed to the government and an insufficient *Upjohn* warning was given, the individual may be able to prevent disclosure leading to the loss of eligibility for cooperation credit. On the other hand, the individual may want to reveal privileged material, in opposition of the corporation's interest, in order to receive cooperation credit for his or her own case. To avoid the above situation, counsel must give clear and well-documented *Upjohn* warnings to interviewed individuals. The cost of possibly losing the candidness of an individual is outweighed by the likely negative consequences of an insufficient *Upjohn* warning.

E.   Avoid Failing to Preserve Records and Electronically Stored Information

Another common mistake is the failure to retain records and electronically stored information. Failing to do so can increase the cost of the investigation and result in sanctions. Individuals should be notified in writing of the potentially responsive documents to the investigation so that they can be properly preserved. Counsel should be knowledgeable about the steps his or her client took to locate, preserve and produce responsive documents. Individuals should be questioned about possible third parties who may possess responsive documents, which should also be preserved. Records of document preservation should be kept in order to facilitate

---

[1174] An *Upjohn* warning should clearly inform the employee that corporate counsel does not represent the employee and that any privileged material derived from the conversation belongs solely to the corporation, not the employee. The purpose of the warning is so that the employee cannot later argue that he or she believed corporate counsel to be representing both the corporation and employee. *Upjohn v. United States,* 449 U.S. 383 (1981).

negotiations with government investigators and to add credibility
to the corporations' and individuals' efforts.

VIII. CONCLUSION

There has been a serious shift in focus on prosecuting individuals,
altering the considerations that corporations must make in handling
the representation of individuals in government investigations.
Although the government has issued memoranda[1175] before noting
the necessity of holding culpable individuals liable, the sole
objective of the Yates Memo is to address holding individuals
accountable for corporate wrongdoings. Even the United States
Attorneys' Manual was updated to reflect the policies outlined in
the Yates Memo, a serious step taken towards individual
accountability.[1176] A corporation's general counsel must meet the
higher expectations of government investigators for cooperation
credit while dealing with the heightened tensions between a
corporation and its culpable individuals. Conflicts of interest are
more likely to arise between a corporation and its employees,
increasing the likelihood of individuals retaining separate
representation and increasing legal costs. Consequently, balancing
such relationships will be a difficult task since individuals may be
less likely to cooperate with internal investigations. It is important

---

[1175] *See* Memorandum from Eric H. Holder, Jr., Deputy Attorney General, Dep't
of Justice, Bringing Criminal Charges Against Corporations (June 16, 1999),
available at https://www.justice.gov/sites/default/files/criminal-
fraud/legacy/2010/04/11/charging-corps.PDF; Memorandum from Larry D.
Thompson, Deputy Attorney General, Dep't of Justice, Principles of Federal
Prosecution of Business Organizations (Jan. 20, 2003), *available at*
http://www.americanbar.org/content/dam/aba/migrated/poladv/priorities/privilege
waiver/2003jan20_privwaiv_dojthomp.authcheckdam.pdf; Memorandum from
Paul J. McNulty, Deputy Attorney General, Dep't of Justice, Principles of Federal
Prosecution of Business Organizations (Dec. 12, 2006), *available at*
https://www.justice.gov/sites/default/files/dag/legacy/2007/07/05/mcnulty_memo.
pdf; Memorandum from Mark Filip, Deputy Attorney General, Dep't of Justice,
Principles of Federal Prosecution of Business Organizations (Aug. 28, 2008),
available at
https://www.justice.gov/sites/default/files/dag/legacy/2008/11/03/dag-memo-
08282008.pdf.

[1176] Yates Delivers Remarks at the New York City Bar Association White-collar
Crime Conference, *supra* note 4.

to keep these issues in mind while handling a government investigation.

It remains to be seen whether the Yates Memo actually leads to an increase in prosecution of individuals. With more time, the effects of the Yates Memo on government investigations will be clearer. In the interim, corporations should keep their employees aware of their legal rights, obligations and the corporate internal policies regarding how to handle instances of misconduct. Identifying corporate wrongdoing through internal reporting policies and promptly remedying misconduct allows a corporation to be one step ahead of a government investigation. Over time, proactive compliance with regulations and mitigating serious risks of misconduct before a government investigation even begins will benefit a corporation.

Chapter 25

Insider Trading

By: Kevin J. Harnisch and Ilana B. Sinkin[1177]

I. INTRODUCTION

It is a common misperception that the federal securities laws prohibit individuals from engaging in all forms of trading while they are in possession of material,[1178] nonpublic information about a company. The reality is more nuanced. The primary laws used to prosecute illegal insider trading are Section 10(b) of the Securities Exchange Act of 1934 ("Exchange Act") and Rule 10b-5 thereunder. Those general antifraud provisions require, among other things, proof of material misstatements or material omissions (when there is a duty to speak) or deception in connection with the purchase or sale of a security. Thus, as this chapter will explain in more detail, trading on the basis of material, nonpublic information is illegal when done in breach of a fiduciary duty or similar duty of trust and confidence, or in breach of an agreement not to use the information for one's own advantage. Trading, or tipping others who trade, in breach of these obligations can trigger both civil and criminal liability. The Department of Justice ("DOJ") brings criminal prosecutions, while the Securities and Exchange Commission ("SEC") brings civil and administrative proceedings.

[1177] Kevin J. Harnisch is a Partner with Norton Rose Fulbright US LLP in Washington, DC, where he is Head of SEC Enforcement. Ilana B. Sinkin is a Senior Counsel at Norton Rose Fulbright US LLP in Washington, DC, and focuses her practice on white-collar civil and criminal defense. The views expressed by the authors are their own and do not necessarily represent the views of the firm or any of its clients.

[1178] Information is material if there is a substantial likelihood that a reasonable investor would consider it important in making an investment or trading decision. *See TSC Industries, Inc. v. Northway, Inc.*, 426 U.S. 438, 449 (1976); *Basic v. Levinson*, 485 U.S. 224, 231 (1988) (materiality with respect to contingent or speculative events will depend on a balancing of both the indicated probability that the event will occur and the anticipated magnitude of the event in light of the totality of company activity).

This chapter explains the classical and misappropriation theories of insider trading, the scope of tipper and tippee liability, and Rule 10b5-1 plans and other insider trading controls.

II. THEORIES OF INSIDER TRADING: CLASSICAL V. MISAPPROPRIATION

A. The Classical Theory of Insider Trading

The classical theory of insider trading pertains to a situation involving corporate insiders, such as company officers or directors, who trade in their company's stock on the basis of material, nonpublic information. Because such insiders have fiduciary duties to the corporation and its shareholders, thereby preventing them from using information about the company for their own personal advantage, they must either disclose material, nonpublic information prior to trading (which is not realistic, as most companies would prohibit such disclosure) or abstain from trading.[1179]

Insider trading under the "classical" theory is not, however, limited to traditional corporate insiders, such as corporate executives. Indeed, insider trading liability can apply to "temporary insiders" who "have entered into a special confidential relationship in the conduct of the business of the enterprise and are given access to information solely for corporate purposes."[1180] Examples of such insiders include "an underwriter, accountant, lawyer, or consultant."[1181]

[1179] *Chiarella v. United States*, 445 U.S. 222, 228-29 (1980).

[1180] *Dirks v. SEC*, 463 U.S. 646, 655 n.14 (1983).

[1181] *Id.; see also SEC v. Lerner*, 1980 WL 1388, at *1 (D.D.C. Apr. 2, 1980) (holding that attorneys cannot purchase stock of client because they become a temporary insider of a company that hires them); *Quaak v. Dexia*, 445 F. Supp. 2d 130, 150 (D. Mass. 2006) (holding that lender was a temporary insider when the borrower placed its trust in the lender by conveying confidential information to the lender); *SEC v. Ingram*, 694 F. Supp. 1437, 1440 (C.D. Cal. 1988) (holding that stock broker temporarily assumed the duties of an insider).

Subjects of insider trading investigations often argue that, while they may have been in possession of material, nonpublic information at the time they traded, they did not use that information when deciding to trade (*i.e.*, they had other reasons for doing the trades). Federal appellate courts were initially split as to whether the SEC and the DOJ had to prove that the defendants actually used the material, nonpublic information in their possession when making their trading decisions.[1182] In 2000, the SEC adopted Rule 10b5-1 to address this issue. Through Rule 10b5-1, the SEC has defined trading "on the basis of" material, nonpublic information as buying or selling a security while "aware" of the material, nonpublic information. Despite the incorporation of the knowing possession standard into Rule 10b5-1, there remains an argument that, in criminal cases, the DOJ must nevertheless prove that the defendant actually used the information as a basis for the trades.[1183]

B. The Misappropriation Theory of Insider Trading

The misappropriation theory of insider trading pertains to a corporate outsider (who, therefore, does not have a fiduciary duty to the company or its shareholders) who trades on the basis of material, nonpublic information in breach of a duty owed to the source of the information. The Supreme Court adopted the misappropriation theory in *United States v. O'Hagan*.[1184] O'Hagan was an attorney whose firm represented the buyer in an

---

[1182] *Compare United States v. Smith*, 155 F.3d 1051, 1069–70 (9th Cir. 1998) ("government (or the SEC, as the case may be) [must] demonstrate that the suspected inside trader actually used material nonpublic information in consummating his transaction" (citations omitted)); *United States v. Teicher*, 987 F.2d 112, 121 (2d Cir. 1993) (upholding the "knowing possession" standard. An "arbitrageur, who traded while possessing information he knew to be fraudulently obtained, knew to be material, knew to be nonpublic,–and who did not act in good faith in so doing," traded on the basis of that information.).

[1183] *See, e.g.*, R. Glaser and Raymond Bilderbeck, "Use v. Possession in Insider Trading Cases," N.Y.L.J. (July 9, 2012) (discussing the reluctance of many courts to embrace the knowing possession standard to criminal insider trading cases).

[1184] 521 U.S. 642 (1997).

acquisition.[1185] The DOJ charged O'Hagan with insider trading because he purchased call options in the stock of the target company before the deal had been publicly announced.[1186] O'Hagan challenged the charges, claiming that he did not breach any duties to the target company's shareholders because his firm did not represent that company.[1187] The Supreme Court held that O'Hagan violated § 10(b) and Rule 10b-5 by using deceit in connection with his trades. Specifically, O'Hagan misappropriated confidential information of his law firm's client in a manner that deceived "those who entrusted him with access to confidential information."[1188] Under the misappropriation theory, a misappropriator must knowingly violate a "duty of loyalty and confidentiality" to the source of the information and trade to his advantage through that deception.[1189] The Court said, "[t]he deception essential to the misappropriation theory involves feigning fidelity to the source of the information."[1190]

The SEC subsequently adopted Rule 10b5-2 to set forth a non-exhaustive list of situations where a person has a duty of trust or confidence for purposes of the misappropriation theory of insider trading:

Whenever a person agrees to maintain information in confidence;

Whenever the person communicating the material, nonpublic information and the person to whom it is communicated have a history, pattern, or practice of sharing confidences, such that the recipient of the information knows or reasonably should know that the person communicating the material, nonpublic information expects that the recipient will maintain its confidentiality; or

---

[1185] *Id.* at 647.

[1186] *Id.*

[1187] *Id.* At 652-53.

[1188] *Id.* at 652.

[1189] *Id.* at 656.

[1190] *Id.* at 655.

Whenever a person receives or obtains material, nonpublic information from his or her spouse, parent, child, or sibling; *provided*, however, that the person receiving or obtaining the information may demonstrate that no duty of trust or confidence existed with respect to the information, by establishing that he or she neither knew nor reasonably should have known that the person who was the source of the information expected that the person would keep the information confidential, because of the parties' history, pattern, or practice of sharing and maintaining confidences, and because there was no agreement or understanding to maintain the confidentiality of the information.[1191]

While § 10(b) and Rule 10b-5 require a breach of fiduciary duty or a similar relationship of trust and confidence, there is a lower threshold for insider trading violations in the context of a tender offer. Rule 14e-3 prohibits trading while in the possession of material, nonpublic information about a tender offer if that information was obtained from someone who is involved in the tender offer. Therefore, in the context of a tender offer, no breach of duty or misappropriation is required.[1192]

The SEC has expanded its view of the misappropriation theory of liability to those who engage in "shadow trading." Shadow trading is where a person trades in the securities of one company while in the possession of material, nonpublic information from another similarly situated company. In August 2021, the SEC used the shadow trading theory against Matthew Panuwat, a former business development director at Medivation, an oncology pharmaceuticals company.[1193] Panuwat, according to the SEC, traded stock options in another mid-sized oncology pharmaceutical company shortly after learning that Pfizer would acquire Medivation at a significant premium. After the public

---

[1191] 17 C.F.R. § 240.10b5-2.

[1192] *See, e.g.*, SEC Order Instituting Cease-and-Desist Proceedings, *In the Matter of Charles L. Hill, Jr.*, Release No. 74249 (Feb. 11, 2015).

[1193] SEC Complaint, *SEC v. Matthew Panuwat*, No. 4:21-cv-06322 (N.D. Cal. Aug. 17, 2021) *available at* https://www.sec.gov/litigation/complaints/2021/comp-pr2021-155.pdf.

announcement of the transaction, the stock price of the other company similarly increased. The SEC pled that Panuwat breached a duty he held to Medivation by violating Medivation's insider trading policy that expressly forbade Panuwat from using confidential information he acquired at Medivation to trade in the securities of any other publicly-traded company. As of the time of this article, the litigation is continuing.

III.   TIPPER AND TIPPEE LIABILITY

Insider trading liability can attach to a person who provides the material, nonpublic information (a "tipper") to another who then trades on the basis of that information (a "tippee"). Thus, a tipper may be liable even if he or she does not personally trade. In *Dirks v. SEC*, the Supreme Court established that the test for tipper liability is "whether the insider personally will benefit, directly or indirectly from his disclosure. Absent some personal gain, there has been no breach of duty to stockholders. And absent a breach by the insider, there is no derivative breach [by the tippee]."[1194] The concept of personal gain is broad and can include "a pecuniary gain or a reputational benefit that will translate into future earnings," or "a gift of confidential information to a trading relative or friend" where there was a quid pro quo or an intention to benefit the tippee.[1195]

The Supreme Court in *Dirks* also established the following standard for imposing liability on the tippee: a tippee engages in insider trading "only when the insider has breached his fiduciary duty to the shareholders by disclosing the information to the tippee and the *tippee knows or should know that there has been a breach*."[1196] In that case, Raymond Dirks—an analyst at a broker-dealer—received a tip from Ronald Secrist—a former officer of Equity Funding—that Equity Funding was engaged in fraud. Dirks told his clients to sell their Equity Funding stock. The Supreme Court held that Dirks did not illegally tip his clients because

---

[1194] *Dirks*, 463 U.S. at 662.

[1195] *Id.* at 664.

[1196] *Id.* at 660 (emphasis added).

Secrist (the source of the information) did not receive any monetary or personal benefit for revealing the fraud to him and Secrist was not trying to make a gift of valuable information to Dirks. Therefore, as Secrist did not breach a duty to Equity Funding, there was no basis to impose liability on Dirks. Essentially, there was no breach of duty for Dirks to inherit from Secrist.[1197]

One of the cornerstones for tipper and tippee liability is "whether the insider personally will benefit, directly or indirectly from his disclosure."[1198] Whether the insider received a personal benefit became the subject of much litigation after the Second Circuit's decision in *United States v. Newman*.[1199] In *Newman*, the Court held that the government failed to prove that the tippee knew the insider disclosed material, nonpublic information in exchange for a personal benefit that was more than mere friendship or familial relationship. The Court held that the government must establish that there was "a meaningfully close personal relationship that generates an exchange that is objective, consequential, and represents at least a potential gain of a pecuniary or similarly valuable nature."[1200] Following *Newman*, alleged tippees began routinely arguing that the government must prove that tippers received a pecuniary gain or something tangible in return for the tip.

The Supreme Court clarified the issue in *United States v. Salman*.[1201] Salman received material, nonpublic information about impending corporate acquisitions from a close friend who had, in turn, received the information from that person's brother who was an investment banker and who also happened to be Salman's brother-in-law. In upholding Salman's conviction, the Supreme Court explained that "[m]aking a gift of inside information to a

---

[1197] *Id.* at 667.

[1198] *Id.* at 662.

[1199] 773 F.3d 438 (2d Cir. 2014), *cert. denied*, 136 S. Ct. 438 (2015).

[1200] *Id.* at 452.

[1201] *Salman v. United States*, 2016 WL 7078448 (U.S. Dec. 6, 2016).

relative…is little different from trading on the information, obtaining the profits, and doling them out to the trading relative. The tipper benefits either way."[1202] The Court rejected the argument that the tipper must receive something of a "pecuniary or similarly valuable nature" in cases where the tipper gifts information to a "trading relative or friend."[1203] Practitioners should note that Salman involved a narrow issue,[1204] and that the Supreme Court acknowledged that factual circumstances in other cases may present difficulties in assessing whether a tipper intended to provide a gift of material, nonpublic information to the tippee.[1205] Although Salman did not address what constitutes a sufficiently close friendship for the passing of information to be considered a gift, the government historically has brought charges against tippers and tippees when insiders share material, nonpublic information with acquaintances, such as work colleagues and members of the same country club, who then trade on the basis of that information.[1206] It is likely that the government will continue to take an aggressive view on when an acquaintance should be considered a friend such that the government need not prove a tangible benefit to the tipper.

In fact, shortly after the Supreme Court decision, a divided Second Circuit overturned its *Newman* opinion in *United States v.*

[1202] *Id.* at *8.

[1203] *Id.*

[1204] *Id.* at *7 ("We adhere to *Dirks*, which easily resolves the narrow issue presented here.").

[1205] *Id.* at *9 (The Court need not "address those difficult cases" because the facts are "precisely the gift of confidential information to a trading relative that *Dirks* envisioned.") (quotations omitted).

[1206] *See e.g., SEC v. Obus*, 693 F.3d 276 (2d Cir. 2012) (SEC brought insider trading charges against college buddies and fellow country club members); *SEC v. O'Neill and Bray*, No. 1:14-cv-13381 (D. Mass Aug. 18, 2014) (SEC brought insider trading charges against golf buddies); *SEC v. Deskovick*, No. 2:11-CV-01522 (D.N.J. Mar. 17, 2011) (SEC alleged a close personal relationship with person hired to perform services at the home of one Defendant and another closer personal relationship with the other Defendant's business associate).

Martoma.[1207] The majority opinion reasoned that the Supreme Court's *Salman* opinion was inconsistent with *Newman's* requirement that, in the absence of quid pro quo, there be a meaningfully close relationship between the tipper and tippee to support an inference of a gifting of the material, nonpublic information in order for insider trading liability to attach. The majority opinion upheld the insider trading conviction of Mathew Martoma, the former portfolio manager at SAC Capital Advisors LP, despite the nonexistence of a proven close relationship between Martoma and the source of the confidential information. In a lengthy dissent, Judge Pooler explained how the majority ignored precedent and "significantly diminishes the limiting power of the personal benefit rule, and radically alters insider-trading law for the worse."[1208]

Nine months later, on June 25, 2018, the Second Circuit issued an amended opinion in *Martoma*, this time backing away from its criticism of *Newman*.[1209] The majority held "because there are many ways to establish a personal benefit, we conclude that we need not decide whether *Newman's* gloss on the gift theory is inconsistent with *Salman*."[1210] Chief Judge Robert Katzmann, writing for the majority, continued to say that the *Newman* decision provided guidance on the term "meaningfully close personal relationship" holding that it "requires evidence of a 'relationship between the insider and the recipient that suggests a *quid pro quo* from the latter, or an intention to benefit the [latter]."[1211] As a result, the majority held that the jury instructions were incomplete in that it allowed the jury to find a personal benefit based solely on the conclusion that the tip was provided to Martoma to develop or maintain a friendship and lacked any

---

[1207] *U.S. v. Martoma*, 869 F. 3d 58 (2d. Cir. 2017) (hereinafter Martoma I).

[1208] *Id.* at 75.

[1209] *U.S. v. Martoma*, No. 14- 3599, at 14 (2d. Cir. June 25, 2018) (*hereinafter Martoma II*).

[1210] *U.S. v. Martoma*, No. 14- 3599, at 14 (2d. Cir. June 25, 2018) (*hereinafter Martoma II*).

[1211] *Martoma II, supra* note 2, at 2.

suggestion of a quid pro quo. Although the jury instructions were inaccurate, however, the Second Circuit held that the error did not affect the verdict because the government had presented compelling evidence that there was a *quid pro quo* relationship between tipper and tippee.[1212] Judge Pooler dissented a second time, arguing that her colleagues now were attempting to redefine the "meaningfully close personal relationship" test in "subjective rather than objective terms, rendering *Newman* a relic."[1213]

On August 27, 2018, the Second Circuit declined to rehear Mr. Martoma's case.[1214]

The SEC has shown an increasing willingness to pursue insider trading cases connected to the use of evolving technology, such as with respect to alternative data providers,[1215] the Dark Web, and crypotcurrencies.[1216] For example, on July 2021, in *SEC v. Trovias*, the SEC sued Apostolos Trovias, also known as "TheBull", for allegedly selling tips of material, nonpublic information on the Dark Web to over 100 subscribers claiming that the information he was selling consisted of order-book data from a

---

[1212] *Id.* at 34 (holding "on the compelling facts of this case, it is clear beyond a reasonable doubt that a properly instructed jury would have found Martoma guilty" absent the error.).

[1213] *United States v. Martoma*, No. 14-3599, (2d Cir. June 25, 2018) (Pooler, J., dissenting), at 2.

[1214] Order, *United States v. Martoma*, No. 14-3599 (2d. Cir. Aug. 27, 2018).

[1215] The SEC in September 2021 settled a $10 million case against an alternative data vendor for the mobile app industry, App Annie, for securities fraud and making material misrepresentations. Allegedly, App Annie, which sells market data on mobile app performance, sold non-anonymized and non-aggregated data to investment firms despite representing to the companies that their data would aggregated and anonymized. Although this was not an insider trading case, the SEC acknowledged that the data could have contained material, nonpublic information. *See* SEC Order, *In the Matter of App Annie Inc. and Bertrand Schmitt*, Exchange Act Release No. 92975 (Sept. 14, 2021).

[1216] https://www.justice.gov/usao-sdny/press-release/file/1521186/download; https://www.sec.gov/litigation/complaints/2022/comp-pr2022-127.pdf

securities trading firm provided to him from an employee of that firm.[1217]

IV.   SANCTIONS FOR INSIDER TRADING

The potential sanctions for insider trading are severe. Currently, the maximum prison sentence for a criminal insider trading violation is 20 years, and the maximum criminal fine for individuals is $5,000,000. In civil cases, the SEC may order disgorgement of any ill-gotten gains, meaning that the defendant must forfeit the trading profits (or losses avoided), plus interest.[1218] The SEC may also impose a monetary penalty up to three-times the profits (or losses avoided) of the trades.[1219] Additionally, a tipper may be jointly and severally liable for the trades by his or her tippees, as well as the for the trades by anybody that those tippees, in turn, tipped (*i.e.*, downstream tippees).[1220] Typically, when the SEC and DOJ both bring charges, "the SEC usually obtains the disgorgement as part of its resolution and DOJ obtains the penalty. This division of labor and remedies achieve full accountability without regulatory 'double dipping.'"[1221]

V.   RULE 10B5-1 PLANS

It can be challenging for company executives to transact in their company's securities because of the frequency with which they possess material, nonpublic information. For executives that receive stock as a significant part of their compensation, this issue is particularly important as executives often want to diversify their

---

[1217] SEC Complaint, *SEC v. Apostolos Trovias*, No. 1:21-cv-05925 (S.D.N.Y. July 9, 2021) *available at* https://www.sec.gov/litigation/complaints/2021/comp-pr2021-122.pdf.

[1218] 15 U.S.C. §§ 78u-2(e); 78u-3(e).

[1219] 15 U.S.C. § 78u-1(a).

[1220] 15 U.S.C. § 78t-1(c).

[1221] Mary Jo White Speech, Three Key Pressure Points in the Current Enforcement Environment, NYC Bar Association's Third Annual White-collar Crime Institute, SEC.gov (May 19, 2014), *available at* https://www.sec.gov/news/speech/2014-spch051914mjw.html.

stock holdings and/or convert to cash. In order to give individuals a mechanism to engage in securities trades while minimizing the likelihood of becoming the subject of an insider trading investigation, the SEC created what have become known as 10b5-1 plans.

Under Rule 10b5-1, a person's purchase or sale of securities is not considered to be "on the basis of" material, nonpublic information if the person adopted a written plan for trading the securities before becoming aware of the information.[1222] On December 14, 2022, the SEC adopted several amendments relating to Rule 10b5-1 trading plans, including introducing "cooling-off" periods delaying the first trades after a plan is adopted or amended.

A 10b5-1 plan provides an affirmative defense against insider trading allegations, even if the plan holder subsequently becomes aware of material, nonpublic information by the time the trades occur. Under Rule 10b5-1(c), the plan must: (1) specify the amount of securities to be purchased or sold and the price (which may be a limit price) and the date on which the securities are to be purchased or sold; (2) include a written formula or algorithm, or computer program for determining the amount, price and date for the transactions; or (3) not permit the person to exercise any subsequent influence over how, when, or whether to effect purchases or sales, meaning giving the exclusive investment discretion to a third party, such as a broker—provided that the third party with investment discretion must not have been aware of the material, nonpublic information when trading.[1223] The purchase or sale must be pursuant to the written plan, otherwise it will not qualify for the affirmative defense.[1224] A purchase or sale may not alter or deviate from the plan and a person may not enter into an

---

[1222] 17 C.F.R. § 240.10b5-1(c)(A)(3).

[1223] 17 C.F.R. § 240.10b5-1(c)(B)(1)-(3).

[1224] 17 C.F.R. § 240.10b5-1(c)(C).

altered or corresponding hedging transaction or position with
respect to those securities.[1225]

A 10b5-1 plan will not protect the plan holder from insider trading
liability if the person is using the plan as part of a scheme to evade
§ 10(b)'s and Rule 10b-5's prohibitions against insider trading. For
example, the SEC sued Angelo Mozilo, the former CEO of
Countrywide Financial, alleging, among other things, that he
engaged in insider trading in Countrywide securities by
establishing four 10b5-1 sales plans in October, November, and
December 2006 while he was aware of material, nonpublic
information concerning Countrywide's increasing credit risk and
the risk regarding the poor expected performance of Countrywide-
originated loans.[1226] Because Mozilo was in possession of material,
nonpublic information at the time that he created the plans, the
affirmative defense under Rule 10b5-1 was not applicable. Mozilo
ultimately settled all of the SEC's allegations against him by
agreeing to pay $67.5 million.[1227]

A portion of the SEC's complaint against Mozilo included
allegations that he implemented four 10b5-1 plans in three months,
modified one of the plans, and started trading immediately under
some of the plans.[1228] Thus, to reduce the risks of investigations
and potential impropriety, some companies often require a waiting
period between the establishment of a 10b5-1 plan and the
execution of trades pursuant to that plan.

In March 2023, the DOJ indicted, and the SEC sued, a CEO and
Chairman of the Board of Directors of a public company for

[1225] *Id.*

[1226] SEC Complaint at 5, *SEC v. Mozilo, Sambol, and Sieracki*, No. 009-cv-03994
(C.D. Cal. June 4, 2009).

[1227] SEC Press Release, Former Countrywide CEO Angelo Mozilo to Pay SEC's
Largest-Ever Financial Penalty Against a Public Company's Senior Executive,
SEC (Oct. 15, 2010), https://www.sec.gov/news/press/2010/2010-197.htm.

[1228] *Id.* at 45-46.

allegedly misusing 10b5-1 plans as a shield for insider trading.[1229] The DOJ and the SEC alleged that Terren Peizer, the CEO and Chairman of the Board for Ontrak Inc. entered into two 10b5-1 trading plans shortly after learning that the company's largest customer might terminate its contract. Peizer then allegedly began selling stock the day after establishing each plan.

VI.   INSIDER TRADING CONTROLS

In addition to being prudent for companies to develop insider trading controls, the federal securities laws also require that certain types of businesses implement reasonable measures to safeguard material, nonpublic information.[1230] For example, § 15(g) of the Exchange Act requires registered broker-dealers to establish, maintain and enforce written policies and procedures reasonably designed, taking into consideration the nature of the firm's business, to prevent the misuse of material, nonpublic information.[1231] Similarly, § 204A of the Investment Advisers Act of 1940 requires investment advisers to establish and maintain written policies and procedures designed to prevent possible insider trading violations.[1232] By virtue of their business, investment advisers, broker dealers and private equity firms often receive material, nonpublic information and therefore are expected to have proper policies and procedures in place to prevent insider trading.

[1229] DOJ Press Release, CEO of Publicly Traded Health Care Company Charged for Insider Trading Scheme, DOJ (Mar. 1, 2023), https://www.justice.gov/opa/pr/ceo-publicly-traded-health-care-company-charged-insider-trading-scheme; https://www.sec.gov/litigation/complaints/2023/comp-pr2023-42.pdf.

[1230] Rule 10b5-1 also provides an affirmative defense to entities if they can demonstrate that the individual making the investment decision on behalf of the entity was not aware of the material nonpublic information and the entity had implemented reasonable policies and procedures to prevent violations of securities laws. 17 C.F.R. § 240.10b5-1(c)(2).

[1231] 15 U.S.C. § 78o. Prior to the Dodd-Frank Wall Street Reform and Consumer Protection Act, this provision was found in Section 15(f) of the Exchange Act.

[1232] 15 U.S.C. § 80b-4a.

The SEC has increasingly sanctioned broker-dealers, investment advisers and private equity firms for having inadequate controls to prevent the misuse of nonpublic information, even where no instance of insider trading occurred. For example, On May 26, 2020, the SEC announced a settlement with Ares Management LLC, a private equity firm and registered investment adviser, for $1 million for failing to implement and enforce procedures designed to prevent the misuse of material nonpublic information.[1233] The SEC did not allege any improper trading. Instead, the SEC alleged that the company had invested in a public company and authorized the appointment of one of its senior employees to that company's board. The compliance policies allegedly failed to account for the special circumstances of having this employee serve on the board and Ares continued to make trading decisions regarding that company without having inquired whether the board representative or members of his team had material nonpublic information.

In addition, Monness, Crespi, Hardt & Co., Inc. ("MCH"), a broker-dealer, paid $150,000 to settle the SEC's charges that it lacked or failed to adequately enforce its written compliance procedures designed to prevent insider trading.[1234] MCH allegedly failed to enforce two of its insider trading procedures—one requiring MCH to place issuers subject to a research report on a restricted securities list and the other requiring MCH employees to submit a report of securities transactions in which they or their families participated.[1235] Notably, the SEC did not contend that any actual improper trading or tipping occurred. According to the SEC, because of MCH's failures, "the firm was unable to review adequately employee or customer trading to prevent or detect potential market violations, including insider trading and trading in advance of material research changes." The SEC further alleged

[1233] SEC Press Release, *Private Equity Firm Ares Management LLC Charged with Compliance Failures, available at* https://www.sec.gov/news/press-release/2020-123 (May 26, 2020).

[1234] *In the Matter of Monness, Crespi, Hardt & Co., Inc.*, Exchange Act Release No. 72886 (August 20, 2014).

[1235] *Id.* at 1-2.

that MCH violated § 15(g) by not having any written policies related to the firm's "Corporate Access" and "Idea Dinner" programs. In the SEC's view, those programs posed the risk that MCH's analysts or other employees might share material, nonpublic information about upcoming research reports.[1236] Again, there was no allegation that any of those risks actually materialized.

Similarly, Section 13(b)(2)(B) of the Exchange Act requires public companies to devise and maintain internal accounting controls. In September 2021, the SEC brought insider trading charges and internal accounting control charges against the company Cavco Industries and its former CEO.[1237] Allegedly, Cavco, at the CEO's direction, traded in securities of a public company while in merger discussions with that company. Although the company had an investment policy and an insider trading policy, the SEC alleged that Cavco failed to devise a system of internal accounting controls sufficient to provide reasonable assurances that the securities trading would be executed in accordance with those policies.

VII. CONCLUSION

The scope of insider trading liability is broad, but not without limits. The fundamental starting point for any insider trading analysis is determining whether there has been a breach of a duty. Absent a breach of duty, there is no illegal insider trading. In the tipping context, determining whether there has been a breach is a fact-intensive analysis. The DOJ and the SEC often take expansive and aggressive positions as to what constitutes a breach of duty (and when an insider benefits from doing so) and when a person should know that the original source of the material, nonpublic information provided it in breach of a duty. To minimize the risks of insider trading, companies are well-served by implementing trading procedures and controls. Similarly, corporate executives

---

[1236] *Id.* at 4, 6.

[1237] SEC Complaint, *SEC v. Cavco Industries Inc. et al.*, No. 2:21-cv-01507 (D. Ariz. Sept. 2, 2021), available at https://www.sec.gov/litigation/complaints/2021/comp25196.pdf.

who want to trade in their company's securities with regularity may want to consider whether a 10b5-1 plan would protect them from investigative risks related to their trades.

Chapter 26

Computer Forensics: An Investigation Begins

By: John Wilson and Christopher Dixon[1238]

There are two main types of investigations and/or scenarios in which a general counsel may be involved: (1) an internal company investigation, whether preceding litigation or to identify and/or confirm suspicious activities by an employee; and (2) an external investigation involving local, state or federal law enforcement. In either example, there are common elements to ensure that an investigator conducts the data examination in a forensically sound manner. This chapter analyzes best practices for collecting and analyzing digital data and conducting computer forensic investigations.

I.   ASSESS THE SCOPE AND TYPE OF INVESTIGATION: MUNDANE MISBEHAVIOR

We will begin with the most basic types of internal investigations that companies perform relating to electronically stored information ("ESI"). These investigations may involve minor breaches of company policy. Although mostly mundane, these matters can introduce the challenges and complexities involved in more serious investigations.

An investigation of minor misconduct by an employee may lead to quick resolution. For example, if a manager suspects that an employee uses work email for personal business, or accesses a company device to check Facebook, information technology (IT) officers can simply check the company's servers to verify the infraction. Most companies can observe their employees' ESI—up to a point—without needing to hire a forensic expert. For example, a communication sent through a company's email system may be

---

[1238] John Wilson is the Chief Information Security Officer at HaystackID. Christopher Dixon is Senior Forensic Consultant at HaystackID. The views expressed in this chapter are their own and do not necessarily represent the views of the firm.

subject to observation by the company's IT staff, usually without triggering any negative consequences. A "light touch" analysis of the files stored on a company's servers follows the same course of action regarding access verification. Additionally, collaboration platforms such as Slack, MS Teams, or Zoom usually permit monitoring at the enterprise level.

However, even banal problems require a formal resolution process. The manager should include the company's Human Resources department in any investigation. This measure may short circuit an employee claim of harassment or stalking against co-workers or supervisors. Human Resources can also ensure that any action taken comports with the terms of the employee's contracts and agreements and the company's unique policies and handbooks.

Human Resources may also call upon the company's General Counsel to confirm that any steps taken comply with applicable laws governing employee protections that might limit an investigation. Local, state, and federal laws are constantly in flux. Furthermore, there are a cadre of federal and state regulations affecting the processes underpinning each forensic examination. Companies that operate outside of the U.S. may be subject to foreign laws that protect employees on company-owned equipment. Additionally, many U.S. states are enacting their own laws relating to data privacy in the workplace with many more states in the process of ratifying similar legislation.

Managers may avoid the hassle of involving different people in a formal investigation process. Instead, they may choose to simply confront an employee directly about their productivity.

A.   Collecting ESI in a Simple Investigation

Even an internal investigation of minor misbehavior will involve the same factors that challenge investigators in larger investigations.

A company may unknowingly implement data systems and network architecture schemas in ways that can help – or hinder – an investigation. For example, forensic best practices dictate that desktop computers and laptops contain small hard drives to encourage employees to store data on company servers, centralizing the analysis. A common data exfiltration tool, IT policies can restrict the use or require the encryption of USB storage devices to prevent their misuse. Productivity software can track employee behaviour and proactively flag activities that violate company policies. Several archiving systems store copies of all documents after creation and track activity on the documents as they are modified or deleted. DLP (Data Loss Prevention) software can prevent the exfiltration of confidential or important documents from leaving the network.

Simple investigations may become unnecessarily more complicated if these measures are not in place. The hard drive remains a potential source of data proving misconduct even with size limitations. If a manager believes that evidence of minor misconduct exists on the hard drive of an employee's work computer, but there is no sign of the misconduct on the company servers, the manager can always request that IT access the individual's hard drive to verify the misconduct. A full forensic investigation is not always required. For an employee under investigation for a simple infraction of the employee handbook, the company's IT department may only need to collect the necessary information simply by copying files if the misconduct is unlikely to result in a lawsuit.

However, a simpler and more straightforward strategy may be to confront the employee directly. Physically accessing an employee's device can unnerve an employee which could escalate to accusations of harassment.

Investigations become more difficult if employees use their own computers for non-work purposes. In those cases, a company will not have physical access to the device in question. Many companies may ask employees to download information on to personal computers they use for work. Even though the employee is using a personal device, IT staff may implement software to access the contents of the computer in exchange for access to the network. Even if a company has this capability, managers should involve Human Resources, the General Counsel, and IT staff in any process to ensure that an investigation is legal, both under the employee's contract and applicable law.

If a mundane investigation reveals evidence of a more serious problem, investigators should stop immediately to regroup in anticipation of potential litigation or the involvement of law enforcement. Simply opening an electronic document to examine its contents often alters the file in ways that could destroy its value as evidence. (The techniques investigators must use to preserve potentially relevant data are described more fully in the sections of this chapter entitled "Chain of Custody" and "Metadata.")

B.   More Serious Investigations

If an investigation could involve considerable economic loss or lead to a lawsuit, the company should consider hiring a forensic computing professional. If law enforcement is involved, the company should immediately consult with a forensic computing expert.

The most common mistake companies make when they attempt to capture ESI on their own is failing to consult with an expert before irreversible damage occurs. Without the guidance of a forensic computing professional, companies may not uncover evidence of any kind. Most importantly, the evidence resulting from a proper forensic investigation may prove exculpatory. If law enforcement is involved, the company may not find the evidence necessary that may lead to a positive result. Of paramount importance, a computer forensics professional can prevent worst-case scenarios where the company's IT department inadvertently destroys the evidence or metadata, invalidating the data's validity leading to potential spoilation charges.

C.   The Chain of Custody

For the proper authentication of evidence uncovered in an investigation, a litigant's attorney must certify that the data was collected and analyzed in a manner complying with the forensic computing standards. At a minimum, litigants ought to consider engaging a forensic computing professional on a consultative basis early in the process before irreversible mistakes occur.

A litigant's responsibility to preserve electronic documents is a central tenet of computer forensic investigations. An entity must preserve evidence to facilitate defensible authentication. A record of the steps taken in preservation, collection, and analysis must align with the standards of evidence for defensibility purposes. Proper chain of custody documentation confirms that the data has not been damaged or adulterated.

Each piece of evidence must have "chain of custody" documentation describing how and when the work was performed and the identity of the examiner conducting the analysis. For the purposes of testimony, organizations often seek neutral party examiners to analyze data subject to litigation or investigation to prevent their own staff from having to testify. If a company investigates an employee for wrongdoing, the company's IT staff will not fit the profile of "neutral party" because these workers are employed by the company and motivated to protect its wellbeing. Given the inexperience that many IT departments have relating to forensic standards, opposing counsel can often invalidate the authentication of the evidence by claiming evidence tampering by IT, even if inadvertent.

Beyond analysis, chain of custody documentation validates the storage conditions of the collected data at rest. Effectively, chain of custody documentation validates that data gathered in an investigation is in its most pristine form and free from tampering.

D.   Preserving the Data: The Metadata

All computer documents contain more data than meets the eye. Electronic documents also include information called metadata which records key facts, such as the last opened date of a document. The metadata is often the most critical component of authentication.

The seemingly innocent act of opening a document can change its metadata and potentially ruin the data's evidentiary value. It is analogous to permitting the unfettered access of an unauthorized person in a potential crime scene; risking the accidental destruction of evidence or inadvertently adding new material to the crime scene. Even the suggestion that evidence has been damaged, destroyed, or altered raises significant questions about the value of all evidence found.

Computer forensics experts preserve ESI in a manner that must also preserve metadata. For example, experts may make a "bit for bit image" of the related hard drives. This measure preserves the relevant ESI, such as related metadata, deleted files, and hidden portions of the hard drive.

E. Assessing the Value of a Case

Investigations leading to a lawsuit can occupy a difficult middle ground for companies that conduct their own forensic examinations. Companies can choose to leverage their own IT staff to find and preserve the necessary ESI only to find them testifying on the stand at trial and they may be subjected to extensive cross examination on the forensic measures and safeguards taken.

As a way to confront cost concerns in engaging experts, companies can use the economic value of a case as a benchmark to determine a budget for finding and preserving ESI. For instance, an investigation relating to a $10,000 lawsuit should not require a litigant to spend disproportionately more to collect the data. In contrast, if hundreds of thousands—or millions—of dollars are at stake in "bet your company" litigation, companies should not hesitate to spend the amount required to preserve all ESI in a manner certain to protect its potential evidentiary value.

Companies might consider gathering relevant information to a case without hiring a forensic expert if an investigation does not involve law enforcement, the company utilizes effective preservation policies comporting with forensic standards, and the organization follows sound data retrieval procedures. Even conventional software tools can be configured to preserve data in a format that will meet forensic standards. However, the company's IT staff must be sufficiently familiar with these tools to use them properly and carefully follow documented procedures to ensure a sound process. Furthermore, the IT staff must be willing and able to testify as to the steps taken in compliance with forensic standards. It is one thing to have a scalpel. It is an entirely different matter to qualify as a surgeon.

Companies should carefully consider the knowledge and experience of their IT departments before entrusting them with conducting investigations. The General Counsel should question whether the experience the IT staff has in the act of preserving ESI. Furthermore, will the collected ESI meet the established standards of forensic computing?

Some companies regularly perform IT audits to evaluate the performance of their computer systems, procedures, and staff. Annually, a company may randomly select 10 employees as investigation test "subjects" as a practice run for a real investigation. As part of the exercise, the IT staff must identify and preserve critical ESI relating to the employees under "investigation" in a manner that meets forensic computing standards. A company that has successfully performed IT audits such as these will properly and objectively assess the capabilities of its IT staff in successfully completing an actual investigation. If an IT department has never performed this kind of exercise has failed in its efforts, it should never attempt to conduct a real investigation with real economic consequences.

Even the best trained IT in proper ESI preservation may be unprepared to defensibly retrieve all the information necessary to preserve. The IT and Forensic disciplines derive from divergent backgrounds and lead to different results.

Furthermore, many companies notice that a wide gap exists between its codified IT procedures versus how employees behave in practicality. As a result, a company's IT staff may not know actual data storage locations and may lack the training to find it. Simply searching company servers for a few documents can reveal a great deal, including whether document storage practices comply with company procedures. The existence of key data outside its anticipated storage location may prove the actual width of the

IT/Practicality gap and may suggest an engagement with a forensic expert.

In preparation, forensic standards require ascertaining the day-to-day work habits of employees involved in an investigation to identify all potential data sources and custodians possessing relevant ESI, as well as all the devices or storage locations. A custodial interview may uncover these details.

The sections of this chapter entitled "Landscape Surveys" and "Custodians" similarly address these matters in greater detail. If an initial investigation identifies multiple employees possessing and devices containing relevant ESI, it may be a key indicator to engage an external expert.

F. Different Jurisdictions

The company's General Counsel should be involved in every step of an investigation to ensure that any action taken conforms with the legal requirements of the jurisdiction where the investigation is taking place. This measure protects the rights of employees under investigation and ensures compliance with the evidentiary standards and requirements for the jurisdiction.

It is important to understand that data collection rules vary from country to country, and within the United States. This factor can impact the cost of a computer forensics investigation.

Jurisdictions in the United States also have different laws governing the proper procedures for forensically collecting and preserving digital evidence. For example, Michigan and Texas require a private investigators license for any forensic examiner.

In the United States, employees do not own personal information they store on a work computer. Lawmakers in the European Union safeguarded employee data relating to their personal work product in the General Data Protection Regulation ("GDPR"). For example, employees have rights that protect both their personal information and their personal work product, even if stored on a company-owned device. Investigations involving European employees requires adherence strict adherence with GDPR and even stricter member state regulations.

Aside from the European Union, other geographies also have policies that can create difficulties. For example, it can be problematic to bring hard drives and other memory storage devices in and out of countries like China, where the government exerts a significant level of control over the flow of data.

G.   Law Enforcement Investigations

Investigations by law enforcement or regulatory agencies may create a clearer path for companies under investigation. That path should lead directly to a third-party expert to ensure compliance and proper procedure.

Invariably, the company's General Counsel and Human Resources departments play an integral role in every step in the investigation. Their involvement helps ensure that the company satisfies any applicable local, state, federal, or foreign laws in attempting to cooperate with the investigation.

General Counsel can lead in communicating with law enforcement officers to confirm that the company supplies the necessary information. If law enforcement issues a search warrant to investigate, companies should comply. The question, though, is: to what degree? A clearly written warrant will provide the best guidance. For example, the search warrant may be unclear as to whether the company must provide an employee's computer, or whether it need only provide an "image" of the information stored on the computer. In that case, it is incumbent upon the general counsel to receive clarification from the officials who produced the warrant.

Law enforcement officers may put an employee on "legal hold" while the investigation proceeds. While the hold is in place, no one should delete any ESI to which that employee has access. Investigations may continue for a very long time – even years. The company's General Counsel should communicate with law enforcement officers during the investigation's life cycle to confirm whether the legal hold is still necessary and to ensure the company and its employees continue to comply with it.

H. Define the Scope of the Investigation

In any investigation involving law enforcement, a company's primary responsibility is compliance with the terms of search warrants while supplying the requested material in a timely manner.

Compliance can prove to be more complicated than it seems. Often, more employees than first thought either created or maintain relevant ESI requiring preservation. Also, an employee working largely with a single laptop will actually utilize multiple pieces of hardware, such as a laptop, cell phone, tablet, virtual computers and cloud storage. The boundary between personal and corporate devices continues to grow increasingly blurry. The employee may also have access to multiple company- run network servers and may actively utilize cloud storage. Additionally, employees often use systems that store information on remote servers run by other companies.

The first step in scoping an investigation is to identify all the "custodians" who might have possessed ESI pertinent to the investigation requiring preservation. A custodian list should be as comprehensive as possible and will invariably include more people than those named in a search warrant. Individuals relevant to an investigation often work with others who may shed light on the scope of the investigation as well. A list of potential custodians must include the peripheral people in communication with the matter target.

Problems can arise with the omission of potentially key custodians from the list. For example, one company under investigation by federal regulators failed to supply hundreds of relevant emails. The company CEO had hand-written these emails out for his assistant to then type up and send by computer. Acceptable practices necessitate the inclusion of the assistant as a custodian because the emails she recreated contained preservable data relevant to the investigation. The result of her exclusion led to the company's failure to comply.

Law enforcement eventually confronted the CEO about the missing emails. Other companies involved in the investigation had been recipients of several of the CEO's emails and turned their copies over to law enforcement. The company's failure to supply all the relevant information proved costly due to the expedited and expanded scope required to remediate the shortcomings. While federal investigators did not fine the company, law enforcement officers doubted the company's compliance in all segments of the investigation. The company failed to identify the CEO's assistant as a custodian of relevant data, it may have left other custodians off the list as well. As a result, they dramatically widened the scope of data required for collection and production. – The list of custodians exceeded 100 employees, up from the 20 or so custodians on the original list.

I.   "Custodian Interview and Landscape Survey" Identifies Devices and Work Habits

Once the company identifies custodians who may have possessed ESI relevant to an investigation, computer forensics experts create a "custodian interview," which is a set of interview questions asked of each custodian. The interview is meant to identify all the devices or locations where ESI exists that have been kept by these custodians and that requires preservation.

A list of custodial hardware for collection must include laptops, cell phones, and other company-issued devices, which can be identified using a landscape survey with IT. However, the company should also preserve information stored on personal equipment used partially or wholly for work purposes. If a company is cooperating with law enforcement, it should supply relevant data from each of these devices. Entities should instruct their custodians to refrain from deleting or altering data from their personal devices information deemed relevant to the law enforcement investigation. This includes upgrading mobile devices with the custodian's carrier or regularly wiping hard drives.

Custodians may hesitate or even refuse to supply full access to personal devices that they use for work. For example, former U.S. Secretary of State Hillary Clinton used her personally owned computer server, as well as a personal email address, to send and receive emails relevant to her work. After investigators demanded access to those emails, her staff deleted the emails she had identified as personal. Clinton has since repeatedly testified before Congress about her private email setup.

With an investigation involving law enforcement, a subpoena can compel an employee to provide access to personal devices, differing from an internal investigation where a company has less leverage in compelling employees to supply access to data on their own equipment.

The landscape survey should also identify computers and hardware that multiple employees share. A loaner laptop in the IT department supply cabinet may have surprising information on its hard drive. Likewise, the landscape survey should ask custodians pointed questions about how they use systems and software for work because employees may store information in unexpected places.

For example, company policies may stipulate that work emails be preserved for an established amount of time and then deleted. Regulators regularly require banks to keep emails for five years, while other companies may delete emails after a year or two. However, employees tend to save copies of their work emails for longer than the company policy. The company is responsible to provide those emails to investigators – even though the officers of the company may not even know that copies of these older emails exist.

The custodian interview should also identify how employees use outside services such as Instant Messenger, collaboration tools, and cloud services. For example, Wall Street executives involved in insider trading cases used their smart phones and third-party apps to send and receive information. It can be expensive and complicated to retrieve data from these services in a way that meets forensic standards.

J.   Investigating Without a Landscape Survey

An investigation often involves a central custodian unaware of their target status in the investigation. The company may have to identify and preserve this custodian's ESI without alerting the custodian. The company might resolve this challenge by announcing a "routine" audit of its IT systems to collect and preserve the ESI of ten "randomly" selected employees. These employees may include those under investigation. For some companies, IT audits such as this are routine. In fact, some companies perform IT audits as often as once a year to validate their systemic safeguards. However, if it seems likely that an audit would alert the employee, the company may not be able to ask this custodian about how they use systems for work.

Draw a diagram of all the data sources to which this central custodian had access. Depending on the type of investigation, relevant data may exist on servers or accounts not meant to hold the kind of data hidden there. Employees may not use systems within the parameters of their intended purpose, especially if they are intentionally trying to hide evidence of wrongdoing.

Companies that fail to provide all relevant data to law enforcement face increasingly stiff penalties. At a minimum, investigations may drag on for longer as investigators search more deeply for other evidence the company may have failed to provide.

Even if law enforcement is not involved, a company's own investigation can become much more expensive if it uncovers relevant information requiring preservation late in the process. The plaintiff in a lawsuit, for example, only has a set amount of time during discovery to enter data into evidence. If the company finds evidence late in the discovery process, it may have to expedite the inclusion of that data in the lawsuit, resulting in overtime hours for IT staff.

Companies should give computer forensics experts sufficient time and latitude to properly preserve data. Often, a company can work with law enforcement to proactively set up a time when law enforcement can collect the evidence it needs. The company's IT staff can then provide spare machines that will allow employees to continue to work.

Companies should also give employees temporary computers, cell phones and other hardware to use during active collection. This substitution avoids stress if the data collection takes longer than anticipated.

K.   Preserving the Data

The actual steps taken to preserve ESI during a law enforcement investigation will be akin to steps taken for an internal investigation, but with potentially major economic consequences. The steps taken to safeguard potential evidence requires preservation in a format that meets forensic computing standards facilitating more likely acceptance as evidence in a court of law. For example, each piece of information preserved should have a "chain of custody" document proving its authenticity. The process should also preserve the document's metadata, as described earlier.

L.   Reassess the Scope of the Investigation as it Proceeds

Any investigation can change as it proceeds. A law enforcement investigation of one employee may eventually require the company to preserve information relating to an extensive list of associated employees, each of whom might use several devices to electronically store information.

As an investigation gathers information, the seriousness of the investigation can also change. An investigation of a small violation of company procedures may uncover criminal activity – requiring a dramatic change in handling potential evidence.

A company involved in an investigation should regularly reassess the investigation as it progresses to make sure the decisions that seemed appropriate in the beginning of the investigation are still appropriate. This reassessment should include the IT staff, human resources, and the general counsel.

In one case, a company investigated one employee's alleged sexual harassment of another employee, who described the harassment during her exit interview from the company. The infraction could potentially have led to a lawsuit. But when the company's IT professional examined the ESI of the employee accused of harassment, they found illicit and potentially illegal images. The company contacted law enforcement and a forensic expert.

II. PREVENTION: HOW TO MAKE A COMPANY MORE RESILIENT

Long before a company engages in an investigation, it can take steps that might simplify compliance with future law enforcement investigations. The company should have consistent data retention policies and procedures in place that meet industry requirements, necessary business standards, and regulatory compliance for the needs of the organization. Examples include:

- Archiving data like emails. The procedure should be clear to identify preserved and non-preserved data. If possible. systems should also prevent employees from breaking the policy by saving their own copies of emails. A company under investigation by law enforcement should be able to say with certainty what information it can and cannot produce, with as few surprises as possible.

- How employees use devices for work. Employers should configure devices to encourage employees to use them properly. For example, if workers are supposed to save their data onto company servers instead of on their laptop hard drives, then the laptops should not have giant hard drives.

Workplace computers can also be configured not to accept USB drives or other devices that would allow employees to copy and remove large amounts of data. If company policies also restrict what employees can view online, it makes sense to configure computers so that employees can't view prohibited websites.

- Migrating data. When a company changes its system, it should make sure not to lose access to data it has committed to preserve. After the company turns off the last computer using a proprietary system, that act may sever access to the information stored in its archives. A company's IT department may need to keep an older computer in operation to maintain access to information saved in outdated file formats or stored electronically on outdated media. Otherwise, a company may have to spend a considerable amount to recreate outdated systems that can access its archived information.

- Cloud computing. Companies should be aware of the potential expense and difficulty of forensically retrieving information from "cloud" servers in a manner that ensures the information discovered meets the legal standards of evidence and facilitates admissibility. Company procedures should discourage employees from storing data in places where it is effectively impossible to retrieve without massive expense.

For example, it can cost well over $100,000 to retrieve a large volume of data from a cloud server system like Microsoft's SharePoint, along with other proprietary software. A company's IT staff should create a plan to retrieve this kind of data, if necessary, in a forensically sound manner.

Texts sent and received over smart phones can also be difficult to preserve in a format that meets the standards of forensic computing. In several cases of insider trading prosecuted by the federal government, employees exchanged information using texts and other third-party texting apps.

Standard procedures implemented in the ordinary course of business may lend themselves well to accomplishing compliance goals.

- <u>Exit procedures.</u> When an employee leaves the company, the company should have a formal procedure in place to handle the employee's electronically stored information. The company policy should specify preserved vs. non-preserved data in addition to what information the employee may take with them when they leave.

- <u>Regular audits.</u> Companies should test their own procedures through regular self-testing. One method is to randomly select one or more employees to see if it is possible to efficiently collect their data. This kind of test can reveal a great deal about the skills of the IT department, the condition of the company's archives, and the company's IT procedures and their compliance status.

The information a company gains from these audits will be immensely helpful if it is ever confronted with an investigation with more profound consequences.

Chapter 27

DOJ's Focus on Organizational Conduct in 2023

By: Patrick L. Oot[1239]

Since 2020, the Department of Justice (DOJ) has issued a series of updates to its guidance for corporate investigations. In 2022, Deputy Attorney General ("DAG") Monaco issued the "Monaco memo" announcing changes to the way the DOJ would investigate corporate crimes under the Criminal Division's Corporate Enforcement Policy.[1240] Building off the Monaco memo, in January of 2023 Assistant Attorney General ("AAG") Polite gave a speech fleshing out those changes, and the DOJ Criminal Division issued a revised and renamed Corporate Enforcement Policy, the Corporate Enforcement and Voluntary Self-Disclosure Policy[1241] ("the Policy"). Then in March of 2023, the DOJ Criminal Division issued revisions to the Evaluation of Corporate Compliance Programs[1242] ("ECCP") and published a new Pilot Program

---

[1239] Patrick Oot is a Partner at Shook, Hardy & Bacon, LLP in Washington, DC and founder of The Government Investigations & Civil Litigation Institute. Prior to joining the firm, Patrick was Senior Special Counsel in the Office of General Counsel at the Securities and Exchange Commission. Prior to joining the S.E.C., Patrick was Director and Senior Litigation Counsel at Verizon in Washington, DC. Amina Sadural was a summer law clerk at Shook, Hardy and Bacon L.L.P. in the summer of 2023. During her summer clerkship, Ms. Sadural led the editorial update of this chapter for this edition.

[1240] U.S. Department of Justice, Further Revisions to Corporate Criminal Enforcement Policies (September 15, 2022), *available at* https://www.justice.gov/opa/speech/file/1535301/download

[1241] See Chapter 7 "Department of Justice (DOJ) Criminal Division Investigations" for an explanation of the new self-disclosure policies. U.S. Department of Justice, Corporate Enforcement and Voluntary Self-Disclosure Policy (updated January 2023), *available at* https://www.justice.gov/criminal-fraud/file/1562831/download

[1242] U.S. Department of Justice, Evaluation of Corporate Compliance Programs (updated March 2023), *available at* https://www.justice.gov/criminal-fraud/page/file/937501/download

Regarding Compensation Incentives and Clawbacks[1243] ("the Pilot Program"). Additionally, in March 2023 AAG Polite gave a speech specifying new considerations regarding data preservation from electronic device use for Criminal Division investigations. [1244] This Chapter is intended to provide a high-level overview of the changes since 2020, and includes a brief explanation of the DOJ's enforcement efforts in the aftermath of the COVID-19 pandemic.

I.   2022-2023 UPDATES IN COMPLIANCE AND GOVERNMENT INVESTIGATIONS

A.   Department of Justice Evaluation of Corporate Compliance Programs

In March 2023, the DOJ's Criminal Division updated its Evaluation of Corporate Compliance Programs (the "Evaluation"). The Evaluation provides protocols and lines of inquiry to guide prosecutors in their assessments of a company's compliance program. Understanding this updated mode of review will aid counsel in navigating government investigations in 2023.

1.   Executive Compensation & Clawback Provisions

The DOJ Criminal Division has a new focus on executive compensation reflected in the section titled "Compensation Structures and Consequence Management." This section calls upon corporations to develop and maintain a strong compliance culture that increases individual accountability on the part of not only the executives and employees who actually engaged in misconduct, but also those who had supervisory authority over them. These

---

[1243] U.S. Department of Justice, The Criminal Division's Pilot Program Regarding Compensation Incentives and Clawbacks (March 3, 2023), *available at* https://www.justice.gov/criminal-fraud/file/1571941/download

[1244] U.S. Department of Justice, "Assistant Attorney General Kenneth A. Polite, Jr. Delivers Keynote at the ABA's 38th Annual National Institute on White Collar Crime" (March 3, 20230), *available at* https://www.justice.gov/opa/speech/assistant-attorney-general-kenneth-polite-jr-delivers-keynote-aba-s-38th-annual-national

new DOJ policies on compensation are designed to incentivize compliance and disincentivize compliance failures by making sure corporation leaders also have "skin in the game" via the corporation's compensation structures.

Now, when prosecutors are evaluating corporate compliance programs and determining possible criminal resolutions, key factors they may consider are:

1. Whether corporations incentivize compliance with the use of promotions, bonuses, or awards to reward policy-compliant conduct;

2. Whether compensation clawback and reduction provisions tied to misconduct or other compliance violations are included in employment contracts, bonuses, or deferred compensation agreements; whether they are available to management to enforce compliance; and how consistently clawback provisions are enforced across the corporation; and

3. Whether corporations track relevant compliance-related metrics, including the proportion of compensation canceled or recouped due to wrongdoing.

Corporations should prioritize restructuring their compliance programs and compensation systems in light of these new considerations.

2.   Compensation Incentives and Clawback Pilot Program

The DOJ's Pilot Program Regarding Compensation Incentives and Clawbacks ("Pilot Program") will run for a three-year pilot period that began in March of 2023, after which the Criminal Division will determine whether to extend and/or modify it. Thus, at least for these next three years, companies must adequately address the Criminal Division's heightened emphasis on incentivizing compliance through compensation structures, particularly clawback policies.

The Pilot Program mandates that every criminal resolution entered into with the Criminal Division must require the company to implement compliance-related criteria into their compensation and bonus system. A company must also report annually to the Criminal Division about their implementation of these criteria during the resolution term. These criteria can include, but are not limited to:

- A prohibition on bonuses for employees who do not satisfy compliance performance requirements;

- Disciplinary measures for employees who violate applicable law and others who both (a) had supervisory authority over the employee(s) or business area engaged in the misconduct, and (b) knew of, or were willfully blind to, the misconduct; and

- Incentives for employees who demonstrate full commitment to compliance processes.

One potential issue is the lack of clarity from the DOJ regarding what companies should do when employees subject to a clawback requirement are from jurisdictions that do not allow employers to recoup bonuses, or that limit when recoupment is allowed (e.g., China, France, Singapore). The Pilot Program states that prosecutors "will use their discretion in fashioning the appropriate requirements based on the particular facts and circumstances of the case, including, but not limited to, applicable foreign and domestic law." Companies will need to navigate the competing requirements from the DOJ and from applicable conflicting laws in writing or restructuring their compensation structures and clawback provisions.

Companies need to be mindful that the DOJ expects compensation policies to target not only executives and employees who actually engaged in corporate wrongdoing, but also those who had supervisory authority over them or their area of business. Moreover, companies now have to contend with the transaction costs of negotiating contracts with new employees, especially management, containing these clawback provisions, as well as litigation costs when an employee contests their enforcement. Additionally, companies have to navigate how to include both clawback provisions and indemnification clauses in employment contracts.

But the Pilot Program incentivizes the inclusion and enforcement of these clawback provisions in the event of a criminal resolution. When a company fully cooperates with the Criminal Division and timely and appropriately remediates, the Pilot Program will further reduce the company's fines up to the amount of compensation the company claws back during the resolution term. Furthermore, even if a company fails to claw back all of the compensation it said it would recoup, the Pilot Program allows prosecutors to reduce the company's fine up to 25% of the amount of compensation it attempted to claw back, or that the company is likely to successfully claw back not long after the resolution term, provided the company made a good-faith effort. For example, if a company could not claw back all that it sought to recoup and incurred significant litigation costs for shareholders, a prosecutor can take such facts into account and award the company a reduction in its fine according to that attempt. Thus, companies should make every effort to enforce clawback provisions against wrongdoers and their supervisors in the event of a criminal resolution as part of their full cooperation.

3. Data Retention from Electronic Device Use

In 2021, J.P. Morgan Securities LLC (JPMS) was hit with a $125 million penalty by the Securities and Exchange Commission (SEC) for failing its recordkeeping obligations under the Securities Exchange Act Rule 17a-4.[1245] The SEC found that from at least

---

[1245] U.S. Securities and Exchange Commission, "JPMorgan Admits to Widespread Recordkeeping Failures and Agrees to Pay $125 Million Penalty to

January 2018 to November 2020, JPMS employees often communicated about business matters using their personal devices and "off-channel" mediums, especially ephemeral messaging platforms, none of which adequately preserved records of the communications, causing problems in the SEC's ability later to investigate potential violations of federal securities laws. Building off this enforcement action against JPMS, in 2022 the SEC hit 15 other major finance firms with massive penalties totalling $1.1 billion due to their failures to implement and maintain proper controls for business-related communications, including those over "off-channel" mediums.[1246] Data preservation of communications made using ephemeral messaging platforms is now a key concern of the DOJ as well. While the SEC was driven by widespread failure of compliance with recordkeeping obligations, the DOJ is focused on retaining information from communication platforms generally, as well as ensuring companies have appropriate information governance.

Hence, within the "Investigation of Misconduct" section of the March 2023 revised Evaluation is a new subsection explaining how prosecutors should evaluate a corporation's policies and procedures regarding the use of personal electronic devices, ephemeral messaging applications, and other communications platforms. Companies should preserve relevant data for their own internal as well as government investigations, should misconduct occur that necessitates such data. AAG Polite's speech in March 2023 declared that in an investigation, when a company refuses to provide relevant data from ephemeral messaging or other communication platforms, prosecutors will "ask about the company's ability to access such communications, whether they are stored on corporate devices or servers, as well as applicable privacy and local laws," and that the company's response (or lack thereof) "may very well affect the offer it receives to resolve

Resolve SEC Charges" (December 17, 2021), *available at* https://www.sec.gov/news/press-release/2021-262

[1246] Eight firms paid $125 million each, two paid $50 million each, and one firm paid $10 million. U.S. Securities and Exchange Commission, "SEC Charges 16 Wall Street Firms with Widespread Recordkeeping Failures" (September 27, 2022), *available at* https://www.sec.gov/news/press-release/2022-174

criminal liability." Thus, it is crucial to preserve that data to the best of a company's ability in the first place so that it can be easily disclosed as part of a company's cooperation with the DOJ.

The Evaluation states that policies governing such applications and their data "should be tailored to the corporation's risk profile and specific business needs and ensure that, as appropriate and to the greatest extent possible, business-related electronic data and communications are accessible and amenable to preservation by the company." Prosecutors will weigh:

- Whether a company's policies and procedures make relevant data accessible and amenable to preservation (including data from devices subject to a "bring your own device" ("BYOD") program);

- How much non-accessibility hinders the company's ability to implement an effective compliance program and conduct investigations;

- How well the company gives notice to its employees about its data policies and procedures;

- What consequences exist when employees refuse to grant the company access to business-related communications and data; and

- Whether the company regularly and consistently enforces its policies and procedures.

In determining whether a company's policies and procedures make relevant data accessible and amenable to preservation, prosecutors will assess what electronic communication channels employees use for business (whether they are actually allowed or not), what data preservation or deletion settings exist and are in place for these channels, and why such settings were chosen.

Companies, especially multinational companies, may face particular difficulties arising from complying with both the Criminal Division's data preservation and access requirements, but also with all local data privacy laws.

4.   Full List of Added Questions

- Executive Compensation & Clawback Provisions

  o   Human resources process

    - How transparent has the company been with the design and implementation of its disciplinary process?

    - In circumstances where an executive has been exited from the company on account of a compliance violation, how transparent has the company been with employees about the terms of the separation?

    - Is the same process followed for each instance of misconduct, and if not, why?

    - Has the company taken steps to restrict disclosure or access to information about the disciplinary process?

  o   Disciplinary Measures

    - What types of disciplinary actions are available to management when it seeks to enforce compliance policies?

- Does the company have policies or procedures in place to recoup compensation that would not have been achieved but for misconduct attributable directly or indirectly to the executive or employee?

- What policies and practices does the company have in place to put employees on notice that they will not benefit from any potential fruits of misconduct?

- With respect to the particular misconduct at issue, has the company made good faith efforts to follow its policies and practices in this respect?

- Consistent Application

  - What metrics does the company apply to ensure consistency of disciplinary measures across all geographies, operating units, and levels of the organization?

- Financial incentive system

  - Has the company evaluated whether commercial targets are achievable if the business operates within a compliant and ethical manner?

  - What role does the compliance function have in designing and awarding financial incentives at senior levels of the organization?

- What percentage of executive compensation is structured to encourage enduring ethical business objectives?

- Are the terms of bonus and deferred compensation subject to cancellation or recoupment, to the extent available under applicable law, in the event that non-compliant or unethical behavior is exposed before or after the award was issued?

- Does the company have a policy for recouping compensation that has been paid, where there has been misconduct?

o Effectiveness

- How has the company ensured effective consequence management of compliance violations in practice?

- What insights can be taken from the management of a company's hotline that provide indicia of its compliance culture or its management of hotline reports?

- How do the substantiation rates compare for similar types of reported wrongdoing across the company (i.e. between two or more different states, countries, or departments) or compared to similarly situated companies, if known?

- Has the company undertaken a root cause analysis into areas where certain conduct is comparatively over or under reported?

- What is the average time for completion of investigations into hotline reports and how are investigations that are addressed inconsistently managed by the responsible department?

- What percentage of the compensation awarded to executives who have been found to have engaged in wrongdoing has been subject to cancellation or recoupment for ethical violations?

- Taking into account the relevant laws and local circumstances governing the relevant parts of a compensation scheme, how has the organization sought to enforce breaches of compliance or penalize ethical lapses?

- How much compensation has in fact been impacted (either positively or negatively) on account of compliance-related activities?

- Data Retention from Electronic Device Use

  - Communication Channels

    - What electronic communication channels do the company and its employees use, or allow to be used, to conduct business? How does that practice vary by jurisdiction and business function, and why?

- What mechanisms has the company put in place to manage and preserve information contained within each of the electronic communication channels?

- What preservation or deletion settings are available to each employee under each communication channel, and what do the company's policies require with respect to each? What is the rationale for the company's approach to determining which communication channels and settings are permitted?

  o Policy Environment

    - What policies and procedures are in place to ensure that communications and other data is preserved from devices that are replaced? What are the relevant code of conduct, privacy, security, and employment laws or policies that govern the organization's ability to ensure security or monitor/access business-related communications?

    - If the company has a "bring your own device" (BYOD) program,

what are its policies governing
preservation of and access to
corporate data and
communications stored on
personal devices—including data
contained within messaging
platforms—and what is the
rationale behind those policies?

- How have the company's data
  retention and business conduct
  policies been applied and
  enforced with respect to personal
  devices and messaging
  applications?

- Do the organization's policies
  permit the company to review
  business communications on
  BYOD and/or messaging
  applications? What exceptions or
  limitations to these policies have
  been permitted by the
  organization?

- If the company has a policy
  regarding whether employees
  should transfer messages, data,
  and information from private
  phones or messaging applications
  onto company record-keeping
  systems in order to preserve and
  retain them, is it being followed in
  practice, and how is it enforced?

  o Risk Management

  - What are the consequences for
    employees who refuse the
    company access to company

communications? Has the company ever exercised these rights?

- Has the company disciplined employees who fail to comply with the policy or the requirement that they give the company access to these communications?

- Has the use of personal devices or messaging applications— including ephemeral messaging applications—impaired in any way the organization's compliance program or its ability to conduct internal investigations or respond to requests from prosecutors or civil enforcement or regulatory agencies?

- How does the organization manage security and exercise control over the communication channels used to conduct the organization's affairs?

- Is the organization's approach to permitting and managing communication channels, including BYOD and messaging applications, reasonable in the context of the company's business needs and risk profile?

B.   COVID-19 Update

As the nation went through the maelstrom of the COVID-19 pandemic, DOJ enforcement was largely focused on prosecuting fraud schemes relating to government programs providing pandemic relief. The DOJ has continued to prosecute medical professionals, owners of medical businesses, and others for pandemic-related schemes to defraud the Centers for Medicare & Medicaid Services and the Health Resources and Services Administration.[1247] The DOJ has also been a part of prosecuting fraud committed by testing labs, COVID-19 test kit suppliers, and manufacturers and distributors of fake COVID-19 vaccination record cards. As the country recovers from the pandemic, the DOJ's pandemic-related efforts remain committed to combatting fraud, waste, and abuse in federal programs aimed at providing relief.

II.   CONCLUSION

The 2020's have been tumultuous, to say the least. The Biden Administration has demonstrated its commitment to tougher corporate criminal enforcement through its series of updates clarifying and expanding its goals. Heading into the 2024 election year, only time will tell whether President Biden and his administrative state will have four more years to continue with this agenda.

[1247] U.S. Department of Justice, "Justice Department Announces Nationwide Coordinated Law Enforcement Action to Combat COVID-19 Health Care Fraud" (April 20, 2023), *available at* https://www.justice.gov/opa/pr/justice-department-announces-nationwide-coordinated-law-enforcement-action-combat-covid-19

Chapter 28

Introduction to Environmental, Social, and Governance (ESG)

By: Veronica Gromada[1248] and Shannon Schoultz[1249]

ESG typically stands for Environmental, Social and Governance. The term ESG was first coined in 2005 in a landmark study entitled "Who Cares Wins."[1250] The study explained that embedding environmental, social and governance factors in capital markets made good business sense and would lead to more sustainable markets and better outcomes for societies.[1251] ESG at that time was defined by factors to evaluate companies and countries on how far advanced they were with sustainability.[1252] The "Who Cares Win" study showcased the ESG factors as follows[1253]:

[1248] Veronica Gromada is a Partner in the Houston and Washington, DC offices of Shook, Hardy & Bacon LLP. Veronica has direct experience in automotive, consumer goods, food and beverage, pharmaceutical and medical device, software and other health, science and technology industries for world-leading brands, and focuses her practice on offering insight to clients on a variety of business functions including operations, employment, insurance, logistics and supply chain issues heightened by the pandemic.

[1249] Shannon Schoultz is an Associate in the Washington, DC office of Shook, Hardy & Bacon LLP. Shannon has direct experience in data, privacy and eDiscovery and focuses her practice on advising corporations in eDiscovery, data privacy, data security and information governance best practices.

[1250] Kell, George. "The Remarkable Rise of ESG," July 11, 2018. *https://www.forbes.com/sites/georgkell/2018/07/11/the-remarkable-rise-of-esg/?sh=3f580be01695*, accessed on August 9, 2022.

[1251] *See* "Who Cares Wins – Connecting Financial Markets to a Changing World" pgs. i-iv (Dec. 2004).

[1252] *See id.*

[1253] *See id.* at v.

As it has evolved, the ESG rubric now includes a wide array of company policies, culture and commitments related to both internal and external stakeholders, for instance: (1) the health and wellness of employees; (2) diversity and inclusion goals; (3) resource preservation and sustainability; (4) privacy and data security policies; (5) transparency around boardroom governance, investor relations and other director and officer activities; and (6) supply chain and vendor risk mitigation and compliance, among many other facets.

ESG is steadily evolving as organizations continue to integrate ESG factors into investment processes and key decision making. This introduction is not intended to cover all aspects of ESG, but will provide an introductory overview of a multifaceted, complex and evolving topic. Section I of this chapter describes the fundamentals of ESG by defining its guiding principles. Section II details the various forms of ESG compliance and how regulatory, legal and marketplace factors contribute overall to an organization's ESG compliance. Section III offers insight on how to turn ESG aspiration into real world action, while Section IV will preview emerging ESG topics to watch.

I.   ESG PRINCIPLES

ESG principles developed out of investment philosophies surrounding sustainability and socially responsible investing.[1254] Initial ESG principles concentrated on excluding organizations from certain investing portfolios due to their environmental, social or governance concerns and issues. ESG principles then advanced to distinguishing companies that were attributing positive contributions to elements of ESG.[1255] Today, ESG principles are guided largely on the U.S. Securities and Exchange Commission's 2022 proposals regarding disclosure requirements.

As ESG is an evolving and complex area of concentration, there is no single list of ESG principles. Often, ESG principles will overlap, and therefore the three categories of ESG are commonly integrated into an organization's analysis, processes, and decision making.

The "E" for environmental typically refers to carbon emissions, air pollution, water pollution, deforestation, green energy initiatives, waste management, and water usage.[1256] Environmental principles may include corporate climate policies, energy use, natural resource conservation, and treatment of animals.[1257] The principle can also help evaluate any environmental risks an organization might face and how the organization is managing those risks.[1258]

The "S" for social typically refers to employee gender and discrimination, data security, customer satisfaction, sexual harassment policies, human rights at home and abroad, and fair

---

[1254] Bergman, Mark, Deckelbaum, Ariel and Karp, Brad. "Introduction to ESG," August 1, 2020. https://corpgov.law.harvard.edu/2020/08/01/introduction-to-esg/, accessed on August 20, 2022.

[1255] *Id.*

[1256] S&P Global. "Understanding the 'E' in ESG," October 23, 2019. *https://www.spglobal.com/en/research-insights/articles/understanding-the-e-in-esg*, accessed on September 30, 2022.

[1257] *Id.*

[1258] *Id.*

labor practices.[1259] Social principles review the organization's relationships with stakeholders.[1260]

"The G" for governance typically refers to diversity of board members, political constitutions, executive pay, large-scale lawsuits, internal corruption, and lobbying. Governance principles ensure an organization uses accurate and transparent accounting methods, pursues integrity and diversity in selecting its leadership, and is accountable to shareholders.[1261]

ESG principles will inevitably evolve as ESG compliance continues to develop.

II.   ESG COMPLIANCE

ESG compliance has become an increasingly complex and challenging environment for organizations to navigate. Until recently, ESG was often considered to be a public relations function, but consideration of ESG as a set of compliance issues is a recent development. Generally, ESG compliance falls into three broad categories: SEC regulatory compliance, state and federal legal compliance, and marketplace compliance. SEC Regulatory compliance refers to the United States Securities and Exchange Commission's (SEC) rulemaking proposals and new ESG risk disclosure plans for investment funds and advisers. Legal compliance focuses on preventing, finding, and fixing problems stemming from violations of laws. Marketplace compliance guides organizations on non-financial factors relating to sustainability,

---

[1259] Neilan, Jonathan, Reily, Peter, Fitzpatrick, Glenn. "Time to Rethink the S in ESG," June 28, 2020. https://corpgov.law.harvard.edu/2020/06/28/time-to-rethink-the-s-in-esg/, accessed on September 30, 2022.

[1260] Id.

[1261] S&P Global. "What is the 'G' in ESG?," February 24, 2020. https://www.spglobal.com/en/research-insights/articles/what-is-the-g-in-esg, access on August 20, 2022.

social impact and ethics as material considerations for risk
mitigation and growth opportunities.[1262]

A.   SEC Regulatory Compliance

Prior to the Wall Street Crash of 1929, the federal government did
not actively regulate the securities market.[1263] The SEC was
formed when the federal government passed the Securities Act of
1933 and the Securities Exchange Act of 1934.[1264] The purpose of
the SEC formation was to restore the public's faith in capital
markets by providing transparent and reliable information
alongside clear rules of honest dealing.[1265] The mission of the SEC
is to protect investors, maintain fair, orderly and efficient markets,
and facilitate capital formation and the Commission strives to
promote a market environment that is worthy of public trust.[1266]
The SEC oversees stock issuers, securities brokers and dealers,
investment advisors, and mutual funds by bringing civil
enforcement actions each year.[1267]

In 2022, prompted by an influx of corporations marketing
themselves or their products as socially-responsible or sustainable,
the SEC began taking its first steps towards regulating ESG.[1268]

[1262] Intelex Insight Report. "Legal Responsibilities and ESG: What You Need to
Know for the Global Marketplace,"
file:///C:/Users/SSCHOULTZ/Downloads/Legal_Responsibilities__002_%20(1).p
df

[1263] U.S. Securities and Exchange Commission (SEC), "What We Do,"
http://www.sec.gov/Article/whatwedo.html#create, accessed on September 21,
2022.

[1264] Id.

[1265] Id.

[1266] U.S. Securities and Exchange Commission. "About the SEC,"
https://www.sec.gov/about.shtml, accessed on September 21, 2022.

[1267] Id.

[1268] U.S. Securities and Exchange Commission. "Enhanced Disclosures by
Certain Investment Advisers and Investment Companies about Environmental,
Social, and Governance Investment Practices, Securities Exchange Act," Release
No. IA-6034 (May 25, 2022).

The SEC proposed amendments to rules and reporting forms to promote consistent, comparable, and reliable information for investors concerning funds' and advisers' incorporation of ESG factors.[1269] The proposed changes would apply to certain registered investment advisers, advisers exempt from registration, registered investment companies, and business development companies.[1270]

The SEC's proposed amendments seek to standardize disclosures for ESG-related funds and would require specific disclosure pertaining to investment funds and investment advisers who consider ESG factors as part of their investment decisions and strategies.[1271]

The SEC's proposed ESG disclosures have three broad requirements. First, the SEC's proposed ESG disclosures would require any fund that considers ESG factors to provide investors with information regarding what ESG factors the fund considers and what strategies the fund implements.[1272] The disclosure could include whether a fund tracks an index, includes or excludes certain types of assets, what engagement is implemented to achieve the objectives, or the specific impact at which the fund is aimed.[1273] The disclosure requirements would vary depending on the ESG fund type. The proposal would require funds that integrate ESG factors along non-ESG factors in investment decisions, to describe how ESG factors are incorporated into their investment

---

[1269] U.S. Securities and Exchange Commission. "SEC Proposes to Enhance Disclosures by Certain Investment Advisers and Investment Companies About ESG Investment Practices," May 25, 2022. *https://www.sec.gov/news/press-release/2022-92*, accessed on September 21, 2022.

[1270] Soba, Marcelo. "SEC Proposes to Enhance Disclosures by Certain Investment Advisers and Investment Companies About ESG Investment Practices," May 25, 2022. *https://www.fundssociety.com/en/news/regulation/sec-proposes-to-enhance-disclosures-by-certain-investment-advisers-and-investment-companies-about-esg-investment-practices-2/*, accessed on August 30, 2022.

[1271] U.S. Securities and Exchange Commission, *supra* note 17.

[1272] *Id.*

[1273] *Id.*

process.[1274] The proposal would also require ESG-focused funds, or funds for which ESG factors are a significant or main consideration, to provide a detailed disclosure, including a standardized ESG strategy overview.[1275] Lastly, the proposal would require impact funds, which seek to achieve a particular ESG goal, to disclose how it measures its progress.[1276]

Second, the SEC's proposed ESG disclosures would require ESG-focused funds to disclose details about the criteria and data they used to achieve their investment goals and specific information regarding their strategies.[1277] This requirement is aimed at improving the reliability of the fund-provided data.[1278] Further, it also allows investors to reliably compare the data of different funds when choosing in which to invest.[1279]

Third, it would require particular types of ESG-focused funds to disclose relevant metrics. For example, an ESG-focused fund that focuses on or includes the environmental factor would be required to report greenhouse gas emission metrics, the weighted average carbon intensity of the portfolio, and annual progress metrics. This requirement is also aimed at providing investors with reliable data when determining in which fund to invest.

The SEC's proposed amendments are geared towards targeting greenwashing or other types of deception. Greenwashing refers to disinformation disseminated by an organization so as to present an environmentally responsible public image.[1280] As the ESG

[1274] *Id.*

[1275] *Id.*

[1276] *Id.*

[1277] *Id.*

[1278] Id.

[1279] Id.

[1280] Kenton, Will. "What is Greenwashing? How It Works, Examples, and Statistics." March 22, 2022. *https://www.investopedia.com/terms/g/greenwashing.asp*, accessed on August 24, 2022.

regulatory landscape regarding disclosure is rapidly evolving, the SEC's proposed amendments have been met with uncertainty and mixed feelings. Some commentators described the proposal as "too prescriptive" because of the level of detail the proposal requires, while others argue the proposed amendments fall in line with the SEC's mission to protect investors.[1281]

B.　State and Federal Legal Compliance

As ESG issues are moving from a mainly voluntary disclosure-oriented dimension to a regulatory one with significant implications for how ESG information is collected, verified, and acted upon within an organization, managing an organization's legal compliance now includes thinking about ESG considerations. As ESG issues navigate to the forefront of investors' minds, federal administrations and individual states legislatures have begun legislating ESG investments.

While some states lean into the push towards sustainable ESG investments, others states resist and prefer to prioritize their state's preexisting industries and economies. This method has created a patchwork of state laws rather than a single national framework of ESG legislation. Thus, ESG related laws vary state-by-state.

For example, California, Illinois, Maine, Massachusetts, New York, New Jersey, and Oregon have all enacted statutes to decrease their ESG risk factors by considering ESG factors and/or limiting their non-ESG related investments. However, some states limit ESG investment opportunities despite the general marketplace push toward ESG-investment. This legislation is often aimed at promoting that state's economy and established industries, such as the oil and gas industry. For example, Texas amended its Government Code to prohibit state financial

---

[1281] Barbarino, Al. "SEC's ESG Fund Plan Called 'Very Weird,' Too Prescriptive," June 6, 2022. https://www.law360.com/compliance/articles/1499922/sec-s-esg-fund-plan-called-very-weird-too-prescriptive?nl_pk=911503f4-54a6-4615-ac20-d8857f10546e&utm_source=newsletter&utm_medium=email&utm_campaign=compliance&utm_content=2022-06-07, accessed on August 20, 2022.

institutions from investing in businesses that boycott fossil fuels.[1282]

Overall, state legislation regarding utilizing ESG factors in making investment decision-making varies widely state-by-state. While some states prioritize or consider ESG factors in investment decision-making, other states refuse to conduct business with financial institutions that boycott certain industries or prioritize ESG factors over financial factors. Financial institutions doing business in these various states may be met with either open arms or a closed fist depending upon how the institution and the state views ESG-related investment decision-making.

Similarly, recent federal government administrations have varied in their view of ESG legal compliance. In general, the Trump Administration was more hostile and hesitant to ESG efforts than the Biden Administration. Specifically, Trump's Department of Labor passed multiple regulations seeking to limit fiduciaries' consideration of ESG in investment decision-making. In contrast, Biden's Labor Department refused to enforce the prior regulations and found ESG factors key to investment decision-making.

ESG lies at the intersection of legal and compliance. As ESG continues to develop, an organization's legal department will need to take the lead in ensuring that the ESG factors are considered when examining, analyzing and reviewing their organization's legal compliance strategies.

C.   Marketplace Compliance

Another key area of developing focus on ESG issues relates to the standards for reporting by organizations regarding ESG compliance. As a practical matter, organizations can anticipate that necessary stakeholders, both internal and external, will increasingly look to organizations' disclosures to evaluate whether

---

[1282] Tex. Gov't Code Ann. § 809.

64

those organizations have embraced ESG principles. Internal stakeholder may include:

- Legal;

- Human Resources;

- Marketing;

- Investor Relations;

- Government Relations;

- Public Policy;

- Supply Chain;

- Sustainability;

- Corporate Secretaries;

- Disclosures Committee;

- Accounting and Finance; and

- Compliance.

External stakeholders may include:

- Partners;

- Consumers/Customers;

- Communities in which you do business;

- Financial Investors; and

- Activist Investors.

665

Organizations should have a compliance plan and an organizational governance framework ready for the inevitable new regulations. A materiality matrix is a way for an organization to establish their ESG organizing framework. A materiality matrix can be viewed as the library of structures, processes, and activities leading companies to engage in to manage ESG risks and opportunities, and is organized the way leaders manage their organizations.

The below sample matrix provides guidance on how an organization may frame their materiality matrix subject to size and scale of the organization, specific industry considerations, and whether it is a privately held or publicly traded organization. The combination of these factors could significantly impact the need for a far more detailed and complex matrix approach.

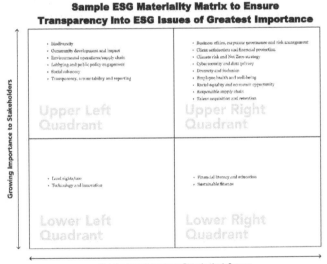

Materiality matrixes are typically organized by four quadrants. The Upper Right Quadrant may generally reflect:

- Business ethics, corporate governance & risk management;

- Client satisfaction & financial protection;

- Climate risk & Net Zero strategy;

- Cybersecurity & data privacy;

- Diversity and inclusion;

- Employee health & well-being;

- Racial equality & economic opportunity;

- Responsible supply chain; and

- Talent acquisition & retention.

The lower right quadrant may generally reflect:

- Financial literacy & education and

- Sustainable finance.

The lower left quadrant may generally reflect:

- Land rights/use and

- Technology & innovation.

The upper left quadrant may generally reflect:

- Biodiversity;

- Community development & impact;

- Environmental operations/supply chain;

- Lobbying & public policy engagement;

- Social advocacy; and

- Transparency, accountability & reporting.

ESG factors cover a wide range of initiatives that may or may not be relevant to an organization's particular business, and as such the maturity model is meant to be used as a guide for organizations as they review and analyze their organization's ESG principles and processes.

III. HOW TO TURN ESG IDEAS INTO REAL WORLD ACTION

As new regulatory and compliance obligations emerge, the need to embed ESG factors into business practices will continue to become necessary beyond corporate responsibilities. The following can shift ESG ideas into real world action:

- Reviewing internal ESG commitments and crafting ESG policy in step with current regulations and other considerations;

- Vetting ESG statements for accuracy at the same level public relations statements are reviewed;

- Educating stakeholders on emerging ESG disclosure requirements; and

- Measuring the organization's ESG goals and implementing cross-functional programs.

One industry that is rapidly turning ESG principles and ideas into real world action is grocery retailers. The emergence of new ESG challenges has forced grocery retailers to adapt their strategies and operations.[1283] Grocery retailers have increased their emphasis on sustainability as consumers have become more aware of the

---

[1283] Supermarket News Staff. "New ESG reporting standard earmarked for grocers,' August 1, 2022. *https://www.supermarketnews.com/sustainability/new-esg-reporting-standard-earmarked-grocers*, accessed on September 28, 2022.

consequences of their purchasing behaviors.[1284] This emergence of socially conscious consumers has forced the grocery industry to act on ESG principles in a way that is tangible, measureable and transparent.

For example, Kroger aims to end hunger and eliminate waste in its communities by 2025, and Albertsons has committed to making 100 percent of its Own Brands packaging recyclable, reusable, or industrially compostable by 2025.[1285] Organizations are recognizing the connection between the result of activities from assets beyond an organization's operations and global supply chain and are reevaluating operations and ESG principles simultaneously to enhance resilience while decreasing their carbon footprint.[1286] Rather than being nebulous, consumers expect definitive, easily discernable commitments that are specific and time bound for accountability.

IV.   EMERGING ESG TOPICS TO WATCH

ESG remains a multifaceted, complex and evolving area for today's organizations. As organization's look ahead to 2023 and beyond, the following are emerging ESG topics to watch.

[1284] Aull, Bill, Coggins, Becca, Kohli, Sajal, and Marohn, Eric. "The state of grocery in North America," May 18, 2022. *https://www.mckinsey.com/industries/retail/our-insights/the-state-of-grocery-in-north-america-2022*, accessed on September 28, 2022.

[1285] *See* Kroger. "Kroger Celebrates Zero Hunger | Zero Waste Momentum in 2020," April 20, 2021. *https://ir.kroger.com/CorporateProfile/press-releases/press-release/2021/Kroger-Celebrates-Zero-Hunger--Zero-Waste-Momentum-in-2020/default.aspx*, accessed on September 27, 2022. *See also* Mohan, Anne Marie. "Albertsons pledges to reduce the use of plastics in its 2,300 stores." *https://www.packworld.com/news/sustainability/news/13377520/albertsons-pledges-to-reduce-the-use-of-plastics-in-its-2300-stores*, accessed September 29, 2022

[1286] Aull, *supra* note 32.

A.   The SEC's Regulatory Interventions

The SEC is likely to require more enhanced disclosures by certain investment advisers and investment companies about ESG investment practices.[1287] As previously discussed, the SEC's current 2022 proposed changes could apply to registered investment advisers, advisers exempt from registration, registered investment companies, and business development companies. The 2022 proposed amendments seek to broaden the scope of disclosure requirements, causing funds and advisers to provide more specific disclosures in fund prospectuses, annual reports, and adviser brochures based on the ESG strategies they pursue. If the proposals are approved, organizations can expect SEC regulatory intervention to increase in coming years.

B.   A Rise in ESG-skilled Corporate Boards and Government Leaders

As SEC regulations increase, investors are likely to mandate greater accountability from leaders with a heightened focus on ESG principles. Shareholder activism in this area has already increased in 2022, including votes against directors for lack of credible climate action plans.[1288] This trend is likely to increase, creating pressure on corporate boards and government leaders to enhance their ESG knowledge bank and skillset to ensure they are adequately equipped to understand and oversee ESG issues. Moreover, board members may be required to focus and commit more time on EGS-related issues to meet their fiduciary duties.

C.   Preventing Greenwashing to Avoid Litigation

As noted above, greenwashing refers to disinformation disseminated by an organization so as to present an

---

[1287] Soba, *supra* note 18.

[1288] Mattison, Richard. "Key trends that will drive the ESG agenda in 2022," January 31, 2022. *https://www.spglobal.com/esg/insights/featured/special-editorial/key-esg-trends-in-2022*, accessed on September 28, 2022.

environmentally responsible public image.[1289] As ESG becomes the subject of new laws and regulations, organizations will spend more time and resources on ESG pledges and initiatives. This development may lead to an increase in greenwashing related litigation. Greenwashing litigation suits are still relatively new and allegations can vary widely.[1290] Examples of greenwashing cases involving ESG-related misrepresentations include ESG-focused investment funds, environmental hazards and safety, sustainability and environmental benefits of a product, and business risks of climate change.[1291] The increase in SEC regulations may impact greenwashing securities litigation as consumer activist groups take more and more action.

D.   Net Zero Transitions

In 2022, the number of government and large corporations setting goals to reach net zero emissions by 2050 grew exponentially,

---

[1289] Kenton, *supra* note 28.

[1290] Barton, Roger. "The Greenwashing Wave Hits Securities Litigation," September 22, 2022. *https://www.reuters.com/legal/legalindustry/greenwashing-wave-hits-securities-litigation-2022-09-22/*, accessed on September 30, 2022.

[1291] *See e.g., In the Matter of BNY Mellon Investment Adviser, Inc.*, SEC Administrative Proceeding File No. 3-20867 (May 23, 2022) (n May 2022, the SEC charged investment firm BNY Mellon with making ESG-related material misstatements and omissions); *SEC v. Vale S.A.*, 1:22-cv-02405 (E.D.N.Y. Apr. 28, 2022) (In April 2022, the SEC charged Vale S.A., a publicly traded mining company based in Brazil, with securities fraud, claiming that Vale knew about the risks pertaining to the compromised integrity of the dam, but knowingly manipulated data and concealed information from dam safety auditors); *In re Danimer Scientific, Inc. Securities Litigation*, 1:21-cv-02708 (E.D.N.Y. May 14, 2021) (Investors filed a class action suit against Danimer Scientific, Inc., a bioplastics company that went public via a business combination with a special purpose acquisition company (SPAC) in 2020. Investors accused Danimer of greenwashing by making materially false and misleading statements regarding the environmentally friendly attributes and sustainability of its product); *Ramirez v. Exxon Mobil Corporation et al*, 3:16-cv-03111 (N.D. Tex. Nov 7, 2016) (n an amended complaint filed in Texas in July 2017, shareholders alleged that Exxon made materially false and misleading statements by overstating the value and amount of its proved oil and gas reserves (i.e., petroleum that is "technologically and commercially feasible to recover")).

creating a snowball effect that may encourage others to join.[1292]
Net zero offers a goal of climate stability and an accounting system
to measure progress towards that goal.[1293] As net-zero rapidly
becomes the standard for government and corporate commitments,
organizations should begin considering net-zero transition. In
2023, organizations can likely anticipate that shareholders and
other stakeholders will increase pressure on organizations to
develop concrete, near-term plans, and implement near-term
actions to reach this seemingly long-term 2050-goal.

V.   CONCLUSION

While environmental, social and governance matters are not new
areas of consideration for many organizations, ESG principles and
factors have surged in recent years. In a post pandemic world,
economic, public health and social justice issues have only
intensified many organization's ESG-related focuses. As
organizations continue to grapple with their ESG policies,
strategies, and processes, ESG principles, compliance and the
above 2023 predicted emerging topics should remain top of mind.

[1292] Mattison, Richard. "Key trends that will drive the ESG agenda in 2022,"
January 31, 2022. *https://www.spglobal.com/esg/insights/featured/special-
editorial/key-esg-trends-in-2022*, accessed on September 28, 2022.

[1293] World Economic Forum. "Net-zero: the risks and benefits for companies
pledging to save the climate," February 28, 2022.
https://www.weforum.org/agenda/2022/02/net-zero-risks-benefits-climate/,
accessed on September 30, 2022.

Chapter 29

Employment Investigations

By: William C. Martucci[1294]

I.   INTRODUCTION

The modern workplace is subject to myriad regulations, and with that, the oversight of a variety of governmental entities that conduct workplace investigations. In particular, the Equal Employment Opportunity Commission (EEOC) and the Department of Labor (DOL) promulgate regulations that affect employers and could subject employers to investigations.

II.   THE EQUAL EMPLOYMENT OPPORTUNITY COMMISSION

The EEOC enforces many of the federal laws prohibiting workplace discrimination in the United States. These laws include Title VII of the Civil Rights Act of 1964, the Age Discrimination in Employment Act, the Americans with Disabilities Act, the Equal Pay Act, and the Genetic Information Non-Discrimination Act. These laws prohibit workplace discrimination on the bases of race, color, religion, sex, national origin, age, disability, and genetic information, as well as retaliation.

The EEOC is headquartered in Washington, D.C., has 15 enforcement districts, and operates through a network of district, field, area, and local offices. It has authority to investigate administrative charges made against covered employers, issue

---

[1294] William Martucci is an Executive Partner at Shook, Hardy, & Bacon, L.L.P. in Kansas City. William has been a charter member with the American Employment Counsel since 1993. William has also served in academia, as an adjunct professor of employment law with the University of Missouri Law School from 1988 to 1995 and a professor of multinational business policy and the global workplace with Georgetown University since 2008. Prior to joining the firm, William was a partner at Spencer, Fane, Britt & Browne.

findings, and pursue litigation if it finds reasonable cause to believe discrimination occurred.

In recent years, the EEOC has pursued its "systemic initiative," an agency-wide priority to strengthen its approach to investigating and litigating systemic, or company-wide, cases. The EEOC defines systemic cases as "pattern or practice, policy, or class cases where the alleged discrimination has a broad impact on an industry, profession, company or geographic area." Through this initiative, the EEOC is bringing bigger cases, addressing broader issues, affecting more people, and getting more media attention. The systemic initiative raises the stakes for employers and heightens their interest in staying out of the EEOC's sights, as defending systemic cases is costly, time-consuming, and often involves publicity.

A.   Overview of the EEOC's Systemic Initiative

The EEOC's systemic initiative began in 2005 with the creation of a special task force convened to examine the EEOC's existing systemic program and recommend new strategies. The Task Force concluded that combating systemic discrimination should be a top priority for the EEOC and that the agency is uniquely able and uniquely positioned to do so. Against this background, the systemic initiative was adopted in 2006.

Since implementation of the initiative, the EEOC has become increasingly aggressive in its pursuit of systemic cases using a "national law firm model." In December 2012, the EEOC rededicated itself to the goals set out by the Task Force, including that systemic enforcement be nationwide, coordinated, adequately resourced, and supported by the agency broadly. At the end of fiscal year 2021, the agency maintained 505 active systemic investigations. In that same period, the agency reported $21,175,337 in total conciliation amounts recovered. Today, lead systemic investigators, systemic coordinators, and the National Systemic Program Manager meet regularly to coordinate investigations, explore strategies, and share information.

B.   Strategies the EEOC Uses to Pursue High-Profile Systemic Cases

The EEOC uses a variety of strategies to advance its systemic initiative and increase its inventory of systemic investigations and lawsuits. Those strategies include:

- Merging the investigation and litigation phases

- Transforming a single charge into a systemic action

- Making nationwide requests for data, including broad e-discovery and HR system data

- Using subpoenas and subpoena enforcement actions to obtain nationwide information from employers

- Partnering with other agencies (like the DOL) to share information

These strategies have been effective for the EEOC in many instances, but employers are more frequently challenging them and succeeding in limiting the agency's expansive investigative efforts. For example, in *EEOC v. Burlington Northern Santa Fe Railroad Company*, 669 F.3d 1154 (2012), the Tenth Circuit rejected the agency's use of its subpoena power to build a systemic case. The court found the subpoena for nationwide employment records was "not relevant" to a case that initially involved just two claims of disability discrimination, both from employees in Colorado.

C.   The EEOC's Leading Enforcement Areas in Systemic Cases

In addition to its strategy of pursuing larger cases, the EEOC has given particular focus to certain enforcement areas in recent years, many of which lend themselves easily to the systemic initiative. According to the EEOC's own publication, it focuses on the following practices and policies in considering systemic enforcement: [1295]

- Hiring, Promotion, Assignment, Referral

  o Criminal/credit background checks

  o Recruitment practices such as favoring or limited to word-of mouth

  o Tap-on-the-shoulder promotion policies

  o Steering of applicants to certain jobs or assignments based on race or gender

  o Historically segregated occupations or industries

  o Job ads showing preference ("young," "energetic," "recent graduate," "men only," "women only")

  o Customer preference

  o Big data: using algorithm to sort through applications

  o Personality or customer service tests; physical ability or capacity tests; cognitive tests

  o No rehire of retired workers or hiring of currently employed persons only

- Mandatory Practices

[1295] *See* EEOC website, *available at* https://www.eeoc.gov/systemic-enforcement-eeoc (last visited September 20, 2022).

- o Mandatory religious practices by employers who do not qualify as religious organizations

- o Paternal leave policies that do not give the same benefits for men and women

- o Mandatory maternity leave

- o Fetal protection policies

- o English only rules

- o Age-based limits on benefits or contributions to pension or other benefits

- Lay-Offs, Reductions in Force, Discharge Policies

- o Mandatory retirement

- o Layoffs, reorganizations, and RIFs (disparate treatment and disparate impact based on protected characteristics)

- o Waivers that may prevent employees from filing complaints or assisting the EEOC

- Americans with Disabilities Act and Genetic Information Nondiscrimination Act Issues

- o "No fault" attendance policies

- o Non-accommodation for medical leave

- o Light duty policies for only work-related injuries

- o 100% healed return-to-work requirements

- o Pre-employment medical inquiries

D. Compliance Strategies

The convergence of the EEOC's systemic initiative and its heightened focus on a limited set of enforcement priorities creates an opportunity for employers to focus on a few high-priority areas and assess existing policy and procedure for potential change. Below are compliance strategies for employers to consider in readying themselves for anticipated EEOC activity in the coming years.

- Hiring Practices

  - Undergo a privileged self-analysis of decision-making and adverse action of the hiring process to determine any disparate impact areas to be addressed.

  - Evaluate each step in the hiring process to ensure each is needed and consistently applied.

  - Ensure job descriptions are current and accurately describe the required qualifications.

  - Consider revisions to or elimination of no rehire policies.

  - Exercise caution in using criminal background information—only when necessary based on the job position.

  - Ensure that criminal history information used to bar an applicant from employment is strongly related to the job the applicant is seeking.

- Pay and Promotions

o Conduct a privileged self-audit to identify areas of potential concern or disparate impact and steps that might be taken to address those areas.

o Consider a hybrid approach to pay and promotions that incorporates both uniform and individualized standards.

- Gender Discrimination

  o Review policies relating to gender-specific activities like breastfeeding and pregnancy.

  o Consider policy updates that ensure fair treatment for gender-specific activities.

- Disability Discrimination and Leave Policies

  o Amend leave policies calling for "automatic" dismissal after a certain amount of leave is used.

  o Ensure that return to work and dismissal procedures involve an individualized assessment.

  o Always engage in a meaningful "interactive process" and account for the ever-expanding definition of "reasonable accommodation."

E.   Strategies for Responding to EEOC Investigation

If your company should find itself facing the scrutiny of the EEOC in a systemic investigation, there are a few considerations to bear in mind. First, if you receive a broad request for information, attempt to gain an understanding of the reason for the request and cooperatively narrow it. Second, consider providing information to the EEOC in a phased manner and highlight information that may be important, but not requested. Third, if you receive a subpoena from the EEOC, remember there is a very short five-day response time. Fourth, be alert to preservation obligations and provide early notice of the need to maintain broad categories of information. Fifth, involve experienced legal counsel in responding to charges involving a systemic focus—information and documents provided at the outset will influence the course of the investigation and any litigation that may result.

III.   THE DEPARTMENT OF LABOR

Headquartered in Washington, D.C., the United States Department of Labor operates through a number of offices and agencies that are organized into broad program initiatives. Particularly relevant in the context of employment investigations are the Office of Federal Contract Compliance Program (OFCCP) and the Wage and Hour Division (WHD).

A.   OFCCP

The OFCCP is comprised of six regional offices. It works to ensure that entities who do business with the federal government (*i.e.*, federal contractors and subcontracts) comply with federal affirmative action requirements and anti-discrimination laws. In this regard, the OFCCP conducts compliance evaluations and complaint investigations of federal contractors and subcontractors' personnel policies and procedures, monitors contractors and subcontractors' progress in fulfilling the terms of their agreements through periodic compliance reports, and recommends enforcement actions to the Solicitor of Labor. Like the EEOC, the OFCCP focuses its resources on finding and resolving systemic discrimination. Employers who are federal contractors or subcontractors should anticipate an OFCCP compliance review to include data requests, document review, and interviews with company officials. The contractor may have an opportunity to engage with the OFCCP through its Early Resolution Procedures (ERP), which the OFCCP implemented in November 2018 to promote early and efficient compliance. Through the ERP program, the investigation is intended to be more streamlined, with the OFCCP proposing potential remedies to ensure and promote compliance.

B.   WHD

The WHD regulates and enforces wage and hour laws, including minimum wage, overtime, and child labor laws. The WHD may conduct a workplace investigation to (a) determine applicability of various regulations to the employer, and/or (b) verify that workers are paid and employed properly.

Many WHD investigations are initiated by worker complaints. Additionally, the WHD focuses investigation on certain industries even without worker complaints (such as, for example, low-wage industries, industries that more often employ vulnerable workers, or industries that have seen rapid growth or decline). Although the investigator may advise the employer prior to opening an investigation, the WHD does not require the investigator to announce an investigation, and the investigator may initiate an unannounced investigation to observe normal business operations.

1.   FLSA Investigations

The WHD may conduct investigations under any of the laws it enforces. The Fair Labor Standards Act (FLSA) is the primary federal law that proscribes wage and hour requirements applicable to most employers. Section 11(a) of the FLSA permits the DOL to gather information from an employer regarding wages, hours, and employment practices, inspect an employer's premises and records, and interview employees to evaluate FLSA compliance. The investigator may first review records to determine which laws and exemptions apply (including, *e.g.*, financial records showing annual dollar volume of business transactions, involvement in interstate commerce, and work on government contracts). The investigator will also review records to determine compliance with applicable laws, including payroll records, time data, job descriptions, and personnel records. Interviews are also frequently conducted during the investigation. Following the investigation, the employer will be informed of any findings and corrective remedies. The investigator may request payment of back wages and assess penalties if wage and hour violations are discovered.

2. Post-Investigation Procedures

The WHD is authorized to supervise the payment of back wages (including unpaid minimum wages or unpaid overtime compensation) to employees. The WHD may obtain back wages, liquidated damages, and civil penalties through pre-litigation settlements with the employer. Alternatively, the WHD may file a lawsuit in federal court on behalf of employees. The WHD may seek injunctive relief to restrain violations (including improper pay practices or failure to maintain records). Additionally, an employee may file a private lawsuit to recover damages, fees, and costs against his or her employer.

Retaliation is explicitly prohibited under the FLSA. Therefore, employees who have complained to the WHD or provided information to an investigator cannot be treated adversely or discharged because of such activity. If retaliation occurs, the employee or the Secretary of Labor may file suit for relief (including reinstatement to the employee's job, payment of lost wages, and other damages).

C. Considerations for DOL Investigations

In terms of compliance and efforts to avoid intrusive investigations, it is important that employers review their wage and hour practices and policies on a regular basis. Take time to conduct routine review of time punch data and payroll records to ensure general compliance (*e.g.*, that overtime pay is being properly calculated and paid, that time punch rounding works both ways so that it generally evens out, and that meal and rest periods are being taken and recorded). If the entity is a federal contractor or subcontractor, ensure you maintain thorough documentation of compliance with all EEO requirements.

Similar considerations that apply to EEOC investigations apply to DOL investigations. Should your company by subject to such an investigation, be cooperative, but attempt to narrow and focus the investigation to the core issues that are the subject of the investigation. Also be alert to preservation obligations should a lawsuit follow the investigation.

Finally, if an internal investigation occurs prior to or contemporaneous with a government investigation, keep in mind confidentiality considerations. If a company lawyer is involved, an *Upjohn* warning may be used to keep internal interviews confidential.[1296] Any notes or draft reports that are prepared during an internal investigation should be marked as confidential, privileged, and/or attorney work product. Additionally, those documents should be maintained separate from other non-confidential business records, and care should be taken so that they are not provided to third parties absent conferral with counsel.

[1296] *See Upjohn Co. v. United States*, 449 U.S. 383 (1981). The *Upjohn* warning informs employees that: (1) counsel is the company's lawyer, not the employee's; (2) communications between counsel and the employee are protected by the attorney-client privilege, but the company may choose to weigh that privilege (a choice that is not uncommon, especially when the government is involved); and (3) the employee should not disclose his or her conversations with counsel to a third party except for his or her personal attorney.

Chapter 30

Protection of Investigatory Materials under Public Records Laws

By: Amy Pritchard Williams[1297] and Abbey M. Thornhill[1298]

Responding to a civil investigative demand from a state or federal agency can be a complicated endeavor. A company's response must be strategic: it must fit within the larger plan for navigating the agency's investigation. Some responses also require voluminous production of documents. Once produced and taken into the hands of a government agency, a company's documents may become the subject of public records requests. Indeed, all fifty states, the District of Columbia, and the federal government have public records laws that allow individuals and businesses alike to request government agency records. As documents are reviewed and prepared for production, a business should take careful stock of the type and nature of the information it is producing to an agency. Then it must take all necessary steps to ensure that any confidential and commercially sensitive information receives the best possible protection from disclosure. This chapter provides an overview of considerations and practical guidance in protecting investigatory productions from disclosure to third parties under state and federal freedom of information laws.

[1297] Amy Pritchard Williams is a partner in the Regulatory Investigations, Strategies + Enforcement Practice Group at Troutman Pepper Hamilton Sanders LLP. She focuses her practice on consumer financial services, government enforcement, and bankruptcy, representing banks and other financial institutions in connection with False Claims Act and Financial Institutions Reform, Recovery and Enforcement Act actions, internal investigations, subpoena responses and government investigations.

[1298] Abbey Thornhill is an associate in the Regulatory Investigations, Strategies + Enforcement Practice Group. She focuses her practice on the representation of clients at the intersection of enforcement actions, investigations, and civil litigation.

I.   HOW PRIVATE RECORDS BECOME PUBLIC

A.   The Freedom of Information Act ("FOIA")

The Freedom of Information Act ("FOIA"), 5 U.S.C. § 552, is the federal public records law that governs the disclosure of information held by federal agencies. Passed in 1966, FOIA's purpose is "to ensure an informed citizenry, vital to the functioning of a democratic society, needed to check against corruption and to hold the governors accountable to the governed."[1299] FOIA achieves this goal by "piercing the veil of administrative secrecy and . . . opening agency action to the light of public scrutiny."[1300] FOIA generally requires federal agencies to disclose any public records requested under the statute unless they fall under one of nine statutory exemptions or three statutory exceptions. FOIA does not define the term "public records." FOIA instead instructs agencies to operate under a "presumption of openness." An agency should only withhold information if it "reasonably foresees that disclosure would harm an interest protected by an exemption" or "disclosure is prohibited by law."[1301]

In 1974 Congress amended FOIA, strengthening its disclosure requirements in several respects. For example, Congress added a statutory segregation requirement which instructs an agency to "take reasonable steps necessary to segregate and release nonexempt information."[1302] This means that whenever an agency decides that full disclosure of a particular document is improper, it must consider whether partial disclosure of the document is possible. The D.C. Circuit, the primary source of appellate law interpreting and enforcing FOIA, has explicitly held that "a district court errs when it approves the government's withholding of information under FOIA without making an express finding on

---

[1299] *Anderson v. Dep't of Health & Human Servs.*, 907 F.2d 936, 941 (10th Cir. 1990) (quoting *NLRB v. Robbins Tire & Rubber Co.*, 437 U.S. 214, 241 (1978)).

[1300] *Id.* (quotation omitted).

[1301] 5 U.S.C. § 552(a)(8)(A)(i).

[1302] *Id.* § 552(a)(8)(A)(ii).

segregability."[1303] Generally, "non-exempt portions of a document must be disclosed unless they are inextricably intertwined with exempt portions."[1304] Whether information is "inextricably intertwined" is determined by "look[ing] at a combination of intelligibility and the extent of the burden in 'editing' or 'segregating' the nonexempt material."[1305] "For example, if only ten percent of the material is non-exempt and it is interspersed line-by-line throughout the document," it may be unreasonable for the agency to segregate and produce.[1306] Meanwhile, "if a large portion of the information in a document is non-exempt, and it is distributed in logically related groupings," absent some argument that the non-exempt material would "indirectly reveal the exempt information," the agency would likely be required to make the partial production.[1307]

Submitting a request for documents is simple. FOIA instructs "each agency, upon any request for records which (i) reasonably describes the records and (ii) is made in accordance with published rules stating the time, place, fees (if any), and procedures to be followed, shall make the records promptly available to any person."[1308] Today, most agencies post clear instructions for submission of FOIA requests on their websites, providing forms for requests with all the required information, or even options to submit requests electronically through the website. Agencies also, as instructed by FOIA, allow requesters to specify the format in which he or she would like to receive the records (e.g., printed or in electronic form), and, assuming the record is readily

---

[1303] *PHE, Inc. v. Department of Justice*, 983 F.2d 248, 252 (D.C. Cir. 1993).

[1304] *Mead Data Cent., Inc. v. United States Dep't of the Air Force*, 566 F.2d 242, 260 (D.C. Cir. 1977).

[1305] *Yeager v. DEA*, 678 F.2d 315, 322 n.16 (D.C. Cir. 1978).

[1306] *Mead Data Cent.*, 566 F.2d at 261.

[1307] *Id.*

[1308] 5 U.S.C. § 552(a)(3)(A).

reproducible by the agency in that specified format, the agency will comply with the request.[1309]

B.   FOIA Exemptions

1.   Overview

While as a general rule the public has access to all documents held by government agencies, there are some notable exceptions. FOIA enumerates certain exemptions and exclusions to the general disclosure rule.

There are nine statutory "exemptions" which authorize agencies to withhold information when it falls within the scope of a records request. The types of information protected by the exemptions include:

1.   Classified matters of national defense or foreign policy;

2.   Internal personnel rules and practices of an agency;

3.   Information that is prohibited from disclosure by another federal statute;

4.   Trade secrets, commercial, or financial information obtained from a person that is privileged or confidential;

5.   Certain privileged communications within or between agencies (e.g., deliberative process privilege, attorney-client privilege);

6.   Personal information affecting an individual's privacy;

[1309] *Id.* § 552(a)(3)(B).

7. Investigatory records complied for law
    enforcement purposes;

8. Records of financial institutions; and

9. Geographical and geophysical information
    concerning wells.[1310]

Courts are instructed to construe these exemptions "narrowly."[1311]

Congress has also provided special protection for three narrower
categories of information. These are the three "exclusions" to
FOIA. While the exemptions allow an agency to withhold
otherwise requestable information, the "exclusions" identify
certain types of information that are simply not subject to the
requirements of FOIA. These categories of information include:

1. Ongoing criminal law enforcement investigation
    materials when the subject of the investigation is
    unaware that it is pending and disclosure could
    reasonably be expected to interfere with
    enforcement proceedings;

2. Informant records held by criminal law
    enforcement agencies where the informant's status
    has not been confirmed; and

3. Foreign intelligence or counterintelligence records
    held by the FBI and international terrorism records
    when the existence of such records is
    classified.[1312]

[1310] *Id.* § 552(b).

[1311] *Anderson*, 907 F.2d at 941.

[1312] *Id.* § 552(c).

## 2.	Exemption 4

Of all these exemptions and exclusions, there is one that is particularly relevant to a company producing documents in an investigation: Exemption 4.[1313] Exemption 4 provides that the requirements for disclosure will not apply to "trade secrets and commercial and financial information obtained from a person and privileged or confidential."[1314] Thus, the exemption has two parts.

First, Exemption 4 protects "trade secrets" from agency disclosure. FOIA does not define the meaning of trade secret in the text of the exemption. And, as the D.C. Circuit Court noted in *Public Citizen Health Research Group v. Food & Drug Admin*, "[t]he legislative history of the FOIA" is "unhelpful."[1315] Congress made clear at the statute's enactment that Exemption 4 was meant generally to cover materials such as "business sales statistics, inventories, customer lists, [and] scientific or manufacturing processes or developments," but it did not offer guidance as to the meaning of "trade secret" within the Act.[1316] Typically, as the D.C. Circuit has explained, where no definition of a term is provided by the statute, courts should turn to the common law definition of the phrase to determine its meaning.[1317] The problem with the term "trade secret" is that courts have been inconsistent in their definition of the phrase, some defining it quite broadly and others defining it

---

[1313] Exemption 6 will also be of particular relevance to banks, financial services companies and other companies whose productions contain consumer personally identifiable information or confidential medical information that is protected from disclosure under other statutes. *See, e.g.,* Department of Justice Guide to the Freedom of Information Act

Exemption 6, https://www.justice.gov/oip/page/file/1207336/download#page=4.

[1314] *Id.* § 552(b)(4).

[1315] 704 F.2d 1280, 1286 (D.C.C. 1983).

[1316] H.R. Rep. No. 1497, 89th Cong., 2d Sess. 10.

[1317] *Pub. Citizen Health*, 704 F.2d at 1286.

more narrowly.[1318] The *Public Citizen Health* court ultimately settled on a definition, announcing:

> [W]e define trade secret, solely for the purpose of FOIA Exemption 4, as a secret, commercially valuable plan, formula, process, or device that is used for the making, preparing, compounding, or processing of trade commodities and that can be said to be the end product of either innovation or substantial effort.[1319]

This definition remains the primary definition used by agencies today.

Second, Exemption 4 protects confidential commercial information. Historically, courts held that Exemption 4 and its confidential commercial information prong allowed agencies to withhold any commercial or financial information if (1) a private entity supplied it to the government under some express or implied promise of confidentiality,[1320] or (2) whenever the circumstances presented an objective expectation of confidentiality.[1321] But such broad protection was seen to be in conflict with the idea that exemptions should be construed narrowly. Thus, in *National Parks & Conservation Association v. Morton*, the D.C. Circuit made qualification for protection under the confidential commercial information prong much more difficult.[1322] The court announced a two-part test. Under *National Parks*, agencies could only withhold information if disclosure would: (1) "impair the Government's ability to obtain necessary information in the future," or (2) would

---

[1318] *Id.*

[1319] *Id.* at 1288.

[1320] *See, e.g., GSA v. Benson*, 415 F.2d 878, 881 (9th Cir. 1969)

[1321] *See, e.g., M.A. Shapira & Co. v. SEC*, 339 F. Supp. 467, 471 (D.D.C. 1972).

[1322] 498 F.2d 765 (D.C.C. 1974).

"cause substantial harm to the competitive position of the person from whom the information was obtained."[1323]

But after years of inconsistent application and confusion, the Supreme Court overhauled the *National Parks* test in 2019. In *Food Marketing Institute v. Argus Leader Media*, the Court criticized the *National Parks* decision for expanding the definition of "confidential" beyond the term's "ordinary meaning,"[1324] and adopted a much more straightforward definition. Under *Argus Leader*, information is generally considered confidential if it is kept private or secret.[1325] As the Court elaborated, information communicated to another remains confidential whenever it is customarily kept private, or at least closely held, by the person imparting it."[1326] Information might also be considered confidential "if the party receiving it provides some assurance it will remain secret."[1327] In sum, "[a]t least where commercial or financial information is both customarily and actually treated as private by its owner and provided to the government under an assurance of privacy, the information is 'confidential' within the meaning of Exemption 4."[1328]

C.   State Public Records Laws

A comprehensive overview of all fifty state public records laws is beyond the scope of this chapter, and it is essential to take into account the state's public records laws when producing documents to a state agency. For example, Florida has a policy that public records "are open for personal inspection and copying by any person" and "[p]roviding access to public records is a duty of each

---

[1323] *Id.* at 770.

[1324] 139 S. Ct. 2356, 2364 (2019).

[1325] Id. at 2363.

[1326] Id.

[1327] Id.

[1328] *Id.* at 2366.

[state, county, and municipal] agency."[1329]   Many state statutes
define the types of records that are considered "public records"
very broadly.[1330]   As explained below, some state agencies are
willing to enter into protective orders or nondisclosure agreements
and this should always be explored in the first instance. However,
the agreements should be paired with invoking applicable statutory
exemptions to the public records laws. In addition, not all states or
agencies will agree to such agreements, and in these instances,
invoking exemptions when producing documents is necessary to
protect documents from subsequent public disclosure.

II.   STRATEGIES FOR PROTECTING INVESTIGATORY MATERIALS FROM DISCLOSURE

A.   Production to State Agencies

When companies submit information to *state* agencies, they often
try to ensure that the government agency will properly protect its
information by asking the agency to enter a stipulated protective
order or nondisclosure agreement. These voluntary agreements
might, among other things, set forth (1) the way in which
confidential information should be identified at the time of
production; (2) protection extended to designated information and
how it may or may not be used or disclosed; and (3) applicable
procedures if a state receives a public-records request. These
agreements cannot protect documents or data from disclosure that
is properly subject to production pursuant to a public-records
request, but they provide protection and the ability to object to
disclosure pursuant to a public records request.

In some jurisdictions, it is not possible to enter into such
agreements or it is unlikely that such agreements will be enforced

---

[1329] Fla. Stat. § 119.01(1).

[1330] *See, e.g.*, Va. Code § 2.2-3701 (public records are writings and recordings "in
the possession of a public body or its officers, employees or agents in the
transaction of public business"); Cal. Gov't Code § 6252(e), (c) ("any writing
containing information relating to the conduct of the public's business prepared,
owned, used, or retained by any state or local agency").

by the courts.[1331] In Florida, for example, protection from automatic subsequent disclosure can be asserted by labeling productions, if appropriate, as containing or consisting of "'trade secrets' under Fla. Stat. §§ 812.08(1)(c) and 688.002(4) and Florida Rules of Civil Procedure 280.1(c)(7)" and a legend that the materials are "exempt from public disclosure under the Florida Public Records Act pursuant to Fla. Stat. § 815.045." No assertion can guarantee that the materials will ultimately be found to be trade secrets under the Florida statutory scheme, but without the assertion, it will be far more difficult to protect against subsequent public disclosure.

It is also often necessary or advisable to assert or request protection in the production cover letter. The cover letter should reference applicable state statutes, but sample generic language can read as follows:

> Respondent requests that the Office afford this letter and the accompanying materials confidential treatment under federal law, state law, and any court or administrative order that may be issued in any related legal or administrative proceeding. Without limiting the Office's obligation to afford this letter and the enclosed materials confidential treatment, Respondent expressly seeks the protections outlined below.
>
> ***Trade Secret and Confidential or Financial Information Protections***. This letter and the enclosed materials include confidential, proprietary, competitively sensitive, and trade-

---

[1331] *See, e.g., NCAA v. AP*, 18 So. 3d 1201, 1208-09 (Fla. 1st Dist. Ct. App. 2009) ("A public record cannot be transformed into a private record merely because an agent of the government has promised that it will be kept private. Nor is it material that [one] had an expectation that the documents would remain private. . . . '[A] private party cannot render public records exempt from disclosure merely by designating information it furnishes a governmental agency confidential.' The right to examine these records is a right belonging to the public; it cannot be bargained away by a representative of the government." (second alteration in original) (citations omitted)).

secret information. The disclosure of the aforementioned information would result in substantial harm to Respondent's competitive position. This letter and the enclosed materials should therefore be afforded confidential, trade-secret treatment.

Personal Information Protections. This letter and the enclosed materials include information of a personal nature, the public disclosure of which would constitute a clearly unwarranted invasion of personal privacy. This letter and the enclosed materials should therefore be afforded confidential treatment.

Inadvertent Production. If Respondent inadvertently produces any material protected by the attorney-client, work-product, or other applicable privilege, immunity, or protection from disclosure, such production shall in no way prejudice or otherwise constitute a waiver of any claim of attorney-client, work product, or other privilege, immunity, or protection from disclosure.

Notice Requested. Before this letter or the enclosed materials are disclosed to any third party, as part of any judicial proceeding, or in any other context, Respondent requests that the Office provide Respondent with prior, written notice and an opportunity to challenge the anticipated disclosure.

Return Requested. Respondent requests that this letter and the enclosed materials be returned to Respondent, pursuant to this written request, when the proceedings arising out of this investigation have been completed or this investigation has otherwise closed.

These strategies improve the likelihood that sensitive information produced to state agencies are protected from subsequent public disclosures.

B.   Federal Productions

Typically, a federal agency will *not* agree to enter a protective order or nondisclosure agreement with the subject of an investigation. Instead, producing parties should comply with the applicable agency's procedures created pursuant to Executive Order 12,600.

In 1987, President Ronald Reagan issued Executive Order 12,600 requiring federal agencies to establish certain pre-disclosure notification procedures to afford basic procedural protections to all persons or entities who submit "confidential commercial information" to the government.[1332] The EO defines "confidential commercial information" as "records provided to the government by a submitter that arguably contain material exempt from release under Exemption 4 of the [FOIA] because disclosure could reasonably be expected to cause substantial competitive harm."[1333]

Under EO 12,600, the process for each agency should look something like this:

1.   The business submitter has the opportunity to designate certain documents provided in the investigation with the "confidential" tag.

2.   If the federal agency receives a FOIA request for information that encompasses the documents marked as "confidential," it must notify the business submitter of the request prior to making any disclosure of the information.

[1332] Exec. Order No. 12,600, 3 C.F.R. 235, *reprinted in* 5 U.S.C. § 552 note.

[1333] *Id.*

3. Upon receiving such notification, the business submitter is afforded a reasonable period of time in which to object to the disclosure of any specified portion of the information, stating all grounds upon which disclosure is opposed.

4. The agency gives "careful consideration to all such specified grounds for nondisclosure" before making an administrative determination of whether the information is exempt from disclosure under Exemption 4.

5. If the agency decides the information does not meet the standard for exemption under Exemption 4, the agency must "give the submitter a written statement briefly explaining why the submitter's objections [were] not sustained." To the extent permitted by law, this written statement should be delivered to the submitter a reasonable number of days prior to the disclosure of the information.

Thus, agencies will not typically agree to enter protective orders or other agreements because they are already required to have specific procedures related to disclosure of confidential commercial business information. Accordingly, if a business becomes the subject of a federal agency investigation and hopes to keep certain information confidential, it should take several steps.

C.   **Identify Documents Containing Trade Secrets or Confidential Commercial Information.**

A producing party should carefully identify which documents it will mark as "confidential." As the business collects documents responsive to requests in a civil investigative demand or subpoena, it should carefully review each document to determine whether it contains information the business would like to keep confidential, and if that information could be considered a trade secret or confidential commercial information under Exemption 4.

D. Identify the Agency's EO 12,600 Rules

Second, the business should identify the agency's EO-mandated rules. Not every agency will follow the same procedures. While EO 12,600 provides some general requirements for the rules the agencies must adopt, the agency has the ability to dictate the exact procedures it will follow. It is important to determine whether the agency has specified any particular mechanism for marking and submitting documents.

For example, the Securities and Exchange Commission's Rule 83[1334] asks submitters to (1) segregate the materials for which confidential treatment is being requested; (2) mark each page of the documents or segregable portion of the documents with the phrase "Confidential Treatment Requested by [name]"; (3) include a written request for confidential treatment[1335] which specifies the information as to what type of confidential treatment is protected (e.g., trade secret or "confidential commercial information"); and (4) send a copy of the request (but not the record) by mail to the Office of Freedom of Information and Privacy Act Operations with a legend clearly titled as "FOIA Confidential Treatment Request."[1336] The SEC's Rule 83 acknowledges that compliance with this procedure may at times be difficult: "In some circumstances, such as when a person is testifying in the course of a Commission investigation or providing a record requested in the course of a Commission examination or inspection, it may be impracticable to submit a written request for confidential treatment at the time the record is first given to the Commission."[1337] But that does not excuse compliance. The SEC instructs that "[i]n no circumstances can the need to comply with the requirements of [Rule 83] justify or excuse any delay in submitting any record to

---

[1334] 17 C.F.R. § 200.83.

[1335] The written statement should identify the relevant documents with an identifying number or code such as a Bates-stamped number. *Id.* § 200.83(C)(2).

[1336] 17 C.F.R. § 200.83(C)(1)–(3).

[1337] *Id.* § 200.83(C)(4).

the Commission."[1338] The submitter must inform the SEC "at the time the record is submitted or as soon thereafter as possible" that it is requesting confidential treatment.[1339]

As the SEC's Rule 83 makes apparent, it is important for a business to understand an agency's rules for designating confidential information so that it can comply with such rules at the time of submission.

E. Submit Documents In Compliance with Agency Rules

Third, the business should comply as precisely as possible with the agency's rules because failure to do so can lead to a failure of protection. For example, as the Environmental Protection Agency ("EPA") provides in its EO 12,600 rules, when information is submitted to the agency in an improper form and without the required documentation regarding its confidentiality, a business may still seek to retroactively designate the information, but protection is simply not as feasible. Its regulation provides:

> If a claim covering the information is received after the information itself is received, EPA will make such efforts as are administratively practicable to associate the late claim with copies of the previously-submitted information in EPA files . . . . However, EPA cannot assure that such efforts will be effective, in light of the possibility of prior disclosure or widespread prior dissemination of the information.[1340]

A business should work with its counsel to carefully examine the text of the agency's rules to create a precise process for production of its confidential information. Further, counsel should not be afraid to consult with the agency. The agency does not necessarily

---

[1338] *Id.*

[1339] *Id.*

[1340] 40 C.F.R. § 2.203(c).

have adverse interests to a business when it comes to protecting confidential commercial information and trade secrets. Proper compliance with its rules helps the agency remain in compliance with federal law. An agency may welcome requests for direction as to how the company should go about designating confidential information. It could save the agency significant time and effort down the road if the information becomes the subject for a FOIA request by helping the agency identify potentially exempt information and avoiding expensive conflict between the agency and the business of the nature described below.

F.   Object to Disclosure

If a business has properly designated its confidential documents and receives notification from the agency that its information falls within the scope of a FOIA request, it should object to the disclosure. Again, this will involve paying close attention to the agency's rules for direction as to the form of such objections and the timeline for submission. As for the substance of the submission, it should conduct careful legal research to explain *why* its information should be withheld. As explained *supra*, while the definition of "trade secret" has remained consistent over the last few decades, the Supreme Court's relatively recent overhaul of the *National Parks* test has left room for development in the meaning of "confidential commercial information." Courts are continuing to grapple with the scope of protection this prong of Exemption 4 provides. Generally, however, "[t]he takeaway from cases in the wake of *Argus Leader* . . . is that a company cannot readily ward off disclosure simply by 'invoking the magic words'— 'customarily and actually kept confidential.'"[1341] Instead, a company must "adequately describe the steps it takes to keep the information at issue confidential" and "[t]hose steps must seem reasonable to the producing agency."[1342] Further, the "company must attest that they have succeeded in maintaining the

---

[1341] *New York Times Company v. U.S. Food and Drug Administration*, 529 F. Supp. 3d 260, 284-85 (S.D.N.Y. 2021) (citing *Am. Small Bus. League v. United States Dep't of Defense*, 411 F. Supp. 3d 824, 832 (N.D. Cal. 2019)).

[1342] *Id.* at 285.

information's confidentiality."[1343] Companies and their outside counsel should carefully monitor the development of this caselaw to make the best possible case for keeping their information confidential.

G.   File a "Reverse FOIA" Suit

Objecting to an agency's notice is in many circumstances effective in actually stopping disclosure. Agency personnel responding to a third party's request for information may not be familiar with the business or the sensitive nature of its information. Communication of the business's legal positions with respect to Exemption 4 can be helpful to the agency in determining how to respond to the request. But in the event a business's objection does not persuade the agency from withholding the requested information, there remains one last option for a company seeking to prevent disclosure

As noted above, once an agency decides it will not withhold the requested information, it must provide the business with a written explanation of its decision a "reasonable number of days" prior to the actual disclosure. Within that "reasonable number of days," a business can file what is known as a "reverse FOIA" suit, seeking a court order that the agency should withhold the information under Exemption 4.[1344]

[1343] *Id.*

[1344] It is important for a business to wait until the agency has made a final determination as to whether the information should be disclosed, as courts have held that they lack jurisdiction to hear reverse FOIA suits prior to such time. *See, e.g., Doe v. Geneman*, 380 F.3d 807, 814–15 (5th Cir. 2004) (reversing injunction after finding that the district court had "exceeded its jurisdiction" by enjoining release of information prior to agency decision); *United States v. N.Y. City Bd. of Educ.*, No. 96-0374, 2015 WL 1949477, at *1 (E.D.N.Y. Aug. 15, 2005) (holding that court "did not have jurisdiction to enjoin disclosure of" requested documents until "a final determination to disclose the documents" had been made by the agency).

In a "reverse FOIA" suit, the party seeking to prevent disclosure assumes the burden of justifying the nondisclosure.[1345] And that burden is, in most cases, substantial. In *Chrysler Corp. v. Brown*, the Supreme Court held that the Administrative Procedure Act's predominant scope and standard of judicial review—review on the administrative record according to an arbitrary and capricious standard—should "ordinarily" apply to reverse FOIA actions.[1346] The D.C. Circuit has since elaborated that judicial review in reverse FOIA cases should be based on the administrative record, but if a court finds that the agency's administrative procedures were "severely defective," it may conduct a de novo review.[1347] Thus, in most cases, the district court utilizes a "deferential standard of review [that] only requires that a court examine whether the agency's decision was 'based on a consideration of the relevant factors and whether there has been a clear error of judgment.'"[1348] "An agency is not required to prove that its predictions of the effect of disclosure are superior."[1349] "It is enough that the agency's position is as plausible as the contesting party's position."[1350]

[1345] *Martin Marietta Corp. v. Dalton*, 974 F. Supp. 37, 40 n.4 (D.D.C. 1997); *accord Frazee v. United States Forest Serv.*, 97 F.3d 367, 371 (9th Cir. 1996) (finding that the "party seeking to withhold information under Exemption 4 has the burden of proving that the information is protected from disclosure"); *Occidental Petroleum Corp. v. SEC*, 873 F.2d 325, 342 (D.C. Cir. 1989) (noting that the "statutory policy favoring disclosure requires that the opponent of disclosure" bear the burden of persuasion); *TRIFID Corp. v. Nat'l Imagery & Mapping Agency*, 10 F. Supp. 2d 1087, 1097 (E.D. Mo. 1998) (same).

[1346] 441 U.S. 281, 318 (1979).

[1347] *Nat'l Org. for Women v. SSA*, 736 F.2d 727, 745 (D.C. Cir. 1984) (per curium) (McGowan & Mikva, JJ., concurring in result).

[1348] *McDonnell Douglas Corp. v. NASA*, 981 F. Supp. 12, 14 (D.D.C. 1997) (quoting *Citizens to Preserve Overton Park v. Vlope*, 401 U.S. 402, 416 (1971)), rev'd on other grounds, 180 F.3d 303 (D.C. Cir. 1999).

[1349] *McDonnell Douglas Corp. v. U.S. Dep't of Air Force*, 215 F. Supp. 2d 200, 205 (D.D.C. 2002) (citing *CAN Fin. Corp. v. Donovan*, 830 F.2d 1132, 1155 (D.C. Cir. 1987)), *aff'd in part & rev'd in part*, 375 F.3d 1182 (D.C. Cir. 2004), *reh'g en banc denied*, No. 02-5342 (D.C. Cir. Dec. 16, 2004).

[1350] *Id.*

In sum, winning a reverse FOIA suit can be an uphill battle. It is therefore important that a business take the administrative objection process very seriously. The best opportunity to stop disclosure of privately held information in by properly designating materials as "confidential" and robustly objecting to an agency's disclosure, but reverse FOIA suits do provide a last-ditch effort to protect information and hold agencies accountable for the proper administration of their EO 12,600-mandated rules.

III.   TAKEAWAYS

When preparing to produce documents in response to state or federal demands, a business must engage with the requesting agency at the outset and prior to production to determine the appropriate steps and process for protecting documents containing sensitive information from public disclosure. When producing to a state agency, a nondisclosure agreement may be available, but should be pared with an invocation of available state exemptions or protections from disclosure. When dealing with federal agencies, a business should closely comply with the agency-specific rules for designating applicable FOIA exemptions. If these designations are challenged, then it is important to respond promptly and put forth a well-developed explanation for why the exemption should apply.

Chapter 31

Conclusion

By: The GICLI Advisory Board

While navigating regulatory investigations remains a complex endeavour, adequate understanding of the nature and structure of agencies and their investigatory processes, effective collaboration, and close knowledge of the key issues and considerations in the regulatory context are critical in moving towards a successful resolution of the matter. These have been major themes throughout this volume. Irrespective of the nature of the agency involved or the alleged corporate malfeasance at hand, continued emphasis on and attention to these themes will be of substantial benefit to corporate legal teams of all types.

As the regulatory landscape has shifted in response to changes by the Biden Administration, as the continued growth of big data provides challenges in discovery, security and privacy, and as federal and state governments continue to vary their regulatory focus, the contributions to this Guide are expected to be revised and expanded accordingly, making this Guide an ever-useful and timely reference. Moreover, as the Government Investigation Reference Model (GIRM) is adopted and implemented, providing for innovation and improved management and efficiency in responding to government investigations, those best practices, lessons, and frameworks will surely be incorporated in this Guide. One can hope that the GIRM will be as useful and as widely adopted an iterative framework as the Electronic Discovery Review Model (EDRM), now an industry standard and recognized set of guidelines for navigating the electronic discovery process.

In short, this volume is a distillation of the key concepts of government investigations from litigators and seasoned professionals, and we hope that you will continue to turn to the pages of this Guide as a useful reference and guide.

The Board hopes to see you at the GICLI Annual Meeting.

APPENDIX A: Enumerated Consumer Protection Laws[1351]

Federal Consumer Financial Statutes Enforced by the CFPB:

- Alternative Mortgage Transaction Parity Act (12 U.S.C. § 3801 et seq.)

- Consumer Financial Protection Act (Title X of Dodd-Frank) (12 U.S.C. § 5481 et seq.)

- Consumer Leasing Act (15 U.S.C. § 1667 et seq.)

- Electronic Fund Transfer Act (15 U.S.C. § 1693 et seq. – excluding § 920)

- Equal Credit Opportunity Act (15 U.S.C. § 1691 et seq.)

- Fair Credit Billing Act (15 U.S.C. § 1666 et seq.)

- Fair Credit Reporting Act (15 U.S.C. § 1681 et seq. – excluding §§ 1681m(e) and 1681w)

- Fair Debt Collection Practices Act (15 U.S.C. § 1692 et seq.)

- Federal Deposit Insurance Act (in part) (12 U.S.C. § 1831t(b) – (f))

- Gramm-Leach-Bliley Act (15 U.S.C. §§ 6802-6809 – in part)

- Home Mortgage Disclosure Act (12 U.S.C. § 2801 et seq.)

[1351] Although not listed in the Dodd-Frank Act, Congress subsequently gave the CFPB enforcement authority.

- Home Owners Protection Act (12 U.S.C. § 4901 et seq.)

- Home Ownership and Equity Protection Act (15 U.S.C. § 1601 note)

- Interstate Land Sales Full Disclosure Act (15 U.S.C. § 1701)

- Military Lending Act (10 U.S.C. § 987)*

- Omnibus Appropriations Act, 2009, Section 626 (Public Law 111-8)

- Real Estate Settlement Procedures Act (12 U.S.C. § 2601 et seq.)

- S.A.F.E. Mortgage Licensing Act (12 U.S.C. § 5101 et seq.)

- Truth in Lending Act (15 U.S.C. § 1601 et seq.)

- Truth in Savings Act (12 U.S.C. § 4301 et seq.)

Selected Consumer Financial Regulations Enforced by the CFPB:

- Regulation B – Equal Credit Opportunity (12 C.F.R. part 1002)

- Regulation C – Home Mortgage Disclosures (12 C.F.R. part 1003)

- Regulation D – Alternative Mortgage Transaction Parity (12 C.F.R. part 1004)

- Regulation E – Electronic Fund Transfers (12 C.F.R. part 1005)

- Regulation F – Fair Debt Collection Practices (12 C.F.R. part 1006)

- Regulations G and H – S.A.F.E. Mortgage Licensing (12 C.F.R. parts 1007, 1008)

- Regulations J, K, and L – Interstate Land Sales Registration Program (12 C.F.R. parts 1010, 1011, 1012)

- Regulation M – Consumer Leasing (12 C.F.R. part 1013)

- Regulation N – Mortgage Acts and Practices – Advertising (12 C.F.R. part 1014)

- Regulation O – Mortgage Assistance Relief Services (12 C.F.R. part 1015)

- Regulation P – Privacy of Consumer Financial Information (12 C.F.R. part 1016)

- Regulation V – Fair Credit Reporting (12 C.F.R. part 1022)

- Regulation X – Real Estate Settlement Procedures (12 C.F.R. part 1024)

- Regulation Z – Truth in Lending (12 C.F.R. part 1026)

- Regulation DD – Truth in Savings (12 C.F.R. part 1030)

- Telemarketing Sales Rule (16 C.F.R. part 310)

- Credit Practices Rule (16 C.F.R. part 444)

Selected Consumer Financial Regulations Enforced by the FTC:

- INFORM Consumers Act (15 U.S.C. § 45f)

- Fraud and Scam Reduction Act (Pub. L. No. 117-103, 136 Stat. 49, Division Q, Title I, §§ 101-122)

- No Surprises Act of the 2021 Consolidated Appropriations Act (Pub. L. No. 116-260, 134 Stat. 1182, Division BB, § 109)

- Protecting Children in the 21st Century Act (15 U.S.C. § 6552-53)

- Economic Growth, Regulatory Relief, and Consumer Protection Act (Pub. L. No. 115-174, codified in relevant part primarily at 15 U.S.C. 1650, 1681c, 1681c-1, 1681i and 42 U.S.C. 405b)

- Patient Right to Know Drug Prices Act (Pub. L. No. 115-263, 132 Stat. 3673, codified in relevant part at 21 U.S.C. § 355 note)

- FAA Reauthorization Act of 2018 (Pub. L. No. 115-254,132 Stat.3314, codified in relevant part at 49 U.S.C. § 44801 note)

- Controlling the Assault of Non-Solicited Pornography and Marketing Act of 2003 (CAN-SPAM Act) (15 U.S.C §§ 7701-7713)

- Consumer Review Fairness Act (15 U.S.C. § 45b)

- Motor Vehicle Information and Cost Savings Act (Pub. L. No. 92-513, 86 Stat. 947, now codified in relevant part at 49 U.S.C. §§ 32908, 32912-32913, and 32918, and 42 U.S.C. § 6363)

- <u>Military Lending Act</u> (10 U.S.C. § 987)

Made in the USA
Columbia, SC
03 November 2024

45217388R00407